CRIMINAL JUSTICE 92/93

Sixteenth Edition

Editor

John J. Sullivan
Mercy College, Dobbs Ferry, New York

John J. Sullivan, professor and chairman of the Department of Law, Criminal Justice, and Safety Administration at Mercy College, received his B.S. in 1949 from Manhattan College and his J.D. in 1956 from St. John's Law School. He was formerly captain and director of the Legal Division of the New York City Police Department.

Editor

Joseph L. Victor
Mercy College, Dobbs Ferry, New York

Joseph L. Victor is professor and assistant chairman of the Department of Law, Criminal Justice, and Safety Administration at Mercy College, and coordinator of Criminal Justice Graduate Study at the Westchester Campus of Long Island University. Professor Victor has extensive field experience in criminal justice agencies, counseling, and administering human service programs. He earned his B.A. and M.A. at Seton Hall University, and his Doctorate of Education at Fairleigh Dickinson University.

Cover illustration by Mike Eagle

Annual Editions
A Library of Information from the Public Press

The Dushkin Publishing Group, Inc.
Sluice Dock, Guilford, Connecticut 06437

The Annual Editions Series

Annual Editions is a series of over 55 volumes designed to provide the reader with convenient, low-cost access to a wide range of current, carefully selected articles from some of the most important magazines, newspapers, and journals published today. Annual Editions are updated on an annual basis through a continuous monitoring of over 300 periodical sources. All Annual Editions have a number of features designed to make them particularly useful, including topic guides, annotated tables of contents, unit overviews, and indexes. For the teacher using Annual Editions in the classroom, an Instructor's Resource Guide with test questions is available for each volume.

VOLUMES AVAILABLE

Africa
Aging
American Government
American History, Pre-Civil War
American History, Post-Civil War
Anthropology
Biology
Business and Management
Business Ethics
Canadian Politics
China
Comparative Politics
Computers in Education
Computers in Business
Computers in Society
Criminal Justice
Drugs, Society, and Behavior
Early Childhood Education
Economics
Educating Exceptional Children
Education
Educational Psychology
Environment
Geography
Global Issues
Health
Human Development
Human Resources
Human Sexuality
International Business
Japan
Latin America

Life Management
Macroeconomics
Management
Marketing
Marriage and Family
Microeconomics
Middle East and the Islamic World
Money and Banking
Nutrition
Personal Growth and Behavior
Physical Anthropology
Psychology
Public Administration
Race and Ethnic Relations
Social Problems
Sociology
Soviet Union (Commonwealth of Independent States and Central Europe)
State and Local Government
Third World
Urban Society
Violence and Terrorism
Western Civilization, Pre-Reformation
Western Civilization, Post-Reformation
Western Europe
World History, Pre-Modern
World History, Modern
World Politics

Library of Congress Cataloging in Publication Data
Main entry under title: Annual editions: Criminal justice. 1992/93.
    1. Criminal Justice, Administration of—United States—Periodicals.
I. Sullivan, John J., comp. II. Victor, Joseph L., comp. III. Title: Criminal justice.
HV 8138.A67   364.973.05   LC 77-640116
ISBN: 1-56134-082-0

Sixteenth Edition

Manufactured by The Banta Company, Harrisonburg, Virginia 22801

To the Reader

In publishing ANNUAL EDITIONS we recognize the enormous role played by the magazines, newspapers, and journals of the *public press* in providing current, first-rate educational information in a broad spectrum of interest areas. Within the articles, the best scientists, practitioners, researchers, and commentators draw issues into new perspective as accepted theories and viewpoints are called into account by new events, recent discoveries change old facts, and fresh debate breaks out over important controversies.

Many of the articles resulting from this enormous editorial effort are appropriate for students, researchers, and professionals seeking accurate, current material to help bridge the gap between principles and theories and the real world. These articles, however, become more useful for study when those of lasting value are carefully *collected, organized, indexed,* and *reproduced* in a *low-cost format*, which provides easy and permanent access when the material is needed. That is the role played by *Annual Editions*. Under the direction of each volume's *Editor*, who is an expert in the subject area, and with the guidance of an *Advisory Board*, we seek each year to provide in each *ANNUAL EDITION* a current, well-balanced, carefully selected collection of the best of the public press for your study and enjoyment. We think you'll find this volume useful, and we hope you'll take a moment to let us know what you think.

During the 1970s, criminal justice emerged as an appealing, vital, and unique academic discipline. It emphasizes the professional development of students who plan careers in the field, and attracts those who want to know more about a complex social problem and how this country deals with it. Criminal justice incorporates a vast range of knowledge from a number of specialties, including law, history, and the behavioral and social sciences. Each specialty contributes to our fuller understanding of criminal behavior and of society's attitudes toward deviance.

In view of the fact that the criminal justice system is in a constant state of flux, and because the study of criminal justice covers such a broad spectrum, today's students must be aware of a variety of subjects and topics. Standard textbooks and traditional anthologies cannot keep pace with the changes as quickly as they occur. In fact, many such sources are already out of date the day they are published. *Annual Editions: Criminal Justice 92/93* strives to maintain currency in matters of concern by providing up-to-date commentaries, articles, reports, and statistics from the most recent literature in the criminal justice field.

This volume contains units concerning crime and justice in America, victimology, the police, the judicial system, juvenile justice, and punishment and corrections. The articles in these units were selected because they are informative as well as provocative. The selections are timely and useful in their treatment of ethics, punishment, juveniles, courts, and other related topics.

Included in this volume are a number of features designed to make it useful for students, researchers, and professionals in the criminal justice field. These include a topic guide, for locating articles on specific subjects; the table of contents abstracts, which summarize each article and feature key concepts in bold italics; and a comprehensive bibliography, glossary, and index. In addition, each unit is preceded by an overview that provides a background for informed reading of the articles, emphasizes critical issues, and presents challenge questions.

We would like to know what you think of the selections contained in this edition. Please fill out the article rating form on the last page and let us know your opinions. We change or retain many of the articles based on the comments we receive from you, the user. Help us to improve this anthology—annually.

John J. Sullivan

Joseph L. Victor
Editors

Contents

Unit 1

Crime and Justice in America

Eight selections focus on the overall structure of the criminal justice system in the United States. The current scope of crime in America is reviewed; topics such as criminal behavior, drugs, and organized crime are discussed.

The concepts in bold italics are developed in the article. For further expansion please refer to the Topic Guide, the Index, and the Glossary.

Unit 2

Victimology

Seven articles discuss the impact of crime on the victim. Topics include the rights of crime victims, the consequences of family violence, and the legal definition of rape.

Unit 3

Police

Seven selections examine the role of the police officer. Some of the topics discussed include police response to crime, utilization of policewomen, and managing police corruption.

The concepts in bold italics are developed in the article. For further expansion please refer to the Topic Guide, the Index, and the Glossary.

Unit 4

The Judicial System

Eight selections discuss the process by which the accused are moved through the judicial system. Prosecutors, courts, the jury process, and judicial ethics are reviewed.

Unit 5

Juvenile Justice

Six selections review the juvenile justice system. The topics include effective ways to respond to violent juvenile crime, juvenile detention, female delinquency, and the impact of teenage addiction.

Unit 6

Punishment and Corrections

Nine selections focus on the current state of America's penal system and the effects of sentencing, probation, overcrowding, and capital punishment on criminals.

The concepts in bold italics are developed in the article. For further expansion please refer to the Topic Guide, the Index, and the Glossary.

Charts and Graphs

The concepts in bold italics are developed in the article. For further expansion please refer to the Topic Guide, the Index, and the Glossary.

Topic Guide

This topic guide suggests how the selections in this book relate to topics of traditional concern to students and professionals involved with the study of criminal justice. It is useful for locating articles that relate to each other for reading and research. The guide is arranged alphabetically according to topic. Articles may, of course, treat topics that do not appear in the topic guide. In turn, entries in the topic guide do not necessarily constitute a comprehensive listing of all the contents of each selection.

TOPIC AREA	TREATED IN:	TOPIC AREA	TREATED IN:
Attorneys	24. Public Defenders 25. Abuse of Power in the Prosecutor's Office 27. Convicting the Innocent	Crime	1. Overview of the Criminal Justice System 2. What Is Crime? 3. Are Criminals Made or Born? 4. Crime's Impact on Blacks 5. High Cost of Crime
Battered Families	11. Hunted 12. Vicious Cycle	Crime Victims	See Victimology
Boot Camp	43. "Boot Camp Programs" Grow in Number and Scope	Criminal Behavior	3. Are Criminals Made or Born?
Children	See Juveniles	Criminal Justice	1. Overview of the Criminal Justice System 2. What Is Crime? 24. Public Defenders 25. Abuse of Power in the Prosecutor's Office 28. Improving Our Criminal Justice System
Community Policing	21. Not Just Old Wine in New Bottles		
Computers	8. Computer Ethics		
Constitutional Rights	26. These Clients Aren't Fools 27. Convicting the Innocent 28. Improving Our Criminal Justice System 30. Criminal Rulings Granted the State Broad New Power	Death Penalty	41. Life Without Parole 44. 'This Man Has Expired' 45. No Reversal of Fortune for Blacks on Death Row
		Defense Counsel	24. Public Defenders
Corrections	35. Correcting Juvenile Corrections 37. Sentencing and Corrections 38. Women in Jail: Unequal Justice 39. You're Under Arrest—AT HOME 41. Life Without Parole 42. U.S.: World's Lock-'Em-Up Leader 43. "Boot Camp" Programs Grow in Number and Scope	Delinquency	See Juveniles
		Discrimination	4. Crime's Impact on Blacks 42. U.S.: World's Lock-'Em-Up Leader 45. No Reversal of Fortune for Blacks on Death Row
Courts	23. Judicial Process 24. Public Defenders 25. Abuse of Power in the Prosecutor's Office 26. These Clients Aren't Fools 27. Convicting the Innocent 28. Improving Our Criminal Justice System 29. Alternative Sentencing	Drugs	6. Men Who Created Crack 34. Teenage Addiction
		Ethics	8. Computer Ethics 25. Abuse of Power in the Prosecutor's Office
		Family Violence	11. Hunted 12. Vicious Cycle

TOPIC AREA	TREATED IN:	TOPIC AREA	TREATED IN:
Fear of Crime	9. Fear of Crime 36. Kids Who Kill	**Probation**	39. You're Under Arrest—AT HOME 40. Difficult Clients, Large Caseloads Plague Probation, Parole Agencies
House Arrest	39. You're Under Arrest—AT HOME	**Prosecution**	23. Judicial Process 25. Abuse of Power in the Prosecutor's Office
Jails	38. Women In Jail: Unequal Justice		
Judges	23. Judicial Process 28. Improving Our Criminal Justice System 29. Alternative Sentencing	**Public Defender**	24. Public Defenders
		Punishment	*See* Corrections
Juveniles	31. Handling of Juvenile Cases 32. Evolution of the Juvenile Justice System 33. Girls' Crime and Woman's Place 34. Teenage Addiction 35. Correcting Juvenile Corrections 36. Kids Who Kill	**Rape**	*See* Sex Offenders
		Sentencing	29. Alternative Sentencing: A New Direction for Criminal Justice 37. Sentencing and Corrections 41. Life Without Parole
Life Without Parole	41. Life Without Parole	**Sex Offenders**	12. Vicious Cycle 13. Tougher Laws Mean More Cases Are Called Rape 14. Even the Victim Can Be Slow to Recognize Rape
Murder	15. Unbearable Loss		
Narcotics	*See* Drugs	**Supreme Court**	26. These Clients Aren't Fools 30. Criminal Rulings Granted the State Broad New Power
Organized Crime	6. Men Who Created Crack 7. Mobster Who Could Bring Down the Mob	**Victimology**	9. Fear of Crime 10. Implementation of Victims' Rights 11. Hunted 12. Vicious Cycle 13. Tougher Laws Mean More Cases Are Called Rape 14. Even the Victims Can Be Slow to Recognize Rape 15. Unbearable Loss
Parole	40. Difficult Clients, Large Caseloads Plague Probation, Parole Agencies 41. Life Without Parole		
Police	16. Police Response to Crime 17. Police in the United States 18. Cops Under Fire 19. Law and Disorder 20. New Faces, and New Roles, for the Police 21. Not Just Old Wine in New Bottles 22. Law Enforcement Officers Killed	**Women**	11. Hunted 13. Tougher Laws Mean More Cases Are Called Rape 14. Even the Victim Can Be Slow to Recognize Rape 33. Girls' Crime and Woman's Place 38. Women in Jail: Unequal Justice
Prisons	41. Life Without Parole 42. U.S.: World's Lock-'Em-Up Leader 43. "Boot Camp" Programs Grow in Number and Scope		

Crime and Justice in America

The United States is still plagued by a crime problem. The court dockets are overcrowded, police are understaffed, and the prison population is swelling. The economic cost of crime is crippling and the human cost even worse.

Drugs are an ever-present source of the problems for the criminal justice system, and the number of people participating in drug traffic is increasing—despite our efforts to curtail them.

The articles presented in this section are intended to serve as a foundation for the materials presented in subsequent sections. "An Overview of the Criminal Justice System" charts the flow of events in the administration of the criminal justice system. The definition and characteristics of the more serious crimes can be found in "What Is Crime?"

Why do people commit crimes? The answer to this question still evades us. There are many opinions concerning the causative factors of criminal behavior, and the article "Are Criminals Made or Born?" presents some thoughts for further contemplation.

Racial issues are considered in "Crime's Impact on Blacks Makes for a Bleak Picture," and the economic impact of crime is discussed in "The High Cost of Crime."

How did crack get into our midst? "Men Who Created Crack," reveals the shrewd marketing strategy of several drug lords. However, "The Mobster Who Could Bring Down the Mob" tells of the government's hope to bring down some organized crime groups through the testimony of a former hit man.

Computers have become a way of life in our society and, as with any new device, there are those who find ways to use them for criminal activity. "Computer Ethics" discusses the criminal and unethical use of these devices.

Looking Ahead: Challenge Questions

What is crime?

What is the sequence of events in the criminal justice system?

Is the criminal justice system racially biased?

An Overview of the Criminal Justice System

The response to crime is a complex process that involves citizens as well as many agencies, levels, and branches of government

The private sector initiates the response to crime

This first response may come from any part of the private sector: individuals, families, neighborhood associations, business, industry, agriculture, educational institutions, the news media, or any other private service to the public.

It involves crime prevention as well as participation in the criminal justice process once a crime has been committed. Private crime prevention is more than providing private security or burglar alarms or participating in neighborhood watch. It also includes a commitment to stop criminal behavior by not engaging in it or condoning it when it is committed by others.

Citizens take part directly in the criminal justice process by reporting crime to the police, by being a reliable participant (for example, witness, juror) in a criminal proceeding, and by accepting the disposition of the system as just or reasonable. As voters and taxpayers, citizens also participate in criminal justice through the policymaking process that affects how the criminal justice process operates, the resources available to it, and its goals and objectives. At every stage of the process, from the original formulation of objectives to the decision about where to locate jails and prisons and to the reintegration of inmates into society, the private sector has a role to play. Without such involvement, the criminal justice process cannot serve the citizens it is intended to protect.

The government responds to crime through the criminal justice system

We apprehend, try, and punish offenders by means of a loose confederation of agencies at all levels of government. Our American system of justice has evolved from the English

What is the sequence of events in the criminal justice system?

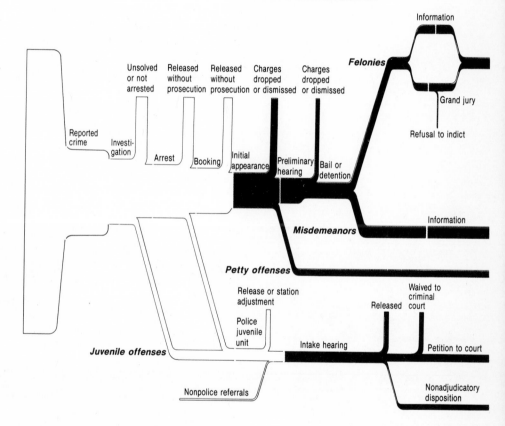

Note: This chart gives a simplified view of caseflow through the criminal justice system. Procedures vary among jurisdictions. The weights of the lines are not intended to show the actual size of caseloads.

common law into a complex series of procedures and decisions. There is no single criminal justice system in this country. We have many systems that are similar, but individually unique.

Criminal cases may be handled differently in different jurisdictions, but court decisions based on the due process guarantees of the U.S. Constitution require that specific steps be taken in the administration of criminal justice.

The description of the criminal and juvenile justice systems that follows portrays the most common sequence of events

From *Report to the Nation on Crime and Justice*, Bureau of Justice Statistics, U.S. Department of Justice, March 1988, pp. 56-60.

in the response to serious criminal behavior.

Entry into the system

The justice system does not respond to most crime because so much crime is not discovered or reported to the police. Law enforcement agencies learn about crime from the reports of citizens, from discovery by a police officer in the field, or from investigative and intelligence work.

Once a law enforcement agency has established that a crime has been committed, a suspect must be identified and apprehended for the case to proceed through the system. Sometimes, a suspect is apprehended at the scene; however, identification of a suspect sometimes requires an extensive investigation. Often, no one is identified or apprehended.

Prosecution and pretrial services

After an arrest, law enforcement agencies present information about the case and about the accused to the prosecutor, who will decide if formal charges will be filed with the court. If no charges are filed, the accused must be released. The prosecutor can also drop charges after making efforts to prosecute (nolle prosequi).

A suspect charged with a crime must be taken before a judge or magistrate without unnecessary delay. At the initial appearance, the judge or magistrate informs the accused of the charges and decides whether there is probable cause to detain the accused person. Often, the defense counsel is also assigned at the initial appearance. If the offense is not very serious, the determi-nation of guilt and assessment of a penalty may also occur at this stage.

In some jurisdictions, a pretrial-release decision is made at the initial appearance, but this decision may occur at other hearings or may be changed at another time during the process. Pretrial release and bail were traditionally intended to ensure appearance at trial. However, many jurisdictions permit pretrial detention of defendants accused of serious offenses and deemed to be dangerous to prevent them from committing crimes in the pretrial period. The court may decide to release the accused on his/her own recognizance, into the custody of a third party, on the promise of satisfying certain conditions, or after the posting of a financial bond.

In many jurisdictions, the initial appearance may be followed by a preliminary hearing. The main function of this hearing is to discover if there is probable cause to believe that the accused committed a known crime within the jurisdiction of the court. If the judge does not find probable cause, the case is dismissed; however, if the judge or magistrate finds probable cause for such a belief, or the accused waives his or her right to a preliminary hearing, the case may be bound over to a grand jury.

A grand jury hears evidence against the accused presented by the prosecutor and decides if there is sufficient evidence to cause the accused to be brought to trial. If the grand jury finds sufficient evidence, it submits to the court an indictment (a written statement of the essential facts of the offense charged against the accused). Where the grand jury system is used, the grand jury may also investigate criminal activity generally and issue indictments called grand jury originals that initiate criminal cases.

Misdemeanor cases and some felony cases proceed by the issuance of an information (a formal, written accusation submitted to the court by a prosecutor). In some jurisdictions, indictments may be required in felony cases. However, the accused may choose to waive a grand jury indictment and, instead, accept service of an information for the crime.

Adjudication

Once an indictment or information has been filed with the trial court, the accused is scheduled for arraignment. At the arraignment, the accused is informed of the charges, advised of the

Source: Adapted from *The challenge of crime in a free society.* President's Commission on Law Enforcement and Administration of Justice, 1967.

1. CRIME AND JUSTICE IN AMERICA

rights of criminal defendants, and asked to enter a plea to the charges. Sometimes, a plea of guilty is the result of negotiations between the prosecutor and the defendant, with the defendant entering a guilty plea in expectation of reduced charges or a lenient sentence.

If the accused pleads guilty or pleads *nolo contendere* (accepts penalty without admitting guilt), the judge may accept or reject the plea. If the plea is accepted, no trial is held and the offender is sentenced at this proceeding or at a later date. The plea may be rejected if, for example, the judge believes that the accused may have been coerced. If this occurs, the case may proceed to trial.

If the accused pleads not guilty or not guilty by reason of insanity, a date is set for the trial. A person accused of a serious crime is guaranteed a trial by jury. However, the accused may ask for a bench trial where the judge, rather than a jury, serves as the finder of fact. In both instances the prosecution and defense present evidence by questioning witnesses while the judge decides on issues of law. The trial results in acquittal or conviction on the original charges or on lesser included offenses.

After the trial a defendant may request appellate review of the conviction or sentence. In many criminal cases, appeals of a conviction are a matter of right; all States with the death penalty provide for automatic appeal of cases involving a death sentence. However, under some circumstances and in some jurisdictions, appeals may be subject to the discretion of the appellate court and may be granted only on acceptance of a defendant's petition for a *writ of certiorari*. Prisoners may also appeal their sentences through civil rights petitions and writs of habeas corpus where they claim unlawful detention.

Sentencing and sanctions

After a guilty verdict or guilty plea, sentence is imposed. In most cases the judge decides on the sentence, but in some States, the sentence is decided by the jury, particularly for capital offenses such as murder.

In arriving at an appropriate sentence, a sentencing hearing may be held at which evidence of aggravating or mitigating circumstances will be considered. In assessing the circumstances surrounding a convicted person's criminal behavior, courts often rely on presentence investigations by probation agencies or other designated authorities. Courts may also consider victim impact statements.

The sentencing choices that may be available to judges and juries include one or more of the following:
• the death penalty
• incarceration in a prison, jail, or other confinement facility
• probation—allowing the convicted person to remain at liberty but subject to certain conditions and restrictions
• fines—primarily applied as penalties in minor offenses
• restitution—which requires the offender to provide financial compensation to the victim.

In many States, State law mandates that persons convicted of certain types of offenses serve a prison term.

Most States permit the judge to set the sentence length within certain limits, but some States have determinate sentencing laws that stipulate a specific sentence length, which must be served and cannot be altered by a parole board.

Corrections

Offenders sentenced to incarceration usually serve time in a local jail or a State prison. Offenders sentenced to less than 1 year generally go to jail; those sentenced to more than 1 year go to prison. Persons admitted to a State prison system may be held in prisons with varying levels of custody or in a community correctional facility.

A prisoner may become eligible for parole after serving a specific part of his or her sentence. Parole is the conditional release of a prisoner before the prisoner's full sentence has been served. The decision to grant parole is made by an authority such as a parole board, which has power to grant or revoke parole or to discharge a parolee altogether. The way parole decisions are made varies widely among jurisdictions.

Offenders may also be required to serve out their full sentences prior to release (expiration of term). Those sentenced under determinate sentencing laws can be released only after they have served their full sentence (mandatory release) less any "goodtime" received while in prison. Inmates get such credits against their sentences automatically or by earning it through participation in programs.

If an offender has an outstanding charge or sentence in another State, a detainer is used to ensure that when released from prison he or she will be transferred to the other State.

If released by a parole board decision or by mandatory release, the releasee will be under the supervision of a parole officer in the community for the balance of his or her unexpired sentence. This supervision is governed by specific conditions of release, and the releasee may be returned to prison for violations of such conditions.

The juvenile justice system

The processing of juvenile offenders is not entirely dissimilar to adult criminal processing, but there are crucial differences in the procedures. Many juveniles are referred to juvenile courts by law enforcement officers, but many others are referred by school officials, social services agencies, neighbors, and even parents, for behavior or conditions that are determined to require intervention by the formal system for social control.

When juveniles are referred to the juvenile courts, their *intake* departments, or prosecuting attorneys, determine whether sufficient grounds exist to warrant filing a petition that requests an *adjudicatory hearing* or a request to transfer jurisdiction to criminal court. In some States and at the Federal level prosecutors under certain circumstances may file criminal charges against juveniles directly in criminal courts.

The court with jurisdiction over juvenile matters may reject the petition or the juveniles may be diverted to other agencies or programs in lieu of further court processing. Examples of diversion programs include individual or group counseling or referral to educational and recreational programs.

If a petition for an adjudicatory hearing is accepted, the juvenile may be brought before a court quite unlike the court with jurisdiction over adult offenders. In disposing of cases juvenile courts usually have far more discretion than adult courts. In addition to such options as probation, commitment to correctional institutions, restitution, or fines, State laws grant juvenile courts the power to order removal of children from their homes to foster homes or treatment facilities. Juvenile courts also may order participation in special programs aimed at shoplifting prevention, drug counseling, or driver education. They also may order referral to criminal court for trial as adults.

Despite the considerable discretion associated with juvenile court proceedings, juveniles are afforded many of the due-process safeguards associated with adult criminal trials. Sixteen States permit the use of juries in juvenile courts; however, in light of the U.S. Supreme Court's holding that juries are not essential to juvenile hearings, most States do not make provisions for juries in juvenile courts.

The response to crime is founded in the intergovernmental structure of the United States

Under our form of government, each State and the Federal Government has its own criminal justice system. All systems must respect the rights of individuals set forth in court interpretation of the U.S. Constitution and defined in case law.

State constitutions and laws define the criminal justice system within each State and delegate the authority and responsibility for criminal justice to various jurisdictions, officials, and institutions. State laws also define criminal behavior and groups of children or acts under jurisdiction of the juvenile courts.

Municipalities and counties further define their criminal justice systems through local ordinances that proscribe additional illegal behavior and establish the local agencies responsible for criminal justice processing that were not established by the State.

Congress also has established a criminal justice system at the Federal level to respond to Federal crimes such as bank robbery, kidnaping, and transporting stolen goods across State lines.

The response to crime is mainly a State and local function

Very few crimes are under exclusive Federal jurisdiction. The responsibility to respond to most crime rests with the State and local governments. Police protection is primarily a function of cities and towns. Corrections is primarily a function of State governments. More than three-fifths of all justice personnel are employed at the local level.

	Percent of criminal justice employment by level of government		
	Local	State	Federal
Police	77%	15%	8%
Judicial (courts only)	60	32	8
Prosecution and legal services	58	26	17
Public defense	47	50	3
Corrections	35	61	4
Total	62%	31%	8%

Source: *Justice expenditure and employment, 1985,* BJS Bulletin, March 1987.

Discretion is exercised throughout the criminal justice system

Discretion is "an authority conferred by law to act in certain conditions or situations in accordance with an official's or an official agency's own considered judgment and conscience."[1] Discretion is exercised throughout the government. It is a part of decisionmaking in all government systems from mental health to education, as well as criminal justice.

Concerning crime and justice, legislative bodies have recognized that they cannot anticipate the range of circumstances surrounding each crime, anticipate local mores, and enact laws that clearly encompass all conduct that is criminal and all that is not.[2] Therefore, persons charged with the day-to-day response to crime are expected to exercise their own judgment within *limits* set by law. Basically, they must decide—
• whether to take action

• where the situation fits in the scheme of law, rules, and precedent
• which official response is appropriate.

To ensure that discretion is exercised responsibly, government authority is often delegated to professionals. Professionalism requires a minimum level of training and orientation, which guides officials in making decisions. The professionalism of policing discussed later in this chapter is due largely to the desire to ensure the proper exercise of police discretion.

The limits of discretion vary from State to State and locality to locality. For example, some State judges have wide discretion in the type of sentence they may impose. In recent years other States have sought to limit the judges' discretion in sentencing by passing mandatory sentencing laws that require prison sentences for certain offenses.

Who exercises discretion?

These criminal justice officials...	...must often decide whether or not or how to—
Police	Enforce specific laws Investigate specific crimes Search people, vicinities, buildings Arrest or detain people
Prosecutors	File charges or petitions for adjudication Seek indictments Drop cases Reduce charges
Judges or magistrates	Set bail or conditions for release Accept pleas Determine delinquency Dismiss charges Impose sentence Revoke probation
Correctional officials	Assign to type of correctional facility Award privileges Punish for disciplinary infractions
Paroling authority	Determine date and conditions of parole Revoke parole

1. CRIME AND JUSTICE IN AMERICA

More than one agency has jurisdiction over some criminal events

The response to most criminal actions is usually begun by local police who react to violation of State law. If a suspect is apprehended, he or she is prosecuted locally and may be confined in a local jail or State prison. In such cases, only one agency has jurisdiction at each stage in the process.

However, some criminal events because of their characteristics and location may come under the jurisdiction of more than one agency. For example, such overlapping occurs within States when local police, county sheriffs, and State police are all empowered to enforce State laws on State highways.

Congress has provided for Federal jurisdiction over crimes that—
• materially affect interstate commerce
• occur on Federal land
• involve large and probably interstate criminal organizations or conspiracies
• are offenses of national importance, such as the assassination of the President.[3]

Bank robbery and many drug offenses are examples of crimes for which the States and the Federal Government both have jurisdiction. In cases of dual jurisdiction, an investigation and a prosecution may be undertaken by all authorized agencies, but only one level of government usually pursues a case. For example, a study of FBI bank robbery investigations during 1978 and 1979 found that of those cases cleared—

• 36% were solved by the FBI alone
• 25% were solved by a joint effort of the FBI and State and local police
• 40% were solved by the State and local police acting alone.

In response to dual jurisdiction and to promote more effective coordination, Law Enforcement Coordinating Committees have been established throughout the country and include all relevant Federal and local agencies.

Within States the response to crime also varies from one locality to another

The response differs because of statutory and structural differences and differences in how discretion is exercised. Local criminal justice policies and programs change in response to local attitudes and needs. For example, the prosecutor in one locality may concentrate on particular types of offenses that plague the local community while the prosecutor in another locality may concentrate on career criminals.

The response to crime also varies on a case-by-case basis

No two cases are exactly alike. At each stage of the criminal justice process officials must make decisions that take into account the varying factors of each case. Two similar cases may have very different results because of various factors, including differences in witness cooperation and physical evidence, the availability of resources to investigate

and prosecute the case, the quality of the lawyers involved, and the age and prior criminal history of the suspects.

Differences in local laws, agencies, resources, standards, and procedures result in varying responses in each jurisdiction

The outcomes of arrests for serious cases vary among the States as shown by Offender-based Transaction Statistics from nine States:

	% of arrests for serious crimes that result in...		
	Prose-cution	Convic-tion	Incarcer-ation
Virginia	100%	61%	55%
Nebraska	99	68	39
New York	97	67	31
Utah	97	79	9
Virgin Islands	95	55	35
Minnesota	89	69	48
Pennsylvania	85	56	24
California	78	61	45
Ohio	77	50	21

Source: Disaggregated data used in *Tracking offenders: White-collar crime,* BJS Special Report, November 1986.

Some of this variation can be explained by differences among States. For example, the degree of discretion in deciding whether to prosecute differs from State to State; some States do not allow any police or prosecutor discretion; others allow police discretion but not prosecutor discretion and vice versa.

What is crime?

Crimes are defined by law

In this report we define crime as all behaviors and acts for which a society provides formally sanctioned punishment. In the United States what is criminal is specified in the written law, primarily State statutes. What is included in the definition of crime varies among Federal, State, and local jurisdictions.

Criminologists devote a great deal of attention to defining crime in both general and specific terms. This definitional process is the first step toward the goal of obtaining accurate crime statistics.

To provide additional perspectives on crime it is sometimes viewed in ways other than in the standard legal definitions. Such alternatives define crime in terms of the type of victim (child abuse), the type of offender (white-collar crime), the object of the crime (property crime), or the method of criminal activity (organized crime). Such definitions usually cover one or more of the standard legal definitions. For example, organized crime may include fraud, extortion, assault, or homicide.

What is considered criminal by society changes over time

Some types of events such as murder, robbery, and burglary have been defined as crimes for centuries. Such crimes are part of the common law definition of crime. Other types of conduct traditionally have not been viewed as crimes. As social values and mores change, society has codified some conduct as criminal while decriminalizing other conduct. The recent movement toward increased "criminalization" of drunk driving is an example of such change.

New technology also results in new types of conduct not anticipated by the law. Changes in the law may be needed to define and sanction these types of conduct. For example, the introduction of computers has added to the criminal codes in many States so that acts such as the destruction of programs or data could be defined as crimes.

What are the characteristics of some serious crimes?

Crime	Definition	Facts
Homicide	Causing the death of another person without legal justification or excuse, including UCR crimes of murder and nonnegligent manslaughter and negligent manslaughter.	• Murder and nonnegligent manslaughter occur less often than other violent UCR Index crimes. • 58% of the known murderers were relatives or acquaintances of the victim. • 20% of all murders in 1985 occurred or were suspected to have occurred as the result of some felonious activity.
Rape	Unlawful sexual intercourse with a female, by force or without legal or factual consent.	• Most rapes involve a lone offender and a lone victim. • About 32% of the rapes recorded by NCS in 1985 were committed in or near the victim's home. • 73% of the rapes occurred at night, between 6 p.m. and 6 a.m. • 58% of the victims of rape in 1985 were under 25 years old.
Robbery	The unlawful taking or attempted taking of property that is in the immediate possession of another, by force or threat of force.	• Robbery is the violent crime that most often involves more than one offender (in almost half of all cases in 1985). • About half of all robberies reported by NCS in 1985 involved the use of a weapon.
Assault	Unlawful intentional inflicting, or attempted inflicting, of injury upon the person of another. Aggravated assault is the unlawful intentional inflicting of serious bodily injury or unlawful threat or attempt to inflict bodily injury or death by means of a deadly or dangerous weapon with or without actual infliction of injury. Simple assault is the unlawful intentional inflicting of less than serious bodily injury without a deadly or dangerous weapon or an attempt or threat to inflict bodily injury without a deadly or dangerous weapon.	• Simple assault occurs more frequently than aggravated assault. • Most assaults involve one victim and one offender.

(continued on next page)

What are some other common crimes in the United States?

Drug abuse violations—Offenses relating to growing, manufacturing, making, possessing, using, selling, or distributing narcotic and dangerous nonnarcotic drugs. A distinction is made between possession and sale/manufacturing.

Sex offenses—In current statistical usage, the name of a broad category of varying content, usually consisting of all offenses having a sexual element except for forcible rape and commercial sex offenses, which are defined separately.

Fraud offenses—The crime type comprising offenses sharing the elements of practice of deceit or intentional misrepresentation of fact, with the intent of unlawfully depriving a person of his or her property or legal rights.

Drunkenness—Public intoxication, except "driving under the influence."

Disturbing the peace—Unlawful interruption of the peace, quiet, or order of a community, including offenses called "disorderly conduct," "vagrancy," "loitering," "unlawful assembly," and "riot."

Driving under the influence—Driving or operating any vehicle or common carrier while drunk or under the influence of liquor or drugs.

From *Report to the Nation on Crime and Justice,* Bureau of Justice Statistics, U.S. Department of Justice, March 1988, pp. 2-3, 8-9.

1. CRIME AND JUSTICE IN AMERICA

Liquor law offenses—State or local liquor law violations, except drunkenness and driving under the influence. Federal violations are excluded.

Gambling—Unlawful staking or wagering of money or other thing of value on a game of chance or on an uncertain event.

Kidnaping—Transportation or confinement of a person without authority of law and without his or her consent, or without the consent of his or her guardian, if a minor.

Vandalism—Destroying or damaging, or attempting to destroy or damage, the property of another without his or her consent, or public property, except by burning, which is arson.

Public order offenses—Violations of the peace or order of the community or threats to the public health through unacceptable public conduct, interference with governmental authority, or violation of civil rights or liberties.

Weapons offenses, bribery, escape, and tax law violations, for example, are included in this category.

How do violent crimes differ from property crimes?

The outcome of a criminal event determines if it is a property crime or a violent crime. Violent crime refers to events such as homicide, rape, and assault that may result in injury to a person. Robbery is also considered a violent crime because it involves the use or threat of force against a person.

Property crimes are unlawful acts with the intent of gaining property but which do not involve the use or threat of force against an individual. Larceny and motor vehicle theft are examples of property crimes.

In the National Crime Survey a distinction is also made between crimes against persons (violent crimes and personal larceny) and crimes against

households (property crimes, including household larceny).

How do felonies differ from misdemeanors?

Criminal offenses are also classified according to how they are handled by the criminal justice system. Most jurisdictions recognize two classes of offenses: felonies and misdemeanors.

Felonies are not distinguished from misdemeanors in the same way in all jurisdictions, but most States define felonies as offenses punishable by a year or more in a State prison. The most serious crimes are never "misdemeanors" and the most minor offenses are never "felonies."

What is organized crime?

Although organized crime has been considered a problem throughout the century, no universally accepted definition of the term has been established. The President's Commission on Organized Crime, for example, defines the criminal group involved in organized crime as "a continuing, structured collectivity of persons who utilize criminality, violence, and a willingness to corrupt in order to gain and maintain power and profit."

Some characteristics of organized crime are generally cited:
- **Organizational continuity:** Organized crime groups ensure that they can survive the death or imprisonment of their leaders and can vary the nature of their activities to take advantage of changing criminal opportunities.
- **Hierarchical structure:** All organized crime groups are headed by a single leader and structured into a series of subordinate ranks, although they may vary in the rigidity of their hierarchy. Nationwide organizations may be composed of multiple separate chapters or "families," each unit generally headed by its own leader who is supported by the group's hierarchy of command. Intergroup disputes, joint ventures, and new membership are generally reviewed by a board composed of the leaders of the most powerful individual chapters. For example, La Cosa Nostra currently is estimated to include 24 individual "families" all under the general authority of a "National Commission" comprised of an estimated nine bosses.
- **Restricted membership:** Members must be formally accepted by the group after a demonstration of loyalty and a willingness to commit criminal acts. Membership may be limited by race or common background and generally

What are the characteristics of some serious crimes?

Crime	Definition	Facts
Burglary	Unlawful entry of any fixed structure, vehicle, or vessel used for regular residence, industry, or business, with or without force, with the intent to commit a felony or larceny.	• Residential property was targeted in 2 out of every 3 reported burglaries; nonresidential property accounted for the remaining third. • In 1985, 42% of all residential burglaries occurred without forced entry. • About 37% of the no-force burglaries were known to have occurred during the day between 6 a.m. and 6 p.m.
Larceny-theft	Unlawful taking or attempted taking of property other than a motor vehicle from the possession of another, by stealth, without force and without deceit, with intent to permanently deprive the owner of the property.	• Less than 5% of all personal larcenies involve contact between the victim and offender. • Pocket picking and purse snatching most frequently occur inside nonresidential buildings or on street locations. • Unlike most other crimes, pocket picking and purse snatching affect the elderly about as much as other age groups.
Motor vehicle theft	Unlawful taking or attempted taking of a self-propelled road vehicle owned by another, with the intent of depriving him or her of it, permanently or temporarily.	• Motor vehicle theft is relatively well reported to the police. In 1985 89% of all completed thefts were reported. • The stolen property is more likely to be recovered in this crime than in other property crimes.
Arson	The intentional damaging or destruction or attempted damaging or destruction by means of fire or explosion of property without the consent of the owner, or of one's own property or that of another by fire or explosives with or without the intent to defraud.	• Single-family residences were the most frequent targets of arson. • 16% of all structures where arson occurred were not in use.

Sources: BJS *Dictionary of criminal justice data terminology*, 2nd edition, 1981. BJS *Criminal victimization in the U.S.*, 1985. FBI *Crime in the United States 1985*.

Organized crime includes many traditional crimes as well as offenses such as racketeering

involves a lifetime commitment to the group, which can be enforced through violent group actions.

• **Criminality/violence/power:** Power and control are key organized crime goals and may be obtained through criminal activity of one type or in multiple activities. Criminal activity may be designed directly to generate "income" or to support the group's power through bribery, violence, and intimidation. Violence is used to maintain group loyalty and to intimidate outsiders and is a threat underlying all group activity. Specific violent criminal acts include, for example, murder, kidnaping, arson, robbery, and bombings.

• **Legitimate business involvement:** Legitimate businesses are used to "launder" illegal funds or stolen merchandise. For example, illegal profits from drug sales can be claimed as legitimate profits of a noncriminal business whose accounting records have been appropriately adjusted. Legitimate business involvement also elevates the social status of organized crime figures.

• **Use of specialists:** Outside specialists, such as pilots, chemists, and arsonists, provide services under contract to organized crime groups on an intermittent or regular basis.

Organized crime groups often are protected by corrupt officials in the government and private sector

Such officials include inspectors who overlook violations, accountants who conceal assets, financial officers who fail to report major cash transactions, law enforcement officers who provide enforcement activity information to drug traffickers, and attorneys who have government witnesses intimidated to change their testimony. The public also supports organized crime by sometimes knowingly or unknowingly purchasing illegal goods and "hot" merchandise.

Organized crime groups are involved in many different activities

In addition to its well known involvement in illegal drugs, organized crime is also involved in prostitution, gambling, and loan sharking operations and has been shown to have infiltrated legitimate industries such as construction, waste removal, wholesale and retail distribution of goods, hotel and restaurant operations, liquor sales, motor vehicle repairs, real estate, and banking.

How much does organized crime cost?

A recent survey for the President's Commission on Organized Crime estimates that 1986 net income from organized crime activity ranged between $26.8 billion (a low estimate) and $67.7 billion (the high estimate).

The indirect costs of organized crime affect all consumers through increased consumer prices. Kickbacks, protection payments, increased labor and material costs, and lack of competition in industries controlled by organized crime all increase consumer costs. Unpaid taxes on illegal activities result in higher tax burdens for legal wage earners.

Racketeer Influenced and Corrupt Organization (RICO) statutes are key tools in the fight against organized crime

The Federal RICO statute was enacted in 1970 and was amended most recently in 1986. Unlike other existing statutes that address individual criminal acts such as murder or robbery, the RICO statute was specifically designed to target the overall and continuing operations of organized crime organizations. Specifically, the act prohibits the use of racketeering activities or profits to acquire, conduct, or maintain the business of an existing organization or "enterprise." Racketeering activities are defined to include any act or threat involving murder, kidnaping, gambling, arson, robbery, bribery, extortion, dealing in narcotic or dangerous drugs, fraud, and other crimes. The act also provides for forfeiture of illegally obtained gains and interests in enterprises.

Twenty-three States had enacted RICO statutes by 1986. Most of them are very similar to the Federal statute.

The government also has other tools to fight organized crime, including witness protection programs, electronic surveillance procedures, and immunity statutes.

There is much debate about how to define "white-collar" crime

Reiss and Biderman define it as violations of law "that involve the use of a violator's position of significant power, influence or trust . . . for the purpose of illegal gain, or to commit an illegal act for personal or organizational gain." Another researcher, Sutherland, defines white-collar crime as "a crime committed by a person of respectability and high social status in the course of his occupation." Edelhertz defines it as "an illegal act or series of illegal acts committed by nonphysical means and by concealment or guile to obtain money or property, to avoid the payment or loss of money or property, or to obtain business or personal advantage."

Although specific definitions vary, the term is generally construed to include business-related crimes, abuse of political office, some (but not all) aspects of organized crime, and the newly emerging areas of high-technology crime. White-collar crimes often involve deception of a gullible victim and generally occur where an individual's job, power, or personal influence provide the access and opportunity to abuse lawful procedures for unlawful gain.

Specific white-collar crimes include embezzlement, bribery, fraud (including procurement fraud, stock fraud, fraud in government programs, and investment and other "schemes"), theft of services, theft of trade secrets, tax evasion, and obstruction of justice.

Unlike violent crimes, white-collar crimes do not necessarily cause injury to identifiable persons

White-collar crime instead can cause loss to society in general as in cases of tax evasion, for example. For this reason, white-collar crimes, unlike violent crimes, may not always be detected and are more difficult to investigate.

Little data are available on the extent of white-collar crime

Measuring white-collar crime presents special problems:

• **No uniform definitions** exist that define either the overall scope of white-collar crime or individual criminal acts.

• **Wide variations** in commercial recordkeeping procedures make it difficult to collect and classify data on the loss.

• **Uncertainty over the legal status** of financial and technical transactions complicates the classification of data.

White-collar crime refers to a group of nonviolent crimes that generally involve deception or abuse of power

• **Computer technology** can conceal losses resulting from computer crimes.
• **Crimes may not be reported** to protect consumer confidence.

Almost three-fourths of the white-collar crimes prosecuted at the State level resulted in convictions

A study of 8 States and the Virgin Islands found that 12% of the white-collar crime cases that originated with an arrest and for which dispositions were reported in 1983 were not prosecuted. The study defined white-

collar crimes as forgery/counterfeiting, fraud, and embezzlement.

Prosecution rates for white-collar crimes were similar to those for violent crimes (murder, rape, robbery, kidnaping, and assault), property crimes (stolen vehicles, burglary, and arson), and public order crimes (drug and weapons offenses and commercial vice). Because the study focused on white-collar crime cases that were reported through the criminal justice system, the sample does not take into account the large number of white-collar crimes that were not discovered, not reported to authorities, or did not result in an arrest.

The study also found the conviction rate for cases prosecuted to be about 74%, slightly higher than for violent crimes (66%) and public order crimes (67%) and about the same as for property crimes (76%).

About 60% of the persons convicted for white-collar crime vs. about 67% of those convicted for violent crimes were sentenced to prison. Eighteen percent of white-collar offenders sentenced to prison were sentenced to more than 1 year (about the same as persons convicted of public order offense) vs. 39% of violent offenders.

ARE CRIMINALS MADE OR BORN?

Evidence indicates that both biological and sociological factors play roles.

**Richard J. Herrnstein and
James Q. Wilson**

*Richard J. Herrnstein is a professor of psychology
and James Q. Wilson a professor of government at
Harvard.*

A revolution in our under-standing of crime is quietly over-throwing some established doctrines. Until recently, criminologists looked for the causes of crime almost entirely in the offenders' social cir-cumstances. There seemed to be no shortage of circumstances to blame: weakened, chaotic or broken families, ineffective schools, antisocial gangs, racism, poverty, unemployment. Criminologists took seriously, more so than many other students of social behavior, the famous dictum of the French sociologist Emile Durkheim: Social facts must have social ex-planations. The sociological theory of crime had the unques-tioned support of prominent editorialists, commentators, politicians and most thoughtful people.

Today, many learned journals and scholarly works draw a dif-ferent picture. Sociological fac-tors have not been abandoned, but increasingly it is becoming clear to many scholars that crime is the outcome of an interaction between social factors and cer-tain biological factors, par-ticularly for the offenders who, by repeated crimes, have made public places dangerous. The idea is still controversial, but in-creasingly, to the old question "Are criminals born or made?" the answer seems to be: both. The causes of crime lie in a com-bination of predisposing bio-logical traits channeled by social circumstance into criminal be-havior. The traits alone do not inevitably lead to crime; the cir-cumstances do not make crim-inals of everyone; but together they create a population respon-sible for a large fraction of America's problem of crime in the streets.

Evidence that criminal behavior has deeper roots than social circumstances has always been right at hand, but social science has, until recent years, overlooked its implications. As far as the records show, crime everywhere and throughout history is disproportionately a young man's pursuit. Whether men are 20 or more times as likely to be arrested as women, as is the case in Malawi or Brunei, or only four to six times as likely, as in the United States or France, the sex difference in crime statistics is universal. Similarly, 18-year-olds may sometimes be four times as likely to be criminal as 40-year-olds, while at other times only twice as likely. In the United States, more than half of all arrests for serious property crimes are of 20-year-olds or younger. No-where have older persons been as criminal as younger ones.

It is easy to imagine purely social explanations for the effects of age and sex on crime. Boys in many societies are trained by their parents and the society itself to play more roughly and aggressively than girls. Boys are expected to fight back, not to cry,

Intelligence and temperament have heritable bases and influence behavior.

and to play to win. Likewise, boys in many cultures are denied adult responsibilities, kept in a state of prolonged dependence and confined too long in schools that many of them find unrewarding. For a long time, these factors were thought to be the whole story.

Ultimately, however, the very universality of the age and sex differences in crime have alerted some social scientists to the implausibility of a theory that does not look beyond the accidents of particular societies. If cultures as different as Japan's and Sweden's, England's and Mexico's, have sex and age differences in crime, then perhaps we should have suspected from the start that there was something more fundamental going on than parents happening to decide to raise their boys and girls differently. What is it about boys, girls and their parents, in societies of all sorts, that leads them to emphasize, rather than overcome, sex differences? Moreover, even if we believed that every society has arbitrarily decided to inculcate aggressiveness in males, there would still be the greater criminality among *young* males to explain. After all, in some cultures, young boys are not denied adult responsibilities but are kept out of school, put to work tilling the land and made to accept obligations to the society.

But it is no longer necessary to approach questions about the sources of criminal behavior merely with argument and supposition. There is evidence. Much crime, it is agreed, has an aggressive component, and Eleanor Emmons Maccoby, a professor of psychology at Stanford University, and Carol Nagy Jacklin, a psychologist now at the University of Southern California, after reviewing the evidence on sex differences in aggression, concluded that it has a foundation that is at least in part biological. Only that conclusion can be drawn, they said, from data that show that the average man is more aggressive than the average woman in all known

societies, that the sex difference is present in infancy well before evidence of sex-role socialization by adults, that similar sex differences turn up in many of our biological relatives—monkeys and apes. Human aggression has been directly tied to sex hormones, particularly male sex hormones, in experiments on athletes engaging in competitive sports and on prisoners known for violent or domineering behavior. No single line of evidence is decisive and each can be challenged, but all together they convinced Drs. Maccoby and Jacklin, as well as most specialists on the biology of sex differences, that the sexual conventions that assign males the aggressive roles have biological roots.

That is also the conclusion of most researchers about the developmental forces that make adolescence and young adulthood a time of risk for criminal and other nonconventional behavior. This is when powerful new drives awaken, leading to frustrations that foster behavior unchecked by the internalized prohibitions of adulthood. The result is usually just youthful rowdiness, but, in a minority of cases, it passes over the line into crime.

The most compelling evidence of biological factors for criminality comes from two studies—one of twins, the other of adopted boys. Since the 1920's it has been understood that twins may develop from a single fertilized egg, resulting in identical genetic endowments—identical twins—or from a pair of separately fertilized eggs that have about half their genes in common—fraternal twins. A standard procedure for estimating how important genes are to a trait is to compare the similarity between identical twins with that between fraternal twins. When identical twins are clearly more similar in a trait than fraternal twins, the trait probably has high heritability.

There have been about a dozen studies of criminality using twins. More than 1,500 pairs of twins have been studied in the

United States, the Scandinavian countries, Japan, West Germany, Britain and elsewhere, and the result is qualitatively the same everywhere. Identical twins are more likely to have similar criminal records than fraternal twins. For example, the late Karl O. Christiansen, a Danish criminologist, using the Danish Twin Register, searched police, court and prison records for entries regarding twins born in a certain region of Denmark between 1881 and 1910. When an identical twin had a criminal record, Christiansen found, his or her co-twin was more than twice as likely to have one also than when a fraternal twin had a criminal record.

In the United States, a similar result has recently been reported by David Rowe, a psychologist at the University of Oklahoma, using questionnaires instead of official records to measure criminality. Twins in high school in almost all the school districts of Ohio received questionnaires by mail, with a promise of confidentiality as well as a small payment if the questionnaires were filled out and returned. The twins were asked about their activities, including their delinquent behavior, about their friends and about their co-twins. The identical twins were more similar in delinquency than the fraternal twins. In addition, the twins who shared more activities with each other were no more likely to be similar in delinquency than those who shared fewer activities.

No single method of inquiry should be regarded as conclusive. But essentially the same results are found in studies of adopted children. The idea behind such studies is to find a sample of children adopted early in life, cases in which the criminal histories of both adopting and biological parents are known. Then, as the children grow up, researchers can discover how predictive of their criminality are the family histories of their adopting and biological parents. Recent studies show that the biological family his-

tory contributes substantially to the adoptees' likelihood of breaking the law.

For example, Sarnoff Mednick, a psychologist at the University of Southern California, and his associates in the United States and Denmark have followed a sample of several thousand boys adopted in Denmark between 1927 and 1947. Boys with criminal biological parents and noncriminal adopting parents were more likely to have criminal records than those with noncriminal biological parents and criminal adopting parents. The more criminal convictions a boy's natural parents had, the greater the risk of criminality for boys being raised by adopting parents who had no records. The risk was unrelated to whether the boy or his adopting parents knew about the natural parents' criminal records, whether the natural parents committed their crimes before or after the boy was given up for adoption, or whether the boy was adopted immediately after birth or a year or two later. The results of this study have been confirmed in Swedish and American samples of adopted children.

Because of studies like these, many sociologists and criminologists now accept the existence of genetic factors contributing to criminality. When there is disagreement, it is about how large the genetic contribution to crime is and about how the criminality of biological parents is transmitted to their children.

Both the twin and adoption studies show that genetic contributions are not alone responsible for crime — there is, for example, some increase in criminality among boys if their adopted fathers are criminal even when their biological parents are not, and not every co-twin of a criminal identical twin becomes criminal himself. Although it appears, on average, to be substantial, the precise size of the genetic contribution to crime is probably unknowable, particularly since the measures of criminality itself are now so crude.

We have a bit more to go on with respect to the link that transmits a predisposition toward crime from parents to children. No one believes there are "crime genes," but there are two major attributes that have, to some degree, a heritable base and that appear to influence criminal behavior. These are intelligence and temperament. Hundreds of studies have found that the more genes people share, the more likely they are to resemble each other intellectually and temperamentally.

Starting with studies in the 1930's, the average offender in broad samples has consistently scored 91 to 93 on I.Q. tests for which the general population's average is 100. The typical offender does worse on the verbal items of intelligence tests than on the nonverbal items but is usually below average on both.

Criminologists have long known about the correlation between criminal behavior and I.Q., but many of them have discounted it for various reasons. Some have suggested that the correlation can be explained away by the association between low socioeconomic status and crime, on the one hand, and that between low I.Q. and low socioeconomic status, on the other. These criminologists say it is low socioeconomic status, rather than low I.Q., that fosters crime. Others have questioned whether I.Q. tests really measure intelligence for the populations that are at greater risk for breaking the law. The low scores of offenders, the argument goes, betray a culturally deprived background or alienation from our society's values rather than low intelligence. Finally, it is often noted that the offenders in some studies have been caught for their crimes. Perhaps the ones who got away have higher I.Q.s.

But these objections have proved to be less telling than they once seemed to be. There are, for example, many poor law-abiding people living in deprived environments, and one of their more salient characteristics is that they have higher I.Q. scores than those in the same environment who break the law.

Then, too, it is a common misconception that I.Q. tests are invalid for people from disadvantaged backgrounds. If what is implied by this criticism is that scores predict academic potential or job performance differently for different groups, then the criticism is wrong. A comprehensive recent survey sponsored by the National Academy of Sciences concluded that "tests predict about as well for one group as for another." And that some highly intelligent criminals may well be good at eluding capture is fully consistent with the belief that offenders, in general, have lower scores than nonoffenders.

If I.Q. and criminality are linked, what may explain the link? There are several possibilities. One is that low scores on I.Q. tests signify greater difficulty in grasping the likely consequences of action or in learning the meaning and significance of moral codes. Another is that low scores, especially on the verbal component of the tests, mean trouble in school, which leads to frustration, thence to resentment, anger and delinquency. Still another is that persons who are not as skillful as others in expressing themselves verbally may find it more rewarding to express themselves in ways in which they will do better, such as physical threat or force.

For some repeat offenders, the predisposition to criminality may be more a matter of temperament than intelligence. Impulsiveness, insensitivity to social mores, a lack of deep and enduring emotional attachments to others and an appetite for danger are among the temperamental characteristics of high-rate offenders. Temperament

is, to a degree, heritable, though not as much so as intelligence. All parents know that their children, shortly after birth, begin to exhibit certain characteristic ways of behaving — they are placid or fussy, shy or bold. Some of the traits endure, among them aggressiveness and hyperactivity, although they change in form as the child develops. As the child grows up, these traits, among others, may gradually unfold into a disposition toward unconventional, defiant or antisocial behavior.

Lee Robins, a sociologist at Washington University School of Medicine in St. Louis, reconstructed 30 years of the lives of more than 500 children who were patients in the 1920's at a child guidance clinic in St. Louis. She was interested in the early precursors of chronic sociopathy, a condition of antisocial personality that often includes criminal behavior as one of its symptoms. Adult sociopaths in her sample who did not suffer from psychosis, mental retardation or addiction, were, without exception, antisocial before they were 18. More than half of the male sociopaths had serious symptoms before they were 11. The main childhood precursors were truancy, poor school performance, theft, running away, recklessness, slovenliness, impulsiveness and guiltlessness. The more symptoms in childhood, the greater the risk of sociopathy in adulthood.

Other studies confirm and extend Dr. Robins's conclusions. For example, two psychologists, John J. Conger of the University of Colorado and Wilbur Miller of Drake University in Des Moines, searching back over the histories of a sample of delinquent boys in Denver, found that "by the end of the third grade, future delinquents were already seen by their teachers as more poorly adapted than their classmates. They appeared to have less regard for the rights and feelings of their peers; less awareness of the

need to accept responsibility for their obligations, both as individuals and as members of a group, and poorer attitudes toward authority."

Traits that foreshadow serious, recurrent criminal behavior have been traced all the way back to behavior patterns such as hyperactivity and unusual fussiness, and neurological signs such as atypical brain waves or reflexes. In at least a minority of cases, these are detectable in the first few years of life. Some of the characteristics are sex-linked. There is evidence that newborn females are more likely than newborn males to smile, to cling to their mothers, to be receptive to touching and talking, to be sensitive to certain stimuli, such as being touched by a cloth, and to have less upper-body strength. Mothers certainly treat girls and boys differently, but the differences are not simply a matter of the mother's choice — female babies are more responsive than male babies to precisely the kind of treatment that is regarded as "feminine." When adults are asked to play with infants, they play with them in ways they think are appropriate to the infants' sexes. But there is also some evidence that when the sex of the infant is concealed, the behavior of the adults is influenced by the conduct of the child.

Premature infants or those born with low birth weights have a special problem. These children are vulnerable to any adverse circumstances in their environment — including child abuse — that may foster crime. Although nurturing parents can compensate for adversity, cold or inconsistent parents may exacerbate it. Prematurity and low birth weight may result from poor prenatal care, a bad diet or excessive use of alcohol or drugs. Whether the bad care is due to poverty, ignorance or anything else, here we see criminality arising from biological, though not necessarily genetic, factors. It is now known that these babies are more likely than normal babies to be the victims of child abuse.

We do not mean to blame child abuse on the victim by saying that premature and low-birth-weight infants are more difficult to care for and thus place a great strain on the parents. But unless parents are emotionally prepared for the task of caring for such children, they may vent their frustration at the infant's unresponsiveness by hitting or neglecting it. Whatever it is in parent and child that leads to prematurity or low birth weight is compounded by the subsequent interaction between them. Similarly, children with low I.Q.s may have difficulty in understanding rules, but if their parents also have poor verbal skills, they may have difficulty in communicating rules, and so each party to the conflict exacerbates the defects of the other.

THE STATEMENT that biology plays a role in explaining human behavior, especially criminal behavior, sometimes elicits a powerful political or ideological reaction. Fearful that what is being proposed is a crude biological determinism, some critics deny the evidence while others wish the evidence to be confined to scientific journals. Scientists who have merely proposed studying the possible effects of chromosomal abnormalities on behavior have been ruthlessly attacked by other scientists, as have those who have made public the voluminous data showing the heritability of intelligence and temperament.

Some people worry that any claim that biological factors influence criminality is tantamount to saying that the higher crime rate of black compared to white Amer-

icans has a genetic basis. But no responsible work in the field leads to any such conclusion. The data show that of all the reasons people vary in their crime rates, race is far less important than age, sex, intelligence and the other individual factors that vary within races. Any study of the causes of crime must therefore first consider the individual factors. Differences among races may have many explanations, most of them having nothing to do with biology.

The intense reaction to the study of biological factors in crime, we believe, is utterly misguided. In fact, these discoveries, far from implying that "criminals are born" and should be locked up forever, suggest new and imaginative ways of reducing criminality by benign treatment. The opportunity we have is precisely analogous to that which we had when the biological bases of other disorders were established. Mental as well as physical illness — alcoholism, learning disabilities of various sorts, and perhaps even susceptibilities to drug addiction — now seem to have genetic components. In each case, new understanding energized the search for treatment and gave it new direction. Now we know that many forms of depression can be successfully treated with drugs; in time we may learn the same of Alzheimer's disease. Alcoholics are helped when they understand that some persons, because of their predisposition toward addiction to alcohol, should probably never consume it at all. A chemical treatment of the predisposition is a realistic possibility. Certain types of slow learners can already be helped by special programs. In time, others will be also.

Crime, admittedly, may be a more difficult program. So many different acts are criminal that it is only with considerable poetic license that we can speak of "criminality" at all. The bank teller who embezzles $500 to pay off a gambling debt is not engaging in the same behavior as a person who takes $500 from a liquor store at the point of a gun or one who causes $500 worth of damage by drunkenly driving his car into a parked vehicle. Moreover, crime, unlike alcoholism or dyslexia, exposes a person to the formal condemnation of society and the possibility of imprisonment. We naturally and rightly worry about treating all "criminals" alike, or stigmatizing persons whom we think might become criminal by placing them in special programs designed to prevent criminality.

But these problems are not insurmountable barriers to better ways of thinking about crime prevention. Though criminals are of all sorts, we know that a very small fraction of all young males commit so large a fraction of serious street crime that we can properly blame these chronic offenders for most such crime. We also know that chronic offenders typically begin their misconduct at an early age. Early family and preschool programs may be far better repositories for the crime-prevention dollar than rehabilitation programs aimed — usually futilely — at the 19- or 20-year-old veteran offender. Prevention programs risk stigmatizing children, but this may be less of a risk than is neglect. If stigma were a problem to be avoided at all costs, we would have to dismantle most special-needs education programs.

Having said all this, we must acknowledge that there

is at present little hard evidence that we know how to inhibit the development of delinquent tendencies in children. There are some leads, such as family training programs of the sort pioneered at the Oregon Social Learning Center, where parents are taught how to use small rewards and penalties to alter the behavior of misbehaving children. There is also evidence from David Weikart and Lawrence Schweinhart of the High/Scope Educational Research Foundation at Ypsilanti, Mich., that preschool education programs akin to Project Head Start may reduce later deliquency. There is nothing yet to build a national policy on, but there are ideas worth exploring by carefully repeating and refining these pioneering experimental efforts.

Above all, there is a case for redirecting research into the causes of crime in ways that take into account the interaction of biological and social factors. Some scholars, such as the criminologist Marvin E. Wolfgang and his colleagues at the University of Pennsylvania, are already exploring these issues by analyzing social and biological information from large groups as they age from infancy to adulthood and linking the data to criminal behavior. But much more needs to be done.

It took years of patiently following the life histories of many men and women to establish the linkages between smoking or diet and disease; it will also take years to unravel the complex and subtle ways in which intelligence, temperament, hormonal levels and other traits combine with family circumstances and later experiences in school and elsewhere to produce human character.

Crime's Impact on Blacks Makes for a Bleak Picture

The future for America's young blacks is increasingly bleak, according to the picture painted by several recent reports on everything from life expectancy to incarceration rates.

Among the barrage of sobering statistics are these:

• In some areas, a young black man faces a greater chance of dying from homicide than a U.S. soldier in Vietnam faced of being killed during his tour of duty.

• More than half of all murder victims in the United States in 1989 were black.

• Black babies born in 1988 have a life expectancy of just 69.2 years, compared to 75.6 years for white people.

• The incarceration rate for black males in the United States is four times that of South Africa.

Taken together, the statistics represent a staggering challenge for this country's social services. In particular, black-on-black violence is a growing problem for the law enforcement community.

Just how quickly that violence is increasing is demonstrated by a study from the Federal Centers for Disease Control. That study found the homicide rate for black men between the ages of 15 and 24 rose 66 percent from 1984 to 1988.

One in a thousand young black males died in a homicide in 1988, a rate six times that of the rest of the population.

More than 95 percent of the increase in black homicides was found to be due to the rate at which young black men were killed by guns, and the death rate among young males was ris-ing fastest for those 15 to 19 years old.

Homicide rates for blacks increased most dramatically in Florida, which saw an 88 percent jump from 1984 to 1987; New York, 84 percent; Michigan, 78 percent; California, 71 percent; the District of Columbia, 40 percent; and Missouri, 22 percent.

"Violence has become a way of life," said Charles Norman, who works with Los Angeles gangs. "Homicide has gotten to the point where it's almost a recreation."

Social, Economic Causes

The report said several factors have contributed to the dramatic increases nationwide, including easy access to firearms, drug trafficking, alcohol and drug abuse, poverty, racial discrimination and cultural acceptance of violent behavior.

Other studies and criminal justice experts cited similar causes for the crime and violence reflected by the statistics.

Authorities responded to reports that for the first time more blacks than whites were murdered in 1989 by pointing out that crackdowns on drug dealers often result in turf wars fought out on inner-city streets, leading to an atmosphere in which violence becomes accepted.

Los Angeles County Sheriff Sherman Block said, "What troubles me is the apparent tolerance of violence that we have developed in this community." He said reporters don't respond to reports of violence if they think it is a "routine murder."

"There doesn't seem to be the level of outrage I think there should be at these events," he said.

Black Imprisonment

The statistics show that blacks are both the victims and the perpetrators of violent crime in disproportionate numbers. A review of international incarceration rates by the Sentencing Project found that 455,000 of the 1 million prison and jail inmates in the U.S. are black. It also reported that for every 100,000 black males in the country, 3,109 are imprisoned, compared to 729 in South Africa.

A report by USA Today also found that while 41 percent of those arrested on drug charges in 1989 were black, just 15 percent of the drug-using population is black.

Several experts said the disproportionate numbers of blacks in prison are due to factors such as social and economic problems, as well as increased police presence in high crime areas such as inner cities.

Representative John Conyers of Michigan said, "We can build all the jails we think we need and slam the doors down on thousands of people, but it won't make a bit of difference until we address the fundamental causes of crime."

Barry Krisberg of the National Council on Crime and Delinquency said the high rate of crime in black neighborhoods isn't surprising. "Any group of people exposed to [this] social stress would manifest high rates of interpersonal violence."

Marc Mauer, author of the Sentencing Project report, said the high arrest rates for black men is a result of the war against drugs. "The actual impact of our drug-war policy has been to lock up young black men," he said.

From *Law Enforcement News*, February 14, 1991, pp. 1, 9. *Law Enforcement News*, a publication of John Jay College of Criminal Justice, CUNY.

His study recommended more research into the root causes of crime, repealing mandatory sentencing laws and expanding alternatives to prison terms, as well as shifting more funds from enforcement efforts to prevention and treatment.

Dr. Robert Froehlke, principal author of the Federal Centers for Disease Control report, urged major efforts to curb the skyrocketing homicide rates for blacks by addressing the issue of access to firearms. While homicide is not a "disease in the classic sense," he said it is ravaging the black community.

"If there were a disease that was causing 40 percent of deaths in a group that should be at the peak of physical health and if there were a substantial increase in the rate of deaths in that disease caused by a particular agent almost all the time, there would be substantial public health and other agency efforts in trying to address it."

Froehlke's study indicates the problems continue to grow. While his report analyzed figures through 1987, he said FBI figures through the first half of 1990 show further increases.

Police Lieut. Arthur Carroll of Richmond, Va., said police in cities like his, which set a new record for homicides in 1990, know the worst is yet to come. "It's like in Saudi Arabia. We're sitting there and we almost, almost know what's going to happen."

The high cost of crime

Although states have spent millions to rid their streets of crime, the criminal justice system remains overcrowded and severely underfinanced.

Kevin P. Morison

Kevin P. Morison is public information officer for the Illinois Criminal Justice Information Authority. The Illinois authority has released a major report [1990] focusing on criminal justice financing,. For more information on the report, Trends and Issues 90: Criminal and Juvenial Justice in Illinois, *contact the Illinois Criminal Justice Information Authority, 120 S. Riverside Plaza, Chicago, IL 60606 or call (312) 793-8550.*

As state and local governments throughout the country redouble their efforts against illegal drugs and drug-related crime, many find themselves in the same situation: they are devoting more of their resources to criminal justice, but are finding it almost impossible to keep up with escalating demands.

In Illinois, state and local government spending on criminal justice rose 15 percent faster than the rate of inflation between 1978 and 1988.

But during the same period, reports of serious crime in the state increased 20 percent, felony case filings shot up 59 percent and the prison population nearly doubled. Drug arrests alone soared 93 percent among adults.

"The bottom line, in Illinois and throughout the country, is that resources for criminal justice aren't keeping pace with the system's needs," said J. David Coldren, executive director of the Illinois Criminal Justice Information Authority.

"Spending on practically every component of the criminal justice system is up, even after you account for inflation. The problem is that workloads are up even more," Coldren said.

According to the Bureau of Justice Statistics, federal, state and local governments spent $61 billion on criminal and civil justice in 1988. That's about 40 percent more than they spent in 1979 when measured in inflation-adjusted dollars. And unlike the trend of the early 1980s, increases in justice spending since 1985 have exceeded increases in total spending on all government activities.

But while overall spending on criminal justice is up, much of the new money is going to the back end of the system, to prisons and jails. Per capita spending on corrections in the United States increased 65

Spending on prison construction is on the rise across the United States. Shown is the Western Illinois Correctional Center in Mt. Sterling, Ill.
Photo courtesy of the Illinois Department of Corrections

percent in constant dollars between 1979 and 1988, compared with increases of 34 percent for legal services and prosecution, 34 percent for public defense and 17 percent for the courts.

G. Albert Howenstein, executive director of California's Office of Criminal Justice Planning, said there are reasons why spending on prison construction has soared in the last decade and why increased spending on prison operations has followed.

Incarceration wasn't the predominant answer to crime problems in the 1960s and 1970s, and there weren't a lot of facilities built, Howenstein said. "But as crime continued to grow, as violence continued to grow, and there was an incarcerative response, then there was a necessity to build," he said.

"Of course, building prisons is extremely expensive. And when you build them, you must staff them, and that's extremely expensive," Howenstein said.

But even with the construction boom — more than 300,000 bed spaces were added to the state and federal prison systems during the 1980s — there still isn't enough room in most states to handle the influx of inmates, many of whom are staying in prison longer under tougher determinate sentencing laws enacted over the last 15 years.

At the beginning of this year, 41 states plus the District of Columbia, Puerto Rico and the Virgin Islands were under court order to reduce crowding or remedy prison conditions, according to the American Civil Liberties Union's National Prison Project. That figure is up from 37 states in 1987. Overall, state prisons were operating at 127 percent of capacity at the end of 1989, according to Bureau of Justice statistics.

With the emphasis on facilities, governments are spending fewer of their corrections dollars on probation, parole and pardon activities. In 1977, these programs accounted for nearly 18 percent of all state and local spending on corrections. By 1988, that figure had fallen to 11 percent.

"What's really hurting in terms of resources are community correctional programs," said Phillip Renninger, director of the Bureau of Statistics and Policy Research at the Pennsylvania Commission on Crime and Delinquency. "If we had a couple of million dollars to devote to community corrections in Pennsylvania, that would have an impact. But right now, the money just isn't out there," he said.

New money also seems to be lacking for the front end of the system — police protection. Although law enforcement still accounts for nearly half of all justice expenditures in the United States, per capita spending on police protection increased only 3 percent between 1979 and 1988. Reported index crimes rose more than 15 percent during this period, and drug crimes, which aren't included in the index, soared.

In some cities, such as Chicago and Detroit, constant-dollar spending on police actually declined in the 1980s, while in other cities (New York, Dallas and Minneapolis, for example) increases in crime have exceeded increases in police funding.

With no real growth in spending on police, which is primarily a local function, and huge increase in spending on corrections, which is primarily a state function, there has been a dramatic realignment of who is paying for criminal justice services. Local governments still account for more than half of the country's justice expenditures, but the states are catching up.

Between 1979 and 1988, state government expenditures for criminal justice rose nearly 60 percent in constant dollars. And the increases in state spending haven't been limited to corrections. State governments are increasingly taking on a larger share of spending on the courts, prosecution, public defense and local jails.

In 1988, the states accounted for nearly half of all state and local expenditures on the courts. That's up from 27 percent in 1971. Similarly, states in 1988 were responsible for more than 42 percent of all non-federal spending for public defense,

up from about 35 percent in 1979.

"Local governments are so incredibly strapped that at the same time that states are making up for what gaps might be created by the feds dropping back, they're also moving to help cities and counties with major expenditure, like court costs," said Gwen Holden, executive vice president of the National Criminal Justice Association.

Holden said a larger state role creates opportunities for better coordination of efforts, improved information sharing and increased accountability. "The great downside, of course, is that it's just an incredible financial burden for the

States are losing ground in keeping up with rising criminal costs.

states, and one that I think is only going to get worse," she said.

Finding money to pay for these services, at the state or local level, may be all the more difficult as jurisdictions consider and pass anti-tax initiatives.

"No one is out there hollering for higher taxes," said David Schroot, director of the Governor's Office of Criminal Justice Services in Ohio.

Some jurisdictions have turned to special public safety surcharges as an alternative to higher property, sales or income taxes. In New Orleans, for example, an $8-per-person public safety tax raised $13 million in 1988. And in Illinois, more than 130 jurisdictions have approved telephone surcharges, ranging from $0.75 to $1.50 a month, to pay for enhanced 911 emergency services.

Other jurisdictions have expanded the use of offender fees, fines and victim restitution, often in combination with correctional industry programs.

Help also is coming from the federal government, at least in the critical area of drug enforcement. Congress last fall approved more than $450 million for state and local drug enforcement, which is more than it awarded in the three previous years combined. Many states have used the federal money to fund task forces and other programs that are difficult to organize and finance.

But Richard Harris, director of the Department of Criminal Justice Services in Virginia, warned that down the road, states must be prepared to pick up the funding of some of the programs started with federal money. "Right now in Virginia, there are no gulps of state money, except perhaps for prisons," he said.

The system is in a perpetual state of crisis management. "State and local administrators are desperately trying to match up limited resources with seemingly unlimited demands," Coldren of Illinois said, "but the system continues to lose ground. And we're losing ground not just in our day-to-day workload. We're also losing ground in our investments in technology, training and other efficiency measures that could relieve some of the pressure down the road."

THE MEN WHO CREATED CRACK

*A shrewd marketing strategy by several groups
of drug traffickers flooded the nation with this deadly
form of cocaine and left many U.S. cities blighted*

GORDON WITKIN WITH MUADI MUKENGE, MONIKA
GUTTMAN IN LOS ANGELES, ANNE MONCREIFF ARRARTE IN MIAMI,
KUKULA GLASTRIS IN CHICAGO, BARBARA BURGOWER IN HOUSTON
AND AIMEE L. STERN IN NEW YORK

The most amazing thing about crack cocaine is that it did not begin rotting America's urban landscape sooner. It has been recognized as a scourge in cities—and none too few suburban and rural areas—for only five years. But the supercharged cocaine, sometimes called "rock," wasn't really new. References to the recipe that used heat and baking soda to turn cocaine hydrochloride, or powder, into the smokable form of freebase called crack appear throughout the 1970s in underground literature, media interviews and congressional testimony. It did not catch on back then, researchers believe, because it was not as pure as other, more processed forms of freebase. Freebasers, who fancied themselves connoisseurs in those bygone days, called it "garbage rock."

What turned crack into a craze was mass marketing that would have made McDonald's proud. Crack was not invented; it was created by a sharp crowd of sinister geniuses who took a simple production technique to make a packaged, ready-to-consume form of the product with a low unit price to entice massive numbers of consumers. Cocaine powder required an investment of at least $75 for a gram, but a hit of crack cost as little as $5. Equally alluring was crack's incredible "high"—an instantaneous euphoria because it was smoked—that could create addicts in weeks.

There were three classes of criminals who created the crack epidemic. The first was composed of anonymous kitchen chemists and drug traffickers in the Caribbean and later in the United States, who used rudimentary science and marketing savvy to help hundreds of small-time criminals set up crack operations. The second was made up of indigenous crime organizations, common in most medium and large American cities, which began to seize local markets from the smaller operators. The third consisted of gangs from both coasts that franchised crack operations into every corner of the country.

The story of how crack infiltrated America is one of daring and enterprise. It also raises distressing questions about the capacity of police agencies to detect and combat massive criminal infiltration into the nation's neighborhoods. It contains lessons for Americans confronting an impending flood of heroin and Europeans tackling a cresting tsunami of cocaine. And it is a cautionary tale about what happens when hopelessness grips whole communities—how it lays them open to the allure of easy money and unspeakable violence.

CHAPTER 1

Early days: smoking coca paste

Two products, coca paste and cocaine freebase made with ether, came before crack—and led indirectly to its debut. Coca paste is an inexpensive, first-stage creation in cocaine processing that sells for as little as $1 a gram. First reports of its use came from Peru in 1971. By 1974, Lima faced a paste-smoking epidemic; by 1980, the practice had spread to

Colombia, Bolivia, Ecuador and Venezuela.

Soon after, Colombia initiated a temporarily successful effort to cut off importation of ether, the primary solvent used to process coca paste into cocaine hydrochloride powder. At the same time, intensified law enforcement efforts began to seal off the Colombia-Florida cocaine pipeline. The result was the widespread transshipment of unrefined coca paste to various Caribbean islands, and then South Florida, for refinement into powder, according to Miami researcher James Hall and University of Delaware criminologist James Inciardi.

Colombian traffickers promoted the idea of cocaine smoking through this new distribution network, hoping to expand sales. Dominican dealers in New York have told sociologist Terry Williams that Colombian wholesalers would include paste in kilo-size shipments of cocaine powder and tell them to give it away free to see how the customers liked it. Paste never did take hold in America, in part because of its harshness. Its future in the Caribbean, though, was bright.

CHAPTER 2
Getting closer: the freebase era

In the early 1970s, American consumers who had seen coca-paste smoking in Latin America apparently came upon the recipe for cocaine freebase through trial and error. Recreational smoking of this type first appeared in 1974 in California. Freebase is created through a chemical process that "frees" base cocaine from the cocaine hydrochloride powder. Crack is a form of freebase, but back in those early days, most freebase was made not from the easy baking-soda recipe but from

a more volatile chemical process involving ether and elaborate paraphernalia, such as acetylene or butane torches. This process created freebase purer than crack, and cocaine aficionados mistakenly believed that the purity made it healthier. It was a big hit in Hollywood in the mid-to-late-1970s, helped along by a burgeoning industry that sold pipes, chemicals and extraction kits. By 1980, experts believed between 10 and 20 percent of all cocaine users were doing freebase exclusively, though others resisted it as too complicated and dangerous.

Their fears were confirmed on the night of June 9, 1980, when comedian Richard Pryor set himself on fire while freebasing at his San Fernando Valley home. Pryor suffered third-degree burns over his entire upper torso and parts of his face. It appears likely that the Pryor incident sent many drug users searching for a safer way to freebase, and thus led to wider dissemination of the simpler and safer, though less pure, baking-soda method for making freebase—the recipe that came to be used for crack.

The final and most important force behind the push for crack was the growing street demand for a simple form of smokable cocaine. By 1982, in New York City selling or "copping" zones, as many as 80 percent of the customers wanted "base," according to sociologist Williams, whose book "The Cocaine Kids" provides a riveting window into Gotham's crack culture. That meant the dealers had to cook it up batch by batch for the customers, while they cooled their heels in the dealers' apartments—a level of sustained exposure to outsiders that dealers loathed. One example was Tony, a 29-year-old dealer observed by New York anthropologist Ansley Hamid of the John Jay College of Criminal

HOUSTON. *Johnny Binder and Martha Preston*

■ THE MAN. Prosecutors say he was the "king" of crack in Houston, but he seems to have had more than nine lives. By the time he was 34, Binder had been arrested 34 times but rarely convicted. He even had a government pardon to his credit. Binder had a front tooth with a gold star, and a diamond necklace that hung to his navel. Now 37, he claims to be an honest music promoter and still maintains his innocence. Authorities alleged his partner was Martha Marie Preston, now 42, a charming, well-connected businesswoman. She, too, says she is not guilty and claims to have been railroaded by federal officials.

■ THE OPERATION. Authorities say this pair joined forces in 1983 and parlayed their connections and charisma into a massive crack operation. They say Binder operated crack houses on the southeast side of town and Preston ran the show in the northeast. Together, authorities contend, they controlled 60 to 80 percent of the crack business in Houston, and their operation reaped at least $7,000 a day in profits.

■ STATUS. Binder and Preston were convicted in September 1989 of aiding and abetting in the distribution of cocaine. Both are now serving 40-year sentences.

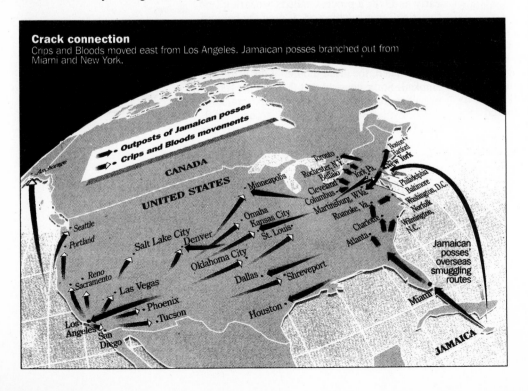

Crack connection
Crips and Bloods moved east from Los Angeles. Jamaican posses branched out from Miami and New York.

Justice. "The change in consuming preference placed a fresh burden upon Tony," Hamid wrote in the Spring 1990 issue of *Contemporary Drug Problems*. "Now he was obliged to suffer even larger throngs of customers to remain in his apartment while he, like a crazed apothecary, cooked up their purchases of powder into freebase."

The result of this pressure to handle customers quickly prompted dealers to search for a new product. "They tried to figure out an efficient way to create large batches of cocaine freebase and then package it in such a way that it could be sold at retail in a market they didn't necessarily interact with directly," according to researcher Bruce Johnson of New York-based Narcotic and Drug Research Inc. Crack was the answer.

CHAPTER 3

The Caribbean test market

Offshore, there were other forces driving the development of crack. Researchers believe that residents of the Netherlands Antilles, after experimenting with coca paste, came up with a crack prototype around 1980 — a conversion of paste using baking soda, water and rum that came to be known there as "roxanne," "base-rock" or "baking-soda base." In the early 1980s, reports of "rock" began to surface regularly in the southern Caribbean. Dr. Charles Wetli, deputy medical examiner for Dade County, Fla., remembers hearing about it during a trip to the Turks and Caicos Islands as part of a teaching team sponsored by the Drug Enforcement Administration: "A local cop asked about a drug that looked like a pebble, and people would smoke it and go crazy. None of us had ever heard of it."

Meanwhile, rumblings of a similar nature were shaking the Bahamas. By the early 1980s, the vast share of cocaine destined for the United States was being transshipped through the Bahamas' 700 islands and 2,000 cays, with a hefty chunk of it being diverted and consumed by the local population. In 1979, the freebasing of cocaine rock made its debut, and the practice slowly gathered momentum over the next three years.

In the fall of 1983, Bahamian rock abuse surged, especially in the poorer neighborhoods of New Providence and Grand Bahama islands. At Princess Margaret Hospital's community psychiatry department, 35 patients were treated for cocaine addiction in all of 1983; in the first six months of 1984, the total was more than 200. Stumbling addicts, rail thin and malnourished, congregated to smoke rock in tattered abandoned buildings on Grand Bahama, Andros and New Providence islands—in places that came to be known as "base houses," the forerunner of crack houses on the mainland.

Public-health officials groping for answers turned to a burly Bahamian named Chris Finlayson. Dr. David Allen, the islands' leading drug-abuse expert, had met Finlayson

when he came in for treatment after claiming his clothes spoke to him during an acute freebase psychosis. Allen helped the personable and fast-talking Finlayson beat his rock problem temporarily, and then followed as his former patient led him deep into the Bahamas' base house culture.

Finlayson convinced Allen and Dr. James Jekel, a Yale Medical School epidemiologist, that the rock epidemic had been caused by a fundamental switch in marketing strategy by local drug pushers. The doctors already knew that in early 1983, the glut of cocaine powder in the Bahamas had dropped the street price per gram to only one fifth of its previous level. Finlayson told them that at that same time, "the pusher man switched to pushing only rock," relates Dr. Jekel. "You couldn't get powder on the street." Other addicts confirmed Finlayson's story. "The pushers knew that crack addicts keep coming back for more and more, so figured, 'Let's create a demand by getting people to go to crack,'" says Jekel. "How do you get them to go to crack? They figured, 'Let's just sell that and nothing else.' It was a marketing decision."

For Finlayson, that was lethal. He succumbed to drugs on a boat trip and died in 1986. His dying words to Allen in Princess Margaret Hospital were: "When the world tastes this, you're going to have a lot of trouble." Allen and Jekel tried to sound the alarm to a wider audience in the United States, but no one seemed particularly alarmed.

CHAPTER 4

Rock arrives in Los Angeles

While the Caribbean story was unfolding, crack was beginning to show up in California. Addicts reported in Los Angeles that as early as 1978, a process called "smearing" or "pasting" was catching on. It used the baking-soda formula. "Instead of letting it form a rock, you would pour it out on a mirror and take a finger and smear it," recalls one former addict. Then, the dried mound of the drug was smoked. Some contend that this was the transitional product between freebase and crack.

Rock made its L.A. debut around 1980, mostly because it was a faster, easier way for addicts to get their kicks. By 1982, Los Angeles hospital emergency rooms reported the nation's greatest increase in cocaine overdoses, a 90 percent rise over the previous year, according to the National Institute on Drug Abuse, due to "more and more users shifting from snorting to injecting or freebasing." By early 1983, the *Los Angeles Sentinel,* the south central neighborhood's community paper, was reporting a problem with "rock houses"—residences used for dealing crack.

But no one was really prepared for what happened in 1984, when sales of $25 rocks swept south central Los Angeles. Dozens of rock houses "went up overnight," says former LAPD Capt. Noel Cunningham, many of them so fortified that the police for a

DETROIT. *Billy Joe and Larry Chambers*

■ **THE MEN.** The Chambers brothers were originally from Marianna, Ark. They crafted a corporate look-alike organization that dominated the Motor City's crack trade.

■ **THE OPERATION.** Founded in 1983, the Chambers brothers gang just a few years later was running some 200 crack houses that employed up to 500 people, according to police, and was tallying profits of $1 million a week. Many of the workers were teenagers recruited from their native Marianna, a dirt-poor rural hamlet of 7,000 set amid cotton and rice fields 60 miles from Memphis. Twelve-hour shifts and round-the-clock crack sales were the norm. Rules, often posted on crack house walls, were strict: no crack and money to be carried at the same time, no speeding while driving and no lavish automobiles used for business purposes. Quality-control managers posed as crack buyers to keep an eye on the product. Rule breakers were referred to the so-called wrecking crew, which, officials say, exacted discipline by tossing violators out a window.

■ **STATUS.** Billy Joe and Larry were both convicted of running a continuing criminal enterprise. Larry is serving a life sentence; Billy Joe netted 29 years.

while used a 14-foot steel battering ram attached to an armored personnel carrier to break in. Teenagers, many of them gang members working for older, tougher former members, openly dealt rock at dozens of hot spots like 98th Street between Avalon Boulevard and Main Street, making thousands of dollars in the process.

Authorities now believe several below-the-surface developments helped crack's rapid ascent. The big Colombian smugglers were responding to increasing heat in Florida by bringing more and more cocaine over the Mexican border into Los Angeles. They found it convenient to tap into the existing gang structure because gang-ridden areas already had heavy concentrations of drug users and because the gangs had experience manufacturing and selling other drugs like PCP. Finally, the market had been thrown wide open by the December 1983 arrest of Thomas (Tootie) Reese, south central's pre-eminent drug kingpin for the previous two decades.

While all these sands were shifting, law enforcement had something else on its mind: planning for the 1984 Summer Olympics. "There was an awful lot of organizational focus on just keeping the city safe from terrorists," says the DEA's William Coonce. "I think the normal law enforcement took a second seat." Ex-LAPD official Cunningham agrees.

CHAPTER 5

Storming the Miami coast

In the late 1970s and early 1980s, South Florida was already reeling under a deluge of cocaine powder. "Cocaine cowboys" were shooting it out for control of the trade. Hidden behind the mayhem was the conversion of some of the street-level cocaine business from powder to base. The steady flow of Caribbean peoples to Miami, heightened by the early-1980s flood of fleeing Haitians, brought with it the burgeoning knowledge of how to convert paste into "baking-soda base." Crack wasn't far behind.

One early inkling came in November 1982, as researcher Inciardi interviewed a prostitute on a bench near the Miami Marina. "She started talking about something called 'garbage freebase,'" he relates. "Suddenly it clicked. That was an old San Francisco term from the '70s for a rock variety of freebase."

The biggest clue that crack had arrived came around 1982, when a Miami Police Department street narcotics unit busted five drug houses and apartments in the city's Little River and Liberty City neighborhoods, all of them run by a Caribbean-island immigrant who called himself Elijah. He bragged to police that he'd invented rocks, and though the claim is impossible to confirm, former Sgt. Mike Ahearn, who ran the unit, says those were the first rocks he saw. Ahearn recalls the first bust of one of those houses: "I couldn't believe it, there were 30 people in this house, and they didn't look like junkies. These were people with jobs—white, black,

upper class, lower class, young girls. I remember thinking, 'What the hell have we got here?' They said they were doing rocks. They called it a 'rock house.'" By 1984, crack had spread more widely to poor neighborhoods like Overtown and Liberty City, selling for as little as $10, sometimes under brand names like "Rambo" or "Miami Vice." Most of the crack retailers were American blacks, small-scale dealers who bought cocaine powder and picked up the crack recipe from Caribbean wholesalers whom they had first met in the marijuana business. Many Caribbean people were attracted to the illicit economy of the crack trade because their illegal-immigrant status cut them off from legitimate jobs.

CHAPTER 6

The New York flood

Authorities think there was probably a race between Californians and Caribbeans to see who got to introduce crack to the New York market the fastest. The first official to spot its arrival was Bill Hopkins, a former Bronx narcotics cop who headed a state "street research unit" set up to monitor drug trends. As he drove up Arthur Avenue in the Tremont section of the Bronx in December 1983, Hopkins recognized some of the drug abusers in Crotona Park and stopped to hear the men talking about two other abusers who had "freaked out." "You know what that was, don't ya?" asked one man.

"Yeah, that was that crack," said the other.

"My ears perked up, because this was something new, and that's rare," recalls Hopkins. "They said it was 'rock cocaine.'" It was almost another year before Hopkins got a firsthand look at a man who was smoking it. "I learned for the first time it was done with baking soda, not ether," says Hopkins. "And I examined what he had, and it was in vials. I knew we had something new on the market." Within a year, crack had saturated the city.

Nowhere did crack grab hold as tightly as it did in the northern Manhattan area called Washington Heights, a teeming neighborhood with a distinctly Caribbean flavor. When night fell, "copping" zones like West 168th Street or 174th Street and Amsterdam Avenue became choked with traffic. Some 70 to 80 percent of the consumers powering the market were white professionals or middle-class youngsters from Long Island, suburban New Jersey or New York's affluent Westchester County—all of whom could easily drive into the community. The neighborhood was diverse enough ethnically, says Hopkins, that "a white guy could come into that neighborhood without standing out like a sore thumb."

Though several groups lived in the Heights, it was Dominicans who came to dominate the crack trade. The drug-dealing Dominicans, like their many legitimate shopkeeping counterparts, proved to be ambitious and well organized. They delivered consistently high-quality crack, and they proved adept at moving easily in both black

NEW YORK. *Santiago Luis Polanco-Rodríguez*

■ **THE MAN.** Police say Polanco-Rodríguez, a street-savvy Dominican immigrant in his mid-20s, was the marketing genius behind the spread of crack in New York's Washington Heights, the city's first big market.
■ **THE OPERATION.** In a hotly competitive atmosphere, Polanco-Rodríguez fostered intense customer loyalty by delivering high-quality crack in vials marked "Based Balls," according to authorities. He hatched the idea while selling cocaine powder, which he named "Coke Is It." He switched to crack in the summer of 1985. Over the next two years, the "Based Balls" ring grew, employing up to 100 people and dealing as many as 10,000 red-capped vials each day. Employees even passed out business cards labeled "Based Balls—Cop and Go" that listed retail sales outlets. Police contend that millions in profits were laundered through a full-time accountant and sent back to the Dominican Republic. A finance company was established there to make investments. The take: about $36 million annually.
■ **STATUS.** Polanco-Rodríguez was among 29 people charged in 1987 in a 57-count federal indictment. He is a fugitive and believed to be in the Dominican Republic.

and white worlds. Most important, perhaps, the cocaine wholesalers—Colombians from Jackson Heights, Queens—preferred doing business with them rather than with American blacks. They had already established links with the Dominicans through earlier marijuana trafficking, and they shared a common language.

The market in 1985 and early 1986 was still in its formative stages, however—marked not by massive organizations but by hundreds of cash-hungry young entrepreneurs. They worked out of apartments, using kitchen utensils. "Anyone could buy the cocaine and make crack," says the city's special narcotics prosecutor, Sterling Johnson. "Back then, there was no General Motors of crack, just a lot of mom and pop operations."

CHAPTER 7

The feds finally catch on

In October 1985, when Robert Stutman took over as the special agent in charge of the federal Drug Enforcement Administration's New York office, one of the first things he heard about was crack. After reading a host of intelligence reports and getting a four-hour briefing from a DEA chemist, he decided to start rattling some cages at headquarters. But Stutman's reputation stood in the way of his cause. DEA Administrator Jack Lawn liked his New York man, but others at headquarters were jealous and suspicious of Stutman's yen for publicity—a trait that earned him nicknames like "Stuntman." As a result, much of what he said about crack in those early days was viewed skeptically in Washington.

Federal officials also had a hard time figuring out how widespread the crack problem had become because they couldn't decode street lingo. Was crack the same as the "rock" the DEA was hearing about in California? Were cocaine rocks the same as "rock cocaine"? The confusion "probably slowed down the law enforcement response," says William Alden, DEA's chief of congressional and public affairs. "It's difficult to establish a strategy when you can't define the target correctly."

Disagreement also raged over whether crack deserved to be treated as something new and different—or simply as a subset of the war on cocaine. "The thing that weighed most heavily against a massive response was the argument that to solve crack, you had to first solve the overall cocaine problem because crack was just a marketing technique," recalls David Westrate, then DEA's assistant administrator for operations. "If this was a completely new drug, we might have had a different response." Others felt crack was an issue better addressed by state and local law enforcement, while the DEA followed its mandate to focus on large traffickers.

Still, Stutman finally prevailed. On June 19, 1986, Lawn and a handful of headquarters brass flew an agency plane to New York for an all-day briefing by DEA agents and chemists, New York police and private treatment providers. As the meeting broke up, news arrived of the sudden death of University of Maryland basketball star Len Bias. Those at the meeting immediately suspected cocaine."When Jack [Lawn] left," recalls Stutman, "he said, 'You've convinced me we've got to do more.' "

For the next few months, however, the federal effort remained confused. As late as July 15, 1986, Westrate was testifying to Congress that "at this time there is no comprehensive analysis of the crack problem, either from a health or enforcement viewpoint." A DEA intelligence review two months later, while acknowledging crack's availability in 12 cities, nonetheless called it "a secondary rather than primary problem in most areas." Just days later, though, the National Drug Enforcement Policy Board, a multiagency group then directing federal strategy, said the "present crack situation, in short, is bleak."

Lawn himself did follow through. Early that fall, he made an emergency request for $44 million to fund 200 agents who would organize a host of state and local crack task forces nationwide. However, the Justice Department's budget monitors, acting on behalf of Ronald Reagan's budget office, denied the request. "[The budget officials] didn't treat it like a major issue," says Lawn, especially under the tight antideficit strictures of the Gramm-Rudman-Hollings law. Stephen Trott, who chaired the Justice Department's budget board, declined comment.

The DEA's next move was to jury-rig a few special crack programs using its existing budget and some new funds from the Anti-Drug Abuse Act of 1986. In 15 cities across the United States, the agency created two-person crack teams to assist local police. Some feel the effort was inadequate. "Then, as now, there is not the same type of commitment to crack as one would see with cocaine generally," says Democratic Rep. Charles Rangel of New York, chairman of the House Select Committee on Narcotics. "In my opinion, that's because it's in the poorer, minority communities."

CHAPTER 8

Bigger organizations muscle in

By the fall of 1986, the National Cocaine Hotline estimated that 1 million Americans had tried crack, in large part because the drug's marketing structure was changing and distribution was expanding. The outlandish profits and inevitable elbowing over turf led to the creation of larger crack organizations that began to overshadow the small-time operators. Some grew by simply dominating a territory and gradually forcing out competitors, through intimidation if necessary. Others were born of mergers. Either way, organization brought structure—CEOs, lieutenants, distributors, lab operators, runners, enforcers and street dealers. The business even went high tech as telephone beep-

SEATTLE. *Derrick Hargress and the Crips gang's branch operations*

■ **THE MAN.** Now 29, "Vamp" Hargress was a member of a Crips gang "set" known as the Nine-Deuce Hoovers (named after the streets where they hung out). Police think he was the mastermind of the Crips' movement from Los Angeles to Seattle in the late 1980s.

■ **THE OPERATION.** Hargress brought eight cohorts with him from Southern California to Seattle in early 1987. Each week, they transported 15 to 20 ounces of crack from Los Angeles, while running three crack houses that made $6,000 a day. According to Seattle prosecutors, "They also brought with them a level of violence and an element of organization previously lacking in drug distribution in this city." In early 1988, Hargress decided to branch out by sending several of his crew to operate half a dozen crack houses in Oklahoma City. One gang member told Oklahoma City detective Charles McIntyre that they had test-marketed the area first. "He said he used to sell vacuum cleaners door-to-door, and it was very similar," reports McIntyre.

■ **STATUS.** Hargress pleaded guilty in 1988 to selling crack near a school and using a gun to further his drug business. He was sentenced to 25 years in Leavenworth.

ers became tools of the trade. Finding the workers for these groups wasn't difficult. Many inner-city teens felt shut off from legitimate economic opportunity and came to see drug dealing as the only path to prosperity.

Once crack selling became big business, it created operations that finally were sophisticated enough to merit extensive attention from federal law enforcement authorities. Many of these home-grown organizations came to be dominated by charismatic supercriminals who ruled with an iron hand. One city that saw the rise of a highly structured organization was Houston, where prosecutors say Johnny Binder and Martha Marie Preston became the "king" and "queen" of the city's crack business (box, **Page 25**). In Detroit, brothers Billy Joe and Larry Chambers emerged from humble backgrounds to craft a disciplined empire that grew to dominate Motown's lucrative crack trade (box, **Page 26**). And in New York, the pre-eminent early figure was a canny street tough named Santiago Luis Polanco-Rodríguez, an immigrant from the Dominican Republic who used marketing savvy to rule Washington Heights (box, **Page 27**).

CHAPTER 9

Gangs up: Crips and Bloods

As bad as the indigenous organizations were, the spread of gangs was truly disastrous. America was caught in a pincer movement; Los Angeles street gangs moved east and Jamaican posses moved west from the East Coast, and between them, by the end of the decade, they had introduced much of the rest of the country to crack.

The chief Los Angeles gangs were the Crips (approximately 30,000 strong now) and the Bloods (about 9,000). Their expansion took off in 1986. Earlier this year, the Justice Department said that investigative reports had placed Crips and Bloods in 32 states and 113 cities. Their reach extended to places as small as Hobbs, N.M., and Ashton, Idaho. Some experts think the L.A.-based gangs now control up to 30 percent of the crack trade.

While the movement conjures up images of a master plan, authorities say it was really more a matter of happenstance. Neither gang is rigidly hierarchical. Both are broken up into loosely affiliated neighborhood groups called "sets," each with 30 to 100 members. Many gang members initially left Southern California to evade police. Others simply expanded the reach of crack by setting up branch operations in places where they visited friends or family members and discovered that the market was ripe—and the prices they could charge were higher than those in locations where the market was saturated. When authorities unraveled an L.A. ring that introduced crack to York, Pa., they discovered not a grand plan but a lovestruck Crip named Benjamin West, who had followed his L.A.-based girlfriend to York, where she was visiting her mother on a summer vacation. Since crack hadn't yet come to York, authorities say, West stayed to set up his own operation.

Compared with Los Angeles, other cities were easy pickings, especially for "rollers" or "OGs"—older gang members in their 20s—with a thirst for more-serious cash and existing connections to Colombian suppliers. "Gang members candidly concede that they choose their new homes because of market conditions and perceived weakness in the community's ability to deal with them," says a government sentencing memo in one Seattle gang case. "The word that a particular community is an easy mark spreads by word of mouth." Some Los Angeles gang members also struck out for new territory because they had hit the glass ceiling back home. "If you're a third stringer in L.A., you may figure you'll never reach the heights there, but somewhere else you can be the biggest and baddest," says the DEA's James Forget.

Portland and Seattle proved to be two of the most inviting targets. The march from L.A. to Seattle began in early 1987, masterminded by Derrick "Vamp" Hargress, an older member of a Crips set known as the Nine-Deuce Hoovers (box, **Page 28**). They brought an unprecedented level of violence and a strong criminal infrastructure to Seattle's drug trade, authorities there say. In Portland, police weren't sure what it meant when a Northside apartment raid in December 1987 turned up a man who said he was a Blood from Los Angeles. But they found out soon enough. By mid-1988, some 100 L.A. gang members were in Portland dealing crack, and they attracted at least 230 Portland youths to the gang lifestyle, turning north and northeast Portland into veritable free-fire zones.

CHAPTER 10

Jamaican posses

From the other coast, the great crack sales-branching scheme was put together by transplanted Jamaicans in the mid-1980s. The discovery of it came in one of those classic investigations that begin with a small piece of evidence and grow like kudzu. In the spring of 1984, Agent J. J. Watterson of the Bureau of Alcohol, Tobacco and Firearms was asked to investigate the origins of a dozen smuggled guns found in shipping containers at the port of Kingston, Jamaica. When he began checking gun store records in Dade and Broward counties in Florida, Watterson found the guns were part of a larger purchase; 50 to 75 weapons had been bought by Jamaicans. The few purchasers who could be tracked—many had given false addresses—seemed to live in virtual fortresses, and it wasn't unusual for a Mercedes or BMW to be parked outside. Pretty soon, the guns began turning up in drug and murder cases in Washington, D.C., New York, Detroit, Miami, Chicago and Los Angeles. "It was an amazing scenario," says Watterson. "We had murders everywhere."

What Watterson had discovered were Jamaican "posses": a network of mobile Jamai-

MIAMI. *Jamaicans Vivian Blake and Lester Coke*

■ **THE MEN.** These characters are alleged to be the leaders of the largest Jamaican trafficking group, the Shower posse. Blake operated from Miami; Coke lived in Jamaica but often traveled to the States. Together, they purportedly were major drug and firearms traffickers.

■ **THE OPERATION.** After dealing primarily in marijuana for three years, according to federal authorities, the Shower posse expanded into cocaine around 1985. The posse grew to a membership of about 5,400 in more than a dozen cities. Its primary drug distribution locations included New York City, Rochester, N.Y., Washington, D.C., Detroit and Toronto. The Showers took their name from the fierce gun battles they initiated: They "showered" the area with blood and body parts. In one shootout with a rival posse at a New Jersey picnic, Shower members fired more than 700 rounds.

■ **STATUS.** In September 1988, a federal grand jury indicted 34 members of the Shower posse, including Blake and Coke. The 62-count indictment charged Blake with illegal arms purchases and racketeering that involved nine murders. Blake and Coke are both fugitives, believed to be in either Kingston, Jamaica, or London.

can gangs that came to dominate gun trafficking and crack dealing over wide swaths of the United States, leaving a trail of bloodspattered bodies wherever they turned up. The posses take their name from American Westerns. Today, approximately 40 of the posses, with an estimated membership of 22,000, operate in the United States. ATF officials think they control a third of America's crack trade. The posses are believed to be partly rooted in Jamaican marijuana trafficking groups and were nurtured in the grinding poverty in Kingston and the violence-soaked politics of the island in the period around 1980.

Seeing crack's profit potential, Jamaican traffickers moved quickly. They focused first on the large Caribbean populations in Miami and New York. By mid-1987, at least five groups were operating in South Florida, led by the notorious Shower posse, so named for firefights that showered an area with bullets. The posse was run by a couple of smart but cutthroat gangsters named Vivian Blake and **Lester Coke (box, Page 29).** It began by smuggling marijuana but turned to cocaine in 1985, and, according to authorities, grew to 5,400 members nationwide. In New York, the Jamaican traffickers came to be particularly dominant in Brooklyn. One of the biggest and toughest groups there was the Renkers posse, run by an especially ruthless character named Delroy Edwards, better known as "Uzi" for his taste in weapons (box, Page 31).

Nearly all the posses displayed an extraordinary penchant for violence. On August 4, 1985, a feud between two posses resulted in a frenzied shootout at an Oakland, N.J., picnic attended by some 5,000 Jamaicans. Shower posse members fired well over 700 rounds; three people were killed and 13 wounded. In New York, a man who tried to steal $20 worth of crack from two members of the Spangler posse was kicked unconscious, placed in a bathtub, decapitated and dismembered. The following morning, a street person found the victim's head in the garbage and began kicking it down the street. Since 1985, the ATF has documented more than 3,000 posse-related homicides nationwide. Gun running, meanwhile, has become a lucrative sideline.

Often, the posses were able to establish new beachheads because it took local authorities some time to figure out what was happening. It hardly seemed unusual when Dallas detective P. E. Jones was rousted from a deep sleep at 2:30 a.m. on July 20, 1985, to investigate a murder at the Kool Vibes Club on Second Avenue; it was Saturday night, after all, in a tough neighborhood. But the victim, Howard Gordon, 28, was Jamaican, and the ensuing investigation turned up scores of out-of-town Jamaican drug connections. The homicide probe led to much more. By the time investigators were finished, they had uncovered 500 to 700 Jamaicans—many of them teenagers called "street worms"—involved in 27 Jamaican drug rings

that operated 75 crack houses turning $400,000 in profits a day.

Kansas City was much the same story. In that heartland city, the Jamaicans, with their dreadlocks and accents, stuck out plainly. They were being arrested on drug charges in significant numbers as early as 1983, all of them with phony IDs and passports. But no one knew quite what it meant. By 1986, investigations of a string of 15 murders involving Jamaicans showed police that the posses had brought 450 members into town and were operating at least 50 crack houses. The brains behind the Kansas City invasion were members of the Waterhouse posse (who came from the Waterhouse region of Kingston), which was led by a creative yet vicious thug named **Errol "Dogbite" Wilson (box at right).**

Other cities showed similar patterns. Prodded by Watterson and his Florida cohorts, ATF launched a national investigation of the posses in January 1987. Since then, the effort has resulted in the prosecution of approximately 1,200 Jamaican defendants. "We made some significant cases, but the fight isn't over," says ATF's Chuck Sarabyn.

By late 1987, two other groups had also gotten involved in interstate trafficking. Dominicans, from their base in New York, moved into New England, dominating the crack trade in places like Providence, R.I., and Stamford, Conn. And migrant farm workers—many of them Haitian—took the crack recipe from Florida into Georgia, North Carolina, southern Delaware, western Michigan and the Dayton, Ohio, area.

Today, though the worst may be over, crack still holds at least half a million people in its grasp. The despair pervading America's inner cities, made worse by the blight caused by crack, continues to provide fertile soil for something similar to grow in its place. Anthropologist Philippe Bourgois, who has been studying East Harlem crack dealers for six years, argues that it is unrealistic to expect a youngster growing up in an environment of evil to develop a healthy concept of equal opportunity and personal responsibility. "The 'common sense' emerging among this newest generation is that 'The System' hates them," writes Bourgois in a recent issue of *The American Enterprise.* That is the reason, he says, that so many inner-city blacks believe there is a secret white conspiracy to destroy them and crack is part of it.

But crack's hold on inner-city kids is logic, not conspiratorial hocus-pocus. High-wage, low-skill manufacturing jobs have disappeared from inner cities. Crack selling became rationalized as the only ticket to prosperity. Those who have studied crack operations uniformly say these kids weren't lazy and drifting; many worked back-breaking hours in the drug trade and yearned to make something of themselves. Given half a chance at productive futures, they just might go for it. If not, some other illicit activity will come along—heroin, ice, gun running, something—and this pathological crime cycle will get another jolt.

KANSAS CITY. *Errol Wilson and the Waterhouse posse*

■ **THE MAN.** Wilson, better known as "Dogbite," rose quickly to become the most powerful of the Waterhouse posse members who controlled crack in Kansas City.

■ **THE OPERATION.** The Waterhousers recruited teenagers in the Jamaican communities of Miami and New York, promising an unheard-of wage of $500 a week. Often that kind of money never really materialized. The youths did get plane tickets and a phone number, and were assigned to crack houses, where they worked like slaves. Jamaican females were used as couriers of cocaine powder from Miami as often as six times a week. Some crack houses took in up to $15,000 a day. The dealers even had a catchy marketing pitch: "Stock Up on Mothers Day." That's the first of the month, when welfare checks are mailed. The crack was always top quality, and the Jamaicans sold bigger pieces for the money than anyone else in town. And always, there were guns—high caliber, top-quality guns.

■ **STATUS.** Wilson was indicted in early 1987 on charges of engaging in a continuing criminal enterprise and distributing cocaine. He was a fugitive until last October, when he died in a car accident in Jamaica.

CHICAGO. *Al Capone and the reason why crack was scarce*

■ THE MYSTERY. While crack raced across the country, infecting communities only a half-hour's drive away, it remained nearly nonexistent in Chicago. As late as 1989, the police seized barely 2 pounds during the whole year. Why didn't crack hit Chicago hard?

■ THE THEORIES. The most convincing explanation is rooted in Chicago's rough-and-tumble criminal tradition. Seventy years ago, Al Capone so dominated the city's bootleg-liquor industry that rivals from other cities never managed to penetrate the market, though many died trying. The same is true of the drug trade today. Jamaican posses and gangs from Los Angeles have hardly set foot in Chicago; much of the reason, authorities say, is that local gangs have been fiercely protective of their already lucrative cocaine and heroin markets. The police, too, have been especially vigilant in attacking crack houses as soon as they have appeared.

■ STATUS. Chicago gangs are now peddling more of the drug, spurred perhaps by some growth in demand or competition from smaller entrepreneurs. In 1990, Chicago police seized three times as much crack as they did in 1989. The city's luck may be running out.

NEW YORK. *Delroy Edwards and the Renkers posse*

■ THE MAN. Edwards, now 31, was reputed to be a former street enforcer for the Jamaican Labor Party. Better known as "Uzi" for his taste in weapons, Edwards arrived in America on a tourist visa in the early 1980s. Police say he began his drug career selling marijuana but moved to crack in 1985.

■ THE OPERATION. Authorities contend Edwards headed an especially ruthless posse known as the Renkers, which ran a huge portion of the crack trade in Brooklyn. In one incident, police say, a teenager suspected of stealing money and drugs from the ring was beaten with a baseball bat, scalded with boiling water and then left hanging from a basement ceiling. He later died. At their peak, the Renkers employed 50 workers and made as much as $100,000 a day selling crack in the Bedford-Stuyvesant, Crown Heights and Flatbush sections of Brooklyn. Later the Renkers branched out to Philadelphia, Baltimore and the District of Columbia. Cops contend that Edwards used a portion of the profits to purchase a house in Amityville, Long Island.

■ STATUS. Edwards was convicted in 1989 on 42 federal charges, including six murders. He is serving a life sentence.

The Mobster Who Could Bring Down the Mob

Phil Leonetti has gone from Mafia hit man to Government witness. His next victim may be John Gotti.

Marguerite Del Giudice

Marguerite Del Giudice, a freelance journalist in Philadelphia, is a former staff writer for The Boston Globe *and* The Philadelphia Inquirer.

You have to see Philip Leonetti in action to appreciate why so many people would like to kill him. This Atlantic City gangster with the movie-star looks, who has been testifying with deadpan sincerity about his once-beloved Mafia, makes one deadly witness.

At racketeering trials in Pennsylvania, Connecticut and New York, Leonetti, possibly the most damaging Mafia informant since Joseph Valachi, has been detailing the grim pastimes of the underworld with a spellbinding nonchalance, speaking carefully in a voice just this side of high-pitched. Emotionally detached, impeccably groomed, he rocks forward in his seat, making eye contact with the jury and exuding the shy respectfulness of the nice Catholic schoolboy he once was. Leonetti, hands clasped, elbows resting on the witness-box ledge, comes across as a man with nothing to hide—he wants to be understood. It's this understated prowess that makes him so dangerous, and so endangered, as he warms up for the main event—the coming murder and racketeering trial of John Gotti.

The "Teflon Don" has been tried and acquitted three times in five years, swaggering in and out of courtrooms in his florid silk ties and mono-grammed see-through socks,

bantering with the press and taunting prosecutors. But this time, the Feds claim to have flawless tape recordings from bugged mob clubhouses. And this time they have Leonetti, once "the under," or under-boss, of the Philadelphia–South Jersey family, now one of the highest-ranking gangsters in the history of organized crime to break the Mafia's code of silence and turn state's evidence. Leonetti has told a Manhattan grand jury that Gotti admitted, in his presence, to arranging the 1985 sidewalk murder of Paul Castellano (which subsequently made room for Gotti on the throne). He will also be called on to establish Gotti as the head of the Gambino crime family—the basis of the sweeping Federal racketeering statute under which he has been charged, and which has led to the jailing of Mafia bosses across the country.

Leonetti has already established himself as a formidable witness. Three trials at which he testified last year in Pennsylvania resulted in convictions. This April, in a union corruption case involving a local in Atlantic City, the defendants pleaded out before he had a chance to take the stand. Later that month, defense attorneys in a window-contract rigging case in Brooklyn didn't

even bother to cross-examine him. And there he was again in May in Hartford, captivating a packed courtroom at a racketeering trial, still in progress, with chilling tales of murder and secret initiation rituals.

The Feds are betting that with Leonetti, they'll finally be able to put away the self-proclaimed zipper and plumbing-and-heating-supply salesman from Queens. Leonetti is betting that an effective performance against Gotti will make the difference when the time comes for his own 45-year sentence for murder and racketeering to be reconsidered. What's at stake for him, at 38 years of age, is a shot at living the second half of his life outside prison.

Leonetti decided to cooperate and enter the Federal witness-protection program after a 1988 Federal trial decimated the Philadelphia mob with 17 convictions, including his own and that of the family boss, Leonetti's now-jailed uncle, Nicodemo (Little Nicky) Scarfo—a vicious, vindictive man who ran his organization by killing anyone who offended him. Leonetti was Scarfo's constant companion, his right-hand man, his confidant. They were like father and son: wherever Scarfo went, whomever he met with, Leonetti was standing at his uncle's side, silent as a stone, absorbing everything.

The Feds portray him as having been lured into the underworld by his Napoleonic Uncle Nick, a small man, dangerously touchy about his size and prone to allergies and stomach complaints, who took the place of Leonetti's absent father and groomed him from a tender age to do his bidding without remorse. Otherwise, he had been an ordinary, happy-go-lucky youth. He dated, went to parties, served as homeroom treasurer and played guard on the Holy Spirit High School varsity basketball team in Absecon, N.J.

The people who knew him before he was a hood, like William Checchio, his homeroom teacher, were "absolutely stunned" to discover how he turned out. "He was no—what do they always say?—he was no 'loner who kept to himself,' " says Checchio. Yet this is what he more or less turned into: a quiet mobster, who has now confessed to two murders by his own hand, eight other murder conspiracies, union corruption, shakedowns and hammer and blackjack beatings.

His deeds may be inexcusable; but the circumstances of Leonetti's wasted life provide a window into the making, and breaking, of a third-generation hit man and gangster.

PHILIP LEONETTI LIVED out his early boyhood in South Philadelphia on a narrow, watchful block of brick row houses with white marble stoops out front, sunken in the middle from wear. It was a neighborhood of close-knit families. In Leonetti's, the Mafia roots ran generations deep. His maternal grandparents were Philip Scarfo, a Uneeda biscuit bakery man, and Philip's wife, Catherine, a seamstress with three brothers who were active in the local mob. The Scarfos had two children, Nicodemo and Nancy. Nancy married a bookmaker, restaurateur and jeweler named Pasquale Leonetti, and the couple had a son, Philip.

But Pasquale Leonetti was out of the picture early on. He and his wife parted when Philip was a boy; he eventually moved to Florida and has since died. Nancy's brother, Nick — by then "connected" through his uncles — filled in as a father figure. During the trial of a confederate last year, Leonetti recounted his earliest criminal memory.

Q: When did you first become involved in criminal activity with your uncle?
A: Ten, 11 years old.
Q: And what was the first thing that you could remember happening?
A: Well, he — he just killed somebody and they buried the guy. They used this pickup truck to dump the body, and he brought the truck back with him to Atlantic City and he picked me up. . . . He told me so it wouldn't look too suspicious because he had a little kid in the truck.

Leonetti testified that he was aware of "an organization" even earlier. When he was "8 or 9, or 6 or 7," his great-grandmother died and an impressive-looking man arrived at the wake "with two guys on the side. . . . He looked

like the President of the United States coming in."

Leonetti asked his uncle who it was.

"That's Angelo Bruno," Scarfo said, identifying the revered boss of the local mob — the man whose assassination would one day lead to Scarfo's rise.

At that time Scarfo was a Mafia functionary with a reputation as a moody hothead, apt to fly off the handle at any perceived slight, particularly any aimed at his bantamweight 5-foot-5 frame. In 1963 he stabbed a longshoreman to death in a fight over a diner booth in South Philadelphia and served a short jail stint. As punishment, Angelo Bruno banished Scarfo to Atlantic City, then the Siberia of the underworld — a dying seaside resort with high unemployment, a small population and no one with any money to blow.

Scarfo moved his family to the Ducktown section, where his mother bought a small apartment complex on North Georgia Avenue — a short, close-set block of modest houses and businesses right off the main drag — and the exiled Scarfo squeaked by for years with a little bookmaking, a little loan-sharking, a little prostitution.

Young Philip, meanwhile, was cutting his basketball teeth at St. Michael's, an elementary school a block away. He played on preteen Biddy church teams and in the Catholic Youth Organization league, and he played guard his junior and senior years for the Holy Spirit Spartans, a decent enough team noted for its hustle.

His high-school graduation picture shows a vulnerable young man with an ample nose, much more prominent then because he hadn't filled out. His looks greatly improved with age.

The following assessment comes from a court stenographer: "I came upstairs after his testimony and I said to people, 'Wow, did I do a double take on that guy!' He had jet-black hair, dark complexion — I don't know if he was tan or naturally dark — and

what looked like green eyes. I mean, what a combination! I don't know, I guess I expected some big duh-duh-duh guy. But he's not. And his voice: it was very soft.

"I found him to be very convincing," she says. "I tell you, he was just as cool as, I don't know. I sat to the right of the witness box, about a foot away from him, and he was so calm. His voice never broke, he never got excited. Only once, when one defense attorney challenged him about his religion — that he's a Catholic but he kills people."

AFTER HIGH SCHOOL, Leonetti could have gone either way with his life. With no specific career in mind, he enrolled in junior college.

Then Uncle Nick started to need him.

In June 1971, Scarfo was imprisoned on a contempt citation, and Leonetti was called on to shuttle his mother and grandmother back and forth to the jail for visits. "Little by little," Leonetti testified, Scarfo started giving him "messages to bring back" to the underboss and other associates. When Scarfo got out of prison in 1973 he proposed that his nephew and others be brought into the family. Scarfo let it be known, said Leonetti, that "if any work had to be done, like any murders or beatings, that we were there waiting to do them, because we wanted to be 'made' members."

Leonetti complied willingly and happily, flattered by his uncle's patronage. People respected his uncle. Leonetti looked up to him as he would a father. Would your own father steer you wrong?

"He never had a chance to be whatever he intended to be," says Harold I. Garber, a former Atlantic City lawyer of Scarfo's. "He never even had a chance to have an intention. Philip, I don't believe, was his own man."

Nor did his mother or grandmother intervene. They went along with the natural flow of generations. They encouraged him.

Nancy Leonetti was "in a way, Philip's mentor," says Dick Ross of Linwood, N.J., who was assigned to the F.B.I.'s office in Atlantic City from 1979 to 1990. "They were very close."

And the grandmother, Catherine Scarfo?

"She's a stone racketeer," says Ross. "She promoted Nicky. She was delighted when he became boss." Ross's informers in the Mafia tell him she's the best wise guy of them all — in her 80's now, but still feisty and sharp-witted. "Shrewd and tough," Ross says of her. "Taught him everything he knew. She's got the money now."

Catherine Scarfo still lives on North Georgia Avenue in the big apartment house, a brown brick and stucco thing with bay windows and wide concrete steps painted bright green. At the top, a scrawled note is taped inside a glass door: "This door must be closed at all times for everyone's safety."

Before I have a chance to knock, a short older woman with reddish hair beckons me in. We stand in the foyer, before what looks like a huge dining room — cozy, tasteful, muted — with a long table in the center. She is cordial, businesslike. "Yes, I'm Catherine Scarfo," she says with clasped, proper hands. But when she learns the purpose of the visit, her voice rises; her exasperation shows her pain. The words tumble out.

"This is *my* family," she says and presses her palms to her chest. "This is *my* problem. This is *my* heartache. I don't have to broadcast it."

Her chin comes forward, proudly, defiantly, and she digs her hands into the low front pockets of her sleeveless cotton smock.

"Save your breath."

The devastation of Catherine Scarfo's life is well documented: a son in prison for life. Philip in prison and informing on the mob. A daughter and great-grandson relocated with new identities. Three other grandsons cast hither and yon: Scarfo's oldest boy has cut off most contact with his father and changed his name. His middle son, Nicky Jr., shot up in a restaurant on Halloween 1989, is under indictment for racketeering in New Jersey. And his youngest son, Mark, has been in a deep coma since November 1988, when he hanged himself during his father's murder and racketeering trial. He was 17. Investigators say that schoolmates were taunting him and that he was ashamed of his father. The boy's horrified mother cut him down in time to save his life but little else.

Leonetti told investigators that Scarfo dismissed his son with an obscene epithet, calling him "weak." He himself "couldn't stop crying" after he read the suicide note, he says. His voice dripping with disgust, Leonetti testified, "A 17-year-old kid hung himself because he don't want to be involved with the mob, O.K.? He wanted to be a normal kid."

He saw it could have been his own son, who had been best friends with Mark Scarfo — still could be his own son, a teen-ager who has been relocated in the witness-protection program.

Q: What do you hope to get out of this when it's all over?
A: That my son goes to college.

And, it goes without saying, a reduced sentence.

ONCE LEONETTI WAS ONE of the boys, his world was populated with men named Faffy and Shotzie and Long John; Pat the Cat, Chicken Noodle, Nicky Crow, Reds and Scoops; Sam the Barber, Nick the Blade and Harry the Hunchback. Tommy Spats, Hawaiian Joe, Sam Cobblestones, Two Fingers Brown, Pappy, Sparky and Spike.

It was a world of double-crosses, triple-crosses and quadruple-crosses; of slapping people around on street corners in front of witnesses, shaking down other crooks, delivering "messages" with baseball bats, and, 90 percent of the time, hanging around. In restaurants, on the boardwalk, at private clubhouses. Sitting on a milk crate in the sun outside some little variety store, and at night frequenting hot spots where the vendors were too afraid to charge.

Watching them pace around with their hands in their pockets, their hands in their belts, was like watching "a skit from 'Saturday Night Live,'" says Frank Friel, a former Philadelphia police captain. Grown men with no visible source of income who have never progressed past the stage of hanging on the corner, plotting deadly capers: How to lure the victim to where you're going to kill him. What weapon to use. Where to get it. How to get away. Who drives. What to do with the body. These were guys with way too much time on their hands.

Q: Now, what is La Cosa Nostra, or the Mafia?
A: Well, it's a secret criminal organization.
Q: What's the purpose of that organization?
A: To make money.
Q: Make money how?
A: Any way we can. Threats, you know, extortions, gambling, murder.

Less than 10 years out of high school, the happy-go-lucky treasurer of Mr. Checchio's homeroom at Holy Spirit had developed a notorious deadly silence and icy stare. His vacant, fearless gaze suggested a man capable of unspeakable acts, and an Atlantic City radio broadcaster was inspired to tag him "Crazy Phil." Leonetti wanted to sue, but Scarfo said he should be glad: "Do you know how many guys would pay to have a nickname like that?" To this day, Leonetti detests it.

Q: Mr. Leonetti, how many people did you say you've killed?
A: Personally?
Q: Personally.
A: Two, sir.

The first one, in 1976, was Louis DeMarco.

"Spaced out on drugs," De-Marco had robbed some numbers houses run by a mob higher-up and had tied up and "abused" an older woman who ran one of them, Leonetti testified.

"So we caught him down in Atlantic City at a motel," said Leonetti, and "I killed him."

Leonetti shot him five times.

Vincent Falcone, a cement contractor from Margate, N.J., was with Leonetti that day. They were friends. In December 1979, Leonetti also killed *him*. Falcone, godfather to Scarfo's youngest son, had bad-mouthed Scarfo as "crazy" to Scarfo's cousin and wisecracked that he wanted $500 a week just to hang around with him. "When my uncle heard that," Leonetti testified, "he wanted to kill him."

Leonetti was acquitted, with others, of the murder but has since confessed and described the circumstances of Falcone's death at a Margate apartment.

Q: O.K. And tell us exactly what happened then, when you got Falcone inside?
A: My uncle was watching TV, and he was making drinks, and I shot him.
Q: Then your uncle checked his breathing?
A: Yes, sir.
Q: And what did he say to you?
A: 'Shoot him again.'
Q: And what did you do?
A: I shot him again.

Leonetti was represented in the 1980 Falcone trial by an Atlantic City lawyer, Edwin J. Jacobs Jr., who remembers Leonetti as "perceptive," "intelligent" and "very charming, not artificially charming as a lot of organized-crime people are."

He was the kind of guy, says Jacobs, who couldn't stand noise and who preferred quiet evenings at home with his girlfriend, Gina. (Leonetti had married when he was young; the couple had a son but were soon estranged.) Gina has been re-located in the witness-protection program. She was a teen-ager dating Vincent Falcone when Leonetti killed him.

IN THE LATE 1970'S, CAsino gambling got the go-ahead in Atlantic City. Overnight, the depressed seaside resort was transformed into a potential underworld bonanza. Scarfo was in the thick of it, and Angelo Bruno's popularity after 21 years was on the wane. Underlings regarded him as an old-fashioned taskmaster who wouldn't keep up with the times: he wanted drug trafficking kept to a minimum. He closed the books on admitting new family members. Rather than "claim" Atlantic City, he diplomatically left it "open" to the more powerful New York families. Ambitious young men in his own clan seethed.

Angelo Bruno had to go, and in March 1980, as he sat in a parked car talking with a man he thought was a friend, he was put away with a single shotgun blast behind his right ear. Thus began an internecine war that Leonetti estimated claimed 20 to 30 lives in mob-related murders.

About a month after Bruno was killed, two of the men believed responsible were found tortured to death. One of them, Bruno's *consigliere*, or counselor, had been stabbed, bludgeoned, garroted and shot 13 times before being stuffed naked into the trunk of a car in the South Bronx that was littered with torn-up $20 bills, an allusion to his greed. Two more senior members were then wiped out: a cousin of Bruno's, who turned up in a wooded area of Staten Island, the back of his head shot away, and a major loan shark, who was found wrapped in trash bags in a South Philadelphia parking lot.

It was at the onset of these heady times that Leonetti, having "made his bones" by carrying out two mob murders, was formally initiated into La Cosa Nostra, *this thing of ours*.

The ceremony took place in

June 1980 at a South Philadelphia row house owned by a *capo* named Johnny Capella. Leonetti was summoned into the middle of a circle of men by Bruno's successor as boss, Philip (Chicken Man) Testa. Testa pointed to a gun and a knife on a table and said, "Would you use this gun or this knife to help anybody if they had a problem?"

Leonetti said, "Yeah, sure I would."

Testa said, "I know you would. I know you since you've been a baby."

Scarfo, by then the *consigliere* and Leonetti's sponsor, took an old-fashioned diamond tie tack and drew blood from Leonetti's trigger finger. He wiped the blood on a tissue, placed the tissue in Leonetti's cupped hands and told him to make believe he was holding a picture of a saint. Scarfo lighted the tissue and Leonetti juggled the fire between his hands. "May I burn like this saint if I betray my friends," he said, and rubbed the ashes into his palms. He was 27, he was "made" and his Uncle Nick was less than a year away from being the boss.

Scarfo's promotion came in the spring of 1981, after Testa was blown up on his porch by a bomb packed with nails. Exactly one year later, the bullet-riddled body of the man believed to have detonated the bomb, a South Philadelphia pizza-parlor owner and family associate named Rocco Marinucci, was discovered stuffed in a garbage bag, his hands bound, his face beaten and his mouth symbolically stuffed with unexploded firecrackers. Three months later, a young Philadelphia waiter named Theodore DiPretoro, fearing for his life, turned himself in and confessed to the murder of Testa. And the month after that, July 1982, Testa's son, Salvatore, was shotgunned from a passing car as he sat on a crate in the Italian Market. (He survived the attack.)

With the old guard murdered off, the organization was fast changing into what one Federal prosecutor de-

scribed as a "me-generation" mob, made up of inexperienced, rash, self-absorbed men, who, after being held back for too long, were inclined to squabble among themselves and bungle hits.

During this time of messy, generational flux, Nick Scarfo emerged as boss almost by default. He had been "dead-out broke" until then, Leonetti testified. Now he was determined to have his pot of gold, and his most trusted confederate throughout would be Philip Leonetti.

By the summer of 1981, Leonetti was a *capo*, and the law was all over Scarfo. They kept finding ways to lock him up — possession of a firearm by a convicted felon, associating with known criminals — and when he was away, Leonetti was one of the members left in charge.

Business prospered. In addition to their lucrative gambling operations, Scarfo's boys were shaking down independent drug dealers, loan sharks and bookmakers and demanding a cut of their action.

The other primary source of income, Leonetti testified, was Local 54 of the hotel and restaurant workers' union, the largest and most powerful union in the casino industry. According to Leonetti, all appointments, jobs, union cards or other favors were subject to the approval of Scarfo, who also collected about $20,000 a month skimmed from the union welfare fund.

Eventually Scarfo amassed enough wealth to buy a getaway in Fort Lauderdale, Fla., called Casablanca South. It featured a giant wrought-iron flamingo fountain and a cabin cruiser named the Usual Suspects.

THROUGHOUT SCARfo's reign, the New York families, having taken advantage of Angelo Bruno's decision to leave Atlantic City "open," were going about their business. Of course there were interfamily disputes, and Scarfo traveled to New York on numerous occasions to air his gripes

and exchange information — first with Paul Castellano and later with John Gotti.

Leonetti accompanied him; in November 1989, he described these meetings in some detail before a Manhattan Federal grand jury looking into the murders of Castellano and his bodyguard, Thomas Bilotti. The following information is based on a transcript of Leonetti's secret grand-jury testimony.

The first time Leonetti met Castellano was in the summer of 1981. Scarfo had just become the boss in Philadelphia, Leonetti testified, "and he wanted to meet Paul Castellano as the boss." Introductions were made all around; they kissed, and Castellano thanked Scarfo for arranging the murder of a Trenton mobster — "an outlaw," Leonetti called him — named Frank (Frankie Stale) Stillitano, who, Philadelphia police say, killed the son of a Gambino-family soldier named Nick Russo in 1979.

By mid-1985 Scarfo and Castellano would meet at least four more times with Leonetti present. Favors were discussed, disputes settled, underworld gossip exchanged. They met for the last time — Leonetti said he couldn't remember why — the summer before Castellano was gunned down in front of Sparks Steak House in midtown Manhattan in December 1985. At Antonio's Restaurant in Trenton about a week later, Salvatore (Sammy the Bull) Gravano, who had been a Gambino family soldier, was telling Leonetti and Scarfo that he had been made a captain, and that "John Gotti is the boss now and Frankie DeCicco is the underboss." (DeCicco was later blown up in his car.)

Soon after, Scarfo and Leonetti took off for Fort Lauderdale, where they ran into a Gambino family member who described John Gotti as "a great guy," according to Leonetti's testimony. "He was telling my uncle, 'Just like you, Nick, he's a real gangster, always for the underdog.'"

By "gangster" he meant that Gotti was "not like Paul Cas-

tellano," Leonetti said. "Paul Castellano was considered a businessman. John Gotti is considered a gangster, because — well, you know — he kills people. ... You do something over there ... if you're wrong and you keep doing it, you're going to have a big problem with him. He don't hem and haw with you."

When Leonetti and his uncle returned to Atlantic City from Florida early in 1986, they were paid a visit by a Gambino soldier named Arnold Squittieri. John Gotti wanted to see Scarfo. He "wanted to meet my uncle as a boss," Leonetti testified. "He was going around at this time meeting all the bosses."

The first meeting took place in February 1986, at what Leonetti understood was the home of Gravano's brother-in-law, Edward Garafola. Gravano had driven them there in a gray Lincoln Continental after meeting them at a Bagel Nosh on Staten Island a few blocks away. Several men were seated inside at a table.

According to Leonetti's testimony: "Gravano said, 'Nick, this is our boss, John Gotti.' And he said, 'John, this is Nicky Scarfo. He's the boss of the Philadelphia family.'"

The first thing John Gotti said to Scarfo, before he even had a chance to sit down, Leonetti testified, was, "I got the O.K. from the Commission to kill Paul Castellano." The Commission has been described by Leonetti as the Mafia's "Supreme Court," a group of underworld bosses, dominated by the five New York families, who make the rules and adjudicate interfamily disputes. "He says, 'I just want you to know that, Nick. I did everything the right way.'"

Scarfo replied: "I know, John. I'm sure you did," Leonetti testified. .

Gotti then went on to describe the size and scope of his family — "about 500 guys," Leonetti testified — and his efforts to identify everybody, figure out who they reported to and who Castellano's captains were, so he could take them down and put in his own men.

At one point Scarfo got up

to go to the bathroom, and Leonetti, Gotti and Gravano struck up a conversation about Mafia management styles. Gravano commented to Gotti that Leonetti was young for an underboss, meaning it as a compliment.

"Yeah, you know, there's a lot of guys in my family, these older greaseballs," Gotti said. "They resent me, because I'm so young and I'm a boss."

"Well, look," said Leonetti, "Al Capone was a boss, he was 29, and Lucky Luciano was a boss when he was young. I mean, as long as you know what you're doing, there's nothing wrong with being young. A lot of them guys are like that, that's the way they think, them old greaseballs. Like Angelo Bruno. If we would go to him to ask him a favor to try to get into a business, he would say, 'No, it's a bad idea,' and then, behind our back, he would send his son-in-law or his cousin to get the deal." But, Leonetti continued, "if he wanted to kill somebody, he would know who to come to, he would use us."

"Jesus, Paul was the same way, the same type of guy," Gotti said to Gravano, referring to Castellano. He turned back to Leonetti. "He did the same thing with us. He wouldn't let us make a living, and on top of everything else, he wanted to kill me."

About a week later, Scarfo and Leonetti returned to New York. They wanted to check out Gotti's claim that the Commission had approved the Castellano hit, and the man they called on was Genovese family *consigliere*, Louis (Bobby) Manna, a close Scarfo ally. Scarfo talked to Manna privately and reported to Leonetti later that Manna had said, "Yes, he did get the O.K.; he did everything the right way," Leonetti testified.

BY THE MID-1980'S, IN-vestigators were sure that Scarfo was grooming his nephew to succeed him as boss. The two men no longer flew on the same plane and had taken to conducting their business with extreme

discretion. There were bugs everywhere — cars, houses, lamp posts — so they never talked business on the phone. (Scarfo didn't even have a phone.) And when they talked business in Scarfo's house they'd turn on two televisions and a radio and then whisper in front of the radio.

Scarfo's paranoia deepened as the years passed and eventually flew off the charts. You never knew what was going to make him want to kill somebody. Subsequent murder and racketeering trials brought it all out. One soldier was eliminated for "dereliction of duty" — not showing up at a hit. When a man who testified against Scarfo was out of reach, Scarfo ordered that his innocent father pay the price. One venerated mobster was killed for showing disrespect, another was shot to death in front of his mother and an entire family faction was ordered exterminated because its leader, a stooped, bald, greedy mob elder named Harry (The Hunchback) Riccobene, refused to share his booty with Scarfo, whom he viewed as an upstart.

Riccobene survived two attempts on his life and eventually went to prison for murder. But other relatives did not survive. One of them, Riccobene's nephew, Enrico, provided the saddest footnote to that war. When Scarfo's men knocked on the door of his Philadelphia jewelry store and smiled through the glass, he stepped into his walk-in safe and shot himself to death.

Eventually Scarfo started ordering the deaths of loyal followers — chief among them Salvatore Testa, the young son of Scarfo's one-time mentor, Philip Testa. Scarfo had thought enough of young Salvy to make him a *capo* when he was in his mid-20's. But Salvy worked so hard that he soon distinguished himself as the rising star of the Philadelphia crime family, and Scarfo began to think of him as a rival. After Salvy jilted his fiancée, the daughter of the underboss, Scarfo decided he

had shown disrespect, and he approved his murder.

By January 1986 Scarfo even suspected that his cousins, the Merlino brothers, were out to get him; he wanted them dead. Other members intervened, however, and in a rare reversal, Scarfo merely demoted both brothers to the rank of soldier and elevated his nephew to the position of underboss.

At 32, Philip Leonetti had reached the apex of his career. But at the same time the dark fairy tale he and his confederates had been living was going up in gunsmoke. Everything was coming unhinged. It was becoming evident to everyone that Scarfo killed not just for business reasons, but for personal affronts. He killed to send a message. He killed, said one Mafia informant, because "he just loves it."

Leonetti told one investigator that Scarfo even considered killing his own wife, Dominica. Scarfo learned during his racketeering trial, Leonetti testified, that "little by little" Dominica had robbed him of "around $400,000." She was gambling at the Trump Plaza.

Scarfo's suspicious nature ultimately brought him down. With the body count rising, the men below him could no longer sustain the fiction that they wouldn't be next to get whacked. Unbelievably, "made" members — all of them "me-generation" gangsters initiated in the 80's — started to defect and inform on the mob. The first two were Thomas (Tommy Del) Del-Giorno, who told investigators that Scarfo had marked him for death, and Nicholas (Nicky Crow) Caramandi, who had been involved in a bold attempt to extort $1 million from the real-estate magnate Willard G. Rouse 3d, who was trying to develop the Philadelphia waterfront. Rouse went to the F.B.I.; Caramandi went to jail, and once Caramandi realized that Scarfo was wrongly blaming him for fouling up the Rouse extortion, he, too, went to the F.B.I.

The two men started testi-

fying against their own, and, in November 1988, Scarfo, Leonetti and 15 others were convicted of Federal murder and racketeering charges in the biggest roundup of bad guys since the days of Eliot Ness and the Untouchables.

Before sentencing, two more members defected — one of them the demoted *capo* Lawrence (Yogi) Merlino, who is also available to testify against Gotti. And, soon after receiving his 45-year sentence in May 1989, Leonetti flipped, too.

His mother arranged the negotiations.

"Imagine the guy under Saddam Hussein," says Leonetti's Philadelphia lawyer, Frank DeSimone. "He's loyal till he gets away from him. Then what do you do? You see the light. Philip saw the light, and he acted."

"He realized," says Louis Pichini, a Federal prosecutor in the November 1988 trial, "that the world he was in wasn't 'The Godfather' anymore. It was 'Goodfellas.' It changed from a perverted romantic ideal of what the mob was into the harder reality of treacheries and deceitfulness."

The Government immediately relocated Leonetti's mother, his girlfriend and his teen-age son, who was whisked out of Holy Spirit, academic records and all. According to investigators, Scarfo, 62, fumed in his maximum-security cell in Marion, Ill., when he heard.

He now refers to his beloved Philip as "my faggot nephew."

THE RESIDENTS OF North Georgia Avenue in Atlantic City remain on their guard. Scarfo's gone. Leonetti's gone. Everybody's gone. But still, no one utters a discouraging word. The woman at Cathy's Beauty Salon, as she stacks cash on a table in the rear: "I'm in business, you understand? I like everybody. Everybody is my friend." The owner of Angeloni's Restaurant, while laying tile in the bathroom: "They were the best customers I had." The pharmacist, from behind his counter, with a sly, reflective smile: "I just feel sorry for the mother. That's my only comment."

And Scarf Inc., a cement contracting company owned by Leonetti and once the mob's Atlantic City headquarters, is now just another of Catherine Scarfo's apartments. A young, good-looking guy comes to the door in tight jeans and a white T-shirt with a small "Surf Boards by Dewey Weber" logo over the breast and says, "Really, I don't know anything." He swallows hard, and his Adam's apple bobs up and down his throat. "I'm just a tenant, I'm just a tenant." He waves his arm, shifts his weight on his stocking feet. He doesn't want to be impolite, but. . . .

Philip Leonetti says it bothers him now that he killed people. He says he's sorry for their families and tries not to think about how he felt when he pulled the trigger. He has told his lawyer he believed he was doing the right thing by punishing those who violated the laws of a society they voluntarily joined and whose rules they were familiar with. He was punishing men like himself.

John Gotti is evidently next. He has been sitting in his cell at the Metropolitan Correctional Center in Manhattan ever since he was picked up last December along with his *consigliere*, Gravano; his underboss, Frank (Frankie Loc) Locascio; and Thomas Gam-

bino, a *capo*. Under RICO, the Racketeer Influenced and Corrupt Organizations statute, Gotti has been charged with heading a criminal enterprise, income-tax evasion, obstruction of justice, gambling, loan-sharking and ordering four mob murders, including Castellano's.

The date of his trial in the Federal District Court in Brooklyn has yet to be set — in part because prosecutors have been jockeying to have Gotti's defense team removed from the case, claiming they are "house counsels" for the Gambino crime organization and guilty of "improper conduct." One of the lawyers representing the lawyers says that Gotti's main attorney, Bruce Cutler,

is just too good at proving Gotti's innocence, and that's why the Government wants to get rid of him.

In the past, prosecutors have had an impossible time convincing jurors that John Gotti is not a romantic, godfatherly sort of gangster, but a cold-blooded menace who should be locked away. They may have had evidence, but they lacked the emotional Robin Hood appeal to "the little people" that Gotti radiates.

Well, the Feds are determined that the charismatic Dapper Don will not strut away from justice again and that by the time their star witness is through with him, it will be Philip Leonetti who emerges as the folk hero.

Computer Ethics

J. Thomas McEwen

J. Thomas McEwen is Principal Associate at the Institute for Law and Justice, Inc., in Alexandria, Virginia.

*T*hree members of the "Legion of Doom" recently pled guilty in Federal court to charges involving theft of computer access codes from BellSouth Corporation. The Legion of Doom is a nationwide group of hackers who exchange information about computer systems and techniques to break into them. According to the Government's evidence, the three entered various BellSouth computer systems without permission and obtained computer access codes. They then distributed the codes to other computer hackers for use in illegally accessing computer systems. The corporation estimates its losses at $372,000 in software and services and $800,000 in credit card losses.

Hacking is just one example of a computer crime. Others include creating computer viruses that infect and sometimes destroy computer systems, altering programs to perform unauthorized functions, creating accounts to advance embezzlements and frauds, and making copies of proprietary software for resale or giveaway. Such crimes and other unethical use of computers are growing rapidly throughout the country as new technology makes computers smaller, cheaper, and more accessible.

The lines dividing ethical, unethical, and illegal practices in using computers, their hardware, software, and data files are not always easy to distinguish.

Consider these situations:

◆ A parent offers to copy a computer program for a school that cannot afford to buy the program.

◆ An employee maintains a small data base on his employer's computer as part of a sideline business.

◆ An individual uses someone else's computer account number and password to view the contents of a data base.

◆ A customer gives his telephone number as part of a sales transaction at a store. The store enters the number into a computerized data base and later sells the data base to a telemarketing firm.

◆ A school system's computer programmer develops a program to schedule students and classes. The programmer accepts a job with another school system and leaves with a copy of the program.

◆ An inadvertent error in entering data into a police department's computer leads to the temporary detainment of an innocent person.

Which of the foregoing scenarios describes illegal activity? Unethical activity? Acceptable activity?

In most States, the first three are illegal actions. Copying a proprietary program is software piracy. Maintaining personal information on a business computer is misuse of a computer. And viewing files with another person's account number and password is illegal access.

The last three scenarios do not deal with actions that are illegal, but they raise other questions regarding privacy and the need to deal accurately and responsibly with information affecting another's welfare. They illustrate the kinds of situations businesses, schools, and public agencies must address in developing standards for ethical, responsible computer use.

Criminal justice administrators, corporate executives, and academic leaders are beginning to focus on doing this and imparting the knowledge to computer users at home, in school, and in the workplace.

Criminal justice agencies, in particular, have a stake in preventing people, particularly young computer enthusiasts, from sliding into computer crime as they become proficient in accessing and manipulating data.

NIJ-sponsored meeting explores ethics issues

In recognition of these problems, the National Institute of Justice, in cooperation with the Department of Education, sponsored a 2-day meeting in Washington, D.C., to examine the overlapping issues of computer laws and the responsibilities of individuals, schools, and businesses to adhere to acceptable standards for computer use.

The meeting brought together educators, business representatives, and criminal justice personnel to discuss "responsible computing"—the rules of conduct that can keep individuals, workers, and students within both the letter and spirit of the law. This article presents key issues from the meeting's discussions and working papers.

Criminal justice perspectives

A recent National Institute of Justice

From *National Institute of Justice Reports*, January/February 1991, pp. 8-11. *National Institute of Justice Reports*, published by the U.S. Department of Justice, Washington, D.C. 20531 survey of police departments illustrates the attention now being paid to computer crime. Nearly half the police respondents in large metropolitan areas said they had received reports of computer crimes and confiscated computers during 1989.

Charles Testagrossa, head of the rackets bureau in the prosecutor's office in New York City, notes, "We're starting to see computerization of records in all sorts of operations—larcenies, gambling, narcotics."[1]

In 1989, the National Institute of Justice sponsored three computer crime studies: one examined different organizational approaches for computer crime investigation and prosecution, another documented the experiences of several dedicated computer crime units, and the third developed a handbook for computer crime investigation.

One conclusion from the studies is that persons involved in computer crimes acquire their interest and skills at an early age. They are introduced to computers in school, and their usual "career path" starts with illegally copying computer programs. Serious offenders then get into a progression of computer crimes including telecommunications fraud (making free long-distance calls), unauthorized access to other computers (hacking for fun and profit), and credit card fraud (obtaining cash advances, purchasing equipment through computers).

Most important, young hackers' beliefs about computers and information come from associations with other hackers, not from family members and teachers. Few schools teach computer ethics, and parents of arrested hackers are usually unaware that their children have been illegally accessing computer systems.

What hackers believe

Investigators worry about the career path that leads young people from hacking into systems to using computers to commit serious offenses. They note that these young hackers hold unconventional beliefs about computers and information. For instance, hackers believe that:

◆ Computerized data are free and should be accessible to anyone.

◆ Passwords and other security features are simply obstacles to be overcome in obtaining data that should already be available.

◆ While data should never be destroyed, there is nothing wrong with viewing and transferring data for one's own use.

One member of the Legion of Doom has said, "Hackers will do just about anything to break into a computer except crashing a system. That's the only taboo."[2]

Criminal justice professionals believe computer abuses will steadily increase. There is a growing need for police, prosecutors, and judges to focus on controlling computer crime and preventing it through joint efforts with educators and business leaders.

Protecting corporate data

The business community has not yet reached a consensus about what "responsible computing" means, according to corporate representatives at NIJ's meeting. However, businesses agree that the information managed by computers needs to be protected. This task is made difficult by the accessibility and impersonality of computer files.

Accessibility. Employees in many businesses and government agencies once feared that computers would replace them. That has not happened. Indeed, businesses require more employees than before to maintain systems, enter data, generate reports, and perform other functions associated with information systems. This makes corporate files more accessible than ever. Previously, ledger sheets and other valuable company papers were kept in a safe, with only a few trusted employees knowing the combination. Today that same information resides in a data base accessible to anyone with a password.

Impersonality. Persons working with the data base should feel a sense of responsibility for protecting the password and the data base information. But the intangible nature of the system makes that responsibility more difficult to accept, business leaders say. Placing valuable papers in a safe establishes a more concrete sense of

responsibility than simply safeguarding a password for a computer system.

Threat to accuracy. The impersonality of computerized information also threatens the accuracy of data base information. Adding, editing, and deleting records are common but impersonal transactions, accomplished through a monitor and keyboard communicating with a computer that may not be in the same building or even the same city.

Universities are victims of unethical computer practices

Businesses feel that employees come to them without the proper education about their responsibilities with computers and information. Colleges and universities seldom include computer use and abuse in their courses, arguing that this is the responsibility of the schools. On the other hand, many secondary school educators are unsure about what should be taught and are, in any case, reluctant or unable to add to the many subjects in the curriculum.

Educational institutions have a stake in developing student awareness of ethical computer behavior, for they have themselves been frequent victims of computer abuses. For instance:

◆ The University of Tennessee expelled several students last year who invaded the university's computer system and changed grades.

◆ Robert Morris, Jr., while a graduate student at Cornell University, created a virus that infected more than 6,000 computers, many of which were university computers.

◆ A virus attacked the file server of the computer lab at the University of New Mexico's Center for Technology and Education. The lab closed for 2 days while the staff tried to reconstruct damaged files and reload software programs.

Student computer ethics

On a smaller, day-to-day scale, some students have already taken the first step toward a career in computer crime. One university professor offers examples of what he has observed:

◆ A student systems operator used

systems privileges to copy other students' homework.

◆ A student with academic problems generated bogus grade sheets.

◆ A student deliberately destroyed the work files of other students.

Finally, a hacker's publication last year devoted a major portion of a quarterly issue to a detailed description of New York's University Applications Processing Center (UAPC). UAPC connects more than 100 public high schools in New York with computer applications for entering grades, tracking attendance, scheduling classes, and generating transcripts and other reports. The article contained enough information for experienced hackers to break into the system.

First steps in developing awareness of ethical issues

During the 1980's, school districts introduced microcomputers into classrooms to teach computer literacy. Instruction included simple programming concepts and uses of computers with only brief discussions, if any, of privacy and security issues, computer crime, and computer responsibility.

Textbooks on computer literacy rarely mention computer abuses and individual responsibilities. In many schools, computer training is no longer a separate topic but instead is integrated into other course work. There is general agreement that responsible computing behavior should be taught along with the other material, and not as a separate offering.

Educators and software developers have worked together in the important area of preventing software piracy within educational institutions. In 1987, the Software Copyright Committee of the International Council for Computers in Education (ICCE)[3] developed a policy to guide educators. The policy calls on school districts to teach staff the provisions of the copyright law and both staff and students the ethical and practical implications of software piracy. This policy has been adopted by many school districts across the country.

Action items

To expand on these first steps, partici-

pants in the NIJ meeting prepared a series of "action items" to carry out in their businesses, schools, and communities. They based these items on two propositions:

1. *Raising awareness of ethical issues in computer technology is a first step toward engendering ethical behavior.*

2. *Information ethics programs, including codes of computer ethics, need to be accepted by businesses and governments.*

Action on these propositions has started. For example:

◆ The National Institute of Justice and the Department of Education have teamed up for an interagency project to promote the responsible use of technology in the schools.

◆ The National School Boards Association has published an article about the need to alert students and parents about the growing problem. "NIJ opened our eyes to an area that schools have ignored or missed," the article said; it called on school districts to share their experiences and develop a unified approach to the problem. The Association for Educational Communications and Technology published a similar article.

◆ Another initiative is tied to "Computer Learning Month" sponsored by the Computer Learning Foundation in October each year. School districts across the country focus on computer topics during this month. In 1990, the Foundation, in cooperation with IBM, sponsored separate competitions for students and for educators on the subject of responsible computing. Students submitted storybooks on the subject and educators submitted ideas on how to teach responsible computing in schools. From the entries, materials are being developed for use in schools.

These action items will further the steps businesses, schools, and associations have already taken to develop an awareness of the ethical dimensions of computer activity.

Some businesses, for instance, have established information ethics programs. The core of such programs consists of published guidelines regarding data base privacy and security. Posters, meetings, and classes

More Information

The National Institute of Justice has published several reports of NIJ-sponsored studies of computer crime. All are available from the National Institute of Justice/ NCJRS.

Organizing for Computer Crime Investigation and Prosecution

Highlights the range of existing approaches to handling cases of computer crime—from the single-investigator method to formal computer crime units and regional networks—to help local officials choose the best approach for their jurisdictions. NCJ 118216. Free.

Write the National Institute of Justice/NCJRS, Box 6000, Rockville, MD 20850, or call 800–851–3420 or 301–251–5500.

Dedicated Computer Crime Units

For jurisdictions that are considering establishing computer crime units, provides guidance on how to set up and operate the units. Reviews 9 existing law enforcement and prosecution units and describes 11 computer crime cases. Also includes an overview of State laws on computer crime. NCJ 118215. Free.

Contact NCJRS (see above).

Computer Crime: Criminal Justice Resource Manual

Provides more than 300 pages of comprehensive training and reference material for investigators and prosecutors. This second edition updates a manual published 11 years ago, reflecting the enormous changes that have taken place over the past decade. NCJ 118214. $16.50.

Contact NCJRS (see above).

supplement the guidelines and stress the importance of the program.

Experience indicates that greater success is achieved if the programs are specific to the organization, modest in scope, and involve management and staff in their implementation.

Several associations have codes of ethics they are willing to share with other organizations.[4]

Prospects for the future

Computers are a permanent fact of life in workplaces and classrooms across the country. The need to be vigilant about potential computer abuse is not likely to abate.

More businesses are likely to incorporate in their employee orientation and training programs policies on information access and confidentiality, and on adherence to copyright laws.

For their part, many schools and universities, responding to pressure from within and outside their walls, will be refining understanding of computer ethics and integrating the topic into their courses.

For the criminal justice community, computer crime, which already poses special challenges in detection and prosecution, will require more and more attention. To prevent future computer crime, enlightened criminal and juvenile justice agencies must look for ways to help parents, teachers, and employers sensitize the computer-using community to the importance of ethical computer behavior.

The National Institute of Justice will be monitoring these developments as it keeps computer crime prominent in criminal justice research priorities.

Notes

[1] "Police Filch Faxes To Snare a Gambling Ring," by Joseph P. Fried, *The New York Times,* June 3, 1990.

[2] "The Terminal Men," by Willie Schatz, *The Washington Post,* June 24, 1990.

[3] In June 1989, ICCE merged with the International Association for Computing in Education (IACE) to form the International Society for Technology in Education (ISTE).

[4] Examples are the Data Processing Management Association, the Association for Computing Machinery, the Institute of Electrical and Electronics Engineers, the Institute for Certification of Computer Professionals, the Information Systems Security Association, and the International Council for Computers in Education.

Victimology

The crime victim, traditionally the forgotten person in the criminal justice system, is now the center of attention for those who want to change the system. Indeed, historians might call the 1980s the decade in which a move was finally made toward acknowledging victims of crime as central characters in the criminal event, worthy of compassion and concern.

From 1981 to 1990 Presidents Reagan and Bush have proclaimed a National Victims of Crime Week annually with a view to focusing attention on the problems and concerns of crime victims. In December 1982 the President's Task Force on Victims of Crime published a 144-page report on the treatment of crime victims throughout the country. This publication contained 68 recommendations for addressing the problems of victims. While studying the experiences of crime victims, the task force recognized that family violence is often more complex in its causes and solutions than crime committed by unknown perpetrators.

Victims of crime have also been the subject of legislation during the 1980s. For example, the 1982 Omnibus Victim and Witness Protection Act requires the use of victim impact statements at sentencing in federal criminal cases, and provides for greater protection of federal victims and witnesses from intimidation. The Comprehensive Crime Control Act and the Victims of Crime Act of 1984 authorize federal funding for state victim compensation and victim assistance programs.

Comprehensive legislation that protects the interests of the victim has been enacted in more than 35 states. State victim compensation programs have continued to expand, as have victim assistance services in the community.

Thus, recent developments have been supportive of the crime victim.

The articles in this unit provide sharper focus on some key issues. From the lead essay, "The Fear of Crime," we learn that the fear of being victimized is pervasive among people, including some who have never been victims of crime. This article addresses the effects of crime on its victims.

Andrew Karmen's essay, "The Implementation of Victims' Rights: A Challenge for Criminal Justice Professionals," maintains that how criminal justice agents respond to victims' demands will resolve many controversies and generate new ones.

The horror of family violence is clearly seen in "Hunted." The essay "A Vicious Cycle" maintains that the abused child often becomes an abusive parent; however, with the right ingredients, the cycle can be broken.

"Tougher Laws Mean More Cases Are Called Rape" focuses on acquaintance rape as does the article, "Even the Victims Can Be Slow to Recognize Rape."

"The Unbearable Loss" by Chip Brown, reflects upon the increase in child murders in the United States. Many of the victims' families are seeking channels for their grief as well as new legal rights.

Looking Ahead: Challenge Questions

Is the fear of crime realistic?

What life-style changes might you consider to avoid becoming victimized?

Are you familiar with victim service programs in your area?

How does crime affect the victim's psyche?

The Fear of Crime

The fear of crime affects many people, including some who have never been victims of crime

How do crime rates compare with the rates of other life events?

Events	Rate per 1,000 adults per year*
Accidental injury, all circumstances	242
Accidental injury at home	79
Personal theft	72
Accidental injury at work	58
Violent victimization	31
Assault (aggravated and simple)	24
Injury in motor vehicle accident	17
Death, all causes	11
Victimization with injury	10
Serious (aggravated) assault	9
Robbery	6
Heart disease death	4
Cancer death	2
Rape (women only)	2
Accidental death, all circumstances	.5
Pneumonia/influenza death	.3
Motor vehicle accident death	.2
Suicide	.2
Injury from fire	.1
Homicide/legal intervention death	.1
Death from fire	.03

These rates approximate your chances of becoming a victim of these events. More precise estimates can be derived by taking account of such factors as your age, sex, race, place of residence, and lifestyle. Findings are based on 1982–84 data, but there is little variation in rates from year to year.

*These rates exclude children from the calculations (those under age 12–17, depending on the series). Fire injury/death data are based on the total population, because no age-specific data are available in this series.

Sources: *Current estimates from the National Health Interview Survey: United States, 1982,* National Center for Health Statistics. "Advance report of final mortality statistics, 1983," *Monthly Vital Statistics Report,* National Center for Health Statistics. *Estimates of the population of the United States, by age, sex, and race: 1980 to 1984,* U.S. Bureau of the Census. *The 1984 Fire Almanac,* National Fire Protection Association. *Criminal victimization 1984,* BJS Bulletin, October 1985.

The chance of being a violent crime victim, with or without injury, is greater than that of being hurt in a traffic accident

The rates of some violent crimes are higher than those of some other serious life events. For example, the risk of being the victim of a violent crime is higher than the risk of death from cancer or injury or death from a fire. Still, a person is much more likely to die from natural causes than as a result of a criminal victimization.

About a third of the people in the United States feel very safe in their neighborhoods

The fear of crime cannot be measured precisely because the kinds of fears people express vary depending on the specific questions asked. Nevertheless, asking them about the likelihood of crime in their homes and neighborhoods yields a good assessment of how safe they feel in their own immediate environment.

In the Victimization Risk Survey, a 1984 supplement to the National Crime Survey, most people said that they felt at least fairly safe in their homes and neighborhoods. Yet, the people who said that they felt "fairly safe" may have been signaling some concern about crime. Based on a "very safe" response, a little more than 4 in 10 people felt entirely safe in their homes and about 1 in 3 felt totally safe in their neighborhoods—
• homeowners felt safer than renters
• people living in nonmetropolitan areas felt safer than those living in cities
• families with incomes of $50,000 or more were most likely to report their neighborhoods were very safe from crime.

The Victimization Risk Survey found that—
• 9 in 10 persons felt very or fairly safe in their places of work
• few persons—about 1 in 10—felt in danger of being a victim of a crime by a fellow employee, but persons working in places that employ more than 50 people were more likely to express fear of possible victimization.

The groups at the highest risk of becoming victims are not the ones who express the greatest fear of crime

Females and the elderly generally express a greater fear of crime than do people in groups who face a much greater risk. The Reactions to Crime project found that such impressions are related to the content of information about crime. Such information tends to emphasize stories about elderly and female victims. These stories may influence women and the elderly in judging the seriousness of their own condition. Perhaps groups such as females and the elderly reduce their risk of victimization by constricting their activities to reduce their exposure to danger. This behavior would account, at least in part, for their high levels of fear and their low levels of victimization.

Relatives, friends, and neighbors who hear about a crime become as fearful as the victim

When one household in a neighborhood is affected by a crime, the entire neighborhood may feel more vulnerable. This suggests that people who have not been victimized personally may be strongly affected when they hear about how others have been victimized. The Reactions to Crime project found that

From *Report to the Nation on Crime and Justice,* Bureau of Justice Statistics, U.S. Department of Justice, March 1988, pp. 24-25.

How does crime affect its victims?

indirect reaction to crime is often very strong.

$13 billion was lost from personal and household crimes in 1985

The direct cash and property losses from personal robberies, personal and household larcenies, household burglaries, and privately owned motor vehicle theft in 1985 was slightly more than $13 billion. This NCS finding probably underestimates the amount covered by insurance because the claims of many respondents had not been settled at the time of the NCS interview.

UCR data show that in 1985 losses from reported robberies, burglaries, and larceny/theft surpassed $5.9 billion. Among the many economic consequences of crime are lost productivity from victims' absence from work, medical care, and the cost of security measures taken to deter crime.

Other costs of crime include the economic costs of the underground economy, lowered property values, and pain and suffering of victims, their families, friends, and neighbors.

The economic impact of crime differs for different groups

The cost of crime is borne by all segments of society, but to different degrees. A study on the economic cost of crime using NCS data for 1981 shows that the dollar loss from crimes involving money, property loss, or destruction of property rises with income.

• Median losses were higher for households with incomes of $15,000 or more than for households with incomes of

less than $7,500 from burglary ($200 vs. $100) and from motor vehicle theft ($2,000 vs. $700).

• Median losses from personal crimes were higher for blacks ($58) than for whites ($43).
• Median losses from household crimes were higher for blacks ($90) than for whites ($60).
• More than 93% of the total loss from crime was in crimes without victim-offender contact (such as burglary, theft without contact, and motor vehicle theft).

Many victims or members of their families lose time from work

Along with injuries suffered, victims or other members of their household may have lost time from work because of a violent crime. Lost worktime was reported in 15% of rapes and 7% of assaults (11% of aggravated assaults, 6% of simple assaults).

Violent crimes killed 19,000 and injured 1.7 million in 1985

NCS data for 1985 show that of all rape, robbery, and assault victims—
• 30% were injured
• 15% required some kind of medical attention
• 8% required hospital care.

The likelihood of injury was—
• greater for females than males even when rape was excluded from the analysis
• about the same for whites and blacks
• greater for persons from lower than from higher income households.

Who is injured seriously enough to require medical attention?

An analysis of NCS data for 1973–82 found that—
• Female victims are more likely than male victims to be injured, but they have about the same likelihood of requiring medical attention (13% of female vs. 12% of male victims).
• Blacks are more likely than whites to require medical attention when injured in violent crimes; 16% of black violent crime victims and 16% of the victims of all other racial groups required medical attention, while 11% of white victims required such care.

How seriously a victim is injured varies by type of crime

	Percent of all violent victimizations requiring:			Median stay for those hospitalized overnight
	Medical attention	Treatment in hospital emergency room	Overnight hospital stay	
Rape	24%	14%	3%	4 days
Robbery	15	7	2	5
Assault	11	5	1	5
Aggravated	18	9	3	5
Simple	7	3	—	2

—less than .5%

Source: BJS National Crime Survey, 1973–82.

THE IMPLEMENTATION OF VICTIMS' RIGHTS: A CHALLENGE FOR CRIMINAL JUSTICE PROFESSIONALS

Andrew Karmen

The victories of the victims' rights movement have led to the enactment of many pledges of fair treatment and of opportunities to participate in the criminal justice process. Evaluations are now needed to determine whether criminal justice officials and agencies are implementing these recently gained rights in good faith. Such evaluations could help to clarify continuing concerns, such as whether the system can ever be reformed to operate in the best interests of victims, how the observance of victims' rights can be guaranteed, whether all victims can be treated fairly, and how often victims might opt for non-punitive resolutions of their conflicts with offenders.

INTRODUCTION

The struggle to gain formal, legal rights has been a powerful moving force throughout history. The concept of "rights" suggests both an escape from oppression and exploitation plus an achievement of independence and autonomy. A number of social movements seeking freedom, liberation, empowerment, equality, and justice have sought greater rights for their constituencies. The most well-known include civil rights, workers' rights, students' rights, children's rights, women's rights, gay rights' and prisoners' rights movements. The victims' rights movement of the late 1970s and 1980s falls within this tradition. The underlying objective of the victims' rights movement is to assure that certain standards of fair treatment towards victims are adopted and respected as their cases are processed within the criminal justice system.

The criminal justice system is a branch of the government that routinely comes under scathing criticism from many different quarters. Conservative advocates of "law and order" find fault with its alleged permissiveness. Liberal proponents of procedural egalitarianism decry the system's apparent discriminatory inequities. Radical activists denounce the system's suspected role as an instrument of ruling class domination. Crime victims, the system's supposed "clients," "consumers," or "beneficiaries", complain that standard procedures fail on a most basic level to deliver "justice".

In recent years, the victims' movement has won a number of impressive victories in its struggle for formal rights within the criminal justice process. Some of these rights have been enacted by statutes passed on the municipal, county, and state level, often as part of a legislative package called a "Victim's Bill of Rights." Others have been derived from case law based on court decisions. In some jurisdictions, certain police chiefs, district attorneys, or judges have taken it upon themselves to grant victims certain privileges and prerogatives not required by law or precedent. (For the full scope of proposals and recent gains, see the President's Task Force, 1982; NOVA, 1988; and Stark and Goldstein, 1985).

The rights that victims have fought for - and won - have become so numerous and complex, and vary so dramatically from place to place that they need to be categorized or classified. One way to group them is by the stage or phase in the criminal justice process at which these standards of fair treatment ought to be implemented. For example, some rights of victims must be respected by the police, while others should be observed by prosecutors, judges, corrections officials, or parole boards. But a better way of grouping these new rights is by asking "At whose expense were they gained?" Given the conflicts between individuals, groups, and classes, the rights gained by one side strengthen their position vis-a-vis their real or potential adversaries. Some recently enacted rights of victims clearly were secured to the detriment of "offenders" - or more accurately: suspects, defendants, and prisoners. For example, under the so-called "Son of Sam" statutes, victims in most states are enabled to lay claim to any royalties and fees paid by movie producers or media outlets to convicts who profit from their notoriety by selling the rights to their "inside story". But other rights, such as the right "to be informed" - an obligation on the part of police departments and prosecutors' offices to keep victims posted of any progress and developments in their cases - come at the expense of the privileges and conveniences of criminal justice officials and the budgets of their agencies. The most widely enacted rights of this kind are listed Part A of Chart One. A third group of rights that empower victims to directly participate to some degree in the criminal justice decision-making process, such as allocation before sentencing, may come at the expense of "offenders" or "officials", depending upon what victims seek as they exercise their new chance to have some input (see Karmen, 1990). The most common statutes of this sort are listed in Part B of Chart One.

CHART ONE: PART A

Informational Rights Gained At The Expense of Criminal Justice Agencies and Officials

1) To be read one's "rights": to reimbursement of losses - from state compensation funds, court ordered offender restitution, insurance coverage, civil lawsuits, or tax deductions; to referrals - to counseling programs, self-help support

From *Issues in Justice*, Chapter 4, pp. 46-57, edited with contributions by Roslyn Muraskin, 1990. Reprinted by permission of Wyndham Hall Press, Inc., Bristol, IN.

groups, shelters for battered women, rape crisis centers, and other types of assistance; and to be told of one's obligations - to attend line-ups, appear in court, be cross-examined under oath, and to be publicly identified and the subject of media coverage.

2) To be informed of the wherabouts of the (accused) offender: at large; or in custody (jail or prison); escaped from confinement; or released back to the community (on bail, or due to dropped and dismissed charges, or because of acquittal after a trial, or out on appeal, probation, furlough, parole, or after an expired sentence).

3) To be kept posted about key decisions: arrests, the granting of bail, rulings at evidentiary hearings, negotiated pleas, verdicts at trials, sentences, and parole board deliberations.

4) To receive assistance in the form of intercession by an official in behalf of a victim with an employer or creditor; advance notification and facilitation of court appearances; and expeditious return of recovered stolen property.

CHART ONE: PART B

Participatory Rights Gained At The Expense Either of Offenders (Suspects/Defendants/Convicts) or Agencies and Officials

1) To be consulted when the terms and conditions of bail are being determined (as a protection against harassment and reprisals for cooperating with the prosecution).

2) To be consulted about the offers made during plea negotiations.

3) To be permitted to submit a victim impact statement, detailing how the crime caused physical, emotional, and/or financial harm, as part of the pre-sentence report, and to submit a statement of opinion suggesting remedies, for the judge's consideration.

4) To be permitted to exercise allocation rights in person, in court, detailing the harm caused by the offender and suggesting an appropriate remedy, before the judge imposes a sentence.

5) To be permitted to bring to the attention of the parole board, either in writing or in person, information about the harm caused by the offender and an opinion about an appropriate remedy.

Source: Karmen, 1990.

Now that a sufficient amount of time has passed since the enactment of these rights, a growing body of data is accumulating about their implementation - or lack of observance - and evaluations are underway (for example, see NIJ, 1989). In fact, legislation introduced before Congress in 1989 called upon the Department of Justice to conduct an annual evaluation of the extent of compliance of federal agencies with the provisions of the Victim and Witness Protection Act of 1982 and the Victims of Crime Act of 1984 ("Bi-partisan Victim Rights Bill," 1989). Thus, it is time to anticipate how the results of these evaluations of pledges about fair treatment might be compiled and interpreted to answer some classical questions that persist within the disciplines of criminal justice, criminology, and victimology.

The findings of evaluation studies, as they accumulate, might either undermine or else lend support to some long-standing suspicions and criticisms about the ways that the criminal justice system operates. It seems worthwhile to hypothesize and speculate about what researchers might discover. If the findings consistently fall into certain patterns, well-grounded answers will emerge for the following questions:

Whose interests are primarily served by the routine operations of the criminal justice system?

The idealistic answer to this question is that the system primarily serves the interests of the whole society in general, and crime victims in particular. Of course, there are many other legitimate sources of input into the decision-making process, and victims are just one of many interested parties. But if indeed victims are truly the clients, customers, consumers, and beneficiaries of a system ostensibly set up to deliver justice to them, then evidence should accumulate that officials and agencies concede their right to participate in the decision-making process. Evaluations should show that victims feel satisfied that their needs and wants were taken into account by decision-makers, even if their requests did not prevail; and that although they were not always "catered to" or "handled with care", they were treated with dignity, respect, and fundamental fairness.

The skeptical, more sociological answer to this question is that a displacement of goals occurs within bureaucratic settings. Unofficial goals, such as minimizing collective effort and maximizing individual and group rewards might be substituted for the official goals of dispensing justice, aiding victims, and serving the public interest. In the context of criminal justice agencies, the hidden agenda behind many official actions might be to dispose of cases in a manner that lightens workloads, covers up mistakes, and curries political favors (McDonald, 1979). Since criminal justice professionals are not directly accountable to victims, either legally or organizationally, they can be inclined to view victims as a resource to be drawn upon, as needed, in the pursuit of objectives such as maintaining high levels of productivity in case processing, and in achieving smooth coordination with other components of the system (Ziegenhagen, 1977). When minor inconveniences to insiders (such as prosecutors, defense attorneys, judges, probation officers, and parole board members) have to be balanced against major inconveniences to outsiders (victims, defendants, witnesses, jurors), insider interests prevail (Ash, 1972). For instance, the courtroom work group of insiders develops a consensus about the "going rate" of appropriate penalties for particular crimes at a given time and place. This work group composed primarily of prosecutors, defense attorneys, and judges tends to resist attempts by outsiders and reformers to alter the penalty structure and disrupt their assembly line processing of cases (Walker, 1989). To the extent that the courtroom workgroup is successful in maintaining their standard operating procedures, victims will find their attempts to influence sentencing (or bail determinations, or plea negotiations, or parole deliberations) an exercise in futility. Their efforts to become involved in the decision-making process will be rebuffed as an intrusion, interference, and a threat to jealously guarded and highly prized professional discretionary authority (see Ranish and Shichor, 1985).

Some preliminary evidence already supports this prediction of "more of the same." Researchers who evaluated the use by victims of their right (since 1982) to allocation in felony cases in California confirmed its ineffectiveness. Plea negotiations which resulted in dismissals of all felony charges or in an understanding of what the sentence would be eliminated the chance for many victims to have any meaningful say in determining the outcomes of their cases. Determinate sentencing laws further eroded victim input. In many cases, officials failed to inform victims of their rights; some of the remaining eligible victims forfeited their chance to appear because of a belief that their appearance before the judge would make no difference in shaping a sentence that was already decided. Of those who exercised their opportunity for allocation, a considerable number felt their recommendations were not heeded. In the opinion of the majority of probation officers and judges, and about half of the prosecutors surveyed, the personal appearances by victims were "minimally, or not at all effective" (Villmoare and Neto, 1987). Similar findings about the difficulty victims have experienced in trying to influence the decision-making process appeared in evaluations of "structured" plea negotiation experiments. Victims who were permitted to attend the negotiation conferences tended to conclude that their presence and the statements they made had no impact on case disposition (Heinz and Kerstetter, 1979; Villmoare and Neto, 1987).

Are some victims more equal than others?

Evaluations might uncover great disparities in the way victims are treated by officials and agencies. A relatively small percentage of privileged people harmed by street criminals might enjoy "first class," "red carpet," or "VIP" treatment - their rights are scrupulously observed - while socially disadvantaged persons experience mistreatment as "second-class complainants." Such a blatant double-standard of justice is not supposed to develop because it violates official doctrines and constitutional guarantees subsumed under the clause "Equal protection under the law", and the pledge, "And justice for all." But many previous studies of case processing indicate that victim characteristics can influence outcomes like decisions to arrest, prosecute, convict, and severely punish offenders (see Myers, 1977; Myers and Hagan, 1979; Paternoster, 1984; Farrell and Swigert, 1986; and Karmen, 1990).

What if evaluations demonstrate that certain categories of victims are more likely to be informed by officials and are more likely to exercise their participatory rights, with demonstrably favorable results? Will the discriminatory treatment in the implementation of informational rights - and especially participatory rights - be correlated with victim characteristics such as race/ethnicity; gender; age; and social class (financial standing; educational attainment; occupational status; reputation in the community)? To state the matter bluntly, will victims drawn from the "right" backgrounds receive better service from the criminal justice system than the vast bulk of underprivileged people routinely preyed upon by street criminals?

Of course, the evaluations might uncover differential treatment on the basis of other factors, as well, which could stimulate considerable debate between officials and victims advocates. For example, should assault victims with "unsavory" backgrounds, such as street gang members, drug abusers, gamblers, and prostitutes be granted the same privileges concerning information and participation as totally innocent, law-abiding victims drawn from other walks of life? If they receive perfunctory responses when they turn to the system for help, would it be justifiable because they are assumed to be offenders in other incidents? Should surrogates and advocates who represent victimized children, and should survivors of murder victims exercise the same rights as direct victims?

What happens when criminal justice professionals violate the rights of crime victims?

The evaluations might expose a thorny problem. What recourse do victims have when their informational and participatory rights are violated? Anticipating the possibility that agencies and officials might fail to inform and involve victims as promised, legislators in many states crafted into their "Victims' Bills of Rights" clauses stating that "nothing in this statute shall be construed as creating a cause of action against the state, a county, municipality, or any of its agents." However, under the separation of powers doctrine, judges might direct officials and agencies to honor their commitments and could authorize injunctive relief for victims who file lawsuits (Stark and Goldstein, 1985). If evaluations turn up widespread non-compliance, additional remedies will be demanded.

Besides inadequate mechanisms for enforcement, evaluations might highlight another related problem: the absence of clear lines of responsibility for implementation. Several different officials and agencies might be held accountable for respecting victims rights. For example, the duty of notifying complainants who served as witnesses for the prosecution of their right to allocation before sentencing might fall to the police, the district attorney's office, the probation department, or a clerk in the office of court administration. All sorts of unanticipated complications might come to light. For example, how many attempts to contact the victim must be made (by phone or mail or in person) before the responsible official can declare that a good faith effort was undertaken to inform and involve the victim in plea negotiations, sentencing recommendations, or parole board deliberations?

Are victims invariably punitive toward offenders?

It is anticipated from common stereotypes, widespread assumptions, and some survey findings (see Hernon and Forst, 1984) that the vast majority of victims will use their newly gained influence to press for the most punitive sanctions permitted under the law. But a significant proportion (how often and under what circumstances?) might argue against lengthy confinement of convicts if alternatives are available. Those victims who do not seek the system's help to exact revenge might expect criminal justice professionals to treat and rehabilitate the persons who harmed them, especially if the offenders are former friends, acquaintances, or relatives. Other victims might place a higher priority on being reimbursed through offender restitution as a condition of probation and parole. Some preliminary reports indicate that when victims are given a full range of options, a significant fraction favor restitution, rehabilitation, and reconciliation over retribution (see Galaway, 1985; Villmoare and Neto, 1987; and Umbreit, 1989).

In conclusion, it is clear that the implementation of victims' rights poses a challenge to criminal justice professionals, especially police administrators, district attorneys, probation officers, judges, corrections officials, and parole board members. How they respond, as revealed by evaluation research, to the demands by victims for fair treatment will resolve many controversies and provoke new ones.

REFERENCES

Ash, M. 1972. "On witnesses: A radical critique of criminal court procedures." Notre Dame Lawyer, 48 (December), pp. 386-425.

"Bi-partisan victim rights bill introduced in U.S. Congress." 1989. NOVA Newsletter 13, 3, pp. 1, 5.

Farrell, R. and Swigert, V. 1986. "Adjudication in homicide:

An interpretive analysis of the effects of defendant and victim social characteristics." Journal of Research in Crime and Delinquency 23, 4 (November), pp. 349-369.

Galaway, B. 1985. "Victim participation in the penal-correction process." Victimology 10, 1, pp. 617-629.

Hernon, J. and Forst, B. 1984. NIJ Research in brief: The criminal justice response to victim harm. Washington, D.C.: U.S. Department of Justice.

Heinz. A. and Kerstetter, W. 1979. "Pretrial settlement conference: Evaluation of a reform in plea bargaining." Law and Society Review, 13, 2, pp. 349-366.

Karmen, A. 1990. Crime Victims: An introduction to victimology. Second edition. Pacific Grove, Ca.: Brooks/Cole.

McDonald, W. 1979. "The prosecutor's domain." In W. McDonald (Ed.), The prosecutor (pp. 15-52). Beverly Hills, Ca.: Sage.

Myers, M. 1977. The effects of victim characteristics on the prosecution, conviction, and sentencing of criminal defendants. Ann Arbor, Mi.: University Microfilms.

_____ and Hagan, J. 1979. "Private and public trouble: Prosecutors and the allocation of court resources." Social Problems, 26, 4, pp. 439-451.

National Institute of Justice (NIJ). 1989. Research in action: The courts- current federal research. Washington, D.C.: U.S. Department of Justice.

National Organization for Victim Assistance (NOVA). 1988. Victim rights and services: A legislative directory - 1987. Washington, D.C.: Author.

Paternoster, R. 1984. "Prosecutorial discretion in requesting the death penalty: A case of victim based racial discrimination." Law and Society Review, 18, 437-478.

President's Task Force on Victims of Crime. 1982. Final Report. Washington, D.C.: U.S. Government Printing Office.

Ranish, D. and Shichor, D. 1985. "The victim's role in the penal process: Recent developments in California." Federal Probation (March), pp. 50-56.

Stark, J. and Goldstein, H. 1985. The rights of crime victims. Chicago: Southern Illinois University Press.

Umbreit, M. 1989. "Violent offenders and their victims." In M. Wright and B. Galaway (Eds.), Mediation and criminal justice: Victims, offenders, and community (pp. 99-112). Newbury Park, Ca.: Sage.

Villmoare, E. and Neto, V. 1987. NIJ Research in brief: Victim appearances at sentencing under California's victims' bill of rights. Washington, D.C.: U.S. Department of Justice.

Walker, S. 1989. Sense and nonsense about crime: A policy guide. (Second edition). Pacific Grove, Ca.: Brooks/Cole.

Ziegenhagen, E. 1977. Victims, crime, and social control. New York: Praeger.

HUNTED

THE LAST YEAR OF APRIL LaSALATA

She thought the criminal-justice system would protect her from her ex-husband. But the system was no match for his lethal rage.

Richard C. Firstman

Richard C. Firstman is a contributing writer of
The Newsday Magazine.

Her body a pattern of scars, April LaSalata stared up at the young woman standing uneasily at her bedside.

"How old are you?" April asked warily.

Frances Radman, a 27-year-old assistant district attorney with a gentle manner, had heard that one before. "How old are *you*?" she asked gamely.

April laughed; she was feeling better this March day in 1988. But still she worried: It seemed to her that the prosecutor was as vulnerable as she was. For her part, Radman hadn't expected April to be so tiny, just 85 pounds and barely five feet tall. When April displayed the scars that split her upper body in two, Radman was amazed that such a delicate woman had managed to survive so brutal an attack.

"He won't get out of jail, will he?" April asked.

Knowing the events of the past months, now seeing this torn body before her, Radman knew this was not a trivial question.

"No," she said, "he won't."

Four months before, in the fall of 1987, a Suffolk County judge had signed the papers terminating the marriage of April and Anthony LaSalata, high school sweethearts from Brentwood. To the mind of her ex-husband, April had been the winner in this divorce; he had been the loser. She got the kids, the house and freedom from a calamitous marriage. He got a trailer and a court order barring him from menacing his ex-wife. It had been the kind of divorce that had produced almost monthly police reports: domestic dispute, 110 McKinley.

On the ninth call to the Third Precinct, in February, the police had found Anthony LaSalata trying to get into the house with a crowbar. They had arrested him for harassment. Then he had been released.

After work on Friday, Feb. 26, April, as was her custom, drove to her mother's house to pick up her sons, Justin, 10, and Anthony Jr., 4. She decided to leave Anthony overnight and drove the few blocks home with Justin. They scanned the front lawn, then walked into the house. The phone in the kitchen, the red one with "911" written on it, was ringing. Justin answered; it was his grandmother, checking to see that they had gotten home all right. Justin said they were fine.

And then, the closet door flew open.

April screamed. Justin cried out, "Dad, what are you doing here?" His father told him to be quiet and then cut the telephone cord. The receiver fell onto a sweater on the floor.

LaSalata, according to the police, pushed his son into a bedroom and closed the door. He grabbed April, dragged her downstairs and started stabbing her. He twisted the knife inside her abdomen. She screamed to Justin to get out of the house, and Justin bolted and began banging on the doors of neighbors.

When LaSalata heard Justin leave, he looked up reflexively, stabbed April a third time, and stopped. He left her bleeding in the basement and fled the house. April dragged herself to the basement phone. After all her instructions to Justin about how to call for emergency help, it was Gerard, her brother who lived 25 miles away, whom she called first.

"Whatsa matter? Whatsa matter?" Gerard screamed into the phone. In his house, a room full of guests stood horrified. April was describing her wounds to her brother. "Close your arms around them! Hold them tight!" Gerard yelled into the phone. When rescue came, April was bleeding so relentlessly that she kept sliding off the stretcher.

She was in surgery through the night. The doctors did not believe she would live — her wounds suggested to them an autopsy had already been performed. But somehow, she reached the recovery room. She spent the next week on life-support machines.

LaSalata was charged with attempted murder and held in the Riverhead jail.

No, Fran Radman told April in the hospital room, he would not get out. His lawyer was arguing that LaSalata was not competent to stand trial, and so there would be no bail until there was a decision on that issue. Or so Radman thought.

TWO weeks later, in what Radman would later describe as a critical bureaucratic "mix-up," Judge Morton Weissman set cash bail at $25,000 while she was appearing in another court on another case. Kevin Fox, LaSalata's attorney, told Radman not to worry: LaSalata would never raise that kind of money.

But five months later, in midsummer, LaSalata's parents decided to mortgage their house to get him out of jail. And from that day forward, as her life was defined by a collection of motions and briefs, April LaSalata came to know on the deepest level that she would not survive.

On New Year's Eve, 1988, when a radio announcer reported on the second woman in Suffolk County in three days to be killed by her estranged husband, despite orders of protection, April turned to her oldest friend and said, "Sharon, I'm next."

* * *

April LaSalata, 34 at her death, was not an anonymous victim crying in the dark. In her world, she was surrounded by many people who cared a great deal about her, a prosecutor who fought for her, a cop who tried to protect her.

And still, she died.

The questions raised by her death a year ago have less to do with why some men are driven to such desperate acts of domestic terrorism than with why the legal system sometimes fails to protect the women they kill. April LaSalata's case played to the fears of all women who saw her death as a confirmation of a terrible truth: that even at its best, the system is not designed to keep a hunted woman alive.

Her case is closed now, her onetime husband having seen to that with five shots from

'WHAT APRIL SAW WAS THAT HE WAS SO MACHO.'

a rifle last January, three to her, two to himself. But her death touched so many lives — people who knew her intimately, others who were more familiar with her case file — and they struggle still for acceptable explanations, to place blame on someone or something other than Anthony LaSalata alone.

April's family is suing the Suffolk County Police Department for failing to protect her, but others argue that the police did all they could. An examination of the last year of her life shows that many factors contributed to her death, including miscalculations by some members of the criminal justice system, perhaps an insensitivity by others, and some ambiguities born of the bureaucracy itself.

In the end, despite the depth of April's fears and the brutality of the stabbing attack, Anthony LaSalata was just another defendant awaiting trial on a charge of attempted murder. The case dragged on as many cases do. LaSalata was released on bail as many defendants are.

And April LaSalata was left to wonder on what night in the near future her ex-husband would come again to kill her.

* * *

April Principio, a bricklayer's daughter, was in the eleventh grade at Brentwood High when she met Tony LaSalata, a senior. April liked to read and Tony liked to fix cars, but they shared ethnic background and neighborhood ties, and April was not attracted to gentle boys. Among the things she found appealing about Tony was the strength of his wrists: She liked the way he shifted his car. When he was 18, LaSalata acquired a tattoo: *Live and Let Die.*

"Tony was the first person who paid attention to her," recalled Sharon Millard, April's close friend. "What April saw was that he was so macho, in total control, which she felt she needed, someone to guide her."

But Tony's control bordered on compulsion. If April was out with a girlfriend, Tony was likely to turn up agitated, demanding her return to his car. April was ambivalent about Tony's tyrannical tendencies. Of course, she found them annoying — his jealousy became so much a part of her daily life that she was moved to write about it, prophetically if with some bemusement, in her yearbook inscription to Millard, her friend since kindergarten:

I'll never forget the time [we] had to hide on wet grass behind Debbie Mann's car because LaSalata was passing, and many more of those "times" to come.

But in her innocence, April took Tony's attentions as a sign of love. "You get all sorts of attention from someone and it makes you feel good," Millard said. "You go on the assumption that it's true love. Tony was her first one, and that was it."

Her parents were so opposed to the rela-

'SHE SLEPT WITH THE DRESSER IN FRONT OF THE BEDROOM DOOR.'

tionship that they begged her to go away to college. But April was headstrong, a lifelong trait, and at the time reasonably rebellious. Despite her parents' urgings, she cast her lot with Tony. She went to work in a bank, Tony got a job on the pie line at Entenmann's Bakery, and in June, 1975, they were married.

In those early years, April and Tony continued the rancor that often marked their courtship. In an interview with a court-appointed psychiatrist after his arrest in 1988, LaSalata said: "The only complaint she ever had about me and our marriage early on was that I smoked too much pot. Other than that there were no other complaints except me yelling at her."

She had one other complaint, however: Tony's employee file was getting thick with reprimands and warnings for missing work and for not getting along with co-workers. April felt at times that she was doing more than her share of supporting the family.

The turning point in the marriage — the point from which it would deteriorate beyond hope of repair — came in 1982, when April and Tony went to the wedding of a friend from high school. April wasn't feeling well and left early with a friend of theirs, and when Tony came home and found the friend in the house, he believed that April had been unfaithful to him. April insisted that she had not.

Whatever happened that night, the incident became so much a point of contention in the marriage that nearly everyone who knew the LaSalatas — their friends, their relatives and ultimately the corps of lawyers, prosecutors and psychiatrists who would populate their lives — would hear a version of it.

WAS always angry with her," LaSalata told the psychiatrist in 1988. "I wouldn't let that night go. She swore she didn't, then she said if she did or didn't, she would swear that she didn't. That one incident for over five years has been constantly on my thoughts. I keep asking friends and they are all sticking together and telling me I was crazy. It was like a conspiracy. When they all looked at my wife, I know they all wanted her. They all wanted to take turns with my wife. They didn't give a —— if I was their friend, they just wanted her."

April would later tell Radman, "You'd think I was Christie Brinkley, the way he was acting."

In 1983, LaSalata was fired from Entenmann's. He found work at Fairchild Republic, and later at Grumman. Down in the basement, which he had finished himself, he also cooked up get-rich-quick schemes. The marriage grew more acrimonious, and then abusive. April would vilify Tony for not working, Tony would bring up the wedding incident. And Jus-

tin would follow his mother around with a bow and arrow to protect her. April taught him how to dial 911.

Finally, in 1986, April decided to see a lawyer about divorcing Tony. The following April, she called the police for the first time. She said that Tony was threatening her. She went to court and was granted an Order of Protection.

"He would be mean one day, begging her the next," said Millard. "Some days he stuck to her like glue. He would follow her around the house. She hated that. She couldn't wait to go to work."

The couple slept in separate rooms, but a few times April woke up with Tony standing over her. For a while, she slept with the dresser in front of the bedroom door. At one point, she told friends, Tony put a gun to her head and threatened to kill her. During the divorce proceedings April called the police eight times.

April decided to move with her sons to her mother's house, but her lawyer advised her to move back in so she would be on firmer ground when she asked the judge to award her the house.

But when she moved back in, she told friends and Radman, her husband raped her. Her lawyer, William Griffin, says April never told him this.

The divorce was granted in the fall of 1987, with April getting custody of the children and sole occupancy of the house. Family Court Judge John Dunn gave LaSalata 60 days to find another place to live, leaving a bitterly divorced couple living under the same roof.

In December, LaSalata moved into a $90-a-month house trailer in Bay Shore. But the terms of the divorce decree only seemed to intensify his violent tendencies. When April gave her brother Gerard a shotgun for Christmas, he told her, "You're the one that needs this."

It is difficult to learn much about LaSalata's view of what was happening in his life because nearly all of his friends and relatives declined to be interviewed for this article. But one friend said that LaSalata had become fixated on April's refusal to sell the house and split the money.

"The guy was strapped," said the friend, who asked not to be identified. "He was working nights at Grumman, he was living in this dinky trailer, he couldn't even watch TV except for Channel 12 because he couldn't afford an antenna. He wanted some money so he could start his life over."

Wary of LaSalata, Gerard Principio, who taught martial arts, arranged for one of his students, Billy Woods, to live in the basement apartment Tony had finished. Billy was 25, slightly built and wore longish hair and an earring. He worked as a maintenance man for Slomin's fuel oil. April was glad to have someone else in the house. Billy was glad to know April. Soon they became involved, and Woods' mission took on greater importance.

April had iron gates installed over the front door.

One late night in February, 1988, LaSalata went to the house and found Woods' fuel truck parked outside. When he saw Woods in the house, he tried to break through the gates with a crowbar. April called the police and Tony was arrested for harassment. Out on bail, he called her and said he would shoot her.

In a few days, April was scheduled to go to court for a stronger Order of Protection. But Tony had other ideas.

"Tony told me that if the judge didn't modify his decision, it was time for this," an acquaintance of LaSalata's said in a statement to police. "As he said this, he picked up a big Rambo-type knife off the table. Tony said that he was going to 'kill the bitch.' . . . Tony then said that he was at the house a few nights before to kill April, that he had cut the telephone lines and then he changed his mind. . . . I got in touch with April and told her what Tony had said. April told me that she would be careful."

SHE came in dead," recalls Dr. Alexander Melman, the surgeon at Southside Hospital in Bay Shore who sewed April back together on the night of Feb. 26. "She had no blood pressure, she had wounds to the lungs and the diaphragm and part of her liver was sticking out. The son of a bitch turned the blade, an old trick to create more injuries. It reminded me of a wartime injury."

April spent six days on life-support systems as her hospital room filled with flowers, balloons, cards and visitors. Members of the Long Island Women's Coalition came to offer their help, but April didn't feel a part of them, didn't feel they were living in her world. To April this was not a political issue. This was *her* issue.

"I thought I was going to die," she told Newsday reporter Dan Fagin, who was preparing a story on how local police respond to domestic violence. "It's been getting worse and worse, but I never thought it would come to this. I'm terrified. You can't imagine what it's like to be living with this every day."

Another visitor was Vincent O'Leary. He had known April since high school, and now he was a police detective, working in their home precinct, the Third. He was assigned to her case. Though such a convenience has the ring of a cheap trick by a screenwriter, in this true story O'Leary was the friend on the force. But it did not seem to relieve April's fear. "I just think of what his jail sentence is going to be and him getting out and getting me," she told Fagin.

LaSalata was initially charged by police with first-degree assault and held on $25,000 bail by District Court Judge Francis Caldeira.

From jail, he wrote a letter to his older son:
Dear Justin,

I am writing you this letter to tell you how sorry I am about what happened to your mother. If you hate me now and never want to see me again I can understand why. I just wanted to tell you that I was very very sick that night and that I did not know what I was doing. I hope and pray to God that you and your mother can forgive me. I wish that there was some way that the pain that your mother has in her body now can somehow be transformed into my body . . . I miss you and Anthony so much. Take care and be a good boy. Please send me a letter. I wish there was something that I could send you but right now I have nothing to send you other than my love. I love you Justin!

On the same day that LaSalata wrote the letter, he was served in jail with this County Court decree: "It is ordered that the above named defendant observe the following conditions of behavior: Stay away from the home, school, business, or place of employment of: April LaSalata."

The next day, LaSalata appeared before County Court Justice Morton Weissman, to whose court the case was transferred after a grand jury indicted him on a charge of attempted murder. Kevin Fox, LaSalata's attorney, indicated he would argue that his client was not competent to stand trial, and Weissman, as is customary when a competency issue is raised, held him without bail.

Fran Radman was brand new to the district attorney's family crimes bureau when she was handed a pile of cases from a departing prosecutor. She had been handling drunk-driving and misdemeanor, child sex-abuse cases in the District Court bureau, and People vs. Anthony LaSalata would be her biggest case to date. A couple of years out of Brooklyn Law School, she had joined the district attorney's office because she felt that was where she could do the most good. Her sympathies lay with victims of crime.

Radman's inexperience was disquieting to April and her family. But what she lacked in seasoning she would try to make up for with dedication. Like April, she was the daughter of a working-class family, had grown up in western Suffolk County and had never wandered far. Now, Radman was living with her parents in East Northport. And when she met April for the first time in the hospital, she felt more than the usual compassion.

"She said that even in the hospital she was afraid he would come get her," Radman recalls. "But she was composed. She always was. Usually she would be kidding, smiling, pleasant, but when it was about being afraid, she got very straight-faced. I thought when I walked out, Wow, that is some strong woman."

* * *

Thursday, April 7, 1988, was a very busy day in the Suffolk County criminal courts.

Radman was scheduled to present evidence to a grand jury on a sex abuse case that day, so she asked another member of the bureau, Gaetan Lozito, to stand in for her at a conference with Judge Weissman on the LaSalata case. Radman's primary concern — for April's peace of mind, as well as her own — was that LaSalata remain in jail. And Fox, she says, had assured her in a phone conversation that he wouldn't be making a bail application. So Radman didn't regard the conference as key.

But there was a crack, after all, and April was about to fall through it.

Weeks before, Dr. Allen Reichman, a psychiatrist who judges the competency of defendants in Suffolk's criminal cases, had found that LaSalata did, in fact, understand the charges against him and was capable of aiding his defense. Now, in the conference in the judge's chambers, a kind of dress rehearsal for open court, Fox told Weissman and Lozito that he would seek to have his own psychiatrist contradict that finding, and also advance his defense of mental impairment on the night of the attack. At Radman's instruction, Lozito told Weissman that April was afraid that her ex-husband would be released, and showed photographs of the weapon he had used.

Then Lozito had to leave for another case. She handed the file over to Matthew Parella, an assistant district attorney who had never seen the case but who was covering Weissman's courtroom for the major crimes bureau. "Nothing's going to happen," he says Lozito told him.

In the courtroom, Fox repeated his intentions for the record. Then Weissman surprised everyone.

"Do you have a bail application?" he asked Fox, according to a transcript of the session.

"No," Fox said, "we reserve it."

"You never made a bail application before this?" Weissman persisted. He seemed to be indicating he wanted to set bail.

Fox was unprepared, but he took his shot. He asked that bail be set at $25,000, the same amount as when the charge was assault.

Weissman looked at Parella. "We'll ask that no bail be continued until the results of the defense psychiatric exam," Parella said.

"No, I won't do that," Weissman said. "Give me a monetary recommendation."

Parella asked for $100,000, but he did not present arguments for the higher bail.

"Hundred thousand bond, twenty-five thousand cash," Weissman said.

To this day, Radman sees that moment as the "mix-up" that made the job of protecting April much more difficult. She says that had she been been there, she would have argued strenuously that the bail wasn't high enough. But now she was stuck with it.

Later, she called Fox. "You said you weren't going to make a bail application," she recalls telling him. Fox explained the circumstances, then said, "Don't worry, Fran, he'll never make that kind of bail."

(Asked to comment for this article, Weissman said he could not recall the case and, anyway, did not discuss cases he had handled.)

MEANWHILE, Fox was finding that his client was still obsessed with his divorce. "Obviously [in retrospect] there was something boiling inside, but it didn't show," he said. "He seemed very subdued, polite, sort of defeated. He wasn't a raving lunatic."

In the spring, April went back to work in the credit department at J.C. Penney, but she was still in pain from her wounds and preoccupied by the court case against Tony. She believed in the *victim's* right to a speedy trial.

The case was transferred to Judge Rudolph Mazzei, and on Aug. 5, a conference was scheduled. April told Radman she wanted to be there.

Also in attendance that day were John and Otille LaSalata, Tony's father and mother. They were like a lot of parents of accused criminals — they were sick over it. And in their sadness, they had an inverted view of the situation. To them, Tony was the victim, April the victimizer.

Afterward, as April walked toward her car with Gerard and Radman, John LaSalata drove up beside them. Throughout, April feared him as much as she feared Tony.

"You slut!" LaSalata screamed at April, according to Radman. "You're the reason my son's in jail!"

John LaSalata was charged with harassment, and although it was later dismissed at April's behest, the incident set the tone for his son's defense.

"His parents saw their son as being sick, and they felt she was one of the causes," said Charles Russo, Fox' law partner. "They didn't say [the stabbing] was justified, but they didn't understand why the criminal justice system was involved. They wanted to get help."

Three days after the incident in the parking lot, and 163 days after their son went to jail, the LaSalatas decided to mortgage their home to get him out.

In April's world, alarms went off. Vinnie O'Leary was the first to call: *He's out.* April couldn't believe it, and when Radman called, the prosecutor found a very nervous woman on the other end of the line.

"Do you have any place to go?" Radman asked.

"*Any place to go?*" April repeated angrily. "He did this to me, and now I have to change my whole life? I live here. My kids go to school here."

A siege mentality set in as word of LaSalata's release spread. Radman had a portable panic button delivered to April's house; she could wear it around her neck and summon the police instantly. And a tape recorder was installed on her kitchen phone. When Det.

Frank Fallon came to install the tape machine, April showed him a picture of her wounds after surgery. "Every noise, every sound, a car or somebody starting a lawn mower, made her nervous," Fallon recalls. "She didn't sleep at night. I told her, 'That's a hell of a way to live. Why don't you move?' "

At home, Justin took to following his mother around with a baseball bat. "He follows me everywhere," April told Radman. "It drives me crazy."

At work, April was allowed to park in the fire zone directly outside the store. A security guard escorted her to her car each night after work.

And at the district attorney's office, the case took on the qualities of a cause. The family crimes unit was staffed mainly by young women whose caseloads were dominated by crimes against women and children, usually involving sexual and physical abuse. It was not unusual for the prosecutors to become emotionally involved with their "clients," and this was especially true of the case of April LaSalata. Radman, whose office was decorated with artwork by victims of child abuse, felt that this time she carried the burden of keeping the victim alive. And she would not play it safe.

Among prosecutors, Mazzei had a reputation, justified or not, as a "defendant's judge." In late August, with Mazzei on vacation, Radman went to Judge Charles Cacciabaudo to try to have LaSalata returned to jail, at a higher bail. To do this, she needed some new evidence. She told Cacciabaudo that April had been receiving "unusual phone calls," since her ex-husband's release, related the incident involving his father, and said that LaSalata had been found competent to stand trial.

Kevin Fox told the judge that LaSalata, suffering from depression, would be voluntarily admitted to South Oaks Hospital in Amityville on that day.

Cacciabaudo rejected Radman's bail request. Then he looked at LaSalata and warned him not to go near his ex-wife.

"Yes, sir," LaSalata said.

As LaSalata underwent psychiatric treatment in South Oaks, Radman pushed for a trial date. To impress upon Mazzei the seriousness of the case, she showed him the photographs of April after the attack. This was an off-the-record move not generally regarded as proper. But LaSalata was due to get out of South Oaks in 60 days, and Radman wanted to jar Mazzei into action. The judge said the case ought to come up soon. But he gave no commitments.

On Sunday, Oct. 16, as Tony's stay in South Oaks was drawing to a close, April was outside the house with Justin and Anthony when a gray car slowed as it passed. In the passenger seat, April was sure, was Tony, wearing a red shirt she had bought him years before.

April called the police, who said they couldn't make an arrest because Tony hadn't come close enough. But Radman said it was enough for her, and had two detectives go to South Oaks to pick him up on charges of criminal contempt.

Radman took the case to District Court

Judge William Bennett. But there was one problem: Fox produced a letter from Dr. Nicholas Samios, LaSalata's physician at South Oaks, saying that the record showed LaSalata had not left the hospital on the day in question.

Radman went to see Bennett in his chambers. "Judge, he's going to kill her," Radman says she told Bennett. "He should be nowhere near this house. We're trying to protect her."

But Bennett said his hands were tied — LaSalata had an alibi. He released him on his own recognizance.

Radman was furious. "His defense [in the stabbing] was mental defect," she says now. "He wasn't saying he didn't do it. So why not keep him in jail? Why not be safe? The problem is we don't have preventative detention in New York and we should."

In New York, as in most other states, the purpose of bail is to insure that a defendant will appear for trial. There, a cornerstone of the criminal justice system, the presumption of the accused's innocence, comes in conflict with the victim's presumption of danger.

After Bennett's decision, Radman called and visited April frequently, if only to let her know she wasn't alone. "I was so afraid," she said. "I don't know if she knew that. Now what do we do? I was afraid that this aggravated everything. April was angry, afraid and wiped out."

In her anxiety, knowing Tony was about to be released from South Oaks, did April imagine seeing him that Sunday? Or did Samios assume that because there was no record of his absence LaSalata must have been in the hospital?

Radman decided to take the South Oaks case to a grand jury and let April tell her story. The grand jury indicted LaSalata, but on Nov. 15, Mazzei, clearly angered at Radman, called it "the proverbial ham sandwich indictment" — referring to a legal truism that prosecutors can lead a grand jury to indict anybody for anything. Mazzei refused to impose bail.

A few weeks before, while Radman was planning her strategy on the South Oaks incident, she had asked Mazzei to move the attempted-murder case up on the calendar. When Mazzei refused, Radman suggested April come to court to make a personal pitch. That day, Radman asked Mazzei again to raise or revoke bail. Mazzei again rejected the request. Then April approached the bench. She spoke softly and nervously.

"I just would like to know how long it's going to take to get a court date. I mean, from Aug. 7 since he's been out on bail, I have been living in fear. I have an 11-year-old son walking around with a baseball bat."

"I understand your concern," Mazzei told her. "The problem is at the present time there are more than 35 defendants who are in custody on murder charges and attempted murder charges who have to be given preference and they have been in custody over a year. Constitutionally that's the way I have to do it."

One factor in the waiting time was the temporary transfer of four criminal court judges to the civil part in April, 1988, to relieve a backlog there. They would not return until December. But another factor that might have been working against April was the trial record of the judge assigned to her case.

AMONG some lawyers, Mazzei is a jurist who has a reputation for delaying or avoiding trials. In 1988, the year the LaSalata case was before him, Mazzei presided over just two trials, according to the court clerk's office. The year before, he had three. In terms of numbers of trials, this placed him 14th among the 15 County Court judges working in Suffolk during those two years.

Mazzei declined to be interviewed for this article, saying through a secretary that he was too busy.

At every turn, Radman felt she was coming up against a rigid legal system whose arbiters were insensitive to the peril that was consuming a woman's life and unresponsive to the urgings of a young, female prosecutor.

"It's still the old boys' network," she said. "I'm little, I'm young. You can sense they treat you differently."

Indeed, her adversaries, Fox and Russo, agree that a different prosecutor might have gotten an earlier trial date. But they lay some of the blame on the district attorney's office for assigning the case to a young prosecutor working in a bureau with a relatively low profile in the office.

"Fran became very involved," Fox said. "She did a good job, but somebody with more authority could have pushed things along." Some of April's family felt likewise. But a former member of the family crimes unit, who asked not to be identified, said a more experienced prosecutor might not have fought as hard: "Fran did more than any other prosecutor would have. She saw the injustice and she went in to Mazzei and kept fighting. A lot of people would have been afraid to."

Chief Assistant District Attorney Mark Cohen added that Radman was well supervised and took counsel from others. "The attention and dedication that assistant paid to the case are beyond question," he said. "To suggest that she was 'inexperienced' and somehow that becomes a logical connection to what happened is misplaced."

As Radman struggled with the system, Fox had troubles of his own. In recent months, LaSalata's parents had been insisting that their son's defense be based on his ex-wife's character. In effect, they wanted Fox to blame April for pushing Tony too far. In October after a series of heated arguments with John LaSalata, Fox took the unusual step of asking to be released from the case. Mazzei granted the request. Fox's withdrawal would delay matters further, as a new attorney would have to be appointed by the court.

Mazzei took the opportunity to remind Anthony LaSalata about the Order of Protection. "I don't want you to go anywhere near your wife," Mazzei said, apparently unaware that they were no longer married.

"No sir," LaSalata said.

But despite his courtroom passivity, it is clear now that LaSalata remained a man possessed. "Some people's self-involvement is so unreasonable that they have enormous trouble dealing with rejection," Dr. Reichman, the court-appointed psychiatrist who examined LaSalata, said in an interview.

April knew this better than anyone. All these months, Fran Radman fought for her and Vinnie O'Leary checked on her. Pictures of LaSalata were kept in the Third Precinct's sector cars. But April told friends she was sure she would not survive Tony's rage. She wrote her will and selected an urn to hold her ashes.

"She *knew* he was going to kill her," Billy Woods said. "She told everybody. Her mother, her brother. She told me every day."

Despite her resignation, April's determination was seen in the way she lived her last months. She went to work in the credit department, shepherded her children to soccer practice, cared for her plants, mowed her mother's lawn.

"A lot of people would have given in," said Kevin Mack, a family friend. "But that was not April's way. She was resolute. She loved her boys and worked hard. And she didn't want to hide. People would say, 'Go away for a while,' or 'Carry a weapon.' "

"We all approached her," Radman said. "I knew she had relatives in New Jersey. But all I got was screaming: 'Here I am, raising two kids, why should we have to leave?' Was it worth it more to her to maintain her life here? Hard question. I think she felt that no matter where she went he would find her. I suggested Ridge, where her brother lives. And she said, 'It's all wide open spaces, he can get me from anywhere.' "

APRIL went to court in Riverhead on Dec. 20. She sat on the opposite side of the room from LaSalata. The defense asked for a three-week adjournment, setting a trial date of Jan. 11. April slipped into the next courtroom to watch the proceedings there. It was the murder trial of Matthew Solomon, accused of strangling his wife the previous Christmas.

The next day, Tony LaSalata went to Edelman's Sporting Goods store in Farmingdale and bought a .22-cal. Marlin rifle, the same model he'd carried with him the night he stabbed April. He filled out the requisite form, which asked, "Are you under indictment . . .?" LaSalata wrote, "No."

On Dec. 26, Lydia Grohoski was shot to death by her estranged husband, Joseph, in the basement of their home in Cutchogue. An Order of Protection was in effect at the time. On Dec. 29, Elizabeth Croff was shot by her estranged husband, William, in front of a cookie factory in Islip. An Order of Protection was in effect at the time. Both men then killed themselves.

On New Year's Eve, Sharon Millard brought her children to April's house for dinner. From the radio in the kitchen they heard a newscaster discussing the cases of Grohoski and Croff. April looked squarely at her oldest friend.

"Sharon," she said. "I'm next."

On the evening of Tuesday, Jan. 3, LaSalata left his parents' house in his mother's car. He said he was going to visit a woman friend. He was wearing his red-and-black hunter's jacket.

At the holidays, he had been feeling low, detectives would learn later. He was living with his parents, was about to come to trial, but was still obsessed with his divorce.

LaSalata drove to 110 McKinley St. He began walking back and forth out front. Justin and

Anthony were inside with their grandmother, who was preparing dinner. The television was on, the volume high. The boys were waiting for Woods to come home with two mice for their pet boa constrictor. Woods had a last-minute call from Slomin's, so he couldn't meet April at work and escort her home, as he liked to do.

April arrived on McKinley Street about 6:30. As she reached the concrete steps in front of her door, LaSalata came out from behind some shrubs. He aimed his sawed-off rifle at her chest and fired. Then he stood over her body and shot her twice in the head. Inside, Justin and Anthony watched television and their grandmother cooked dinner. Their mother lay in the bushes until Woods came home and found her.

"Frannie," Mary Werner, the chief of the family crimes bureau, told Radman over the phone an hour after the fatal shots were fired, "they got April." Radman cried; she didn't sleep for three days. "I kept thinking of her children, of the little boy coming to my office saying he'll do anything to help his mother."

In the end, Radman realized she was part of a system that couldn't help enough. "I had tried to be optimistic," she said. "Gerard wanted to get a gun. I said no, don't do that. I should have told him, yeah. Going to law school, you think the system works, but here's someone I knew and liked and she's dead."

People in the office asked Radman if she'd request a transfer out of family crime, but she felt that would be letting April down somehow. Now, she takes some comfort from the belief that judges in her part of the world seem to be setting higher bails in domestic abuse cases. And in the year since the murders of April and the two other women, reports and arrests for family violence increased dramatically in Suffolk County. But still, when battered women descend the stairs to her basement office and sit before her, it is April whom Radman sees in her mind. And she worries for them.

"We all feel part of it," said Charles Russo, Fox' partner. "When you wake up in the morning and hear, 'April LaSalata is killed,' you feel part of the system. . . . You can't help but have this big empty hole in you."

It was, Mazzei said a day after the murder, "a judge's nightmare."

On Jan. 6, the police discovered LaSalata's frozen corpse slumped in the front seat of his mother's car at a rest stop beyond Exit 52 of the Long Island Expressway. There were two gunshot wounds.

Two days later, more than 100 people crowded into St. Luke's Church in Brentwood for April's funeral mass. "She will never be forgotten," a friend told a reporter. "She will be in our hearts forever." April was cremated, her ashes placed in the urn she had picked out.

In the spring, LaSalata's family petitioned for guardianship of Justin and Anthony, who were living with their grandmother Lillian Principio. April's friends gathered 2,000 names on petitions opposing the idea, and in the fall the petition was withdrawn.

Last month, over the airwaves of radio station WBLI came the voice of Steve Harper, the afternoon disc jockey.

"We've got a special request right now for two little guys, Anthony and Justin, who've had a very tough year. And I understand . . . they're on their way to New York City to see the tree at Rockefeller Center. And we want to wish them all the best. We've got a song for them."

He played "This One's for the Children."

A VICIOUS CYCLE

The abused child often becomes an abusive parent. But as this case shows, caring can replace hostility; the cycle can be broken.

Michael D'Antonio

Michael D'Antonio is a Newsday *staff writer.*

OROTHY settled down on the bathroom floor and pulled her legs up into fetal position. The cool white tile felt good on her large, soft body. She lay there, closed her eyes and refused to answer Jim, who was on the other side of the door pleading for her to come out. The bathroom was a safe hiding place, a ceramic cave where Dorothy sought refuge, wedging herself into the corner by the pedestal sink.

She wasn't coming out.

Of course, the memory was in there with her, still scratching at her consciousness like a rat scraping at the corner of a door. The door to her mind, so long closed, was as heavy as a ship's steel bulkhead. The tiny noise of this memory was faint. But it was always with her—tiny claws scratching furiously at the edge of her carefully sealed past. Dorothy could not name the source of her depression. But she wondered if it had something to do with Jennifer.

Jennifer, brown-eyed and beautiful, was a January baby. She was also a fussy baby. She slept fitfully and cried often. When she cried, Dorothy fed her and changed her and then put her down, reminding herself: Don't spoil her. Don't spoil her.

As the months went by, Dorothy found ways to care for Jennifer with a minimum of contact. She rarely played with her. And she held her just long enough to complete a feeding or help her clear a bubble from her stomach. Dorothy found cuddling revolting. She was repelled by Jennifer and her needs.

The hitting started when Jennifer, not yet 1, was taking her first, wobbly steps. She was still a fussy and demanding child. On some days the crying would get to be too much and Dorothy would just slap her or push her. Jennifer would shudder in disbelief and then wail.

Child abuser. It was not a phrase anyone who knew Dorothy would have used to describe her.

A computer analyst for a state agency, she had a master's degree from an Ivy League university and a respectable middle-class income. She lived in a clean, well-maintained house on Long Island's South Shore, not far from the water. She seemed, to her friends and family, to be sane, sober and, most of all, competent, balancing the demands of work and mothering, of home and career. She conjured no automatic images of Hedda Nussbaum or Joel Steinberg, the monstrous and pitiful objects of the New York child-abuse case that had filled the media for much of the last year. But, then, everyday child abuse is a much more ordinary tragedy.

This is the story of one woman's search for the reasons behind her mysterious violent outbursts and her struggle to stop. Her intensely personal discoveries reveal the intricate patterns that seem to apply to the lives of most child abusers. As an entire generation of researchers and clinicians has discovered, child abuse is almost never a single isolated problem. Asking only that their names be changed to protect young children, Dorothy and her adult relatives have told their story in hopes that it will help others.

Dorothy had compartmentalized her life, placing boundaries between herself and others and blotting out huge chunks of her memory. She remembered everything from eighth grade to the present. But the time before then was a blur of images; fragments of memories.

It was the same with her relationships with friends and relatives. She would later describe them as fragments of friendship and intimacy. Although she had friends, no one really knew her. She kept others at arm's length. Her obesity, which had appeared when she turned 13, helped keep them away. Now, at age 30, she kept even Jim, whom she had married seven years before, on the outside. They had coexisted that way, with Jim's two teenage daughters, until the baby arrived.

"I had no patience at all. I would just lose control and knock her down, actually, by hitting her," Dorothy would explain a year later. "On the worst times, I would slap her in the face. I would immediately feel bad and I couldn't really explain what had happened. But then, on those times, I'd want to hold her. I felt I could hold her. It was the only time when I thought it was OK. I don't suppose I thought about it as child abuse, but I did feel something was wrong."

Dorothy didn't know it at the time, but her hidden truth was in the unspoken memory that drove her into her bathroom sanctuary that night in December, 1987. She lay on the tile and tried, again, to shut down her mind, to make herself numb to an ache that had begun when she was 11 years old. On the other side of the door, Jim grew frightened.

"She stopped answering me and just stayed in there for a long time," he would recall a year later. "I tried yelling and then I sort of pleaded. But she just wouldn't come out. She wouldn't get up. It frightened me. I knew I had to get some help."

Don-David Lusterman was perhaps the only person who might help. A psychologist, Lusterman had been seeing Janet, Jim's 14-year-old middle daughter, for several months. She had been referred for counseling by her school when her grades began to fall and she was caught shoplifting. Lusterman seemed like a kind person. Dorothy liked him. And, besides, where else could Jim turn? He called. Even a year later, Lusterman could recall every detail of what happened that night, including Jim's words and Dorothy's condition.

"Doc, you've gotta come over right away," came Jim's voice from the other end of the telephone line. He began by pleading, then started demanding. "She's wedged into a corner of the bathroom and she won't come out, she won't even talk. You gotta come, Doc."

"All right, I understand," Lusterman replied. "I'm coming."

It was dark when Lusterman drove up to the house. The glowing lights in the living room gave the place a soft cozy ap-

pearance. Lusterman walked down a concrete path to a side door where Jim, a smallish man with receding black hair, met him.

"She's in the bathroom. I can't get her to move. She won't even answer me."

Lusterman, tall with graying hair and a relaxed, open face, went to the bathroom door and called softly: "Dorothy."

He paused to listen and then called again, "Dorothy."

No answer.

"It's Don-David. Doctor Lusterman. May I come in?"

"OK," came a faint reply.

Lusterman went in, shut the door and sat on the edge of the bathtub. He was shocked by what he saw.

"Here was this woman who had always seemed like superwoman, so competent, so together, collapsed on the floor," Lusterman would say when he described the scene later. "She had never given me any hint there could be something so wrong." No one had ever mentioned Dorothy's blow-ups with baby Jennifer. Janet, the 14-year-old, was supposed to be the problem in the family.

"I'm all alone. I'm alone," Dorothy sobbed when the bathroom door was closed behind Lusterman.

"I'm here with you and I'm not going to leave you," Lusterman answered. They stayed together, in silence, for more than an hour. Dorothy eventually sat up. Then she began to talk.

"There's something wrong with me. I can feel it, but I don't know what it is. Something just snapped for me tonight and I couldn't take it any more. Now I wish the floor would swallow me up. There is something terrible going on with me. I feel it, but I can't say what it is."

THE terrible thing remained a mystery that night. "I had too much concern and respect for her to push her," Lusterman recalls. He helped Dorothy leave the bathroom, and the two agreed to meet again the next day. But the terrible thing couldn't be named the next day, either. Dorothy talked about her life, revealing the frustrations she felt with Janet and hinting at the abuse she directed at Jennifer. But she couldn't explain the collapse, except to say, "I felt overloaded, like I couldn't take it any more."

Over the first few weeks of meetings, Dorothy described problems with her husband and her work. But when Lusterman asked her about her past, she said she was unable to remember much before high school. She couldn't explain the gap in her

memory. But she knew that the more she struggled to remember, the more depressed she felt.

As the months went by Dorothy slowly described, in small puzzle pieces, a childhood of betrayal and isolation. She would struggle through days of depression and anxiety before a dream, or one of Lusterman's questions, would bring a new bit of information up from the depths of her memory. During one session, she said her father was an alcoholic who had rarely been home. And when he was home, she said, he demanded silent obedience. To her, he was only someone to be feared.

"I had never thought about it as a child," Dorothy would say later. "You come to think your family is normal, good, because it's the only one you know."

DURING another session, Dorothy said her mother had beaten her or one of her four brothers almost every day as they were growing up. She said her mother used her hands at first, but then, as the children got older, used sticks. One of her favorite weapons, Dorothy recalled, was a whippy, inch-thick dowel that had once been the handle for a child's push toy.

"I thought the beatings and the outbursts were normal," said Dorothy.

She told Lusterman that, as a child, she had assumed everyone's mother ripped phones out of the wall and hurled them across the room. She thought everyone's mother yanked draperies down in fits of rage. "In a way, what was worse was the coldness," Dorothy recalled during a joint interview with Lusterman and a reporter. "Even when I was a very little child, I wasn't hugged or kissed. My parents were very withdrawn, very cold. They just didn't get involved with us. They thought it would spoil you to let you know they loved you." In her sessions with Lusterman, Dorothy described horrible scenes from her life in the same detached way a reviewer might recount the scenes from a film. She didn't seem angry or outraged. She didn't cry. "She seemed to have what I call a religious belief against crying," Lusterman recalled. "It was as if she was describing someone else."

Gradually, with Lusterman's help, Dorothy was able to remember much of her early life and came to understand the ways she had been carefully taught to abuse her own child. "I was never shown what normal parents did with their children. I had no role model," she would say. But she still couldn't completely stop neglecting Jennifer. She remained frustrated and anxious, and her depressions came more often and more intensely.

As revelations came, one after another,

Dorothy became more and more depressed and detached, except when she slept. When she slept she was haunted by a recurring nightmare. There was a razor, her wrists, and the seemingly seductive peace of suicide. The dreams were so disturbing, so lifelike, that she tried to avoid sleep. As sleepless nights piled upon one another, she became desperate. Eventually, Lusterman referred Dorothy to a doctor who prescribed large doses of a tranquilizer. But the pills didn't help much. It seemed that as Dorothy remembered, and struggled to get better, the waves of pain came faster and stronger.

"The breakthrough came one day when she came in and announced she had remembered something," says Lusterman. Dorothy had remembered that, when her uncle died, she felt very confused. She had worked with him in her father's bakery when she was 11 and 12 years old, but had never been close to him. Yet, when he died, she was overwhelmed by emotions. She couldn't stop crying at the funeral. She felt mournful, angry, relieved and anxious. "The way I carried on, you would have thought I was his wife or something," she said. She couldn't understand why.

"But, as I was talking, I remembered something more, something awful," Dorothy said as she repeated the story later. "I thought that in the bakery, in the storeroom, I had seduced him."

The way Dorothy saw it, she had seduced a middle-aged man — her uncle, no less — into a romantic, sexual relationship. It had begun with him kissing her lightly. Over the course of many weeks it progressed to passionate necking, fondling and more. The encounters, child molesting actually, went on nearly every weekend for two years. And Dorothy was convinced that her father, who was a minor partner in the business, had seen the kissing and known what was going on.

"The most amazing thing about it was, she felt as if she seduced him. Here she was

Talking It Out

THE eight women who filled the homey meeting room at the school in Deer Park greeted each other as old friends. Some hugged, others laughed loudly as they talked about their children, who were in the playground just outside.

After drawing coffee from a big silver urn, they sat on the old sofas and easy chairs that formed a circle in the middle of the room. As they settled in, the room grew silent when first one, then others talked about hitting, slapping, shoving, humiliating and neglecting children. The stories sounded the same, whether the women were talking about the way they treated their own children or the way they had themselves been reared. Telling them at the weekly mothers' support group run by the Family Service League helps parents break the cycle of abuse.

"I remember being very sure, when I was maybe four or five, that I was hated. It was something I was certain about and I was sure I deserved it," began Doris, a woman in her mid-30s who had long brown hair and wore a heavy, deep green sweater. She brushed her hair from her forehead and thought for a moment about her own three children. "I know I used that kind of anger against my kids. I was doing what was done to me, and it made me feel crazy. I saw them look at me the way I know I looked at my parents. I didn't want them to grow up feeling like a piece of garbage, like I did. I had to stop it."

Beverly, a young woman dressed in faded jeans and a white cotton sweater, said: "My father used to hit people, hit furniture, hit the walls, and I found myself feeling like doing the same things. He even told me to do the same with my son. He says, 'Just swat him. Break his leg if you need to. That'll just teach him.' Sometimes I did what he said."

"The fact is, as adults, we repeat the kind of parenting that we experienced as children," explained Adrea Seligsohn, a social worker who helps supervise the support group. Children, whose very survival depends on their parents, find it impossible to believe that the mother or father who is hitting them is doing something wrong, said Seligsohn. "So the child grows up believing she deserves it, that it's appropriate, and she can be become a parent who does it, too."

The Deer Park program is one of a handful of experimental projects funded by the state to provide comprehensive services to families at risk of violence. Twenty-nine families participate in the project, which offers free day care, individual and group counseling and classes in effective, nonviolent parenting. The Deer Park project is part of the state Department of Social Service's effort to stem a rising tide of child abuse reports. The number of reported cases of child abuse is generally believed to be just a small fraction of the actual abuse taking place.

Child abuse is still largely a private matter. Police rarely get involved even though abuse, neglect and incest are crimes. Victims rarely consider calling the authorities. Nevertheless, public awareness of the child-abuse problem has risen in this decade, spurred by the publicity around infamous cases such as Lisa Steinberg's. Reported cases have doubled in this decade, reaching 2.2 million reports nationwide in 1988.

Nearly 200,000 child abuse cases were reported in New York State in last year, with 11,000 on Long Island. The fastest-growing category of abuse reports is sexual abuse. The proliferation of child-abuse reports reflects what experts believe is both an increased awareness of the problem and an increased incidence. They say that child abuse is more common today because families are under more stress.

"Child abuse occurs usually when someone is under great stress," said Adrea Seligsohn. "That's when people seem to react instinctively to a crisis and their first impulse is to do what their parents did to them. Most people don't understand that. Many haven't even come to understand the truth of their own childhood because we all seem to create a very rosy, 'Brady Bunch' fantasy in our minds about childhood. It's as if people need to believe they had a great childhood, so they make one up, even if it wasn't real."

WHEN abusive parents recognize how they were abused as children, they can begin to see the reasons why they seem to explode in anger. "Then it's much easier to stop the cycle, to bring it under control," Seligsohn said.

As the women in the mothers' support group recounted stories from their own tortured pasts and talked about their own children, they provided vivid illustrations of the cycle of abuse and neglect. "The worst part was when I realized what I was teaching my children. My father had taught me to be violent," explained Beverly. "He taught me to hate him and to hate myself. When I got older, I knew I shouldn't feel that way but I did. It got so my feelings weren't really based on reality. I had trouble even telling what was real."

In her group meetings, Beverly discovered she is not the only one who grew up believing she deserved to be abused. She found she's not the only one who loathes her parents and, at the same time, fears she's becoming like them. "I know I didn't deserve what I got, and my kids don't deserve it, either," she said. — *Michael D'Antonio*

11 years old, a child, and he's an adult, but she's the one who felt guilty," Lusterman said. "She was very confused about what had happened. Most victims of this kind of abuse are very confused."

Years later Dorothy recalled that she had, indeed, been very confused by her uncle's advances. On one level, she was frightened by what was happening and what would happen if her family knew everything that was happening. On another level, she felt betrayed. How could her uncle do this? Why didn't her father protect her? Couldn't he tell something was happening in the storeroom? Finally, she felt guilty because she liked the attention. She was a lonely, isolated, unhappy child. No one had ever paid so much attention to her. In a certain way, she would later admit, she liked it.

It took several months before Dorothy came to see herself as a victim of sexual abuse, not the cause of it, she said as she described the process. Slowly, she came to believe her parents had abandoned her so thoroughly that she was a victim waiting to be abused. She had felt so isolated that there was not a single adult, not even her own parents, whom she could trust.

Repeated studies have shown that child abuse occurs in every class and race. A child abuser is, more often than not, white, middle class and seemingly stable. And child abuse is not an isolated rampage or an unexplainable, random phenomenon. "Abusers are people like us. They are the people we know, maybe the people next door or the people reading this magazine," says Barbara Applebaum, one of the psychologists who would eventually help Dorothy. "And abuse doesn't occur by accident. There is a reason why they do it, a reason that's hidden in the abuser's past and it is usually very difficult to find, which is why it's so hard to stop."

Like most stories of abuse, Dorothy's is a tragic three-act drama that begins when an abused child learns to deny the truth of her own suffering. A parent's abuse is often too disturbing for the child to accept as real, so he learns to repress the memories of the violence, the abandonment and humiliation. The truth stays hidden until she has children of her own. Then the pattern re-emerges, only this time the child victim becomes the abusive parent. Abuse becomes a way of life, a legacy handed from one generation to the next. But the legacy can be broken.

As Dorothy came to understand what had happened to her, she was flooded with feelings of shame and rage. Lusterman recommended she join a support group for women who had been caught in the same cycle of abuse. She went and discovered that each of them had herself been abused

or molested as a child and had grown up to be an abusive or neglectful mother. The group was sponsored by North Shore Child and Family Guidance Center in Manhasset. It was guided by counselor Barbara Applebaum.

"Dorothy's story is unique and at the same time typical," Applebaum explained one afternoon as she and Dorothy reviewed her case for a reporter. Nearly all abused children come to believe they have good reason to hide what was done to them, either because it's too painful to acknowledge or because they feel responsible for what happened.

"Dorothy's situation was typically complex. She had been seduced as a child and had, at the same time, felt some gratification from it because she was so lonely and had been neglected for so long. There are so many difficult feelings in something like this—betrayal, shame, guilt—that you begin to deny it."

Denial is a child's strongest defense against an ugly reality. She can use it to blot out the feelings of exploitation, abandonment or shame that may be too painful to bear. "The problem is, with this kind of denial, the memory gets pushed back into your subconscious so far that it's not real to you. You begin to think that it didn't happen." But the memory doesn't go away, Applebaum says. It is almost always stirred when an abused child becomes an adult and has children.

When Dorothy had a child of her own, Jennifer, her memory was stirred. For the first time, she was involved with a little child again—one not unlike the innocent child she had once been. "I was so confused by her," Dorothy said. "I would hold back my affection and then I would hit her. Then I would immediately hate myself and be terrified by what I did. It was awful."

The hitting stopped when Dorothy discovered the source of her rage, relived her own abuse and joined a support group for abusive mothers, one of several that gather each week at counseling centers around Long Island. There she found other women who had sought help because they were abusing their own children. They, too, had been victims of abuse themselves and, as mothers, turned their rage on their children.

Dorothy used her group meetings, and her individual counseling sessions with Lusterman, to reach the same kind of understanding. The more she explored her past, the more clearly she saw the way child abuse had been passed to her in the manner of an inheritance. She also saw how her own mother had been tragically scarred in her childhood in a way that made it all but inevitable that she would be an abuser.

"My mother was illegitimate and her mother abandoned her," she said. "Her father took her and gave her to his parents.

He said he couldn't handle her. So she was raised by her grandparents, who told her she was illegitimate and that they hated her mother. They hated her, too. When it thundered they would tell my mother, 'That's God coming to punish you.' As a little kid, she believed it.

"The worst must have been when there was a chance that my mother could have gotten out of there when her father remarried and started a new family. But he never took her back, never let her be in his family. Can you imagine how that felt? First your mother abandons you, then your father. Then, when he could take you back, he just doesn't?"

When Dorothy's mother married and had children, she re-created the lonely family of her childhood. Her husband, who spent six nights a week out drinking, was just as neglectful as her father. Her home was as empty of love as her childhood home. And her children became co-victims of her past.

"Of course, no one ever talked about it this way; no one really even acknowledged anything was wrong in our family," said Dorothy. "We acted like everything was normal, as if everyone lived this way."

When she moved out on her own, Dorothy followed the script handed down by her family. Jim, her husband, it turned out, was an alcoholic — often withdrawn and cold. A computer analyst in private industry, Jim described his own childhood in an interview as years of neglect spent on the streets of Brooklyn, where he was twice molested by men. "I ran the streets, which at the time I thought was normal," he now says. "But I was a very isolated kid and I never learned how to be involved with anyone, how to even be nice." Jim never told anyone about the molesting or his life on the streets. He learned, instead, to detach from the reality of his own life and from other people. Now sober, Jim still has problems communicating with his wife and children.

"I'm not the kind of person who can be very warm very easily," he explained one afternoon as he flicked the switches on the TV set in the living room. One corner of the room was packed with computer equipment, which Jim used for moonlighting. He said he can spend hours lost in his computer work. "It's easier for me than coping with people sometimes," he said. While he talked, Dorothy sat beside him on the couch, Janet relaxed in a big easy chair and Jennifer, now 3, puttered around the living room.

"I guess you could say I was an abusive parent," Jim volunteered as he stopped changing channels and sat on a sofa. He has also undergone extensive psychotherapy and belongs to a support group for men who have been caught in the cycle of abuse. "I used to hit the kids pretty good, back when I had them by myself," he said.

2. VICTIMOLOGY

"There were lots of times when I lost control and didn't know why." Jim had spent several years as a single parent and during that time used force to discipline Janet and her older sister, Patti. When Patti was old enough, she ran away to live with her mother. Janet stayed with her father, his new wife and their baby.

ATTI got the worst of it, I have to say," Jim admitted. "But, when this one was little, I'd kick her too," he added, pointing to his daughter, who sat curled up in an arm chair. "She'd go sailing across the floor like a football. It was pretty bad."

"You did not," Janet answered, denying she had been abused, just as Dorothy had once denied it. "That never happened, Dad, c'mon."

The experts — Lusterman, Applebaum and Seligsohn — predict that many of today's abused children will be tomorrow's child abusers. The most recent study of the intergenerational nature of child abuse was done at the University of Colorado Medical School. The researchers identified abuse as physical and emotional abuse, which included denying a child love and comfort, and actively humiliating or berating a child. They found that one-third of abused children themselves become child abusers.

The phenomenon is most pronounced among those who were abused or neglected at an early age, and in families that were emotionally cold and secretive. That was the case with Dorothy and it could have been the case with Janet. But now the family secrets are out in the open. Janet now knows that child abuse could be a family legacy. That knowledge, and Dorothy's attempt to fashion a new kind of family, could break the chain.

Dorothy has also begun to explore her past with her parents and her brothers. The process began when she invited her mother to a meeting with Lusterman. The three talked for an hour about Dorothy's childhood and about the repeated molestation that took place in the family bakery. "When it was over," Dorothy recalls, "my mother got up and said, 'Well, I'm sorry about what happened, but I'm glad it was nothing we did, Dorothy.' " It was only the faintest glimmer of understanding, but Dorothy took it as a beginning. She recently repeated the process with her father. Although he has not discussed Dorothy's past since the meeting with Lusterman, Dorothy's mother, Anne, has used the opening with her daughter to begin, at last, to tell the truth about herself. For the first time she told Dorothy about her own growing up and about feeling trapped and unable to cope as the mother of five young children.

Anne's early life story was so filled with abuse that she kept it hidden out of shame and fear. "I was beaten in ways my children never experienced and made to feel absolutely worthless," she recalled in an interview.

Anne said her grandparents, forced to take her in when her mother abandoned her, treated her icily. "I got no affection and, if there was any little problem, they would do something to me." The some-things included beatings with switches or the emotional torture of a trip to a nearby orphanage where her grandparents would pretend to abandon her again. The nightmare of her childhood brought Anne to her own nervous breakdown — not unlike Dorothy's crisis in the bathroom — and the apparent escape of an early marriage. That marriage, to a man she described as aloof and alcoholic, soon recreated her hellish past.

"I married a man who was as cold as my grandparents," Anne says. "He was so inside himself I could never communicate with him. I was working, trying to keep a spotless house and raising five kids, all with really no help. So, when push came to shove, I hit the kids. It was very bad sometimes. But I didn't know any other way. I had never seen any other way.

"But, when the hitting happened, I just hated myself. It got so that I was going to kill myself if I couldn't stop." At that time she sought help from her pastor, who is also a psychotherapist. "He taught me that I was a worthwhile person, that there was a chance for me. That was the beginning of the change."

After Dorothy brought the child abuse of her past into the open with her parents, she also discussed it with her brothers. She gathered them together last New Year's to share her discoveries and was surprised to find they had long suspected their family was deeply disturbed. They had been five strangers, growing up under the same roof. "We finally talked about Mom and Dad and life back then. And we talked about the way we act now. All of us have problems now.

"We finally talked about some of this stuff and I think, for the first time, we felt close that day," said Dorothy. "At least it was a beginning."

OROTHY'S brother Daniel said said he was more impressed by his parents' coldness than by their violence. "Loving things just weren't expressed," he said. One of his most poignant memories is of an autumn afternoon when he was throwing a football with his brother. "My father came out the door and put his hands up. I asked him if he wanted to catch it. I was shocked. He had never played catch with me before, and I was 17 years old."

Not long ago, Dorothy spent an hour and a half in Lusterman's office, recounting the past year. Just talking about it was draining. In the past year she had admitted she was an abusive mother and relived a painful past that had been so awful she had kept it locked away in her subconscious for nearly 20 years. And then she had begun the painful process of healing.

Standing outside Lusterman's office, on a bright afternoon, Dorothy paused to let the sun warm her face. She brushed her brown hair back and looked up at a small flock of sparrows passing in the sky.

"You know, when they tell stories like this they usually end with the person making the decision that they need help, as if that's all there is. That's not the way the story should end. That's really only the beginning. There's a lot of pain you have to go through to get better, the pain of remembering. Even now, I still get depressed. But the pain belongs mostly to my past, to the 13-year-old girl who kept silent for so long. It's better, now that I have let her speak."

Dorothy took a few steps toward her car and pulled some keys from her pocket. She paused again. "It takes a long time," she said before turning away. "But I know I'm getting better. I can't get enough of hugging my daughter and I don't feel so out of control anymore."

Where to Find Help

Child Abuse Hotline	(800) 342-3720
Parents Helpline	(516) 473-1747
Response Hotline	(516) 751-5700
Victims Information Bureau (Suffolk)	(516) 360-3606
North Shore Child and Family Guidance Center	(516) 626-1971
Child Abuse Prevention Service	(516) 621-0552
Parents Anonymous	(800) 462-6404

Tougher Laws Mean More Cases Are Called Rape

Tamar Lewin

Under liberalized state laws, prosecutors have grown more willing to pursue rape charges in cases in which women have been attacked not by strangers but by acquaintances. And criminal justice experts say that rapes by acquaintances are by far the most common type.

"Prosecutors have historically been more comfortable pursuing stranger rape, but that is changing by leaps and bounds," said Laura X, director of the National Clearinghouse on Marital and Date Rape in Berkeley, Calif. "Very serious criminal charges are now routinely filed in cases involving acquaintance rape. The whole atmosphere has changed, as more people come to understand that 'no' means 'no.' "

But acquaintance rape still presents special legal challenges.

Many Situations Are Involved

"Where it's his word versus hers, the discretion is totally in the hands of the prosecutor and the police, to decide whether the woman is credible," said Mary Ann Largen, executive director of the National Network for Victims of Sexual Assault.

"There are crimes of acquaintance rape being reported these days that just would not have been reported 10 years

---

Prosecution is now more likely when the accused is known.

---

ago," Ms. Largen said. She said more women believe the legal system will do more on their behalf.

Acquaintance rape is a broad term, encompassing many different situations. In recent years, on many campuses, there have been notorious incidents in which a student, often drunk, is forced to have sexual intercourse with her date, and sometimes his teammates or fraternity brothers.

But acquaintance rape also happens to older women off campus. The victim can easily be a 50-year-old widow who asked the man next door to repair her toaster or a single 35-year-old who drove home with an office colleague.

The rape case against William K. Smith, based on charges by a woman who said he attacked her at the Kennedy family estate in Palm Beach, is typical, in that it concerns two people who were social companions, and in that it seems likely to come down to a woman who says she said 'no' and a man who says he heard 'yes.'

A study of 2,291 adult working women from Cleveland, published this year, and an earlier study of 3,187 women at 32 colleges, found that 15 percent of the college women and 20 percent of the working women said they had been raped. Eighty percent of the rape victims in both studies knew their attackers while half of the rapists were dates or men with whom they have been intimate, said Prof. Mary P. Koss, of the University of Arizona, who conducted the studies.

"Women worry about a man jumping from behind a bush, when they should be worrying about their date," Ms. X said.

Crime statistics do not distinguish between stranger rape and acquaintance rape, and many rapes are never reported to the police, so there are no reliable official statistics on the incidence of acquaintance rape.

But David Beatty, the public policy director of the National Victim Center, an advocacy group in Washington, said: "There is no question that acquaintance rape is more common than stranger rape. No one has the exact numbers, but the consensus is that probably in 80 to 85 percent of all rape cases, the victim knows the defendant."

More Than 100,000 Reported

And last year, the number of rapes reported to the authorities in the United States rose to 100,433, according to a Senate Judiciary Committee report.

Until the 1970's, rape laws in most states covered only those situations in which a man forced a woman to have sexual intercourse under the threat of bodily injury, she resisted strenuously, and there was outside corroboration.

In the early 1970's, when New York had a very strict rape law, requiring outside corroboration of every element of the crime, there were typically only 18 rape convictions a year statewide out of more than a thousand rape complaints.

Now, most state laws include several degrees of rape charges and cover a broader range of situations.

Most states have made marital rape a crime as well.

"In most states, you still have to show some kind of force or threat, and the woman's non-consent," Ms. Largen said. "What's changed is how force is defined, which can now include verbal threats or physically overpowering the woman. The other thing that's changed is that the victim's word has far more weight with police and prosecutors."

2. VICTIMOLOGY

Shield Laws in Every State

Every state has also adopted some kind of rape shield law, protecting most rape victims from being questioned about their past sexual conduct. But those laws, too, vary considerably, particularly regarding evidence that the victim previously had consensual sexual relations with the defendant.

"Rape laws are a moving target right now," said Stephen Schulhofer, a criminal law professor at the University of Chicago. "I think we're in for a period of even more change, because there's such enormous diversity of cultural messages out there about what is and isn't acceptable behavior."

Rape laws generally do not treat acquaintance rape any differently from rape by a stranger. But because of variations in wording, rape by an acquaintance is easier to prosecute in some states than in others.

Florida's rape law is fairly typical: Its most serious charge requires proof of penetration, non-consent, use or display of a deadly weapon, or the use or threat of physical force likely to cause serious injury. And the least serious charge, under which Mr. Smith was charged, requires proof of physical force or violence not likely to cause serious injury.

But in Michigan, a state that has a wider definition of rape, prosecutors charging the most serious crime, first-degree criminal sexual conduct, must prove penetration and injury to the victim or a threat of physical force, coercion, concealment or surprise.

"The language about coercion, concealment or surprise covers the most typical date-rape scenarios, where the woman suddenly finds a man on top of her, and while there is no gun or knife, she is taken by surprise and can't get out," Ms. Largen said. "In Florida, that would be much harder to prosecute."

Silence Can Mean 'No'

Michigan, like many of the states with broader statutes, also has a crime of criminal sexual contact, covering situations in which women have been forcibly grabbed but not raped.

Some states go further, eliminating any requirement of force. In Wisconsin, for example, a man can now be found guilty of third-degree sexual assault, a felony, if he has sexual intercourse with a woman who has not agreed to it, even if she remained silent and he used no force.

"In the most liberal states, it is a crime to have intercourse without consent, and consent is interpreted as a knowing and affirmative expression of willingness," Professor Schulhofer of the University of Chicago said. "That means if the woman is silent, or crying, or too drunk to give knowing consent, it's a 'no.' "

But Wisconsin prosecutors say such cases are difficult to win, and rarely taken to trial.

The proposed Federal Violence Against Women Act, introduced by Senator Joseph R. Biden, Jr., Democrat of Delaware, would take a different approach than state laws. It would declare rape a "hate crime" based on sex bias and allow victims to bring private civil rights lawsuits against their attackers.

Still, many prosecutors remain wary of acquaintance rape cases, feeling that juries are unlikely to convict unless the victim suffered physical injury.

'Beyond the Usual Limits'

"I was consulted just this week on a case where two guys had sex with a woman, but the prosecutor won't take it because the woman had been drinking," Professor Koss of Arizona said in a recent interview. "There's virtually no chance of winning an acquaintance rape case unless you can show the jury some physical injury. The expectation is that men will be aggressive about sex and women will be reticent, so the jury wants to see that his assertiveness went beyond the usual limits."

Cheryl Calcagno, director of victim services in the Wayne County, Mich., prosecutor's office, estimated that the conviction rate is about 40 percent in acquaintance rape cases, as against 60 percent in stranger rapes.

"Whether or not there's a conviction depends a lot on how the victim presents herself in court, whether she's got a job, and her life style," said Ms. Calcagno, adding that about 80 percent of the rape cases her office handles involve acquaintances.

Linda Fairstein, who heads the sex crimes unit in the Manhattan District Attorney's office, said her unit successfully tries many cases involving women's lovers or husbands in which there is no injury, but she agrees that such cases are harder to win.

In a recent week, she said, six new cases in her unit involved acquaintance rape, including a mother-in-law assaulted by her son-in-law, a couple that had been dating for five months, and a young woman raped by two men she met at a club.

"She presents herself very well, and is completely forthright about liking to party, liking to drink and sometimes do cocaine, but not being promiscuous about sex, and I think she'll do just fine in court," Ms. Fairstein said of the young woman. "There's this idea that you can't win that kind of case, but last week, one of my young assistants, for her first case, tried and won a rape conviction where the victim was a crack addict-prostitute who had previously had consensual sex with the rapist. She did have minor injuries from being hit with a chair leg."

Even the Victim Can Be Slow to Recognize Rape

Jane Gross

Special to The New York Times

SAN FRANCISCO, May 27—Lori Slicton-Williams did not call what happened to her "rape" until many years later.

She figured she had made a stupid mistake by agreeing to drive a fellow student home from a party. She wondered if she had led him on by going into his house.

She asked herself if she could have fought back more vigorously when he threw her to the bed and forced her to have sexual intercourse. And when the attack was over, she felt embarrassed rather than angry and apologized for "not wanting sex."

Victims Blame Themselves

"I put the burden on myself," Ms. Slicton-Williams said recently, recounting that night eight years ago, when she was a freshman at a community college in the small Sierra Nevada town where she was raised. "I thought it was all my fault."

Counselors and other rape experts say that in blaming herself first, and only gradually deciding that she had been raped, Ms. Slicton-Williams is typical of women who say they have been sexually assaulted by men they know.

This is borne out by the accounts of eight women introduced to a reporter by counselors familiar with their cases, which date back 11 months to 20 years. The women, now ranging in age from 21 to 56 years old, described social encounters that began pleasantly, often at a party or in a bar, with no hint of the violence to come. They described men who seemed to have double personalities, changing in the blinking of an eye from someone they liked and trusted to a surly attacker.

They described their cries of protest and struggle while the attack continued and their amazement afterward when the man behaved as if nothing extraordinary had happened. And, they described a counseling process, often taking months or years, in which using the term "rape" helped them recover, even if the force used against them and their level of resistance might not have met the legal standards of rape, which differ from state to state.

Rape Definition Broadens

Public attitudes and legal definitions of rape are changing to encompass a wide range of sexual events, with varying degrees of violence, submissiveness and injury, but all involving women having sex against their will. At the same time that society is developing a broader view of rape, many more women are availing themselves of counseling, experts say, and struggling to take the onus off themselves and put it on the man. The majority of these cases involve acquaintance rape, an offense that has gained attention lately because of the charges in Palm Beach, Fla., against William K. Smith. A 29-year-old woman has charged that Mr. Smith raped her at the Kennedy family estate after she drove him home from a Palm Beach bar.

Of the eight women interviewed for this article, five asked to be identified to better demonstrate the wide range of women who have been raped and the varying circumstances of what they regard as acquaintance rape. The other three requested some measure of anonymity to protect their privacy or their families.

Many of them said they had helped set the stage for rape by going places and doing things that made them uncomfortable rather than confronting or insulting the men they were with who were making strong sexual advances.

Michele Hughes, for instance, allowed a man to sleep at her San Francisco apartment after a long night of drinking and wound up raped and infected with gonorrhea. She invited him in, Ms. Hughes said, because she did not want to hurt his feelings, was worried he had no way to get home and was too tired to continue bickering at the door about whether he could come inside.

Ms. Hughes, now a 26-year-old administrative assistant in a small office, was celebrating her 21st birthday the night of her attack. She said she told the man, who walked her home after they had met in a bar, that there would be no sex and had made up a couch for him in a separate room. She awoke hours later, still fuzzy from alcohol, to find him raping her.

Experts note that the lack of assertiveness can also affect how women act after they have been forced to have sex. That was the case with Ms. Slicton-Williams—now an anthropology graduate student, married to her high school boyfriend and expecting her first child—who practically apologized to her rapist for not being more cooperative.

"You think I'm stupid for not wanting sex, don't you?" she recalls asking him.

The man nodded affirmatively.

Of the women interviewed, only two, who were subject to extreme violence by their assailants, said they knew at the time that they had been raped.

A 'Buddy' Is Guilty of Rape

One, June Williams, was strangled to the point of unconsciousness, beaten and sexually abused for four hours by her cousin, Michael Mumphrey, with whom she had been drinking and smoking cocaine after a family barbecue last July 4. Mr. Mumphrey, whom Ms. Williams had considered her closest "buddy," pleaded guilty to rape this month and is awaiting sentencing.

The other six women described periods of self-doubt and guilt, nightmares and emotional problems before deciding, usually guided by counselors, that a rape had occurred.

Ms. Hughes, who did not immediately seek help, said she was withdrawn, bulimic and prone to sudden tears after her attack. "I staved it off for a while, the emotions and stuff," she said. "But four years later I was still thinking and writing about it."

Eventually, Ms. Hughes sought counseling and regained her self-esteem. Like many other women who go through such counseling, she now volunteers at a rape hotline.

The healing process was similarly slow for Jackie Serena, who was 50 years old when she was attacked during a New Year's Eve date that she had tried to cancel because she had had oral surgery and "wasn't in shape for the traditional midnight kiss."

Ms. Serena, who had been going out with the man for several months before the attack, was so traumatized after-

Women often blame themselves when attacked by men they trust.

ward that she moved to another town, changed jobs five times in six years and gained 50 pounds. Now, after counseling, she is working as a secretary in a hospital, has lost weight and has regained her equilibrium.

But she still refuses to date. "I do not feel safe anywhere," Ms. Serena said.

Ms. Serena, who has four daughters and several grandchildren, met her attacker when he was sent by a union to organize the office where she did clerical work. They hit it off immediately and began dating.

"We had been intimate," she said shyly. "But he always treated me like such a lady." When she told him about the surgery, for example, he assured

her that "sex is not the only reason to be together."

But that night, when they were together briefly in a bedroom, he grabbed her. When Ms. Serena tried to break free and run, he threw her against the wall and yelled, "Where do you think you're going?"

At that moment, Ms. Serena said, her "will to fight was gone." She said she realized "the person I was facing was not the man I'd known before." He had "changed from one person to another," she said, asserting, "I was dealing with a monster."

Other women also noted the dramatic transformation of a gentle man. One woman, who was a 21-year-old college student when she was attacked by a former neighbor whom she met on the street and invited home for a cup of coffee, recalled "that look he all of a sudden got in his eye."

Another woman told of the time when, as a young single mother living in a poor neighborhood, she went home with a man to see his art work after several pleasant encounters outside a market. He had always been polite and garrulous, the woman said. But in his apartment, the man suddenly turned silent and mean. Over the course of several hours, he hogtied and sodomized her, without speaking a word.

"It was like he had become someone else," she said.

Several women described men who ignored their resistance and tears before and during sexual intercourse and acted afterward as if nothing untoward had happened. Typical was Jenifer W., an undergraduate at the University of San Francisco, who said she had been raped by a medical student. Jenifer met the man while studying the bulletin board in the student union in search of an apartment. She was impressed by his English accent and flattered by his attention.

After Rape, Promising to Call

Alternately charming and hectoring in a series of telephone calls, the man

persuaded her to invite him to her dormitory. When he arrived, the girl said she told him, "I have no desire to have sex with you." During the attack, she cried, pushed him away and begged him to stop, "but that didn't faze him." Afterward, apparently immune to her distress, the man said, "I'll give you a call," as he headed out the door.

Jenifer, who came to the realization that she had been raped over the next several days, then notified the police about the attack but law-enforcement officials told her there was not enough evidence to pursue a case. Most of the women did not notify the authorities, saying they doubted anyone would believe them since they were willingly in the company of the men who attacked them.

But counselors encourage women to take the position that sex without an explicit "yes" is not consensual, even between people who have had sexual intercourse in the past. That was the case with K. Kaufman, a 38-year-old freelance writer, who allowed a man to sleep in the same bed after he promised not to "bother" her. Later that night, he forced her to have sex, she said.

Ms. Kaufman noted that calling what happened to her rape was likely to prompt disdain. "But what people don't understand is powerlessness," she said. "They don't understand the amount of sex women submit to because it's easier than saying no."

Several of the women said they were assaulted by men who were very drunk and subsequently passed out, thus enabling them to flee. Ms. Serena, for instance, recalled pulling the man's limbs off her and inching to the door, terrified that her footsteps or the click of the latch would rouse him. At home, she said she "showered and showered but couldn't get clean, no matter how hot the water or how stiff the brush."

Ms. Serena said that people who hear her story often inquire if the man had a weapon. "They ask, 'Did he have a knife? Did he have a gun?' I guess you had to be there to understand."

THE UNBEARABLE LOSS

With the rise in child murders,
victims' families are seeking new legal rights
and channels for their grief

CHIP BROWN

Life is arrested in the quilt. The muddy pictures of the dead stare out like faces in a yearbook. Some squares have bric-a-brac or heartfelt verse below the dates of birth and death. *Forever in our hearts.* Under Raynell Muskwinsky's picture, her mother, Gilda, satin-stitched a yellow rose of Texas; the faint red stain is lipstick from where she bit the thread.

Glen Enright, who would have taken over his father's business, smiles from his parents' family room. Kimberly Strickler is settled happily on the knee of a department-store Santa. Daniel Ward beams at the camera in a picture taken a month before his father shot him in the head. The photo of Elena Semander comes from the session she hoped would show her potential as a model; she was strangled by a serial killer. The youngest face belongs to Sam McClain Jr., murdered with his mother, Linda, six weeks after his first birthday. She was found on the floor of the living room, Sam in the kitchen freezer, frozen solid, with many small cuts on the soles of his feet.

The keeper of the quilt is Shirley Parish, mother of Kimberly. Shirley is a warm and hospitable woman, a former nurse, but in parts of Fort Bend County, where her only daughter was shot in the trunk of a car in January 1979, she is known as "the crazy lady." For ten years she has made no secret of her determination to see the state of Texas execute Roger Leroy DeGarmo, the con-

victed killer of her daughter, a man who testified at his own trial that the guilty verdict was correct, and that, furthermore, the jury should put him to death because if he ever got out he was going to track them all down and kill them too—and if they were sleeping he would wake them up first.

Many pictures on the quilt are all the more poignant because they were never envisioned as images of commemoration. Some of the parents Shirley asked for photos were reluctant to part even temporarily with what had become their most precious possessions. A Houston T-shirt shop called Street Smart agreed to transfer the pictures onto fabric for free, and Shirley got a book of quilting patterns. She picked out a blue border with a calico backing. A year ago last February she started sewing. By the fall she had filled twenty-seven of the thirty spaces. She laid the squares out boy, girl, boy, girl, like a dinner party, but the pattern didn't hold, because there were too many murdered men.

On the second Tuesday of every month Shirley removes the quilt from her bed and bundles it downtown to St. Paul's United Methodist Church, where she hangs it on a stand in a room on the second floor of the youth building. As people drift in they gather around it. Some fall to reminiscing cheerfully. Others just stand there in a kind of stone communion, as if they were staring into an abyss. The people arriving are mostly white middle-

aged women, but there are a number of men and some younger faces, and you would not know from their disparate looks and backgrounds what they have in common, why they are all here—not until the meeting starts and everyone takes a seat in the circle of folding chairs, and a grave ceremony commences.

"We will begin tonight by introducing ourselves and telling our stories. I'm Gilda Muskwinsky, president of the Houston Chapter of Parents of Murdered Children. My daughter, Raynell, was murdered August 15, 1984."

Gilda turns to her left.

"I'm Paul E. Martin and my son, Todd, was murdered November 26."

"I'm Linda Kelley and on August 29, 1988, my two children were murdered by an ex-con who came into a pawnshop and shot them in the head. My two children are gone and my life is destroyed."

"I'm Gloy Redden. James Goss was my son. I didn't say anything at the last meeting."

And so they go around the room telling their stories, quilt songs, rote summaries of privation and grief. Now it is the turn of an attractive young Korean woman.

"My name is Caroline Min and my younger brother, Walter, was killed by two men."

It is only her second meeting, and she begins to lose her composure. As a new member, she has been cited in the September newsletter piled on the table: "Into our circle of friends we cordially welcome..." Shirley Parish has already had

2. VICTIMOLOGY

The Supreme Court is considering whether to allow "victim-impact statements," telling the jury of a family's suffering.

Walter's picture inked onto cloth, and she has presented the square to Caroline. Now, with forty pairs of eyes on her, Caroline starts to weep. She clutches the quilt square like a handkerchief she can't use.

"He was supposed to graduate from high school..." she says. Her last words come out in a vehement sob. "They didn't just kill my brother, they killed a part of my life!"

For all the lives that terminate in the quilt, the quilt is a point of departure, the place from which survivors can start back from the dead. It is a long road. That nothing is harder to bear than the death of a child is axiomatic, but the truth is the death of a child by homicide is a hundred times worse. "You can't prepare for it," Shirley Parish told me one day. "One minute you're waving good-bye, expecting to see your child at home that night, the next you're looking at a tag on a toe." These years after Kim's death, she still cannot stop herself from running after a stranger in the mall because a flashing resemblance makes her think it's Kim.

Scarcely ten years ago, family members who had been victimized by a violent crime often felt injured twice—once by the crime and a second time by the criminal-justice system. Judges excluded them from courtrooms lest they prejudice juries. Prosecutors dropped charges or fashioned plea bargains without notifying them. Their emotional losses were not taken into account. They were shunned, perhaps out of some superstitious fear of murder, or judged morally defective when they voiced the natural desire for revenge. Grieve, but privately, was the message. Express your anger, but not too loudly. Seek justice, but don't get in the way of the law.

With nowhere to turn, they turned to one another.

The Parents of Murdered Children was founded in 1978 by a Cincinnati couple whose daughter had been murdered. Today the organization claims 30,000 members in seventy chapters. P.O.M.C. is one of a raft

of groups in the victims'-rights movement, which has improved the treatment of the survivors of violent crimes. In death-penalty cases, the Supreme Court is reconsidering whether to allow "victim-impact statements" that describe for juries the suffering of a victim's family. Many states have adopted restitution laws and passed victims' bills of rights. Many prosecutors now make a point of keeping families apprised of legal developments. "I was one of the very first parents allowed to be present at the trial in Texas," Shirley Parish recalled.

But these victories have been won in the face of greater losses. Murder rates continue to rise, and in the late eighties criminal homicide was the second-most-common cause of death for Americans between the ages of fifteen and twenty-four. Congress, which will declare August 12 to 18 National Parents of Murdered Children Week, has been locked in debate over a more substantive response to violence in America. The Brady Bill, passed by the House, would impose a waiting period on handgun purchases. And President Bush has submitted a crime bill that would expand the use of the death penalty, limit legal appeals for death-row inmates, and permit "good faith" exceptions to existing restrictions on the use of evidence by police and prosecutors.

Congressman Charles Schumer, the New York Democrat who chairs the House subcommittee on crime, believes that P.O.M.C. is a valuable outlet and hopes the commemorative legislation will "generate a broader base of support and assistance."

In Houston, where there's a murder every fifteen hours, P.O.M.C. has one of its most active branches. A core of about forty people regularly attend meetings. Newcomers are referred by police and victims'-assistance officers. Active members canvass the morgue and drop brochures off at funeral homes. ("A lot of men think we just sit around and cry," said one member.) The format is not for everybody, and the attrition rate is high.

"Nobody can tell you what to do," said Jack Enright, sitting in the office that had once belonged to his thirty-two-year-old son, Glen, murdered in the summer of 1989. "We needed help and we knew it. We were going in all crazy directions. My wife and I went to one meeting of Parents of Murdered Children and we didn't get a lot out of it, but I stuck it out, and she started coming,

too. It's the best thing we've done. They don't perform miracles, but they can help you mentally or with things you don't know about."

The purpose of the meetings is "to give sorrow words," but often parents unburden themselves of darker emotions that can't be expressed anywhere else in public. They voice their rage, the violence in themselves that tempts them to take the law into their own hands. They are bound as much by the effort to articulate a loss that beggars description as by their special suffering. Their stories, repeated month after month, acquire a kind of liturgical power. As in the text of a Mass, the language is both literal and symbolic. Even at the extremes of despair, the ritual of telling the tale reflects some faith in the power of the word. In saying what happened, somehow there's hope.

And so that night newcomers and long-standing members alike were introduced to Terri Jeffers: "I'm Terri Jeffers and my son, Daniel, was murdered by my ex-husband while I listened on the telephone."

A few days later, I visited her at her home in an apartment development twenty miles north of Houston. Now thirty-seven, she works as a scrub technician for an ophthalmologist, and lives alone with ten-year-old Melissa, her daughter from her first marriage. James Ward was her second husband, and at the time, they had been divorced a month. He had three-year-old Daniel. She had attached a tape recorder to the phone, trying to get proof that he was dangerous. She played the tape of the phone call for me.

Ward's voice is flat and purposeful, and filled with calmly insane logic. She is sobbing and screaming as she pleads for the life of their son.

"Honey, I do love you," he said.

"Don't kill my baby. How could you threaten to kill my baby?" she said.

"You want to tell him good-bye?"

"You're going to kill him?"

"Yes I am. Here he is."

"I'm Terri Jeffers and my son was murdered by my ex-husband while I listened on the telephone."

"Don't you dare!"

"You made the decision. You called my bluff."

"Don't you dare!"

"Huh?"

"Don't you dare touch my baby!"

"Hey, you're the one who called the cops. You thought you were cool, bitch. You did what you thought was right, huh? Think about it."

Then two light, flat pops that on the tape sound almost inconsequential. Terri shut off the recorder and removed the tape. It was raining outside. I didn't know what to say.

She had met James Ward in May 1983 through friends of friends. He was a carpenter, and as she wrote in notes made after Daniel's death, "He seemed to be everything I wanted—hard worker, family man, churchgoer, [and he] liked Melissa." She said that his temper surfaced eight months later. He drank caseloads of beer. Extremely jealous, he accused her of being a whore, and threatened to cut her hands off. Eventually she moved out; they reconciled when he agreed to see a counselor. In February 1988 he smashed her against the headboard of their bed, and she fled to a women's shelter and filed for divorce. He received the news with what seemed to her to be "an eerie calm," and persuaded the court to let him have visitation rights. While she believed he might try to kill her, and Melissa too, she was sure he would not harm Daniel. When Daniel kept saying "Daddy's got a gun and he's going to kill me," she reassured him, "No, Daniel, Daddy loves you."

At the hospital on August 6, 1988, Terri held her son's hands. He was brain-dead, but his heart flailed on at two hundred beats a minute. She cradled him until the organ-donor team arrived.

Now, two years later, in her bedroom, she pulled down the books of Daniel, four blue volumes of photographs showing Daniel being born, Daniel standing up, Daniel wearing a fire hat with a siren in the crown. Terri paged through his short life: "This is when he was three—he was so proud that he was tall enough to jump up and turn off the light switch. And here he's bobbing for apples. And this is Daniel at his last birthday, at Show Biz pizza. I bought him a banjo and his cowboy hat, and some six-shooters because I had them as a kid. That's Jim loading them with caps."

The last pages are filled with pictures of the funeral: three days after Daniel died, she was spending money she didn't have to buy him a white shirt, a double-breasted navy blazer with gold buttons, and a bow tie. She bought him shoes too, even though no one would be able to see his feet in the casket.

Melissa came through the living room. Terri stopped me from opening a manila envelope until Melissa left. "She's never seen it." Inside was Daniel's autopsy photograph: one of those pictures that register before you mean to look. A .22-caliber slug smashed open a raw red crater of tissue and blood in Daniel's forehead. Jim Ward recovered from his self-inflicted wound. Six months after his son's death, he was convicted of murder. He is serving a life sentence, and in 2003 he may be eligible for parole.

"I just don't think I can forgive him," Terri said. "If it was a drowning, or something accidental, but to deliberately pull a gun and pull the trigger—to say 'I've got him now and I'm going to hurt you'...I believe in God, but I'm angry at God because he'd let somebody like Jim go to heaven. If he repents, he can go to heaven. There's something terribly wrong with that. My heart has been ripped out. All the plans I had, all the love—you raise your child, you teach them, you nurse them, you stay up at night when they're sick. Daniel never got to play baseball. He never got to go to AstroWorld. One of my last vivid memories is of him standing in the bathtub, saying, 'I love you, Mama.' It's all I've got...."

She began to cry. Every time she opened the newspaper she found more evidence of man's depravity. And now the atrocities were impossible to ignore: "Christopher Kalmbach—his mother's boyfriend poured pepper down his throat. Tommy Lott—he was tortured to death in 1981. I just wrote the parole board. A man just got fifty years for raping an eight-month-old baby—she had semen in her chest cavity, her chest cavity had been penetrated. Another child was thrown out a window and died, and the man who did it got ten years. A father shot his two kids in the head; that was on the one-year anniversary of Daniel's death. I listen to all the little details. Just last week a mother stabbed her daughter twenty-seven times because she broke a music box. There's a lot of us in Parents of Murdered Children who are considered crazy because we're talking about what happened, because we're not afraid to say how we feel. I just get this rage—how can these people do this and get away with it? I'm stunned. I can't believe it. There are some people in this world that are evil."

She was stunned, and that rage which had given her strength also threatened to consume her. It had eroded her faith. She used to read lessons at Mass, but after Daniel's death biblical homilies made her restless, and the doctrine of forgiveness, the axis of the New Testament, outraged her sense of justice. She had bought a .38 with a four-inch barrel —a present to herself one Christmas. There was a bullet-riddled target taped to the back of her closet.

Parents of Murdered Children helped channel her feelings. She'd toured death row with members from the group. Campaigning to make child murder a capital offense, she'd taken her autopsy photo to Austin to show to state legislators. She'd played the tape of her son's execution on TV talk shows. Now she'd shown the picture to me, and played the tape for me, and as I stood up to leave she thanked me profusely.

Was it simply that she needed someone to hear her out? To help her come to terms with the evil she had encountered, the grief, the pointlessness of her days, which made her not care if she got fat or ever met anyone again?

It was more than that. One could venture that she was stuck in her story, telling it over and over, but not getting anywhere. She was still devoured by rage at what people did—what your own family could do. Such feelings were only human, but they had trapped her. Anyone who listened had to know there was a plea for help in her confidences, her willingness to review the most harrowing episodes. There was an appeal not that one endorse her bitter feelings but that perhaps one could show her the way beyond them. There had been meaning and purpose in the days before Daniel was killed. There had been peace of mind too. Whatever rage might accomplish (and she had sworn to return violence for violence if the occasion should arise), it could not beget peace of mind. However much vengeance might satisfy her, it did not contain the germ of new life. She could not build happiness around brutal newsclips and a .38, and yet she could not get her mind around forgiveness, the untenable idea that the murderer, who once had been her husband, had a place in heaven with her son. The rain had quit, and the air on the

2. VICTIMOLOGY

Families often felt injured twice—once by the crime and a second time by the criminal-justice system.

front porch was fresh. We shook hands, and Terri thanked me again. Then she summoned Melissa inside, pulled the door, and threw the lock.

If Terri Jeffers was stuck, her friend Sam McClain had moved on, or at least seemed to. He had made a new life for himself. He had remarried. He had a new son. His days had been redeemed, and yet he still viewed his life through the prism of the past, and on the second Tuesday of the month, sometimes accompanied by his new wife, he went to the Parents of Murdered Children meeting, where he said, "My name is Sam McClain and my wife and son were murdered and no one was ever caught."

A few days later I drove out to see him at his house in northeast Houston. He let me in while Jumbo, his black "bark-and-hide" lapdog, bounded about like a keyed-up cat. His new wife, Kerry, was holding their boy, Ricky, born four months earlier. On the living-room shelf were pictures of Sam's first wife, Linda Annette Flora, and his first son, Sam junior.

At twenty-seven Sam was younger than most members in the group, lanky and soft-spoken, with large liquid eyes. Two years ago he had been living with Linda and Sam junior in a house in Woodland Acres, a short drive away. He worked as a machinist; Linda had a job at a Wal-Mart store. They had been together for a year and a half, but had dated since high school. The baby had been born prematurely, and pulled through only after five dicey weeks in neonatal intensive care.

Shortly after two on the afternoon of August 7, 1988, Sam returned from a trip to Trinity County. The door was shut but not latched. The stereo was playing, the air-conditioning was on. Linda was sprawled on the floor on top of some of baby Sam's toys. By the eerie pallor of her legs and the glazed, milky color of her eyes, Sam knew the situation was dire. Baby Sam was nowhere to be found. Sam called the police.

At eight that night, after the cops had combed the house, a patrolman on guard noticed a couple of loaves of bread on top of the refrigerator. On a hunch, he opened the freezer. Sam junior's naked body was curled up in the fetal position, frozen solid. It had to be pried out. The morgue was unable to type the blood, and the coroner noted evidence of torture: thirty-three cuts on the boy's feet and buttocks, abrasions on his penis, fractures on both sides of his head.

"I went in to see him for ten or fifteen seconds," Sam recalled in a soft, halting voice. "I had to see him—I couldn't let them take this object off under a blanket and me accept it. It was a gruesome sight, but if I hadn't seen it, I might have trouble believing it."

For a week he was a suspect. He was interviewed by detectives all night, and several days later took six hours of polygraph tests. No money or jewelry was missing, and there was no sign of forced entry. The horror of being a suspect himself scarcely registered as he struggled to come to grips with the annihilation of his family. "If the police were suspicious of me, I didn't care. Their deaths were such a giant idea. It was so big you couldn't conceive of it all at once in your mind. I'd go home and pick a little piece of it to think about."

Eventually the police ruled out Sam. They videotaped the funeral, but turned up few clues. Today the case remains unsolved.

A month after the murder, Sam went to a neighborhood hangout called the Junction with Linda's brother. He met Kerry, who had read about the case, but didn't recognize him. She sympathized. She let him go on. Not long afterward, he asked her to go with him to a meeting of Parents of Murdered Children. He felt out of place among the older members of the group, who were in their forties and fifties, but he could relate to Terri Jeffers. Their children were killed on the same day.

Two months after Sam met Kerry, he gave her an emerald ring. "You helped me," he said. "You were there to talk to. You weren't involved."

"I had some reservations about getting married," she recalled now, shifting little Ricky to her shoulder. "I knew he wasn't over it, I know now he'll never be over it. There are some people at Parents of Murdered Children whose children died twelve years ago and they're not over it. I just thought, This is

what he wanted. I knew I loved him, I knew it was going to be tough, and he told me he needed me."

"Most people at the meetings are able to tell their stories," Sam said. "What I say is: 'My wife and son were murdered and I have had a hard time.' It's easier to avoid it than to say my little boy was cut up and Linda was stabbed eleven times. When I try to wonder what Linda felt, all I can feel is panic. . . . Sometimes I get real mad. I drove by the house once; a lady with a little kid was sitting outside. Part of me wanted to stop and say, 'Do you know what happened here? How can you live here?' But I've had a second chance. It's harder on an older person. If I'd have been twenty years older, I would have lost out. I had Sam for thirteen months. That's not a long time. I'm wondering how these people whose children are my age, how they manage. It's not like somebody being sick. It's just all of a sudden, boom, like lightning striking. Everything in my whole life changed the moment I walked through that door. I lost my wife, I lost the person I talk to, I lost my son, I lost the place I lived. It took everything. I almost feel it took part of my life sometimes."

A year after the murder Sam and his brother Jim had leaflets printed up offering a $1,500 reward. On the night of the first anniversary of the murders, Sam stayed up all night assembling a model of a gold Jeep. Kerry slept beside him on the living-room floor. He is afraid of losing his new family, and insists Kerry spend the night at her mother's if he has to go out of town. For months he used to time her trips to the Laundromat. He moved Ricky's crib away from the window. He always phones before he comes home, not wanting to enter an empty house. He'll check the closets. For months it was impossible for him to open the refrigerator and get ice.

His keepsakes are few: two pairs of baby shoes, one outfit, and the blue scrub suit he wore in the delivery room —the smock stamped with his son's inky footprint. And photographs, including the pictures of Linda and Sam that Shirley Parish sewed into the quilt. And there is the videotape: baby Sam's first birthday, June 26, 1988, at Pistol Pete's Pizza in Pasadena. We watched it that night, laughed about all the *p*'s as Sam slipped the cassette into the VCR. Suddenly baby Sam's face appeared on the screen, prodigally

More than anyone I met in Parents of Murdered Children, Harriett Semander has divined meaning in her daughter's death.

smiling. He was dressed in a red-striped shirt and shorts and a party hat. Kerry glanced at her husband's face and at the video. The camera zoomed in on Linda.

"She's perfect now," Kerry said. "I can never be that perfect person."

Jumbo climbed off the couch. On the screen, the party unrolled with no dramatic developments. "This is probably pretty boring for you," Sam said to me.

"Not at all."

"Look at this part. He's on a merry-go-round and somebody calls his name, and he almost falls off trying to look back over his shoulder. He'd just started walking. He was killed four days after he took his first steps."

On the sound track a voice called, "Sam! Sam! Sam!"

"He's smiling a lot."

"He'd smile at anything. You see him there, and then what happened...You wonder how anybody could...It's two totally different deals...I wonder..."

Little Ricky began to fuss in the other room. "I better throw a bottle in the microwave," said Kerry, getting up.

"It's really helped since he came along," said Sam.

When Kerry was pregnant, she had a baby shower; Terri Jeffers came. She gave them Daniel's stroller.

"Two and a half years ago," said Sam, "if somebody showed me a picture of where I'd be now I'd say, 'No, that's not me, that's somebody else...'"

His voice trailed off; he seemed embarrassed by his frailty. In some ways he would never catch up to the events that had engulfed him; he would always be dislocated by his life's violent turn, and the tenacity of grief, and the mystery of never having answers, much less the satisfaction of justice. Perhaps he would always struggle with the miracle of deliverance too, as the possibility of happiness now hovered before him in the form of his new wife and son.

The camera zoomed in on baby Sam and then panned to Linda, who was holding up a large yellow T-shirt, a gift

to the birthday boy from Pistol Pete's. She looked into the camera and said, "One of these days it'll fit."

Last fall many parents in the Houston Chapter were outraged when two federal judges ordered inmates released from the county jail to ease a severe overcrowding problem. When the release date approached, Shirley Parish stayed on the phone all week mustering a crowd to protest; Jack Enright called local TV and radio stations, and even the White House. He had the idea to form a human chain around the jail. Also, he was hunting around for a coffin, the idea being to dramatize the impact of violent crime by having the parents fill it with copies of their children's death certificates.

By the time Harriett Semander got to the jail on Friday night an angry crowd had assembled, and sheriff's deputies had established a cordon between the protesters and the prisoners coming out. Some parents had taped pictures of their murdered children to plastic Halloween tombstones, although the inmates being released were not murderers, or even felons, but people like the guy who'd been in jail a week awaiting trial for driving with a suspended license.

Someone handed Harriett Semander a Marks-A-Lot and some poster board. She didn't know what to put on her placard, and so in big letters she scrawled a message that had less to do with the issues of overcrowded jails than with her own imprisonment and the story of her daughter Elena, who was strangled to death eight years ago by a serial killer named Coral Watts. Her message was simply: NO, NO, NO!

And yet more than anyone I met in Parents of Murdered Children, more than Sam McClain and surely more than Terri Jeffers, Harriett Semander has divined meaning in her daughter's death. If her conclusions betray the compulsion to twist and bend inscrutable events so that they fit some pattern in our heads, her efforts have at least produced a kind of reckoning. The journal she kept traces her struggle.

Holy Week April 1982: The similarity of Christ's death and Elena's was revealed to me—the humiliation, the nakedness, pain, beatings, and in the end, both were wrapped in a sheet and taken away. This was on Holy Thursday. Holy Friday was confusing—whose funeral, Elena's or Christ's?

Elena was the oldest of the four kids Harriett raised with her husband, Zack. Zack taught math, and Harriett worked in the office at an exclusive Houston private school. Elena was educated there, a whiz in math, with a talent for sculpture and drawing. She also excelled at sports, enough to earn a field-hockey scholarship to the University of Denver. She had gorgeous chestnut hair, and was flirting with the idea of being a model.

On the night of February 6, a night cold enough for her to have worn her rabbit jacket, she stopped by a friend's apartment. He wasn't home. It was after midnight. As she was getting back in her car, she was jumped by Coral Watts, a twenty-eight-year-old mechanic who had been under surveillance by Houston police as a suspect in a number of other killings. Six months later, when he confessed that hers was the fifth of nine murders he had committed in the Houston area, Watts told the story of Elena's death.

"Did she fight?" detectives asked him. "Yeah."

"Was she still wearing that coat?"

"Yeah."

"Remember what she said during the struggle?"

"No."

"Then what happened? What was this that you choked her with?"

"My hands."

"O.K., then what happened?"

"Then I took her coat and her pants and shirt off.... I tied the shirt around her neck and one end around her leg."

"What did you do this for?"

"I don't know."

"...All right, then what did you do?"

"Picked her up and put her in the Dumpster."

"Remember what the Dumpster looked like? What color was it?"

"Gray, I believe."

"Was it a tall Dumpster?"

"A short one."

"Was she heavy to lift?"

"Yeah."

Stripped and hog-tied, Elena was discovered that morning by a garbageman. Harriett was able to identify the body when she recognized her daughter's crooked toe. The only reason Watts was caught three months after Elena's murder was that a woman he had tied up escaped while he was busy trying to drown another woman in a bathtub. In exchange for telling police where nine of his victims were, the state of Texas allowed him to plead guilty to one

2. VICTIMOLOGY

She mapped out the sequence of killings, drawing up an elaborate chart, annotating news accounts, digging for information.

count of burglary. He was sentenced to 60 years; because the judge found that the water in the bathtub was the equivalent of a deadly weapon and therefore an aggravating factor, Watts would not be eligible for parole for twenty years.

Mother's Day 1982: Love never dies, it just grows. I felt Elena's love on Mother's Day and she felt mine. Our love continues to grow throughout eternity. What a glorious resurrection it will be when we are all again united. I wonder if Elena's murderer celebrated Mother's Day and what kind of woman his mother is?

Harriett had survived the first years pretending Elena was away at college. She would sign Elena's name to Christmas presents for her other kids. Once, she sat by a pool for four hours watching a twelve-year-old girl who looked like Elena at that age. Even picking up an apple could trigger grief: it reminded her of Elena, who was afraid of red apples because of what had happened to Snow White.

The second year, she started to harness her feelings. She opened files on Watts. She tried to contact the mothers of some of his other victims. She mapped out the sequence of killings, drawing up an elaborate chart, annotating news accounts, digging for information from the police. She worked for four years to audit a tape of his confession. She attended his sentencing. And in August 1989 she and Zack won a $1.1 million wrongful-death judgment against him. (They were represented by Shirley Parish's husband, whom they had met through Parents of Murdered Children.)

"I was at the beginning of the victims'-rights movement, and the police and the district attorney didn't know what to do with me. I was asking for things no other parents had asked for. They thought I was crazy, my husband thinks I'm crazy, but it was part of the grief I had to deal with."

When Watts was sentenced, Harriett

thought she could move on. In July 1987 she wrote in her journal: "I find myself moving out of the 'justice' stage to the more healing area of 'acceptance' by sharing Elena's story. . . . The type of built-in anger that I can't seem to shake is giving way to an inner voice that tells me life is too short."

Then in August 1989 she called the Board of Pardons and Paroles and learned the astonishing news that Watts was eligible for parole. The judicial finding that a deadly weapon—the water in the bathtub—had been used in the commission of the burglary had been overturned on appeal, and though it was unlikely that Watts would be released on parole, he nevertheless qualified for review.

"My husband and I are getting old," she said. "We'd like to do something together in the five or ten years of good health we have left. Then one fatal phone call and I'm back in it." She alerted the national headquarters of Parents of Murdered Children to put out the word, and more than one thousand letters arrived decrying the possibility of parole. The experience impressed upon her the necessity of unceasing vigilance.

June 4, 1986: I was reading through my journal meditation from 1979 to 1981. So many prayers were written for Elena to find a meaningful Christian relationship with a boyfriend! I never understood why the Lord didn't answer that prayer for me before she died, when tonight it suddenly dawned on me that He did answer those prayers. Every boy Elena dated has probably given their relationship Christian meaning since her death. There is no time element with God.

The Semanders are Greek Orthodox; like Terri Jeffers, a Roman Catholic, they are as troubled by the doctrine of forgiveness as by God's purpose in taking their child's life. They have struggled to reconcile religious precepts on life's sanctity with their personal experience of evil, which has made them advocates of the death penalty.

As they are Greek-Americans, I asked if they had read Nicholas Gage's book *Eleni*, which tells the story of how the author returned to Greece and tracked down the man who had murdered his mother. In the climactic scene Gage stands over his mother's murderer with a gun but does not pull the trigger. They had read the book, and had in fact dis-

cussed that very scene with the author when he came to Houston to speak.

"I went up to him afterwards," Harriett said. "I said, 'My daughter's been a murder victim, and there's something bothering me. Do you regret not shooting him?' He said there were moments when he wakes up and wishes he had. In God's eyes he did the right thing, but I don't know how he did it. How did he control himself? If Coral Watts was in this room I would start beating on him. It's not hate—it's an uncontrollable urge to fight back, to protect, to revenge.

"The first time we went to church after Elena's death, we had to kneel down and thank Him for everything good and bad. I had to thank Him for Elena's death. I couldn't do it, not at first. It took a couple of years. I had a list of people to pray for, the living and the dead, and I had to put Coral Watts in the living list and Elena in the dead."

Her husband was staring at a classical clay bust on the den table—Elena had made it. "Wiping Watts out of my mind, I don't know if I could do that," said Zack.

"When I think of Elena, I think of Watts," said Harriett. "I know his birthday. I think about his daughter. I would like to go back to school someday and study painting; I'm interested in portraits, and one of the first I would do is Coral Watts. His face is embedded in my mind. He's part of my family."

Could there be a more wrenching introduction to our condition as pawns of fate than having to cope with homicide? Two cases I heard about seem now to exemplify the beginning and the end of what is a long procession of wounded people struggling to go on. A few years ago, a woman in the Houston Chapter came to the meetings mourning her murdered daughter. She seemed to be mending on schedule, and then suddenly she took her own life on her daughter's grave.

And then there was the late Kitty Yonley, who stands out as the only person anyone can think of in the Houston Chapter who was opposed to capital punishment. She forgave the man who had stabbed her daughter, Nina, to death in August 1979. She sent him a copy of the Bible.

Some parents are stuck; some adjust.

Vengeance would never be blind. It was personal. It was, in a strange way, like family.

Some cannot pick up the burden of catastrophe; others are able to find grace, a balance between the yearning to remember and the need to forget. A lot of success has to do with ritualizing a connection with the murdered child. For ten years after Kim's death, Shirley Parish, who had never smoked before, would start her day smoking one of her daughter's brand of cigarettes.

Success also often seems to depend on what sort of understanding parents can reach about the people who killed their children. To understand is not necessarily to make peace or to forgive. Time, which according to the platitude heals all wounds, has in many cases turned parents into ferocious advocates of capital punishment. Nearly two-thirds of P.O.M.C. members support the death penalty. In Texas, a fair number would relish the chance to start the lethal solution dripping into the vein of the condemned. They know the appeal-laden process of imposing the death penalty can be more expensive than committing a murderer to life in prison. They know the New Testament injunctions against killing, the plea for forgiveness. They know Camus's famous argument that no murderer's deed can compare with the evil of capital punishment, ''the most premeditated of murders.''

To Camus, many parents would reply that, however great the agony of the condemned, no doubt exists about what debt is being paid. A condemned man knows why he is to die; their children did not. In advocating capital punishment, what many parents seem to be seeking is not so much the extermination of a killer as an equivalency of feeling:

they want their suffering communicated and shared. They want the people who murdered their children to know the torture of their loss. The desire for revenge is the ugliest emotion in the human psyche, but it often collapses into something almost poignant—the longing to find a shred of conscience in people whose moral capacity is grotesquely diminished. Why did you do this? they ask, and they pore over criminal records and family histories, hunting for answers, for any trace of that sympathetic faculty by which one person can know and even suffer another's pain.

Murder ultimately was a measure of *their* moral capacity. Many found themselves wanting. Their innocence had been stripped away; their values and beliefs had been badly gouged, if not wrecked. For most parents, murder ruptured the idea of unalloyed goodness. But for others, honest or brave enough to look within, it ruptured the idea of unalloyed evil too. Evil was nothing apart from them anymore—no longer ''the Other.'' It had stolen into their homes and seeped into their hearts. They had to live with the vengeful impulse to return death for death, and, conversely, had to find the resolve to hold themselves back. In their extremes of emotion, nothing was black-and-white; the world was a palette of grays. One could as glibly pay sanctimonious lip service to the idea of forgiveness as join the ignorant masses clamoring for the executioner. Forgiveness would never come cheap for parents, but then, vengeance would never be blind. It was personal. It was, in a strange way, family.

So they marched on courthouses and mailed off Bibles and stitched together quilts. They did something because they needed to *do* something, if only to fend off the full experience of loss. More than from grief, they needed to save themselves from their own powerlessness. If murder was a book of lessons in fragility, ephemeral happiness, the irrevers-

ible arrow of fate, the hardest lesson of all was that life is not organized around human needs; for every one thing they could control there were a million they could not.

After Captain Bill Edison from the Houston Homicide Division gave a little talk, and somebody joked that maybe they should get Charles Bronson to speak at the next meeting, and after the group rejected the idea of putting the names of the killers on the quilt below their victims (''Why would you want that scum on the quilt?'' ''We can make another quilt and let it burn''), and after Terri Jeffers made a pitch for the fifteen-dollar heart-shaped lockets, the proceeds to go to the national organization, and after some discussion as to what might be done to counteract the anti-death-penalty slant of a new movie on Home Box Office (resolved to write a letter to HBO), and after more discussion as to whether the chapter ought to include a rose when distributing brochures to funeral homes, the September meeting broke up.

''Y'all remember to bring your death certificates next meeting,'' said Gilda Muskwinsky as the circle of friends dispersed. The cake plates and the truth-in-sentencing petitions were packed up. The quilt came down. Shirley Parish carried it out to her car. The air after the rain was clean and sweet. Caroline Min would return the cloth square fixed with Walter's face, and tomorrow or the next day, or sometime soon, Shirley would sew it into the Houston Chapter's tapestry of phantoms. They'd likely seen the last of Caroline. She was moving back to Seattle to be with her parents—heartbroken immigrants from Korea. Walter was their American future. Walter was going to be a lawyer...Face after face, story after story. It had occurred to Shirley as the quilt came together that it could never be finished. It could only be kept up-to-date.

Police

The police officer of today faces a wide range of problems that were not the concern of the police a generation ago. The criminal is more violent and heavily armed, and drug use is on the increase, bringing with it more violent crime. As the police turn to new technologies, new methods of patrolling, and so forth, the human impact of the tensions of the work load are being felt.

The articles in this section address several aspects of the role of the police in society. "Police Response to Crime" traces the primary and secondary roles of the police in the enforcement of the law. It is interesting to note just how small a proportion of crime is actually dealt with by the police. The diverse nature of police organizations is outlined in "The Police in the United States," and the article "New Faces, and New Roles, for the Police" indicates the changing ethnic and sexual composition of these agencies.

"Cops Under Fire" and "Law and Disorder" deal with the pressures the police are exposed to and the results of those pressures on the individual. Are the recent incidents of reported cases of police brutality caused in part by stress?

As crime increases, the police seek new ways to combat it. Crime prevention, always an elusive goal for the police, is now one of the main targets and police departments are returning to the "cop on the beat" concept, now called "community policing." "Not Just Old Wine in New Bottles" discusses the relationship between community policing and crime prevention.

"Law Enforcement Officers Killed, 1980–1989" reviews a decade of statistics relating to officers who died in the line of duty. An analysis of these statistics may help define new methods of reducing the number of such incidents.

Looking Ahead: Challenge Questions
Can stress be a cause of deviant behavior by a police officer?

Should police officers be more heavily armed to combat crime?

Should the police be involved with community matters not directly concerned with crime?

Unit 3

Police Response to Crime

The system responds directly to a fraction of crime

Most crime is not reported to police

. . . [O]nly about a third of all crimes are reported to police. The crimes most likely to be reported are those most serious in terms of injury and economic loss.

The criminal justice system responds to crimes brought to its attention by reports from citizens or through direct observation by law enforcement officers. Crimes are reported most often by the victim or a member of the victimized household. Police discover 3% of reported personal crimes and 2% of reported household crimes.

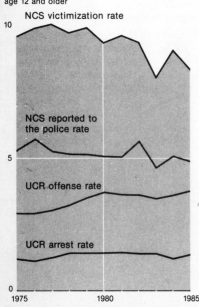

Aggravated assault rate per 1,000 persons age 12 and older

NCS victimization rate

NCS reported to the police rate

UCR offense rate

UCR arrest rate

Most reported crimes are not solved by arrest. For that reason the proportion of crimes handled directly by the criminal justice system through the processing of suspects is relatively small. Indirectly, the criminal justice system may be dealing with more crime than appears from arrest data because the offenders who are processed may have committed much more crime than that for which **they are arrested.**

Fallout for the crime of aggravated assault is shown in this chart:

The first contact with the criminal justice system for most citizens is the police dispatcher

In many cities citizens can report crimes through a universal number, such as 911. In other cities the citizen must call the police directly. The dispatcher will ask for facts about the crime, such as what happened, where, when, whether or not it involved injury or loss. This information helps the police to select the most appropriate response.

Law enforcement is one of several police roles

The roles of police officers are—
• **Law enforcement**—applying legal sanctions (usually arrest) to behavior that violates a legal standard.
• **Order maintenance**—taking steps to control events and circumstances that disturb or threaten to disturb the peace. For example, a police officer may be called on to mediate a family dispute, to disperse an unruly crowd, or to quiet an overly boisterous party.

• **Information gathering**—asking routine questions at a crime scene, inspecting victimized premises, and filling out forms needed to register criminal complaints.
• **Service-related duties**—a broad range of activities, such as assisting injured persons, animal control, or fire calls.

Wilson's analysis of citizen complaints radioed to police on patrol showed that—
• 10% required enforcement of the law
• more than 30% of the calls were appeals to maintain order
• 22% were for information gathering
• 38% were service-related duties.

Most crime is not susceptible to a rapid police response

A study by the Police Executive Research Forum suggests that police response time is important in securing arrests only when they are called while the crime is in progress or within a few seconds after the crime was committed. Otherwise, the offender has plenty of time to escape.

In a study of response time in Kansas City, only about 6% of the callers reported crimes in progress. Where discovery crimes are involved (those noticed after the crime has been completed), few arrests may result even if citizen reporting immediately follows discovery; by this time the offender may be safely away. If a suspect is arrested, the length of delay between the offense and arrest may crucially affect the government's ability to prosecute the suspect successfully because of the availability of evidence and witnesses.

From *Report to the Nation on Crime and Justice,* Bureau of Justice Statistics, U.S. Department of Justice, March 1988, pp. 62-63, 66.

A variety of public agencies provide protection from crime

Today, police officers do not always respond to calls for service

Based on research and the desire for improved efficiency, many police departments now use a number of response alternatives to calls for service. The type of alternative depends on a number of factors such as whether the incident is in progress, has just occurred, or occurred some time ago and whether anyone is or could be injured. Police officers may be sent, but the call for service may also be responded to by—
• **Telephone report units** who take the crime report over the telephone. In some departments, more than a third of the calls are initially handled in this way.
• **Delayed response** if officers are not needed at once and can respond when they are available. Most departments state a maximum delay time, such as 30 to 45 minutes, after which the closest unit is assigned to respond.
• **Civilian personnel** trained to take reports; they may be evidence technicians, community service specialists, animal control officers, or parking enforcement officers.
• **Referral to other noncriminal justice agencies** such as the fire department, housing department, or social service agencies.
• **A request for a walk-in report** where the citizen comes to the police department and fills out a report.

Law enforcement evolved throughout U.S. history

In colonial times law was enforced by constables and a night watch made up of citizens who took turns watching for fires and unruly persons. By the beginning of the 19th century, most citizens who could afford it paid for someone else to take their watch.

The first publicly supported, centralized, consolidated police organization in the United States was established in New York in 1844. It was modeled after the London Metropolitan Police created in 1829 by Sir Robert Peel. Other major American cities adopted the same system soon after. Today, more than 90% of all municipalities with a population of 2,500 or more have their own police forces.

Rural policing in the United States developed from the functions of sheriffs

The office of sheriff, a direct import from

17th century England, was used primarily in the rural colonies of the South. As elected county officials, sheriffs had detention and political functions along with law enforcement responsibilities.

Originally responsible for large, sparsely populated areas, many sheriffs were faced with big city law enforcement problems because of urban growth after World War II. In some counties the sheriff's office has retained its detention functions, but law enforcement functions are handled by county police departments. In other counties the sheriff's office resembles many big city police departments. There are more than 3,000 sheriff's departments in the United States today.

Traditionally, the police function has been dominated by local governments

• In 1986 there were 11,743 municipal, 79 county, and 1,819 township general-purpose police agencies in the United States. Together, they employ 533,247 full-time equivalent employees.
• Other State and local law enforcement groups include State agencies such as the 51 State police and highway patrols and some 965 special police agencies including park rangers, harbor police, transit police, and campus security forces. Along with their independent responsibilities, these agencies often support local law enforcement on technical matters such as forensics and identification.
• The Federal Government employs 8% of all law enforcement personnel. Among the more than 50 Federal law enforcement agencies are the Federal Bureau of Investigation (FBI), the Drug Enforcement Administration (DEA), the Bureau of Alcohol, Tobacco, and Firearms (BATF), the Secret Service, and the Postal Inspection Service.

Urbanization and social change have had great impact on policing

• The dramatic shift in population to urban areas since World War II has had great impact on the demand for police service. The percentage of police officers employed in urban areas rose from 68% in 1977 to 82% in 1982.
• During the recent period of increasing concern about employment discrimination against women and minorities, mostly white, male police departments have added women and minorities to their ranks. The proportion of sworn

officers who were women went from 2% in 1971 to almost 7% in 1985. The proportion of police officers and detectives who were black went from 9% in 1983 to 12% in 1985.

Professionalism and advanced technology have also transformed policing in the past half century

• In 1982, 79% of police officers in a sample survey conducted by the FBI reported that they had done some college work. 23% of the respondents had received baccalaureate degrees.[1] Basic and in-service training is now regarded as indispensable. More than 670 training academies now exist in the United States.[2]
• In 1964 only one major police department was using automated data processing.[3] More recent surveys suggest that virtually all jurisdictions of 50,000 or more population were using computers by 1981.[4]
• In 1922 less than 1,000 patrol cars were in use in the entire country.[5] At that time, only one city had radio-equipped cars. Today, the patrol car has almost replaced the "beat cop" and police communications enable the patrol officer to have access to citizen calls for service as well as data banks on a variety of critical information, including outstanding warrants and stolen property.

Private security continues to grow

After public police agencies were formed in the mid-1800s, organized pri-

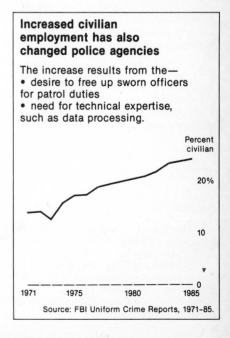

Increased civilian employment has also changed police agencies

The increase results from the—
• desire to free up sworn officers for patrol duties
• need for technical expertise, such as data processing.

Source: FBI Uniform Crime Reports, 1971–85.

Private security plays an important role in crime control

vate law enforcement developed in response to—
• the lack of public police protection in the expanding West
• problems with interstate jurisdiction
• development of the railroad
• increased industrialization.

The first private security officer, Allan Pinkerton, had a tremendous impact on private security through his work with the railroads and through his establishment of the first private security firm. Owing to the lack of a Federal law enforcement agency, Pinkerton's security agency was hired by the Federal Government in 1861. More recently there has been increased need for private security, particularly to protect defense secrets and defense supplies provided by the private sector. More recent growth in private security is in response to growth of crime and security needs in businesses.

The private security industry protects private concerns against losses from accidents, natural disasters, or crime

This for-profit industry provides—
• personnel, such as guards, investigators, couriers, bodyguards
• equipment, including safes, locks, lighting, fencing, alarm systems, closed circuit television, smoke detectors, fire extinguishers, and automatic sprinkler systems
• services, including alarm monitoring; employee background checks and drug testing; evacuation planning; computer security planning; and polygraph testing.

Private security is provided either by direct hiring (proprietary security) or by hiring specific services or equipment (contract security).

1.1 million people are estimated to be employed in private security

Proprietary security	448,979
Guards	346,326
Store detectives	20,106
Investigators	10,000
Other workers	12,215
Manager and staff	60,332
Contract security	**640,640**
Guards and investigators	541,600
Central alarm station	24,000
Local alarm	25,740
Armored car/courier	26,300
Security equipment	15,000
Specialized services	5,000
Security consultants	3,000
Total	1,100,000

Source: Cunningham and Taylor, *Private security and police in America: The Hallcrest report* (Portland, Oreg.: Chaneller Press, 1985).

The authority of private security personnel varies among States and localities

Many States give private security personnel authority to make felony arrests when there is "reasonable cause" to believe a crime has been committed. Unlike sworn police officers, private personnel are not obligated to tell arrestees of their rights. Private security usually cannot detain suspects or conduct searches without the suspect's consent. In some States laws give private security authority to act as "special police" within a specific jurisdiction such as a plant, a store, or university campus.

Many private security firms are licensed or regulated

In some jurisdictions both State and local requirements must be met to obtain a license to provide private security.

At the State level—
• 35 States license guard and patrol firms.
• 22 States and the District of Columbia require the registration of guards.

• 37 States license private investigators.
• Alarm companies must obtain a license in 25 States and are regulated in 10 States.
• 8 States license armored car companies and 6 States license couriers.
• In fewer than 12 States, the same agency or board regulates alarm companies and armored car firms, as well as guard, patrol, and investigative firms.
• 3 States have independent regulatory boards; 6 States have such boards in State agencies.
• Private security is regulated by the department of public safety or State police in 15 States, the department of commerce or occupational licensing agency in 7 States, and the department of state in 5 States.

Public police are often employed by private security firms

Some police officers "moonlight" as private security officers in their off-duty hours. According to the Hallcrest survey, 81% of the surveyed police departments permit moonlighting, but most estimated that 20% or less of their officers are working as private security personnel. Acting like a contract security firm, some police departments provide personnel to private concerns and use the revenue for the department.

Private security has continued to outnumber public police since the 1950s

Public police protection grew most rapidly in the late 1960s and early 1970s in response to increasing urbanization and crime rates. Public police protection has stabilized in the 1980s, but private security has continued to grow. Further growth of the private security industry is expected, particularly in relation to products using high technology, such as electronic access control and data encryption units for computer security systems.

Notes

1. FBI, *A study of factors influencing the continuing education of police officers,* LeDoux and Tully, July 1982.
2. O'Leary and Titus, *Monograph,* vols. I and II, National Association of State Directors of Law Enforcement Training (Columbia: South Carolina Criminal Justice Authority, 1986).

3. Kent Colton, "Police and computers: Use, acceptance, and impact of automation," in *The municipal yearbook, 1972* (Washington: International City Management Association, 1972).
4. *Survey of police operational and administrative practices 1978* (Washington: Police Executive Research Forum, 1978).

5. Herbert G. Locke, "The evolution of contemporary police service," in *Local government police management,* 2nd edition, Bernard L. Garmine, ed. (Washington: International City Management Association, 1982).

The Police in The United States

Beverly Sweatman and Adron Cross

Beverly R. Sweatman is public affairs assistant to the chief of INTERPOL and Adron Cross is assistant chief , Interpol /State Liasion Program. Both Sweatman and Cross work at the Interpol National Central Bureau in Washington, D.C.

The United States police system is neither as complicated nor as confusing as it might appear on the surface. It is, however, vast and complex, and involves more than 20,000 separate and distinct law enforcement agencies that employ more than half a million people. The differences between these law enforcement agencies are generated primarily by the jurisdictional authority or boundaries under which they operate and the specific laws they are empowered to enforce.

The U.S. does not have a national police force. Instead, the United States is served by a multi-layered network of police jurisdictions that include town, city, county, and state police, as well as federal law enforcement agencies.

One reason for this diverse structure lies at the foundation of the Nation's governmental system. The U.S. Constitution provides for a federal system of government, which is a two-level structure consisting of distinct and separate state governments functioning under a central national government.

Federal jurisdictions encompass crimes of interstate and international proportions, such as the illegal transporting of persons or property across state borders and crimes that endanger national security or affect the integrity of the U.S. monetary system or national borders.

At the state level, law enforcement becomes a bit more complex since each state has the right to govern itself within the parameters of the Constitution and must enforce its own law enforcement agency, which in most cases is a state police force. The states themselves are further divided into counties, metropolitan areas, cities and towns, and each of these divisions enacts its own local ordinances. Enforcing these ordinances and maintaining local law and order are thousands of county sheriffs, city and county police, and town marshals. These men and women are the first in line of law enforcement in all U.S. communities, and citizens look primarily to them for protection from criminal activity.

HISTORICAL BACKGROUND

To fully understand the police system in the United States, it is helpful to look back in colonial days in America. Many natural differences existed between the early colonies, such as size, location, population, commerce, and industry. Because of the independent nature of these colonies and the vast territory that separated them, each one developed its own system of order and authority to meet its particular needs. There was no central authority with power over all the colonies to enact or enforce laws and regulations.

The methods used to provide protection for citizens and maintain order against criminal activities varied between the colonies. For example, early in the seventieth17th century Boston established a system of nightwatchmen to supplement their military guard. New Amsterdam (later New York) and Philadelphia soon adopted a similar system. Throughout the colonies, an assortment of law

From *C.J. International,* January/February 1989, pp. 11-18. Originally appeared in *International Criminal Police Review,* official publication of Interpol. Reprinted by permission.

3. POLICE

enforcement officials such as constables, marshals, and sheriffs gradually developed.[1]

When the original thirteen colonies joined together to form the United States of America, they established the aforementioned federal system of government whereby power was distributed between a central national government and separate state governments. The individual states were not willing to turn over complete authority to the federal government, and they stringently guarded their rights to govern themselves within the parameters of the Constitution and to enact and enforce their own laws. Consequently, the federal government was granted jurisdiction only as set forth by the Constitution, as interpreted by the courts, and all other jurisdictions remained with the states. This action worked against the establishment of a national police force.

Development of police entities that met the specific needs of the towns and cities continued. In 1838 Boston supplemented its nightwatch with a day police force. Other cities followed, and in 1844 the New York legislature passed a law authorizing creation of "the first unified day and night police" force. Philadelphia soon followed suit and by the late nineteenth century most major American cities had municipal police forces. These forces were commanded by a chief or commissioner who was either elected or appointed. Appointments sometimes required the consent of a city council.

Thus, the mid-nineteenth century saw the emergence of the main structural elements of American policing. These

Police check on a highway in the United States.

included municipal (city or town) police, supplemented by county sheriffs in rural areas. The gradual addition of two other elements, state police and federal agencies, complete the present-day system. [3]

The Texas Rangers, created in 1835 to supplement Texas military forces, were the forerunners of today's state police forces. Other states followed after the turn of the century. Some state police agencies are restricted to enforcing traffic laws and protecting life and property on the highways. Others, however, have general policing authority in criminal matters throughout the state. [4]

In keeping with its constitutional authority to regulate international and interstate commerce and to protect U.S. property both at home and abroad, Congress enacted

federal laws against a wide range of criminal activity, and the federal government slowly expanded its police capacity.

The Revenue Cutter Service was established in 1789 to help prevent smuggling, and thirteen U.S. marshals were appointed by the president, concurrent with enactment of

Alabama State Police patrol car and helicopter

the Judiciary Act, which created the original court system for the United States. In 1836 agents responsible for investigating infringements involving postal matters were added to the staff of the Postmaster General, and in 1865, the U.S. Secret Service was formed to investigate counterfeiting that was rampant during the Civil War. Later in the century, inspectors with law enforcement powers joined the Immigration and Naturalization Service. Among the more important law enforcement responsibilities later recognized by Congress were internal revenue investigations and narcotics control. Investigators hired by the Department of Justice in late 1800 became the Bureau of Investigation in 1908, and later, in 1930, became the present day Federal Bureau of Investigation.

For some crimes, such as espionage, federal law stands alone. For others, such as arson, bank robbery, counterfeiting, or possession of illegal drugs, federal as well as state and local authorities have concurrent jurisdiction. [5]

None of the federal law enforcement agencies of today has unlimited jurisdiction over all federal laws. Each agency was created to "enforce specific laws and cope with particular situations." [6] In addition, "Federal police agencies have no particular rank order or hierarchy of command or responsibility, and each reports to the specific department or bureau to which it is responsible." [7]

Federal authority is divided primarily between two major departments of the executive branch of government - the Department of the Treasury and the Department of Justice. Other Federal organizations, such as the various inspector general offices that investigate crime within the government itself, and the U.S. Coast Guard, an agency within the Department of Transportation, which is responsible for enforcing maritime laws, all have important roles in law enforcement. The Postal Inspection Service is the law enforcement arm of the postal service and handles all postal crimes such as mail fraud and assaults upon postal employees while exercising their duties. In 1986, the State Department's Bureau of Diplomatic Security was granted law enforcement authority to investigate matters involving passport and visa fraud and special internal matters within that agency.

In addition to the civilian law enforcement authority listed above, federal statutes also grant law enforcement authority to military operations and security and crimes committed against U.S. military personnel or property or by U.S. military personnel. The three separate military investigative agencies are the Naval Investigative Service, the Air Force Office of Special Investigation, and the Army

ATF officers at the scene of a bombing

Criminal Investigation Command. Military agencies are forbidden to enforce civilian laws.

STATE LAW ENFORCEMENT (Police Agencies)

It is not possible within the scope of this article to present a description of the police structure in each of the 50 states and the District of Columbia (Washington, D.C.). Instead, we will provide an overview of the police structure of one representative state. This overview, with minor variations, is reflective of many of the police departments throughout the United States.

POLICE JURISDICTIONS IN THE STATE OF ILLINOIS

Within the state of Illinois, there are 793 town and city (municipal) police departments, employing more than 25,000 full- and part-time sworn police officers who investigate all types of crimes and enforce local ordinances of the towns and cities as well as state laws, with implicit authority to arrest for violations of federal laws. Approximately 12,000 of these sworn officers are employed by the Chicago Police Department.

The state has 102 county sheriff departments, which employ more than 3,300 sworn officers. These officers, also investigate all types of crime and have the same arrest authority as the municipal officers.

The Illinois State Police Department, which has police powers throughout the state, employs 2,168 full-time sworn

officers. There are other state agencies, such as the Secretary of State, which is responsible for driver licensing and vehicle registrations and employs 170 sworn officers who are responsible for fishing, hunting, forestry, and boating laws. These agencies, too, enforce state laws with implicit authority to arrest for violations of federal laws.

The total of 31,475 sworn officers described above does not include the officers of railroads, airports, hospitals, park districts, forest preserves, colleges, and universities that maintain law enforcement agencies of their own.

Although each of the aforementioned officers has taken an oath to enforce local ordinances as well as county, state, and federal laws, their powers of arrest are restricted to the jurisdictional boundaries of the police departments that employ them.

Illinois also has more than 700 licensed private security and detective agencies that provide guard, patrol and investigative services to businesses, corporations, and private individuals (celebrities). These private agencies must confine their services to the properties of their employers.

JURISDICTIONAL BOUNDARIES

A police officer's powers of arrest are restricted to the geographical boundaries of his employer, whether it is a town, city, state or other police department, such as airport, university, etc.

The cities of Normal, Illinois, and Bloomington, Illinois, as well as Illinois State University and Bloomington Municipal Airport, have distinct corporate and municipal boundaries. Police officers employed by these entities, therefore, are restricted to investigating crimes and enforcing laws within their respective boundaries.

The above-mentioned entities are located in the county of McLean. McLean county has a county sheriffs depart-

Arrest of a fugtive by two U.S. Marshals

ment to investigate crimes and enforce all laws in the unincorporated areas outside the jurisdiction of the cities of Normal and Bloomington, Illinois State University and the Bloomington Airport Authority. However, the sheriff's officers have full arrest powers anywhere within McLean County, including the cities of Normal and Bloomington, the university and the airport.

3. POLICE

The Illinois State Police have full arrest powers within the 102 counties that comprise the state of Illinois, including all municipal communities.

An Illinois State Supreme Court ruling has stipulated that a local police officer has no authority to make an arrest outside his jurisdiction without the aid of an arrest warrant that is valid anywhere in the state of Illinois. The various law enforcement agencies, by utilizing mutual assistance agreements, multi-jurisdictional aid compacts, and state laws, effectively assist each other in arresting criminals who have travelled from one jurisdiction to another.

Federal law enforcement agencies such as the FBI, the DEA, the U.S. Secret Service, the U.S. Customs Service, the U.S. Marshals Service, etc., have the authority to initiate arrests in any state or U.S. territory for offenses that are a violation of federal law, specifically, offenses such as bank robbery, flight to avoid prosecution, kidnapping, counterfeiting, and treason, to name a few. This is especially true when the criminal travels across a state boundary into another state jurisdiction. For example, in the case of a bank robbery, local police would respond to the initial alert and notify the FBI, subsequently releasing control of the investigation to them. Mutual assistance agreements between federal and state agencies, however, enable both agencies to join resources and collectively pursue the investigation of the bank robbery. This type of cooperation diminishes jurisdictional problems between town, city, county, state and federal police agencies.

Cooperation is further enhanced through the task force concept, a system whereby the various municipal, state and federal agencies combine information and investigative resources to address a specific criminal problem in a specific area.

FUNCTIONS OF A POLICE DEPARTMENT

Municipal police departments range in size from one- or two-man offices, such as Smithsburg, Maryland, and Ridgeway, South Carolina, to elaborate and extensive facilities, such as the cities of New York, Chicago, and Los Angeles, which, together, employ more than 46,000 police officers, according to figures reported in the 1986 *Uniform Crime Report* published by the FBI.

The departments are operationally structured to meet the needs of the town or city in which they are located. For example, larger departments generally assign squads to address specific types of crimes, while the smaller departments, which experience lower crime rates, handle whatever type of crime or investigation arises. Assistance is always available should a situation extend beyond the capability of the police entity involved.

FEDERAL LAW ENFORCEMENT AGENCIES

Division of law enforcement authority at the federal level is not only between major departments but within them as well. As indicated earlier, each federal law enforcement agency reports to the head of the specific department to which it is responsible. The heads of these departments comprise a segment of the president's cabinet.

The Department of the Treasury, for example, has four distinct law enforcement agencies: the Bureau of Alcohol, Tobacco, and Firearms, the U.S. Customs Service, the U.S. Secret Service, and the Internal Revenue Service. Each has specific duties and jurisdictions related to the mission of the U.S. Treasury.

Computerized file of missing persons in the state of Alabama

For instance, the Bureau of Alcohol, Tobacco, and Firearms, also known as ATF, enforces federal laws pertaining to the manufacture, sale, and possession of firearms and explosives and uses these laws to investigate the use of firearms or explosives to commit violent crimes. Since federal laws require that manufacturers and dealers keep records on all sales of firearms and explosives, ATF is the nation's leading agency for tracing such weapons for domestic and international law enforcement agencies.

ATF also investigates major arson cases, particularly interstate arson-for-profit schemes, and initiates joint federal, state, and local anti-arson task forces. At the same time, ATF collects federal taxes on alcohol and tobacco products, suppresses illegal traffic in these commodities, and regulates alcohol industry trade practices.

Like ATF, the U.S. Customs Service is an agency with many responsibilities. Foremost among these is the collection of import duties and taxes at more than 300 ports of entry, from both individuals and commercial carriers. At the same time, the Customs Service detects and intercepts illegal drugs, counterfeit consumer goods, and other contraband entering the United States and prevents strategic high technology from being smuggled out of the country. Recent seizures of boats, planes and other vehicles used to transport illegal drugs into the United States have received widespread media attention and are an integral part of the federal government's efforts to stem the drug trade in America.

The U.S. Secret Service is best known for its role of protecting the president and vice president and their families, as well as other elected officials and foreign heads of state visiting the United States. But, as an agency of the Treasury Department, the Secret Service also investigates crimes related to the U.S. monetary system, such as counterfeiting of currency, coins, stamps, and bonds, forgery of government checks, and credit card fraud. And, together with the FBI, the Secret Service works to stem the growing tide of computer fraud in the United States.

The Internal Revenue Service is the nation's primary revenue-collecting agency, responsible for enforcing the revenue laws and tax statutes. However, because of drug smuggling, organized crime, and other criminal operations that involve large sums of undeclared income, the Internal Revenue Service is often included in investigations in these areas.

Two officers guard a suspect

Within the Department of Justice, law enforcement also falls primarily within four agencies: the FBI, the Drug Enforcement Administration, the U.S. Marshals Service, and the Immigration and Naturalization Service. And occupying a unique category all its own is IP-Washington, the U.S. National Central Bureau for Interpol.

The FBI focuses on organized crime activities, among them racketeering, corruption, bank robbery, pornography, and prostitution. The FBI also investigates "white collar" crimes - crimes that rely on deceit and concealment rather than force or violence. As the primary agency responsible for investigating terrorist activity in the United States, the FBI also trains special antiterrorist teams to prevent and respond to terrorist attacks and tracks foreign intelligence agents and their activities within the United States. In addition, the FBI operates an extensive forensic science laboratory and a computerized fingerprint identification service that performs identifications for federal, state and local law enforcement agencies, and maintains the National Crime Information Center (NCIC), which provides investigators with data on everything from known criminals and stolen property to missing persons and unsolved violent crimes.

The Drug Enforcement Administration, or DEA, spearheads the United States' intensifying war on illegal drugs. As part of its activities, the DEA conducts surveillance operations and infiltrates drug rings. The agency also tracks illicit drug traffic, registers manufacturers and distributors of pharmaceutic drugs, tracks the movement of chemicals used to manufacture illegal drugs, and leads the nation's domestic marijuana eradication program.

The U.S. Marshals Service was created in 1789 with the appointment of thirteen federal marshals by President George Washington. Today, in addition to ensuring the security of court facilities, U.S. marshals apprehend most federal fugitives and execute federal arrest warrants. In addition, they operate the Witness Security Program, ensuring the safety of endangered witnesses. The Marshals Service has its own Air Wing to transport federal prisoners to court appearances and then to prison. At the same time, the Marshals Service is responsible for handling the seizure and disposal of property resulting from criminal activity.

The Immigration and Naturalization Service (INS) controls the entry of aliens along thousands of miles of land and sea borders, and investigates smuggling rings that bring thousands of illegal immigrants into the country each year. The INS also facilitates certification of naturalized citizens and entry of qualified aliens into the country.

IP-Washington, known in the United States as the USNCB, is also an agency within the Department of Justice. It fulfills a unique position in the U.S. police structure by coordinating investigative request for international assistance from both domestic and foreign police. Through the USNCB, state, and local police departments, as well as federal law enforcement agencies, are able to pursue international investigative leads. Conversely, foreign police seeking criminal investigative assistance anywhere in the United States can do so by contacting the USNCB through their own Interpol National Central Bureau. To meet the demands of both the domestic and foreign police communities, the USNCB makes wide use of computerization and the latest modern communications technology, effectively tying together the more than 20,000 state, local, and federal agencies and their foreign counterparts.

COOPERATION AND TRAINING

The success of American law enforcement efforts can be attributed to numerous formal and informal programs of cooperation and training. Chief among the formal cooperative programs are the special task forces mentioned earlier, such as the Organized Crime/Drug Enforcement Task Forces operating throughout the United States. These task forces bring together the expertise of state and local law enforcement authorities and federal agencies in a concentrated effort against organized crime, illicit drug operations, and other areas of mutual interest and concern. Most often, U.S. attorneys are included as important members of the task forces.

Numerous training programs offered by both federal and state agencies keep police officers current with the latest

3. POLICE

A Massachusetts State Police officer

investigative techniques and equipment. For example, the Federal Law Enforcement Training Center (FLETC) at Glynco, Georgia, is an interagency training facility serving sixty federal law enforcement organizations. The major training effort at the center is in the area of basic programs to teach common areas of law enforcement skills to police and investigative personnel. The center also conducts advanced programs and provides the facilities and support services for other agencies to conduct advanced training for their own law enforcement personnel. In addition, the center offers selective, highly specialized training programs to state and local officers.

The FBI National Academy at Quantico, Virginia, is open to senior law enforcement officers from federal, local, and state agencies as well as foreign police departments. The academy offers a wide array of course curricula covering police management, police science, firearms, forensic science, crisis management, legal problems of police administrators, fitness for police officers, and applied criminal psychology. Also, specialized courses are provided concerning death investigations, crime scenes, identification, photography, and fingerprint science. The FBI Academy also offers college credit to police officers through its affiliation with the University of Virginia.

The U.S. Secret Service offers courses to state and local police officers in the examination of questioned (forged) documents. In addition, they train firearms instructors at the James J. Rowley Training Center in Beltsville, and offer briefings in protective techniques to state and local police who are engaged in the protection of their local dig-

nitaries. These briefings better enable the state and local police to work with the Secret Service when that agency's protectees visit their areas.

On the state level, a police agency may have its own training facility for the training of officers. In addition, municipalities with a population of 100,000 or more also offer a basic training program for new officers, and this can result in a particular state having several police academies.

To ensure uniformity in the degree and quality of training given to police at the academies, most of the 50 states have local training boards that are responsible for the establishment of training standards. Course curricula to be presented to the officers must be approved by the training board prior to being offered. The basic curriculum generally consists of courses in criminal law, humanities, first aid, weapons, self defense, and investigative procedures, to name but a few. The length of the training programs varies within each state, from a minimum of 10 weeks to a maximum of 18 weeks.

Periodic inservice and specialized training is provided to all law enforcement officers by the training academies within the states. A minimum of forty hours per year has been set as a standard requirement.

Other police training institutions within the United States include the Northwestern Traffic Institute, Southern Police Traffic Institute, the Institute of Police Technology and Management, and the San Luis Obispo Training Facility, all of which provide specialized training for supervisors and managers of police agencies.

In addition to programs within agencies, professional associations, such as the International Association of Chiefs of Police and the National Sheriff's Association, offer law enforcement executives a forum for sharing ideas and provide the spark for many successful law enforcement programs.

States also form associations among themselves, such as the Association for State Criminal Investigative Agencies, which meets twice annually to share common problems and solutions and to work toward the betterment of state investigative agencies. This association's membership numbers approximately 24 states whose state police agencies have been given general policing authority throughout the state and carry out criminal investigative functions.

The states also sponsor training sessions for law enforcement personnel throughout their state that address specific types of criminal activity. For example, the Colorado Springs Police Department, in conjunction with the District Attorney's office in that district, recently hosted a seminar to address the problems of fugitives and missing persons and the law enforcement response to these problems. This seminar, with more than 200 attendees, was open to police at all levels -- municipal, county, state, and federal. In addition, the South Carolina Law Enforcement Officers Association meets annually for a retraining conference at which seminars covering various topics are held.

The Kansas Sheriffs Association, the Kansas Peace Officers Association and the Kansas Association of Chiefs of Police, recently held their second annual Joint Law Enforcement Conference for the purpose of strengthening ties between that state's various police agencies and offering workable solutions to problems of mutual interest.

A Michigan State Police Officer

Similar conferences include, to name but a few: the Western States Crime Conference, sponsored by the Arizona Department of Public Safety; the New England State Police Administrator's Conference, which is a meeting of commissioners and other representatives of six New England States, including Connecticut, Maine, Massachusetts, New Hampshire, Rhode Island, and Vermont; and the California Attorney General's Annual Criminal Intelligence Training Conference, hosted by the California Department of Justice.

These meetings, seminars, and conferences provide excellent opportunities for sharing ideas and new programs, and enhance the effectiveness of police throughout the country.

Other formal efforts include periodic crime reports that give law enforcement personnel reliable information on criminal activities and trends. For example, the Bureau of Justice Statistics (BJS) within the Department of Justice collects, analyzes, publishes, and disseminates statistical information on crime, victims of crime, criminal offenders, and the operations of justice systems at all levels of government. BJS also provides financial and technical support to state statistical agencies and analyzes national information policy on such issues as the privacy, confidentiality, and security of data and the interstate exchange of criminal records.

The National Institute of Justice (NIJ) is the primary federal sponsor of research on crime and justice. Its goal is to answer real world questions about crime control and

ensure that this new knowledge is disseminated to those who can use it. NIJ publishes *Issues and Practices* reports and research summaries to highlight findings for busy criminal justice policy makers. NIJ's National Criminal Justice Reference Service (NCJRS) gives the criminal justice community access to a data base of over 83,000 reference materials.

The Bureau of Justice Assistance (BJA) administers the Department of Justice's state and local justice assistance program to improve criminal justice operations. BJA sets priorities for and awards discretionary grants, makes block awards to the states and territories, and administers the Public Safety Officers' Benefits Program.

These and innumerable other programs provide the U.S. law enforcement community with the means to obtain their mutual objectives of enforcing laws and protecting citizens.

The activities enumerated in this article by no means include every function and activity associated with law enforcement operations in the United States. They do, however, present a brief overview of the variety and types of interaction practiced by the members of the law enforcement community, whether they represent a federal, state, or local agency.

Despite its vastness and complexity, the American police system works. It successfully serves more than 235 million people in a country that covers more than 3.5 million square miles, a monumental task by any standard.

REFERENCES

The writers gratefully acknowledge the cooperation of all those who provided them with access to the reference sources listed below and, in particular, that of the Bureau of Alcohol, Tobacco, and Firearms in granting permission to use excerpts from their video *Teamwork and the Law,* and that of Dr. David Lester of Stockton State College in Pomona, New Jersey, who provided the excerpts from **Introduction to Criminal Justice.**

Encyclopedia of Crime and Justice, McMillan & Free Press, New York, 1984 (References Nos. 1, 3 and 5).

Joseph J. Senna, L.J. Siegel, **Introduction to Criminal Justice,** West Publishing Co., St. Paul, Minn., 1981 (References Nos. 2, 4, 6 and 7).

Illinois Criminal Justice Information Authority Illinois Revised Statutes.

Illinois Department of Transportation.

Inbau, **Criminal Law for Police.**

O. Wilson, **Police Administration.**

Annual Report of the Attorney General of the U.S., 1986.

U.S. Government Manual, 1988.

COPS UNDER FIRE

Their adversaries are more heavily armed and more arrogant than ever. Their 'allies' include an army of second-guessers. The job can't get much tougher

The Crime Surge
Nearly 36 million Americans were victims of serious crimes in 1989, including nearly 19,000 who were murdered. In the first six months of 1990, reported violent crimes increased by 10 percent over the comparable period last year.

It's a steamy Thursday night in central Dallas, and officers John Weiss and Jay James have been mired for 6 hours in an exasperating routine that belies the drama-saturated TV images of police. They have plodded through minor fender benders, stolen-car reports, false burglar alarms and disturbance calls in which little was disturbed. A small victory comes when they arrest a man in a baseball cap for possession of two tenths of a gram of crack: It takes them off the streets for more than an hour to book and process the hapless prisoner at the county jail. But at 10 p.m., the radio crackles with reports of a drive-by shooting, the by-product of bad blood between the Eastside Locos and the Wayne Street Boys. As James and Weiss pull up and begin coaxing information from a wailing Hispanic woman and angry bystanders, the red truck from which the shots were fired zooms by.

The chase is on. James throws the patrol car into a transmission-shattering reverse. Tires spin and smoke. Within seconds, James and Weiss rocket down a side street, slam on the brakes at a stop sign and lay down rubber as they catapult onto a crowded thoroughfare. Moments later, they are careening in and out of traffic at 80 miles per hour, before the chase skids to a halt in a parking lot. As two other police cars converge, Weiss and James dive from their car, throwing open doors for protection while they draw and aim their guns in a single fluid motion. Meanwhile, to their surprise, other officers run right

up to the truck—that "old John Wayne BS," James will say later—and yank a chunky youth from the cab, hurling him to the pavement, their guns at his head. It is a typical weekday night shift in central Dallas. The weekends, of course, are more dangerous.

Being a cop today is a stop-and-go nightmare. It has never been easy. But all the debilitating leitmotifs of police work in past generations— the danger, the frustration, the family disruptions—have been made geometric-orders worse by the drug war in the nation's streets. There are more violent criminals, armed with more potent weaponry, showing more contempt for the men and women in blue than at any time in history.

Police work on inner-city streets is a domestic Vietnam, a dangerous no-win struggle fought by confused, misdirected and unappreciated troops. They are racking up impressive arrest and imprisonment statistics without much changing the situation on the ground. Increasingly, police feel trapped between rising crime rates and an angry citizenry demanding immediate solutions to intractable problems. The FBI says reported violent crime rose 5 percent in 1989, even as law-enforcement officers made 7 percent more arrests than in 1988. And in the first half of 1990, big-city murder rates surpassed the record year of 1970. Murders in New York City totaled 1,077 for the first six months of 1990, up from 837 for the first half of 1989; Chicago's total—406 murders—was up 21 percent.

From *U.S. News & World Report*, December 3, 1990, pp. 332-334.

COPS AND CRIME

COPS UNDER FIRE

There appears to be little correlation between the number of police on city streets and the rate of serious crime.

Washington, D.C., with some 4,700 police officers, has the highest proportionate police presence of any major city — 7.8 cops for every 1,000 citizens. But its crime rate, 103 crimes for every 1,000 persons, is higher than the rate in many major cities with smaller relative police strength. Among them: New York, Los Angeles, Philadelphia, Milwaukee and Baltimore.

Similarly, Dallas has more cops per 1,000 residents than Houston (2.8 vs. 2.4), but Dallas's crime rate is much higher.

San Francisco has 1,800 police officers serving its 750,000 residents, a relatively low ratio of 2.4 cops per 1,000 citizens. But its crime rate of 90.2 per 1,000 citizens is one of the lowest among the nation's largest cities.

Here are the 10 cities with the largest police forces:

New York	25,465
Chicago	11,500
Los Angeles	8,450
Philadelphia	6,800
Washington	4,700
Detroit	4,700
Houston	4,104
Baltimore	2,868
Dallas	2,750
Boston	2,053

Being in the midst of such carnage exacts a toll on police that is impossible to overstate. In these American versions of Beirut, cops are asked to be peacekeepers among street warriors, buffers between frightened black neighborhoods and young black criminals — who commit much of the violent urban crime — and social workers for families chronically in crisis. The latest example of how police are being asked to minister to whole communities came in Atlanta last week, when a curfew for those under 17 went into effect. Police were given the power to lodge criminal charges against parents whose children repeatedly stay out after 11 p.m. on weekdays and midnight on weekends. Undergirding these tensions is the explosive potential for racial strife. While most big-city police departments have increased integration in the past generation, it is still often the case that white cops who live in the suburbs are patrolling minority communities. In some cities, relations between black communities and white cops have worsened in recent years after highly publicized incidents of police brutality took place or shootings by police were twisted by provocateurs into racial morality plays.

The response to exploding crime in some areas has been to call for more troops — most recently in New York, which plans to hire 6,500 more cops. However, many law-enforcement experts believe the cops' ability to affect crime rates is limited. "We're asking the police to deal with social conditions by applying laws, and you really cannot correct conditions by applying laws," says former New York City cop James Fyfe, now a professor of justice, law and society at American University. Some cities that have added police in recent years, like Phoenix and Los Angeles, have actually seen the number of reported crimes go up. In Atlanta, reported crimes jumped from 67,171 in 1987 to 88,536 in 1989, even as the number of police went from 1,346 to 1,518.

It is much more often the case, though, that police are being asked to do more with less. A recent Justice Department study showed that big-city police departments employed about 2.3 officers per 1,000 residents in 1987, compared with 2.4 a decade earlier; over the same period of time, crime climbed by 22 percent. Cleveland's force has dropped from a high of 2,456 officers in 1971 to 1,661 today; the city's crime rate, meanwhile, is now 35.6 percent higher than it was two decades ago. Despite near-record crime levels, the New York City Police Department has 6,200 fewer officers today than during 1970, even though the addition of 5,300 civilians to get cops out of desk jobs and back on the street has taken up some of the slack.

Meanwhile, despite population losses in many big cities, calls for police service have remained high or even increased, especially with the proliferation of 911 emergency numbers. New York police responded to 2.7 million calls in 1980; last year they answered more than 4 million. In some cities, it is an unwritten police policy that minor incidents like purse snatchings have to be put aside, lest they take cops away from more serious crimes. At 2:30 a.m. one summer Saturday,

police in the South Dallas police district had 83 calls backed up. Some nonemergency calls were not answered for 10 hours. By then, the incidents were over, the assailants had disappeared — and the callers were furious.

Experts now think police and politicians made a major mistake in promoting 911 numbers with the promise of immediate response. "With that kind of increase in the tyranny of 911, cops lost the time to take any initiative or get to know the community," says University of Maryland criminologist Lawrence Sherman. So police work has come to be almost exclusively reactive. Some departments are trying to change that through "community policing," which takes cops out of their cars and puts them back on the foot beat, getting to know their neighborhoods while emphasizing precrisis problem solving. But weaning the public off 911 will be tough — almost as tough as getting the public to develop a better appreciation for what cops are asked to face.

The drug war

The new terror on America's streets is inseparable from the explosion of the drug trade. When Dallas Sgt. David McCoy first worked the narcotics beat in the early 1970s, "a pound of pot was a lot of stuff, and you never saw cocaine in Dallas." But when he returned to drug work five years ago, "the difference was like night and day. Cocaine was everywhere. People carried it around in candy dishes."

Nationwide, drug arrests by state and local police forces jumped from 559,000 in 1981 to 1,155,200 in 1988. But despite recent claims of progress in the drug war by federal officials, many cops and city dwellers are hard pressed to see any effect. The struggle looks especially hopeless from the ground-level view of a patrol car on the streets of central Dallas. Officers Weiss and James can easily point out myriad crack dens, but by the time James leaps from the car in an attempt to nab a seller, lookouts have yelled "Headache!" to signal the arrival of the police, and the dealer has disappeared into an apartment complex. Typically, other apartment dwellers claim to have seen nothing. "The next guy who hollers 'Headache!' — I'm gonna kick his ass," sputters a winded James before climbing back into the patrol car and slamming the door.

Drug profits have also made the lure of corruption more tantalizing than ever. "Ten or 20 years ago, when you talked about a bribe, it was a $20 bill in a matchbook," says Sheldon Greenberg, associate director of the Police Executive Research Forum, which studies police issues. "Today, you have people in the drug culture saying, 'There's 10 grand in the bag, and it's yours if you let me go.'" In California, seven members of the Los Angeles County sheriff's narcotics squad went on trial last month, charged with skimming $1.4 million in seized drug money.

The 1980s have also seen the resurgence of street gangs, many of which profit from narcotics and enforce their own ruthless brand of law with drive-by shootings and turf wars that leave the real lawmen ducking for cover. The Crips and the Bloods, originally Los Angeles street

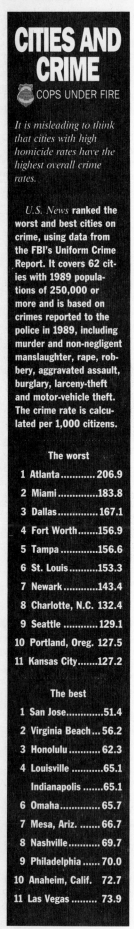

CITIES AND CRIME

COPS UNDER FIRE

It is misleading to think that cities with high homicide rates have the highest overall crime rates.

U.S. News ranked the worst and best cities on crime, using data from the FBI's Uniform Crime Report. It covers 62 cities with 1989 populations of 250,000 or more and is based on crimes reported to the police in 1989, including murder and non-negligent manslaughter, rape, robbery, aggravated assault, burglary, larceny-theft and motor-vehicle theft. The crime rate is calculated per 1,000 citizens.

The worst

1 Atlanta	206.9
2 Miami	183.8
3 Dallas	167.1
4 Fort Worth	156.9
5 Tampa	156.6
6 St. Louis	153.3
7 Newark	143.4
8 Charlotte, N.C.	132.4
9 Seattle	129.1
10 Portland, Oreg.	127.5
11 Kansas City	127.2

The best

1 San Jose	51.4
2 Virginia Beach	56.2
3 Honolulu	62.3
4 Louisville	65.1
Indianapolis	65.1
6 Omaha	65.7
7 Mesa, Ariz.	66.7
8 Nashville	69.7
9 Philadelphia	70.0
10 Anaheim, Calif.	72.7
11 Las Vegas	73.9

gangs, have now spread to more than 100 cities and total more than 40,000 members, according to the FBI. And cops say the modern-day bad guys seem more willing than ever to tangle with the law. "You used to go to a party and say, 'Break it up,' and they would break it up," says Cleveland detective Robert Zak, a 25-year veteran. "Now they throw beer bottles at you and smash the windows of your patrol car."

The arming of America

The new bellicosity has been frighteningly punctuated by the appearance in recent years of high-powered, rapid-fire weapons like MAC-10s and Tec-9s, which spew up to 30 rounds in a minute. No one keeps track of gun sales nationwide, but production figures illustrate the trend; street punks today want 9-mm semiautomatic pistols that reload quickly and carry more bullets. In 1980, the U.S. gun industry produced 1.6 million revolvers and just 764,000 pistols. By 1989, the industry was turning out 1.4 million pistols, but only 629,000 revolvers.

Street cops, meanwhile, feel more and more constrained in responding to this growing criminal firepower. Though a host of departments are now arming their officers with 9-to-18-shot semiautomatic pistols, many still carry six-shot revolvers that are hardly a match for the weapons many street criminals are packing. "Every situation I go through I assume right away I'm going to be outgunned," says Cleveland patrolman Matt Pompeani, Jr., 29, a second-generation cop and father of three small children. For Pompeani and his colleagues in Cleveland, bulletproof vests—though optional—are as much a part of the uniform these days as a badge. "I tell him to keep the vest on every day," says his father, Matt, Sr., now a detective.

In December, 1988, Dallas officer McCoy watched as his partner, undercover narcotics cop Larry Cadena, was shot to death by drug dealers. One assailant walked up to Cadena, pulled out a Tec-9, and without a word, swiftly shot him seven times in the chest. "I can't think of words to describe how coldblooded it was," says McCoy, who then got into a frenzied shoot-out with the assailants, wounding three.

It's not that more cops are killed these days. Indeed, those numbers have stabilized in recent years—146 in 1989, 155 in 1988, 148 in 1987—thanks to better training and widespread use of bulletproof vests. But the attitudes, the weapons and the unpredictable stimulant effect of crack have created a volatile mix that leaves cops feeling more vulnerable. On a recent meal break at a well-lit, cheery, family-style restaurant, Dallas officers Chris Nabors, 27, and Rodney Neely, 28, made it a point—as they always do—to sit opposite one another. "That way," says Nabors, "he can watch my back and I can watch his." On each call that Friday night, Nabors stepped to the side before knocking on the front door, thereby avoiding the possibility of a bullet in response.

In addition, many cops are frustrated by rampant gunrunning, which renders even the toughest local gun-control laws virtually useless. New York City, for instance, has one of the nation's strictest antigun measures, so weapons needed by criminals there are simply purchased in states with little regulation, like Georgia, Texas, Virginia and Florida—then driven north to New York. Analysis of 315 guns seized by police in New York from October, 1988, through January, 1989, showed that 79 were bought in Virginia, 60 in Texas and 30 in Florida. Only 15 came from New York. One exasperated Bureau of Alcohol, Tobacco and Firearms agent complains that "half the guns in Brooklyn" come from a single gun store in Richmond, Va.

Meanwhile, policies on how police may use their weapons have grown more restrictive. One reason is a landmark 1985 Supreme Court case, *Tennessee v. Garner,* which helped to establish a national standard that allows police to shoot only when lives are endangered. Also, most urban police may now shoot only to apprehend a violent felon; they cannot take aim at just any fleeing suspect. Finally, in determining whether a shooting is justified, many departments today consider not only the split-second decision to fire but just how the officer got into a situation that left him no choice.

Most law-enforcement experts and community leaders feel these specific guidelines make good sense, but many street officers disagree. A recent New York City study showed that instances of officers there being fired upon without returning fire rose 33 in 1981 to 76 in 1989. "Before, we used to have the edge," says Cleveland patrolman Pompeani, Jr. "Now I have to see a weapon, I have to wait for action to take action, and that 1 or 2 seconds might cost me my life."

The second-guessers

Today's cops are under far more scrutiny than their predecessors were, thanks in part to governmental soul-searching suggesting that police behavior had much to do with touching off the race riots of the late 1960s. Today, more than 75 percent of the major metropolitan police departments have some sort of civilian review agency. And top cops are watching more closely, too. "It's unbelievable how they Monday-morning quarterback you," says Dallas officer James, who underwent a vigorous internal investigation last spring after he fired at, but missed, a man who pointed a gun at him. "I'm out there sweating bullets, my heart's going 95 miles per hour and some guy is sitting in an air-conditioned office telling me what I should have done."

Part of that scrutiny is rooted in departmental efforts to head off lawsuits. Cops have presented an increasingly inviting target for litigation. For example, in 1972, the City of Los Angeles paid $553,340 in judgments and settlements for the actions of its police department. Last year, Los Angeles paid $6.4 million.

The fear of being sued is never far from officers' minds. It certainly wasn't for FBI agent Ed Mireles, the hero of the bureau's bloody 1986 Miami shoot-out in which two agents were killed and five were wounded. Before the shooting

DRUGS AND CRIME
 COPS UNDER FIRE

The use of drugs, especially cocaine, among crime suspects has become pervasive.

In San Diego and Philadelphia last year, 4 of every 5 men arrested tested positive, according to the National Institute of Justice's Drug Use Forecasting (DUF) program.

The percentage of men in other cities who tested positive for drugs when they were arrested:

New York .... 79 percent

Chicago .... 74 percent

Los Angeles ... 70 percent

Miami .... 70 percent

New Orleans   69 percent

In all cities surveyed, more than half of arrested males tested positive.

At least 45 percent of all the female suspects in the cities surveyed also tested positive for use of one or more drugs:

Washington .... 83 percent

Philadelphia ... 82 percent

San Diego ...... 77 percent

Kansas City .... 74 percent

Phoenix .... 70 percent

Some encouraging signs have surfaced recently. During the final quarter of 1989, seven cities found the lowest drug use among male arrestees since 1987, and seven of the 17 cities testing females reported the same. Washington, D.C.'s percentage of arrestees testing positive fell from 67 percent in 1989 to 56 percent in August of 1990.

GUNS AND CRIME
 COPS UNDER FIRE

Perhaps the most important new complaint from cops is that the latest generation of criminals routinely carries weapons. Many of the criminals have more firepower at their disposal than the police themselves are allowed.

Of the guns traced by the U.S. Bureau of Alcohol, Tobacco and Firearms in police investigations in 1987, 6.5 percent were assault weapons. By 1989, the proportion had increased to 9.9 percent.

Police in New York City seized 16,214 guns in 1989, up from 14,008 in 1986.

More than 3 of every 5 murders are committed with guns, mostly handguns. But contrary to widespread belief, the number of murders committed with firearms has remained fairly steady for at least 15 years.

Murders with guns:

	All firearms	Handguns
1989	11,832	9,013
1986	11,381	8,460
1983	10,895	8,193
1980	13,650	10,012
1974	12,470	9,334

Knives or other cutting instruments were the next most common murder weapon:

1989	3,458
1986	3,957
1983	4,075
1980	4,212
1974	3,228

AGE, RACE AND CRIME
 COPS UNDER FIRE

Violent crime is a young person's activity. The racial makeup of criminal suspects is mixed.

The crime wave has followed the baby-boom generation. From 1980 to 1989, the number of persons under 18 arrested for crimes dropped 6.5 percent. But during the same period, arrests of those 18 and over jumped by 37 percent.

Of all those arrested for major crimes in 1989, here are the percentages of arrestees who were under the age of 25:

Total crimes: 46%

Murder: 49%

Rape: 44%

Robbery: 60%

Assault: 41%

Burglary: 65%

Auto theft: 73%

Of the estimated 11.3 million persons arrested last year for serious crimes, 67 percent were white. But for some crimes, such as murder and robbery, the proportion and number of blacks arrested far exceeded those for whites. For example, during 1989, 56 percent of those arrested for murder and 65 percent of those arrested for robbery were black.

In proportion to their population, nonwhites are still arrested for nearly all crimes at a much higher rate than are whites. But between 1965 and 1989, for all violent crimes, the arrest rate soared 197 percent for whites and 67 percent for nonwhites.

VICTIMS OF CRIME
 COPS UNDER FIRE

Those at greatest risk of being crime victims are males, younger persons, blacks, Hispanics, residents of central cities and the poor.

The average age of murder victims has remained fairly stable since the '70s, at about 35 for all men and women. But nonwhite victims, both male and female, tend to die younger than do whites.

From 1979 to 1986, blacks suffered higher rates of both violent and household crimes than whites, relative to their populations. And the violent crimes committed against blacks tended to be more serious than those against whites.

Blacks are far more likely than whites to fall victim to certain crimes. For every white who is a victim of the following, here's how many black victims there will be:

Robbery: 2.4

Rape: 2

Auto theft: 1.6

Aggravated assault: 1.5

Burglary: 1.5

Yet, whites are 1.2 times more likely than blacks to be victims of simple assault.

Specific crime rates fluctuate with the seasons. Many kinds of personal and household crimes occur most often during warmer months when people spend more time outdoors, making them — and their homes — more vulnerable.

began, the car in which Mireles rode was crashing and banging against the vehicle driven by the two alleged bank robbers. Mireles could almost reach out and touch the driver. "Even today, I keep running that back," he says. "Knowing what I know now, I would have brought my 12-gauge shotgun to bear on those two sons of bitches, and taken them out right there. What flashed through my mind was the legal ramifications, the liability issue. But that would have ended the whole thing before it got started." As it turned out, two of his fellow agents were slain before a wounded Mireles killed both assailants.

The police melting pot

Efforts to integrate women and minorities into urban police departments have provided another fertile source for tension and suspicion in the squad room. Some 40 large police agencies nationwide are operating under agreements with the Justice Department governing improvements in minority hiring and promotion. Cleveland's department worked under a court-supervised decree from 1977 to 1985 and is still under a modified decree. The agreement, says Lt. Martin Flask, "has caused a lot of strain on officers, black and white, male and female. The camaraderie that existed at one time was at least partially broken down."

Suits challenging such agreements are increasing, thanks to a 1989 Supreme Court ruling that persons adversely affected by the decrees could later contest them. Over the past two years, four suits alleging reverse discrimination have been filed against the Dallas Police Department by groups of largely white officers. In the back-room whispering at the Cleveland Police Department, promotions of minorities were sometimes derisively referred to as "gimmes" or "affirmative-action babies." "I agree there was a problem years ago, and this is a way for government to alleviate it," says Cleveland patrolman Jeffrey Martin, who is black. "But I'd rather be looked at based on my abilities.

In recent years, these strains have been further exacerbated by the presence of more female officers, whose ranks in major departments grew from just 2 percent in 1972 to 9 percent by the end of 1986. Many veteran male officers retain a stereotypical suspicion that women officers cannot handle the physical demands of the job.

Departments respond

For too many of the men in blue, attempts to cope with the stress boil down to a bar and a bottle with the boys—a pattern of after-work drinking and ventilating known as "choir practice." A variety of studies suggest that as many as 1 in 4 cops may be a "problem" drinker.

Under these circumstances, a serene family life is frequently elusive. Many police still work rotating shifts, which disrupt eating and sleeping patterns while wreaking havoc on the body's natural rhythms. Fear is also a constant in police families. "We have an unwritten rule that Chris will never go to work with us angry at each other," adds Dallas cop Nabors's wife Gayle

matter-of-factly. "It might be the last time we ever see each other." And when Cleveland patrolman Pompeani, Jr., works the overnight shift, his wife Nadine can't sleep. Many cops try to shield their spouses, but often the wives feel frozen out and a gulf develops. Police have divorce rates as high as twice the norm.

Psychologists feel many of the personal problems suffered by cops are linked by a common underpinning: Pressure to maintain a rock-hard, superhero image that keeps their emotions bottled up until the lid blows off. "The thing that disrupts personal relations more than anything is this 'image armor,' the need to look tough," says James Reese of the FBI's behavioral science unit. In the view of Ed Donovan, a former Boston cop, "We've got to teach cops that fear is a natural emotion." Donovan himself tried to deny his fright, numbing it with alcohol and drugs, until he found himself trembling outside Boston's Fenway Park one afternoon in 1969, slowly inserting a pistol barrel in his mouth as he contemplated suicide. Eventually, he sought counseling from fellow officers—and then became a pioneer in helping cops cope with stress.

As the accretion of stress on cops has reached the breaking point, a number of progressive departments have begun to respond. A typical stress-management program starts with interviews and a battery of psychological tests for applicants, to weed out would-be cops who can't handle the pressure or who see the job as a macho power trip. It continues with at least a few hours of training at the police academy: Talking with recruits about the tensions of their work, alerting them to warning signs and teaching basic relaxation techniques. Recruits are also advised to lower their expectations. "I tell them if they're coming into police work to stop crime, they're in the wrong profession," says Al Somodevilla, psychologist for the Dallas Police Department.

In Davie, Fla., Donovan and Ed Benedict, a former deputy sheriff and New York City firefighter, have taken the concept one step further. They have designed Seafield 911, a substance-abuse treatment center specifically for law-enforcement officers. For many, it represents a last-ditch effort to save their jobs—and their lives. The concept behind Seafield is that cops have trouble prospering in programs for the general population. They believe others don't understand what they're going through. "I wouldn't have trusted anyone else," says one Seafield graduate. "You realize that officers have the same problems everywhere," adds another.

The program, usually 30 days long, combines individual and group therapy, nutritional counseling and a fitness regimen with the stress-management plan developed by Donovan in Boston. Formal sessions are enhanced by long, sometimes weepy walks and back-porch bull sessions among peers, which help defuse cops' paranoia.

Not everyone likes the approach. The FBI's Reese wonders whether having cops treat cops worsens an unhealthy us-against-them mentality. "One of the major problems cops have is isolation," says Reese. "Then you get into a place to seek help, and you're surrounded by more badges. Well, good Lord, at what point do we start teaching people about the real world? I admire what they're doing, but I think a healthier stance may be to integrate, not isolate."

Nevertheless, Seafield staffers claim a 91 percent success rate since opening in July, 1989, and the Joint Commission on Accreditation of Healthcare Organizations recently commended the program for "outstanding organizational performance." Seafield staffer Joe Daniels argues: "This place is saving cops' lives from the most common cop-killer. It's not the gun-wielding maniac. It's the bottle."

Police departments are also making strides against the tension caused by the gun-wielding maniac. The most promising approach is "critical-incident management"—helping officers ease the stress of a traumatic event like a plane crash or a shooting incident. In the hours, days and months that follow such incidents, headaches, nausea, insomnia, memory loss, nightmares, flashbacks and depression are all common. Handled improperly or not at all, traumatic events can cripple an officer's psyche. Many end up retiring prematurely.

But in the more progressive departments, a psychologist quickly debriefs the involved officer, then conducts follow-up sessions. In Rochester, N.Y., for instance, the police department has a mandatory, three-visit post-trauma program. Dallas officer McCoy talked to a psychologist the night of his shooting, "and that got me off on the right foot," he says. "The key thing was the reassurance that what I was feeling was not unusual." The problem for many officers in the nation's 15,000-odd law-enforcement agencies, though, is that there is no stress-management program at all. "The police mind resists change," says Msgr. Joseph Dunne, former chaplain for the New York City Police Department.

An even bigger problem is that the criminal-justice system itself is now designed to break cops' hearts. For every 100 felony arrests, 43 are typically dismissed or not prosecuted. Of the remaining 57, 54 are disposed of by guilty plea. Only 3 go to trial, and of those, 1 is acquitted and 2 are found guilty. And of the 56 convicted, 22 typically get probation, 21 are sentenced to a year or less of prison and only 13 are sentenced to prison for more than a year.

"We're not making a dent," concludes Dallas officer Nabors. The greatest lift the nation could give its police is the promise that when they do their jobs well, it *will* amount to something. This is a war the nation can't walk away from.

By Gordon Witkin
with Ted Gest and Dorian Friedman

Law and Disorder

For cops, fear and frustration are constants. Sometimes even the best of them snap under the pressure.

RICHARD LACAYO

To watch the videotape of Los Angeles policemen kicking and clubbing Rodney King was to suddenly explore a dark corner of American life. For many police officers who fear that the incident could undermine their image of cool professionalism, the case quickly became an occasion for dismay, soul searching and a measure of defensiveness. For many citizens, particularly blacks and other minorities, it brought back bitter memories of their own rough encounters with police. George Bush bluntly summarized the prevailing shock: "What I saw made me sick."

The sickening glare from that grisly scene has thrown light upon police brutality all across the country. Was the beating an aberration, as Los Angeles police chief Daryl Gates insists? Or did it affirm yet again that many cops resort to violence, and even deadly force, when no threat to their safety can justify it? Is racism so pervasive among police that the fight against crime all too often becomes a war on blacks? Has the criminal-justice system, which permits too many criminals to go free after serving only token sentences or none at all, become so ineffectual that officers feel the need to play judge and jury on the spot? Has police work become so dangerous that even well-meaning officers can snap under the pressure?

Those questions became more urgent last week as evidence grew that the officers involved in King's beating might have expected their behavior to be winked at, at least in their own department. In tapes of radio calls and computer records of police communications on the night of the attack, some of the officers involved could be heard swapping racist jokes and boasting to other cops about the beating. Their lighthearted exchanges, which they knew were being recorded, sound nothing like the words of men who fear they have done something reprehensible—or even something out of the ordinary. Two nurses at Pacifica Hospital, where King was taken after the beating, testified to a grand jury last week that the officers who assaulted King showed up later at the hospital room to taunt him. One allegedly told the victim, "We played a little hardball tonight, and you lost."

In the eyes of many outraged citizens in Los Angeles and elsewhere, responsibility for the beating rests with Chief Gates. Though he has rebuffed demands that he resign, a citizens' group last week began a push for a special election to undo what practically amounts to his lifetime appointment as leader of the nation's third largest police department. Almost unique among police chiefs, Gates cannot be dismissed by Los Angeles Mayor Tom Bradley, himself a former L.A.P.D. lieutenant, or by a five-member police commission, except "for cause"—misconduct or willful neglect of duty.

Los Angeles is far from the only place where police play hardball, dispensing curbside justice with disturbing regularity, especially in crime-plagued ghetto neighborhoods and to people whose only offense is the color of their skins. Those who live outside such areas can usually ignore that reality. Fed up with violent street crime, they are often content to send in the police force and demand that it do whatever is necessary while they look the other way. But the Los Angeles beating has shaken such head-in-the-sand attitudes. A spate of brutality cases that normally would have attracted little attention made national news last week:

▶ In New York City five officers were indicted on murder charges in the Feb. 5 death by suffocation of a 21-year-old Hispanic man suspected of car theft. The officers were accused of having hit, kicked and choked Federico Pereira while he lay face down and perhaps hog-tied—his wrists cuffed behind his back while another set of cuffs bound his hands to one ankle.

▶ In Memphis a black county sheriff was convicted Friday of violating civil rights laws in the June 1989 choking death of Michael Gates, 28, a black drug suspect. Gates' body was covered with bruises in the shape of shoe prints.

▶ In Plainfield, N.J., 50 people demonstrated outside police headquarters, charging that a policeman beat Uriah Hannah, a 14-year-old black. Last Sunday Hannah and his friends were playing with a remote-controlled toy car on a sidewalk near his home. A motorist stopped short at the spot where the boys were playing, and a police cruiser ran into the rear of his car. Hannah's parents, whose older son allegedly committed suicide in police custody last year, charged that the officer jumped from his car, accused the teenager of obstructing traffic and at one point tried to choke him. His parents were arrested when they tried to intervene.

Skull-drumming tactics have an enduring and dismal place in police history, not least in the U.S., where accusations of brutality commonly accompany charges of racism. Many of the ghetto riots of the 1960s were prompted by police incidents. More recently, Miami has suffered five street uprisings in 10 years, all ignited by episodes of perceived police brutality.

Spotty record keeping makes it hard to measure the frequency of police misconduct. Departments often refuse to disclose the number of complaints they receive. Citizens often bring their accusations to civil rights or police-watchdog groups, which complicates attempts to compile a comprehensive count. Allegations of misconduct can also multiply in the wake of reforms that make it easier for citizens to report abuses.

In the end, many cases doubtless go unreported, especially in cities where complaints have to be filled out at the station house that is the home base of the very officers against whom the charge is being brought. "The general feeling out on the streets is that you can't get justice when a cop mistreats you," says Norman Siegel, executive director of the New York Civil Liberties Union. Many blacks believe, with considerable cause, that if the King beating had not been recorded, complaints about the case would have been discounted.

But while the experts cannot agree on whether abuses are up or down, few dispute that they are common—and sadly predictable. Even in the best of times, police work is dangerous and stressful, and an officer can face several life-or-death decisions during a single eight-hour watch. The pressures have mounted in recent years as crack has poured into the inner cities, giving rise to drug-dealing gangs armed with automatic weapons—and the hairtrigger temperament to use them.

In New York City, which has highly restrictive guidelines for when police may use their guns, the number of people shot by local cops soared in the past three years from 68 to 108. At the same time, police have been fired on by suspects in greater numbers every year since 1980. Though the number of officers killed nationally has fallen from 104 in 1980 to 66 in 1989, that is partly the result of wider use of bulletproof vests. "It used to be that arrested suspects got right into the patrol car," sighs Boston policeman John Meade, who heads the department's bureau of professional standards. "Now they put up a fight. Weapons suddenly turn up. Just like that, everything explodes."

As inner cities have degenerated into free-fire zones, many officers have become more aggressive, if only in self-defense. Danger "is something you get used to," says Officer Dennis Rhodes, a

20-year veteran of the L.A.P.D., "but every time you check in for a shift, you don't really know if you're going to go home that night." Two weeks ago, a suspected car thief pointed a 9-mm pistol at Rhodes' partner in the squad car, who then fired a shot at the gunman, forcing him to drop his weapon. "The whole incident took a minute and a half," says Rhodes, "and what raced through my mind was . . . the fact that I was going to get killed in the front seat of my car."

The temptation to administer streetcorner sentences is sometimes reinforced by the frustration of knowing that many of those the police collar will get off on plea bargains or serve mockingly short sentences.

Beyond those factors, police have been saddled with a task for which they are singularly ill-equipped. Most authorities believe that urban street crime arises from a combination of poverty, poor education and a lack of opportunity in inner-city neighborhoods, problems that the police can do nothing about. Officers, who tend to be recruited from places far from the neighborhoods they will patrol, often have little in common with the citizens they must serve and protect. "The bulk of police forces are white males of the middle class," says Ron DeLord, head of the Combined Law Enforcement Associations of Texas. "Yet we send them into large urban centers that are black and Hispanic and poor, with no understanding of the cultural differences, to enforce white, middle-class moral laws. Doesn't that create a clash?"

Law-abiding residents of crime-infested neighborhoods are desperate for police protection. They, after all, are the ones most likely to fall victim to muggers or drive-by shooters. But they also want the police's use of force kept in check, especially in poor neighborhoods where everyone is apt to be treated like a suspect. Even though many police departments have abandoned the official use of so-called drug-dealer profiles, officers may continue to carry racial stereotypes in their heads. To them, virtually any young black male with a gold chain is a potential drug courier. Any well-dressed black man in an expensive car might be a big-time dealer.

As a result, middle-class blacks, including celebrities like actor Blair Underwood, one of the stars of *L.A. Law,* complain that they have been harassed, and worse, during simple encounters with the law. At the University of Massachusetts, Boston, last week, the ACLU sponsored a conference that attracted 500 people to discuss the topic of police and local communities. "Over and over, black youngsters stood up and talked about how scary and demeaning it is to be stopped and searched," says ACLU state executive director John Rob-

MARCH 3, 12:39 A.M. AFTER BREAKING UP A QUARREL THAT REPORTEDLY INVOLVED BLACKS, LOS ANGELES POLICEMEN LAURENCE M. POWELL AND TIMOTHY E. WIND USE THEIR PORTABLE COMMUNICATIONS COMPUTER TO CONTACT A TEAM OF OFFICERS ON A BURGLARY STAKEOUT:

"Sounds almost exciting as our last call . . . It was right out of *Gorillas in the Mist.*"

THE STAKEOUT TEAM REPLIES:

"Hahahaha . . . let me guess who be the parties."

12:47 A.M. THE POLICE RADIO DISPATCHER ALERTS NEARBY SQUAD CARS THAT THE CALIFORNIA HIGHWAY PATROL IS PURSUING A WHITE HYUNDAI AT HIGH SPEED. MINUTES LATER POWELL AND WIND HELP APPREHEND THE DRIVER AND TWO PASSENGERS.

12:56 A.M. L.A.P.D. SERGEANT STACEY C. KOON NOTIFIES THE NIGHT WATCH COMMANDER AT THE FOOTHILL POLICE HEADQUARTERS THAT ONE SUSPECT HAS BEEN BEATEN BY THE ARRESTING OFFICERS:

"You just had a big-time use of force . . ."

THE WATCH COMMANDER REPLIES:

"Oh well . . . I'm sure the lizard didn't deserve it . . . haha."

1:12 A.M. POWELL AND WIND HAVE ANOTHER COMPUTER CHAT WITH THEIR FRIENDS ON THE BURGLARY STAKEOUT:

"Ooops."

"Ooops, what?"

"I haven't beaten anyone this bad in a long time."

"Oh not again . . . Why for you do that . . . I thought you agreed to chill out for a while . . ."

erts. "Even good kids now see police as the enemy. They shun cops."

Hassled cops, in turn, often retreat into a bipolar outlook: us vs. them. "Police see the sorry side of it all," says Mark Clark, former president of the Houston Police Officers Association. "A policeman can start out bright-eyed and bushy-tailed, but it goes away quickly on the street. It takes a mature officer not to stereotype people." Immersion into the police culture can quickly strip away a rookie's idealism. Says Hubert Williams, president of the Police Foundation: "Many officers will say, the moment I graduated from the police academy my partner told me, 'Forget all that stuff they told you at the academy; this is the real world.' "

Many of the best cops are no longer willing to pay the physical and psychological costs. Take Paul Wyland, who is planning to quit the Washington force after 20 years. "How many dead bodies have you seen?" he asks. "I've lost count. I'm not burned out. But you look at yourself and you say, 'How long can I keep doing this and not get messed up?' " Partly because so many seasoned officers have retired, departments around the nation have found themselves seriously understaffed. Others have expanded too rapidly, filling their ranks with inexperienced—and sometimes poorly trained—officers. Because the L.A.P.D. grew from 6,282 to 8,382 in the past three years, 38% of its field officers and 36% of its sergeants have less than three years on the force.

Experts on police psychology insist that most officers are attracted to police work by the opportunity to protect and serve. But a certain number of rotten apples, predisposed to brutality, make it through psychological testing that can be woefully inadequate. Ed Donovan, who runs a counseling service in Plymouth, Mass., for police suffering from stress, warns that police supervisors—and other officers—must be trained to be on the lookout for misfits as they move through the ranks. "Police are out there looking for troubled people," he says. "They ought to be able to spot troubled cops."

Writing on the Wall

Two years before the videotaped beating of Rodney King, television viewers were shocked by footage of a white patrolman in Long Beach, Calif., apparently ramming a black man's head through a plate-glass window. The victim was Don Carlos Jackson, who has devoted himself to exposing police racism since he himself retired from the police force of Hawthorne, Calif., in 1989.

Jackson has assembled a collection of bigoted materials he has found in police departments. Among them: an "Official Running Nigger Target," depicting a grossly caricatured nude black male, posted in a station house in Glendale, Calif.; and a memorandum he found in Los Angeles reading, "Effective immediately, Negroes are no longer to be called 'niggers' or 'jigs'—but seagulls. They cruise all night, squawk all day, s___ on everybody. And are protected by the Federal Government."

Jackson argues that for many officers, "the definition of a criminal suspect is almost synonymous with a black male face." Most departments have rules forbidding the display of racist materials. All too often those regulations are ignored.

A few cities have revamped their training and supervision to make abuses less likely. Since 1988, all 2,400 police officers on the Metro-Dade county force have undergone violence-reduction training to school themselves in ways to defuse potentially violent situations and to avoid overreaction to typical confrontations.

Critics of the police say that legal-damage suits are a more useful deterrent to police brutality and that they would work even better if jury awards were paid out of individual officers' pockets instead of by city treasuries. While courts have decided that public employees are not individually liable for most of their actions on the job, taxpayer concern about the rising cost of lawsuits has revived the popularity of civilian review boards. Such panels are at work in 26 of the nation's 50 largest cities, up from 13 seven years ago. The boards save municipal dollars by providing complainants with an alternative to the courts. They can also help departments identify and weed out problem officers before they strike again.

Rodney King, the victim of the Los Angeles beating, is bringing a $56 million civil suit against the L.A.P.D.—according to his lawyer, $1 million for each blow against him. As it happens, Chief Gates appeared before the city council last week to testify about the sums being paid by Los Angeles—about $10.5 million in 1990—to successful plaintiffs in police-misconduct suits. One was a $265,000 judgment to an 18-year-old white youth who was dragged from a car and beaten severely enough to suffer permanent ear damage. Although a civil-court jury found six officers at fault, Gates told the council that after a nine-month investigation, his department could not determine which officer had actually done the beating. "If you can't identify them, it's difficult to discipline them," he insisted. Members of the council were incredulous.

In the end, discipline must come from rank-and-file police with courage enough to break the so-called Blue Code, which prohibits one officer from ratting on another. A few encouraging signs exist that some officers are abandoning the tradition of blind loyalty to one another in misconduct cases. In Houston more than half of all complaints now come from other officers. During the King beating, two California highway-patrol officers reportedly took down the names of those involved from their breast-pocket name tags. They have since testified to investigators.

Episodes of police brutality are likely never to vanish entirely. But they could be significantly curtailed if more officers concluded that as long as their fellow police take the law into their own hands, there is no law at all.—**Reported by Cathy Booth/Miami, Sylvester Monroe and Edwin M. Reingold/Los Angeles**

New Faces, and New Roles, for the Police

Timothy Egan

Twenty years ago, the average American police officer was a white man from a military background, without any college education. The handful of female officers were not even allowed to ride in patrol cars after dark in some major cities.

Today the police are more representative of the nation's racial makeup than many institutions, including Congress. They are better educated than the typical worker. And women do almost every job that men do. But those are not the only things that have changed about police work.

The nature of the job has undergone a revolution, and, contrary to public perception, statistics show that the streets of America are considerably less deadly for police officers today than they were 20 years ago.

Last year 65 officers were killed in the line of duty—the lowest number since 1968 and about half the peak rate of 120 officers a year in the early 1970's. And now a typical police officer's day is spent settling family disputes and doing other kinds of social work, answering calls that may go nowhere, untangling traffic and filling out paperwork, said Comdr. Hugh Holton of the Chicago Police Department, reflecting a sentiment expressed by other police officers interviewed around the nation.

"Police work used to be like a laborer's job," said Commander Holton. "The only real requirement was you had to be tough. Now, that's not what we're looking for. You don't spend that much of your time actually fighting crime, I'd say only 4 percent of the job."

As the nature of the job has changed, so has the typical police officer.

Image vs. Reality

According to studies by two police research agencies, the proportion of officers with college degrees has more than quintupled in two decades: to 23 percent, from less than 4 percent in 1970. And they are paid more money than the average American worker—with a median annual salary of $29,066 last year, as against $21,580 for wage-earners as a whole, the Labor Department says. Police officers widened that gap over the last decade.

"The job has become more complicated," Commander Holton said. "People are demanding more. They want all kinds of services from us. It's come a long way from the us-versus-them days."

While the streets are indeed less deadly for officers, police officials say a single killing is too much. And there are variations from place to place: Some cities have indeed become more violent. But in interviews around the nation, officers and experts said nightly television images of military-style drug busts, and constant talk about a "war" on crime has created an impression that does not reflect modern reality among most of the nation's 500,000 police officers.

The war image has also been used in defense of the videotaped beating of Rodney G. King, the black motorist who was clubbed and kicked by white police officers in Los Angeles last month.

With the spread of crack and the violence that has accompanied its sale and distribution, the police are threatened as never before, the argument goes in cities that experience a particularly high level of violence.

"There is a very thin line between the complete chaos of some of our cities and civilization, and that thin line is our Police Department," said Father Robert Rankin, who is the parish priest for Sgt. Stacey C. Koon, one of four Los Angeles police officers charged in the beating of Mr. King.

Disputed Military Image

There are just as many police officers now per crime as there were 10 years ago. And for all the talk about proliferation of semiautomatic assault weapons, most police officers are still killed by ordinary handguns. Last year 48 of the 65 police shooting deaths were from small pistols. More officers were killed by knives and fists than by shotguns.

"To cast the modern American police force in a military way—as in the war on drugs—is wrong," said Darrel Stephens, director of the Police Executive Research Forum, a nonprofit group that studies police issues. "It's not a proper characterization."

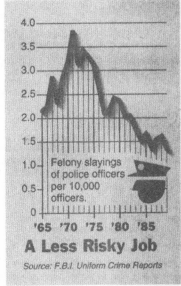

Felony slayings of police officers per 10,000 officers.

A Less Risky Job

Source: F.B.I. Uniform Crime Reports

The New York Times

When Commander Holton, a Vietnam veteran who has a master's degree, started in police work in 1969, most police officers in Chicago were Irish-American. Now, nearly 25 percent of the Chicago force is black.

'Everybody Called Us Pigs'

"It didn't matter what color you were, everybody called us pigs when I started out," said Commander Holton, who is black. "We had to swallow a lot of insults."

Nationwide, Labor Department figures show that 13.5 percent of police officers are black, higher than the civilian labor force average of 10.1 percent.

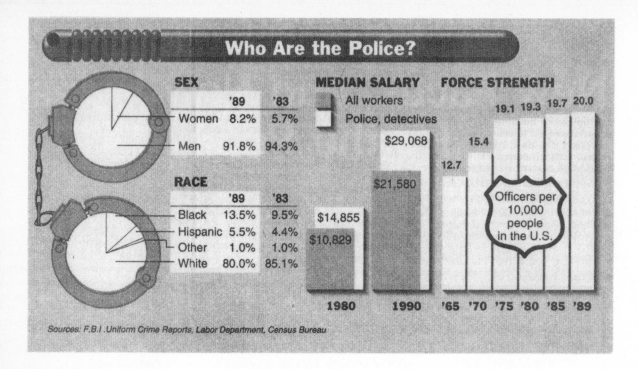

Who Are the Police?

SEX

	'89	'83
Women	8.2%	5.7%
Men	91.8%	94.3%

RACE

	'89	'83
Black	13.5%	9.5%
Hispanic	5.5%	4.4%
Other	1.0%	1.0%
White	80.0%	85.1%

MEDIAN SALARY

All workers
Police, detectives

$29,068
$21,580
$14,855
$10,829

1980   1990

FORCE STRENGTH

12.7 15.4 19.1 19.3 19.7 20.0

Officers per 10,000 people in the U.S.

'65 '70 '75 '80 '85 '89

Sources: F.B.I .Uniform Crime Reports, Labor Department, Census Bureau

Hispanic officers make up 5.5 percent of the police departments in the nation, as against 7.5 percent of the labor force.

There are very few Asian police officers, less than 1 percent, except in cities like San Francisco and Seattle, where Asians are the dominant minority group. Even then, it is difficult to recruit them.

"Among Asians, police work is not very well thought of," said a Chinese-American officer, Ignatius Chinn, a 20-year veteran of the Oakland Police Department, who is beginning a new police job with the state of California.

'We Are the Community'

Police officers say they are no more or less racist than American society as a whole. "Most cops are not rednecks," said Ed Striedinger, a homicide detective in Seattle. "We are the community, whatever that racial makeup might be."

After interviewing 125 Chicago police officers for her new book, "What Cops Know," (Villard Books), Connie Fletcher, a journalism professor at Loyola University, found that police officers tend to develop prejudices against whatever ethnic group commits most of the crimes in their precinct.

"One cop told me they end up with biases against the poorest people in whatever town, be it blacks in Chicago, Hispanics in Los Angeles or Indians in the West," she said.

Mr. Striedinger said: "People don't call us when things are good. So all we see is the bad stuff—people doing aw-

ful things to each other. It's tough to maintain a fair perspective."

Mr. Stephens, of the research forum, said the videotaped beating of Mr. King created an impression that, "most police officers are brutal and racist, and that nothing has changed over the last 25 years." But he added, "That's clearly not the case."

Reducing Danger

3.0
2.5
2.0
1.5
1.0
0.5
0

People killed by police officers in the U.S., per million people.

'70 '75 '80 '85

Sources: F.B.I .Uniform Crime Reports

The New York Times

Expanded Role of Women

Another change has taken place among police departments; there are

now enough women on police forces nationwide to fill a stadium: 41,148, according to the 1989 Federal survey. But law enforcement is still a man's world. Women make [up] only about 8 percent of police officers.

As late as the mid-1970's, women had to wear heeled shoes on the job, were only allowed to work with juvenile offenders, and in many cities, like Chicago, they could not ride in patrol cars after dark. Often, they were kept out of more dangerous police work because of minimum height, weight and strength requirements, most of which have been replaced with tests that measure endurance.

Now women serve on paramilitary police tactical squads, patrol in the most crime-plagued parts of cities and make every sort of arrest. Their presence has changed police work, many experts say. Along with the college graduates entering police work, women are less likely to go along with the so-called Blue Wall, the code of silence that keeps officers from testifying against one another in cases of wrongdoing, according to people who study police behavior.

"Police recruiters used to be looking for somebody out of 'Starsky and Hutch,'" said Rona Sampson, a former New York police officer who is a research consultant on police affairs. "Now that police agencies realize that 95 percent of the job has nothing to do with actually making arrests, they've come to value women more."

But women are not immune from using excessive force. Ms. Fletcher identified a tendency by some rookie female officers to over-react, trying to live up to a tough image. "The cops call it the Dirty Harriet or Jane Wayne Syndrome," she said. "You'll find that most brutality cases are with rookies, although not necessarily women. They want to impress the older guys."

The ratio of police officers to citizens, about 2.1 officers for every 1,000 people, has stayed the same over the last 10 years, reflecting the hiring surge that has kept up with population growth. But recruiters say that in contrast to 10 or 15 years ago, they are looking for a different type of person.

Recruiting Has Changed

"We used to use recruiting posters showing cops chasing somebody, advertising that it was an exciting job," said John Stedman, a former police commander in Alexandria, Va. "But 97 percent of the job has nothing to do with that. It's all about knowing how to talk to people. We screen for drug use, criminal background, but we don't do much screening for people who can get along with other people."

Ms. Fletcher said, "What everybody kept telling me was that 99 percent of the job is jawboning—a good cop knows how to defuse the situation by talking it out."

Still, the occasional adrenaline surge that comes with risk and pursuit are what keeps many officers on the job, said Mr. Chinn, who until a few months ago was an undercover agent in the most dangerous part of Oakland.

"No matter what anyone tells you about being burned out, or bored, cops like the adrenaline rush," said Mr. Chinn. "The kind of job I had, even when I thought I was going to get my head blown off, can be a lot of fun."

Higher Demand for Jobs

Perhaps because police work is unique, or because the pay has continued to rise above the national average, there are far more job applicants than positions. Nationwide, less than 10 percent of all people who apply for police work are chosen. In Chicago last year, 30,000 people applied for 600 police jobs.

After passing civil service and physical endurance tests, police recruits are sent to academies, where they may spend from 6 to 26 weeks learning about guns, legal rights, investigative techniques and arrest procedures. In most cities, rookies are placed on one-year probation. In the first three years on the job, there is a high attrition rate, which personnel managers attribute to the gulf between what a recruit expects of the job and the drudgery of daily work. There is far less glamor or excitement than most recruits expect.

Police officers talk of receiving a "street degree," which comes only after years on patrol. They say they develop their own world view, looking with suspicion on people who fit a particular demographic profile, feeling that nobody really understands them except other officers.

"They say that if you spend seven years as a cop, you can never really do anything else," said Commander Holton, whose father was also a police officer. "Even if you leave the department, you're a cop for life."

Not Just Old Wine in New Bottles

The Inextricable Relationship Between Crime Prevention and Community Policing

Peter Horne

Peter Horne, Ph.D., Criminal Justice Program Coordinator, Mercer County Community College, Trenton, New Jersey

AT THE OUTset, it is important to clarify the two terms in the title of this article. The formal definition of crime prevention is fairly straightforward: "The anticipation, recognition and appraisal of a crime risk and the initiation of some action to remove or reduce it."[1] While this definition is good as far as it goes, it doesn't go far enough. Fear reduction is also a significant aspect of crime prevention. Even if crime prevention efforts are only marginally effective in diminishing crime, they may help to reduce the citizen's *fear* of crime and thus enhance his sense of security.

Crime prevention *per se* is not new; on the contrary, Sir Robert Peel, the founder of the London Metropolitan Police in 1829, clearly viewed crime prevention as one of the basic tenets of policing. But the contemporary, more formalized and structured emphasis on crime prevention in American policing is a fairly recent occurrence that can be traced to the 1971 establishment of the National Crime Prevention Institute (NCPI) at the University of Louisville.

The definition of community policing is not nearly as simple and direct as that of crime prevention. *Community Policing,* an excellent new book by Trojanowicz and Bucqueroux, provides an in-depth examination of this complex phenomenon. The first paragraph of the page-long definition of community policing reads as follows:

Community policing is a new philosophy of policing, based on the concept that police officers and private citizens working together in creative ways can help solve contemporary community problems related to crime, fear of crime, social and physical disorder and neighborhood decay. The philosophy is predicated on the belief that achieving these goals requires that police departments develop a new relationship with the law-abiding people in the community, allowing them a greater voice in setting local police priorities and involving them in efforts to improve the overall quality of life in their neighborhoods. It shifts the focus of police work from handling random calls to solving community problems.[2]

Some law enforcement experts argue that community policing is simply a return to the 19th-century British and American systems built around officers on foot whose primary responsibility was maintaining order. But contemporary community policing is more than just "old wine in new bottles." It is really a new way of thinking about policing, suggesting that police officers are creative, intelligent individuals who can do more than just respond to incidents. By working with the people who live and work in an area, they can both identify the underlying problems and determine the best strategy to solve those problems.

Herman Goldstein's problem-oriented policing (POP) concept is an essential component of community policing. Basically, POP is a department-wide proactive strategy aimed at solving persistent crime-related community problems. Police are asked to identify, analyze and respond to the underlying circumstances that create incidents.[3]

Crime Prevention and Community Policing

Obviously, crime prevention and community policing are inextricably related. Crime prevention is the cornerstone of community policing. Internationally, "community-based crime prevention is the ultimate goal and centerpiece of community-oriented policing."[4]

One critical element common to both concepts is citizen input and participation; police crime prevention programs rely on the cooperation and voluntary involvement of individuals and groups in the community. True community policing acknowledges that the police cannot succeed without the community's operational and political support. The premise is that citizens will develop a sense of shared responsibility with the police to carry on an effective crime-fighting effort.[5]

What are the Weaknesses?

An in-depth examination of crime prevention and policing today reveals a number of weaknesses in the approach most police departments have taken to crime prevention. While in some departments crime prevention plays a greater role than ever before, too many agencies have erected a facade with no real substance behind it. Many police chiefs give lip service to the concept, particularly in their talks with the community, but then sabotage it (either consciously or unconsciously) through poor management practices.

In practice, crime prevention units often operate as separate entities within the department, never fully integrated into the police milieu. In the organizational scheme, the crime prevention unit is usually in the service track rather than the operations bureau, meaning the jobs are manned by staff and not line officers. The result is that crime prevention often is viewed as "arts and crafts" by patrol officers and detectives. Crime prevention officers tend not to be considered "real cops" who handle crime and disorder on a daily basis. This is particularly true since the 1980s, as many police agencies have done away with separate police-community relations units and merged them and their functions into crime prevention units.

Unfortunately, crime prevention units tend to be viewed as "dumping grounds" for all kinds of programs and miscellaneous assignments. Crime prevention officers are often responsible for a whole host of functions, including crime prevention, community relations, public relations, media relations and anything else the chief can think of. Because of the structure of the crime prevention unit, the nature of its daily activities and the scope of its responsibilities, crime prevention officers are often looked upon as public relations flak-catchers.

Although community policing is in its relative infancy in American law enforcement, problems similar to those confronting crime prevention have emerged in this country and overseas. As Skolnick and Bayley note:

Departmental segregation has by now become an almost predictable problem of community policing. Community policing activities are assigned to newly created, specialized units—crime prevention branches, mini-station commands and community relations squads. Community police personnel . . . 'do their own thing' and are not integrated into traditional patrol or criminal investigation activities. Police departments are composed of jealous fiefdoms that don't want to . . . share their responsibilities with community policing units . . . . Community policing becomes another specialized function, distinct from other ongoing department activities.[6]

What are the Remedies?

As Dr. Forrest Moss, director of NCPI, has stated, "Crime prevention is still woefully underutilized, underappreciated and . . . has not made it 'to the line' in terms of . . . real organizational commitment."[7] If these shortcomings are to be overcome, then crime prevention must become totally integrated into police

agencies. Specialist positions in crime prevention have to be reduced or eliminated altogether. Just like community relations, crime prevention must become part of the repertoire of full-fledged street cops in the community.

If there are to be specialist crime prevention units, they should be kept small and used as consultants to the generalist units, rather than as staff to carry out operational activities. Crime prevention units should be part of the line organizational structure, where they can coordinate the roles of patrol officers who, in essence, act as the field staff for crime prevention. The crime prevention specialist must assume the role of a planner, trainer, evaluator and supportive resource —an "enabler" rather than a primary "doer."[8]

All officers should undergo meaningful and practical training regarding the myriad activities of crime prevention. Also, just as in POP, field officers must be trained and encouraged to identify and analyze a present or potential crime or public disorder problem and work toward its reduction or elimination. A critical analysis of problems is needed to formulate crime-specific tactics and avoid a "shotgun" approach to problem solving. This analysis should be undertaken with community members; after corrective actions (e.g., counseling, arrest) have occurred, there must be evaluation and assessment of the success or failure of the actions.

"Rule of thumb" and "gut-level" impressions have no place in crime prevention. All crime prevention efforts must undergo critical scrutiny by both the police and the public. Comprehensive evaluations should also consider crime displacement issues, as well as citizen perceptions and levels of fear.

It may be unrealistic, though, to expect the police to devise and implement new strategies, as well as evaluate their impact. This would be particularly true in small and medium-sized police departments. After all, the priorities of the police are operational and "their expertise in evaluation limited . . . . The responsibility for evaluating program results should be shouldered by agencies outside the police."[9]

Two other issues should be briefly noted. One has to do with the concept referred to as "crime prevention through environmental design" (CPTED). CPTED, which should become an integral part of every department's crime prevention efforts, seeks to integrate natural approaches to crime prevention into building design and neighborhood planning. The formal definition of CPTED as de-

veloped by NCPI is that the "the proper design and effective use of the built environment can lead to a reduction in fear and the incidence of crime, and an improvement in the quality of life."[10] CPTED embodies the true value of crime prevention in that it is a proactive rather than a reactive approach to the crime problem.

If crime prevention is going to become part of all officers' everyday routines, it is important to consider performance evaluation. An ongoing dilemma in policing concerns how supervisors can best measure officer performance. Traditional quantitative measures—number of arrests, tickets issued, reports written, etc.—do not directly address such activities as crime prevention, problem solving or maintaining order. If officers are going to be motivated to engage in comprehensive crime prevention actions, then qualitative as well as quantitative measures must be developed to "provide an important barometer of officer activity and success, as well as a measure of organizational goals."[11] And since rewards continue to be powerful motivators, a reward system that recognizes officer achievements in nontraditional areas such as crime prevention must be created.

Just as community policing and crime prevention share many common problems, they also share many common remedies. Police officers will have to be adequately trained in community policing for them to understand the concept and how it is to be implemented. Performance evaluation issues will have to be addressed in community policing, as will crime analysis and assessment issues.

Community policing may be viewed by many as a radical and unproven police strategy. While it is true that community policing is still in its formative stage in such communities as Houston, Texas, Madison, Wisconsin, and Baltimore County, Maryland, considerable success has been experienced with this concept in Great Britain, Japan and Singapore. Whether community policing is a radical approach depends on one's perspective and view of policing. A critical examination of community policing and full understanding of the philosophy behind it make it seem far less radical. Skolnick and Bayley note that "it is critically important to emphasize that community policing represents a change in the practices—but not the objectives—of policing. Too often, the debate about community policing is couched in terms of 'hard' versus 'soft' policing and crime fighting versus crime prevention."[12]

But what is important to understand is that community policing does not require an "either/or" choice regarding "hard" versus "soft" policing. Indeed, it is absolutely imperative that both types of police tactics coexist in the same department. Officers trained in special weapons and tactics will still be needed in the same police agency as officers trained in crime prevention and engaged in foot patrol. Centralized strategic police efforts will be needed to effectively deal with individual offenders such as serial murderers or career criminals and criminal associations such as organized crime families, gangs and drug distribution networks. Therefore, community policing represents only a change in *means* rather than *ends*—public safety and security are still the bottom line.

Conclusion

Crime prevention is here to stay; it is more than just the latest fad in policing. The contemporary police crime prevention movement is 20 years old this year, and there are no signs of it waning. But while law enforcement has increased its utilization of crime prevention programs and strategies, it is at a crucial midpoint in the process. Too many police administrators talk a good game about crime prevention, but their follow-through is inadequate at best. They are more concerned with appearances than reality.

Some administrators jump on the crime prevention bandwagon simply because to do so is "progressive" and makes for good public relations. They also recognize that crime prevention provides a rationale for urging the public to support the police. "Without necessarily being consciously cynical, such leaders tend to develop one-directional [police to the community] outreach programs. They form specialized media relations units, undertake much-publicized programs in community education and organize Neighborhood Watch groups. But these programs are tacked onto existing operations."[13] Thus, crime prevention in its typical form rarely touches operational practices, nor does it open up the police to a true partnership with the community.

Crime prevention must be seen as more than just an "add-on" to existing police operations. It must become more broadly utilized and more fully integrated into the day-to-day lives of street cops. It is important for law enforcement to move ahead regarding crime prevention. If policing remains stagnant and clings to the status quo, then neither the police nor the public will reap the complete benefits of crime prevention.

Crime prevention can and does thrive in both traditional and community-oriented police departments. Of course, one hopes that community policing catches on and becomes part of the mainstream of policing, since inherent within the notion of community policing is the concept of crime prevention. Indeed, community policing presupposes that crime prevention efforts are an integral, institutionalized part of police management and operations. But, even if community policing does not become the norm in American law enforcement, there still is a vital and productive role for crime prevention in traditional-style police agencies.

Although crime prevention has enjoyed a certain amount of success in its short life span, the potential exists for much greater success in the future. It appears that

> . . . the greatest potential for improved crime control may not be in the continued enhancement of response times, patrol tactics and investigative techniques. Rather, improved crime control can be achieved by (1) diagnosing and managing problems in the community that produce serious crimes; (2) fostering close relations with the community to facilitate crime solving; and (3) building self-defense capabilities within the community itself.[14]

Crime prevention in conjunction with community policing can help diminish crime and enhance security in the neighborhoods of our nation. American law enforcement would do well to strive toward this objective.

---

[1]National Crime Prevention Institute, *Understanding Crime Prevention* (Boston, MA: Butterworths, 1986), p. 2.

[2]Robert Trojanowicz and Bonnie Bucqueroux, *Community Policing: A Contemporary Perspective* (Cincinnati, OH: Anderson, 1990), p. 5.

[3]Herman Goldstein, *Problem-Oriented Policing* (New York, NY: McGraw-Hill, 1990), pp. 3, 32.

[4]Jerome Skolnick and David Bayley, *Community Policing: Issues and Practices Around the World* (Washington, DC: National Institute of Justice, May 1988), p. 4.

[5]Lee P. Brown, *Community Policing: A Practical Guide for Police Officials—Perspectives on Policing*, No. 12 (Washington, DC: National Institute of Justice, U.S. Department of Justice and Harvard University, September 1989), p. 8.

[6]Skolnick and Bayley, pp. 62-63.

[7]Forrest Moss, "Director's Message," *NCPI Hotline*, December 1989, pp. 1, 11.

[8]National Crime Prevention Institute, p. 34.

[9]Skolnick and Bayley, pp. 68-69

[10]Timothy Crowe, "An Ounce of Prevention: A New Role for Law Enforcement," *FBI Law Enforcement Bulletin*, October 1988, p. 19.

[11]Trojanowicz and Bucqueroux, p. 178.

[12]Skolnick and Bayley, p. 90

[13]*Ibid.*, p. 33

[14]Mark Moore, Robert Trojanowicz and George Kelling, *Crime and Policing—Perspectives on Policing*, No. 2 (Washington, DC: National Institute of Justice, U.S. Department of Justice and Harvard University, June 1988), p. 2.

Law Enforcement Officers Killed 1980-1989

VICTORIA L. MAJOR

Mrs. Major is a supervisor assigned to the Uniform Crime Reporting Section, Federal Bureau of Investigation, Washington, D.C.

The Federal Bureau of Investigation began to maintain and to publish statistics on law enforcement officers killed in 1961. The data collected over the years are a sad legacy of the dedicated men and women of this Nation's police forces who lost their lives protecting others. Yet, at the same time, the information provides an insightful look into this heinous crime. This article gives an overview of law enforcement officers killed during the years 1980-1989.

The 1980s

During the decade of the 1980s, 801 law enforcement officers were feloniously killed in the line of duty. Officer deaths were recorded in 46 States; the District of Columbia; the U.S. territories of American Samoa, Guam, the Mariana Islands, Puerto Rico, and the Virgin Islands; and Mexico. Of the slain officers, 442 were employed by city police departments, 208 by county police and sheriff's offices, and 84 by State agencies. Twenty-three Federal agents and 44 territorial officers were also slain.

The 1980s total was 30 percent lower than that of the 1970s, when 1,143 officers were slain. The highest annual total during the past decade was in the first year, 1980, when 104 officers were killed. The lowest totals were in 1986 and 1989, when each year registered 66 officers killed. This figure represents the lowest annual total since records have been kept.

Victims

Of the 801 officers killed from 1980 through 1989, 783 were male and 18 were female. Seventy-seven officers were under 25 years of age; 515 were aged 25 to 40; and 209 were over 40 years old. By race, 703 of the slain officers were white; 96 were black; and 2 were of other races.

The law enforcement officers killed during the past decade averaged 9 years' law enforcement experience. Veterans of more than 10 years accounted for 34 percent of the victim officers. Thirty-three percent had from 5 to 10 years of service; 29 percent, from 1 to 4 years of service; and 5 percent, less than 1 year of experience.

The average height of officers killed during the 10-year period was 5 feet 11 inches. Seven of every 10 were in uniform when slain.

Circumstances

Arrest situations resulted in the deaths of law enforcement officers more frequently than any other activity during the 1980s. Two of every 5, or 327, of the officers slain were attempting an arrest when killed.

Among the remaining victims, 132 were killed upon responding to disturbance calls (man with gun, bar fights, family quarrels); 117 were investigating suspicious persons or circumstances; 107 were conducting traffic pursuits or stops; 71 were ambushed; 34 were handling,

Reprinted with permission from the *FBI Law Enforcement Bulletin*, U.S. Department of Justice, Federal Bureau of Investigation, May 1991, pp. 2-5.

transporting, or maintaining custody of prisoners; and 12 were handling mentally deranged individuals. One officer was slain during a civil disorder.

Types of Assignment

Patrol officers accounted for nearly two of every three officers slain throughout the decade. Detectives or officers on special assignment accounted for 23 percent of the victims, and 12 percent were off duty but acting in an official capacity when slain.

Of those killed while on patrol, 78 percent were assigned to one-officer vehicles, 20 percent to two-officer vehicles, and 2 percent to foot patrol. Fifty-three percent of the patrol officers were alone and unassisted at the time of their deaths, while 30 percent of the victim officers on other types of assignment were alone and unassisted.

Weapons

Firearms claimed the lives of 92 percent or 735 of the 801 officers killed in the line of duty from 1980 through 1989. Seventy percent of the murders were committed by the use of handguns, 13 percent by rifles, and 9 percent by shotguns.

The most common types of handguns used against officers were the .38 caliber and .357 magnum. These two weapons jointly accounted for nearly two of every three handgun deaths.

More than one-half of the officers killed by gunshots during this same timeframe were within 5 feet of their assailants at the time of the attack. Fifty-four percent of the firearm fatalities were caused by wounds to the upper torso, while 42 percent resulted from wounds to the head.

Of the 735 officers killed with firearms, 120 or 16 percent were killed with their own weapons. Handguns accounted for 118 of the service weapons used against the officers; shotguns for 2. Among the service handguns, 9 of 10 were those using .357- or .38-special cartridge types.

Weapons other than firearms claimed the lives of 66 officers during the 10-year period. Thirty-three officers were intentionally struck with

Law Enforcement Officers Killed 1980-1989

- 801 were feloniously killed in the line of duty
- 104, the highest annual total, were killed in 1980
- 66, the lowest annual total, were killed in both 1986 and 1989
- 783 were male
- 18 were female
- 515 were aged 25 to 40
- 327 were attempting an arrest when killed
- 735 officers were killed by firearms
- 120 were killed with their own weapons
- 157 of those killed by firearms were wearing protective armor
- 7 out of every 10 were in uniform when killed
- 2 out of every 3 were patrol officers

vehicles, 17 were knifed, 7 were beaten with blunt objects, 5 were beaten with personal weapons (hands, fists, feet), 2 were burned, 1 was drowned, and 1 was asphyxiated.

Body Armor

Of the 735 officers slain with firearms during the 1980s, 157 were wearing protective body armor. Wounds to the head resulted in the deaths of 94 officers wearing protective armor. Thirty-two officers were killed when bullets entered between the panels of the vests or through the arm openings. Thirteen were killed by wounds to the upper torso outside the area of the vests, and 12 by gunshot wounds below the vest area. Six officers were slain when bullets penetrated their protective vests.

In addition to the 157 officers shot and killed while wearing vests, 12 victims wearing vests were killed by weapons other than firearms. Eight officers wearing vests were intentionally struck by vehicles, three were stabbed, and one was pushed to his death.

Places

The most populous region, the Southern States, recorded 46 percent of the officer fatalities in the 1980s. The Western States recorded 18 percent of the deaths; the Midwestern States, 17 percent; the Northeastern States, 13 percent; and U.S. territories, 5 percent.

A comparison of regional totals for the two periods, 1980-1984 and 1985-1989, showed that the number of officers killed during the latter 5-year span declined in all regions.

Among the 50 States, Texas lost more officers to line-of-duty deaths than any other during the decade. Four States recorded no felonious killings during the 10-year period—Delaware, New Hampshire, Rhode Island, and Vermont.

Law enforcement agencies in the Nation's largest cities, those with more than 250,000 inhabitants, lost more officers to line-of-duty deaths than departments in municipalities of any other size. These cities collectively recorded 24 percent of all felonious killings in the decade. Following were suburban county law enforcement agencies, registering 16 percent of the slayings.

Times

In the past decade, 62 percent of the incidents resulting in officers' deaths occurred from 6:01 p.m. to 6:00 a.m. The figures show the 6:01 a.m. to 8:00 a.m. period to be the hours when the fewest officers were slain, while the hours from 8:01 p.m. to 10:00 p.m. were those during which the highest totals were recorded.

Daily figures for the decade show more officers were slain on Thursdays than on any other day of the week. The fewest fatalities were recorded on Sundays. January was the month during the 10-year span that registered the highest total, 91; August showed the lowest total, 53.

Assailants

Ninety-eight percent of the 801 slayings of law enforcement officers during the 1980s have been cleared. Of the 1,077 suspects identified in connection with the murders, 1,034 were male and 43 were female. Fifty-six percent of those identified were white, 42 percent were black, and 2 percent were of other races. Sixty-two percent of the assailants were younger than 30 years old.

Seven of every 10 suspects identified had previous arrests, and 5 of 10 had a prior conviction. The records also show that 3 of every 10 had a prior arrest for a violent crime. Twenty-four percent of those identified were on parole or probation at the time of the killings.

Of the 1,077 persons identified, 879 have been arrested by law enforcement agencies. One hundred forty-three were justifiably killed, 48 committed suicide, 6 are still at large, and 1 was murdered in an unrelated incident.

Disposition

Based on available disposition information, 70 percent of those arrested and charged in connection with the killings of law enforcement officers during the 1980s were found guilty of murder. Eight percent were found guilty of a lesser offense related to murder, and 4 percent were found guilty of some crime other than murder. Two percent of those charged were committed to psychiatric institutions, and 1 percent died in custody before final disposition. Ten percent of the suspects were acquitted or had the charges against them dismissed. Disposition is pending for 6 percent of the arrestees, the majority of whom were arrested in 1988 and 1989.

Accidental Deaths

In addition to those feloniously killed during the decade, 713 law enforcement officers lost their lives accidently while performing their official duties. The lowest annual total of the decade was in 1980 with 61 deaths recorded. The last year of the decade, 1989, registered the highest count, 79.

Automobile accidents were the leading cause of accidental deaths, accounting for 312 fatalities during the decade. Following were accidents where officers were struck by vehicles at traffic stops, road blocks, while directing traffic or assisting motorists, etc. (160); aircraft accidents (89); accidental shootings (60); motorcycle accidents (49); and other types of accidents, such as falls, drownings, etc., (43).

Geographically, the Southern States recorded 312 accidental deaths; the Western States, 168; the Midwestern States, 116; the Northeastern States, 101; Puerto Rico, 10; and Guam, 2. An additional four officers were accidentally killed in the line of duty while in foreign countries.

Conclusion

Many officers paid the ultimate price in the performance of their duties. They accepted the challenges of their profession freely and faced each challenge unselfishly. Hopefully, the statistics compiled on officer deaths can be used to protect those who continue to enforce the laws of this country and protect its freedom.

The Judicial System

Our system of criminal justice is an adversarial system and the protagonists are the state and the criminal defendant. The courtroom is where the drama is played out, and we look to the courts to preserve our liberties and assure a fair trial.

"The Judicial Process: Prosecutors and Courts" outlines the roles of prosecutors, defense counsel, and the courts in the criminal justice process. "Public Defenders" discusses the role of the public defender.

"Abuse of Power in the Prosecutor's Office" is a critical analysis of the office of prosecutor. The article is presented, not as an indictment of all prosecutors, but to stimulate discussion as to the potential for abuse. "Convicting the Innocent" also raises questions concerning the adequacies of some defense counsels.

"These Clients Aren't Fools" tells of three prisoners who, acting as their own attorneys, managed to get their cases heard by the U.S. Supreme Court. The argument is made in "Improving Our Criminal Justice System" that the current system is archaic and that we should look to other models.

Charles Colson, former special counsel to President Richard Nixon and a leading figure in the Watergate scandal, in "Alternative Sentencing: A New Direction for Criminal Justice," urges that the courts consider alternatives other than sentencing to prison as a means of handling nondangerous offenders.

The Supreme Court of the United States is the ultimate forum for interpreting the Constitution and guaranteeing our rights. Each term of the Court involves several cases that impact on the criminal justice system and concern issues relating to confessions, right to counsel, search and seizure, the death penalty, and so forth. "Criminal Rulings Granted the State Broad New Power" reviews some of the decisions of the Supreme Court during the 1990–1991 term.

Looking Ahead: Challenge Questions

Should the American court system be overhauled?

What can be done to assure fairness in the prosecutor's office?

Is the current Supreme Court of the United States too biased in favor of law enforcement?

The Judicial Process: Prosecutors and Courts

The courts participate in and supervise the judicial process

The courts have several functions in addition to deciding whether laws have been violated

The courts—
• settle disputes between legal entities (persons, corporations, etc.)
• invoke sanctions against law violations
• decide whether acts of the legislative and executive branches are constitutional.

In deciding about violations of the law the courts must apply the law to the facts of each case. The courts affect policy in deciding individual cases by handing down decisions about how the laws should be interpreted and carried out. Decisions of the appellate courts are the ones most likely to have policy impact.

Using an arm of the State to settle disputes is a relatively new concept

Until the Middle Ages disputes between individuals, clans, and families, including those involving criminal acts, were handled privately. Over time, acts such as murder, rape, robbery, larceny, and fraud came to be regarded as crimes against the entire community, and the State intervened on its behalf. Today in the United States the courts handle both civil actions (disputes between individuals or organizations) and criminal actions.

An independent judiciary is a basic concept of the U.S. system of government

To establish its independence and impartiality, the judiciary was created as a separate branch of government co-equal to the executive and the legislative branches. Insulation of the courts from political pressure is attempted through—
• the separation of powers doctrine
• established tenure for judges
• legislative safeguards
• the canons of legal ethics.

Courts are without the power of enforcement. The executive branch must enforce their decisions. Furthermore, the courts must request that the legislature provide them with the resources needed to conduct their business.

Each State has a system of trial and appeals courts

Generally, State court systems are organized according to three basic levels of jurisdiction:

• **Courts of limited and special jurisdiction** are authorized to hear only less serious cases (misdemeanors and/or civil suits that involve small amounts of money) or to hear special types of cases such as divorce or probate suits. Such courts include traffic courts, municipal courts, family courts, small claims courts, magistrate courts, and probate courts.

• **Courts of general jurisdiction**, also called major trial courts, are unlimited in the civil or criminal cases they are authorized to hear. Almost all cases originate in the courts of limited or special jurisdiction or in courts of general jurisdiction. Most serious criminal cases are handled by courts of general jurisdiction.

• **Appellate courts** are divided into two groups, intermediate appeals courts, which hear some or all appeals that are subject to review by the court of last resort, and courts of last resort, which have jurisdiction over final appeals from courts of original jurisdiction, intermediate appeals courts, or administrative agencies. As of 1985, 36 States had intermediate appellate courts, but all States had courts of last resort.

The U.S. Constitution created the U.S. Supreme Court and authorized the Congress to

From *Report to the Nation on Crime and Justice*, Bureau of Justice Statistics, U.S. Department of Justice, March 1988, pp. 81-82, 71-72, 74-75.

establish lower courts as needed

The Federal court system now consists of various special courts, U.S. district courts (general jurisdiction courts), U.S. courts of appeals (intermediate appellate courts that receive appeals from the district courts and Federal administrative agencies), and the U.S. Supreme Court (the court of last resort). Organized on a regional basis are U.S. courts of appeals for each of 11 circuits and the District of Columbia. In Federal trial courts (the 94 U.S. district courts) more than 300,000 cases were filed in 1985; there was one criminal case for every seven civil cases. In 1985 more than half the criminal cases in district courts were for embezzlement, fraud, forgery and counterfeiting, traffic, or drug offenses.

Court organization varies greatly among the States

State courts of general jurisdiction are organized by districts, counties, dual districts, or a combination of counties and districts. In some States the courts established by the State are funded and controlled locally. In others the court of last resort may have some budgetary or administrative oversight over the entire State court system. Even within States there is considerable lack of uniformity in the roles, organization, and procedures of the courts. This has led to significant momentum among States to form "unified" court systems to provide in varying degrees, for uniform administration of the courts, and, in many cases, for the consolidation of diverse courts of limited and special jurisdiction.

Most felony cases are brought in State and local courts

The traditional criminal offenses under the English common law have been adopted, in one form or another, in the criminal laws of each of the States. Most cases involving "common law" crimes are brought to trial in State or local courts. Persons charged with misdemeanors are usually tried in courts of limited jurisdiction. Those charged with felonies (more serious crimes) are tried in courts of general jurisdiction.

In all States criminal defendants may appeal most decisions of criminal courts of limited jurisdiction; the avenue of appeal usually ends with the State supreme court. However, the U.S. Supreme Court may elect to hear the case if the appeal is based on an alleged violation of the Constitutional rights of the defendant.

Courts at various levels of government interact in many ways

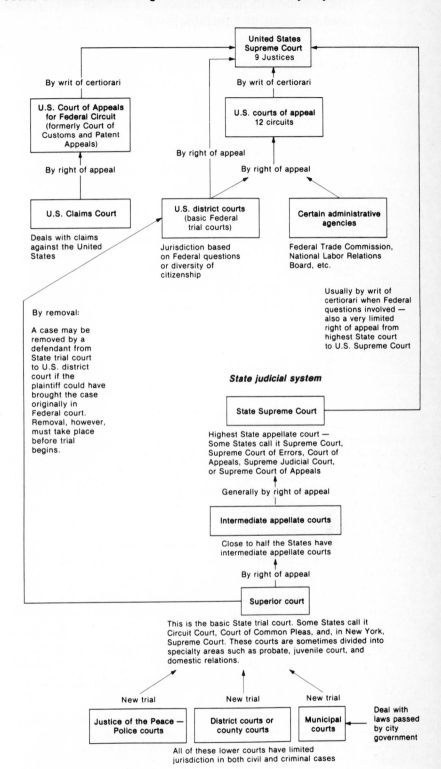

State courts process a large volume of cases, many of them minor

In 1983, 46 States and the District of Columbia reported more than 80 million cases filed in State and local courts. About 70% were traffic-related cases, 16% were civil cases (torts, contracts,

Differences in how prosecutors handle felony cases can be seen in 4 jurisdictions

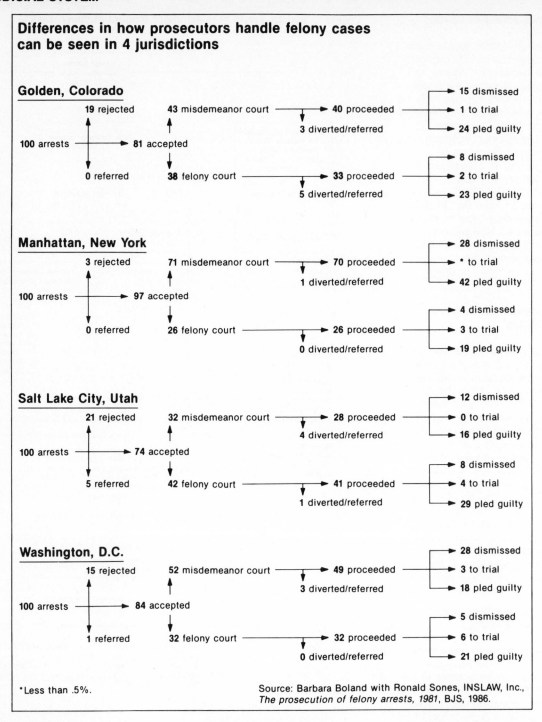

Golden, Colorado

	19 rejected	43 misdemeanor court ──→ 40 proceeded ──→	15 dismissed / 1 to trial / 24 pled guilty
		3 diverted/referred	
100 arrests ──→ 81 accepted			
	0 referred	38 felony court ──→ 33 proceeded ──→	8 dismissed / 2 to trial / 23 pled guilty
		5 diverted/referred	

Manhattan, New York

	3 rejected	71 misdemeanor court ──→ 70 proceeded ──→	28 dismissed / * to trial / 42 pled guilty
		1 diverted/referred	
100 arrests ──→ 97 accepted			
	0 referred	26 felony court ──→ 26 proceeded ──→	4 dismissed / 3 to trial / 19 pled guilty
		0 diverted/referred	

Salt Lake City, Utah

	21 rejected	32 misdemeanor court ──→ 28 proceeded ──→	12 dismissed / 0 to trial / 16 pled guilty
		4 diverted/referred	
100 arrests ──→ 74 accepted			
	5 referred	42 felony court ──→ 41 proceeded ──→	8 dismissed / 4 to trial / 29 pled guilty
		1 diverted/referred	

Washington, D.C.

	15 rejected	52 misdemeanor court ──→ 49 proceeded ──→	28 dismissed / 3 to trial / 18 pled guilty
		3 diverted/referred	
100 arrests ──→ 84 accepted			
	1 referred	32 felony court ──→ 32 proceeded ──→	5 dismissed / 6 to trial / 21 pled guilty
		0 diverted/referred	

*Less than .5%.

Source: Barbara Boland with Ronald Sones, INSLAW, Inc., *The prosecution of felony arrests, 1981*, BJS, 1986.

small claims, etc.), 13% were criminal cases, and 1% were juvenile cases. Civil and criminal cases both appear to be increasing. Of 39 States that reported civil filings for 1978 and 1983, 32 had increases. Of the 36 States that reported criminal filings for both years, 33 showed an increase in the volume of criminal filings.

In the 24 States that could report, felony filings comprised from 5% to 32% of total criminal filings with a median of 9%.

Victims and witnesses are taking a more significant part in the prosecution of felons

Recent attention to crime victims has spurred the development of legislation and services that are more responsive to victims.
• Some States have raised witness fees from $5–10 per day in trial to $20–30 per day, established procedures for victim and witness notification of court proceedings, and guaranteed the right to speedy disposition of cases

• 9 States and the Federal Government have comprehensive bills of rights for victims

• 39 States and the Federal Government have laws or guidelines requiring that victims and witnesses be notified of the scheduling and cancellation of criminal proceedings

• 33 States and the Federal Government allow victims to participate in criminal proceedings via oral or written testimony.

The prosecutor provides the link between the law enforcement and adjudicatory processes

The separate system of justice for juveniles often operates within the existing court organization

Jurisdiction over juvenile delinquency, dependent or neglected children, and related matters is vested in various types of courts. In many States the juvenile court is a division of the court of general jurisdiction. A few States have statewide systems of juvenile or family courts. Juvenile jurisdiction is vested in the courts of general jurisdiction in some counties and in separate juvenile courts or courts of limited jurisdiction in others.

The American prosecutor is unique in the world

First, the American prosecutor is a public prosecutor representing the people in matters of criminal law. Historically, European societies viewed crimes as wrongs against an individual whose claims could be pressed through private prosecution. Second, the American prosecutor is usually a local official, reflecting the development of autonomous local governments in the colonies. Finally, as an elected official, the local American prosecutor is responsible to the voters.

Prosecution is the function of representing the people in criminal cases

After the police arrest a suspect, the prosecutor coordinates the government's response to crime—from the initial screening, when the prosecutor decides whether or not to press charges, through trial. In some instances, it continues through sentencing with the presentation of sentencing recommendations.

Prosecutors have been accorded much discretion in carrying out their responsibilities. They make many of the decisions that determine whether a case will proceed through the criminal justice process.

Prosecution is predominantly a State and local function

Prosecuting officials include State, district, county, prosecuting, and commonwealth attorneys; corporation counsels; circuit solicitors; attorneys general; and U.S. attorneys. Prosecution is carried out by more than 8,000 State, county, municipal, and township prosecution agen-

cies.[1] In all but five States, local prosecutors are elected officials. Many small jurisdictions engage a part-time prosecutor who also maintains a private law practice. In some areas police share the charging responsibility of local prosecutors. Prosecutors in urban jurisdictions often have offices staffed by many full-time assistants. Each State has an office of the attorney general, which has jurisdiction over all matters involving State law but generally, unless specifically requested, is not involved in local prosecution. Federal prosecution is the responsibility of 93 U.S. attorneys who are appointed by the President subject to confirmation by the Senate.

The decision to charge is generally a function of the prosecutor

Results of a 1981 survey of police and prosecution agencies in localities of over 100,000 indicate that police file initial charges in half the jurisdictions surveyed. This arrangement, sometimes referred to as the police court, is not commonly found in the larger urban areas that account for most of the UCR Index crime. Usually, once an arrest is made and the case is referred to the prosecutor, most prosecutors screen cases to see if they merit prosecution. The prosecutor can refuse to prosecute, for example, because of insufficient evidence. The decision to charge is not usually reviewable by any other branch of government.

Some prosecutors accept almost all cases for prosecution; others screen out many cases

Some prosecutors have screening units designed to reject cases at the earliest possible point. Others tend to accept most arrests, more of which are dismissed by judges later in the adjudication process. Most prosecutor offices fall somewhere between these two extremes.

Arrest disposition patterns in 16 jurisdictions range from 0 to 47% of arrests rejected for prosecution. Jurisdictions with high rejection rates generally were found to have lower rates of dismissal at later stages of the criminal process. Conversely, jurisdictions that accepted most or all arrests usually had high dismissal rates.

Prosecutorial screening practices are of several distinct types

Several studies conclude that screening

decisions consider—
- evidentiary factors
- the views of the prosecutor on key criminal justice issues
- the political and social environment in which the prosecutor functions
- the resource constraints and organization of prosecutorial operations.

Jacoby's study confirmed the presence of at least three policies that affect the screening decision:
- Legal sufficiency—an arrest is accepted for prosecution if, on routine review of the arrest, the minimum legal elements of a case are present.
- System efficiency—arrests are disposed as quickly as possible by the fastest means possible, which are rejections, dismissals, and pleas.
- Trial sufficiency—the prosecutor accepts only those arrests for which, in his or her view, there is sufficient evidence to convict in court.

The official accusation in felony cases is a grand jury indictment or a prosecutor's bill of information

According to Jacoby, the accusatory process usually follows one of four paths:
- arrest to preliminary hearing for bindover to grand jury for indictment
- arrest to grand jury for indictment
- arrest to preliminary hearing to a bill of information
- a combination of the above at the prosecutor's discretion.

Whatever the method of accusation, the State must demonstrate only that there is probable cause to support the charge.

The preliminary hearing is used in some jurisdictions to determine probable cause

The purpose of the hearing is to see if there is probable cause to believe a crime has been committed and that the defendant committed it. Evidence may be presented by both the prosecution and the defense. On a finding of probable cause the defendant is held to answer in the next stage of a felony proceeding.

The grand jury emerged from the American Revolution as the people's protection against oppressive prosecution by the State

Today, the grand jury is a group of ordinary citizens, usually no more than 23, which has both accusatory and investigative functions. The jury's proceedings are secret and not adversarial so that most rules of evidence for trials do not apply. Usually, evidence is presented by the prosecutor who brings a case to the grand jury's attention. However, in some States the grand jury is used primarily to investigate issues of public corruption and organized crime.

Some States do not require a grand jury indictment to initiate prosecutions

Grand jury indictment required	Grand jury indictment optional
All crimes	Arizona
New Jersey	Arkansas
South Carolina	California
Tennessee	Colorado
Virginia	Idaho
	Illinois
All felonies	Indiana
Alabama	Iowa
Alaska	Kansas
Delaware	Maryland
District of Columbia	Michigan
Georgia	Missouri
Hawaii	Montana
Kentucky	Nebraska
Maine	Nevada
Mississippi	New Mexico
New Hampshire	North Dakota
New York	Oklahoma
North Carolina	Oregon

Ohio	South Dakota
Texas	Utah
West Virginia	Vermont
	Washington
Capital crimes only	Wisconsin
Connecticut	Wyoming
Florida	
Louisiana	**Grand jury lacks authority to indict**
Massachusetts	
Minnesota	
Rhode Island	Pennsylvania

Note: With the exception of capital cases a defendant can always waive the right to an indictment. Thus, the requirement for an indictment to initiate prosecution exists only in the absence of a waiver.
Source: Deborah Day Emerson, *Grand jury reform: A review of key issues*, National Institute of Justice, U.S. Department of Justice, January 1983.

The secrecy of the grand jury is a matter of controversy

Critics of the grand jury process suggest it denies due process and equal protection under the law and exists only to serve the prosecutor. Recent criticisms have fostered a number of reforms requiring due process protections for persons under investigation and for witnesses; requiring improvements in the quality and quantity of evidence presented; and opening the proceeding to outside review. While there is much variation in the nature and implementation of reforms, 15 States have enacted laws affording the right to counsel, and 10 States require evidentiary standards approaching the requirements imposed at trial.

The defense attorney's function is to protect the defendant's legal rights and to be the defendant's advocate in the adversary process

Defendants have the right to defend themselves, but most prefer to be represented by a specialist in the law. Relatively few members of the legal profession specialize in criminal law, but lawyers who normally handle other types of legal matters may take criminal cases.

The right to the assistance of counsel is more than the right to hire a lawyer

Supreme Court decisions in *Gideon* v. *Wainwright* (1963) and *Argersinger* v. *Hamlin* (1972) established that the right to an attorney may not be frustrated by lack of means. For both felonies and misdemeanors for which jail or prison can be the penalty, the State must provide an attorney to any accused person who is indigent.

The institutional response to this Constitutional mandate is still evolving as States experiment with various ways to provide legal counsel for indigent defendants.

Public Defenders

AGNES A. SERPE

Agnes A. Serpe is a student at Creighton University in Omaha, Nebraska. She is pursuing Creighton's Three Plus Three program, a combination Business Administration/Law program.

They [public defenders] are a fraternity of righteous, these low-paid lawyers, dogmatists of the criminal justice system, who often find themselves lining up on the sides of rapists, murderers, child-molesters, and drug dealers.[1]

A public defender is an attorney appointed to aid indigent persons, usually in cases involving possible imprisonment. Because the Supreme Court guarantees that all persons accused of felonies, regardless of their ability to pay for counsel, have the right to a publicly provided defense lawyer during police questioning, pretrial hearings, the trial, and appeal, the public defender is a busy attorney.[2]

With the rate of crime in the United States continuing to rise, the demand for defense counsel increases. Public defenders are expected to begin research and representation early on in their cases, and they are expected to follow through to the appeals stages and probation revocation hearings.[3] The problem is that there are more cases in need of public defense counsel than there are attorneys with the time, money, and expertise to handle such cases. The result is that cases involving indigent clients are often delayed or expedited, hampering the public defender in effectively representing his client.[4]

Although the problems facing public defense counsel in the United States today are severe ones, the present judicial system has a strong foundation. The U.S. bases its whole judicial system on the fundamental principle ". . . laid down by the greatest English judges . . ."[5] The system holds that it is better to let many guilty persons escape than it is to let one innocent person be imprisoned.[6]

Since the primary goal of the judicial system is to protect the innocent, the system holds that every individual has the right to counsel. In 1791, Congress passed the Sixth Amendment to the Constitution, guaranteeing in all criminal prosecutions, the accused person has the right to a ". . . speedy and public trial, by an impartial jury of the state and district wherein the crime shall have been committed. . . and to have the assistance of counsel for his defense."[7] According to the Sixth Amendment, 'counsel' does not include lay persons, but rather refers only to persons authorized to practice law.[8]

Despite the amendment, flaws still remained in the system. Only until after 1961 did the Supreme Court rule that the guarantees found in the Sixth Amendment apply to the state trial courts as well as the federal trial courts.[9] Also, court-appointed attorneys were expected to serve the public without compensation, burdening the practicing bar of attorneys and forcing the judges to appoint young, inexperienced counsel.[10] Moreover, a public defender program was not established until the early 1920's.[11]

History

At first, public defenders were part of the legal aid societies that were supported by charities. The society handled both civil and criminal cases and had the authority to accept or reject cases. The earliest legal aid society was Der Deutsche Rechtsshutz

Verein (the German Legal Defense Society) which was organized in 1876 to help German immigrants. Later, in 1888, New York City created the New York Legal Aid Society, and Chicago established the Chicago Bureau of Justice.[12]

Early legal aid societies, such as the ones in New York and Chicago, did not take many criminal cases because they lacked the time, money, and personnel to conduct criminal investigations and absorb the trial work.[13] By 1962, the burden of criminal caseloads shifted from the legal aid societies to the 110 newly established public defender offices across America. The number of public defender offices was very few in proportion to the population of the country, but enough to provide minimal service in some major cities. Accordingly, the offices were noted for being understaffed.[14]

Furthermore, up until 1963, any legal assistance providing defense services for indigent criminals had been a matter left up to the judge to decide, depending heavily upon the charitable time and money contributions from the bar association. The demand for sufficient funding resulted in the Ford Foundation's decision to create the National Defender Project in 1964. Donating $6,000,000 to the National Legal Aid and Defender Association over a five-year period, the foundation provided the funds that were needed to improve and establish organized defense systems in over sixty cities across the nation.[15]

The Ford Foundation's sudden display of generosity occurred immediately after the landmark court case Gideon v Wainwright in 1963. In this case, Clarence Earl Gideon, the defendant, who was tried and convicted in a Florida state court, committed the felony of breaking and entering (a poolroom) with the intent to commit a misdemeanor theft. When he requested an attorney for his trial, the judge refused him. The judge claimed that he could not assign an attorney to Gideon because Gideon was not charged with a capital offense (that is, one punishable by death). Since the judge did have the power to appoint counsel, the judge had made an obvious mistake.[16] As a result, the Supreme Court ruled that Gideon's quality of defense was inadequate

and "about as well as could be expected from a layman."[17]

Therefore, the outcome of Gideon v Wainwright was an emphasis on what the Sixth Amendment is all about. "The right to legal representation must be granted to all indigent defendants in all felonies."[18]

"This noble idea [right to counsel] cannot be realized if the poor man charged with crime has to face his accusers without a lawyer to defend him," stated Mr. Justice Black, who was in harmony with the majority opinion in Gideon v Wainwright.[19]

Although there was a time when public defenders were paid a great deal less than the state's prosecuting attorney, today the difference between the public defender's salary and the state's prosecuting attorney's salary has decreased.

Thus, the Gideon v Wainwright decision came at the right time, prompting the Ford Foundation to donate money. Also, the case proved that ". . . lawyers in criminal courts are necessities, not luxuries."[20] The foundation had heard the pleas for the funding and had solved some problems for the time being.

Later, in 1964, The Criminal Justice Act was passed, making the federal government provide funds for judges to pay attorneys to represent indigent defendants. At first, however, these funds were available only to attorneys who defended federal crimes, not state crimes. The earliest response was from the state of New Jersey which enacted a state-wide public defender program.[21]

Public Defenders Today

Generally, there are two main means of appointing defense counsel in the U.S. One is the ad hoc, or random, appointment of counsel, and the other is the coordinated assigned counsel program.[22] With ad hoc appointments, the more predominant of the two methods, attorneys are appointed case by case rather than in accordance with an organized plan. The attorneys who are appointed to a case are often the ones who just happen to be in the courtroom at the time of the client's arraignment. As a result the allocation of the burdens placed on defense attorneys is often unfair, and often denies the accused person competent and prepared defense counsel.[23]

On the other hand, the coordinated assigned counsel programs have systematic methods and procedures for the assignment of defense counsel. Some of the programs have loosely structured control over appointments; whereas, others maintain a strict level of control.[24] The coordinated assigned counsel system may be administered by the organized bar, as in San Mateo County, California;[25] a defender office, as in the state of New Jersey;[26] the county, as in King County, Washington;[27] an independent agency, as in the state of Wisconsin;[28] a judge or other court official who provides a rotating list of attorneys;[29] or a client who selects his own attorney, as in Ontario, Canada.[30]

It seems clear that lawyers join the public defender's office to gain trial experience and to make a positive contribution to society through public service.[31] However, the number of attorneys interested in this type of work is declining because of low salaries, and also due to the attraction of big law firms and corporate law,[32] and the extensive and specialized expertise needed for public defender work.[33] As a result, all too often the poor accused of crimes in our country do not receive the fair trial and the full attention to which they are entitled.

Problems and Solutions

Nowadays, the public defender's problem with money is not so much related to salary as it is the lack of sufficient funding for research provided by the federal government. Although there was a time when public defenders were paid a great deal less than the state's prosecuting attorney, today the difference between the public defender's salary and the state's prosecuting attorney's salary has decreased.[34] For example, in 1931, the public defender's salary was $300 per year; whereas, the state's attorney's salary was $1,000 per year. However, in 1984, public defenders were paid approximately $29,863 per year; and the state's attorneys were paid approximately $30,680

per year—a difference of only $817.[35] That is to say that public defenders no longer are justified to complain about the major salary difference between themselves and the state's attorneys.

On the other hand, public defenders are justified in complaining about the difference between their salaries and the salaries of young lawyers who enter legal aid groups. An entry level attorney at a legal aid group will be guaranteed a salary of at least $32,500 per year, along with some extra help with paying back student loans. Although the entry level attorney's pay at legal aid groups is under one-half of what entry level attorneys at major law firms earn, it is still higher than the public defender's salary.[36]

Furthermore, many salaried public defenders, like the ones in New York City and St. Louis, Missouri,[37] have valid reasons to complain about heavy caseloads because the federal government does not provide the necessary funds required for the adequate defense of indigents.[38] Even though public defenders are tireless and dedicated workers, they lack the resources and government funding needed for their overwhelming caseload.[39] For example, in 1983 in St. Louis, Missouri, twenty-two public defenders handled 12.000 cases on a budget of $695,000. At the same time, forty-five attorneys in the state prosecutor's office had a budget of $2.4 million.[40] Therefore, all too often, the public defender does not or cannot find the time and the money to spend researching and preparing a client's case to the best of his ability. Accordingly, indigent clients often do not receive adequate representation.

A second problem that hinders a public defender from effectively defending his client is the lack of manpower. Even though about one-half of all criminal cases in New York City and St. Louis, Missouri, involved defendants who were too poor to pay for their counsel, state and federal levels failed to support the proposed increase in the staff of the public defender office in both these cities.[41]

Furthermore, the problems stem from the attorneys themselves who do not want to become public defenders. The American Bar Association reports that 17.7% of our nation's 659,000 private attorneys practice pro bono work. In Los Angeles, Public Counsel—a group that provides the poor with legal assistance—has lost its participation from outside law firms. The total drop in participation from outside law firms is 30% since 1986.[42] The point is that not enought attorneys are willing to spend their time and money representing the poor free of charge, even though a held belief of the profession is that all lawyers should devote part of their time to pro bono work in either a public defender's office or legal aid society.[43]

Accordingly, Circuit Court Judge, Byron Kinder of Jefferson City, Missouri, subpoenaed 100 lawyers who work for Missouri agencies based in Jefferson City—the state's capital—to press them into service as public defenders for indigent criminal defendants. The U.S. Constitution guarantees a lawyer to all poor defendants. However, Cole County—the county in which Jefferson City is located—has only one public defender. Also, the county has run out of money to pay private attorneys to help out.[44]

One solution to the lack of attorneys is to make pro bono work mandatory for all private attorneys. The proposed system would allow courts, legislatures, and bar associations to force attorneys into donating their time to public defense. However, in some cases, attorneys may avoid their service obligation by paying a fee. Recently, a mandatory pro bono program has been imposed in Westchester County, New York, and El Paso, Texas.[45]

The problem with mandatory pro bono work is that its requirements are not fair to small law practices. Solo practitioners and small law firms, unlike large law firms with many young associates who can be assigned to meet pro bono requirements, will find it nearly impossible to meet pro bono quotas.[46]

Moreover, mandatory pro bono work is a problem for the indigent defendant as well as the solo practitioner. For example, some legal aid attorneys testify that 'drafting' attorneys is not the answer because it may lead to the attorney's lack of conviction and/or his lack of legal skills needed to defend the poor.[47]

The third and final problem contributing to ineffective defense counsel in the U.S. is

that few attorneys possess the expertise needed to defend the poor and carry out the functions of a public defender. All public defenders need special skills and knowledge, an unorthodox philosophy, and patience. All too often, the defense counsel in the U.S. is lacking in one or more of the aspects of expertise, resulting in ineffective public counsel for the poor.[48]

To begin with, law school students gain practical trial experience working for public defender organizations and legal aid departments. As a result, clients may be getting help from students rather than professional counsel who have acquired skill through past experience.[49] Also, the past few years, younger lawyers tend to serve people who are too poor to afford their own lawyers—especially poor persons accused of narcotics law violations. The accused person's defense in drug-related crimes requires technical statutes and procedures that many lawyers are not familiar with. Therefore, young attorneys are the ones who tend to handle the bulk of these cases, resulting in questionable representation.[50]

Furthermore, effective defense counsel need skills and knowledge to deal with the problems of the indigent. As one attorney explains, "Your clients have no funds. . . no witnesses. . . only have one name. . . hang out on the streets. . . don't have phones. . . don't have a life like the rest of us."[51]

Adding to the problem, most of the accused are not articulate and tend to be less intelligent and more sociopathic than the general population.[52] Thus, the public defender needs special skills for dealing with the poor.

Second, the problem with the lack of expertise is the lack of attorneys who are capable of having an unconventional philosophy. Since the basis of legal ethics is loyalty to the client, public defenders have ethics which are practically opposite of what is commonly understood to be ethical. If, in fact, the client did commit a crime, the defense attorney is supposed to prevent the "coming out" of the crime and the jury's recognition of the crime.[53] In other words, it would be legally unethical for a defense attorney to refrain from doing everything in his power to protect his client. For example, even when a lawyer knows that his client is a thief, the public defender must attempt to prevent the search for the victim's stolen property.[54] Because justice under the law is not always the same as true justice, public defenders often find it difficult to uphold and believe in their legal ethics. James S. Kunen, a former public defender who found it difficult to believe in legal ethics, stated the following:

> . . . my job was to get what my client wanted. . . [Judge Ugast] flew into one of his daily earnest, rages, upbraiding me for being 'an idealist' with abstract notions of legal duty and no contact with reality, adding that I typified everything that was wrong with the Public Defender Service. I was pleased . . . because. . . I shared the judge's preference for doing what you think is right, as opposed to what you are supposed to do . . . .[55]

If public defenders find it difficult to believe in legal ethics, then what are their motives to defend the indigent criminal? Aside from striving to "legitimize themselves as professionals," the public defenders' motives stem from the belief that a person is innocent until proven guilty beyond reasonable doubt. Also, they believe that it is right to defend the guilty client because—although he is guilty—he needs protection from police, prosecutorial, and judicial abuse.[56]

Finally, the third essential to defense expertise is patience. The rest of the judicial system—that is, the police, the prosecuting attorney, and the judges—along with the clients and the general public, all test the patience of the public defender.

For instance, not only must a public defender accept that he will probably not win his cases,[57] but also, he must deal with the habitual postponements of his cases. Public defenders' cases get postponed more often than cases involving private defense attorneys.[58] Some judges act as if they are being considerate of private attorneys by calling their cases before public defenders' cases because "time is money for the private attorney."[59]

In reality, some of these judges lack respect for the public defender. All too often judges are "prosecution-minded and. . . generally tougher on the defense attorney."[60] They tend to treat public defenders as "second-class lawyers."[61] One public

defender explains just how some judges treat public defenders:

> [Judges] view the public defenders very similar to how they view court clerks. We are gophers, we run for things. Whenever there's something the judge needs done, if there is not a clerk available, the judge gives it to the public defender and has him do it. They would never think of having the state's attorney do it. But public defenders have to do the silly stuff.[62]

Not only do public defenders need patience with the judicial system, but they need to have patience with their clients.

Not only do public defenders need patience with the judicial system, but they need to have patience with their clients. Clients often doubt the public defender's ability as a trial lawyer. As a result, public defenders are continually swallowing their pride for their clients—most of whom lack faith in the legal profession. One public defender protested, "I am a real lawyer, I went to a real law school, I passed a real bar exam!"[63]

Because of unappreciative clients, public defenders believe, and have the right to believe, that the people in their community do not appreciate them as competent attorneys.[64] Even though a small portion of the population does respect public defenders, the profession has clearly been degraded time and time again:

> Public defenders in America have been both maligned and idealized. Some [people] view them as champions of individual rights, the defenders of the poor and down trodden. Others see them as 'cop-out' artists who are too quick to bargain away the precious rights of their underprivileged clients.[65]

Furthermore, the public defender has the problem of developing the expertise of patience with a judicial system that delays cases to the point where witnesses disappear, and expedites trials so that the defense is at a disadvantage.[66]

Conclusion

The search for an improved public defender program continues. The ideal program would have adequate staffing and more than enough funding to assign cases to attorneys according to their experience and workload. The primary goals of the program would be efficiency, effectiveness, and productivity.[67]

The productivity measurement would include a high quality of service, which will be the most difficult to render.[68] However, despite the rocky history and recent beginning of the public defender program, the level of expertise that exists among attorneys now is much better than it was a few years ago. Therefore, the office of the public defender—although it has major problems—is improving, and will continue to improve as long as it attempts to solve its problems.

Thirty years ago the public defender office seemed to be little more than a beneficient (though ultimately benign) gesture, on the part of a few county governments, toward poor people in trouble with the law. . . But. . . public defenders today play such an important role in the administration of criminal justice that without them, the work of our urban criminal courts especially would come to a standstill.[69]

[1] Lisa McIntyre, *The Public Defender* (Chicago, Illinois: The University of Chicago Press, 1987), p. 86.

[2] "Public Defenders," *Funk and Wagnalls New World Encyclopedia,* 1983.

[3] William McDonald, *The Defense Counsel* (Beverly Hills, California: Sage Publications, 1983), p. 79.

[4] "Public Defenders Assail Felony Judges' New Rules to Speed Court Cases," *Milwaukee Journal,* October 28, 1988, p. A1, Col. 1–6.

[5] James Kunen, *How Can You Defend Those People?* (New York: Random House, 1983), p. vii.

[6] *Ibid.,* p. vii.

[7] United States Constitution, Amendment 6.

[8] *Ibid.,* p. 314.

[9] McIntyre, p. 21.

[10] McDonald, p. 76.

[11] Robert Janosik, *Encyclopedia of the American Judicial System* (New York: Charles Scribner's Sons, 1972), p. 645.

[12] *Ibid.,* p. 645.

[13] *Ibid.,* p. 645.

[14] *Ibid.,* p. 646.

[15] McDonald, p. 81.

[16] McIntyre, p. 21.

[17] *Ibid.,* p. 21.

[18] *Ibid.,* p. 21.

[19] McDonald, p. 76.

[20] McIntyre, p. 21.

[21] Janosik, p. 645.

[22] McDonald, p. 85.

[23] *Ibid.,* p. 86.

[24] *Ibid.,* p. 87.

[25] *Ibid.,* p. 87.

[26] *Ibid.,* p. 88.

[27] *Ibid.,* p. 88.

[28] Richard J. Phelps, *Office of the State Public Defender Biennial Report* (Madison, Wisconsin: 1987), p. 5.

[29] McDonald, p. 89.

[30] *Ibid.,* p. 89.

[31] McIntyre, p. 86.

[32] R. Lacayo, "The Sad Fate of Legal Aid," *Time,* June 20, 1988, p. 59.

[33] B. Kinder, "Lawyer Round-up in Jeff City," *Time,* May 4, 1981, p. 44.

[34] McIntyre, p. 90.

[35] *Ibid.,* p. 90.

[36] Lacayo, p. 59.

[37] Janosik, p. 645.

[38] Denise Shekerjian, *Competent Counsel: Working With Lawyers* (New York: Dodd, Mead, and Co., 1985), p. 55.

[39] *Ibid.,* p. 55.

[40] Janosik, p. 645.

[41] *Ibid.,* p. 645.

[42] Lacayo, p. 59.

[43] *Ibid.,* p. 59.

[44] Kinder, p. 44.

[45] Lacayo, p. 59.

[46] *Ibid.,* p. 59.

[47] *Ibid.,* p. 59.

[48] Kinder, p. 44.

[49] Henry Poor, *You and the Law* (New York: Reader's Digest, 1984), p. 733.

[50] *Ibid.,* p. 736.

[51] McIntyre, p. 144.

[52] *Ibid.,* p. 144.

[53] James Kunen, "How Can You Defend Those People?" *Harper's,* April, 1982, p. 83.

[54] *Ibid.,* p. 86.

[55] *Ibid.,* p. 82.

[56] McIntyre, p. 169.

[57] *Ibid.,* p. 162.

[58] Kunen, p. 83.

[59] McIntyre, . 87.

[60] *Ibid.,* p. 87.

[61] *Ibid.,* p. 87.

[62] *Ibid.,* p. 88.

[63] *Ibid.,* p. 89.

[64] *Ibid.,* p. 87.

[65] McDonald, p. 67.

[66] Kunen, p. 83.

[67] McDonald, p. 299.

[68] *Ibid.,* p. 299.

[69] McIntyre, p. 1.

ABUSE OF POWER IN THE PROSECUTOR'S OFFICE

Bennett L. Gershman

Bennett L. Gershman is professor of law at Pace University. He is the author of Prosecutorial Misconduct *and several articles on law dealing with such topics as entrapment and police and prosecutorial ethics. For ten years, he was a prosecutor in New York.*

The prosecutor is the most dominant figure in the American criminal justice system. As the Supreme Court recently observed, "Between the private life of the citizen and the public glare of criminal accusation stands the prosecutor. [The prosecutor has] the power to employ the full machinery of the State in scrutinizing any given individual." Thus, the prosecutor decides whether or not to bring criminal charges; whom to charge; what charges to bring; whether a defendant will stand trial, plead guilty, or enter a correctional program in lieu of criminal charges; and whether to confer immunity from prosecution. In jurisdictions that authorize capital punishment, the prosecutor literally decides who shall live and who shall die. Moreover, in carrying out these broad functions, the prosecutor enjoys considerable independence from the courts, administrative superiors, and the public. A prosecutor cannot be forced to bring criminal charges, or be prevented from bringing them. Needless to say, the awesome power that prosecutors exercise is susceptible to

abuse. Such abuses most frequently occur in connection with the prosecutor's power to bring charges; to control the information used to convict those on trial; and to influence juries.

The prosecutor's charging power includes the virtually unfettered discretion to invoke or deny punishment, and therefore the power to control and destroy people's lives. Such prosecutorial discretion has been called "tyrannical," "lawless," and "most dangerous." Prosecutors may not unfairly select which persons to prosecute. But this rule is difficult to enforce, and the courts almost always defer to the prosecutor's discretion. In one recent case, for example, a prosecutor targeted for prosecution a vocal opponent of the Selective Service system who refused to register, rather than any of nearly a million nonvocal persons who did not register. The proof showed that the defendant clearly was selected for prosecution not because he failed to register but because he exercised his First Amendment rights. This was a legally impermissible basis for prosecution. Nevertheless, the courts refused to disturb the prosecutor's decision, because there was no clear proof of prosecutorial bad faith. Many other disturbing examples exist of improper selection based on race, sex, religion, and the exercise of constitutional rights. These cases invariably are decided in the prosecutor's favor. The reasoning is circular. The courts presume that prosecutors act in good faith, and that the prosecutor's expertise, law enforcement plans, and priorities are ill suited to judicial review.

Unfair selectivity is one of the principal areas of discretionary abuse. Another is prosecutorial retaliation in the form of increased charges after defendants raise statutory or constitutional claims. Prosecutors are not allowed to be vindictive in response to a defendant's exercise of rights. Nevertheless, proving vindictiveness, as with selectiveness, is virtually impossible. Courts simply do not probe the prosecutor's state of mind. For example, prosecutors often respond to a defendant's unwillingness to plead guilty to a crime by bringing higher charges. In one recent case, a defendant charged with a petty offense refused to plead guilty despite prosecutorial threats to bring much higher charges. The prosecutor carried out his threat and brought new charges carrying a sentence of life imprisonment. The court found the prosecutor's conduct allowable. Although the prosecutor behaved in a clearly retaliatory fashion, the court nevertheless believed that the prosecutor needed this leverage to make the system work. If the prosecutor could not threaten defendants by "upping the ante," so the court reasoned, there would be fewer guilty pleas and the system would collapse.

Finally, some prosecutions are instituted for illegitimate personal objectives as opposed to ostensibly valid law enforcement objectives. Such prosecutions can be labeled demagogic and usually reveal actual prosecutorial malice or evil intent. Telltale signs of demagoguery often include the appearance of personal vendettas, political crusades, and witch hunts. Examples of this base practice abound. They have involved prosecutions based on racial or political hostility; prosecutions motivated by personal and political gain; and prosecutions to discourage or coerce the exercise of constitutional rights. One notorious example was New Orleans District Attorney James Garrison's prosecution of Clay Shaw for the Kennedy assassination. Other examples have included the prosecutions of labor leader James Hoffa, New York attorney Roy Cohn, and civil rights leader Dr. Martin Luther King.

HIDING EVIDENCE

A prosecutor's misuse of power also occurs in connection with legal proof. In the course of an investigation, in pretrial preparation, or even during a trial, prosecutors often become aware of information that might exonerate a defendant. It is not unusual for the prosecutor to have such proof, in view of the acknowledged superiority of law enforcement's investigative resources and its early access to crucial evidence. The adversary system relies on a fair balance of opposing forces. But one of the greatest threats to rational and fair fact-finding in criminal cases comes from the prosecutor's hiding evidence that might prove a defendant's innocence. Examples of prosecutorial suppression of exculpatory evidence are numerous. Such conduct is pernicious for several reasons: It skews the ability of the adversary system to function properly by denying to the defense crucial proof; it undermines the public's respect for and confidence in the public prosecutor's office; and it has resulted in many defendants being unjustly convicted, with the consequent loss of their liberty or even their lives.

Consider the following recent examples. Murder convictions of Randall Dale Adams in Texas, James Richardson and Joseph Brown in Florida, and Eric Jackson in New York all were vacated because the prosecutors hid crucial evidence that would have proved these defendants' innocence. The Adams case—popularized by the film *The Thin Blue Line*—depicts Texas "justice" at its worst. Adams was convicted in 1977 of murdering a policeman and sentenced to die largely on the testimony of a juvenile with a long criminal record who made a secret deal with the prosecutor to implicate Adams, and the testimony of two eyewitnesses to the killing. The juvenile actually murdered the policeman, as he later acknowledged. At Adams' trial, however, the prosecutor suppressed information about the deal and successfully kept from the jury the juvenile's lengthy record.

The prosecutor also withheld evidence that the two purported eyewitnesses had failed to identify Adams in a line-up, and permitted these witnesses to testify that they had made a positive identification of Adams. A Texas court recently freed Adams, finding that the prosecutor suborned perjury and knowingly suppressed evidence.

Richardson—whose case was memorialized in the book *Arcadia* was condemned to die for poisoning to death his

tor misrepresented to the jury that ballistics evidence proved the defendant's guilt, when in fact the prosecutor knew that the ballistics report showed that the bullet that killed the deceased could not have been fired from the defendant's weapon.

Eric Jackson was convicted of murder in 1980 for starting a fire at Waldbaum's supermarket in Brooklyn in which a roof collapsed and six firefighters died. Years later, the attorney who repre-

---

Abuses most frequently occur in connection with the prosecutor's power to bring charges, to control the information used to convict those on trial, and to influence juries.

---

seven children in 1967. The prosecutor claimed that Richardson, a penniless farm worker, killed his children to collect insurance. A state judge last year overturned the murder conviction, finding that the prosecutor had suppressed evidence that would have shown Richardson's innocence. The undisclosed evidence included a sworn statement from the children's babysitter that she had killed the youngsters; a sworn statement from a cellmate of Richardson's that the cellmate had been beaten by a sheriff's deputy into fabricating his story implicating Richardson; statements from other inmates contradicting their claims that Richardson confessed to them; and proof that Richardson had never purchased any insurance.

Brown's murder conviction recently was reversed by the Eleventh Circuit. Brown was only hours away from being electrocuted when his execution was stayed. That court found that the prosecutor "knowingly allowed material false testimony to be introduced at trial, failed to step forward and make the falsity known, and knowingly exploited the false testimony in its closing argument to the jury." The subornation of perjury related to the testimony of a key prosecution witness who falsely denied that a deal had been made with the prosecutor, and the prosecutor's misrepresentation of that fact to the court. In addition, the prosecu-

sented the families of the deceased firemen in a tort action discovered that one of the prosecutor's expert witnesses at the trial had informed the prosecutor that the fire was not arson related, but was caused by an electrical malfunction. At a hearing in the fall of 1988, the prosecutor consistently maintained that nothing had been suppressed and offered to disclose pertinent documents. The judge rejected the offer and personally inspected the prosecutor's file. The judge found in that file two internal memoranda from two different assistant district attorneys to an executive in the prosecutor's office. Each memorandum stated that the expert witness had concluded that the fire had resulted from an electrical malfunction and had not been deliberately set— and that the expert's conclusion presented a major problem for the prosecution. None of this information was ever revealed to the defense. On the basis of the above, the court vacated the conviction and ordered the defendant's immediate release.

To be sure, disclosure is the one area above all else that relies on the prosecutor's good faith and integrity. If the prosecutor hides evidence, it is likely that nobody will ever know. The information will lay buried forever in the prosecutor's files. Moreover, most prosecutors, if they are candid, will concede that their inclination in this area is not to reveal information that might damage his or her case. Ironically, in this important area in which the prosecutor's fairness, integrity, and good faith are so dramatically put to the test, the courts have defaulted. According to the courts, the prosecutor's good or bad faith in secreting evidence is irrelevant. It is the character of the evidence that counts, not the character of the prosecutor. Thus, even if a violation is deliberate, and with an intent to harm the defendant, the courts will not order relief unless the evidence is so crucial that it would have changed the verdict. Thus, there is no real incentive for prosecutors to disclose such evidence.

Hopefully, in light of the recent disclosures of prosecutorial misconduct, courts, bar associations, and even legislatures will wake up to the quagmire in criminal justice. These bodies should act vigorously and aggressively to deter and punish the kinds of violations that recur all too frequently. Thus, reversals should be required automatically for deliberate suppression of evidence, and the standards for reversal for nondeliberate suppression relaxed; disciplinary action against prosecutors should be the rule rather than the exception; and legislation should be enacted making it a crime for prosecutors to willfully suppress evidence resulting in a defendant's conviction.

MISBEHAVING IN THE COURTROOM TO SWAY THE JURY

Finally, the prosecutor's trial obligations often are violated. The duties of the prosecuting attorney during a trial were well stated in a classic opinion fifty years ago. The interest of the prosecutor, the court wrote, "is not that it shall win a case, but that justice shall be done. As such, he is in a peculiar and very definite sense the servant of the law, the twofold aim of which is that guilt shall not escape or innocence suffer. He may prosecute with earnestness and vigor—indeed, he should do so. But, while he may strike hard blows, he is not at liberty to strike a foul one."

Despite this admonition, prosecutors continually strike "foul blows." In one leading case of outrageous conduct, a prosecutor concealed from the jury in a murder case the fact that a pair of undershorts with red stains on it, a crucial piece of evidence, was stained not by blood but by paint. In another recent case, a prosecutor, in his summation, characterized the defendant as an "animal," told the jury that "the only guarantee against his future crimes would be to execute him," and that he should have "his face blown away by a shotgun." In another case, the prosecutor argued that the defendant's attorney knew the defendant was guilty; otherwise he would have put the defendant on the witness stand.

The above examples are illustrative of common practices today, and the main reason such misconduct occurs is quite simple: It works. Indeed, several studies have shown the importance of oral advocacy in the courtroom, as well as the effect produced by such conduct. For example, a student of trial advocacy often is told of the importance of the opening statement. Prosecutors would undoubtedly agree that the opening statement is indeed crucial. In a University of Kansas study, the importance of the opening statement was confirmed. From this study, the authors concluded that in the course of any given trial, the jurors were affected most by the first strong presentation that they saw. This finding leads to the conclusion that if a prosecutor were to present a particularly strong opening argument, the jury would favor the prosecution throughout the trial. Alternatively, if the prosecutor were to provide a weak opening statement, followed by a strong opening statement by the defense, then, according to the authors, the jury would favor the defense during the trial. It thus becomes evident that the prosecutor will be best served by making the strongest opening argument possible, thereby assisting the jury in gaining a better insight into what they are about to hear and see. The opportunity for the prosecutor to influence the jury at this point in the trial is considerable, and many prosecutors use this opportunity to their advantage, even if the circumstances do not call for lengthy or dramatic opening remarks.

An additional aspect of the prosecutor's power over the jury is suggested in a University of North Carolina study, which found that the more arguments counsel raises to support the different substantive arguments offered, the more the jury will believe in that party's case. Moreover, this study found that there is not necessarily a correlation between the amount of objective information in the argument and the persuasiveness of the presentation.

For the trial attorney, then, this study clearly points to the advantage of raising as many issues as possible at trial. For the prosecutor, the two studies taken together would dictate an "action-packed" opening statement, containing as many arguments as can be mustered, even those that might be irrelevant or unnecessary to convince the jury of the defendant's guilt. The second study would also dictate the same strategy for the closing argument. Consequently, a prosecutor who through use of these techniques attempts to assure that the jury knows his case may, despite violating ethical standards to seek justice, be "rewarded" with a guilty verdict. Thus, one begins to perceive the incentive that leads the prosecutor to misbehave in the courtroom.

Similar incentives can be seen with respect to the complex problem of controlling evidence to which the jury may have access. It is common knowledge that in the course of any trial, statements fre-

dence on the decisions of jurors. The authors of the test designed a variety of scenarios whereby some jurors heard about an incriminating piece of evidence while other jurors did not. The study found that the effect of the inadmissible evidence was directly correlated to the strength of the prosecutor's case. The authors of the study reported that when the prosecutor presented a weak case, the inadmissible evidence did in fact prejudice the jurors. Furthermore, the judge's admonition to the jurors to disregard certain evidence did not have the same effect as when the evidence had not been mentioned at all. It had a prejudicial impact anyway.

However, the study also indicated that when there was a strong prosecution case, the inadmissible evidence had little, if any, effect. Nonetheless, the most significant conclusion from the study is that inadmissible evidence had its most prejudicial impact when there was little other evidence upon which the jury could base a decision. In this situation, "the controversial evidence becomes quite salient in the jurors' minds."

Finally, with respect to inadmissible evidence and stricken testimony, even if

---

In one leading case of outrageous conduct, a prosecutor concealed from the jury in a murder case the fact that a pair of undershorts with red stains on it, a crucial piece of evidence, was stained not by blood but by paint.

---

quently are made by the attorneys or witnesses despite the fact that these statements may not be admissible as evidence. Following such a statement, the trial judge may, at the request of opposing counsel, instruct the jury to disregard what they have heard. Most trial lawyers, if they are candid, will agree that it is virtually impossible for jurors realistically to disregard these inadmissible statements. Studies here again demonstrate that our intuition is correct and that this evidence often is considered by jurors in reaching a verdict.

For example, an interesting study conducted at the University of Washington tested the effects of inadmissible evi-

one were to reject all of the studies discussed, it is still clear that although "stricken testimony may tend to be rejected in open discussion, it does have an impact, perhaps even an unconscious one, on the individual juror's judgment." As with previously discussed points, this factor—the unconscious effect of stricken testimony or evidence—will generally not be lost on the prosecutor who is in tune with the psychology of the jury.

The applicability of these studies to the issue of prosecutorial misconduct, then, is quite clear. Faced with a difficult case in which there may be a problem of proof, a prosecutor might be tempted to try to sway the jury by adverting to a matter that might be highly prejudicial. In this connection, another study has suggested that the jury will more likely consider inadmissible evidence that favors conviction.

Despite this factor of "defense favoritism," it is again evident that a prosecutor may find it rewarding to misconduct himself or herself in the courtroom. Of course, a prosecutor who adopts the unethical norm and improperly allows jurors to hear inadmissible proof runs the risk of jeopardizing any resulting conviction. In a situation where the prosecutor feels that he has a weak case, however, a subsequent reversal is not a particularly effective sanction when a conviction might have been difficult to achieve in the first place. Consequently, an unethical courtroom "trick" can be a very attractive idea to the prosecutor who feels he must win. Additionally, there is always the possibility of another conviction even after an appellate reversal. Indeed, while a large number of cases are dismissed following remand by an appellate court, nearly one-half of reversals still result in some type of conviction. Therefore, a pros-

moral standards, the problem of courtroom misconduct will inevitably be tolerated by the public.

Moreover, when considering the problems facing the prosecutor, one also must consider the tremendous stress under which the prosecutor labors on a daily basis. Besides the stressful conditions faced by the ordinary courtroom litigator, prosecuting attorneys, particularly those in large metropolitan areas, are faced with huge and very demanding caseloads. As a result of case volume and time demands, prosecutors may not be able to take advantage of opportunities to relax and recover from the constant onslaught their emotions face every day in the courtroom.

Under these highly stressful conditions, it is understandable that a prosecutor occasionally may find it difficult to face these everyday pressures and to resist temptations to behave unethically. It is not unreasonable to suggest that the conditions under which the prosecutor works can have a profound effect on his attempt to maintain high moral and ethical standards. Having established this hy-

An unethical courtroom "trick" can be a very attractive idea to the prosecutor who feels he must win.

ecutor can still succeed in obtaining a conviction even after his misconduct led to a reversal.

An additional problem in the area of prosecutor-jury interaction is the prosecutor's prestige; since the prosecutor represents the "government," jurors are more likely to believe him. Put simply, prosecutors are the "good guys" of the legal system, and because they have such glamor, they often may be tempted to use this advantage in an unethical manner. This presents a problem in that the average citizen may often forgive prosecutors for ethical indiscretions, because conviction of criminals certainly justifies in the public eye any means necessary. Consequently, unless the prosecutor is a person of high integrity and able to uphold the highest

pothesis, we see yet another reason why courtroom misconduct may occur.

WHY PROSECUTORIAL MISCONDUCT PERSISTS

Although courtroom misconduct may in many instances be highly effective, why do such practices continue in our judicial system? A number of reasons may account for this phenomenon, perhaps the most significant of which is the harmless error doctrine. Under this doctrine, an appellate court can affirm a conviction despite the presence of serious misconduct during the trial. As one judge stated, the "practical objective of tests of harmless error is to conserve judicial resources by enabling appellate courts to cleanse the judicial process of prejudicial error without becoming mired in harmless error."

Although this definition portrays harmless error as having a most desirable consequence, this desirability is undermined when the prosecutor is able to misconduct himself without fear of sanction. Additionally, since every case is different, what constitutes harmless error in one case may be reversible error in another case. Consequently, harmless error determinations do not offer any significant precedents by which prosecutors can judge the status of their behavior. Moreover, harmless error determinations are essentially absurd. In order to apply the harmless error rule, appellate judges attempt to evaluate how various evidentiary items or instances of prosecutorial misconduct may have affected the jury's verdict. Although it may be relatively simple in some cases to determine whether improper conduct during a trial was harmless, there are many instances when such an analysis cannot be properly made but nevertheless is made. There are numerous instances in which appellate courts are deeply divided over whether or not a given error was harmless. The implications of these contradictory decisions are significant, for they demonstrate the utter failure of appellate courts to provide incentives for the prosecutor to control his behavior. If misconduct can be excused even when reasonable judges differ as to the extent of harm caused by such misbehavior, then very little guidance is given to a prosecutor to assist him in determining the propriety of his actions. Clearly, without such guidance, the potential for misconduct significantly increases.

A final point when analyzing why prosecutorial misconduct persists is the unavailability or inadequacy of penalties visited upon the prosecutor personally in the event of misconduct. Punishment in our legal system comes in varying degrees. An appellate court can punish a prosecutor by simply cautioning him not to act in the same manner again, reversing his case, or, in some cases, identifying by name the prosecutor who misconducted himself. Even these punishments, however, may not be sufficient to dissuade prosecutors from acting improperly. One noteworthy case describes a prosecutor who appeared before the appellate court on a misconduct issue for the third time, each instance in a different case.

Perhaps the ultimate reason for the ineffectiveness of the judicial system in curbing prosecutorial misconduct is that prosecutors are not personally liable for their misconduct. During the course of a trial, the prosecutor is absolutely shielded from any civil liability that might arise due to his or her misconduct, even if that misconduct was performed with malice. To be sure, there is clearly a necessary level of immunity accorded all government officials. Without such immunity, much of what is normally done by officials in authority might not be performed, out of fear that their practices would later be deemed harmful or improper. Granting prosecutors a certain level of immunity is reasonable. Allowing prosecutors to be completely shielded from civil liability in the event of misconduct, however, provides no deterrent to courtroom misconduct.

For the prosecutor, the temptation to cross over the allowable ethical limit must often be tremendous, because of the distinct advantages that such misconduct creates with respect to assisting the prosecutor to win his case by effectively influencing the jury. Most prosecutors must inevitably be subject to this temptation. It takes a constant effort on the part of every prosecutor to maintain the high moral standards necessary to avoid such temptations. Despite the frequent occurrences of courtroom misconduct, appellate courts have not provided significant incentives to deter it. Inroads will not be made in the effort to end prosecutorial misconduct until the courts decide to take a stricter, more consistent approach to this problem.

These Clients Aren't Fools

Representing themselves, three prisoners have taken their cases to the U.S. Supreme Court

Colorado state inmate No. 48201 is not your typical killer.

On the high prairie east of Pueblo, along the tracks of the Union Pacific, Richard S. Demarest does his prison time differently from most of the other 985 burglars, embezzlers and assorted felons. They mop, they cook, they exercise. Demarest, by contrast, spends 12 hours a day in the law library—as clerk, computer jockey and self-made Darrow. Though he has yet to overturn his conviction for murdering a roommate—he's still working on that—Demarest has put the time to impressive use: 18 months ago he wrote his own petition to the U.S. Supreme Court, challenging an ancient federal policy against paying prisoners who testify in court the same fee received by all other witnesses. This term, the justices agreed to hear the appeal.

That by itself was an achievement for Demarest. Of the roughly 5,000 petitions filed every year with the high court, only 130 or so are accepted to fill the seven-month calendar. While most of these petitions are written by hired lawyers, several hundred are prepared directly by the aggrieved parties—usually prisoners—who obviously have the most to gain from a successful appeal. These are called *pro se* cases, literally, "for himself." Only if the justices grant review does a real attorney get involved. The court appoints someone to write a full brief and argue the case in person. But very few are accepted. In each of the four terms before 1990–1991, for example, just one pro se case made the cut. Most of the others, says a former court clerk, "just spout gibberish."

This term, in an unexplained and unexpected development, the justices agreed to hear five pro se appeals, all

from inmates. One was subsequently dismissed on technical grounds; another, NEWSWEEK discovered, wasn't really written by the prisoner. The other three, though, represent notable curiosities in an era where litigation has become a team sport. Whatever their crimes, Richard Demarest, along with Dawud Mu'min of Virginia and John J. McCarthy of Kansas, are lone warriors. Their stories show the tenacity of three men who have made good on the ultimate legal pledge: by Jove, we'll take this case all the way to the Supreme Court.

The pro se tradition is rooted in the most fundamental of American constitutional birthrights—the right to be heard. It extends even to the freedom of jailhouse lawyers to represent other inmates (box). The tradition was mythologized in "Gideon's Trumpet," the 1964 classic by Anthony Lewis about an obscure felon who handwrote a plea to the Supreme Court. Clarence Gideon had been convicted of larceny, without a lawyer because he couldn't afford one. His legal beef: the Sixth Amendment ought to guarantee counsel. The justices took the case and went on to issue a landmark ruling.

Dawud Mu'min, on death row in southern Virginia, is determined to be another Gideon. Mu'min, 38, was first sent to prison in 1973 for murder. On Sept. 22, 1988, while on a work detail,

---

The Law in Their Own Hands

Jailhouse lawyers start out pleading their own cases. Some go on to build practices behind the walls.

Caryl Chessman: The most famous death-row inmate of the 1950s, Chessman battled execution for 12 years. Before lawyers came to his aid, he wrote his own appeals—and a best-selling autobiography. In 1960, he died in the California gas chamber.

Clarence Gideon: Imprisoned for petty theft, the 51-year-old drifter made history with a handwritten appeal to the U.S. Supreme Court. In 1963, the court overturned his Florida conviction; the case gave indigent defendants the right to have lawyers.

Jerry Rosenberg: Serving a life sentence for participating in the 1962 killing of two policemen, the eighth-grade dropout has earned two law degrees and helped numerous New York convicts in their legal battles.

Doyle Williams: In 10 years on Missouri's death row, he has won five trials involving prisoners' rights, despite having to argue before juries while wearing leg irons. A day before his scheduled execution last month, Williams won a stay.

Mu'min slipped away to a local carpet store, where he attacked the owner, stabbing her 17 times with a screwdriver he kept in his shirt pocket. The trial received lots of attention in the local press. Concerned about the adverse effects of pretrial publicity, Mu'min's trial lawyer sought to examine prospective jurors in detail about what they had heard of the case. The judge limited him to vague and general questions. Only one member of the jury pool was dismissed. Mu'min was convicted of capital murder and the Virginia Supreme Court upheld the verdict. "I started thinking about an appeal the moment the jury came back," Mu'min says, sitting in the visitors' lounge at the Mecklenburg Correctional Center.

Thanks to a local judge who attended the trial out of personal interest and passed along advice, Mu'min focused on the questions to the prospective jurors. He and his mother tried to find counsel, even calling a relative who had worked for F. Lee Bailey. They had no luck. Mu'min, who earned a correspondence college degree in prison, started doing the research himself, spending 10 hours a week in the prison law library, the maximum permitted. In addition he got help from a lawyer paid by the state to assist inmates. Mu'min had never read a court decision. "Law is very confusing," he says. "If you write in ordinary language, you're not going to get anywhere." While Mu'min maintains his innocence, his petition was based on procedural errors. "How can you find out what sort of preconceived ideas a juror might have if you can't even ask the questions?" he says. The court is expected to rule by July. "If they deny it, I'll be back in the law library," he vows in

a voice mixed with fire and resignation and fear. "My life is at stake."

John McCarthy, 36, has now taken up residence in the Leavenworth federal penitentiary in Kansas. He is serving a 10-to-20-year sentence for stealing $42,000 worth of silverware from a Connecticut home. In fact, McCarthy is technically a prisoner of that state who was transferred for disciplinary reasons. A run-in with Connecticut guards is the basis for his day in the Supreme Court. Claiming they used excessive force in moving him from one cell to another, McCarthy filed a civil-rights suit seeking damages. The case was referred to a magistrate who dismissed his claim. On appeal, McCarthy argues that he was entitled to a trial before a regular judge.

Hitting the stacks was McCarthy's only chance at vindication. "I could have waited 10 years before getting counsel," he says. "So I started reading things like 'Criminal Law in a Nutshell.' I can research anything." It would appear so. McCarthy, who has an eighth-grade education, speaks the lingo of the law and understands its byways. "The trouble with a lot of lawyers," he observes, "is that they know they have no case and they file anyway." About his own challenge, McCarthy is an optimist and a cynic. "I believe in the principles of Rocky Marciano—you never quit," he says. "But I don't think the courts follow justice. The government wins and the rules are drawn that way."

Quickie divorces: Unlike Mu'min or McCarthy, the 43-year-old Demarest has an interest in the law beyond its potential to free him. Indeed, even though Demarest in January won a unanimous decision from the Supreme

Court, it had nothing to do with his underlying conviction, for which he isn't eligible for parole until 2001; all he stands to receive is $300. "It's the principle," Demarest says. "I was called to testify about another inmate. The statute said I was entitled to $30 a day."

A high-school graduate with two years of college, he is now an encyclopedia of legal decisions and can recite last month's developments as readily as others describe yesterday's box scores. He has become a legend in the Colorado penal system. In the last 30 months alone, he has handled 70 name changes and 300 divorces for inmates. "My quickie divorces take six minutes," he says. He's created Apple databases for tax returns, estate filings and even a digest of Supreme Court precedents. If he can raise $9,000, he plans to enroll in a correspondence law school. Officials have consulted Demarest before designing law libraries. "Working in the library has been a godsend," he says. "It's a job I'll never master."

His brief to the Supreme Court on the arcane subject of witness fees was so good that the firm appointed to present it to the high court (Washington's Arnold & Porter, whose founding partner, Abe Fortas, represented Gideon) hardly needed to do more work. At the oral argument, Justice Byron White admiringly asked counsel, "Did Mr. Demarest think up this claim by himself?"

Congress may get the last laugh in the case. Already legislation has been introduced to undo the Supreme Court decision. That doesn't faze Demarest. "I won," he beams. "When I called my parents to tell them, they were so proud. I changed American law." That sure beats breaking it.

David A. Kaplan and Bob Cohn

Convicting the Innocent

JAMES McCLOSKEY

James McCloskey is Director of Centurion Ministries, Inc, Princeton, N.J.

On most occasions when it has been discovered that the wrong person was convicted for another's crime, the local law enforcement community, if it has commented at all, has assured the public that such instances are indeed rare and isolated aberrations of a criminal justice system that bats nearly 1,000 percent in convicting the guilty and acquitting the innocent. And this view is shared, I think, not only by the vast majority of the public but also by almost all of the professionals (lawyers and judges) whose work comes together to produce the results.

I realize that I am a voice crying in the wilderness, but I believe that the innocent are convicted far more frequently than the public cares to believe, and far more frequently than those who operate the system dare to believe. An innocent person in prison, in my view, is about as rare as a pigeon in the park. The primary purpose of this article is to delineate why and how I have come to believe that this phenomenon of the "convicted innocent" is so alarmingly widespread in the United States. Although no one has any real idea of what proportion it has reached, it is my perception that at least 10 percent of those convicted of serious and violent crimes are completely innocent. Those whose business it is to convict or to defend would more than likely concede to such mistakes occurring in only 1 percent of cases, if that. Regardless of where the reader places his estimate, these percentages, when converted into absolute numbers, tell us that thousands

and even tens of thousands of innocent people languish in prisons across the nation.

Allow me to outline briefly the ground of experience on which I stand and speak. For the past eight years I have been working full time on behalf of the innocent in prison. To date, the nonprofit organization I founded to do this work has freed and vindicated three innocent lifers in New Jersey. Another, on Texas's death row, has been declared "innocent" by a specially appointed evidentiary hearing judge, who has recommended a new trial to Texas's highest court. Currently we are working on ten cases across the country (New Jersey, Pennsylvania, Virginia, Louisiana, Texas, and California). We have received well over 1,000 requests for assistance and have developed extensive files on more than 500 of these requests, which come to us daily from every state of the nation from those who have been convicted, or from their advocates, proclaiming their innocence. We serve as active advisors on many of those cases.

Besides being innocent and serving life or death sentences, our beneficiaries have lost their legal appeals. Their freedom can be secured only by developing new evidence sufficient to earn a retrial. This new evidence must materially demonstrate either that the person is not guilty or that the key state witnesses lied in critical areas of their testimony. We are not lawyers. We are concerned only with whether the person is in fact completely not guilty in that he or she had

nothing whatsoever to do with the crime. When we enter the case it is usually five to fifteen years after the conviction. Our sole focus is to reexamine the factual foundation of the conviction -- to conduct an exhaustive investigation of the cast of characters and the circumstances in the case, however long that might take.

We find and interview as often as necessary anyone who has knowledge about the case and/or the people who are related to the case. We search for documentation and employ whatever forensic scientific tests are available that in any way shed light on, point to, or establish the truth of the matter. While developing this new information, we retain and work with the most suitable attorney in seeking judicial relief for our clients. We raise and disburse whatever funds are required to meet the legal, investigative, and administrative costs of seeking justice for these otherwise forgotten and forsaken souls buried in our prisons all across the land.

Appellate Relief for the Convicted Innocent

As all lawyers and jurists know, but most lay people do not, innocence or guilt is irrelevant when seeking redress in the appellate courts. As the noted attorney F. Lee Bailey observed, "Appellate courts have only one function, and that is to correct legal mistakes of a serious nature made by a judge at a lower level. Should a jury have erred by believing a lying witness, or by drawing an

Reprinted from *Criminal Justice Ethics*, Vol. 8, No. 1 (Winter/Spring 1989), pp. 2, 54-59. Reprinted by permission.

attractive but misleading inference, there is nothing to appeal." So, if the imprisoned innocent person is unable to persuade the appellate judges of any legal errors at trial, and generally he cannot, even though he suffered the ultimate trial error, he has no recourse. Nothing can be done legally to free him unless new evidence somehow surfaces that impeaches the validity of the conviction. Commonly, the incarcerated innocent are rubber-stamped into oblivion throughout the appeals process, both at the state and at the federal level.

So where does that leave the innocent person once he is convicted? Dead in the water, that's where! He is screaming his head off that he is innocent, but no one believes him. One of our beneficiaries standing before his sentencing judge told him, "Your Honor . . . I will eat a stone, I will eat dust, I will eat anything worse in the world for me to prove my innocence. I am not the man. I am innocent. I am not the man." The jury didn't believe him. The judge didn't. Certainly the prosecutor didn't, and more important than all of these put together, neither did his trial attorney nor his appellate lawyer. And so it goes for the convicted innocent. Their cries of innocence will forever fall on deaf ears and cynical minds.

Once he is convicted, no one in whose hands his life is placed (his lawyer and the appellate judges) either believes him or is concerned about his innocence or guilt. It is no longer an issue of relevance. The only question remaining that is important or material is whether he "legally" received a fair trial, not whether the trial yielded a result that was factually accurate. Appellate attorneys are not expected to, nor do they have the time, inclination, and resources to, initiate an investigation designed to unearth new evidence that goes to the question of a false conviction. Such an effort is simply beyond the scope of their thinking and beyond the realm of their professional responsibility. It is a rare attorney indeed who would dare go before any American appellate court and attempt to win a retrial for his client based on his innocence. That's like asking an actor in a Shakespearian tragedy to go on stage and pretend it's a comedy. It is simply not done.

Causes of Wrongful Conviction

But enough of this post-conviction appellate talk. That's putting the cart before the horse. Let's return to the trial and discuss those elements that commonly combine to convict the innocent. Let me state at the outset that each of these ingredients is systemic and not peculiar to one part of the country or one type of case. We see these elements as constant themes or patterns informing the cases that cross our desks. They are the seeds that sow wrongful convictions. After one has reflected on them individually and as a whole, it becomes readily apparent, I think, how easy it is and how real the potential is in every courthouse in America for wrongful convictions to take place.

(a) *Presumption of Guilt* The first factor I would like to consider is the "presumption-of-innocence" principle. Although we would all like to believe that a defendant is truly considered innocent by those who represent and judge him, this is just not so. Once accusations have matured through the system to the point at which the accused is actually brought to trial, is it not the tendency of human nature to suspect deep down or even believe that the defendant probably did it? Most people are inclined to believe that where there is smoke, there is fire. This applies to professional and lay people alike albeit for different reasons perhaps.

The innate inclinations of the average American law-abiding citizen whose jury experience is that person's first

Most people are inclined to believe that where there is smoke, there is fire.

exposure to the criminal justice system is to think that law enforcement people have earnestly investigated the case and surely would not bring someone to trial unless they had bona fide evidence against the person. That is a strong barrier and a heavy burden for the defense to overcome. And how about judges and defense lawyers? These professionals, like members of any profession, have a natural tendency to become somewhat cynical and callous with time. After all, isn't it true that the great majority of the defendants who have paraded before them

in the past have been guilty? Why should this case be any different? As far as defense attorneys are concerned, if they really believe in their clients' innocence, why is it that in so many instances they are quick to urge them to take a plea for a lesser sentence than they would get with a trial conviction? So, by the time a person is in the trial docket, the system (including the media) has already tarnished him with its multitude of prejudices, which, of course, would all be denied by those who entertain such prejudices.

(b) *Perjury by Police* Another reason for widespread perversions of justice is the pervasiveness of perjury. The recent District Attorney of Philadelphia once said, "In almost any factual hearing or trial, someone is committing perjury; and if we investigate all of those things, literally we would be doing nothing but prosecuting perjury cases." If he is guilty, the defendant and his supporters would lie to save his skin and keep him from going to prison. That is assumed and even expected by the jury and the judge. But what would surprise and even shock most jury members is the extent to which police officers lie on the stand to reinforce the prosecution and not jeopardize their own standing within their own particular law enforcement community. The words of one twenty-five-year veteran senior officer of a northern New Jersey police force still ring in my ears: "They [the defense] lie, so we [police] lie. I don't know one of my fellow officers who hasn't lied under oath." Not too long ago a prominent New York judge, when asked if perjury by police was a problem, responded, "Oh, sure, cops often lie on the stand."

(c) *False Witnesses for the Prosecution* What is more, not only do law officers frequently lie, but the primary witnesses for the prosecution often commit perjury for the state, and do so under the subtle guidance of the prosecutor. Inveterately, common criminals who are in deep trouble themselves with the same prosecutor's office or local police authority are employed as star state witnesses. In exchange for their false testimony, their own charges are dismissed, or they are given non-custodial or greatly reduced prison sentences. In other words a secret deal is struck whereby the witness is paid for his fabricated testimony with that most precious of all commodities -- freedom!

Such witnesses are usually brought forward by the state to say either that the defendant confessed the crime to them

---

Jailhouse confessions are a total perversion of the truth-seeking process.

---

or that they saw the defendant near the crime scene shortly before it happened, or they saw him flee the scene of the crime as it was occurring. If I have seen one, I have seen a hundred "jailhouse confessions" spring open the prison doors for the witness who will tell a jury on behalf of the state that the defendant confessed the crime to him while they shared the same cell or tier. When the state needs important help, it goes to its bullpen, the local county jail, and brings in one of the many ace relievers housed there to put out the fire. As several of these "jailhouse priests" have told me, "It's a matter of survival: either I go away or he [the defendant] goes away, and I'm not goin'." Jailhouse confessions are a total perversion of the truth-seeking process. Amazingly enough, they are a highly effective prosecutorial means to a conviction. Part and parcel of a jailhouse confession is the witness lying to the jury when he assures them that he expects nothing in return for his testimony, that he is willing to swallow whatever pill he must for his own crimes. (d) *Prosecutorial Misconduct* The right decision by a jury depends largely on prosecutorial integrity and proper use of prosecutorial power. If law enforcement officers, in their zeal to win and convict, manipulate or intimidate witnesses into false testimony, or suppress evidence that impeaches the prosecution's own witnesses or even goes to the defendant's innocence, then the chances of an accurate jury verdict are greatly diminished. Sadly, we see this far too often. It is frightening how easily people respond to pressure or threats of trouble by the authorities of the law. Our insecurities and fears as well as our desires to please those who can punish us allow all of us to be far more malleable than we like to think.

Few of us have the inner strength we

think we have to resist such overreaching by the law. This applies to mainline citizenry as well as to those living on the margins. However, the underclasses are particularly vulnerable and susceptible to police pressure because they are powerless; and both they and the police know it. A few examples will illustrate.

In 1981 three white high school janitors were threatened by the Texas Rangers into testifying that they had seen Clarence Brandley, their black custodial supervisor, walking into the restroom area of the high school where the victim had entered only minutes before she had disappeared. Brandley was convicted and sentenced to death based on the inferential testimony that since he was the last person seen near her, then he must have killed her. Eight years later Brandley was exonerated by the judge who conducted his evidentiary hearing when one of these janitors came forward and told how they had lied in implicating Brandley because of coercion by the investigating law officer.

On the eve of the Rene Santana trial in Newark, New Jersey, which was a year and a half after the crime, the prosecutors produced a surprise "eyewitness" who said he saw Mr. Santana flee the scene of the crime. A decade later that same witness visited Mr. Santana at New Jersey's Rahway State Prison and asked for his forgiveness after admitting to him that he had concocted the "eyewitness" testimony in response to intense pressure from the prosecutor's investigator. Since this "eyewitness" was from Trujillo's Dominican Republic police state, his innate fear of the police made him vulnerable to such police coercion.

Or how about the Wingo case in white, rural northwestern Louisiana? Wingo's common-law wife came forward on the eve of his execution and admitted that she had lied at his trial five years earlier because the deputy sheriff had threatened to put her in jail and forever separate her from her children unless she regurgitated at trial what he wanted her to say.

And in the Terry McCracken case in the suburbs of Philadelphia, a fellow high school student of the caucasian McCracken testified that he saw McCracken flee the convenience store moments after a customer was shot to death during the course of a robbery.

The teenager was induced to manufacture this false eyewitness account after three visits to the police station. Among the evidence that vindicates McCracken are the confessions by the real robber/killers. So, you see, it not only can happen anywhere, it does happen everywhere; and it does happen to all different people, regardless of race and background.

Another common trait of wrongful convictions is the prosecutor's habit of suppressing or withholding evidence which he is obliged to provide to the defendant in the interests of justice and fairness. Clarence Darrow was right when he said, "A courtroom is not a place where truth and innocence inevitably triumph; it is only an arena where contending lawyers fight not for justice but to win." And so many times this hidden information is not only "favorable" to the defendant but it clears him. In Philadelphia's Miguel Rivera case the district attorney withheld the fact that two shopkeepers had seen the defendant outside their shop when the art museum murder was actually in progress. And in the Gordon Marsh case near Baltimore, Maryland, the state failed to tell the defendant that its main witness against him was in jail when she said she saw him running from the murder scene. One has to wonder what the primary objective of prosecutors is. Is it to convict, regardless of the factual truth, or is it to pursue justice?

The prosecution is the "house" in the criminal justice system's game of poker. The cards are his, and he deals them. He decides whom and what to charge for

---

The prosecution is the "house" in the criminal justice system's game of poker.

---

crimes, and if there will be a trial or whether a plea is acceptable. He dominates. Unfortunately, his power is virtually unchecked because he is practically immune from punishment for offenses, no matter how flagrant or miscreant. According to many state and federal courts, prosecutorial misbehavior occurs with "disturbing frequency." When the "house" cheats, the innocent lose. Lamentably, we see prosecutors throughout the nation continually violating the standards set for them by the U.S. Supreme Court in 1935 when it said that the prosecutor's

interest in a criminal prosecution is not that it shall win a case, but that justice shall be done. . . . He is in a peculiar and very definite sense the servant of the law, the twofold arm of which is that guilt shall not escape or innocence suffer. . . . While he may strike hard blows, he is not at liberty to strike foul ones. It is as much his duty to refrain from improper methods calculated to produce a wrongful conviction as it is to use every legitimate means to bring about a just one.

It is human nature to resist any information that indicates that we have made a grievous mistake. This is particularly true of prosecutors when presented with new evidence that impeaches a conviction and goes to the innocence of a person convicted by their office at a prior time, whether it occurred four months or forty years before. Not only are they coldly unresponsive to such indications but they quickly act to suppress or stamp them out. New evidence usually comes in the form of a state witness who, plagued with a guilty conscience, admits that he lied at the trial; or from a person completely new to the case who comes forward with his exculpatory knowledge. Without exception, in my experience, the prosecutor's office will treat that person with total contempt in its usually successful attempt to force the person to retreat into silence. If that doesn't work, it will dismiss such testimony as somehow undeserving of any credibility and blithely ignore it. This prosecutorial impishness reminds me of a little boy holding his hands to his ears on hearing an unpleasant sound.

The Joyce Ann Brown case is a poignant illustration of this kind of prosecutorial posturing. One year after Joyce's 1980 conviction for being one of two black women who had robbed a Dallas, Texas furrier and killed one of the proprietors, the admitted shooter was captured and pleaded guilty while accepting a life sentence. She also told her attorney that the district attorney had convicted the wrong woman (Joyce Brown) as her partner in the crime. She had never known or even heard of that Joyce Brown. With the district attorney fighting her with all of his might, Joyce

sits in prison to this day trying to win a retrial as we try to develop new evidence on her behalf.

(e) *Shoddy Police Work* The police work of investigating crimes, when done correctly and thoroughly, is indeed a noble profession. Law and order are essential to a cohesive and just society. Because police work is fraught with so many different kinds of pressures, it is rather easy for an investigation to go awry. The high volume of violent crime plagues every urban police department. Skilled detectives are few, and their caseloads are overwhelming. The "burnout" syndrome is a well-documented reality within police ranks. Interdepartmental politics and the bureaucracy stifle initiative and energy. The pressure to "solve" a case is intensely felt by the line detective and comes both from his superiors and the

---

If today's climate of "burn or bury them" puts more pressure on the detective to resolve, it also gives him more license to do so by whatever means.

---

community and from his own ambitious need for recognition and advancement. If today's climate of "burn or bury" them puts more pressure on the detective to resolve, it also gives him more license to do so by whatever means.

Too often, as a result of the above factors, police officers take the easy way out. Once they come to suspect someone as the culprit, and this often occurs early within the investigation and is based on rather flimsy circumstantial information, then the investigation blindly focuses in on that adopted "target." Crucial pieces of evidence are overlooked and disregarded. Some witnesses are not interviewed who should be, while others are seduced or coerced into telling the police what they want to hear. Evidence or information that does not fit the suspect or the prevailing theory of the crime is dismissed as not material or is changed to implicate the suspect. Good old-fashioned legwork is replaced by expediency and shortcuts. Coercive confessions are extracted and solid leads are ignored.

Before too long, momentum has gathered, and the "project" now is to put it on the suspect. Any information that points

to the suspect, no matter how spuriously secured, is somehow obtained; and anything that points away from him is ridiculed and twisted into nothingness. The task is made much easier if the suspect has a police record because he should be "taken off the streets" anyhow. That kind of person is not only a prime suspect but also a prime scapegoat. An example of this is Clarence Brandley, who was mentioned earlier. He was arrested in late August four days after the crime and on the weekend before school was to begin. The high school where the rape and murder took place was flooded with telephone calls by scared parents who refused to send their children to school until the murderer was caught. The arrest of Brandley calmed the community, and school started as scheduled. It was after Brandley's arrest that the investigation then spent five hundred hours building the case against him.

(f) *Incompetent Defense Counsel* The wrongly convicted invariably find themselves between the rock of police/prosecutorial misconduct and the hard place of an incompetent and irresponsible defense attorney. While the correct decision by a jury hinges on a fair prosecution, it also depends on dedicated and skilled defendant lawyering. And there is such a paucity of the latter. Not only are there very few highly competent defense lawyers but there are very few criminal defense lawyers, period. They are rapidly becoming an extinct species.

The current Attorney General of New Jersey not too long ago told the New Jersey State Bar Association that finding quality private defense attorneys "may be the most crying need that we have." He also told this same assemblage that unless there is an adequate number of well-trained private defense lawyers, there will be little hope for justice. Of the 30,000 lawyers in New Jersey, the number of those doing primarily criminal defense work is only in the hundreds. At this same conference the First Assistant Attorney General pointed out that 85 percent of New Jersey's criminal cases are handled by the public defender system; and he wondered if there would be a private defense bar by the year 2000.

This means, of course, that 85 percent of those charged with a crime cannot afford an attorney, so they are forced to use the public defender system. As competent as New Jersey's full-time salaried public defenders generally are, their resources (budget and people) are vastly inadequate and are dwarfed by those of their adversaries (the local prosecutor's office). Moreover, they are so overwhelmed by the sheer volume of caseload that no defender can give quality attention to any one of his cases, let alone all of them. So, in response to this shortage, public defender cases are farmed out to "pooled" attorneys, who are paid a pittance relative to what they earn from other clients who retain them privately.

The experience of these pooled attorneys in criminal matters is often limited and scanty. In addition, they do not bring to their new-found indigent client the desired level of heart and enthusiasm for their cases. All of these conditions leave the defendant with an attorney somewhat lacking in will, effort, resources, and experience. Thus, the defendant goes to trial with two strikes against him.

What we have discovered as a common theme among those whose cases we have studied from all over the country is that their trial attorney, whether from the public domain or privately retained, undertakes his work with an appalling lack of assiduity. Communication with the defendant is almost nonexistent. When

---

Eighty-five percent of those charged with a crime cannot afford an attorney.

---

it does take place, it is carried on in a hurried, callous, and dismissive manner. Attempts at discovery are made perfunctorily. Prosecutors are not pressed for this material. Investigation is shallow and narrow, if conducted at all. Preparation meets minimal standards. And advocacy at trial is weak. Cross-examination is superficial and tentative.

Physical evidence is left untested, and forensic experts are not called to rebut whatever scientific evidence the state introduces through its criminalists. I cannot help thinking of the Nate Walker case, where, at Nate's 1976 trial for rape and kidnapping, the doctor who examined the victim the night of her ordeal testified that he found semen in her vaginal cavity. Walker's privately retained attorney had no questions for the doctor when it came time for cross-examination, nor

did he even ask anyone to test the vaginal semen for blood type. Twelve years later, that test was peformed at our request, and Walker was exonerated and immediately freed.

This is not to say, however, that we have not encountered some outstanding examples of vigorous and thorough defense lawyering that left no stones unturned. What a rare but inspiring sight! We could not do our work without the critically important services of the extremely able and dedicated attorneys with whom we team up. If only the preponderance of attorneys would heed the admonition of Herbert Stern, a former U.S. Attorney and U.S. District Court judge in Newark, New Jersey, when he addressed a new crop of attorneys who had just been sworn in. He told them that they were free to choose their own clients. "But," he continued, "once that choice is made, once a representation is undertaken, then that responsibility is as sacred to us as the one assumed by a surgeon in the operating room. You must be as committed and as selfless as any surgeon." He further challenged them to "be an advocate. Represent your clients -- all of them -- fearlessly, diligently, unflinchingly. . . . Withhold no proper legal assistance from any client. And when you do that, you thereby preserve, protect, and defend the Constitution of the United States, just as you have this day sworn to."

(g) *Nature of Convicting Evidence* The unschooled public largely and erroneously believes that convictions are mostly obtained through the use of one form of tangible evidence or another. This naive impression is shaped by watching too many TV shows like Perry Mason or Matlock. The reality is that in most criminal trials the verdict more often than not hinges on whose witnesses -- the state's or defendant's – the jury chooses to believe. It boils down to a matter of credibility. There is no "smoking gun" scientific evidence that clearly points to the defendant. This puts an extremely heavy burden on the jury. It must somehow ferret out and piece together the truth from substantially inconsistent and contradictory testimony between and within each side. The jury is forced to make one subjective call after another in deciding whom to believe and what inferences to draw from conflicting statements.

For example, how can a jury accept a victim's positive identification at trial of the defendant as her assailant when she had previously described her attacker in physical terms that were very different from the actual physical characteristics of the defendant, or when the defense has presented documented information that precludes the defendant from being the assaulter? Several cases come to mind. Boy was convicted of robbing a convenience store in Georgia. The clerk initially told the police that since she was 5 feet 3 inches, was standing on a 3-inch platform, and had direct eye contact with the robber, he must have been about 5 feet 6 inches tall. Boy is 6 feet 5 inches tall. Four teenage girls identified Russell Burton as their rapist on a particular day in Arkansas. Burton introduced evidence that on that day his penis was badly blistered from an operation two days before for removal of a wart. And a Virginia woman was certain that Edward Honaker was her rapist even though her rapist had left semen within her, and Honaker had had a vasectomy well in advance of the assault.

Criminal prosecutions that primarily or exclusively depend on the victim's identification of the defendant as the perpetrator must be viewed with some skepticism unless solid corroborating evidence is also introduced. Traumatized by a crime as it occurs, the victim frequently is looking but not seeing. Victims are extremely vulnerable and can easily be led by the police, through unduly suggestive techniques, into identifying a particular person. The victim in Nate Walker's case, for example, was with her abductor/rapist for two and a half hours with ample opportunity to clearly view him. She told the jury without hesitation eighteen months later that "he's the man." Nate had an ironclad alibi. The jury struggled for several days but in the end came in with a guilty verdict. As mentioned earlier, he was scientifically vindicated twelve years later.

When juries are confronted with a choice between a victim's ringing declaration that "that's the man" and solid evidence that "it couldn't be him," they usually cast their lot with the victim. I suggest that this can be a very dangerous tendency and practice. And this is particularly so when identification crosses racial lines, that is, when a white victim says it was that black person. Future jurors should be aware that identifications can be very unreliable forms of evidence.

Another type of evidence that can be misleading and even confusing to jurors is that offered by laboratory scientists. Results of laboratory tests that are presented by the forensic scientists are not always what they appear to be, although they strongly influence jury decisions. A recent New York Times article pointed out that there is a "growing concern about the professionalism and impartiality of the laboratory scientists whose testimony in court can often mean conviction or acquittal." This article went

---

The reality is that in most criminal trials the verdict more often than not hinges on whose witnesses -- the state's or defendant's -- the jury chooses to believe.

---

on to say that the work of forensic technicians in police crime laboratories is plagued by uneven training and questionable objectivity.

We share this mounting concern because we see instance after instance where the prosecutor's crime laboratory experts cross the line from science to advocacy. They exaggerate the results of their analysis of hairs, fibers, blood, or semen in such a manner that it is absolutely devastating to the defendant. To put the defendants at a further disadvantage, the defense attorneys do not educate themselves in the forensic science in question, and therefore conduct a weak cross-examination. Also, in many cases, the defense does not call in its own forensic experts, whose testimony in numerous instances could severely damage the state's scientific analysis.

One case profoundly reflects this common cause of numerous unjust convictions. Roger Coleman sits on Virginia's death row today primarily because the Commonwealth's Bureau of Forensic Science expert testified that the two foreign pubic hairs found on the murdered victim were "consistent" with Mr. Coleman's, and that it was "unlikely" that these hairs came from someone other than Mr. Coleman. The defense offered nothing in rebuttal, so this testimony stood unchallenged. In a post-convic-

tion hearing Mr. Coleman's new lawyer introduced the testimony of a forensic hair specialist who had twenty-five years of experience with the F.B.I. He testified that "it is improper to conclude that it is likely that hairs came from a particular person simply because they are consistent with that person's hair because hairs belonging to different people are often consistent with each other, especially pubic hairs."

Another problem that we continually observe within the realm of forensic evidence is the phenomenon of lost and untested physical evidence. Often, especially in cases up to the early 1980s, the specimens that have the potential to exclude the defendant have not been tested and eventually get misplaced. At best this is gross negligence on the part of both the police technician and the defense attorney in not ensuring that the tests be done.

Conclusion

We agree with a past president of the New Jersey Division of the Association of Trial Lawyers of America who said that "juries are strange creatures. Even after taking part in many, many trials, I still find them to be unpredictable. The jury system isn't perfect, but it does represent the best system to mete out justice. They're right in their decisions more often than not." Remember when I quoted a former District Attorney who said that "in almost any factual hearing or trial someone is committing perjury." So, a wide margin of error exists when earnest but all too fallible juries are only right "more often than not" and when trial testimony is so frequently and pervasively perjurious. My contention is that at least 10 percent of those convicted for serious, violent crimes are incorrectly convicted because some combination of the trial infirmities described in this article results in mistaken jury determinations.

Everyone will agree that the system is not perfect, but the real question is this: To what extent do its imperfections prevail? I contend that for all the reasons detailed above the system is a far leakier cistern than any among us has ever imagined. Untold numbers of innocents have tumbled into the dark pit of prison. Some of them have eventually gained their freedom, but a majority remain

buried in prison, completely forsaken and forgotten by the outside world.

Other than my own wholly inadequate organization, no person or agency, private or public, exists anywhere that works full time and serves exclusively as an advocate and arm for the innocent in prison. The body of justice that has evolved over the centuries has many members. But not one part that functions within this whole has been created or is properly equipped specifically to secure the freedom of the incarcerated innocent.

Publications Received

Timo Airaksinen, *Ethics of Coercion and Authority: A Philosophical Study of Social Life* (Pittsburgh, PA: University of Pittsburgh Press, 1988), ix + 219 pp.

George F. Cole, *The American System of Criminal Justice* (5th ed) (Pacific Grove, CA: Brooks/Cole Publishing Co., 1989), xxiv + 706 pp.

Joshua Dressler, *Understanding Criminal Law* (New York: Mathew Bender & Co., 1987), xli + 540 pp.

Franco Ferracuti, ed. *Trattato Di Criminologia, Medicina Criminologia E Psichiatria Forense* (Milano: Dott. A. Guiffre Editore, 1988) *IX. Forme di Organizzazioni Criminali e terrorismo* xiii + 403 pp.

Mark S. Gaylord & John F. Galliher, *The Criminology of Edwin Sutherland* (New Brunswick: Transaction Inc., 1988) xiv + 183 pp.

Jean Harris, *"They Always Call Us LADIES": Stories from Prison* (New York: Charles Scribner's Sons, 1988), vii + 276 pp.

Geoffrey C. Hazard, Jr. & Deborah L. Rhode, *The Legal Profession: Responsibility and Regulation* (2nd ed) (Westbury, NY: The Foundation Press, Inc., 1988), viii + 505 pp.

Jack Katz, *Seductions of Crime: Moral and Sensual Attractions in Doing Evil* (New

4. THE JUDICIAL SYSTEM

York: Basic Books, Inc., 1988), viii + 367 pp.

Kelsey Kauffman, *Prison Officers and their World* (Cambridge: Harvard University Press, 1988), ix + 290 pp.

Robert Klitgaard, *Controlling Corruption* (Berkeley & Los Angeles: University of California Press, 1988), xiii + 220 pp.

Richard A. Myren & Carol Henderson Garcia, *Investigation for Determination of Fact: A Primer on Proof* (Pacific Grove, CA: Brooks/Cole Publishing Co., 1988), xv + 240 pp.

David W. Neubauer, *America's Courts and the Criminal Justice System* (3rd ed) (Pacific Grove, CA: Brooks/Cole Publishing Co., 1988), xvi + 464 pp.

Andrew Oldenquist, *The Non-Suicidal So-ciety* (Bloomington & Indianapolis: Indiana University Press, 1986), viii + 263 pp.

Richard Polenberg, *Fighting Faiths: The Abrams Case, the Supreme Court, and Free Speech* (New York: Viking Penguin Inc., 1987), xiv + 431 pp.

Joycelyn M. Pollock-Byrne, *Ethics in Crime & Justice: Dilemmas and Decisions* (Pacific Grove, CA: Brooks/Cole Publishing Co., 1989), xiii + 169 pp.

Curtis Prout & Robert N. Ross, *Care and Punishment: The Dilemmas of Prison Medicine* (Pittsburgh, PA: University of Pittsburgh Press, 1988), x + 276 pp.

Lionel Tiger, *The Manufacture of Evil -- Ethics, Evolution and the Industrial System* (New York: Harper & Row, 1987), 345 pp.

Michael Tonry & Norval Morris, eds. *Crime and Justice: A Review of Research* (Vol. 10) (Chicago: The University of Chicago Press, 1988), x + 343 pp.

UMI, ed. *Criminal Justice Periodical Index* (Vol. 13) (Ann Arbor: University Microfilms Inc., 1988), xi + 391 pp.

H. Richard Uviller, *Tempered Zeal -- A Columbia Law Professor's Year on the Streets with the New York City Police* (Chicago & New York: Contemporary Books, 1988, xvii + 234 pp.

Samuel Walker, *Sense and Nonsense about Crime: A Policy Guide* (2nd ed) (Pacific Grove, CA: Brooks/Cole Publishing Co., 1989), xvi + 276 pp.

Stanton Wheeler, Kenneth Mann, & Austin Sarat, *Sitting in Judgement: The Sentencing of White-Collar Criminals* (New York: Yale University Press, 1988), xii + 199 pp.

Improving Our Criminal Justice System

❧ ❧ ❧ ❧ ❧ ❧

Can We Borrow from Europe's Civil Law Tradition?

Charles Maechling, Jr.

Charles Maechling, Jr., an international lawyer and former State Department official, led a study of European criminal justice systems while a visiting fellow at Wolfson College, Cambridge University, 1985–87. An earlier version of this article appeared in the American Bar Association Journal *(January 1991).*

The American criminal justice system is breaking down. Court calendars and prisons are clogged. It can take years to execute a child murderer or put a rapist behind bars, while an otherwise harmless teenager can get a mandatory 20-year sentence for mere possession of cocaine. One Southern state recently sentenced an ignorant black youth to five years at hard labor for shoplifting a $6 item.

One cause of the simultaneous harshness and ineffectiveness of the U.S. system is something Americans take so for granted that it never occurs to us to question it—the adversarial nature of our courts.

All European countries except Great Britain and Ireland, and nearly all third world countries that have a European cultural heritage, employ variations of the so-called inquisitorial criminal justice method, which grew out of the 2,000-year tradition of the civil or Roman law. Only the Anglo-Saxon countries cling to a judicial parody of the medieval tournament—lawyers for the state and the defense fight for the body of the accused before a judge as umpire and a jury carefully selected for its ignorance of the personalities and issues before it.

In the Anglo-American system, the narrow focus on the accused, coupled with the disproportionate power and authority of the state, necessitates a bristling array of constitutional safeguards and procedural rules to level the jousting field and protect the defendant's rights. The tournament, or trial, is the supreme event. Nothing in the prior stages of the criminal justice process has any validity until proved to the satisfaction of the jury in open court.

Anglo-American trial procedure has a limited purpose—to enforce the tournament rules. The function of the trial is not to establish the truth about the facts of the crime. As any law graduate will attest, it is to provide the prosecution with a forum to convince the jury beyond a reasonable doubt that the accused is guilty of the specific crime he is charged with, and nothing else.

The process requires the prosecution to present its case in the most awkward way possible—through a succession of witnesses, each of whom lifts the curtain on a separate aspect of the events in question. Each witness is held to the confines of his own personal experience; the last thing a witness is allowed to do is tell his story in his own words and give his opinion of what it means.

Moreover, to lend credibility to his testimony and avoid having it discredited on cross-examination, the witness must profess absolute certainty about what he saw or heard. That leaves the veracity of trial testimony always open to question since the police record of statements made by witnesses at the time has no probative value of its own, and the average person cannot, without coaching or prompting, remember the details of events that he witnessed the week before, let alone six months or a year ago.

Another distortion is imposed by the hearsay rule. In the adversarial process the jury is not allowed to hear what the witness says another person told him he heard or saw at the time. The only exception in Britain, Canada, and some other jurisdictions is what the accused told the witness or may have said in the latter's presence. The hearsay rule wipes out a whole area of valuable information that is especially useful in the prosecution of conspiracies, racketeering, and white-collar crime.

An artificial obstacle now more or less unique to the United States is the exclusion of illegally seized evidence. No reasonable person would question that the Fourth Amendment prohibition against unreasonable searches and seizures is an essential freedom of a democratic society. But why it should be allowed to interfere with criminal prosecutions and, under the "fruit of the poisonous tree" doctrine, bar legally obtained evidence as well defies common sense.

There are plenty of remedies, from disciplinary penalties to civil liability judgments, to punish violators of civil liberties without withholding critical information from juries. Former Chief Justice Warren Burger pointed out in a well-known Supreme Court opinion that there is no empirical evidence that the exclusionary rule deters unreasonable searches and seizures. The rule in Canada, Britain, and other Anglo-Saxon countries is that the means of obtaining evidence has no bearing on its admissibility in a criminal trial.

Even more irrational is the way the traditional English prohibition against self-incrimination has been pushed to an extreme by Supreme Court extensions of the Fifth Amendment. This relic of the Star Chamber was intended to protect an accused in a criminal trial from confession under torture or extreme duress. There has never been a sound rationale for allowing the rule to obstruct introduction of testimony given in other forums, such as congressional inquiries.

In Canada, for example, a witness cannot refuse to answer a question on the ground that it may tend to incriminate him, although that specific question and answer may not be used in any trial or civil proceeding where he is a defendant. The most outlandish extension of the Fifth Amendment to date, unwarranted by any ruling of the Supreme Court, was the decision of the Iran-Contra special prosecutor to forbid his staff to read relevant congressional transcripts and newspaper accounts.

The System at Its Worst

The adversarial system is at its worst in the ritual of cross-examination. The witness who tries to give a frank and honest statement of his observations, impressions, and beliefs, with all the necessary qualifications, will find his recollection and indeed credibility challenged at every step. In most cases he will be forced to retract or at least to restate only those portions that he can testify to with precision and absolute certainty. Ostensibly designed to narrow testimony down to a hard core of "fact," cross-examination more often confuses the witness and muddies the record. That is exactly what the cross-examiner intends. His object is to seize on contradictions and uncertainties to discredit the witness.

As noted British criminal law jurist Professor P.A.J. Waddington pointed out last year in a *Times* of London article, "The aim is not to find out how much or in which respects testimony can be relied on. It is a zero-sum game in which evidence must be accepted as wholly true or worthless."

Deprived of a great deal of relevant information, and forced by the rules to receive what is deemed admissible in piecemeal form removed from real-life context, the jury is required to determine guilt or innocence on the narrowest grounds possible.

The choice is not "what, if anything, did the defendant do that was against the law?" but "did the defendant do exactly what the prosecution alleges?" Unless specified in the indictment, there is no possibility, for example, of convicting an accused of arson as well as burglary, no matter how overwhelming the evidence that emerges at trial that he set fire to the house he burgled.

The mock tournament aspects of the accusatorial process are also prejudicial to the accused. Since the prosecution needs to build a bullet-proof case beyond reasonable doubt, it tends to accumulate only information that reinforces the initial presumption of a suspect's guilt, and to disregard or discount information that contradicts or qualifies it. The need to establish criminal intent also puts a premium on over-certainty, pseudo-precision, and one-dimensional interpretation of the evidence by the prosecution.

Two other abuses that spring from the accusatorial process are the plea bargain and the temptation to fabricate evidence. The plea bargain does little damage to the integrity of the system as long as it is limited to one individual. It has the practical benefit of saving the state from the expense and effort of time-consuming trials and appeals that overload the system.

But once transformed into an instrument for convicting conspirators and codefendants, it opens the door to dishonesty and gross injustice. A criminal defendant who breaks with his confederates and succumbs to the lure of a light sentence or no sentence at all is likely to give the prosecution everything it wants—testimony to incriminate others, embellished with all requisite certainty.

Worse, plea bargains are increasingly made with the defendant in the best position to implicate others—not with a minor accomplice to nail the ringleader. In the John Walker espionage case, for example, the mastermind of the ring was allowed to plea-bargain his way to a light sentence, while his hapless brother-in-law, pressed into service virtually against his will, received a sadistic 25-year sentence without parole for turning over one low-grade security item.

Civil law countries reject the plea-bargain practice as tainted and make it a bar to extradition.

Criminal Justice by "Inquiry"

The civil law tradition that governs the countries of Western Europe, and that has been retained in Eastern Europe as well, proceeds from premises so different from the Anglo-Saxon tradition that it can easily delude Americans into imagining the worst.

For starters, the name "inquisitorial" applied to a criminal justice process conjures up "inquisition" rather than the actual derivation from "inquiry." The notion that justice can be served by objective methods of inquiry rather than by pit-bull confrontations in a judicial arena leaves the average American uneasy about his ability to fight back. This is especially true if he assumes that in Europe the accused is presumed guilty until proved innocent.

The inquisitorial process does not make the trial the supreme event in the way the accusatorial process does. It is rather the public finale of an ongoing investigation.

In a felony case the process breaks down into three stages—an initial investigatory phase, conducted by the police; an examining phase, conducted by an examining magistrate; and the trial, conducted by the state prosecutor before a small panel of judges, supplemented in some countries by lay judges or a small jury. The examining phase is both a more detailed investigation and a preliminary *in camera* trial to determine whether the case against a suspect is strong enough to bring him before a more formal tribunal.

The task of the magistrate in the examining phase is to develop and assess all the information surrounding a crime. At issue is not only what is produced by the police during the investigative phase but what is subsequently extracted by the examining magistrate from the witnesses, physical evidence, and information provided from other sources.

Building Up the Record

In the civil law system, the *dossier*, or official record, plays a crucial role. Every relevant scrap of information about the case and the individuals involved in it goes into the *dossier*. The task of the examining magistrate is to sift through this material, weigh it for what it is worth, and decide whether it adds up to a prima facie case.

Well into the examining phase, the focus is likely to be on the event rather than on a particular suspect. Thereafter, the emphasis is on building a coherent case based on all the information available. As the case is built, corroborative evidence pointing to one conclusion is accumulated, but that conclusion is always left open to challenge by new evidence and contradictory testimony.

Hence, a great deal of the examining magistrate's time is taken up in examining and reexamining witnesses and taking supportive affidavits. Since one of the magistrate's principal concerns is resolving contradictions, witnesses are often summoned to directly confront each other or the principal suspect. During the examining phase, a suspect may have his counsel present at any time during questioning, but counsel is not usually allowed to question witnesses himself, although he is free to point out anomalies in their testimony and request lines of questioning on behalf of his client. In some respects the procedure is similar to a congressional committee hearing.

Only after completion of the examining phase and resolution of any ambiguities and uncertainties will the examining magistrate decide whether to bring a suspect to formal trial. By this time all other suspects will have been washed out, and much of the function of the accusatorial trial fulfilled. At this point, the burden of proving innocence does in a sense shift to the accused, since he would not reach the trial stage at all without a strong prima facie case against him. Nonetheless, he is entitled to a public trial to prove his innocence, or, more likely, to show extenuating circumstances.

At the trial, the public prosecutor will present the case against the accused by in effect distilling the *dossier* into coherent form, not in rehashing its content through the testimony of one witness after another. Witnesses may, however, be requested by the defense to refute the information in the *dossier* or by the court to resolve crucial questions or apparent anomalies. The court does the questioning, although the lawyers may cross-examine. All witnesses are the court's witnesses, though either side may propose them.

The function of defense counsel is to make legal arguments to the court, to open and sum up for the accused, and to advise the accused at every stage of the proceedings. He cannot disrupt the proceedings with delaying tactics and frivolous objections on points of procedure.

Rights of the Defendants

In civil law jurisdictions, the rights of suspects and defendants are safeguarded, but not in the same way as here or in other Anglo-Saxon countries. In the civil law world the process itself provides safeguards. As noted, the focus is initially on the event, not the person—first, to determine whether a crime took place and only thereafter to zero in on a particular suspect. The accused has the right to counsel almost from the moment of his arrest and can refuse to answer questions. However, a negative inference may be drawn from his refusal to answer, and anything he does say may be used against him.

The admissibility of all evidence for what it is worth can also work in his favor. Background information that in an adversarial proceeding would be ruled irrelevant until sentencing can be introduced at any stage to show mitigating circumstances. Judicial rulings and sentencing will be the product of the collective judgment of a judicial panel and not dependent on the arbitrary judgment of a single, all-powerful judge.

In the United States, the sanctimonious maxim that "Ignorance of the law is no excuse" puts every citizen at risk. What may have been a sound rule in simpler times, when the catalog of punishable offenses was limited to traditional offenses like murder, robbery, rape, and larceny, becomes a sinister joke when applied to the five-foot shelf of the U.S. criminal code and the even more voluminous statutes of individual states.

Moreover, in the United States a citizen cannot rely on the plain meaning of a statute, or what passes for it. He must retain a lawyer to parse its legislative history and judicial evolution. So many forms of social and economic activity have now been criminalized that the discretionary power of federal and state authorities to pick and choose targets for prosecution has made enforcement utterly arbitrary.

In the case of the tax codes, not one citizen in 10 million can tell whether he has committed a trivial error or subjected himself to the risk of a felony conviction. In addition, by a grotesque inversion of legal principle, the burden is on the taxpayer to prove his innocence.

By contrast, a citizen of Switzerland or Denmark, to name only two examples, keeps on his bookshelf, next to the family Bible, a complete compilation of the civil and criminal codes of his country in a volume no larger than a thick pocket dictionary. Following the Roman tradition, statutory language is terse, uncomplicated, and comprehensible to all. The traditional catalog of crimes is considered adequate for even sophisticated forms of economic malfeasance.

The Abuse of Perjury

Another hazard for the U.S. citizen, rare in civil law countries, is the use of perjury to put an accused behind bars when the evidence is either insufficient or inadmissible to convict him for the charged offense. In civil law countries the oath is of less significance. It is assumed that most people lie or conceal the truth when their vital interests are at stake. In any case it is the totality of corroborative evidence that counts, not the answer to any particular question.

The American version of the accusatorial process, which emphasizes the extortion of "yes" or "no" answers, can easily turn cross-examination under oath into a game of entrapment. Under skilled cross-examination, any witness, denied the opportunity to recount his experience in his own words, is likely to commit perjury not once but several times, especially if the subject matter is complex and the events took place long ago.

The fact that prosecution for perjury is often used to "get" a controversial public figure—Alger Hiss is the classic example—in itself induces public cynicism and suspicion. For the government to fall back on a minor procedural charge when, if credible evidence were available, it would otherwise prosecute the suspect for a serious offense smacks of persecution.

As might be expected from the ancestor of the accusatorial model, the British version shares many of our system's shortcomings. But thanks to English pragmatism, the absence of a written constitution and Bill of Rights, and the high priority the British public gives to law and order, the British system is neither snarled in red tape nor befogged by democratic ideology.

In Britain, the accused is protected from self-incrimination in court, but any statements he makes in other contexts or after a Miranda-type "caution" may be used against him. Since the media are prohibited from publishing any information about a criminal suspect before the trial, the need to disqualify jurors for bias seldom arises.

The nature of the British legal establishment virtually ensures a smooth and expeditious criminal justice process. Trial lawyers for both prosecution and defense are drawn from the same elite pool of qualified barristers. High Court and appeal judges are appointed from the ranks of senior barristers. Procedural rules are straightforward and relatively simple. Barristers owe their primary duty to the court and not to the client. And since everyone plays by the rules, there are none of the disruptive outbursts, histrionics, and dilatory tactics that disgrace American criminal trials.

Furthermore, paperwork is kept to a minimum. Objections and motions are rarely reduced to writing and almost never appealed. If there is a dispute over a point of law, the law books are handed up to the judge, who makes a ruling on the spot. The sentence usually follows immediately after the verdict. The trial transcript is generally considered sufficient for an appeal, which is processed in 90 days or less and, except in unusual circumstances, is confined to review of the evidence.

Can the U.S. System Be Fixed?

Whether the deficiencies of the American adversarial method can be rectified is an open question. Indeed, at first glance, the U.S. Constitution and Bill of Rights do appear to raise insuperable barriers to change.

But closer examination will reveal that many of the anachronisms discussed above are not anchored in the specific language of the Constitution. They are either the products of later interpretation by the Supreme

Court or derive from British precedents that, in turn, trace their origins to medieval abuses and the long struggle for power between Parliament and the Crown. Illustrations abound.

There is, for example, nothing in the Bill of Rights that requires that evidence procured in violation of the Fourth Amendment prohibition against unreasonable searches and seizures be inadmissible in court. On the contrary, the early history of this provision indicates that it was designed to protect private property and the sanctity of the home—to stand on its own feet with its own penalties, rather than to interfere with the prosecution of criminals. The exclusionary rule in federal courts dates back only to 1914, and in state courts to 1961. In 1949 Justice Felix Frankfurter in a Supreme Court opinion invited Congress to overturn the rule.

As another example, the Fifth Amendment prohibition against self-incrimination could be restored by the Supreme Court to its declared purpose of preventing self-incrimination in a criminal case against the accused, and removed as an excuse for allowing a defendant to evade truthful responses in congressional inquiries and other forums.

The archaic rule against admission of hearsay evidence—the kind of information governments and ordinary people use daily to make decisions—finds no mention in the Constitution and could be eliminated at a stroke by legislative fiat.

There is no reason to disqualify the best educated and better informed citizenry from jury duty simply because they have acquired general knowledge of a crime or personality from the news media, as in the Iran-Contra trials. The Sixth Amendment requirement of impartiality need not be a mandate for political illiteracy.

Nor is there any reason why all witnesses in a criminal trial—especially "expert" witnesses now carefully selected by each side for their biases and coached to give slanted testimony—should not be witnesses for the court, chosen and screened for competence and objectivity. Or why most of the questioning of witnesses should not be the function of the judge, with the lawyers only afterwards permitted a limited right of cross-examination.

Finally, there is nothing in the Constitution to prevent limiting criminal appeals to one appeal confined (as in England) to review of the whole record, absent a showing of some gross irregularity at the trial or new evidence. Legislation or judicial ruling could accomplish these and other improvements drawn from the civil law tradition without starting down the futile road of trying to amend the Constitution. The Supreme Court, in an April 1991 decision, has already gone part of the way in limiting capital punishment appeals.

A Question of Guilt or Innocence

In the United States, the criminal justice process is now politicized in a way unknown in other civilized countries. Courts have become arenas of ideological conflict in which the overriding questions of guilt or innocence are eclipsed by disputes over procedure and constitutional safeguards.

There are of course powerful arguments against change. The most instinctive is the fear that any tampering with the structure of the criminal justice system threatens two of its essential features, certainty and predictability. Another weighty objection is that the American version of the adversarial system is uniquely compatible with our federal constitutional structure, the diversity of American society, and the vast dimensions of the country. It is also true that the civil law has no strict *habeas corpus* requirement, thus allowing detention before trial for as long as permitted by statute.

Certainly our federal system, with its reservation of the police power to the states and an independent judiciary at both state and federal levels, is at variance with the continental system of a centralized criminal justice system, uniform criminal code, and a career civil service judiciary with investigative and quasi-prosecutorial functions. Our ethnic diversity, social mobility, and absence of uniform social values make a "government of laws and not of men" under a written constitution essential to assure equality of treatment under the law.

Presumed Innocent

In contrast to the civil law tradition, where the accused is to some extent the prisoner of the process and great trust is vested in the state to winnow the innocent from the guilty, the adversarial system guarantees the U.S. citizen a presumption of innocence right up to the verdict and a chance to challenge the power of the state until the final appeal. Trial by "jury of his peers" satisfies American egalitarian instincts and distrust (often well-founded) of governmental authority. The right of defense counsel to take advantage of every legal artifice, and to base appeals on procedural irregularities and infringement of constitutional safeguards rather than on sufficiency of the evidence, provides the accused with alternative routes of escape not available in other systems.

But whether the American adversarial system best serves the interests of society is another matter. Before making a final judgment, the reader should first take note of the observation of Professor John Merryman of the Stanford University Law School, a leading comparative law scholar: if innocent, he would prefer to be tried by a civil law court, but if guilty, he would prefer to be tried by a common law court.

Given the sanctity of the Constitution, the legalism that pervades American society at every level, and the size and power of the American legal establishment, there is no possibility that this country would ever embrace the whole of the civil law system. But why not consider borrowing from it? Or at least streamlining our own system in accordance with the British model?

ALTERNATIVE SENTENCING:
A New Direction for Criminal Justice

"Diverting the nondangerous offenders from prison to work in community service would ease overcrowding in our institutions, freeing up space for the truly dangerous. . . . "

Charles W. Colson

Mr. Colson, Special Counsel to the President during the Nixon Administration, is chairman and founder of Prison Fellowship Ministries, Washington, D.C.

I never will forget the day I was sentenced. I stood before Judge Gerhard Gesell in a packed Washington, D.C., courtroom while my attorney made a last, impassioned plea on my behalf. Judge Gesell already had told my lawyer that it was his policy to send convicted government officials to prison. Still, I held to the slight hope that he might decide on an alternative punishment or suspend most of my sentence, as he had done with another Watergate defendant.

Gesell lifted his gavel in the air. "The court will impose a sentence of one to three years and a fine of $5,000." The gavel fell. I was going to prison.

So, when former White House aide Oliver North was convicted and awaiting sentencing before Judge Gesell, I was certain he, too, would face a jail term, particularly since one of the counts against him was virtually identical to the one under which the same judge had sentenced me. Courthouse insiders were giving odds that North would get at least five years.

However, Gesell surprised us, suspending prison terms and ordering two years'

probation, 1,200 hours of community service, and a fine of $150,000. I immediately was besieged by the media. Did Judge Gesell let North off easy?, they queried. Was I bitter that I, under the same judge, had served time in prison?

No, I said emphatically. I was elated by the judge's decision. A sentence to work with inner-city youth in the District of Columbia was an appropriate punishment and channel for North's energies. In my view, those convicted of nondangerous offenses should be working to pay back society, rather than sitting idle in expensive cells. My belief is shaped by having seen the criminal justice system from both sides.

As counsel to former Pres. Richard Nixon, I wrote some of his toughest anti-crime speeches. I was a law-and-order conservative then and still am today. Nevertheless, I have come to realize that the traditional "lock-em-up-and-throw-away-the-key" and "build-more-prisons" strategies in the war on crime are punishing taxpayers more than criminals.

I've seen the system up close—as a prisoner and in the hundreds of correctional facilities I have visited since my release in 1975. What I witnessed changed the course of my life. I did not return to law practice. I was a new Christian and felt compelled to found Prison Fellowship, a nonprofit ministry in which church volunteers help prisoners, ex-prisoners, and their families, while promoting biblical standards of justice.

I can testify from firsthand experience over 14 years how our criminal justice system wastes precious cell space and taxpayer resources by locking up nonviolent offenders. Moreover, the system is on the verge of collapse. Unless Americans are willing to re-educate themselves about crime and punishment, our felony rates will continue to spiral upward, our prisons to overflow, and our communities to live in fear.

A failing system

The criminal justice system is failing in four vital respects. First, prisons are not rehabilitating criminals or deterring crime. We jam more and more people into already overcrowded facilities, which, in turn, release more and more rancorous, hostile men and women to commit more crimes. We all agree that prisons are necessary to confine dangerous offenders and protect the public, but half of those currently incarcerated have been convicted of *nonviolent* offenses.

As Gary Smith, a former inmate, said, "You might as well say cologne cures gangrene as to say prisons rehabilitate people. Prisons teach people how to do time." In prison, I saw men convicted of nonviolent offenses lying on bunks, day in and day out, growing bitter. They also are learning tricks of the trade from repeat offenders. That, combined with the bitterness, leads to an obsession to go out and "get even,"

Reprinted from *USA Today Magazine*, May 1991, pp. 64-66. Copyright © 1991 by the Society for the Advancement of Education.

but this time—or so they think—they won't get caught.

Yet, they do get caught. According to the FBI, 74% of released prisoners are rearrested within four years. A recent Bureau of Prisons study found that the re-arrest rate is lowest among those who have spent the least time in prison.

Why have we relied so much on a failing system? Earlier in this century, when liberal enthusiasm about social engineering was at its peak, crime was thought to be an illness caused by social factors such as poverty, unemployment, or racism. Offenders were not considered accountable for their actions, but "victims" who needed to be "cured" of their anti-social behavior. This therapeutic theory led to massive prison building programs.

In the 1970's, the failure of the rehabilitative model became painfully apparent. Thinking about crime shifted dramatically as conservative winds blew. If people couldn't be *cured*, maybe they could be *scared* out of committing crimes.

However, the threat of incarceration—hundreds of big, new prisons across the country—did little to deter. The evidence if incontrovertible. We've built more prisons and locked up more people per capita than any other nation except the Soviet Union and South Africa. Yet, our crime rates are the highest in the Western world and rising—up five percent this year alone.

Victims' rights

Second, the system virtually ignores the victims of crime. A *Washington Post* feature article created a major controversy in the summer of 1989 by providing a grisly illustration of what can happen to victims. In 1973, while Pamela Small was shopping, the store manager suddenly turned on her, smashed her skull with a hammer, stabbed her, and slit her throat. He left her to die, though she survived.

Her attacker, 19-year-old John Mack, served about two years in a county jail, then was released to an awaiting clerk's job with Rep. Jim Wright (D.-Tex.). Mack eventually rose to a senior staff position on Capitol Hill, but Small was left to pick up the pieces of her shattered life. When she revealed her story, many people responded angrily. Why hadn't Mack served more time in prison? As a result of the furor, Mack resigned his $89,000-a-year job with Wright.

Instead of directing the bile at Mack, the outrage should be focused on our criminal justice system. Former Congressman Tony Coelho (D.-Calif.) sounded callous when defending Mack, "Under our system of law, John Mack owed his debt to society, not to this young woman."

Coelho was correct—and that's precisely the problem. As a lawbreaker, Mack

"owed a debt to society." If our system is to dispense real justice, however, it must go further than punishing the offender. It must respect the victim as well.

This used to be the case. The ancient legal codes—Hebrew, Mesopotamian, Greek, Roman, and Anglo-Saxon—held offenders responsible to repay their victims. The view that crime is primarily an offense against individuals was well-established until Henry I declared all crimes an offense against the King. Gradually, government took the place of the individual and the victim was forgotten.

Stories like Pamela Small's remind us how far we have departed from this tradition. We need to return to these principles built into the historical foundations of Western law.

Third, the current system fails to bring peace to our communities. Ninety-nine percent of us can expect to be victims of crime at least once in our lives; 83% will be affected by a *violent* felony. In 1988, 18,269 people were murdered in this country—more American casualties than in Vietnam during the worst year of the war.

The purpose of the criminal justice system is to provide a just order for society. Crime destroys order, shattering the ideal of what the Hebrews once called *shalom*—a righteousness, wholeness, and harmony that was to exist among neighbors. Today's criminal justice system could take a cue from the ancient Hebrews, who felt the proper communal response to crime was for the offender to make financial restitution and for the community to restore right relationships among the affected parties.

Finally, the system fails the taxpayers. It would be one thing if the failure to rehabilitate offenders, restore victims, and provide security for communities was a cheap one. Instead, however, this failure is a budget-busting behemoth.

It costs an average of $15,900 to keep a person in prison for one year. Because of overcrowding, state and Federal governments are building new correctional facilities as fast as they can—to the tune of almost $5,000,000,000 in the last fiscal year. Nevertheless, as fast as new prisons are opened, they are filled to capacity and beyond.

For example, during recent years, California has added 30,000 new prison beds at a cost of $2,000,000,000, financed by a costly bond issue. Yet, the state already has been forced to ask for an additional sum almost equal to the original. California taxpayers will have underwritten 50,000 more beds by 1995, at which point, state officials project, they still will be 30,000 beds short! How long can we afford to continue this insane cycle?

When I was incarcerated, my job was to run the washing machine. Next to me, the

former chairman of the board of the American Medical Association ran the dryer. This skilled doctor could have been sentenced to provide free medical help to the poor, thus contributing to the community, rather than costing taxpayers about $16,000 a year in prison.

Restoring lives

On all four counts, our system is failing us. The road back to sanity starts by rediscovering the root causes of crime, best articulated in a landmark study conducted by Stanton Samenow and Samuel Yochelson. In 1976, they published *The Criminal Personality*, the result of 17 years of clinical analysis. According to conventional wisdom, they expected their subjects' criminal behavior to hinge on factors such as poverty, race, deprivation, or environment.

To their surprise, they found a clear and different trend. Such anti-social behavior came not from external social factors, but from internal moral choices. Criminals, not society, created crime.

Samenow and Yochelson, who were Jewish, used a "Christian" term to describe what could change a criminal—the *conversion* of the wrongdoer to a more responsible lifestyle. Accordingly, the only way to deal with crime and sin is at its root—in the human heart—and it is working. Through Prison Fellowship, I've worked with thousands of inmates over the years, hardened criminals whose lives truly have been transformed.

Prison Fellowship volunteers bring hope to the nearly 600 prisons in which we work. We offer offenders a fresh vision, the opportunity to make correct moral choices. They can find forgiveness for their sins and a new life through a personal relationship with Jesus Christ. Across the country, prisoners are turning their backs on their old habits and becoming responsible citizens.

There is hope as well for restoring our ailing criminal justice system. The tired, old rhetoric may please crowds, but it accomplishes little else. We—politicians, criminal justice officials, and volunteer citizens—need to work toward creative, effective solutions. Let me propose a few.

First, we should divert nondangerous offenders away from penal institutions. Restitution, house arrest, intensive probation, and similar programs protect the community, restore victims, and allow offenders to gain a sense of dignity and self-worth that can contribute to real rehabilitation.

Diverting the nondangerous offenders from prison to work in community service would ease overcrowding in our institutions, freeing up space for the truly dangerous who ought to be confined longer for the public's protection.

Second, we can redirect the criminal justice system to what once was one of its primary purposes—the restoration of victims. When possible, they should be compensated with restitution payments. They should have the right to pursue civil damages as part of the criminal case.

More volunteer-run victim assistance programs can help casualties of crime walk through the trauma of their situations and get back on their feet. Moreover, reconciliation programs can get victims and offenders to meet face to face, with a mediator, and work out a satisfactory restitution agreement. These meetings give victims an opportunity to express anger, fear, and frustration. Yet, as they listen to the offender, they often realize that this person is a human being, not a monster. As offenders are forced to confront the human impact of their crime, they often ask for forgiveness.

Third, instead of spending money on new prisons, we should invest in drug treatment centers. The majority of crimes in this country are drug-related. To solve the problem, we must deal with the root—addiction.

By taking these steps, we can begin to bring order into our criminal justice system—restoring justice, repaying victims for losses and injuries suffered, returning a measure of peace and well-being to our communities, attacking the drug problem at its root, and even restoring hope and a sense of self-worth to criminals themselves.

This latter point is crucial. It is in society's interest to make punishment redemptive. Sitting in a prison cell with nothing to do is demeaning and destructive. Put people to work, and they begin to regain a sense of value.

A dramatic example of the power of prisoner service occurred in one of America's oldest and dreariest correctional facilities. The Maryland Penitentiary is the home of the state's most violent offenders, as well as to any inmate in the corrections system diagnosed with AIDS. The AIDS ward is its own death row. The inmates, waiting for the disease to take its inevitable toll, are isolated from contact with the rest of the institution.

Recently, however, fresh hope came to that unit from some surprising sources. First, a local church in Baltimore raised $7,500 to renovate and furnish a new cell block for the AIDS inmates. Then, a group of non-AIDS prisoners, men whose lives and values had been converted by the power of Jesus Christ, volunteered to be part of a special in-house service project—turning an old, barren cellblock into what has become known as "The Living Room."

Five inmates, who wanted to help others, even those in their midst who were feared and isolated, worked for six weeks in the evenings, refurbishing the block, scraping away grime and dust, and repairing and tiling the floor.

I had the privilege of speaking at the dedication service for The Living Room. The walls of the new quarters were painted bright shades of fuschia. Couches and chairs, a television set and VCR, games, books, and exercise equipment had been donated from church funds.

"I never expected to see anything like this. I feel like a child at Christmas," said one infected inmate. If a hardened offender can learn a new way to live while behind bars, there is hope. If we can apply this same spirit of cooperation, respect, and caring for others in communities across the country, there may be hope for a system otherwise wracked by costly failures and growing frustrations.

Criminal Rulings Granted the State Broad New Power

Ira Mickenberg

Special to The National Law Journal

Mr. Mickenberg is a New York attorney specializing in criminal appeals.

FIVE YEARS ago it would have been inconceivable to suggest that the departure of Thurgood Marshall might have no immediate impact on U.S. Supreme Court rulings in the area of criminal law. Yet if the 1990-'91 term is any indication of trends to come, the replacement of Justice Marshall will only allow the government to win criminal cases by 7-2 and 8-1 majorities, instead of 6-3 and 7-2.

The addition of Justice David H. Souter appears to have created a solid conservative majority, determined to grant the state extensive new authority in criminal law. During the past year, virtually every criminal case of any significance was decided in favor of the government. In some instances, this required overruling decades of precedent. Other cases merely required discarding two or three years of past decisions. In still others, the court reinterpreted old cases in ways that give the state broad new power to search, seize and interrogate its citizens.

If one case epitomizes the court's criminal jurisprudence during 1990-'91, it is *Arizona v. Fulminante.*[1] For decades, it has been a truism that convictions obtained with the aid of coerced confessions must be reversed. The notion of police extracting an involuntary confession from a suspect was deemed so abhorrent to a free society that whenever such a confession is used at trial, the conviction must fall. The use of coerced confessions was viewed so seriously that when the court ruled in 1967 that some constitutional trial errors might be "harmless" — meaning that if the other evidence of guilt was overwhelming, a conviction could still be affirmed — coerced confessions were specifically excepted from "harmless error" analysis.[2]

'Trial Error'

In *Fulminante*, the court overruled years of precedent to hold that if other evidence introduced at trial is strong enough, the use of a coerced confession could be considered harmless and a conviction upheld. Writing for the majority on this issue, Chief Justice William H. Rehnquist ruled that the use of coerced confessions is a "trial error," which occurs "during the presentation of the case to the jury, and which may therefore be quantitatively assessed in the context of other evidence presented in order to determine whether its admission was harmless beyond a reasonable doubt." According to the chief justice, viewing involuntary confessions in this way "promotes public respect for the criminal process by focusing on the underlying fairness of the trial rather than on the virtually inevitable presence of immaterial error."

In many respects, *Fulminante* goes a long way toward explaining the philosophical attitude upon which the court's view of criminal procedure is based. Perhaps the most significant thing about the majority opinion is that it is a document totally devoid of historical context. It views constitutional protections, such as the ban on coerced confessions, as liberal curiosities that have been introduced into the law for no apparent reason, and serve no purpose other than interfering with the truth-seeking function of trials. Nowhere does the majority discuss or even mention the reason for prohibiting involuntary confessions. Nowhere does it address the vital question of whether coercive interrogation is so evil that the need to prevent it transcends the truth-seeking function.

In past decades, the court repeatedly explained its reasons for barring coerced confessions, citing the extraordinary danger posed by police coercion to a democratic society and the manner in which it taints the entire judicial process. In *Payne v. Arkansas*[3] in 1957, for example, the court held that:

[W]here, as here, a coerced confession constitutes a part of the evidence before the jury and a general verdict is returned, no one can say what credit and weight the jury gave to the confession. And in these circumstances this Court has uniformly held that even though there may have been sufficient evidence, apart from the coerced confession, to support a judgment of conviction, the admission in evidence, over objection, of the coerced confession vitiates the judgment.

In the midst of World War II, Justice Hugo Black, writing for the majority in *Ashcraft v. Tennessee*,[4] wrote:

The Constitution of the United States stands as a bar against the conviction of any individual in an American court by means of a coerced confession. There have been and are now, certain foreign nations with governments dedicated to an opposite policy: governments which convict individuals with testimony obtained by police organizations possessed of an unrestrained power to seize persons suspected of crimes against the state, hold them in secret custody, and wring from them confessions by physical or mental torture. So long as the Constitution remains the basic law of our Republic, America will not have that kind of government.

In *Fulminante*, the 1991 court did not even mention these concerns.

Nationally, the problem of police brutality obviously has not gone away. The majority in *Fulminante*, however, acts as though it has. It relegates involuntary confessions to the category of "the virtually inevitable presence of immaterial error," and it makes no attempt to explain why coerced admissions are less abhorrent now than in the past.

Yet, as the *Fulminante* dissenters noted:

[T]he use of coerced confessions, whether true or false, is forbidden because the methods used to extract them offend an underlying principle in the enforcement of our criminal law: that ours is an accusatorial and not an inquisitorial system...The search for truth is indeed central to our system of justice, but certain constitutional rights are not, and should not be, subject to harmless-error analysis because those rights protect important values that are unrelated to the truth-seeking function of the trial.

Gauging Court's Intent

For several reasons, the decision in *Fulminante* provides a good barometer of the court's intentions. First, *Fulminante* demonstrates that the present Supreme Court is willing to jettison even the oldest and most established constitutional protections afforded criminal defendants. Second, the case suggests the manner in which the court intends to proceed in dealing with other constitutional rights.

The court in *Fulminante* did not hold that coerced confessions are admissible. Rather, it said that if the other evidence in the case is strong enough, the use of an involuntary statement may be harmless. By so ruling, the court maintains the appearance of condemning police coercion, while sending a signal to lower courts that if they really want to uphold a tainted conviction, the painless excuse of "harmless error" is always available.

Finally, *Fulminante* suggests that the court is striving to impose an explicit political agenda on the development of criminal law. As any member of the Federalist Society will confirm, the Supreme Court long has operated under the principle that it will decide constitutional questions only when essential to resolving the case before it. In *Fulminante*, there was no need for the court to address the harmless-error issue at all. A majority held that use of the coerced statements was not harmless, and the conviction was reversed.

Thus, the harmless error-holding was completely irrelevant to the determination of this particular case. Nonetheless, the court went out of its way to reach the question and to reverse decades of precedent. This is exactly the kind of "activist" behavior that conservatives long have claimed to be the exclusive province of liberal courts — once again proving that activism is largely a question of whose judicial ox is being gored.

Fulminante grants lower courts a tool for affirming otherwise tainted convictions. A pair of other cases decided in the past term give police officers expanded powers to search people under circumstances previously viewed as dubious.

Searches on Buses

Several years ago, the sheriff's department of Broward County, Fla., adopted a policy of routinely boarding buses at scheduled stops and asking passengers for permission to search their luggage. The officers referred to this duty as "working the buses."

There was no claim that the police had probable cause to search anyone. In fact, the state admitted that they generally had no information at all about the passengers. The technique was so common that one officer testified that he searched more than 3,000 bags in a nine-month period.[5]

Employing a standard that had been used for many years, the Florida Supreme Court held that a reasonable bus passenger accosted by police under these circumstances would not feel free to leave the bus and the officers. Accordingly, it held this form of police action to be the equivalent of seizing the passengers without probable cause. Even if the subject ultimately consented to being searched, that consent did not legitimize the unlawful police action. Any items seized pursuant to such a search were to be suppressed.

In *Florida v. Bostick*,[6] the U.S. Supreme Court reversed the holding of the Florida court and ruled that "The mere fact that Bostick did not feel free to leave the bus does not mean that the police seized him." The majority supported this conclusion by reasoning that:

Bostick was a passenger on a bus that was scheduled to depart. He would not have felt free to leave the bus even if the police had not been present. Bostick's movements were 'confined' in a sense, but this was the natural result of his decision to take the bus; it says nothing about whether or not the police conduct at issue was coercive.

Dissenting, Justice Marshall charged the majority with engaging in sophistry that "trivializes the values that underlie the Fourth Amendment." He wrote:

[A] person's 'voluntary decision' to place himself in a room with only one exit does not authorize the police to force an encounter upon him by placing themselves in front of the exit...By consciously deciding to single out persons who have undertaken interstate or intrastate travel, officers who conduct suspicionless, dragnet-style sweeps put passengers to the choice of cooperating or of exiting their buses and possibly being stranded in unfamiliar locations. It is exactly because this 'choice' is no 'choice' at all that police engage this technique.

Just as the majority in *Fulminante* did not hold that the coerced confession was actually harmless, the majority in *Bostick* did not decide whether the defendant really had been seized. In fact, it remanded the case to the trial court for a hearing on that narrow factual issue.

As in *Fulminante*, however, the majority in *Bostick* used the opportunity to send a clear signal to police departments and trial courts that a previously suspect investigative tactic is now permissible. Given the holding in *Bostick*, encounters with armed officers desiring to question and search random passengers can now become a routine part of travel in America.

POLICE WERE given additional leeway to investigate in *California v. Hodari D.*[7] In that case, a group of youths fled at the approach of a police car. The officers had no information about the "suspects" and no cause to believe that they were committing a crime. In fact, the prosecution conceded that the police did not even have "reasonable suspicion" on which to detain anyone.

Nonetheless, officers pursued the youths, ultimately confronting the defendant, referred to in the decision only as Hodari D., who then discarded a piece of crack cocaine. The California Court of Appeal held that the evidence must be suppressed because Hodari was effectively seized when he saw the police chasing him. Since there was no basis for believing that Hodari was committing a crime, the seizure was illegal. This opinion was unremarkable, and consistent with established views of the Fourth Amendment. The Supreme Court reversed.

Writing for the majority, Justice Antonin Scalia held that the defendant was not seized until the police physically grabbed him. The fact that officers were chasing him without cause, and that his alleged throwing away of the drugs undoubtedly was caused by the pursuit, was irrelevant to the question of whether Hodari had been "seized" for Fourth Amendment purposes:

The narrow question before us is whether, with respect to a show of authority as with respect to application of physical force, a seizure occurs even though the subject does not yield. We hold that it does not...In sum, assuming that [the police] pursuit in the present case constituted a 'show of authority' enjoining Hodari to halt, since Hodari did not comply with that injunction he was not seized until he was tackled.

Dissenting, Justice John Paul Stevens wrote that "the Court now adopts a definition of 'seizure' that is unfaithful to a long line of Fourth Amendment cases...Whatever else one may think of today's decision, it unquestionably represents a departure from earlier Fourth Amendment case law."

Before *Hodari D.*, it was understood — at least since *Terry v. Ohio,*[8] *Katz v. U.S.,*[9] *U.S. v. Mendenhall*[10] and *Florida v. Royer*[11] — that a seizure occurs whenever an objective evaluation of a police officer's show of force conveys the message that the citizen is not entirely free to leave. *Hodari D.*, however, seems to replace this definition with a new standard, holding that a person has not been seized until police have forced the person to submit to their authority by means of physical contact.

This new standard invites police to engage in broad investigative actions that previously had been thought illegal. As Justice Stevens points out, "[i]f carried to its logical conclusion, it will encourage unlawful displays of force that will frighten countless innocent citizens into surrendering whatever privacy rights they may still have."

The dissent further notes that on an even more dangerous level, "the Court assumes, without acknowledging, that a police officer may now fire his weapon at an innocent citizen and not implicate the Fourth Amendment — as long as he misses his target."

The majority decision in *Hodari D.* also provides a hint of things to come in future court terms. Although the *Hodari D.* prosecution conceded that police had no justification to chase a defendant about whom they had no information, Justice Scalia suggested that he may be willing to rule otherwise. Citing Proverbs 28:1 — "The wicked flee when no man pursueth" — he noted that:

California conceded below that Officer Pertoso did not have the "reasonable suspicion" required to justify stopping Hodari...That it would be unreasonable to stop, for brief inquiry, young men who scatter in panic upon the mere sighting of the police is not self-evident, and arguably contradicts proverbial common sense...We do not decide that point here, but rely entirely upon the State's concession [citations omitted].

It would not be shocking, if during the 1991-'92 term, the court were to find an opportunity to hold that flight, without more, is sufficient to justify chase, detention and search. Should that come to pass, a combined reading of *Bostick* and *Hodari D.* would present a curious result.

If a person accosted by police without cause decides to flee, he or she has, by fleeing, created the cause that previously was missing. If, on the other hand, that same person does not flee, he or she may well be considered to have consented to the encounter. The only way to avoid an interrogation and search may be to stand up to an armed police officer and declare, "I will not leave your presence, but I will not consent to be questioned, seized or searched." One wonders how many people would have the courage to take such a stand. One also wonders just how suspicious Justice Scalia would consider such behavior.

Automobile Searches

Having dealt with suspects on foot and in buses, the court turned to those fortunate enough to drive cars.

The question of when police officers may conduct a warrantless search of an automobile long has been one of the most complex to face the court. As a general rule, the Fourth Amendment requires that even when police have probable cause to search, they must first obtain a warrant. The reason for this rule is that the determination of whether sufficient legal cause exists to invade a person's privacy should be made by a neutral magistrate, not a police officer.

The court, however, has carved out several exceptions to this warrant requirement, which allow police to act quickly in situations in which the evidence is likely to disappear before a warrant can be obtained. In *Carroll v. U.S.,*[12] the court created such an exception for searches of moving vehicles, since a car or boat is sufficiently mobile simply to leave the scene while police are waiting for a warrant. This "automobile exception" to the warrant requirement allows officers, when they have probable cause to search a particular car, to conduct the search without first obtaining a warrant.

The extent of the automobile exception was clarified in two more recent cases, *Arkansas v. Sanders*[13] and *U.S. v. Chadwick.*[14] In those matters, the court ruled that the automobile exception to the warrant requirement does not apply to situations in which the target of the search is not the car itself, but a sealed container that the police believe contains contraband and that has been placed in the car.

Thus, if officers had probable cause to believe that drugs were hidden somewhere inside a car, they could search the car for narcotics without a warrant. If officers believed, however, that a package being carried by a defendant contains drugs, and the defendant then places the package in his or her car, the officers might seize the package but had to get a warrant before opening it.

The rationale for this rule was that although a car is mobile, a package is not. Therefore, once the police have seized the package, there is no reason why a judicial determination of probable cause should not be made before opening it and further invading the suspect's privacy.

Standard Overruled

In *California v. Acevedo*[15] and the similar case of *Florida v. Jimeno*,[16] the Supreme Court overruled *Sanders*. The court held that the automobile exception not only covers vehicles but also permits warrantless searches of immobile packages that have been placed in cars.

Acevedo involved a factual situation identical to that of *Sanders*. Police observed the defendant leaving his house, carrying a brown paper bag the size of marijuana packages they had seen earlier. He placed the bag in his car's trunk, and as he drove away, police stopped the car, opened the trunk and seized and opened the bag.

The law is quite clear that had the officers stopped the defendant, Charles Steven Acevedo, before he put the bag in his car, they could have seized the bag but would have had to get a warrant before opening it. Writing for the majority, however, Justice Harry A. Blackmun focused not on the privacy interest one normally has in one's luggage and packages, but on the need for uniformity in allowing searches of vehicles. He determined that it was illogical and unproductive to have different standards for searching a car and searching containers placed in the car:

[B]y attempting to distinguish between a container for which the police are specifically searching and a container which they come across in a car, we have provided only minimal protection for privacy and have impeded effective law enforcement.

While Justice Blackmun's majority opinion only expands the present scope of the warrant requirement, Justice Scalia's concurrence provides a glimpse of where the court is headed in Fourth Amendment jurisprudence:

I would reverse the judgment in the present case, not because a closed container carried inside a car becomes subject to the "automobile" exception to the general warrant requirement, but because the search of a closed container, outside a privately owned building, with probable cause to believe that the container contains contraband, and when it in fact does contain contraband, is not one of those searches whose Fourth Amendment reasonableness depends upon a warrant.

The concurrence includes two radical departures from presently existing search-and-seizure law. First, it virtually would read the warrant requirement out of the Constitution. If the police can approach someone carrying a closed container and search the container without a warrant, it is difficult to foresee circumstances in which officers would be required to get a warrant.

Second, by including the seemingly innocuous phrase "when it in fact does contain contraband," Justice Scalia could be suggesting that in the future, searches might be justified by what they ultimately disclose. Or, put in other terms, it is never reasonable to expect the Fourth Amendment to protect one from the seizure of contraband. This construct at least would have the virtue of clarity, since it would legitimize all police conduct, render all items seized admissible in criminal trials and eliminate the need for time-consuming suppression hearings.

In the span of nine months, the court has authorized police to chase down citizens whom they have no reason to believe have committed a crime, permitted random interrogation and requests to search people who use public transportation, and specifically allowed state legislatures to establish harsh sentencing schemes that are grossly disproportionate to the crimes to which they are applied.[17]

Individual justices have hinted that the future will bring replacement of the Constitution's present warrant requirement with a vague "reasonableness" standard that will permit virtually any police search without benefit of a warrant. In all, the criminal law decisions of 1990-'91 mark the beginning of a significant change in the relationship between the citizens of this country and its police.

(1) 111 S. Ct. 1246 (1991).
(2) See Chapman v. California, 386 U.S. 18 (1967).
(3) 356 U.S. 560, 568 (1957).
(4) 322 U.S. 143, 155 (1943).
(5) See Florida v. Kerwick, 512 So. 2d 347 (Fla. App. 1987).
(6) 59 U.S.L.W. 4708 (June 20, 1991).
(7) 111 S. Ct. 1547 (1991).
(8) 392 U.S. 1 (1968).
(9) 389 U.S. 347 (1967).
(10) 446 U.S. 544 (1980).
(11) 460 U.S. 491 (1983).
(12) 267 U.S. 132 (1925).
(13) 442 U.S. 753 (1979).
(14) 433 U.S. 1 (1977).
(15) 111 S. Ct. 1982 (1991).
(16) 111 S. Ct. 1801 (1991).
(17) Harmelin v. Michigan, 89-7272 (June 27, 1991).

Juvenile Justice

A century ago children found guilty of committing crimes were punished as if they were adults. Since there were few specialized juvenile detention institutions, children were thrown into jails and prisons with murderers, thieves, drunks, tramps, and prostitutes, with no protection and no programs for rehabilitation.

The establishment of a special criminal justice system for the handling of juvenile offenders was hailed in the

1920s by humanitarians, reformers, and social scientists, and accepted, somewhat reluctantly, by the legal profession and the police. Only recently has the cry of dissent been heard.

Judge Ben Lindsay and others who pioneered the juvenile court movement believed that juveniles sinned out of ignorance, because of the growing pains of adolescence, or because they were corrupted by adults. They believed that a juvenile court should concern itself with finding out why a juvenile was in trouble and what society could do to help him or her. They saw the juvenile judge as parental, concerned, and sympathetic, rather than judgmental. They viewed the juvenile justice process as diagnostic and therapeutic, rather than prosecutive and punitive.

The proponents of this system were, of course, thinking of the delinquents of their time—the runaway, the truant, the petty thief, the beggar, the sexual experimenter, and the insubordinate. Now, however, the juvenile in court is more likely to be on trial for murder, gang rape, arson, or mugging. The 1990s also differ from the 1920s in other ways. Juvenile courts are everywhere, as are juvenile police, juvenile probation officers, and juvenile prisons. Literally hundreds of thousands of American juveniles enter this system annually.

It is clear at this time that the winds of change are blowing across the nation's juvenile justice system. Traditional reforms are being replaced by a new and more conservative agenda. This new reform movement emphasizes the welfare of victims, a punitive approach toward serious juvenile offenders, and protection of children from physical and sexual exploitation. Policies that favor diversion and deinstitutionalization are less popular. After many years of attempting to remove status offenders from the juvenile justice system, there are increasing calls for returning truants, runaways, and other troubled youth to juvenile court jurisdiction. In spite of these developments, however, there are many juvenile justice reformers who remain dedicated to advancing due process rights for children and reducing reliance on incarceration.

Clearly, there is conflict and tension between the old

and new juvenile justice reform agendas. The articles in this section evaluate problems with the current juvenile justice system and present some possible solutions.

The first essay, "Handling of Juvenile Cases," draws distinctions between juvenile cases and adult cases, explains the circumstances under which juveniles may be tried in criminal courts, and reveals that juveniles receive dispositions rather than sentences.

In "The Evolution of the Juvenile Justice System," Barry Krisberg explains how the original purpose for the juvenile system when it was first conceived has been altered rather dramatically.

Are existing delinquency causation theories adequate to the task of explaining female delinquency and official reactions to girls' deviance? The answer is clearly no, according to the author of the next essay, "Girls' Crime and Woman's Place." She maintains that the academic study of delinquent behavior usually focuses on male delinquency alone.

"Teenage Addiction" explores information about drug abuse among teenagers. The article reports on treatment techniques, a successful school-based program for adolescent addicts, and recent research studies. The next article in this unit, "Correcting Juvenile Corrections," makes a case for the benefits of community programs over the use of large institutions for most juvenile offenders.

Disputes once settled with fists are now settled with guns, according to the concluding article titled, "Kids Who Kill."

Looking Ahead: Challenge Questions

When the juvenile court was first conceived, what convictions did its pioneers hold about juvenile offenders?

Some argue that the failure of the juvenile court to fulfill its rehabilitative and preventive promise stems from a grossly oversimplistic view of the phenomenon of juvenile criminality. Do you agree? Why or why not?

Do you believe the departure of the juvenile justice system from its original purpose is warranted?

Handling of Juvenile Cases

Cases involving juveniles are handled much differently than adult cases

The juvenile court and a separate process for handling juveniles resulted from reform movements of the late 19th century

Until that time juveniles who committed crimes were processed through the criminal courts. In 1899 Illinois established the first juvenile court based on the concepts that a juvenile was a salvageable human being who needed treatment rather than punishment and that the juvenile court was to protect the child from the stigma of criminal proceedings. Delinquency and other situations such as neglect and adoption were deemed to warrant the court's intervention on the child's behalf. The juvenile court also handled "status offenses" (such as truancy, running away, and incorrigibility), which are not applicable to adults.

While the juvenile courts and the handling of juveniles remain separated from criminal processing, the concepts on which they are based have changed. Today, juvenile courts usually consider an element of personal responsibility when making decisions about juvenile offenders.

Juvenile courts may retain jurisdiction until a juvenile becomes legally an adult (at age 21 or less in most States). This limit sets a cap on the length of time juveniles may be institutionalized that is often much less than that for adults who commit similar offenses. Some jurisdictions transfer the cases of juveniles accused of serious offenses or with long criminal histories to criminal court so that the length of the sanction cannot be abridged.

Juvenile courts are very different from criminal courts

The language used in juvenile courts is less harsh. For example, juvenile courts—
• accept "petitions" of "delinquency" rather than criminal complaints
• conduct "hearings," not trials
• "adjudicate" juveniles to be "delinquent" rather than find them guilty of a crime
• order one of a number of available "dispositions" rather than sentences.

Despite the wide discretion and informality associated with juvenile court proceedings, juveniles are protected by most of the due process safeguards associated with adult criminal trials.

Most referrals to juvenile court are for property crimes, but 17% are for status offenses

Reasons for referrals to juvenile courts

11%	**Crimes against persons**	
	Criminal homicide	1%
	Forcible rape	2
	Robbery	17
	Aggravated assault	20
	Simple assault	59
		100%
46%	**Crimes against property**	
	Burglary	25%
	Larceny	47
	Motor vehicle theft	5
	Arson	1
	Vandalism and trespassing	19
	Stolen property offenses	3
		100%
5%	**Drug offenses**	100%
21%	**Offenses against public order**	
	Weapons offenses	6%
	Sex offenses	6
	Drunkenness and disorderly conduct	23
	Contempt, probation, and parole violations	21
	Other	44
		100%
17%	**Status offenses**	
	Running away	28%
	Truancy and curfew violations	21
	Ungovernability	28
	Liquor violations	23
		100%
100%	Total all offenses	

Note: Percents may not add to 100 because of rounding.
Source: *Delinquency in the United States 1983*, National Center for Juvenile Justice, July 1986.

Arrest is not the only means of referring juveniles to the courts

While adults may begin criminal justice processing only through arrest, summons, or citation, juveniles may be referred to court by law enforcement agencies, parents, schools, victims, probation officers, or other sources.

Law enforcement agencies refer three-quarters of the juvenile cases, and they are most likely to be the referral source in cases involving curfew violations, drug offenses, and property crimes. Other referral sources are most likely in cases involving status offenses (truancy, ungovernability, and running away).

From *Report to the Nation on Crime and Justice*, Bureau of Justice Statistics, U.S. Department of Justice, March 1988, pp. 78-79, 95.

"Intake" is the first step in the processing of juveniles

At intake, decisions are made about whether to begin formal proceedings. Intake is most frequently performed by the juvenile court or an executive branch intake unit, but increasingly prosecutors are becoming involved. In addition to beginning formal court proceedings, officials at intake may refer the juvenile for psychiatric evaluation, informal probation, or counseling, or, if appropriate, they may close the case altogether.

For a case involving a juvenile to proceed to a court adjudication, the intake unit must file a petition with the court

Intake units handle most cases informally without a petition. The National Center for Juvenile Justice estimates that more than half of all juvenile cases disposed of at intake are handled informally without a petition and are dismissed and/or referred to a social service agency.

Initial juvenile detention decisions are usually made by the intake staff

Prior to holding an adjudicatory hearing, juveniles may be released in the custody of their parents, put in protective custody (usually in foster homes or runaway shelters), or admitted to detention facilities. In most States juveniles are not eligible for bail, unlike adults.

Relatively few juveniles are detained prior to court appearance

One juvenile case in five involved secure detention prior to adjudication in 1983. Status offenders were least likely to be detained. The proportion of status offenders detained has declined from 40% in 1975 to 11% in 1983.

All States allow juveniles to be tried as adults in criminal courts

Juveniles are referred to criminal courts in one of three ways—

• **Concurrent jurisdiction**—the prosecutor has the discretion of filing charges for certain offenses in either juvenile or criminal courts
• **Excluded offenses**—the legislature excludes from juvenile court jurisdiction certain offenses usually either very minor, such as traffic or fishing violations, or very serious, such as murder or rape
• **Judicial waiver**—the juvenile court waives its jurisdiction and transfers the case to criminal court (the procedure is also known as "binding over" or "certifying" juvenile cases to criminal courts).

Age at which criminal courts gain jurisdiction of young offenders ranges from 16 to 19

Age of offender when under criminal court jurisdiction	States
16 years	Connecticut, New York, North Carolina
17	Georgia, Illinois, Louisiana, Massachusetts, Missouri, South Carolina, Texas
18	Alabama, Alaska, Arizona, Arkansas, California, Colorado, Delaware, District of Columbia, Florida, Hawaii, Idaho, Indiana, Iowa, Kansas, Kentucky, Maine, Maryland, Michigan, Minnesota, Mississippi, Montana, Nebraska, Nevada, New Hampshire, New Jersey, New Mexico, North Dakota, Ohio, Oklahoma, Oregon, Pennsylvania, Rhode Island, South Dakota, Tennessee, Utah, Vermont, Virginia, Washington, West Virginia, Wisconsin, Federal districts
19	Wyoming

Source: "Upper age of juvenile court jurisdiction statutes analysis," Linda A. Szymanski, National Center for Juvenile Justice, March 1987.

12 States authorize prosecutors to file cases in the juvenile or criminal courts at their discretion

This procedure, known as concurrent jurisdiction, may be limited to certain offenses or to juveniles of a certain age. Four States provide concurrent jurisdiction over juveniles charged with traffic violations. Georgia, Nebraska, and Wyoming have concurrent criminal jurisdiction statutes.

As of 1987, 36 States excluded certain offenses from juvenile court jurisdictions

Eighteen States excluded only traffic, watercraft, fish, or game violations. Another 13 States excluded serious offenses; the other 5 excluded serious offenses and some minor offenses. The serious offenses most often excluded are capital crimes such as murder, but several States exclude juveniles previously convicted in criminal courts.

48 States, the District of Columbia, and the Federal Government have judicial waiver provisions

Youngest age at which juvenile may be transferred to criminal court by judicial waiver	States
No specific age	Alaska, Arizona, Arkansas, Delaware, Florida, Indiana, Kentucky, Maine, Maryland, New Hampshire, New Jersey, Oklahoma, South Dakota, West Virginia, Wyoming, Federal districts
10 years	Vermont
12	Montana
13	Georgia, Illinois, Mississippi
14	Alabama, Colorado, Connecticut, Idaho, Iowa, Massachusetts, Minnesota, Missouri, North Carolina, North Dakota, Pennsylvania, South Carolina, Tennessee, Utah
15	District of Columbia, Louisiana, Michigan, New Mexico, Ohio, Oregon, Texas, Virginia
16	California, Hawaii, Kansas, Nevada, Rhode Island, Washington, Wisconsin

Note: Many judicial waiver statutes also specify offenses that are waivable. This chart lists the States by the youngest age for which judicial waiver may be sought without regard to offense.

Source: "Waiver/transfer/certification of juveniles to criminal court: Age restrictions: Crime restrictions," Linda A. Szymanski, National Center for Juvenile Justice, February 1987.

A small proportion of juvenile cases are referred to criminal court

Recent studies found that most juveniles

referred to criminal court were age 17 and were charged with property offenses. However, juveniles charged with violent offenses or with serious prior offense histories were more likely to be adjudicated in criminal court. Waiver of juveniles to criminal court is less likely where court jurisdiction extends for several years beyond the juvenile's 18th birthday.

offending behavior has been corrected, whichever is sooner.

Of the 45 States and the District of Columbia that authorize indeterminate periods of confinement—
• 32 grant releasing authority to the State juvenile corrections agency
• 6 delegate it to juvenile paroling agencies

fixed range of time for commitment, or mandate a minimum length of stay in a type of placement, such as a secure institution.

Dispositions for serious juvenile offenders tend to look like those for adults

Aggregate statistics on juvenile court

Juveniles receive dispositions rather than sentences

Juveniles tried as adults have a very high conviction rate, but most receive sentences of probation or fines

More than 90% of the judicial waiver or concurrent jurisdiction cases in Hamparian's study resulted in guilty verdicts, and more than half the convictions led to fines or probation. Sentences to probation often occur because the criminal courts view juveniles as first offenders regardless of their prior juvenile record. However, serious violent juvenile offenders are more likely to be institutionalized. In a study of 12 jurisdictions with Habitual Serious or Violent Juvenile Offender Programs, 63% of those convicted were sentenced to prison and 14% to jail. The average prison sentence was 6.8 years.

Correctional activities for juveniles tried as adults in most States occur within the criminal justice system

In 1978, in more than half the States, youths convicted as adults and given an incarcerative sentence could only be placed in adult corrections facilities. In 18 jurisdictions, youths convicted as adults could be placed in either adult or juvenile corrections facilities, but sometimes this discretion was limited by special circumstances. Only 6 jurisdictions restricted placements of juveniles convicted as adults to State juvenile corrections institutions. Generally, youths sentenced in this manner will be transferred to adult facilities to serve the remainder of their sentence on reaching majority.

Juvenile court dispositions tend to be indeterminate

The dispositions of juveniles adjudicated to be delinquent extend until the juvenile legally becomes an adult (21 years of age in most States) or until the

• 5 place such authority with the committing judges
• 3 have dual or overlapping jurisdiction.

Most juvenile cases are disposed of informally

In 1982 about 54% of all cases referred to juvenile courts by the police and other agencies were handled informally without the filing of a petition. About 20% of all cases involved some detention prior to disposition.

Of about 600,000 cases in which petitions were filed, 64% resulted in formal adjudication. Of these, 61% resulted in some form of probation, and 29% resulted in an out-of-home placement.

The juvenile justice system is also undergoing changes in the degree of discretion permitted in confinement decisions

Determinate dispositions are now used in six States, but they do not apply to all offenses or offenders. In most cases they apply only to specified felony cases or to the juveniles with prior adjudications for serious delinquencies.

California imposes determinate periods of confinement for delinquents committed to State agencies based on the standards and guidelines of its paroling agency. Four States have similar procedures, administered by the State agencies responsible for operating their juvenile corrections facilities.

As of 1981 eight States had serious-delinquent statutes requiring that juveniles who are either serious, violent, repeat, or habitual offenders be adjudicated and committed in a manner that differs from the adjudication of other delinquents. Such laws require minimum lengths of commitment, prescribe a

dispositions do not provide an accurate picture of what happens to the more serious offenders because many of the cases coming before juvenile courts involve minor criminal or status offenses. These minor cases are more likely to be handled informally by the juvenile court.

An analysis of California cases involving older juveniles and young adults charged by the police with robbery or burglary revealed more similarities in their disposition patterns than the aggregate juvenile court statistics would suggest. For both types of offenses, juvenile petitions were filed and settled formally in court about as often as were complaints filed and convictions obtained in the cases against adults. The juveniles charged with the more serious offenses and those with the more extensive prior records were the most likely to have their cases reach adjudication. At the upper limits of offense and prior record severity, juveniles were committed to secure institutions about as frequently as were young adults with comparable records.

Most juveniles committed to juvenile facilities are delinquents

	Percent of juveniles
Total	100%
Delinquents	74
Nondelinquents	
Status offenders	12
Nonoffenders (dependency, neglect, abuse, etc.)	14

Source: BJS Children in Custody, 1985, unpublished data.

The outcomes of juvenile and adult proceedings are similar, but some options are not available in juvenile court

For example, juvenile courts cannot

order the death penalty, life terms, or terms that could exceed the maximum jurisdiction of the court itself. In Arizona the State Supreme Court held that, despite statutory jurisdiction of the juvenile courts to age 21, delinquents could not be held in State juvenile corrections facilities beyond age 18.[3]

Yet, juvenile courts may go further than criminal courts in regulating the lifestyles of juvenile offenders placed in the community under probation supervision. For example, the court may order them to—
• live in certain locations
• attend school
• participate in programs intended to

improve their behavior.

The National Center for Juvenile Justice estimates that almost 70% of the juveniles whose cases are not waived or dismissed are put on probation; about 10% are committed to an institution.

THE EVOLUTION OF THE JUVENILE JUSTICE SYSTEM

Barry Krisberg

Barry Krisberg is president of the National Council on Crime and Delinquency. He has written extensively on the subject of juvenile delinquency.

This article is an adaptation of an earlier version published by the National Council on Crime and Delinquency.

In part, perhaps, due to sensational accounts of youth crime which have been highlighted by the media in recent years, a public sentiment that is less than sympathetic to young offenders has become prevalent. Yet, many of the juveniles caught in the wave of "get tough" legislation and calls for sterner measures against young criminals may be losing the opportunity to redeem their lives and their futures. The juvenile justice system has evolved into a system quite removed from the original purpose for which it was conceived—the protection of young people from unwarranted punishment. In what follows, three revolutions in the history of the juvenile justice system will be described, showing how the gap between theory and reality emerged.

The first revolution in juvenile justice culminated in the creation of the juvenile court. As early as 1817, the founding of the Society for the Prevention of Pauperism began a new era in the care of troubled youngsters. This group, which in 1824 was renamed the Society for the Reformation of Juvenile Delinquents, consisted of philanthropists who were committed to religious charity in a secular world. These reformers were philosophically close to the Federalists

in that they rejected the concept of popular democracy and viewed themselves as the moral stewards of their community.[1] The Society for the Prevention of Pauperism conducted investigations into methods of dealing with the poor and ultimately recommended changes in policy and legislation. It led campaigns against the corrupting influences of taverns and theatres. Of special importance was its focus on the linkages between poverty and delinquency.

These early reformers, like those of later generations, decried the housing of children in adult jails. The Society's members believed that harsh jail conditions did not result in the rehabilitation of delinquents. In fact, many of them feared that deplorable jail conditions led juries and judges to acquit young criminals rather than send them to these places. Fundamentally, these early reformers believed that the available penal institutions could not solve the underlying problems of pauperism. They envisioned a special prison for wayward youth that would emphasize education, industry and moral training.[2] The first of these youth prisons, the New York City House of Refuge, was opened in 1825. Within a few years other houses of refuge were established in Philadelphia, Boston and other major cities, and accepted children convicted of crimes as well as destitute youth. These new facilities were preventive institutions designed to accept the children of unfit parents. This new concept immediately brought judicial review to define the limits of the houses of refuge to supercede parental authority. The Pennsylvania Supreme Court carefully examined this matter in *Ex Parte*

Crouse (1838), holding that parental control was not an inalienable right.

The object of charity is reformation by training of inmates; by imbuing their minds with principles of morality and religion; by furnishing them with a means to earn a living; and, above all, by separating them from the corrupting influences of improper associates. To this end, may not the natural parents, when unequal to the task of education, or unworthy of it, be superceded by the *parens patriae* or common guardian of the community?[3]

The *Crouse* case elaborated the key legal doctrine of *parens patriae* that supported the virtually unrestrained powers of later juvenile courts.

While the houses of refuge had many prominent supporters, the new youth prisons also suffered the problems that would plague later juvenile correctional facilities. For example, there is ample evidence of the use of solitary confinement, whipping and other forms of corporal punishment. The labor system within the houses of refuge was managed by outside contractors who sometimes abused the children. There was rarely enough work to keep all of the inmates busy and that which was available was mostly menial in nature. Violence was commonplace in these prisons, and one historian estimates that 40 percent of the children escaped from the institutions or from their post-release placements.[4]

Throughout the nineteenth century, the practice of incarcerating wayward youth expanded. Over the next several

This article appeared in *The World & I*, April 1990, pp. 487-503, and is reprinted with permission from *The World & I*, a publication of The Washington Times Corporation, copyright © 1990.

decades the houses of refuge, which were established by private philanthropic groups, were taken over by state and local governments. The shift from private to public operation was stimulated by the scandals and abuses aforementioned and the growing influence of government in the management of welfare programs. By 1890, every state outside the South had a refuge or reform school and many jurisdictions had separate facilities for males and females.

This rapidly growing youth corrections system also had its critics. Nineteenth century child advocates, including Samuel Gridley Howe and Charles Loring Brace, founded children's aid societies to rescue youth from lives of depravity and crime. The societies emphasized missionary work in urban neighborhoods. Members' personal experiences convinced them that urban poverty was too widespread to be contained by expanding the number of correctional facilities. In particular, Brace asserted that houses of refuge were breeding grounds for crime. To replace them, he advocated solving delinquency by placing urban poor children with families in the West. Brace had traveled to Europe and was impressed with the values and strength of the German farm family. To Brace and his followers, the family was "God's reformatory" and the American farm families of the West seemed to possess the same qualities he found in Germany.

Partly in response to Brace and his followers, many juvenile facilities attempted to reorganize their routines around a "cottage" or "family" system, placing youth in smaller living units of 40 or less with live-in house parents. Corrections officials responded to the claims about the rehabilitative values of farm life by locating new institutions in rural areas and expanding inmate participation in agricultural labor.

Probation was a parallel development during the mid-nineteenth century. In 1841, a Boston shoemaker, John Augustus, began putting up bail money for public inebriates. Although he possessed no formal court position, Augustus soon expanded his efforts to young offenders. He supervised wayward youngsters on bail and provided them with clothing and shelter, in addition to helping them find jobs and often paying their court expenses. As word of Augustus' good works spread, several children's aid societies took up similar activities. By 1869, Massachusetts had

Early reformers envisioned a special prison for wayward youth that would emphasize education, industry, and moral training.

established a system in which representatives of the Board of State Charities assumed responsibility for youths before they appeared in court. Youngsters placed under the custody of the Board of Charities were then released on probation subject to their maintaining proper behavior in the future.

Proponents of correctional facilities and those who stressed the need for community-based services were often engaged in intensely ideological debates, fueled by regular reports of arson and violence in the juvenile prisons, along with continuous accounts of physical abuse of incarcerated children. Moreover, the labor unions objected to the system of contract labor in the reform schools. The rumors of scandal and abuse led to a series of well-publicized investigations. Many states formed special boards and commissions to inspect the youth facilities and to make recommendations for reform. While some hoped that the new state boards would find alternatives to reform schools, the number of incarcerated young people continued to increase.

These historical forces culminated in the Illinois Juvenile Court Law of 1899 —the first comprehensive child welfare legislation in American history. The state of Illinois possessed virtually no specialized institutions for children, for its earlier reform schools had been destroyed by fires. Juvenile justice advocates, who were joined by powerful allies such as the Chicago Bar Association and Chicago Women's Club, decried the practice of holding large numbers of youngsters in the Cook County jail.

The new Illinois juvenile court was mandated to handle delinquent, dependent and neglected children. Court jurisdiction was intentionally made broad and the new "children's court" inherited much of the legal thinking that surrounded the houses of refuge. Juveniles who violated any state law or municipal ordinance could be brought before the court, which was also responsible for controlling

youth charged with truancy, running away and chronic disobedience. The Illinois law gave the court enormous discretion to remove youngsters from their homes or to supervise them in the community. Interestingly, the new law recognized the role of unpaid probation officers to assist the court in its work.

The concept of a separate children's court was quickly adopted by many states. By 1925, all but two states had specialized legal proceedings for young people. Child advocates believed they had ushered in a new model for dealing with wayward youth. The Pennsylvania Supreme Court echoed the earlier sentiments of the *Crouse* case in defending the state's new juvenile court law.

To save a child from becoming a criminal, or continuing a career of crime . . . the legislatures surely may provide for the salvation of such a child, if its parents or guardians be unwilling or unable to do so, by bringing it into one of the courts of the state *without any process at all*, for the purpose of subjecting it to the state's guardianship and protection.[5]

The juvenile court did have its early detractors, many of whom pointed to the large number of children that continued to languish in adult jails. Some legal scholars, including Roscoe Pound and Judge Ben Lindsey, worried about the seemingly unlimited discretion of the children's court. Moreover, many observers noted that urban courts were virtually swamped with children and families whose needs greatly outstripped available court resources. The promise of individualized treatment and close supervision quickly came apart under staggering court dockets that often permitted less than ten minutes per case for hearings.

The founders of the juvenile court movement sought to solve some of these problems by employing the emerging

153

technologies suggested by the new behavioral sciences. Influential reformers such as Julia Lathrop and Jane Addams raised funds to sponsor comprehensive studies of children going through the juvenile courts. The child advocates commissioned Dr. William A. Healy to examine thousands of youngsters using social, psychological and even anthropometric measures. It was Healy's hope that these detailed studies would lead to highly individualized treatment plans for each youth. This early scientific work was heavily influenced by the theories of Freudian psychology and emphasized the importance of the family as the key to delinquent behavior.

Healy's work helped establish child guidance clinics that were attached to most urban juvenile courts. By 1931, there were 232 clinics across the nation, including a traveling child guidance clinic that visited Western rural communities. Most important, the new clinics provided a rationale for the extremely flexible and discretionary operations of the court. The clinic movement led to a de-emphasis on legal principles and increased reliance on "experts" trained in social work and the behavioral sciences. The basic model of the children's court and the child guidance clinic dominated juvenile justice for the next three decades.

JUVENILE JUSTICE

Whereas the first revolution in juvenile justice culminated in a new children's court with expansive powers, the second revolution aimed at reducing the intrusion of the juvenile court into children's lives. Sociologist LaMar Empey[6] has characterized this second transformation of juvenile justice in terms of the "Four D's"—decriminalization, due process, diversion and deinstitutionalization. Before discussing the specific components of the second revolution, it is important to examine the forces that motivated these reform efforts.

During the two decades after World War II, the juvenile justice system faced many intractable problems, including the spread of adolescent drug use and the emergence of violent youth gangs. The court's clients were increasingly minority children and their families, whose cultural backgrounds and experiences differed greatly from those of court staff. The ex-

Throughout the nineteenth century, the practice of incarcerating wayward youth expanded.

tent of urban poverty and social deprivation increased, placing further burdens on the juvenile court's already strained resources.

Critics of the juvenile court became more vocal and more organized. The most politically potent attack on the court charged that judges were overly lenient with violent and serious offenders. Some critics questioned the court's practice of mixing dependent and neglected youth with serious criminal offenders, while others alleged that the court was particularly punitive in handling female status offenders. The mounting attacks on the court were fueled by periodic reports of scandals and child abuse in juvenile correctional facilities.

During the 1960s, growing doubts about the juvenile court led to a series of major U.S. Supreme Court decisions that fundamentally changed the court's character. For example, in *Kent v. U.S.* (1966) the Supreme Court warned juvenile courts against arbitrariness in detention procedures. One year later in *In re Gault* (1967) the Supreme Court specified a detailed list of rights that must be accorded juveniles in court hearings. The *Gault* decision focused on notification of charges, protections against self-incrimination, the right to confront witnesses and the right to have a written transcript of the proceedings. Many juvenile court personnel were opposed to these new rights, claiming that the informal humanitarian juvenile court would be supplanted by an impersonal junior criminal court. Nonetheless, communities across the nation struggled to find methods of providing legal representation for indigent youth and virtually every state was required to redraft its juvenile court codes to conform with the Supreme Court's dictates.

Concurrent with the judicial review of court practices, a professional and political consensus emerged on behalf of limiting formal court intervention in children's lives. The President's Commission

on Law Enforcement and the Administration of Justice (1967), established by President Lyndon Johnson, advocated the expansion of programs to divert youth from the court system and reduce the number of youngsters housed in detention centers and training schools. In 1974 the Congress enacted, by an overwhelming majority, the Juvenile Justice and Delinquency Prevention Act (JJDPA) which provided federal judges to states which agreed to remove status offenders from secure confinement and to separate children from adults in jails.[7] These new federal funds were earmarked for programs of diversion, deinstitutionalization, delinquency prevention and other "advanced practices." Almost immediately, all but a few states voluntarily joined the new federal juvenile justice policies.

Child advocates and federal lawmakers were also strongly influenced by dramatic developments occurring in Massachusetts during the early 1970s. Led by Commissioner Jerome Miller, the Massachusetts Department of Youth Services closed all of the state's training schools —moving nearly 1000 youngsters into a diverse array of small, community-based programs. Encouraged by the apparent successes in Massachusetts and the availability of substantial federal grant funds, juvenile justice reformers hoped to usher in a new age of enlightened juvenile justice practices.

Decriminalization. As states moved to revise their juvenile codes pursuant to the *Gault* decision, the separate status offender category was often included in new statutes. Suddenly there were Children in Need of Supervision (CHINS), Minors in Need of Supervision (MINS) and Unruly Children (UC). A national task force on juvenile justice even recommended the category of Families in Need of Supervision (FINS). Yet many youth advocates were unhappy with the new legal labels. Concerns were voiced that People in Need of Supervision (PINS) were not treated substantially differently than delinquents. For example, there was continued mixing of delinquents and status offenders in secure detention centers. Other critics questioned the logic of moving status offenders into the child welfare systems which were already overloaded with dependency and neglect cases. Also, courts employed their contempt powers to incarcerate status offenders who defied court orders or who ran away from placements.

The National Council on Crime and Delinquency called for the complete elimination of court jurisdiction over status offenders, arguing that community-based programs rather than court services were more relevant to solving the personal and family problems of status offenders.[8]

Despite the impressive array of groups seeking to end court jurisdiction over status offenses, very few states moved in this direction.

Diversion. The 1967 President's Crime Commission had strongly endorsed diversion as a new method of handling status offenders and petty delinquents. Youth were to be diverted from formal juvenile justice processing into community-based services. Diversion could be accomplished either by police agencies or by court intake personnel. The Crime Commission recommended that communities create youth services bureaus that would assist the police and courts in making diversion decisions as well as providing a range of voluntary services. Funding from the United States Department of Justice helped launch hundreds of youth services bureaus across the nation.

The diversion movement soon encountered several problems. As federal funding ended, the community-based youth services bureaus were replaced by diversion programs operated by juvenile justice agencies. Observers expressed the concern that diversion programs were dominated by the interests of law enforcement agencies—who controlled intake into diversion programs, thereby defining which clients they would serve. Diversion programs have been criticized as discriminatory towards female offenders. Some research showed that diversion programs often "widened the net" of social control —drawing clients from youth who previously would have had their cases dismissed or would not even have been referred. Further, other studies indicated that diversion programs that emphasized individual and family counseling produced worse outcomes across several measures

During the 1960s, a series of major U.S. Supreme Court decisions fundamentally changed the Court's character.

than programs which diverted youth to no services.

The aggregate data on the impact of diversion is mixed. The *Uniform Crime Reports* data on juvenile arrests showed a major drop in the volume of juvenile arrests from 1971 to 1981, including a decline in arrests for status offenses. But of those arrested, a higher proportion of youth were taken into custody. The proportion of youngsters referred to noncourt agencies declined. Thus, it appears that the police were not arresting status offenders at the same levels as previously. It is less clear whether this drop in status offense arrests was attributable to diversion programs. During this period there was a significant decline in the overall size of the youth population that could partially explain the drop in status offense arrests. Moreover, some have argued that the movement to decriminalize status offenses may have produced the unanticipated consequence of status offenders being relabeled as delinquents.

During this same period, juvenile court caseloads remained relatively constant. The proportions of court referrals handled via formal versus informal dispositions were largely unchanged—suggesting a minimal impact of diversion at the court level. In the 1980s, fiscal constraints and major retrenchments in federal funding led to the demise of most diversion programs. Diversion programs could not withstand the increasingly shrill political rhetoric to "get tough" with juvenile offenders.

Deinstitutionalization. If youngsters could not be diverted from the juvenile court, at least they could be treated in smaller community-based programs. Developments in Massachusetts and California's Probation Subsidy program had shown the way and the federal Office of Juvenile Justice and Delinquency Prevention (OJJDP) provided funds to encourage the deinstitutionalization process. This juvenile justice reform movement resonated with similar system change efforts in the

treatment of the mentally ill, the dependent and the disabled.[9] The key concepts of this period were "mainstreaming," "normalization" and "community-based care." Advocates of deinstitutionalization asserted that these new programs would avert the many abuses that were regularly occurring in large state-run institutions and that the smaller, localized treatment environments would produce better outcomes for clients.

The deinstitutionalization movement initially produced promising results. For example, admissions to public juvenile correctional facilities declined by 12 percent between 1974 and 1979; the number of confined youth as measured by a series of one day counts also declined slightly. The drop in admissions was largely due to fewer status offenders being sent to detention centers. Admissions to training schools remained fairly constant during this period.

Data on admissions to private juvenile facilities suggest that youth, particularly females, were shifted from public to private facilities, raising questions about the real impact of the deinstitutionalization process. However, it must be recalled that the advocates of deinstitutionalization sought to increase placements in private and community-based programs. In general, private facilities were more likely to be small group homes and half-way houses, whereas public placements mostly consisted of large secure detention centers and training schools. Some critics raised important questions about (1) the quality of care in private programs, (2) the longer average stays in private facilities and (3) the apparent discriminatory tendency to place white youth in private programs and minority youngsters in public facilities.

After 1979, the data on children in juvenile facilities revealed growing numbers of young people in public and private facilities.[10] These increases were primarily caused by lengthening institutional stays. In the late 1970s, most states enacted new legislation designed to harshen the penalties for serious juvenile offenders. States passed laws making it easier to transfer juveniles to adult criminal courts and mandated stiffer penalties in juvenile courts. The policy of the OJJDP urged the passage of tougher sentencing laws and openly questioned the wisdom of deinstitutionalization policies.

Despite the new "get tough" policies of the U.S. Department of Justice and in statehouses across the nation, several states made substantial progress in removing juveniles from large, congregate institutions. In states as diverse as Utah, Pennsylvania, Louisiana, Oklahoma, Colorado, Oregon and Texas, juvenile officials closed down or "down-sized" antiquated juvenile training schools and initiated community-based programs for youthful offenders. These reforms were energized by litigation or the credible threat of court intervention and were stewarded by progressive juvenile justice professionals in these jurisdictions.

As with diversion and decriminalization, the deinstitutionalization movement failed to meet all of its optimistic goals. Overall, the numbers of incarcerated youth continued to rise despite declining rates of juvenile crime. As noted earlier, some observers have raised important concerns about the quality of care in privately-run alternative programs.

Due Process. The final "D" of the second revolution in juvenile stands for due process. The *Gault* case motivated many state legislatures to revamp their juvenile court practices. Later U.S. Supreme Court and other federal appellate court decisions expanded and specified the rights enunciated in *In re Gault.*

In the late 1970s and 1980s, the U.S. Supreme Court began redefining the boundaries of how far legal rights for juveniles extended. These judicial reforms stopped short of key rights accorded adult offenders: (1) the right to jury trials, (2) the right to public proceedings and (3) the right to bail. Some observers have criticized the adequacy of legal counsel for juveniles. The appellate courts have let stand statutory provisions governing juvenile status offenders and have approved the exercise of broad discretion in the preventive detention of children.

In the view of retired Supreme Court Chief Justice Warren Burger:

What the juvenile court system needs is less, not more, of the trappings of legal procedure and judicial formalism; the

A consensus emerged on behalf of limiting formal court intervention in children's lives.

juvenile court needs breathing room and flexibility to survive the repeated assaults on the court. The real problem is not the deprivation of constitutional rights but inadequate juvenile court staffs and facilities.[11]

Former juvenile judge H. Ted Rubin believes the *Gault* case brought about significant advancements. However, he also enumerated a litany of abuses still occurring in the juvenile court. He observed:

The foregoing cases are but a smattering of the abuses of juvenile rights which have occurred in our courts and the juvenile justice agencies in the years since *Gault.* From the defense point of view, actualization of due process and uniformly executed legal safeguards remain, today, more rhetoric than reality.[12]

The divergent opinions expressed by Justice Burger and Judge Rubin exemplify the contemporary debate on how much success the due process movement has achieved.

From the late 1970s into the 1980s, a very different and more conservative political agenda dominated the juvenile justice policy arena. For instance, in 1984 the National Advisory Committee for Juvenile Justice and Delinquency Prevention (NAC) stated that "the time has come for a major departure from the existing philosophy and activity of the federal government in the juvenile justice field."[13] The NAC sharply attacked the previous policy thrust toward deinstitutionalization and diversion. The liberal agenda of reform was pejoratively described as "ideas whose vogue has run far ahead of solid knowledge."[14] The NAC argued for a new federal focus on serious juvenile offenders —with an emphasis on deterrence, just deserts and incarceration of youth. Moreover, new doubts were expressed about the federal government's role in regulating local practices concerning status offenders and children in adult jails.

Conservatives called for (1) vigorous

prosecution of serious and violent juvenile offenders, (2) a new focus on the plight of "missing children," (3) mandatory and harsher sentencing laws for young offenders, (4) national crusades against drugs and pornography and (5) programs to reduce school violence. These themes defined the federal funding priorities throughout the Reagan administration.

Changes in federal policy were also reflected in actions at the state level. Since 1976, legislation was enacted in nearly half of the states which makes it easier to transfer juveniles to adult courts. State lawmakers have moved to lower the age of transfer (Tennessee, Kentucky and South Carolina), have excluded certain serious offenses from juvenile court jurisdiction (Illinois, Indiana, Oklahoma and Louisiana) and have made it easier to prosecute children as adult offenders (Florida and California). In addition, several jurisdictions have stiffened juvenile court responses to serious offenders via mandatory minimum terms of incarceration (Colorado, New York and Idaho) and comprehensive sentencing guidelines (Washington).

In addition to the wave of "get tough" legislation and political calls for sterner measures against young criminals, conservative policies are also reflected in significant state and federal court decisions. For example, the U.S. Supreme Court's majority opinion in *Schall v. Martin* (1984) is a clear indicator of the High Court's more restrictive attitude toward children's rights.

Plaintiffs in *Schall v. Martin* challenged the constitutionality of New York's Family Court Act as it pertained to the preventive detention of juveniles. It was alleged that the law was too vague and that juveniles were denied due process. A federal District Court struck down the statute and its decision was affirmed by the U.S. Court of Appeals. However, the U.S. Supreme Court reversed the lower courts, holding that preventive detention of juveniles for their own protection and to prevent pretrial crimes was a legitimate state action.

DISARRAY IN JUVENILE CORRECTIONS

Although the conservative revolution in juvenile justice was motivated by the concepts of deterrence and deserts, the emergence of a "get tough" philosophy also produced another "D" in the world of juvenile justice—disarray. The juvenile corrections system is confronted with (1) growing levels of overcrowding, (2) increased litigation challenging the abuse of children in training schools and detention centers and (3) increased rates of minority youth incarceration.

These results have occurred despite a declining youth population and a corresponding decline in juvenile arrests. For example, between 1976 and 1985, juvenile arrests for serious crime dropped by 21 percent. While juvenile arrests were declining, police were referring a higher proportion of these cases to juvenile and adult courts. Judges were sentencing a larger share of convicted juvenile offenders to correctional facilities for longer periods of confinement. Because of these new policies, the number of incarcerated youth increased dramatically: between 1974 and 1985, the numbers of children in juvenile facilities rose by almost 10 percent. Other data show that during the 1979 to 1985 period, the number of persons under 18 years residing in prisons rose from approximately 2700 to nearly 4000—an increase of 48 percent.

By 1985, the BJS reported that nearly two-thirds of youth residing in the larger juvenile institutions (those with more than 100 beds) were living in chronically overcrowded facilities. While there was a modest increase in the operating budgets of detention centers, expenditures for training schools barely kept pace with the rate of inflation and seldom have provided resources for increased populations.

Another ominous sign was the growing proportion of minority youths confined in public juvenile correctional facilities. In 1982, more than half (53 percent) of those in public facilities were minority youths, while approximately two-thirds of those confined in private juvenile correctional facilities were white. Between 1979 and 1982 when the number of incarcerated youngsters grew by 6,178, minority youth accounted for 93 percent of this increase. The rise in minority youth incarceration cannot be explained in terms of higher rates of minority youth crime.

Many juvenile correctional agencies have been unable to secure the funding for facility maintenance, increased populations or the provision of basic inmate needs. These pressures have resulted in extensive litigation against juvenile correctional facilities challenging the constitutionality of conditions of confinement.

It is worth recalling that the mounting problems of the juvenile justice system occurred despite declines in the general youth population and juvenile arrests. The demographic trends that produced these declines are now reversing. In the coming decade, there will be a new surge of adolescents going through their high-risk years in terms of criminal behavior. Unless our approach to juvenile justice is restructured now, this new wave of youth will produce even higher future rates of incarceration. It is unrealistic to believe that enough juvenile facilities can be built to stay ahead of this problem.

JUVENILE JUSTICE: POSSIBLE FUTURES

The future of the juvenile court is fraught with uncertainty. Some would question whether it has any future. There have been several calls for the abolition of the children's court. Moreover, criticism of the children's court from both liberal and conservative quarters remains strong. With the reduced caseload of status offenders, the juvenile court has lost its traditional preventive mission. It must now deal with youth who are typically repetitive property offenders, drug offenders and those who have failed in child welfare placements. These youth have very high recidivism rates—making the juvenile court's effectiveness look quite bad. Within this policy environment the court needs a revitalized mission to bolster its image and public support.

One potentially negative future direction would be to reintroduce status offenders into the court's mainstream.

From the late 1970s, a very different and more conservative political agenda dominated the juvenile justice policy arena.

Those who wish to control status offenders allege that the deinstitutionalization movement has failed. They assert that many youth are being victimized and exploited due to lack of proper supervision. Public awareness campaigns have already stimulated great concern over missing children and the sexual abuse of young people. Much has also been heard about the exploitation of children by the pornography industry and the involvement of teenage runaways in prostitution. We are just beginning to hear claims that runaways are at great risk of contracting and transmitting AIDS—although the scientific evidence to support these assertions is absent. The "child as victim" provides a seemingly powerful justification for the court to return to its previous rule as regulator of family life.

State legislatures are considering expanding the court's authority to incarcerate status offenders. Even where state laws limit the confinement of status offenders, growing numbers of runaways and truants are showing up in detention centers. Judges are using the contempt powers of the court to lock up chronic status offenders. The sentence of 30 days in detention is the preferred sanction of many juvenile court judges for female status offenders.

Service gaps do exist for severely troubled youth. Many communities have failed to fund the alternative community-based programs called for by the deinstitutionalization movement. Yet, returning status offenders to detention centers is an inappropriate response to their real needs.

Any proposal to return status offenders to the juvenile justice system must answer serious policy concerns about (1) the commingling of status offenders with serious offenders, (2) the traditional over-reliance on institutional placements versus home-based services and (3) the dangers that status offenders will be unnecessarily drawn further into the juvenile justice process.

As the juvenile court moves toward a punishment model, more attention must be paid to issues of due process, equal protection, and proportionality of sanctions.

Those who seek a more punishment-oriented juvenile court argue that juveniles must be held accountable for their criminal behavior. Even the National Council of Juvenile and Family Court Judges, an advocate of the traditional juvenile court philosophy, has proposed that punishment and just deserts play a larger role in juvenile justice practice.

The emphasis on enhancing punishment has led to an exploration of determinate sentencing for juveniles. As the juvenile court moves toward a punishment model, more attention must be paid to issues of due process, equal protection and proportionality of sanctions. The comprehensive reform of Washington State's juvenile code in 1979 represents a most significant movement toward a determinate sentencing model for juveniles. Soon after the Washington code was implemented, the number of youth in detention and in training schools rose dramatically. The state quickly implemented early release policies to avert severe crowding in its juvenile facilities.

The political environment supporting harsher juvenile court policies and penalties exists in several jurisdictions. These "get tough" policies are popular with politicians who are responsive to persistent public fears about crime. But, the most immediate results of "get tough" policies are overcrowded facilities and demands for increased funding for corrections agencies. There is no evidence that tougher penalties actually reduce youth crime. Until recently, the true costs of enhancing punishments for juvenile offenders have been hidden by the enormous expenditures required by skyrocketing prison and jail populations. The severe problems of the juvenile system have not successfully competed for public attention in most jurisdictions. Even more troubling, the ethos of punishment may have blunted the response of public officials to the continuing legacy of abuses within juvenile facilities. Some juvenile justice officials claim that the public actually supports these abusive practices. While litigation by itself has rarely been sufficient to achieve major juvenile justice reforms, increased legal challenges are crucial in order to hold public officials accountable for minimum standards of decency in the care of troubled youngsters.

RECLAIMING THE JUVENILE COURT'S VISION

A more promising future for the juvenile court would entail the rediscovery and updating of its historic vision. Reforms should pursue the "best interests of the children" by truly implementing individualized treatment plans and expanding the range of dispositional options available to the court. Incarceration should be used as a last resort. Large-scale training schools must be replaced with a continuum of placements and services, including small, service-intensive secure programs for the few violent youth and community-based placements for other offenders. Lower caseloads make possible correctional programming geared to meeting individual youth needs.

Innovative correctional programs emphasize aftercare and preparation for community reentry. In fact, planning for the offender's eventual return to community living starts soon after admission. Upon release from secure programs, violent and chronic offenders should enter highly structured community programs. Those offenders placed in community settings should be supervised very closely. Many of these youth should also attend educationally-based day treatment programs and pay restitution or perform community service.

States as diverse as Massachusetts and Utah have shown that this neo-traditional view of juvenile justice can be actualized. In these states, less than 25 percent of youth committed to state corrections agencies are housed in secure facilities. Research results from these states strongly indicate that their more community-based response to youthful offenders does not endanger public safety.[15]

Massachusetts and Utah are not alone in reducing the over-reliance on incarceration. States such as Maryland, Georgia, Louisiana, Oklahoma, Oregon, Pennsylvania, Texas, Florida and Delaware have adopted similar juvenile justice policy goals. However, only a few states, most notably California, Michigan and Arizona, have embarked on massive programs to build new training schools.

Individualized treatment and "the best interests of the child" do not require a return to the arbitrary and often capricious decision-making that has plagued the juvenile court. It is time to recognize that the values of due process, equal protection and proportionality are in the best interests of children. First and foremost, the juvenile court must be a full-fledged justice court. The excellent work of the American Bar Association and the Institute for Judicial Administration provides a blueprint for court proceedings that are completely consistent with a humane vision of justice for youth. Indeed, it is worth noting that jurisdictions possessing the widest assortment of treatment resources for children are often those that also pay careful attention to protecting the legal rights of young people.

Winning support for an individualized, treatment-oriented future for the juvenile court will be very difficult. The public is frustrated and angry about unacceptably high levels of youth violence and drug abuse. It is the challenge of modern day reformers to garner influential and powerful support for progressive policies that benefit disadvantaged youth. While juvenile justice reform can be justified on humanitarian grounds alone, it will be crucial to demonstrate the societal utility of more enlightened policies.

Besides reforming the juvenile court, the reclaimed vision of justice for youth must confront stark economic and social trends. Nearly 25 percent of all children under the age of 18 are growing up in poverty. The number of homeless families has skyrocketed: In New York City alone, 10,000 children reside in "welfare hotels" on a given day. School dropout rates are at obscenely high levels in urban areas. Job prospects for those at the bottom of the social system have worsened because of basic economic transformations. Our cities contain neighborhoods more disorganized and chaotic than in recent memory. These social trends portend even higher rates of youth crime in the future.

According to criminologists Alden Miller and Lloyd Ohlin:

Delinquency is a community problem. In the final analysis the means for its prevention and control must be built into the fabric of community life. This can only happen if the community accepts its share of responsibility for having generated and perpetuated paths of socialization that lead to sporadic criminal episodes for some youth and careers in crime for others.[16]

A new generation of childsavers may be required to advance the principles of social justice and community reconstruction called for by Miller and Ohlin.

Whether an enlightened concept of juvenile justice will be limited to a few jurisdictions or whether it can achieve wider public acceptance is difficult to predict. In too many communities, abusive and inferior care of troubled and disadvantaged youngsters is still the norm. Now more than ever the redemptive vision of justice symbolized by the juvenile court must be rekindled.

---

1. Pickett, 1969.
2. Mennel, 1973.
3. *Ex Parte Crouse*, 4 Wharton PA 9 (1838).
4. Mennel, 1973.
5. *Commonwealth v. Fisher*, 213 Pennsylvania 48 (1905) (emphasis added).
6. Empey, 1978.
7. In 1980, the JJDPA was amended to require the complete removal of children from jails.
8. NCCD, 1975.
9. Lerman, 1982.
10. BJS, 1986.
11. *In re Winship*, 397 U.S. 358 (1970).
12. Rubin, 1979:211.
13. NAC, 1984:iii.
14. NAC, 1984:8.
15. NCCD, 1987, 1988.
16. Miller and Ohlin, 1985.

CASES CITED

Commonwealth v. Fisher, 213 P.A. 48 (1905)
Ex Parte Crouse, 4 Wharton PA 9 (1838)
In re Gault, 387 U.S. 1 (1967)
In re Winship, 397 U.S. 358 (1970)
Kent v. U.S., 383 U.S. 541 (1966)
Schall v. Martin, 467 U.S. 253

REFERENCES

Bureau of Justice Statistics
1986   *1984 Census of State Adult Correctional Facilities*. Washington, D.C.: Bureau of Statistics.

Empey, LaMar
1978   *American Delinquency: Its Meaning and Construction*. Homewood, IL: Dorsey Press.

Lerman, Paul
1982   *Deinstitutionalization and the Welfare State*. New Jersey: Rutgers University Press.

Mennel, Robert
1973   *Thorns and Thistles*. Hanover, NH: The University of New Hampshire.

Miller, Alden and Lloyd Ohlin
1985   *Delinquency and Community*. Beverly Hills, CA: Sage Publications.

National Advisory Committee for Juvenile Justice and Delinquency Prevention
1984   *Serious Juvenile Crime: A Redirected Federal Effort*. Washington, D.C.: Office of Juvenile Justice and Delinquency Prevention.

National Council on Crime and Delinquency
1988   *Study of the Massachusetts Division of Youth Services: Basic Data Tables*. San Francisco: NCCD.
1987   *The Impact of Juvenile Court Sanctions*. San Francisco: NCCD.

National Council on Crime and Delinquency, Board of Directors
1975   "Jurisdiction Over Status Offenders Should be Removed from the Juvenile Court." *Crime and Delinquency*. Vol. 21, pp. 97-99.

National Probation and Parole Association
1957   *Guides for Juvenile Court Judges*. New York: National Probation and Parole Association.

Pickett, Robert
1969   *House of Refuge: Origins of Juvenile Justice Reform in New York*. Syracuse: Syracuse University Press. pp. 1815-1857.

Rubin, H. Ted
1979   *Juvenile Justice Policy, Practice and Law*. Santa Monica, CA: Goodyear.

Girls' Crime and Woman's Place: Toward a Feminist Model of Female Delinquency

This article argues that existing delinquency theories are fundamentally inadequate to the task of explaining female delinquency and official reactions to girls' deviance. To establish this, the article first reviews the degree of the androcentric bias in the major theories of delinquent behavior. Then the need for a feminist model of female delinquency is explored by reviewing the available evidence on girls' offending. This review shows that the extensive focus on disadvantaged males in public settings has meant that girls' victimization and the relationship between that experience and girls' crime has been systematically ignored. Also missed has been the central role played by the juvenile justice system in the sexualization of female delinquency and the criminalization of girls' survival strategies. Finally, it will be suggested that the official actions of the juvenile justice system should be understood as major forces in women's oppression as they have historically served to reinforce the obedience of all young women to the demands of patriarchal authority no matter how abusive and arbitrary.

Meda Chesney-Lind

Meda Chesney-Lind: Associate Professor of Women's Studies and an Associate Researcher with the Center for Youth Research at the University of Hawaii, Manoa.

I ran away so many times. I tried anything man, and they wouldn't believe me. . . . As far as they are concerned they think I'm the problem. You know, runaway, bad label. (Statement of a 16-year-old girl who, after having been physically and sexually assaulted, started running away from home and was arrested as a "runaway" in Hawaii.)

You know, one of these days I'm going to have to kill myself before you guys are gonna listen to me. I can't stay at home. (Statement of a 16-year-old Tucson runaway with a long history of physical abuse [Davidson, 1982, p. 26].)

Who is the typical female delinquent? What causes her to get into trouble? What happens to her if she is caught? These are questions that few members of the general public could answer quickly. By contrast, almost every citizen can talk about "delinquency," by which they generally mean male delinquency, and can even generate some fairly specific complaints about, for ex-

ample, the failure of the juvenile justice system to deal with such problems as "the alarming increase in the rate of serious juvenile crime" and the fact that the juvenile courts are too lenient on juveniles found guilty of these offenses (Opinion Research Corporation, 1982).

This situation should come as no surprise since even the academic study of delinquent behavior has, for all intents and purposes, been the study of male delinquency. "The delinquent is a rogue male" declared Albert Cohen (1955, p. 140) in his influential book on gang delinquency. More than a decade later, Travis Hirschi, in his equally important book entitled *The Causes of Delinquency,* relegated women to a footnote that suggested, somewhat apologetically, that "in the analysis that follows, the 'non-Negro' becomes 'white,' and the girls disappear."

This pattern of neglect is not all that unusual. All areas of social inquiry have been notoriously gender blind. What is

perhaps less well understood is that theories developed to describe the misbehavior of working- or lower-class male youth fail to capture the full nature of delinquency in America; and, more to the point, are woefully inadequate when it comes to explaining female misbehavior and official reactions to girls' deviance.

To be specific, delinquent behavior involves a range of activities far broader than those committed by the stereotypical street gang. Moreover, many more young people than the small visible group of "troublemakers" that exist on every intermediate and high school campus commit some sort of juvenile offense and many of these youth have brushes with the law. One study revealed, for example, that 33% of all the boys and 14% of the girls born in 1958 had at least one contact with the police before reaching their eighteenth birthday (Tracy, Wolfgang, and Figlio, 1985, p. 5). Indeed, some forms of serious delinquent behavior, such as drug and alcohol abuse, are far more frequent than the stereotypical delinquent behavior of gang fighting and vandalism and appear to cut across class and gender lines.

Studies that solicit from youth themselves the volume of their delinquent behavior consistently confirm that large numbers of adolescents engage in at least some form of misbehavior that could result in their arrest. As a consequence, it is largely trivial misconduct, rather than the commission of serious crime, that shapes the actual nature of juvenile delinquency. One national study of youth aged 15-21, for example, noted that only 5% reported involvement in a serious assault, and only 6% reported having participated in a gang fight. In contrast, 81% admitted to having used alcohol, 44% admitted to having used marijuana, 37% admitted to having been publicly drunk, 42% admitted to having skipped classes (truancy), 44% admitted having had sexual intercourse, and 15% admitted to having stolen from the family (McGarrell and Flanagan, 1985, p. 363). Clearly, not all of these activities are as serious as the others. It is important to remember that young people can be arrested for all of these behaviors.

Indeed, one of the most important points to understand about the nature of delinquency, and particularly female delinquency, is that youth can be taken into custody for both criminal acts and a wide variety of what are often called "status offenses." These offenses, in contrast to criminal violations, permit the arrest of youth for a wide range of behaviors that are violations of parental authority: "running away from home," "being a person in need of supervision," "minor in need of supervision," being "incorrigible," "beyond control," truant, in need of "care and protection," and so on. Juvenile delinquents, then, are youths arrested for either criminal or noncriminal status offenses; and, as this discussion will establish, the role played by uniquely juvenile offenses is by no means insignificant, particularly when considering the character of female delinquency.

Examining the types of offenses for which youth are actually arrested, it is clear that again most are arrested for the less serious criminal acts and status offenses. Of the one and a half million youth arrested in 1983, for example, only 4.5% of these arrests were for such serious violent offenses as murder, rape, robbery, or aggravated assault (McGarrell and Flanagan, 1985, p. 479). In contrast, 21% were arrested for a single offense (larceny, theft) much of

which, particularly for girls, is shoplifting (Sheldon and Horvath, 1986).

Table 1 presents the five most frequent offenses for which male and female youth are arrested and from this it can be seen that while trivial offenses dominate both male and female delinquency, trivial offenses, particularly status offenses, are more significant in the case of girls' arrests; for example the five offenses listed in Table 1 account for nearly three-quarters of female offenses and only slightly more than half of male offenses.

More to the point, it is clear that, though routinely neglected in most delinquency research, status offenses play a significant role in girls' official delinquency. Status offenses accounted for about 25.2% of all girls' arrests in 1986 (as compared to 26.9% in 1977) and only about 8.3% of boys' arrests (compared to 8.8% in 1977). These figures are somewhat surprising since dramatic declines in arrests of youth for these offenses might have been expected as a result of the passage of the Juvenile Justice and Delinquency Prevention Act in 1974, which, among other things, encouraged jurisdictions to divert and deinstitutionalize youth charged with noncriminal offenses. While the figures in Table 1 do show a decline in these arrests, virtually all of this decline occurred in the 1970s. Between 1982 and 1986 girls' curfew arrests increased by 5.1% and runaway arrests increased by a striking 24.5%. And the upward trend continues; arrests of girls for running away increased by 3% between 1985 and 1986 and arrests of girls for curfew violations increased by 12.4% (Federal Bureau of Investigation, 1987, p. 171).

Looking at girls who find their way into juvenile court populations, it is apparent that status offenses continue to play an important role in the character of girls' official delinquency. In total, 34% of the girls, but only 12% of the boys, were referred to court in 1983 for these offenses (Snyder and Finnegan, 1987, pp. 6–20). Stating these figures differently, they mean that while males constituted about 81% of all delinquency referrals, females constituted 46% of all status offenders in courts (Snyder and Finnegan, 1987, p. 20). Similar figures were reported for 1977 by Black and Smith (1981). Fifteen years earlier, about half of the girls and about 20% of the boys were referred to court for these offenses (Children's Bureau, 1965). These data do seem to signal a drop in female status offense referrals, though not as dramatic a decline as might have been expected.

For many years statistics showing

large numbers of girls arrested and referred for status offenses were taken to be representative of the different types of male and female delinquency. However, self-report studies of male and female delinquency do not reflect the dramatic differences in misbehavior found in official statistics. Specifically, it appears that girls charged with these noncriminal status offenses have been and continue to be significantly overrepresented in court populations.

Teilmann and Landry (1981) compared girls' contribution to arrests for runaway and incorrigibility with girls' self-reports of these two activities, and found a 10.4% overrepresentation of females among those arrested for runaway and a 30.9% overrepresentation in arrests for incorrigibility. From these data they concluded that girls are "arrested for status offenses at a higher rate than boys, when contrasted to their self-reported delinquency rates" (Teilmann and Landry, 1981, pp. 74–75). These findings were confirmed in another recent self-report study. Figueira-McDonough (1985, p. 277) analyzed the delinquent conduct of 2,000 youths and found "no evidence of greater involvement of females in status offenses." Similarly, Canter (1982) found in the National Youth Survey that there was no evidence of greater female involvement, compared to males, in any category of delinquent behavior. Indeed, in this sample, males were significantly more likely than females to report status offenses.

Utilizing Canter's national data on the extensiveness of girls self-reported delinquency and comparing these figures to official arrests of girls (see Table 2) reveals that girls are underrepresented in every arrest category with the exception of status offenses and larceny theft. These figures strongly suggest that official practices tend to exaggerate the role played by status offenses in girls' delinquency.

Delinquency theory, because it has virtually ignored female delinquency, failed to pursue anomalies such as these found in the few early studies examining gender differences in delinquent behavior. Indeed, most delinquency theories have ignored status offenses. As a consequence, there is considerable question as to whether existing theories that were admittedly developed to explain male delinquency can adequately explain female delinquency. Clearly, these theories were much influenced by the notion that class and protest masculinity were at the core of delinquency. Will the "add women and stir approach" be sufficient? Are these really theories of delin-

TABLE 1: Rank Order of Adolescent Male and Female Arrests for Specific Offenses, 1977 and 1986

Male				Female			
1977	% of Total Arrests	1986	% of Total Arrests	1977	% of Total Arrests	1986	% of Total Arrests
(1) Larceny-Theft	18.4	(1) Larceny-Theft	20.4	(1) Larceny-Theft	27.0	(1) Larceny-Theft	25.7
(2) Other Offenses	14.5	(2) Other Offenses	16.5	(2) Runaway	22.9	(2) Runaway	20.5
(3) Burglary	13.0	(3) Burglary	9.1	(3) Other Offenses	14.2	(3) Other Offenses	14.8
(4) Drug Abuse Violations	6.5	(4) Vandalism	7.0	(4) Liquor Laws	5.5	(4) Liquor Laws	8.4
(5) Vandalism	6.4	(5) Vandalism	6.3	(5) Curfew & Loitering Violations	4.0	(5) Curfew & Loitering Violations	4.7

	1977	1986	% N Change		1977	1986	% N Change
Arrests for Serious Violent Offenses[a]	4.2%	4.7%	2.3	Arrests for Serious Violent Offenses	1.8%	2.0%	+1.7
Arrests of All Violent Offenses[b]	7.6%	9.6%	+10.3	Arrests of All Violent Offenses	5.1%	7.1%	+26.0
Arrests for Status Offenses[c]	8.8%	8.3%	−17.8	Arrests for Status Offenses	26.9%	25.2%	−14.7

SOURCE: Compiled from Federal Bureau of Investigation (1987, p. 169).
a. Arrests for murder and nonnegligent manslaughter, robbery, forcible rape, and aggravated assault.
b. Also includes arrests for other assaults.
c. Arrests for curfew and loitering law violation and runaway.

quent behavior as some (Simons, Miller, and Aigner, 1980) have argued?

This article will suggest that they are not. The extensive focus on male delinquency and the inattention the role played by patriarchal arrangements in the generation of adolescent delinquency and conformity has rendered the major delinquency theories fundamentally inadequate to the task of explaining female behavior. There is, in short, an urgent need to rethink current models in light of girls' situation in patriarchal society.

To understand why such work must occur, it is first necessary to explore briefly the dimensions of the androcentric bias found in the dominant and influential delinquency theories. Then the need for a feminist model of female delinquency will be explored by reviewing the available evidence on girls' offending. This discussion will also establish that the proposed overhaul of delinquency theory is not, as some might think, solely an academic exercise. Specifically, it is incorrect to assume that because girls are charged with less serious offenses, they actually have few problems and are treated gently when they are drawn into the juvenile justice system. Indeed, the extensive focus on disadvantaged males in public settings has meant that girls' victimization and the relationship between that experience and girls' crime has been systematically ignored. Also missed has been the central role played by the juvenile justice system in the sexualization of girls' delinquency and the criminalization of girls' survival strategies. Finally, it will be suggested that the

official actions of the juvenile justice system should be understood as major forces in girls' oppression as they have historically served to reinforce the obedience of all young women to demands of patriarchal authority no matter how abusive and arbitrary.

THE ROMANCE OF THE GANG OR THE WEST SIDE STORY SYNDROME

From the start, the field of delinquency research focused on visible lower-class male delinquency, often justifying the neglect of girls in the most cavalier of terms. Take, for example, the extremely important and influential work of Clifford R. Shaw and Henry D. McKay who beginning in 1929, utilized an ecological approach to the study of juvenile delinquency. Their impressive work, particularly *Juvenile Delinquency in Urban Areas* (1942) and intensive biographical case studies such as Shaw's *Brothers in Crime* (1938) and *The Jackroller* (1930), set the stage for much of the subcultural research on gang delinquency. In their ecological work, however, Shaw and McKay analyzed only the official arrest data on male delinquents in Chicago and repeatedly referred to these rates as "delinquency rates" (though they occasionally made parenthetical reference to data on female delinquency) (see Shaw and McKay, 1942, p. 356). Similarly, their biographical work traced only male experiences with the law; in *Brothers in Crime,* for example, the delinquent and criminal careers of five brothers were followed for fifteen years. In none of these works was any justification given for the equation of male delinquency with delinquency.

Early fieldwork on delinquent gangs in Chicago set the stage for another style of delinquency research. Yet here too researchers were interested only in talking to and following the boys. Thrasher studied over a thousand juvenile gangs in Chicago during roughly the same period as Shaw and McKay's more quantitative work was being done. He spent approximately one page out of 600 on the five of six female gangs he encountered in his field observation of juvenile gangs. Thrasher (1927, p. 228) did mention, in passing, two factors he felt accounted for the lower number of girl gangs: "First, the social patterns for the behavior of girls, powerfully backed by the great weight of tradition and custom, are contrary to the gang and its activities; and secondly, girls, even in urban disorganized areas, are much more closely supervised and guarded than boys and usually well incorporated into the family groups or some other social structure."

Another major theoretical approach to delinquency focuses on the subculture of lower-class communities as a generating milieu for delinquent behavior. Here again, noted delinquency researchers concentrated either exclusively or nearly exclusively on male lower-class culture. For example, Cohen's work on the subculture of delinquent gangs, which was written nearly twenty years after Thrasher's, deliberately considers only boys' delinquency. His justification for the exclusion of the girls is quite illuminating:

My skin has nothing of the quality of down or silk, there is nothing limpid or flute-like about my voice, I am a total

TABLE 2: Comparison of Sex Differences in Self-Reported and Official Delinquency for Selected Offenses

	Self-Report[a] M/F Ratios (1976)	Official Statistics[b] M/F Arrest Ratio	
		1976	1986
Theft	3.5:1 (Felony Theft) 3.4:1 (Minor Theft)	2.5:1	2.7:1
Drug Violation	1:1 (Hard Drug Use)	5.1:1	6.0:1 (Drug Abuse Violations)
Vandalism	5.1:1	12.3:1	10.0:1
Disorderly Conduct	2.8:1	4.5:1	4.4:1
Serious Assault	3.5:1 (Felony Assault)	5.6:1	5.5:1 (Aggravated Assault)
Minor Assault	3.4:1	3.8:1	3.4:1
Status Offenses	1.6:1	1.3:1	1.1:1 (Runaway, Curfew)

a. Extracted from Rachelle Canter (1982, p. 383).
b. Compiled from Federal Bureau of Investigation (1986, p. 173).

loss with needle and thread, my posture and carriage are wholly lacking in grace. These imperfections cause me no distress—if anything, they are gratifying—because I conceive myself to be a man and want people to recognize me as a full-fledged, unequivocal representative of my sex. My wife, on the other hand, is not greatly embarrassed by her inability to tinker with or talk about the internal organs of a car, by her modest attainments in arithmetic or by her inability to lift heavy objects. Indeed, I am reliably informed that many women—I do not suggest that my wife is among them—often affect ignorance, frailty and emotional instability because to do otherwise would be out of keeping with a reputation for indubitable femininity. In short, people do not simply want to excel; they want to excel as a man or as a woman [Cohen, 1955, p. 138.]

From this Cohen (1955, p. 140) concludes that the delinquent response "however it may be condemned by others on moral grounds has least one virtue; it incontestably confirms, in the eyes of all concerned, his essential masculinity." Much the same line of argument appears in Miller's influential paper on the "focal concerns" of lower-class life with its emphasis on importance of trouble, toughness, excitement, and so on. These, the author concludes, predispose poor youth (particularly male youth) to criminal misconduct. However, Cohen's comments are notable in their candor and probably capture both the allure that male delinquency has had for at least some male theorists as well as the fact that sexism has rendered the female delinquent as irrelevant to their work.

Emphasis on blocked opportunities (sometimes the "strain" theories)

emerged out of the work of Robert K. Merton (1938) who stressed the need to consider how some social structures exert a definite pressure upon certain persons in the society to engage in nonconformist rather than conformist conduct. His work influenced research largely through the efforts of Cloward and Ohlin who discussed access to "legitimate" and "illegitimate" opportunities for male youth. No mention of female delinquency can be found in their *Delinquency and Opportunity* except that women are blamed for male delinquency. Here, the familiar notion is that boys, "engulfed by a feminine world and uncertain of their own identification . . . tend to 'protest' against femininity" (Cloward and Ohlin, 1960, p. 49). Early efforts by Ruth Morris to test this hypothesis utilizing different definitions of success based on the gender of respondents met with mixed success. Attempting to assess boys' perceptions about access to economic power status while for girls the variable concerned itself with the ability or inability of girls to maintain effective relationships, Morris was unable to find a clear relationship between "female" goals and delinquency (Morris, 1964).

The work of Edwin Sutherland emphasized the fact that criminal behavior was learned in intimate personal groups. His work, particularly the notion of differential association, which also influenced Cloward and Ohlin's work, was similarly male oriented as much of his work was affected by case studies he conducted of male criminals. Indeed, in describing his notion of how differential association works, he utilized male examples (e.g., "In an area where the delinquency rate is high a boy who is

sociable, gregarious, active, and athletic is very likely to come in contact with the other boys, in the neighborhood, learn delinquent behavior from them, and become a gangster" [Sutherland, 1978, p. 131]). Finally, the work of Travis Hirschi on the social bonds that control delinquency ("social control theory") was, as was stated earlier, derived out of research on male delinquents (though he, at least, studied delinquent behavior as reported by youth themselves rather than studying only those who were arrested).

Such a persistent focus on social class and such an absence of interest in gender in delinquency is ironic for two reasons. As even the work of Hirschi demonstrated, and as later studies would validate, a clear relationship between social class position and delinquency is problematic, while it is clear that gender has a dramatic and consistent effect on delinquency causation (Hagan, Gillis, and Simpson, 1985). The second irony, and one that consistently eludes even contemporary delinquency theorists, is the fact that while the academics had little interest in female delinquents, the same could not be said for the juvenile justice system. Indeed, work on the early history of the separate system for youth, reveals that concerns about girls' immoral conduct were really at the center of what some have called the "childsaving movement" (Platt, 1969) that set up the juvenile justice system.

"THE BEST PLACE TO CONQUER GIRLS"

The movement to establish separate institutions for youthful offenders was part of the larger Progressive movement, which among other things was keenly concerned about prostitution and other "social evils" (white slavery and the like) (Schlossman and Wallach, 1978; Rafter, 1985, p. 54). Childsaving was also a celebration of women's domesticity, though ironically women were influential in the movement (Platt, 1969; Rafter, 1985). In a sense, privileged women found, in the moral purity crusades and the establishment of family courts, a safe outlet for their energies. As the legitimate guardians of the moral sphere, women were seen as uniquely suited to patrol the normative boundaries of the social order. Embracing rather than challenging these stereotypes, women carved out for themselves a role in the policing of women and girls (Feinman, 1980; Freedman, 1981; Messerschmidt, 1987). Ultimately, many of the early childsavers' activities revolved around the monitoring of young girls', particularly immigrant girls', behavior to prevent their straying from the path.

This state of affairs was the direct consequence of a disturbing coalition between some feminists and the more conservative social purity movement. Concerned about female victimization and distrustful of male (and to some degree female) sexuality, notable women leaders, including Susan B. Anthony, found common cause with the social purists around such issues as opposing the regulation of prostitution and raising the age of consent (see Messerschmidt, 1987). The consequences of such a partnership are an important lesson for contemporary feminist movements that are, to some extent, faced with the same possible coalitions.

Girls were the clear losers in this reform effort. Studies of early family court activity reveal that virtually all the girls who appeared in these courts were charged for immorality or waywardness (Chesney-Lind, 1971; Schlossman and Wallach, 1978; Shelden, 1981). More to the point, the sanctions for such misbehavior were extremely severe. For example, in Chicago (where the first family court was founded), one-half of the girl delinquents, but only one-fifth of the boy delinquents, were sent to reformatories between 1899–1909. In Milwaukee, twice as many girls as boys were committed to training schools (Schlossman and Wallach, 1978, p. 72); and in Memphis females were twice as likely as males to be committed to training schools (Shelden, 1981, p. 70).

In Honolulu, during the period 1929–1930, over half of the girls referred to court were charged with "immorality," which meant evidence of sexual intercourse. In addition, another 30% were charged with "waywardness." Evidence of immorality was vigorously pursued by both arresting officers and social workers through lengthy questioning of the girl and, if possible, males with whom she was suspected of having sex. Other evidence of "exposure" was provided by gynecological examinations that were routinely ordered in virtually all girls' cases. Doctors, who understood the purpose of such examinations, would routinely note the condition of the hymen: "admits intercourse hymen rupture," "no laceration," "hymen ruptured" are typical of the notations on the forms. Girls during this period were also twice as likely as males to be detained where they spent five times as long on the average as their male counterparts. They were also nearly three times more likely to be sentenced to the training school (Chesney-Lind, 1971). Indeed, girls were half of those commit-

ted to training schools in Honolulu well into the 1950s (Chesney-Lind, 1973).

Not surprisingly, large numbers of girls'reformatories and training schools were established during this period as well as places of "rescue and reform." For example, Schlossman and Wallach note that 23 facilities for girls were opened during the 1910–1920 decade (in contrast to the 1850–1910 period where the average was 5 reformatories per decade [Schlossman and Wallach, 1985, p. 70]), and these institutions did much to set the tone of official response to female delinquency. Obsessed with precocious female sexuality, the institutions set about to isolate the females from all contact with males while housing them in bucolic settings. The intention was to hold the girls until marriageable age and to occupy them in domestic pursuits during their sometimes lengthy incarceration.

The links between these attitudes and those of juvenile courts some decades later are, of course, arguable; but an examination of the record of the court does not inspire confidence. A few examples of the persistence of what might be called a double standard of juvenile justice will suffice here.

A study conducted in the early 1970s in a Connecticut training school revealed large numbers of girls incarcerated "for their own protection." Explaining this pattern, one judge explained, "Why most of the girls I commit are for status offenses, I figure if a girl is about to get pregnant, we'll keep her until she's sixteen and then ADC (Aid to Dependent Children) will pick her up" (Rogers, 1972). For more evidence of official concern with adolescent sexual misconduct, consider Linda Hancock's (1981) content analysis of police referrals in Australia. She noted that 40% of the referrals of girls to court made specific mention of sexual and moral conduct compared to only 5% of the referrals of boys. These sorts of results suggest that all youthful female misbehavior has traditionally been subject to surveillance for evidence of sexual misconduct.

Gelsthorpe's (1986) field research on an English police station also revealed how everyday police decision making resulted in disregard of complaints about male problem behavior in contrast to active concern about the "problem behavior" of girls. Notable, here, was the concern about the girls' sexual behavior. In one case, she describes police persistence in pursuing a "moral danger" order for a 14-year-old picked up in a truancy run. Over the objections of both the girl's parents and the Social Services Department and in the face of a written confirmation from a surgeon

that the girl was still premenstrual, the officers pursued the application because, in one officer's words, "I know her sort . . . free and easy. I'm still suspicious that she might be pregnant. Anyway, if the doctor can't provide evidence we'll do her for being beyond the care and control of her parents, no one can dispute that. Running away is proof" (Gelsthorpe, 1986, p. 136). This sexualization of female deviance is highly significant and explains why criminal activities by girls (particularly in past years) were overlooked so long as they did not appear to signal defiance of parental control (see Smith, 1978).

In their historic obsession about precocious female sexuality, juvenile justice workers rarely reflected on the broader nature of female misbehavior or on the sources of this misbehavior. It was enough for them that girls' parents reported them out of control. Indeed, court personnel tended to "sexualize" virtually all female defiance that lent itself to that construction and ignore other misbehavior (Chesney-Lind, 1973, 1977; Smith, 1978). For their part, academic students of delinquency were so entranced with the notion of the delinquent as a romantic rogue male challenging a rigid and unequal class structure, that they spent little time on middle-class delinquency, trivial offenders, or status offenders. Yet it is clear that the vast bulk of delinquent behavior is of this type.

Some have argued that such an imbalance in theoretical work is appropriate as minor misconduct, while troublesome, is not a threat to the safety and well-being of the community. This argument might be persuasive if two additional points could be established. One, that some small number of youth "specialize" in serious criminal behavior while the rest commit only minor acts, and, two, that the juvenile court rapidly releases those youth that come into its purview for these minor offenses, thus reserving resources for the most serious youthful offenders.

The evidence is mixed on both of these points. Determined efforts to locate the "serious juvenile offender" have failed to locate a group of offenders who specialize only in serious violent offenses. For example, in a recent analysis of a national self-report data set, Elliott and his associates noted "there is little evidence for specialization in serious violent offending; to the contrary, serious violent offending appears to be embedded in a more general involvement in a wide range of serious and non-serious offenses" (Elliott, Huizinga, and Morse, 1987). Indeed, they went so far as to speculate that arrest histories that tend to high-light particular types of offenders reflect variations in police policy, practices, and processes of uncovering crime as well as underlying offending patterns.

More to the point, police and court personnel are, it turns out, far more interested in youth they charge with trivial or status offenses than anyone imagined. Efforts to deinstitutionalize "status offenders," for example, ran afoul of juvenile justice personnel who had little interest in releasing youth guilty of noncriminal offenses (Chesney-Lind, 1988). As has been established, much of this is a product of the system's history that encouraged court officers to involve themselves in the noncriminal behavior of youth in order to "save" them from a variety of social ills.

Indeed, parallels can be found between the earlier Progressive period and current national efforts to challenge the deinstitutionalization components of the Juvenile Justice and Delinquency Prevention Act of 1974. These come complete with their celebration of family values and concerns about youthful independence. One of the arguments against the act has been that it allegedly gave children the "freedom to run away" (Office of Juvenile Justice and Delinquency Prevention, 1985) and that it has hampered "reunions" of "missing" children with their parents (Office of Juvenile Justice, 1986). Suspicions about teen sexuality are reflected in excessive concern about the control of teen prostitution and child pornography.

Opponents have also attempted to justify continued intervention into the lives of status offenders by suggesting that without such intervention, the youth would "escalate" to criminal behavior. Yet there is little evidence that status offenders escalate to criminal offenses, and the evidence is particularly weak when considering female delinquents (particularly white female delinquents) (Datesman and Aickin, 1984). Finally, if escalation is occurring, it is likely the product of the justice system's insistence on enforcing status offense laws, thereby forcing youth in crisis to live lives of escaped criminals.

The most influential delinquency theories, however, have largely ducked the issue of status and trivial offenses and, as a consequence, neglected the role played by the agencies of official control (police, probation officers, juvenile court judges, detention home workers, and training school personnel) in the shaping of the "delinquency problem." When confronting the less than distinct picture that emerges from the actual distribution of delinquent behavior, how-

ever, the conclusion that agents of social control have considerable discretion in labeling or choosing not to label particular behavior as "delinquent" is inescapable. This symbiotic relationship between delinquent behavior and the official response to that behavior is particularly critical when the question of female delinquency is considered.

TOWARD A FEMINIST THEORY OF DELINQUENCY

To sketch out completely a feminist theory of delinquency is a task beyond the scope of this article. It may be sufficient, at this point, simply to identify a few of the most obvious problems with attempts to adapt male-oriented theory to explain female conformity and deviance. Most significant of these is the fact that all existing theories were developed with no concern about gender stratification.

Note that this is not simply an observation about the power of gender roles (though this power is undeniable). It is increasingly clear that gender stratification in patriarchal society is as powerful a system as is class. A feminist approach to delinquency means construction of explanations of female behavior that are sensitive to its patriarchal context. Feminist analysis of delinquency would also examine ways in which agencies of social control—the police, the courts, and the prisons—act in ways to reinforce woman's place in male society (Harris, 1977; Chesney-Lind, 1986). Efforts to construct a feminist model of delinquency must first and foremost be sensitive to the situations of girls. Failure to consider the existing empirical evidence on girls' lives and behavior can quickly lead to stereotypical thinking and theoretical dead ends.

An example of this sort of flawed theory building was the early fascination with the notion that the women's movement was causing an increase in women's crime; a notion that is now more or less discredited (Steffensmeier, 1980; Gora, 1982). A more recent example of the same sort of thinking can be found in recent work on the "power-control" model of delinquency (Hagan, Simpson, and Gillis, 1987). Here, the authors speculate that girls commit less delinquency in part because their behavior is more closely controlled by the patriarchal family. The authors' promising beginning quickly gets bogged down in a very limited definition of patriarchal control (focusing on parental supervision and variations in power within the family). Ultimately, the authors' narrow formulation of patriarchal control results in their arguing that mother's work force participation (particularly in high

status occupations) leads to increases in daughters' delinquency since these girls find themselves in more "egalitarian families."

This is essentially a not-too-subtle variation on the earlier "liberation" hypothesis. Now, mother's liberation causes daughter's crime. Aside from the methodological problems with the study (e.g., the authors argue that female-headed households are equivalent to upper-status "egalitarian" families where both parents work, and they measure delinquency using a six-item scale that contains no status offense items), there is a more fundamental problem with the hypothesis. There is no evidence to suggest that as women's labor force participation accelerated and the number of female-headed households soared, aggregate female delinquency measured both by self-report and official statistics either declined or remained stable (Ageton, 1983; Chilton and Datesman, 1987; Federal Bureau of Investigation, 1987).

By contrast, a feminist model of delinquency would focus more extensively on the few pieces of information about girls' actual lives and the role played by girls' problems, including those caused by racism and poverty, in their delinquency behavior. Fortunately, a considerable literature is now developing on girls' lives and much of it bears directly on girls' crime.

CRIMINALIZING GIRLS' SURVIVAL

It has long been understood that a major reason for girls' presence in juvenile courts was the fact that their parents insisted on their arrest. In the early years, conflicts with parents were by far the most significant referral source; in Honolulu 44% of the girls who appeared in court in 1929 through 1930 were referred by parents.

Recent national data, while slightly less explicit, also show that girls are more likely to be referred to court by "sources other than law enforcement agencies" (which would include parents). In 1983, nearly a quarter (23%) of all girls but only 16% of boys charged with delinquent offenses were referred to court by non-law enforcement agencies. The pattern among youth referred for status offenses (for which girls are overrepresented) was even more pronounced. Well over half (56%) of the girls charged with these offenses and 45% of the boys were referred by sources other than law enforcement (Snyder and Finnegan, 1987, p. 21; see also Pope and Feyerherm, 1982).

The fact that parents are often committed to two standards of adolescent behavior is one explanation for such a disparity—and one that should not be discounted as a major source of tension even in modern families. Despite expectations to the contrary, gender-specific socialization patterns have not changed very much and this is especially true for parents' relationships with their daughters (Katz, 1979). It appears that even parents who oppose sexism in general feel"uncomfortable tampering with existing traditions" and "do not want to risk their children becoming misfits" (Katz, 1979, p. 24). Clearly, parental attempts to adhere to and enforce these traditional notions will continue to be a source of conflict between girls and their elders. Another important explanation for girls' problems with their parents, which has received attention only in more recent years, is the problem of physical and sexual abuse. Looking specifically at the problem of childhood sexual abuse, it is increasingly clear that this form of abuse is a particular problem for girls.

Girls are, for example, much more likely to be the victims of child sexual abuse than are boys. Finkelhor and Baron estimate from a review of community studies that roughly 70% of the victims of sexual abuse are female (Finkelhor and Baron, 1986, p. 45). Girls' sexual abuse also tends to start earlier than boys (Finkelhor and Baron, 1986, p. 48); they are more likely than boys to be assaulted by a family member (often a stepfather)(DeJong, Hervada, and Emmett, 1983; Russell, 1986), and as a consequence, their abuse tends to last longer than male sexual abuse (DeJong,Hervada, and Emmett, 1983). All of these factors are associated with more severe trauma—causing dramatic short- and long-term effects in victims (Adams-Tucker, 1982). The effects noted by researchers in this area move from the more well known "fear, anxiety, depression, anger and hostility, and inappropriate sexual behavior" (Browne and Finkelhor, 1986, p. 69) to behaviors of greater familiarity to criminologists, including running away from home, difficulties in school, truancy, and early marriage (Browne and Finkelhor, 1986).

Herman's study of incest survivors in therapy found that they were more likely to have run away from home than a matched sample of women whose fathers were "seductive" (33% compared to 5%). Another study of women patients found that 50% of the victims of child sexual abuse, but only 20% of the nonvictim group, had left home before the age of 19 (Meiselman, 1978).

Not surprisingly, then, studies of girls on the streets or in court populations are showing high rates of both physical and sexual abuse. Silbert and Pines (1981, p. 409) found, for example, that 60% of the street prostitutes they interviewed had been sexually abused as juveniles. Girls at an Arkansas diagnostic unit and school who had been adjudicated for either status or delinquent offenses reported similarly high levels of sexual abuse as well as high levels of physical abuse; 53% indicated they had been sexually abused, 25% recalled scars, 38% recalled bleeding from abuse, and 51% recalled bruises (Mouzakitas, 1981).

A sample survey of girls in the juvenile justice system in Wisconsin (Phelps et al., 1982) revealed that 79% had been subjected to physical abuse that resulted in some form of injury, and 32% had been sexually abused by parents or other persons who were closely connected to their families. Moreover, 50% had been sexually assaulted ("raped" or forced to participate in sexual acts)(Phelps et al., 1982, p. 66). Even higher figures were reported by McCormack and her associates (McCormack, Janus, and Burgess, 1986) in their study of youth in a runaway shelter in Toronto. They found that 73% of the females and 38% of the males had been sexually abused. Finally, a study of youth charged with running away, truancy, or listed as missing persons in Arizona found that 55% were incest victims (Reich and Gutierres, 1979).

Many young women, then, are running away from profound sexual victimization at home, and once on the streets they are forced further into crime in order to survive. Interviews with girls who have run away from home show, very clearly, that they do not have a lot of attachment to their delinquent activities. In fact, they are angry about being labeled as delinquent, yet all engaged in illegal acts (Koroki and Chesney-Lind, 1985). The Wisconsin study found that 54% of the girls who ran away found it necessary to steal money, food, and clothing in order to survive. A few exchanged sexual contact for money, food, and/or shelter (Phelps et al., 1982, p. 67). In their study of runaway youth, McCormack, Janus, and Burgess (1986, pp. 392–393) found that sexually abused female runaways were significantly more likely than their nonabused counterparts to engage in delinquent or criminal activities such as substance abuse, petty theft, and prostitution. No such pattern was found among male runaways.

Research (Chesney-Lind and Rodriguez, 1983) on the backgrounds of adult women in prison underscores the important links between women's childhood victimizations and their later criminal careers. The interviews revealed that virtually all of this sample were the victims of physical and/or sexual abuse as youngsters; over 60% had been sexually abused and about half had been raped as young women. This situation prompted these women to run away from home (three-quarters had been arrested for status offenses) where once on the streets they began engaging in prostitution and other forms of petty property crime. They also begin what becomes a lifetime problem with drugs. As adults, the women continue in these activities since they possess truncated educational backgrounds and virtually no marketable occupational skills (see also Miller, 1986).

Confirmation of the consequences of childhood sexual and physical abuse on adult female criminal behavior has also recently come from a large quantitative study of 908 individuals with substantiated and validated histories of these victimizations. Widom (1988) found that abused or neglected females were twice as likely as a matched group of controls to have an adult record (16% compared to 7.5). The difference was also found among men, but it was not as dramatic (42% compared to 33%). Men with abuse backgrounds were also more likely to contribute to the "cycle of violence" with more arrests for violent offenses as adult offenders than the control group. In contrast, when women with abuse backgrounds did become involved with the criminal justice system, their arrests tended to involve property and order offenses (such as disorderly conduct, curfew, and loitering violations) (Widon, 1988, p. 17).

Given this information, a brief example of how a feminist perspective on the causes of female delinquency might look seems appropriate. First, like young men, girls are frequently the recipients of violence and sexual abuse. But unlike boys, girls' victimization and their response to that victimization is specifically shaped by their status as young women. Perhaps because of the gender and sexual scripts found in patriarchal families, girls are much more likely than boys to be victim of family-related sexual abuse. Men, particularly men with traditional attitudes toward women, are likely to define their daughters or stepdaughters as their sexual property (Finkelhor, 1982). In a society that idealizes inequality in male/female relationships and venerates youth in women, girls are easily defined as sexually attractive by older men (Bell, 1984). In addition, girls' vulnerability to both physical and sexual abuse is heightened by norms that require that they stay at home where their victimizers have access to them.

Moreover, their victimizers (usually males) have the ability to invoke official agencies of social control in their efforts to keep young women at home and vulnerable. That is to say, abusers have traditionally been able to utilize the uncritical commitment of the juvenile justice system toward parental authority to force girls to obey them. Girls' complaints about abuse were, until recently, routinely ignored. For this reason, statutes that were originally placed in law to "protect" young people have, in the case of girls' delinquency, criminalized their survival strategies. As they run away from abusive homes, parents have been able to employ agencies to enforce their return. If they persisted in their refusal to stay in that home, however intolerable, they were incarcerated.

Young women, a large number of whom are on the run from homes characterized by sexual abuse and parental neglect, are forced by the very statutes designed to protect them into the lives of escaped convicts. Unable to enroll in school or take a job to support themselves because they fear detection, young female runaways are forced into the streets. Here they engage in panhandling, petty theft, and occasional prostitution in order to survive. Young women in conflict with their parents (often for very legitimate reasons) may actually be forced by present laws into petty criminal activity, prostitution, and drug use.

In addition, the fact that young girls (but not necessarily young boys) are defined as sexually desirable and, in fact, more desirable than their older sisters due to the double standard of aging means that their lives on the streets (and their survival strategies) take on unique shape—one again shaped by patriarchal values. It is no accident that girls on the run from abusive homes, or on the streets because of profound poverty, get involved in criminal activities that exploit their sexual object status. American society has defined as desirable youthful, physically perfect women. This means that girls on the streets, who have little else of value to trade, are encouraged to utilize this "resource" (Campagna and Poffenberger, 1988). It also means that the criminal subculture views them from this perspective (Miller, 1986).

FEMALE DELINQUENCY, PATRIARCHAL AUTHORITY, AND FAMILY COURTS

The early insights into male delinquency were largely gleaned by inten-

sive field observation of delinquent boys. Very little of this sort of work has been done in the case of girls' delinquency, though it is vital to an understanding of girls' definitions of their own situations, choices, and behavior (for exceptions to this see Campbell, 1984; Peacock, 1981; Miller, 1986; Rosenberg and Zimmerman, 1977). Time must be spent listening to girls. Fuller research on the settings, such as families and schools, that girls find themselves in and the impact of variations in those settings should also be undertaken (see Figueira-McDonough, 1986). A more complete understanding of how poverty and racism shape girls' lives is also vital (see Messerschmidt, 1986; Campbell, 1984). Finally, current qualitative research on the reaction of official agencies to girls' delinquency must be conducted. This latter task, admittedly more difficult, is particularly critical to the development of delinquency theory that is as sensitive to gender as it is to race and class.

It is clear that throughout most of the court's history, virtually all female delinquency has been placed within the larger context of girls' sexual behavior. One explanation for this pattern is that familial control over girls' sexual capital has historically been central to the maintenance of patriarchy (Lerner, 1986). The fact that young women have relatively more of this capital has been one reason for the excessive concern that both families and official agencies of social control have expressed about youthful female defiance (otherwise much of the behavior of criminal justice personnel makes virtually no sense). Only if one considers the role of women's control over their sexuality at the point in their lives that their value to patriarchal society is so pronounced, does the historic pattern of jailing of huge numbers of girls guilty of minor misconduct make sense.

This framework also explains the enormous resistance that the movement to curb the juvenile justice system's authority over status offenders encountered. Supporters of the change were not really prepared for the political significance of giving youth the freedom to run. Horror stories told by the opponents of deinstitutionalization about victimized youth, youthful prostitution, and youthful involvement in pornography (Office of Juvenile Justice and Delinquency Prevention, 1985) all neglect the unpleasant reality that most of these behaviors were often in direct response to earlier victimization, frequently by parents, that officials had, for years, routinely ignored. What may be at stake in efforts to roll back deinstitutionaliza-

tion efforts is not so much "protection" of youth as it is curbing the right of young women to defy patriarchy.

In sum, research in both the dynamics of girls' delinquency and official reactions to that behavior is essential to the development of theories of delinquency that are sensitive to its patriarchal as well as class and racial context.

REFERENCES

Adams-Tucker, Christine. 1982. "Proximate Effects of Sexual Abuse in Childhood." *American Journal of Psychiatry* 193: 1252–1256.

Ageton, Suzanne S. 1983. "The Dynamics of Female Delinquency, 1976–1980.," *Criminology* 21:555–584.

Bell, Inge Powell. 1984. "The Double Standard: Age." in *Women: A Feminist Perspective*, edited by Jo Freeman. Palo Alto, CA: Mayfield.

Black, T. Edwin and Charles P. Smith, 1981. *A Preliminary National Assessment of the Number and Characteristics of Juveniles Processed in the Juvenile Justice System.* Washington, DC: Government Printing Office.

Browne, Angela and David Finkelhor, 1986. "Impact of Child Sexual Abuse: A Review of Research," *Psychological Bulletin* 99:66–77.

Campagna, Daniel S. and Donald I. Poffenberger, 1988. *The Sexual Trafficking in Children,* Dover, DE; Auburn House.

Campbell, Ann. 1984. *The Girls in the Gang.* Oxford: Basil Blackwell.

Canter, Rachelle J. 1982. "Sex Differences in Self-Report Delinquency," *Criminology* 20:373–393.

Chesney-Lind, Meda. 1971, *Female Juvenile Delinquency in Hawaii,* Master's thesis, University of Hawaii.

_____1973. "Judicial Enforcement of the Female Sex Role," *Issues in Criminology* 3:51–71.

_____1978. "Young Women in the Arms of the Law," In *Women, Crime and the Criminal Justice System,* edited by Lee H. Bowker, Boston: Lexington.

_____1986. "Women and Crime: The Female Offender," *Signs* 12:78–96.

_____1988. "Girls and Deinstitutionalization: Is Juvenile Justice Still Sexist?" *Journal of Criminal Justice Abstracts* 20:144–165.

_____and Noelie Rodriguez 1983. "Women Under Lock and Key," *Prison Journal* 63:47–65.

Children's Bureau, Department of Health, Education and Welfare, 1965. *1964 Statistics on Public Institutions for Delinquent Children.* Washington, DC; Government Printing Office.

Chilton, Roland and Susan K. Datesman, 1987, "Gender, Race and Crime: An Analysis of Urban Arrest Trends, 1960–1980," *Gender and Society* 1:152–171.

Cloward, Richard A. and Lloyd E. Ohlin, 1960. *Delinquency and Opportunity,* New York: Free Press.

Cohen, Albert K., 1955. *Delinquent Boys: The Culture of the Gang,* New York: Free Press.

5. JUVENILE JUSTICE

Datesman, Susan and Mikel Aickin, 1984, "Offense Specialization and Escalation Among Status Offenders," *Journal of Criminal Law and Criminology,* 75:1246–1275.

Davidson, Sue, ed. 1982. *Justice for Young Women.* Tucson, AZ; New Directions for Young Women.

DeJong, Allan R., Arturo R. Hervada, and Gary A. Emmett, 1983. "Epidemiologic Variations in Childhood Sexual Abuse," *Child Abuse and Neglect* 7:155–162.

Elliott, Delbert, David Huizinga, and Barbara Morse, 1987, "A Career Analysis of Serious Violent Offenders," In *Violent Juvenile Crime: What Can We Do About It?* edited by Ira Schwartz, Minneapolis, MN: Hubert Humphrey Institute.

Federal Bureau of Investigation, 1987. *Crime in the United States 1986,* Washington, DC; Government Printing Office.

Feinman, Clarice, 1980. *Women in the Criminal Justice System,* New York; Praeger.

Figueira-McDonough, Josefina, 1985. "Are Girls Different? Gender Discrepancies Between Delinquent Behavior and Control," *Child Welfare* 64:273–289.

———1986, "School Context, Gender, and Delinquency," *Journal of Youth and Adolescence* 15:79–98.

Finkelhor, David, 1982. "Sexual Abuse: A Sociological Perspective," *Child Abuse and Neglect* 6:95–102.

———and Larry Baron. 1986. "Risk Factors for Child Sexual Abuse," *Journal of Interpersonal Violence* 1:43–71.

Freedman, Estelle, 1981. *Their Sisters' Keepers,* Ann Arbor; University of Michigan Press.

Geltshorpe, Loraine, 1986. "Towards a Sceptical Look at Sexism," *International Journal of the Sociology of Law* 14:125–152.

Gora, JoAnn, 1982. *The New Female Criminal: Empirical Reality or Social Myth,* New York: Praeger.

Hagan, John, A. R. Gillis, and John Simpson, 1985. "The Class Structure of Gender and Delinquency: Toward a Power-Control Theory of Common Delinquent Behavior," *American Journal of Sociology* 90:1151–1178.

Hagan, John, John Simpson, and A. R. Gillis, 1987. "Class in the Household: A Power-Control Theory of Gender and Delinquency," *American Journal of Sociology* 92:788–816.

Hancock, Linda. 1981. "The Myth that Females are Treated More Leniently than Males in the Juvenile Justice System." *Australian and New Zealand Journal of Criminology* 16:4–14.

Harris, Anthony, 1977. "Sex and Theories of Deviance," *American Sociological Review* 42:3–16.

Herman, Jullia L. 1981. *Father-Daughter Incest.* Cambridge, MA; Harvard University Press.

Katz, Phyllis A. 1979. "The Development of Female Identity," In *Becoming Female: Perspectives on Development,* edited by Claire B. Kopp, New York; Plenum.

Koroki, Jan and Meda Chesney-Lind. 1985, *Everything Just Going Down the Drain.* Hawaii; Youth Development and Research Center.

Lerner, Gerda. 1986. *The Creation of Patriarchy.* New York: Oxford.

McCormack, Arlene, Mark-David Janus, and Ann Wolbert Burgess, 1986. "Runaway Youths and Sexual Victimization: Gender Differences In an Adolescent Runaway Population," *Child Abuse and Neglect* 10:387–395.

McGarrell, Edmund F. and Timothy J. Flanagan, eds. 1985. *Sourcebook of Criminal Justice Statistics—1984.* Washington, DC; Government Printing Office.

Meiselman, Karen. 1978. *Incest.* San Francisco: Jossey-Bass.

Merton, Robert K. 1938. "Social Structure and Anomie." *American Sociological Review* 3(October):672–782.

Messerschmidt, James, 1986. *Capitalism, Patriarchy, and Crime: Toward a Socialist Feminist Criminology,* Totowa, NJ: Rowman & Littlefield.

———1987. "Feminism, Criminology, and the Rise of the Female Sex Delinquent, 1880–1930," *Contemporary Crises* 11: 243–263.

Miller, Eleanor, 1986. *Street Woman,* Philadelphia: Temple University Press.

Miller, Walter B. 1958. "Lower Class Culture as the Generating Milieu of Gang Delinquency," *Journal of Social Issues* 14:5–19.

Morris, Ruth, 1964, "Female Delinquency and Relational Problems," *Social Forces* 43:82–89.

Mouzakitas, C. M. 1981, "An Inquiry into the Problem of Child Abuse and Juvenile Delinquency," In *Exploring the Relationship Between Child Abuse and Delinquency,* edited by R. J. Hunner and Y. E. Walkers, Montclair, NJ: Allanheld, Osmun.

National Female Advocacy Project, 1981. *Young Women and the Justice System: Basic Facts and Issues.* Tucson, AZ; New Directions for Young Women.

Office of Juvenile Justice and Delinquency Prevention, 1985. *Runaway Children and the Juvenile Justice and Delinquency Prevention Act: What is the Impact?* Washington, DC; Government Printing Office.

Opinion Research Corporation, 1982, "Public Attitudes Toward Youth Crime: National Public Opinion Poll." Mimeographed. Minnesota; Hubert Humphrey Institute of Public Affairs, University of Minnesota.

Peacock, Carol, 1981. *Hand Me Down Dreams.* New York: Shocken.

Phelps, R. J. et al. 1982. *Wisconsin Female Juvenile Offender Study Project Summary Report,* Wisconsin: Youth Policy and Law Center, Wisconsin Council of Juvenile Justice.

Platt, Anthony M. 1969. *The Childsavers,* Chicago: University of Chicago Press.

Pope, Carl and William H. Feyerherm. 1982. "Gender Bias in Juvenile Court Dispositions," *Social Service Review* 6:1–17.

Rafter, Nicole Hahn, 1985. *Partial Justice.* Boston: Northeastern University Press.

Reich, J. W. And S. E. Gutierres, 1979, "Escape/Aggression Incidence in Sexually Abused Juvenile Delinquents," *Criminal Justice and Behavior* 6:239–243.

Rogers, Kristine, 1972. "For Her Own Protection. . . . Conditions of Incarceration for Female Juvenile Offenders in the State of Connecticut," *Law and Society Review* (Winter):223–246.

Rosenberg, Debby and Carol Zimmerman, 1977. *Are My Dreams Too Much To Ask For?* Tucson, A. Z: New Directions for Young Women.

Russell, Diana E. 1986. *The Secret Trauma: Incest in the Lives of Girls and Women,* New York: Basic Books.

Schlossman, Steven and Stephanie Wallach, 1978. "The Crime of Precocious Sexuality: Female Juvenile Delinquency in the Progressive Era," *Harvard Educational Review* 48:65–94.

Shaw, Clifford R. 1930. *The Jack-Roller,* Chicago: University of Chicago Press.

———1938. *Brothers in Crime,* Chicago: University of Chicago Press.

———and Henry D. McKay, 1942. *Juvenile Delinquency in Urban Areas,* Chicago: University of Chicago Press.

Shelden, Randall, 1981. "Sex Discrimination in the Juvenile Justice System: Memphis, Tennessee, 1900–1917." In *Comparing Female and Male Offenders,* edited by Marguerite Q. Warren. Beverly Hills, CA: Sage.

———and John Horvath, 1986. "Processing Offenders in a Juvenile Court: A Comparison of Males and Females." Paper presented at the annual meeting of the Western Society of Criminology, Newport Beach, CA, February 27–March 2.

Silbert, Mimi and Ayala M. Pines, 1981. "Sexual Child Abuse as an Antecedent to Prostitution," *Child Abuse and Neglect* 5:407–411.

Simons, Ronald L., Martin G. Miller, and Stephen M. Aigner, 1980. "Contemporary Theories of Deviance and Female Delinquency: An Empirical Test," *Journal of Research in Crime and Delinquency* 17:42–57.

Smith, Lesley Shacklady, 1978. "Sexist Assumptions and Female Delinquency," In *Women, Sexuality and Social Control,* edited by Carol Smart and Barry Smart, London: Routledge & Kegan Paul.

Snyder, Howard N. and Terrence A. Finnegan, 1987. *Delinquency in the United States.* Washington, DC: Department of Justice.

Steffensmeier, Darrell J. 1980 "Sex Differences in Patterns of Adult Crime, 1965–1977," *Social Forces* 58:1080–1109.

Sutherland, Edwin, 1978. "Differential Association." in *Children of Ishmael: Critical Perspectives on Juvenile Justice,* edited by Barry Krisberg and James Austin. Palo Alto, CA: Mayfield.

Teilmann, Katherine S. and Pierre H. Landry, Jr. 1981. "Gender Bias in Juvenile Justice." *Journal of Research in Crime and Delinquency* 18:47–80.

Thrasher, Frederic M. 1927. *The Gang.* Chicago: University of Chicago Press.

Tracy, Paul E., Marvin E. Wolfgang, and Robert M. Figlio. 1985. *Delinquency in Two Birth Cohorts: Executive Summary.* Washington, DC: Department of Justice.

Widom, Cathy Spatz. 1988. "Child Abuse, Neglect, and Violent Criminal Behavior." Unpublished manuscript.

TEENAGE ADDICTION

Chemical dependency is a problem that discriminates against no one, old, young, rich or poor, black or white. Yet, the tragedy of addiction seems more acute when it afflicts our adolescents, those whose bright futures seem threatened by drugs alcohol. In this section, we present three reports: one on the differences in treating teenage and adult chemical dependents; another on a successful school-based program on helping adolescent addicts; and finally, summaries of recent research on adolescent drug and alcohol abuse.

DON'T TREAT CHEMICALLY DEPENDENT TEENAGERS AS ADULTS

Martin N. Buxton, M.D., F.A.A.C.P.

Martin Buxton is director of the Chemical Dependency Program at Carter Westbrook Hospital, Richmond, Virginia and a member of the Editorial Advisory Board of The Addiction Letter.

Despite what they think, teenagers are not adults. Unfortunately, many of us treating chemically dependent adolescents forget that truism and use expertise we developed with adults on teenaged clients. It's not our fault; most training programs use adults as prototype patients, and while there has been an increasing reflection on the child-oriented family as part of the alcoholic system, there is still a dearth of literature on the chemically dependent adolescent patient.

In my experience in treating both adults and teenagers, I have found there are both subtle and not-so-subtle differences between the two groups. Dealing with adolescents requires the use of certain techniques that would be unsuccessful, if not extremely provoca-

tive, if tried on adults. Here are five techniques that I have found successful:

1. Don't treat the adolescent as an adult. This may be obvious, but it is vitally important. I would guess that 98% of the adolescents entering our treatment program are co-dependent, having at least one parent who is either chemically dependent and/or co-dependent themselves. Most come from at least a three-generational chemically dependent family system. Their age-expected developmental denial lulls them into taking risks in using chemicals, thinking "damage can't happen to me." The denial is exacerbated by the fact that as co-dependent, pseudo-adult, pseudo-precocious, omnipotent-thinking adolescents, they and

From *When Children Need Help*, Manisses Communications Group, 1987, pp. 15-27. Published with permission of The Brown University Child Behavior and Development Letter, Manisses Communications Group, Inc., Three Governor Street, P.O. Box 3357, Wayland Square, Providence, RI 02906-0357.

the world often see themselves as being older than they really are. If you aren't careful, you'll be lulled into the same attitude that enables their addiction. You must subtly recognize co-dependent adolescents' need to be friendly in an adult-to-adult fashion and deal with them in a way that does not reject them. At the same time, however, you must softly but realistically identify the fact that there is an age difference and that they are not adults.

2. Encourage them to develop relationships. Alcoholics Anonymous wisely teaches adults not to have a relationship within the first year of recovery, or else they risk an impulsive and ill-timed marriage or commitment. And adolescents, too, during their active co-dependency, may be prone to making serious but unhealthy commitments at a young age. Once this issue is worked out sufficiently, however, adolescents, as part of their healthy identity formation as heterosexual beings, should be encouraged to have involvement in relationships. Your need to see adolescence as a developmental entity distinct from adults requires you to encourage them to have healthy relationships that are not compulsively rife with sexuality or co-dependent caretaking.

3. Intervene more to keep adolescents in therapy. As caregivers, we are very aware of the concept of "parens patriae" which implies that we, who work in an institution or other treatment facility, often function as surrogate parents. But we also recognize the importance of the "Serenity Prayer," accepting the things we cannot change. These notions lead to a "laissez-faire" approach to treating adults, who may need to face more consequences of their addiction before they can be treated successfully.

The nature of chemically dependent adolescents, however, requires a different approach, at least at the beginning of treatment. More often than with adults, chemically dependent adolescents enter treatment not of their own volition but because they either attempted suicide, showed other self-destructive tendencies, or because of trouble with the law. As a result, more heroics and activism must be used by the therapist in order to keep a teenager in treatment, at least until the adolescent becomes enlisted in the therapeutic process.

You cannot go overboard, however, and seduce the adolescent into oppositional resistance. Evoking opposition is one of the dangers of working with adolescents, who often are contrary in order to establish their identity and autonomy. So you must be careful not to let the issues of staying sober and sticking with recovery become involved in the adolescent autonomy struggle, while trying to intervene assertively and clarify identity confusions.

4. Hold marathon sessions. We use this technique in our inpatient unit where we try to undo the alcoholic family types of communication and replace it with healthy family communication. Often, we'll find that a number of the youngsters have know that another has been using drugs or is planning on going AWOL. Yet they did not speak up despite the fact that they themselves are doing well in recovery. As we track this down, we come to understand that the youngsters are recapitulating the unrecovered alcoholic system's communications in that there are coalitions and alliances that do not address the truth of what is happening. We'll "close" the unit and keep the youngsters in a marathon intervention session, perhaps for hours at a time. The enabling denial of the process is addressed and resistance wears down, setting the stage for the reunification of healthy family lines of communication.

5. Use paradoxical intervention. Pioneered by the family systems people in Philadelphia, this technique is invaluable if used delicately. I have found it most helpful, given my personality style, when a youngster is entrenched in a co-dependent position and cannot see it objectively. In such cases, I'll have the co-dependent youngster be in charge of all ashtrays or being responsible for seeing that another youngster is on time for group therapy. It helps show the co-dependent adolescent their tendency to try to take care of people and control things as a way of avoiding their own issues. You must be careful that the patient has enough insight to be able to understand the abstract nature of what is being said and does not take it literally. If a tone of humor, without sarcasm is used, paradox can be a very successful intervention technique.

These aren't the only techniques that are helpful with adolescents. But they should stimulate more ideas in your own practice in dealing with the unique characteristics of adolescents. Certainly, both in a transferential and counter-transferential sense, you may find yourself more of a parent than a friend or counselor. But, as long as you are aware of the complications, you can use it in helping your teenaged patient attain recovery.

SCHOOL: AN AVENUE FOR CHANGE FOR DRUG-USING TEENAGERS

Matthew C. Green, M. Ed., C.A.C.

Matthew C. Green is co-director of the Newton Youth Drug/ Alcohol Program, 100 Walnut Street, Newtonville, MA 02160 (617–552–7679).

Alcohol, drugs, and teenagers have been a troublesome problem for high schools since the 1960's. Whether they used pot, LSD, or cocaine—not to mention the ever-present alcohol—adolescents using chemicals have been a problem for two decades and most communities are frustrated in their inability to stem the tide of drug use on a broad scale.

Since teenagers, by law in most states, are required to participate in some kind of formal education process through the age of 16, schools have a large stake in the drug issue. In most cases, teens bring their drug problems to the schoolhouse door, forcing the school as well as communities and parents to have equal responsibility in dealing with the problem.

In recent years, there has also been an increase in the number of teenagers appearing in courts throughout the country for drug and alcohol-related violations. Most courts send the teenagers to correctional facilities or put them on probation, completely ignoring what created the problem: drugs and alcohol. In addition, physicians, social workers and teachers have seen increasing numbers of adolescents with drug problems. These professionals rarely have adequate training or experience in substance abuse to enable them to feel comfortable and competent in helping teens who abuse drugs.

In Newton, Massachusetts, we have formed an unusual alliance between schools and the courts, the two institutions most important in the life of the drug-abusing teenager. Now in its eighth year, the Newton Youth Drug/Alcohol Program has worked together with court probation departments and public school staff to meet the needs of about 40 adolescents in trouble with drugs each year.

I should note that, in Massachusetts anyway, school administrators are cool towards the concept of alcohol and drug treatment operated through public school. Schools are for education, they believe, not for medical or mental health treatment. School does not own the responsibility for the students' emotional and physical problems, they say.

The Newton community, however, believes that when school is the only constant in an adolescent's life and when children bring their drug and alcohol problems into the school environment, then the educational system is obligated to implement change.

At Least a Year
Students enter the Newton Youth Drug/Alcohol Program either as a condition of probation or as a school requirement. Court-referred teens remain in the program for the duration of their probation, usually one to three years or until they fail to comply with the program's requirements. School-referred students commit themselves for a least one year.

Satisfactory completion of the program means earned high school credit for all participants. Unsatisfactory performance means denial of credit for those

referred from school and surrender and final disposition for those on probation.

Participants must attend either Alcoholics Anonymous and/or Narcotics Anonymous as well as group therapy and individual counseling. Vocational assistance, court liaison and interpretation of events are available to each student. Students are required to attend all meetings on time. Absence and tardiness are not tolerated and result in termination from the program. Furthermore, students must attend meetings sober and free of any mind-altering chemical.

Lack of Limits
The program's philosophy is based on the premise that the lack of limits in an adolescent's life promotes the drug abusing life-style. Adolescents are frightened of the decisions they are forced to make in their teenage years—on values, and life goals—so they respond to firm guidance and strict limits. Program workers are available to students 24 hours per day, seven days per week, and 52 weeks a year in case of crisis.

The program has grown during the past five years. In the 1980–81 school year, the courts referred eight youngsters, seven of whom completed the program and remained in school. None was referred by school officials. During 1984–85, 53 were enrolled in the program, 46 referred by the courts and 7 by the schools. Completing the program last year were 30 of the 46 on probation (40 are still in school) and 5 of the 7 school-referred youths. (All 7 are still in school). Of the 46, 24 were new enrollees while the remainder had continued from the previous year.

The program is designed to provide:
- A framework to help students understand their drug-using behavior.
- Skills for self-awareness.
- A non-threatening environment for discussion.
- Experiences which encapsulate various life situations (through AA, NA, and discussion).
- High school credits as an added incentive for success and a road back for those who dropped out of school.
- A mechanism for the schools and courts to monitor the student/offenders' behavior.

Successful Completion
A student will have successfully completed the program if he or she is able to state thoughts and feelings which lead to abusive drinking and/or drug use; identify moments when the student is beginning to feel out of control concerning alcohol or drugs; list alternatives to use at such moments; and practice skills or alternatives (ways of handling arguments, conflict, tension and boredom) which take control of his or her future, by describing specific actions in his or her personal plan for future development.

Individuals with drug and alcohol problems continually suffer from unrealistic aspirations. Our students learn through discussion the type of risks they usually take. The effect of consistently taking high risks is discussed in our groups, in the context of resolving family disputes, work, recreational activities, driving and abusive drinking and drug use. Our students are encouraged to seek help from other professionals, and to view it as a way of using resources rather than as a weakness or character defect. We emphasize seeking personal change that is realistic and have benchmarks for testing the program periodically. For many students, plans for maintaining sobriety and continued treatment become an essential part of their future plans. The program has had extensive contact with inpatient detoxification and treatment/rehabilitation facilities throughout the Northeast, making referrals as well as being used as an aftercare placement for students coming back from these facilities.

Treatment and prevention are closely allied, and the Newton program combines the two effectively. Once a student is "straight," he or she becomes a staunch advocate of abstinence and an evangelist in approaching their drug-using friends. We have young people—ages 17 to 22—who are teachers by example to their peers. One such group of young people started an NA and AA group of their own in Newton and are speaking to other young adults about alcohol and drug dependency.

The program is broader than the cooperation between schools and courts implies. Students are not only referred by school officials and probation departments but by police and city human services departments. It provides support services to adolescents returning to school from residential chemical dependency programs and to parents and staff who are being trained in the identification of potential problems in adolescence.

All referrals coming from the various community agencies are the same adolescents who are also having difficulties in school. Therefore the Newton program is able to coordinate these groups to provide appropriate services for the adolescent with difficulties, avoiding outside placement and providing early identification of special needs.

Attitudes of disbelief and denial are often found in communities. We are finding kids coming to school either hungover, stoned or tripping; some are even coming to school drunk. For the most part, our students are ingesting their drugs outside of the school building, but are playing out their trip either in the classrooms, the corridors, the washrooms, or the cafeteria. Most often when questioned about their drug problem, these kids don't see it as a problem at all.

One 17-year-old we interviewed provides a stark example. He said he began using drugs and alcohol at the age of 10 and identified his use of illegal substances as "moderate" by the time he reached the age of 12. At that time, he smoked an ounce of marijuana and drank a six-pack of beer daily. He used LSD weekly. He was identified in school and in the community as delinquent because of his occasional criminal behavior and was remanded to the State Department of Youth Services for a two-year period. It was upon incarceration, that he stated, "My drug use then began to get bad."

This case simply exemplifies the attitude of individuals as well as the community surrounding a teenager's use of drugs and alcohol. The outward behavior, criminal activity, is punished, and the root of the problem continues to grow. In addition, teens are often unaware that their drug use or their friends' drug use is dangerous, life-threatening, and producing negative consequences.

The Newton program is set up on the premise that education is the primary tool to break through this denial. Legal controls have proved largely ineffective in controlling alcohol and drug use by youth. Preaching and scare tactics generally have also met with failure.

If the problem of alcoholism and drug abuse is to be managed in the future, it will be because young people have adopted a responsible attitude. They gain this through adult examples of responsible behavior as well as learning all the facts, positive and negative. Programs like the Newton Youth Drug/Alcohol Program, which link education, adjudication and rehabilitation, accomplish this task.

INDIRECT INDICATORS OF CHEMICAL ABUSE

How can we tell whether children are abusing chemicals?

Abusive use itself (being drunk at school, using drugs to get high, etc.) is, of course, a direct indicator of a problem with chemicals. But the Johnson Institute, a Minneapolis training center for addiction professionals, found in a 1984 survey of Minnesota teenagers several other indicators—some related to chemical use, some lacking any apparent connection—that correlated with chemical abuse by teenagers.

The presence of one or two of the following indicators hardly suggests chemical abuse, but the presence of several, perhaps five or more, should at least raise the question of chemical abuse:

- Low grades—a consistent pattern of below average grades or a recent drop in grades. Low grades are three times as likely among heavy users (11%) as among abstainers (4%).
- Absenteeism from school. Heavy users are four times more likely than abstainers to miss school (37% vs. 10%).
- A negative opinion of school. Heavy users are much more likely than abstainers to complain that they don't like school (37% vs. 16%) or to complain that they don't get along with their teachers (18% vs. 6%).

- Cigarette smoking. Two-thirds of heavy users smoke tobacco vs. 6% of infrequent users vs. 3% of abstainers.
- Drinking hard liquor (as opposed to beer or wine).
- Using marijuana.
- Avoiding parties where no chemicals are available or attending parties where drugs other than alcohol are available.
- Drinking in cars (86% of heavy users vs. 13% of infrequent users vs.—of course—0% abstainers).
- Lack of involvement in community activities, organized sports or other school activities. (Heavy users are less likely to have a part-time job or be involved in organized sports. They are much less likely than infrequent users or abstainers to be involved in other school activities (21% vs. 72% vs. 63%).
- The student is a male in grades 10–12.

***

RECENT STUDIES PROVIDE INSIGHT INTO DRUG USE AMONG TEENS

Reflecting the general public's increasing concern about teenagers' use of drugs and alcohol, numerous recent studies attempt to shed light on why adolescents experiment with alcohol and drugs, how use and experiment progress to dependency, and which teenagers are more at risk of developing chemical dependency. Here are several of the more significant recent studies:

The Role of Personality
Does a teenager's personality predict whether he or she will use drugs or alcohol? A recent study by Erich W. Labouvie and Connel R. McGee at Rutgers' Center of Alcohol studies says yes, strongly suggesting that personality may cause later use of alcohol and drugs. The study was published in Journal of Consulting and Clinical Psychology (1986, 54:289–293).

The researchers randomly selected 882 adolescents in three waves in 1979, 1980 and 1981. Initially tested at the ages of 12, 15 and 18, participants in the first two waves were retested after three years at the ages of 15, 18 and 21 years. The researchers asked the teenagers how often and how much they used alcohol, cigarettes, marijuana and cocaine. They also measured whether they used alcohol, cigarettes and illicit drugs as a coping device; their personality attributes; and, finally, their self-esteem.

After testing, researchers divided the sample into three groups, light, moderate and heavy users of substances. They found that male adolescents used marijuana and alcohol more than females, but that females smoke cigarettes more.

Light users in early adolescence tend to use only alcohol by age 21 and to maintain limited usage. Moderate users, by age 15, exhibit fairly regular use of alcohol and cigarettes, and by age 18, regular use of marijuana. Heavy users indulge in marijuana, cigarettes and alcohol by age 15 and use cocaine occasionally by age 21. The heavy users are involved with multiple drugs.

Heavy users scored high on the personality test on autonomy, exhibitionism, impulsivity, and play. They scored low on achievement, cognitive structure and harm avoidance. Light users scored the opposite. The authors suggest strongly that personality causes later alcohol and drug use. Personality changes were not significant over time, they said, indicating that use did not cause the personality characteristics. They found, however, that self-esteem did not correlate with use levels, suggesting that use among today's adolescents may no longer represent deviance or self-rejection. They note that adolescents who scored lower in achievement, cognitive structure and harm avoidance are not only more likely to use substances, but also to underdevelop those characteristics over time.

They caution, however, against concluding that heavy adolescent use predicts adult alcoholism. They hypothesize that the heavy using teenager find the substances as instant gratification for needs of play and impulsivity with little effort or skill expended. Second, the researchers suggest that alcohol and drug use may help the teens express needs for affiliation, autonomy, and exhibitionism. Finally, adolescents with risk-taking attributes are likely to be at odds with their environment and alcohol and drug use would relieve that stress via rebellion and expression of individuality.

Drug Use Begins in Sixth Grade
A longitudinal study of more than 1,100 children in two New England towns, published in the Journal of Drug Education (1986, 16: 203–220), shows that drug use begins as early as sixth grade and that there are critical periods for onset of use that may be helpful in designing effective prevention strategies.

The researchers, Katherine Grady, David L. Snow, and Marion Kessen of Yale University, and Kelin E. Gersick of the California School of Professional Psychology at Los Angeles, first studied the youngsters during their sixth grade and re-evaluated them in their seventh and eighth grades.

They had noted that other studies showed patterns of use that include significant experimentation and use in increasingly early grades. Youths typically move from initial experimentation to increasing experimentation and that they move from beer and wine, then tobacco and hard liquor, then to marijuana and other illicit drugs.

For their study, the authors divided use into four stages: none-use, experimental use (less than once monthly), regular use (one to two times monthly) and heavy use (once a week or more).

The study used a two-part questionnaire: the first asked them how often they had been offered any of ten listed drugs: tobacco, LSD, marijuana, alcohol, amphetamines, barbiturates, heroin, inhalants, cocaine, and other drugs. The second asked them if and how often they had used the drugs.

The study confirmed that alcohol, tobacco, and marijuana are gateway drugs. Sixty-five percent of the sixth graders had at least experimented with alcohol. That increased to 68% in seventh grade, and 74% in eighth grade. Experimentation or use of tobacco increased from 36% in sixth grade to 59% in the eighth. Experimentation and use of marijuana increased from 11% in sixth grade to 38% in the eighth. For other drugs, the study indicated sizable increases in experimentation but not in regular or heavy use over the three years.

Males used more alcohol, marijuana and other substances in the sixth grade, but by the eighth grade, there were no gender differences. Females used tobacco more in seventh and eighth grades. Whites used more than blacks in all grades. Rates of use were higher in the town having a middle school structure than in the town having a K–6, 7–8, and 9–12 system.

Family situations also affected use rates. Students from broken homes used tobacco and marijuana more in all three grades and higher use of alcohol in sixth grade. Students with remarried parents had slightly lower use rates than students reporting separated or divorced parents. Religious background showed little correlation, except for seventh grade tobacco use. Protestants used more than Catholics.

Offer rates were higher than use rates by the eighth grades. By then, 78% had been offered alcohol, 77% tobacco, 58% marijuana, 18% inhalants, 20% amphetamines, 19% barbiturates, and 16% cocaine.

Few students rejected alcohol in all three years, while rejection rates were moderate for tobacco and high for marijuana. Over the three years, the percentage of students rejecting decreases.

The authors concluded that prevention programs in the younger grades may need to focus on boys' use of alcohol and drugs and girls' use of tobacco. Students from broken homes need programs to meet their special needs.

The critical period for initiation into alcohol use occurs prior to the middle school years, they conclude, requiring earlier prevention programs and intensive parent and school involvement. Prevention programs should aim at preventing experimentation and increasing rejection of alcohol when offered.

The critical period for tobacco use seems to be the sixth grade. Prevention programs should include earlier grades with the middle school focus being on increasing the capacity to reject offers of tobacco.

For marijuana the researchers suggest sixth grade as the best time for prevention programs since use is most evident in seventh and eighth grades. Prevention programs for non-gateway drugs need to build on these programs when experimentation with such drugs as amphetamines and cocaine are just beginning.

Polydrug Abusers Seek Pleasure or Escape Pain

A study of 433 high school students, published in Adolescence (1985, 20: 853–861) found that 12% were polydrug users or abusers and that the reason they used drugs was to seek pleasure or escape pain.

Polydrug use, in this case, means that the users used more than one drug at the same time or in close sequence to produce different effects. They researcher, Loyd S. Wright, a psychologist at Southwest Texas State University, noted the dangers of the synergistic effects that polydrug use pose to users and abusers. In his study, seniors at two Texas high schools filled out confidential questionnaires on their drug using habits as well as how they perceived their parents and themselves.

Polydrug users and abusers more likely:

- Were physically abused or in conflict with their parents;
- Rated themselves as lazy, bored, rejected and unhealthy;
- Have serious suicidal thoughts, delinquent behavior, early use of marijuana and alcohol and the tendency to drink more than six alcoholic drinks at a sitting; and
- Agreed with the statements "If something feels good, I usually do it and don't worry about the consequences" and "I try to play as much as possible and work as little as possible."

Wright concluded that the results confirmed the notion that polydrug users seek either relief or pleasure and, therefore, do not see their drug use as a problem. He writes, "a variety of treatment and prevention strategies are necessary. Any drug abuse treatment program that hopes to have an impact on the pleasure seekers must get them to reexamine their basic philosophy, remove their peer support, and provide alternatives that will meet their needs for excitement and adventure."

Model College Drug and Alcohol Treatment Program

A model program to treat drug and alcohol abusers in college was proposed by three researchers after a national study of currently available university-based programs.

James Dean, DMIN, Hannah Dean, RN, Ph.D., and Donna Kleiner, MA, writing in the Journal of Substance Abuse Treatment (1986, 3 95–101), maintain that current use levels and accompanying problems require greater involvement than currently exists.

They propose that each institution form a planning committee to set attainable goals for the institution. Variables would include the extent of alcohol and drug problems, campus and community political climate, available resources and the financial capacity of the school. These factors will dictate the degree of involvement possible on a continuum ranging from no response to crisis intervention, identification and assessment only, or identification, assessment, and treatment. Most universities have counseling services for career, academic and personal needs. Only half have alcohol and drug services, they said.

The structural style of a program will reflect campus size, location, affiliation, student age, financial resources, state and local laws. Off-campus referral might be most applicable for some, while others might better utilize on-campus treatment. On-campus treatment would need to be offered through the counseling center. Friction with traditional psychological counseling service providers can be minimized by considering the chemical problem as central with psychological services potentially available, the authors suggest.

Physical services need to be available in support of alcohol and drug abuse crisis situations. Campus police, residence hall and dean of students' staffs, and crisis response team members need special training.

Treatment philosophy in the national survey was found by the authors to reflect a variety of models including AA/NA, psychoanalytical, behavioral, cognitive, family systems, Gestalt, religious, disease and eclectic approaches. The authors urge avoid use of labels in any model such as "alcoholic" or "drug addict," but rather to focus on the specific problems behavior associated with chemical use.

They note the need for trained staff with alcohol and drug treatment approach as most useful with attention focused on chemical use, on environmental and intrapsychic factors that influence use. They cite the University of North Dakota assessment as most helpful. They collect family and personal history, history of previous treatment, arrests, and psychological disorders. This data is supplemented with tests such as the MMPI and Beck Depression Inventory.

Referral to counseling comes via word of mouth, radio and TV publicity campaigns, and linkage to housing and resident hall disciplinary systems. They note the North Dakota system as most effective. It involves observing the problem behavior, encountering the problem by presenting facts to the student and referral. The student has the choice of accepting assistance or facing disciplinary action. A similar model is used by the Greek system and is run as a peer intervention system.

The authors stress the need for high-level administrative support and financial budgeting. Primary and secondary prevention are both the legitimate concerns of academic institutions to prevent problems before

they occur, and to arrest them before they become serious and disabling, they conclude.

Youth 'Heavy Involvements' in Drugs and Alcohol

More than one-quarter of all senior high school students use marijuana, and one in ten 12th graders used cocaine during the 1985–86 school year, according to the results of a survey conducted for the Parents' Resource Institute for Drug Education (PRIDE) of Atlanta, Georgia.

The survey also reported that, based on interviews with 40,000 students in 17 states in grades 6 through 12, few students use drugs or alcohol during school hours. Only 1% of all students used alcohol, and 2% marijuana, during school hours.

"However, this does not suggest that drug and alcohol abuse is not a school problem. Students who have smoked marijuana while waiting for the bus or who have a hangover from too much alcohol the night before will be less receptive to instruction during the school day," PRIDE said.

PRIDE also reported that alcohol abuse among students was high, with more than one quarter of students in grades 6–8 reporting some use of liquor during the past year, a figure that jumps to 60% for ninth through 12th graders.

Students reported an even higher incidence of beer or wine use, with just under half of all junior high school students, and nearly three quarters of all senior high students admitting to some experience with those products.

Although the incidence of alcohol abuse far outpaced that of drug abuse, PRIDE officials reserved their direst warnings for parents of students using drugs, particularly cocaine.

"Only 1.6% of the junior high students reported any cocaine use while 6.4% of the senior high school students reported cocaine use," the survey's summary reported. Cocaine use increased with age, with 10.4% of 12th grade students admitting to some experience with the drug," the report stated.

Worse, PRIDE reported, cocaine users admitted that, when they used alcohol or marijuana, they did so expressly to get "bombed" or "very high."

Almost half of all students who have used cocaine report that they become intoxicated when using any drug or alcohol products. By comparison, only 4.5% of students who use only beer or wine reported intoxication.

Finally, the report concluded that students—particularly older high school students—abuse drugs and alcohol outside of parents' purview, and, alarmingly, continue to do so while driving. Nine percent of beer and wine drinkers, and 6% of marijuana abusers, are combining substance use with driving.

"This use of alcohol and marijuana outside the home and the reported direct use of these substances in a car suggest a serious problem with teenagers driving under the influence," PRIDE concluded.

(Parents Resource Institute for Drug Education, 100 Edgewood Ave., #1002, Atlanta, GA 30303, 800–241–7946.)

Teens Concerned About
Health Consequences of Drinking

A new study sponsored by the Alcoholism Council of Greater New York, suggests that teenagers are as concerned about the personal health problems associated with heavy drinking as about the social consequences.

The study, by an Albert Einstein College of Medicine researcher, involved 108 adolescents, ages 12 through 18, in three New York City community centers of the Children's Aid Society.

In a questionnaire which never mentions alcohol, the youths were asked to indicate their level of concern about specific health problems (such as acne, cancer, diabetes, and obesity) and behavior problems (peer acceptance, relationship with parents, and so on).

On 34 health issues, 19 represented problems that can be associated with heavy drinking, and 15 were not alcohol-related. All of the 19 behavioral items could be alcohol-related.

In an analysis of the responses, Thomas Ashby Wills, an assistant professor of psychology and epidemiology in Albert Einstein's Department of Epidemiology and Social Medicine, found the youths' concern about health problems "comparable to, and possibly greater than, their level of concern about behavioral problems."

"Concern about health consequences of alcohol may be an effective component of educational programs to reduce rates of alcohol abuse, in addition to the social consequences approach used in current alcohol education," he said.

The study was part of the Alcoholism Council's current Health Awareness Campaign designed to inform the public of alcohol's hidden effects on health, fitness and appearance.

(Alcoholism Council of Greater New York, 133 East 62nd St., New York, NY 10021; 212–935–7075)

Reasons for Drug Use

For teenagers, drugs: serve as rationalization vehicles for otherwise unacceptable behavior, enhance identity states, enable users to find companionship, and fulfill expectations of effects, as a hostility releaser, as a deepening of consciousness, or as an expression of civil disobedience.

These are the conclusions of Craig R. Thorne and Richard R. DeBlassie, who surveyed numerous recent studies and published their findings in Adolescence (1985, 78: 335–347).

According to the researchers, onset of use involves opportunity. At first, the teenager does not use at the first opportunity, but if his or her peer group uses drugs or alcohol, he or she, gradually, will follow suit. Young adults 18–25 years of age are most likely to use illicit drugs—especially if living away from family, alone or with peers. Perceived availability of drugs also influences use, with marijuana being seen as the universally most available, followed, in order, by psychotherapeutic drugs, barbiturates, cocaine, hallucinogens, opiates and heroin.

Marijuana is the most widely used illicit drug among high school seniors with 60% having used it, but alcohol and tobacco are the most widespread with 93% having tried alcohol and 71% having tried tobacco.

Use of illicit drugs occurs in the last three years of high school. Marijuana, alcohol, and tobacco are tried prior to high school. Inhalant use occurs typically prior to 10th grade while illicit drugs excluding inhalant and marijuana use begin after 10th grade. Marijuana use is increasing in all grade levels down to 8th grade, but on a declining curve.

Males and females exhibited difference in frequency of use with males using more of all substances except tobacco. Early aggressiveness and shyness correlate to later substance abuse in males only. Males rank peer and school bonds as primary. Females ranked family and school bonds as most important for them. Strong peer bonds correlates with use. College aspirations correlate with lower rates of illicit drug use. Northeastern American residents have highest rates of use, the Southern, the lowest. Urban areas outscore rural areas on use, except for tranquilizers, sedatives, stimulants, and tobacco which show no association to setting.

Family influence in this report involves older siblings' examples, mothers who smoke and drink moderately. Fathers' use does not appear, according to the authors, to be a significant factor.

Virtually all students perceived parental attitudes to be disapproving of drug use. Peer attitude is closest to the student's attitude toward use.

Prevention programs surveyed have largely focused on the individual, take place in an institutional setting rather than in the community, are directed at the middle-class, white population, aim at prevention of all drug use, and are presented to rather large audiences.

Four models of treatment are prevalent—legal, medical, traditional (AA, abstinence), and emergent (learned behavior/controlled use outcome). Increased opportunity for use relates with gradual increase in use. There is much cause of continuing concern and continued prevention efforts, work in the legal, research, and treatment areas.

The authors cite recognition of our individual and collective attitudes and beliefs as primary elements in overcoming substance abuse worldwide.

Self-image and Alcohol Use

Teenagers' self-images and social images were found to be factors as to whether they drank alcohol, according to researchers Laurie Chassin, Christine Tetzloff, and Miriam Hershey, who published the results of their study in the Journal of Studies on Alcohol (1985, 46: 39–47). They hypothesized that adolescents would drink if their self-concepts were consistent with a drinking image (consistency theory), or if their peers admired a drinking image (impression management theory).

They studied 266 students in a southwestern suburban high school, 51% male, 49% female and 92.5% white, 4.7% Hispanic, 2.4% Indian. The average age was 15 years old.

They were shown slides of youths holding beverage cans—beer or soft drinks—in pairs. Questions were asked on the desirability of the model as a friend, and how much like the model the student was. The Adolescent Alcohol Involvement Scale was given, testing frequency and quantity of use, and social and psychological problems resulting. Finally, adolescents gave intentions for future use.

The social image associated with alcohol use was ambivalent. They saw the adolescent drinker as projecting an image of toughness and precocity—a perceived social asset. It also conveys the association of rebellion against authority. On the negative side, they associated users with being less happy and honest, and more socially rejected regardless of sex of model. Drinking alcohol was noted by the authors as having significantly more social acceptability to adolescents than smoking. The authors suggest that the distress associated with use may be seen as teens viewing drinkers as more likely to bear dysphoric symptoms. They may see use as increasing positive mood states.

Adolescent boys tend to aspire to the drinking image and to believe that the drinker attributes are valued by their peers (toughness and precocity).

Girls who did not misuse alcohol followed this pattern. Significantly, girls who did misuse alcohol had ideal self-images that were less like the drinker image than their actual self-descriptions. The authors infer that these girls may be using alcohol to control mood or reduce stress.

Adolescents of both sexes who saw themselves as similar to a drinking image were more involved with alcohol (consistency hypothesis). Seeing peers as admiring the drinking image correlates with intent to use in the future (impression management hypothesis). Males who saw their ideal self-image as similar to the drinking image used more (self enhancement hypothesis).

The precise mechanics of causes of use by adolescents is unclear. Peer influence, modeling, opportunities, and social reinforcement are all cited as being involved by the authors. More work is needed to provide adequate programs for prevention. Finding ways to work around the social image associated with drug use—finding alternatives—is the course they suggest.

CORRECTING JUVENILE CORRECTIONS

Ira M. Schwartz

Ira M. Schwartz is director of the Center for the Study of Youth Policy at the University of Michigan. His most recent publication is (In)justice for Juveniles—Rethinking the Best Interests of the Child *(Lexington Books, 1989).*

Fighting juvenile crime is a multibillion-dollar business in the United States. State and local politicians and juvenile justice officials will spend approximately $1.5 billion in 1990 just to incarcerate young offenders in detention centers, youth training schools, and juvenile prisons. Hundreds of millions more will be spent on police, prosecutors, defense attorneys, juvenile courts, probation officers, and parole workers.

Public concern about the juvenile crime problem and the widespread availability of drugs promises to push the level of expenditures up significantly in the 90s. Elected public officials, ever sensitive to the demands of their constituents, are advocating tougher and more costly policies to address this issue. Before such policies are enacted, policymakers, juvenile justice officials, and the public-at-large would be well advised to step back and take a hard look at this problem.

Juvenile justice expenditures mushroomed during the period from 1977 to 1987. This was largely due to "get tough" policies that were implemented throughout the country. For example, elected public officials in practically every state supported legislation that allowed more juveniles to be prosecuted as adults and stiffened penalties for those young offenders who were kept in the juvenile system. Despite this, the best available evidence indicates that, at best, we have been able to only hold the line on the juvenile crime problem. For example, the rates of serious juvenile violent and property crimes remained relatively stable during those years.[1] Moreover, most criminologists believe that the stability in the rates is largely the result of the changing demographics of the youth population, not because of state and local juvenile crime control measures.

One clear result of the "get tough" policies of the past decade is that there are significantly more young people incarcerated in juvenile detention centers and correctional facilities.[2] In fact, the increase has been so great that more than half of the juvenile training schools in the country are overcrowded.

Unfortunately, there is no credible evidence that confining more juveniles in large and impersonal correctional facilities is effective in curbing rates of recidivism. In fact, just the opposite appears to be true. The few available careful follow-up studies reveal recidivism rates as high as 75 percent or more. In testimony on October 13, 1989, before a legislative committee in Michigan, L.A. Abrams, the director of the state's youth corrections system, reported that more than 40 percent of the graduates from Michigan's two training schools show up in the state's prison system within five years after release. The Michigan figures do not include the numbers who are sentenced to prisons in other states and the numbers who are convicted of new crimes and placed on probation or sentenced to local county jails.

PROMISING DEVELOPMENTS IN JUVENILE CRIME CONTROL

Approximately fifteen years ago, youth correction officials in Massachusetts embarked on a bold and highly controversial course of action in managing their juvenile offenders. They closed down all of their large juvenile training schools. In their place, they developed a network of small (fifteen- to twenty-bed units) high-security treatment centers for violent and chronic juvenile offenders. Today, there are only 184 secure treatment beds in the state, and they are primarily located in or close to the communities where the youth come from.[3] For all other juvenile offenders committed to the state's Department of Youth Services (DYS), the state youth correction authority, Massachusetts developed a diverse network of community-based programs that provide intensive surveillance and supervision, and enriched educational employment, counseling, and other appropriate services. These programs are largely delivered by private providers under contract with the state.

The Massachusetts youth correction system was recently evaluated by the National Council on Crime and Delinquency. The study indicated that:

● The Massachusetts youth correction reforms did not unleash a juvenile crime wave. In 1985, Massachusetts ranked 46th among the 50 states with respect to their rate of serious juvenile crime[4];

● Juveniles placed in the custody of DYS committed "far fewer offenses after entering DYS," and for those who did commit new offenses "there was a tendency to commit less serious crimes."[5] In particular, "violent and serious property offenders committed to DYS reduced the frequency and severity of their criminal activities"[6];

● The overall rates of recidivism for DYS were as low or lower than any other state that the researchers compared Massachusetts with[7];

● The number of juveniles waived to the adult criminal justice system for prosecution has steadily declined since the reforms were implemented[8];

● "The DYS operated in a cost-effective manner, balancing fiscal concerns with the imperatives of preserving public safety and rehabilitation."[9]

Massachusetts is not an aberration. Elected public officials and juvenile corrections experts in the state of Utah implemented a similar approach beginning in 1980. Prior to 1980, the Utah youth corrections system consisted of one large 275-bed training school, an institution that often housed over 350 youths and provided few community-based programs. Utah now has one ten-bed and two thirty-bed high security treatment units for violent juvenile offenders and chronic repeaters. All other young offenders committed to the state youth correction agency are managed in highly structured community-based programs that are largely run by private providers under contract with the state.

Like Massachusetts, the Utah system was subjected to an independent evaluation. The evaluation revealed that Utah's shift in policies to limit incarceration to those youth who were violent and chronic repeaters and to manage the others in highly structured and individualized community-based programs was cost-effective and did not compromise public safety (National Council on Crime and Delinquency, 1987, 147-48).

JUVENILE CRIME CONTROL POLICIES IN THE 90S

The widespread availability of drugs promises to keep the juvenile crime problem high on the public agenda. While the knee-jerk reaction to build more juvenile prisons and incarcerate greater numbers of young people may be politically popular, such a response is likely to be counterproductive and costly. Before elected public officials and juvenile justice professionals advocate such measures, they would be wise to look carefully at the policies and results in such diverse states as Massachusetts and Utah. Clearly, if Sen. Ted Kennedy's and Sen. Orrin Hatch's home states can agree on a common approach to juvenile corrections policy, then there must be something worthwhile in it for the rest of the country.

1. M.W. Steketee, D.A. Willis, and I.M. Schwartz (1989, November). *Juvenile Justice Trends 1977-1987.* (Ann Arbor: Center for the Study of Youth Policy, 1989).

2. I.M. Schwartz, *(In) Justice for Juveniles: Rethinking the Best Interest of the Child.* (Lexington, Lexington Books, 1989), 47.

3. B. Krisberg, J. Austin, and P.A. Steele. *Unlocking Juvenile Corrections: Evaluating the Massachusetts Department of Youth Services.* San Francisco: National Council on Crime and Delinquency, November, 1989, 4.

4. Krisberg, Austin, and Steele, 14.

5. Krisberg, Austin, and Steele, 19.

6. Krisberg, Austin, and Steele, 22.

7. Krisberg, Austin, and Steele, 27-32.

8. Krisberg, Austin, and Steele, 37.

9. Krisberg, Austin, and Steele.

Additional Reading

L.A. Abrams, Testimony of Director, Office of Children and Youth Services to Michigan House of Representatives Special Ad Hoc Committee on Criminal Justice System, October 13, 1989.

Ira M. Schwartz, *The Impact of Juvenile Court Intervention,* National Council on Crime and Delinquency, San Francisco, January, 1987.

Kids who kill

Disputes once settled with fists are now settled with guns. Every 100 hours, more youths die on the streets than were killed in the Persian Gulf

Kevin's mother was a drug addict, his father a dope dealer. After being taken from them by social workers in his native Massachusetts, Kevin* went to live with his grandparents in Texas. His grandfather, a security guard, let him shoot a .22, and "firing it made me feel like I was on top." By his early teens, he was firing a gun out windows at a nearby day-care center to show off and he had joined a gang. He began carrying a .38-caliber revolver at 14 and obtained guns by burglarizing nearby homes. "I wanted to carry a weapon because I wasn't going to tolerate anything. I was scared and I was mad." At 15, Kevin began working for a Jamaican drug trafficking posse and eventually became an enforcer who did his work by shooting people in the arm.

One day, $2,000 of the Jamaicans' money was lost, and though Kevin says he was innocent, the blame fell on him. Panicking, he confronted an acquaintance whom he suspected of the theft. "I figured if I shot him, the Jamaicans wouldn't think I'd taken the money," he says. "He begged for his life five times. I shot him in the face at point-blank range and killed him instantly. Blood was everywhere, and some parts of his head were laying in the doorway. I didn't have to kill

Names with an asterisk are pseudonyms, required in some cases by legal restrictions.

him. If I'd just pulled the gun, I could have gotten my money. But still I shot him. The man lost his life over nothing."

This is the stone-hearted ethos of an astonishingly large segment of the teenage population. It saturates not only the gang-ridden environment of the cities but the supposedly more benign suburban world as well. Everyday quarrels that used to result in flailing fists and bloody noses—

FIREARM MURDERS COMMITTED BY OFFENDERS UNDER AGE 18

952
1989

615
1987

444
1984

USN&WR
Basic data:
James Alan Fox
of National Crime
Analysis Program
at Northeastern
University

over a bump on the shoulder, a misinterpreted glance, romantic complications or flashy clothes—now end, with epidemic frequency, in gunshots.

The reasons why are clear. Today's kids are desensitized to violence as never before, surrounded by gunfire and stuffed with media images of Rambos who kill at will. For many inner-city youngsters, poverty and hopelessness yield a "what the hell" attitude that provides the backdrop for gunplay. Family breakdowns further fuel the crisis; a survey of Baltimore public-school students showed that 59 percent of the males who came from one-parent or no-parent homes have carried a handgun. But by far the biggest difference in today's atmosphere is that the no-problem availability of guns in every nook of the nation has turned record numbers of everyday encounters into deadly ones.

The datelines change daily, but the stories are chillingly similar. In Washington, D.C., 15-year-old Jermaine Daniel is shot to death by his best friend. In New Haven, Conn., Markiest Alexander, 14, is killed in a drive-by shooting. In St. Louis, Leo Wilson, 16, is robbed of his tennis shoes and Raiders jacket and then shot dead. In New York, a 14-year-old boy opens up with a semiautomatic pistol in a Bronx schoolyard, wounding one youngster and narrowly missing another, apparently in a dispute over a girl.

Those outside the city are no less vulnerable. Within the past fortnight, in an exclusive neighborhood of Pasadena, Calif., police say two teenage boys passed a shotgun between them to shoot three young women to death at close range. Asked why, the suspects reportedly told police they'd had angry words with the victims but couldn't remember what the fight was about. In middle-class Lumberton, N.J., outside Philadelphia, a 14-year-old boy took a revolver from his father's gun cabinet in late February and fatally shot a basketball teammate in the back of the head.

These tales from the streets were punctuated last month by some knee-weakening numbers from the government's National Center for Health Statistics, which analyzed youth firearm death rates from 1979 to 1988. The study showed that gun homicides felled 1,022 teens ages 15 to 19 in 1984; the number spiked to 1,641 in 1988. The picture was especially bleak for young black males 15 to 19, for whom firearm homicides climbed from 418 in 1984 to 955 in 1988. Their homicide rate in 1988 was more than 11 times the rate for their white counterparts. And research by James Alan Fox of Northeastern University shows that the number of black teenage gunmen who have killed has risen sharply, from 181 in 1984 to a record 555 in 1989.

"During every 100 hours on our streets we lose more young men than were killed in 100 hours of ground war in the Persian Gulf," lamented Louis Sullivan, secretary of the Department of Health and Human Services. "Where are the yellow ribbons of hope and remembrance for our youth dying in the streets?"

Amid the carnage, much of the political discussion seems sterile and off the point. Last week, when Ronald Reagan endorsed the Brady bill, a modest mea-

sure that would require a seven-day waiting period to buy a gun, it was heralded by gun-control advocates. In fact, almost all teens who kill with guns *already* get them illegally, and nothing in the bill or George Bush's get-tough crime law will address the existing system that places more and more guns with greater and greater firepower in the hands of kids.

Some communities are taking small steps to halt the tragic cycle of teenage gun violence. But psychologist Charles Patrick Ewing, author of "When Children Kill," argues that the confluence of several trends is foreboding. Among them: the continuing proliferation of guns, increases in numbers of abused and neglected children, hefty juvenile poverty rates and a projected 7.7 percent increase in the population of 5-to-17-year-olds. Ewing predicts this will be "the bloodiest decade of juvenile violence we've ever seen."

The explosion of guns

John* had two requirements for the homes he burglarized around Winston-Salem, N.C.: first, that they belonged to gun owners and, second, that the owners weren't home. For more than a year and a half, at the rate of a house a day, he batted nearly 1.000. John, now 15, traded many of the guns for marijuana and cocaine. Sometimes he sold the guns at school. Either way, they moved. "If somebody knows you have a gun—nobody is going to mess with you," he says.

John's days as a gun burglar ended when the police were tipped off to his activities. He was charged with 15 counts of breaking and entering and two counts of burglary. He spent 14 months at a camp for problem kids, must serve 660 hours of community service and must pay $2,212 in restitution. His court-appointed counselor says John's only remaining problem is truancy, but for John, temptation abounds. "You can get drugs and guns here real easy," he says of school.

It's the presence of so many guns that makes the current atmosphere so volatile. Arrests of kids under 18 for weapons violations jumped from 19,649 in 1976 to 31,577 in 1989. Firearm murders committed by youngsters in that same age bracket leaped from 444 in 1984 to 952 in 1989, according to the National Crime Analysis Program at Northeastern University.

Ask a streetwise kid how tough it is to get a gun, and a smile is often the response—"no problem." The best available estimates indicate that between 150 million and 200 million guns nationwide are in civilian hands. A 1989 poll reported that nearly 3 out of 5 Americans own guns. Domestic firearm production, after dipping in the early

1980s, grew steadily from 3.1 million in 1986 to 4.4 million in 1989.

A 20-state survey of 11,000 adolescents found that 41 percent of the boys could obtain a handgun if they wanted to. An extrapolation of surveys by the National School Safety Center suggested that 135,000 students carried guns to school daily in 1987. Officials at the center think that figure is higher today.

In cities with strong gun-control laws, like Boston, New York and Washington, weapons are imported and resold at a profit by traffickers who purchase them in states that until recently have had few gun-buying restrictions: Florida, Texas, Virginia, Georgia and Ohio. In Los Angeles, two men operating out of a van in a park east of downtown are thought to have sold more than 1,000 handguns over an eight-month period last year, largely to street-gang members, before being arrested. In suburban Chicago last fall, police say, a 16-year-old boy rented a gun from a fellow student for $100, then used it to kill his parents.

There is no mystery about how kids get guns. A survey of Baltimore public-school students showed the four most prevalent sources to be street corners, friends, drug dealers and thefts. Residential burglaries are lucrative pipelines, and mom and dad are often unknowingly a ready supply. A Florida school study found that 86 percent of the guns taken from students were from their homes.

And the trend is toward more powerful guns with higher-capacity magazines, like 9-mm semiautomatic pistols. "You ask a young kid what a '9' is, he knows what you're talking about," says Art Boissiere, 19, who grew up in a tough Oakland, Calif., neighborhood and considered carrying a gun himself. A popular 9-mm gun like a Tec-9 might sell for $300 to $700 on the street. Other, cheaper guns might go for as little as $50.

The gang connection

It began as a typical adolescent dispute—two Texas teenagers talking trash over broken car windows. "And then I pulled out the gun," says Victor,* 15, whose 1984 Cutlass had been damaged. "And he said, 'You ain't going to shoot me,' and I just started shooting, because he didn't think I would. It would have looked stupid if I pulled the gun and then didn't shoot him. I would have looked dumb."

That's the last thing Victor wanted. He joined a gang at 13 "because I thought I'd be accepted better, and they seemed like family." Guns were everywhere. Soon, Victor was participating in drive-by shootings. "My friends would call me their 'little gangster,'" he says. "With the gun, I felt like I couldn't be stopped." Victor and his friends broke into homes and pawnshops to steal guns, sometimes run-

IN 1984-88, THE FIREARM DEATH RATE FOR TEENS 15 TO 19 ROSE A RECORD 43 PERCENT.

A 1989 CHICAGO SCHOOL SURVEY SHOWED THAT 39 PERCENT OF THE CHILDREN HAD SEEN A SHOOTING.

ning pickup trucks right through the front window of a store. Then he'd sell the guns—some 100 in all—to drug dealers and other unsavory acquaintances. In three months, Victor made about $6,000.

Then, in retaliation for a drive-by shooting Victor had taken part in, rival gang members broke the windows in that 1984 Cutlass. After he hunted down the supposed culprits, he fired nine shots, wounding two members. "I just got in the car and sped away," he says. "And then right after that, it started raining, right after I shot them. And it didn't seem like a day where it was going to rain."

Much of the fuel for the growth in youth violence flows from gangs and drugs. Not nearly as many teens would have guns if they hadn't raised the money by dealing drugs, nor would the streets be so violent these days in the absence of drug trade. While there has been progress in the war against casual drug use, some 1.7 million to 2.4 million Americans are still weekly cocaine users. But some authorities think the drug trade today is more deadly than ever precisely because traffickers are tussling over a shrinking pie.

Gangs are growing like a cancer. The Crips and the Bloods began in Southern California about 20 years ago but now have loose affiliations in 32 states and 113 cities. Not only have they absorbed the talents of local toughs, but they've given a twisted kind of haven to confused inner-city kids for whom gangs provide the security, acceptance and protection that are often missing in fragmented homes. The price of that kind of security is horrific. In the Los Angeles area, gangs doubled from 400 with 45,000 members in 1985 to 800 with 90,000 members in 1990. Gang-related killings last year accounted for 690 deaths, 35 percent of the county's homicides.

In this atmosphere, carrying a gun is just keeping up with the Joneses. "The gun is your best friend," says a 15-year-old gang member in south central L.A. One popular local saying: "I'd rather be judged by 12 than carried by six."

Using a gun is often a rite of passage for joining a gang or enhancing a reputation. Recently, a 14-year-old rode by an East L.A. schoolyard on his bike, randomly firing a semiautomatic at the nearly 2,000 children on the playground. "He just wanted to prove to his gang he was worthy," says Capt. Ray Gott of the L.A. County Sheriff's Department.

Los Angeles gang experts have identified three levels of gun-packing gang involvement. "The wannabes are starting to do target practice and get used to holding a gun. They may shoot, but in a lot of cases they won't aim," says Steve Valdivia, director of an outreach program called Community Youth Gang Services.

THE FIREARM DEATH RATE FOR BLACK TEEN MALES WAS 2.8 TIMES THE RATE FOR NATURAL CAUSES IN 1988.

YOUNG BLACKS WERE FIVE TIMES AS LIKELY AS WHITES TO BE HOMICIDE VICTIMS.

"The next level is a gang-involved youth who wants to make his stripes. He's going to kill somebody. But he's not yet seen by his peers as a hard-core crazy person. If they get to that final level, they don't care about themselves or the victim—very random violence, very cold-blooded. These are the guys who will open a casket and shoot a dead body with a semiautomatic until it turns to ketchup. I know that has happened."

The spread of gangs basically followed the interstate highway system. They moved into Minneapolis from Chicago almost 10 years ago and have been building ever since. "The word got out that Minneapolis was easy pickings," says one gang member. "Moneyapolis." The police can identify more than 3,000 gang members, though no one knows for sure. And with the gangs came the guns. Hundreds of them. "They're coming up from Chicago every day," says Ramone,* a member of the Bloods. "My gang holds them until we need them. I say I'm in trouble and they give me a gun." In Hennepin County, the number of juveniles tried as adults for carrying dangerous weapons—mostly guns—jumped from 14 in 1986–87 to 63 in 1990.

In cities like Austin, Texas, gang growth has come from both home-grown groups and infiltration by outsiders. Gang membership there has climbed from just 200 five years ago to some 2,800 today. Last September, after rival gang members taunted each other at a crowded downtown bus stop, a 16-year-old fired a 9-mm pistol, wounding two other teens and a 61-year-old man.

Fear of the criminal-justice system is largely absent in these teens because they realize the system is jammed and know that juvenile penalties lack real bite. In Austin, older gang members call their younger compadres "minutemen" because they'll only be in jail for a minute.

Partly for that reason, the high-stakes hurly-burly of drug trafficking has also drawn scores of youths into gun ownership. Adults hire youngsters to run the drugs because the penalties are so much weaker if they're caught. The danger level, though, is no different. Clarence,* a big-city Texas teen who was clearing $1,200 weekly dealing dope at 15, needed a gun "because people on the corner where I was selling were getting robbed, and you never knew who was coming for you." In February 1989, he saw his best friend get killed for dealing bad dope.

As many as 20 to 25 percent of the kids who shoot people are high themselves—on alcohol or drugs like crack or PCP, all of which are "disinhibitors" that may spur violent behavior. "One time I burst right into this guy's house and shot him," says Shooter, 17, of Los Angeles. "Man, was he surprised. But I wasn't thinking about anything bad happening, because I was doing PCP, and I was all kicked up. It was like he could have shot me, and it wouldn't have mattered."

Lowering the killing threshold

Arthur* is busted now, spending a year at the Hennepin County Home School in Minnetonka, just outside Minneapolis. But he can still wax nostalgic about the small, profitable empire he ran with his younger brother and four others, none older than 16. Drugs gave them money; guns gave them power. "Everybody knew we had them," he says. "Everybody knew not to mess with us." Arthur's gang had some real firepower. "There were just so many coming in," he says. "We had six automatics. We had a .25; a .38; two 9-mm semiautomatic pistols, one of which was a Beretta; a .32 automatic; a 20-gauge shotgun. Some we got out of the newspapers. My brother Dennis* went way out in some suburbs and picked them up. He bought an AK-47 [assault rifle] for $500. It seemed like we were the only ones who were out there with real artillery. You'd hear all that gunfire, and it was all us."

For some kids, drugs, gangs and guns are simply vehicles through which to satisfy more basic yearnings. Teens have always wanted power, attention, respect and a tough-guy reputation. But the prevailing gang ethos has lowered the threshold of violence and sanctioned the replacement of fists with firearms as the way to achieve those goals.

Often, the fast route to attention is through money or material goods. Sneakers, coats or cash—kids want it now, and the gun can get it. For Clarence, at 15, the motivation for dealing dope and carrying guns was this: "I wanted to get paid. I thought money was the world. I'd spend it on my girlfriend, or I'd take all

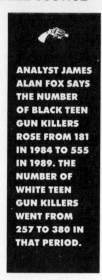

ANALYST JAMES ALAN FOX SAYS THE NUMBER OF BLACK TEEN GUN KILLERS ROSE FROM 181 IN 1984 TO 555 IN 1989. THE NUMBER OF WHITE TEEN GUN KILLERS WENT FROM 257 TO 380 IN THAT PERIOD.

my homeboys out. If you made money that day, you'd pay, and that made me feel like I was the big daddy, the big man with the master plan."

But Clarence also discovered that the gun provided a power and an image all its own. "If you had a gun, and you were with a girl, she'd be thinking, 'He's bad,' " says Clarence. "It made me feel macho, like nobody could touch me, like no one's going to mess with me."

Nothing inflames the extreme narcissism and hypersensitivity of teens more than disrespect—"dissin'," in the language of the streets. Teen killers cite it perhaps most often as the justification for their lethal acts. "If someone disrespects you or your homeboys, you've got to do something about it," says one Los Angeles teen. "You just can't have them doing that and hold your head up."

One byproduct of this arms race is that many basically good kids now carry guns simply because they're terrified or fed up—or both. "I had it for protection," says Derek of Washington, D.C., who bought a gun at age 17 after a friend was shot to death and Derek himself was robbed. "You lose your sense of dignity after a while, and I wasn't going to let that happen again. I figured the gun would prevent it." In a Boston program for kids caught with weapons, a teacher recently asked, "Is there any way to exist without a weapon?" "Yeah," snapped one teen. "Stay in the house."

The schools crack down

Damon* got angry in his Milwaukee school on Valentine's Day. Some friends were teasing him, slapping him in the face. So Damon, 12, decided to get even. "Wait until I get back," he said as he ran off the playground. "I'm going to cap all

of you guys." When Damon returned, he stepped through the opening of the fenced-in playground and pulled from his jacket a silver .25 semiautomatic pistol. He fired it, again and again and again. In an instant, a mass of bluejeans and ponytails was screaming and running toward the school's metal doors. The boy Damon says was slapping him cowered behind a teacher. Damon pointed the gun at him. "I'm going to blow your head off," the teachers quoted Damon as saying. Damon fired five shots, hit nobody and then ran from the schoolyard. Why, he is asked, did he do it? "He slapped me in my face," says Damon, tears rolling down his cheeks. What was Damon thinking? "I don't remember thinking anything," he says. "I just did it."

A Seattle high school uses a breathalyzer to test students suspected of drinking; hundreds of Detroit students pass through metal detectors before entering school, and teachers at Fairfax Elementary School in Mentor, Ohio, signal students to duck from gunfire by yelling "earthquake drill." Welcome to the campus of '91, where "bullies," "deathtraps" and "hole diggers"—commonly known as guns—are often as much the rage as faddish haircuts, team jackets and Air Jordans.

School systems across the country are borrowing heavily from correctional institutions with dress codes, metal detectors and security forces patrolling the hallways. Not surprisingly, more and more schools, especially in America's troubled inner cities, now resemble prisons, with bars across windows, camera monitors and bolted doors. Some school systems are even requiring students to wear identification badges.

At Belvedere Junior High in Los Angeles, where campus aides patrol the hall

IN THE PAST FOUR ACADEMIC YEARS, AT LEAST 65 STUDENTS AND SIX ADULTS WERE KILLED WITH GUNS AT SCHOOL, 201 PERSONS WERE BADLY WOUNDED AND 242 PERSONS WERE HELD AT GUNPOINT.

to maintain order, visitors register name, time and destination with security personnel and are escorted by aides with two-way walkie-talkies. Signs, barely legible through the graffiti, warn against vandalism and trespassing. Seven students, some members of notorious local gangs, have been killed in the past year; two died in one weekend last month. Last fall, a 13-year-old gang member was shot just blocks from the school and died on a sidewalk as his friends gathered around. "This is my fifth year as principal," says Victoria Castro. "The first four years, I lost maybe two children to gang violence. Now we have drive-by shootings onto campus. The only thing I keep hoping is that I have no actual incident on campus."

Even suburban schools are coming face to face with guns and crime. A recent study of Illinois high-school students found that 5.3 percent of them said they had brought a gun to school, and 1 in 12 students confessed to sometimes staying away out of fear.

Communities respond

Exasperated by the ever growing teenage body count, a variety of educators, psychologists, pediatricians and just plain folks are experimenting with ways of stopping the carnage. Among them:
- **Violence prevention**. Several programs attempt to teach children how to prevent violence; most prominent among them is a curriculum for adolescents used in Boston high schools and several other cities, developed by Deborah Prothrow-Stith of the Harvard School of Public Health. The 10-session curriculum tries to reduce the allure of violence, make clear its consequences and show kids alternative avenues for dealing with anger. Most experts are encouraged but think the jury's still out on the curriculum's effectiveness.
- **Gun awareness**. Alarmed by a rise in gun deaths, schools in Dade County, Fla., inaugurated their own gun-safety program in the 1988–89 school year, in cooperation with the Center to Prevent Handgun Violence. The effort employs books, role-playing and videos to "deglamorize and deglorify the possession and use of guns," says coordinator Bill Harris. Early results are promising, but such programs are only a small piece of the puzzle. The National Rifle Association also runs several gun-safety programs tailored to different age groups; one emphasis is the need to secure guns at home.
- **Offender diversion**. For the past four years, every Boston public-school student caught with a weapon has been sent to the Barron Assessment & Counseling Center for a five-to-10-day stay. Students there undergo a detailed psychological and educational assessment, and a plan is devel-

oped for working with them once they are either back in school or in some alternative setting. BACC students also participate in counseling, regular academic work, violence-prevention classes and trips to local detention facilities. The center has serviced more than 1,000 students, and the recidivism rate is about 5 percent. Director Franklin Tucker admits it would be helpful to have the kids for a longer time. But, adds staffer Richard Puckerin, BACC does provide its kids "a timeout, a chance to think and reflect."

■ **Peers.** Teens on Target, an Oakland, Calif., program, is based on the idea that young people are better equipped than adults to attack their violence problem. Student volunteers are trained as violence-prevention "advocates," learning about guns, drugs and family violence, and then sent to schools to teach ways of preventing violence. Officials are enthusiastic; they are scraping up more money for the program.

GUN PRICES ON THE STREET VARY. THE HOTTEST WEAPON, A TEC-9, RETAILS FOR $150-$200 AND GOES FOR UP TO $700 ON THE STREET. THE SMALLER RAVEN P-25s NET UP TO $250 ON THE BLACK MARKET.

Many believe getting the guns off the streets is the only answer. But the existing gun-control debate misses the mark.

Gun-control measures that might help — like personalized combination locks on the gun's safety, allowing only the original owner to use the gun — aren't even part of the current political debate.

Some argue that focusing solely on the weapons obscures the underlying causes of teen gun violence — especially the sense of hopelessness that pervades many inner cities. Yet the national inclination not even to tackle systematically the immediate issue of violence and gun availability suggests there's even less hope that the larger issues will be addressed. And that means the uniquely American tragedy of teens killing teens is likely to continue its record run.

BY GORDON WITKIN WITH STEPHEN J. HEDGES, CONSTANCE JOHNSON, MONIKA GUTTMAN IN LOS ANGELES, LAURA THOMAS IN SAN FRANCISCO AND ANNE MONCREIFF ARRARTE IN MIAMI

Punishment and Corrections

In the American system of criminal justice, the term "corrections" has a special meaning. It designates programs and agencies that have legal authority over the custody or supervision of persons who have been convicted of a criminal act by the courts.

The correctional process begins with the sentencing of the convicted offender. The predominant sentencing pattern in the United States encourages maximum judicial discretion and offers a range of alternatives from probation (supervised conditional freedom within the community), through imprisonment, to the death penalty. Selections in this unit focus on the current condition of the penal system in the United States, and the effects that sentencing, probation, imprisonment, and parole have on the rehabilitation of criminals.

"Sentencing and Corrections" illustrates how society, through sentencing, expresses its objectives for the correctional process. The objectives are deterrence, incapacitation, rehabilitation, retribution, and restitution.

Some 60 percent of inmates released from state and federal lockups return to prison. Recidivism contributes greatly to the overcrowding that plagues prisons throughout the United States. Crowded, tense conditions make survival the principal goal. Rehabilitation is pushed into the background in the effort to manage incipient chaos.

Other issues and aspects of the correctional system—house arrest, women in prison, probation and parole, the high rate of imprisonment in the United States, life sentences without parole, boot camp programs, and the death penalty are other topics in this unit.

Fred Scaglione discusses a new high-tech, yet age-old approach to confinement in "You're Under Arrest—AT HOME." American probation and parole systems are not keeping pace with the challenges presented by rising caseloads of very troubled clients, according to "Difficult Clients, Large Caseloads Plague Probation, Parole Agencies." A life sentence without parole in place of the death penalty is the suggestion made in "Life Without Parole."

The essay that follows, "U.S. World's Lock-'Em-Up Leader," tells of the widespread use of imprisonment as a criminal sanction in this country. Special prison programs for young offenders and nonviolent offenders are the subject of " 'Boot Camp' Programs Grow in Number and Scope." Finally, the most controversial punishment of all is under discussion in "This Man Has Expired" and "No Reversal in Fortune for Blacks on Death Row."

Looking Ahead: Challenge Questions

If you were to argue the pathology of imprisonment, what points would you make? On the other hand, if you were to justify continued imprisonment of offenders, what would you stress?

Some authorities would have us believe that probation and parole are ineffective correctional strategies, and should be abandoned. Others maintain that they have yet to really be tried. What is your view?

If you were a high-level correctional administrator and had the luxury of designing a "humane" prison, what would it be like? What aspects of a traditional prison would you keep? What would you eliminate? What new strategies or programs would you introduce?

What are your feelings about the death penalty? Do you think it is an effective deterrent to murder?

Unit 6

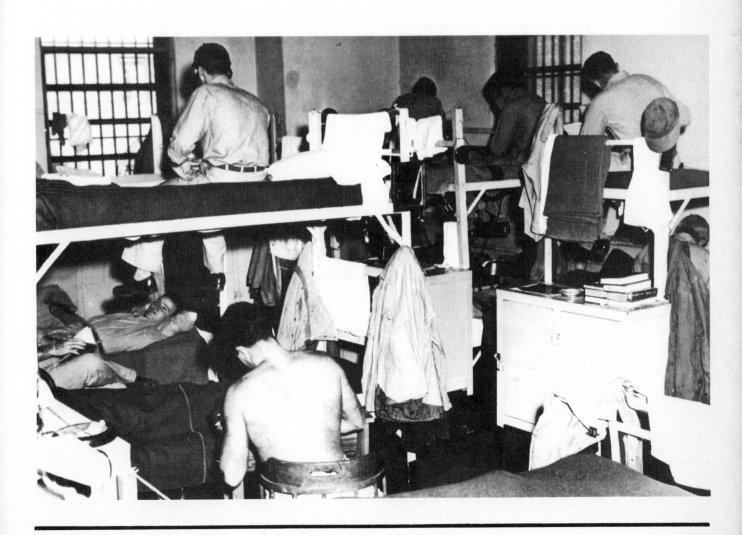

Sentencing and Corrections

Through sentencing, society attempts to express its goals for the correctional process

The sentencing of criminals often reflects conflicting social goals

These objectives are—
• **Retribution**—giving offenders their "just deserts" and expressing society's disapproval of criminal behavior
• **Incapacitation**—separating offenders from the community to reduce the opportunity for further crime while they are incarcerated
• **Deterrence**—demonstrating the certainty and severity of punishment to discourage future crime by the offender (specific deterrence) and by others (general deterrence)
• **Rehabilitation**—providing psychological or educational assistance or job training to offenders to make them less likely to engage in future criminality
• **Restitution**—having the offender repay the victim or the community in money or services.

Attitudes about sentencing reflect multiple goals and other factors

Research on judicial attitudes and practices in sentencing revealed that judges vary greatly in their commitment to various goals when imposing sentences. Public opinion also has shown much diversity about the goals of sentencing, and public attitudes have changed over the years. In fashioning criminal penalties, legislators have tended to reflect this lack of public consensus.

Sentencing laws are further complicated by concerns for—
• **Proportionality**—severity of punishment should be commensurate with the seriousness of the crime
• **Equity**—similar crimes and similar criminals should be treated alike
• **Social debt**—the severity of punishment should take into account the offender's prior criminal behavior.

Judges usually have a great deal of discretion in sentencing offenders

The different sentencing laws give various amounts of discretion to the judge in setting the length of a prison or jail term. In a more fundamental respect, however, the judge often has a high degree of discretion in deciding whether or not to incarcerate the offender at all. Alternatives to imprisonment include—
• probation
• fines
• forfeiture of the proceeds of criminal activity
• restitution to victims
• community service
• split sentences, consisting of a short period of incarceration followed by probation in the community.

Often, before a sentence is imposed a presentence investigation is conducted to provide the judge with information about the offender's characteristics and prior criminal record.

Disparity and uncertainty arose from a lack of consensus over sentencing goals

By the early 1970s researchers and critics of the justice system had begun to note that trying to achieve the mixed goals of the justice system without new limits on the discretionary options given to judges had—
• reduced the *certainty* of sanctions, presumably eroding the deterrent effect of corrections
• resulted in *disparity* in the severity of punishment, with differences in the sentences imposed for similar cases and offenders
• failed to validate the effectiveness of various rehabilitation programs in

changing offender behavior or predicting future criminality.

Recent sentencing reforms reflect more severe attitudes and seek to reduce disparity and uncertainty

Reforms in recent years have used statutory and administrative changes to—
• clarify the aims of sentencing
• reduce disparity by limiting judicial and parole discretion
• provide a system of penalties that is more consistent and predictable
• provide sanctions consistent with the concept of "just deserts."

The changes have included—
• making prison mandatory for certain crimes and for recidivists
• specifying presumptive sentence lengths
• requiring sentence enhancements for offenders with prior felony convictions
• introducing sentencing guidelines
• limiting parole discretion through the use of parole guidelines
• total elimination of discretionary parole release (determinate sentencing).

States use a variety of strategies for sentencing

Sentencing is perhaps the most diversified part of the Nation's criminal justice process. Each State has a unique set of sentencing laws, and frequent and substantial changes have been made in recent years. This diversity complicates the classification of sentencing systems. For nearly any criterion that may be considered, there will be some States with hybrid systems that straddle the boundary between categories.

From *Report to the Nation on Crime and Justice,* Bureau of Justice Statistics, U.S. Department of Justice, March 1988, pp. 90-93.

The basic difference in sentencing systems is the apportioning of discretion between the judge and parole authorities

Indeterminate sentencing—the judge specifies minimum and maximum sentence lengths. These set upper and lower bounds on the time to be served. The actual release date (and therefore the time actually served) is determined later by parole authorities within those limits.

Partially indeterminate sentencing—a variation of indeterminate sentencing in which the judge specifies only the maximum sentence length. An associated minimum automatically is implied, but is not within the judge's discretion. The implied minimum may be a fixed time (such as 1 year) for all sentences or a fixed proportion of the maximum. In some States the implied minimum is zero; thus the parole board is empowered to release the prisoner at any time.

Determinate sentencing—the judge specifies a fixed term of incarceration, which must be served in full (less any "goodtime" earned in prison). There is no discretionary parole release.

Since 1975 many States have adopted determinate sentencing, but most still use indeterminate sentencing

In 1976 Maine was the first State to adopt determinate sentencing. The sentencing system is entirely or predominantly determinate in these 10 States:

California	Maine
Connecticut	Minnesota
Florida	New Mexico
Illinois	North Carolina
Indiana	Washington

The other States and the District of Columbia use indeterminate sentencing in its various forms. One State, Colorado, after changing to determinate sentencing in 1979, went back to indeterminate sentencing in 1985. The Federal justice system has adopted determinate sentencing through a system of sentencing guidelines.

States employ other sentencing features in conjunction with their basic strategies

Mandatory sentencing—Law requires the judge to impose a sentence of incarceration, often of specified length, for certain crimes or certain categories of offenders. There is no option of probation or a suspended sentence.

Mandatory sentencing laws are in force in 46 States (all except Maine, Minnesota, Nebraska, and Rhode Island) and the District of Columbia. In 25 States imprisonment is mandatory for certain repeat felony offenders. In 30 States imprisonment is mandatory if a firearm was involved in the commission of a crime. In 45 States conviction for certain offenses or classes of offenses leads to mandatory imprisonment; most such offenses are serious, violent crimes, and drug trafficking is included in 18 of the States. Many States have recently made drunk driving an offense for which incarceration is mandated (usually for relatively short periods in a local jail rather than a State prison).

Presumptive sentencing—The discretion of a judge who imposes a prison sentence is constrained by a specific sentence length set by law for each offense or class of offense. That sentence must be imposed in all unexceptional cases. In response to mitigating or aggravating circumstances, the judge may shorten or lengthen the sentence within specified boundaries, usually with written justification being required.

Presumptive sentencing is used, at least to some degree, in about 12 States.

Sentencing guidelines—Explicit policies and procedures are specified for deciding on individual sentences. The decision is usually based on the nature of the offense and the offender's criminal record. For example, the prescribed sentence for a certain offense might be probation if the offender has no previous felony convictions, a short term of incarceration if the offender has one prior conviction, and progressively longer prison terms if the offender's criminal history is more extensive.

Sentencing guidelines came into use in the late 1970s. They are—
• used in 13 States and the Federal criminal justice system
• written into statute in the Federal system and in Florida, Louisiana, Maryland, Minnesota, New Jersey, Ohio, Pennsylvania, and Tennessee
• used systemwide, but not mandated by law, in Utah
• applied selectively in Massachusetts, Michigan, Rhode Island, and Wisconsin
• being considered for adoption in other States and the District of Columbia.

Sentence enhancements—In nearly all States, the judge may lengthen the prison term for an offender with prior felony convictions. The lengths of such enhancements and the criteria for imposing them vary among the States.

In some States that group felonies according to their seriousness, the repeat offender may be given a sentence ordinarily imposed for a higher seriousness category. Some States prescribe lengthening the sentences of habitual offenders by specified amounts or imposing a mandatory minimum term that must be served before parole can be considered. In other States the guidelines provide for sentences that reflect the offender's criminal history as well as the seriousness of the offense. Many States prescribe conditions under which parole eligibility is limited or eliminated. For example, a person with three or more prior felony convictions, if convicted of a serious violent offense, might be sentenced to life imprisonment without parole.

Sources: Surveys conducted for the Bureau of Justice Statistics by the U.S. Bureau of the Census in 1985 and by the Pennsylvania Commission on Crime and Delinquency in 1986.

Sentencing guidelines usually are developed by a separate sentencing commission

Such a commission may be appointed by the legislative, executive, or judicial branch of State government. This is a departure from traditional practice in that sentences are prescribed through an administrative procedure rather than by explicit legislation.

In some States the guidelines are prescriptive in that they specify whether or not the judge must impose a prison sentence and the presumptive sentence length. In other States the guidelines are advisory in that they provide information to the judge but do not mandate sentencing decisions.

To determine whether a prison sentence should be imposed, the guidelines usually consider offense severity and the offender's prior criminal record. A matrix that relates these two factors may be used.

6. PUNISHMENT AND CORRECTIONS

Sentencing matrix

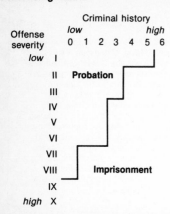

Adapted from *Preliminary report on the development and impact of the Minnesota sentencing guidelines*, Minnesota Sentencing Guidelines Commission, July 1982.

Sentencing guidelines used in the Federal justice system were developed by the United States Sentencing Commission. The guidelines provide for determinate sentencing and the abolition of parole. Ranges of sentence length are specified for various offense classifications and offender characteristics. The judge must provide written justification for any sentence that deviates from the guideline range; sentences that are less severe can be appealed by the prosecution, and sentences that are more severe can be appealed by the defense.

Changes in sentencing have brought changes in correctional practices

Many sentencing reforms have led to changes in the way correctional systems operate:

The proliferation of determinate and mandatory sentences during the past decade, together with dissatisfaction about the uncertainties of indeterminate sentencing (especially the linking of release decisions to rehabilitative progress or predictions of future behavior), have led to modifications in parole decisionmaking. Many States now use parole guidelines, and many have modified their use of "goodtime" and other incentives for controlling inmate behavior and determining release dates.

New administrative requirements, such as collection of victim restitution funds, operation of community service programs, and levying fees for probation supervision, room and board, and other services, have been added to traditional correctional practices.

Changes in sentencing laws and prac-

tices may be affecting the size of the correctional clientele. Such changes include—
• using determinate and mandatory sentencing
• limiting or abolishing parole discretion

• lowering the age at which youthful offenders become subject to the adult criminal justice system
• enacting in a few jurisdictions laws providing for life imprisonment without the possibility of parole.

Forfeiture is a relatively new sanction

What is forfeiture?

Forfeiture is government seizure of property derived from or used in criminal activity. Its use as a sanction aims to strip racketeers and drug traffickers of their economic power because the traditional sanctions of imprisonment and fines have been found inadequate to deter or punish enormously profitable crimes. Seizure of assets aims not only to reduce the profitability of illegal activity but to curtail the financial ability of criminal organizations to continue illegal operations.

There are two types of forfeiture: civil and criminal

• **Civil forfeiture**—a proceeding against property used in criminal activity. Property subject to civil forfeiture often includes vehicles used to transport contraband, equipment used to manufacture illegal drugs, cash used in illegal transactions, and property purchased with the proceeds of the crime. No finding of criminal guilt is required in such proceedings. The government is required to post notice of the proceedings so that any party who has an interest in the property may contest the forfeiture.

• **Criminal forfeiture**—a part of the criminal action taken against a defendant accused of racketeering or drug trafficking. The forfeiture is a sanction imposed on conviction that requires the defendant to forfeit various property rights and interests related to the violation. In 1970 Congress revived this sanction that had been dormant in American law since the Revolution.

The use of forfeiture varies greatly among jurisdictions

The Federal Government originally provided for criminal forfeiture in the Racketeer Influenced and Corrupt Organization (RICO) statute and the

Comprehensive Drug Prevention and Control Act, both enacted in 1970. Before that time civil forfeiture had been provided in Federal laws on some narcotics, customs, and revenue infractions. More recently, language on forfeiture has been included in the Comprehensive Crime Control Act of 1984, the Money Laundering Act of 1986, and the Anti-drug Abuse Act of 1986.

Most State forfeiture procedures appear in controlled substances or RICO laws. A few States provide for forfeiture of property connected with the commission of any felony. Most State forfeiture provisions allow for civil rather than criminal forfeiture. A recent survey responded to by 44 States and territories found that under the controlled substances laws most States provide only for civil forfeiture. Eight States (Arizona, Kentucky, Nevada, New Mexico, North Carolina, Utah, Vermont, and West Virginia), however, have criminal forfeiture provisions.[1] Of the 19 States with RICO statutes, all but 8 include the criminal forfeiture sanction.[2]

What is forfeitable?

Originally most forfeiture provisions aimed to cover the seizure of contraband or modes of transporting or facilitating distribution of such materials. The types of property that may be forfeited have been expanded since the 1970s to include assets, cash, securities, negotiable instruments, real property including houses or other real estate, and proceeds traceable directly or indirectly to violations of certain laws. Common provisions permit seizure of conveyances such as airplanes, boats, or cars; raw materials, products, and equipment used in manufacturing, trafficking, or cultivation of illegal drugs; and drug paraphernalia.

How long does it take to determine if property can be forfeited?

In most cases some time is provided before the actual forfeiture to allow persons with an interest in seized property to make a claim. Seized property is normally kept for 6 months to 1 year before being declared forfeit and disposed of. Contraband or materials that are illegal *per se*, such as drugs, are disposed of relatively quickly. Cars, airplanes, boats, and other forms of transportation are usually kept for about 6 months before disposal. Real property is often kept for longer periods. Administrative forfeitures usually take less time than ones that require judicial determination.

Because of the depreciation in value of many assets over time and the cost of storing or caring for such assets, forfeiture may result in a cost rather than revenue to the prosecuting jurisdiction.

What happens to forfeited property?

The disposition of forfeited property is controlled by statute or in some States by their constitutions. In many cases, the seizing agency is permitted to place an asset in official use once it has been declared forfeit by a court. Such assets are usually cars, trucks, boats, or planes used during the crime or proceeds of the crime.

For assets that are sold, the proceeds are usually used first to pay any outstanding liens. The costs of storing, maintaining, and selling the property are reimbursed next. Some States require that, after administrative costs are reimbursed, the costs of law enforcement and prosecution must be paid. More than half the States provide that any outstanding balance go to the State or local treasury, or a part to both.

In eight States law enforcement agencies can keep all property, cash, or sales proceeds. If the State constitution governs distribution, the receiving agency is usually the State or local school system. Some States have specified the recipients to be special programs for drug abuse prevention and rehabilitation.

In 1984 the Federal Government established the Department of Justice Assets Forfeiture Fund to collect proceeds from forfeitures and defray the costs of forfeitures under the Comprehensive Drug Abuse Prevention and Control Act and the Customs Forfeiture Fund for forfeitures under customs laws. These acts also require that the property and proceeds of forfeiture be shared equitably with State and local law enforcement commensurate with their participation in the investigations leading to forfeiture.

Women in Jail: Unequal Justice

An unprecedented influx of female inmates leaves prisons overcrowded and overwhelmed

Californians call it The Campus, and with its low-lying, red-brick buildings set against 120 acres of dairy land, the California Institution for Women at Frontera looks deceptively civilized. The illusion ends inside. Constructed in the early 1950s as a repository for 800 or so wayward ladies, Frontera today holds more than 2,500 women at any given moment. The convicts complain that guards spy on them while they're showering or using the toilet. Inspectors have found rodent droppings and roaches in the food. In a lawsuit against the state, inmates charged that shower drains get so backed up, they have to stand on crates to avoid the slime.

A continent away, New York City's Rose M. Singer jail stands as a testimony to penal enlightenment. Because most inmates are young and sometimes high-spirited, the jail can feel a bit like a boarding school for girls. But the starkly lit hallways and pervasive smell of disinfectant are constant reminders of the true purpose of the place. And even though it was completed only two years ago, it is already seriously overcrowded—a dining room has been turned into a dorm. Above all, the inmates hate the lack of privacy. Says Carmen Gonzalez, who is serving nine months for selling crack, "I wish I was in a cell."

Stiff penalties: For years, the ranks of convicted criminals have been swelling steadily, bringing the nation's prison system perilously close to an overload. The vast majority—94.4 percent—of those inmates are men. But even in jail, women are breaking down the barriers to equal achievement. The Bureau of Justice Statistics reported last week that the female prison population jumped 21.8 percent from 1988 to 1989—the ninth consecutive year that

the rate of increase at women's institutions far outstripped the men's. The number of women doing time has doubled to 40,000 in the last five years (chart). The main reason is drugs. Stiffer penalties are on the books throughout the country and women, who have turned to crack in a way they never embraced other narcotics, have been caught in the sweep. Judges have also shown a greater willingness to incarcerate women than in the past, when chivalry extended even to lawbreakers. "Courts used to look at it as if they were sentencing a mother," says Gary Maynard, Oklahoma's corrections director. "Now they look at it as if they are sentencing a criminal."

Prisons have been largely unprepared to handle the unique problems of their growing female populations. "We assumed that they could benefit from the same programs as men," says Dan Russell, administrator of Montana's division of corrections. "But women have a lot of psychological and medical needs" that men do not. Often, children are at the heart of the matter. Three quarters of the women are mothers, and many of them single parents. In recent years, a number of prisons have created programs to provide greater contact between kids and inmate moms (box). And public officials have begun to acknowledge—sometimes nudged along by lawsuits—that prisons do not provide women with the same rehabilitation or educational programs as men. Inequities in the correctional system, says Washington, D.C., Superior Court Associate Judge Gladys Kessler, "are a mirror of the sex discrimination that occurs in the nonprison population."

Fed by steamy, seamy '50s movies like "Reform School Girl," Americans have had a long fascination with women behind bars. The reality is a good deal more disturb-

ing—and pathetic. The typical offender, according to a 1988 national study conducted for the American Correctional Association, is a young minority mother. In general, she is slightly better educated and less violent than her male counterpart. Many inmates were victims themselves—of poverty, physical violence or sexual abuse. Though most poor people are obviously law abiding, some analysts say more

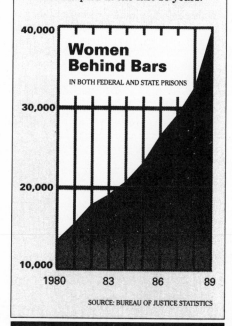

Filling Prisons

The number of women inmates has almost tripled in the last 10 years.

Women Behind Bars

IN BOTH FEDERAL AND STATE PRISONS

40,000

30,000

20,000

10,000

1980   83   86   89

SOURCE: BUREAU OF JUSTICE STATISTICS

'Dear Mommy, How Are You Doing?'

It is Mother's Day at the Lorton Correctional Complex outside Washington, D.C., and Michael, 10, is waiting impatiently as the women in camouflage pants file into the gym. Finally, Jennifer Nimmons, who is serving 18 months on a drug charge, arrives and Michael rushes into her arms. He has brought his mother a present: a cutout of a dancing bear with a letter on its stomach, which he reads aloud. "Dear Mommy, How are you doing in the hospital? Have a happy mother's day, this is a poem for you. 'Roses are red, Violets are blue, You are the best mother, I ever wrote to'." Then he asks: "Is this a hospital?"

Confused, enraged, hurt—children like Michael are innocent victims of their mothers' crimes. Until recently, prison officials didn't recognize that a child's emotional dependence doesn't stop just because his mother lands behind bars. Now attitudes are changing: institutions around the country have put programs in place to foster that vital relationship.

Some of the most innovative begin at birth. Federal prisons separate mothers and newborns after 24 hours, and few state pens allow inmates to spend time with infants. The Rose M. Singer Center on Rikers Island is a heartening contrast. The mothers' cells surround the glass-walled nursery on three sides, and an intercom system keeps them in constant touch. If kids cry, moms can rush to their aid—the cells are never locked. Because a female federal prisoner is likely to do time far from home, a program called PACT (Parents and Children Together) is designed to improve long-distance parenting. "We counsel inmates to get as involved as possible by calling teachers on a regular basis," says Jaretta Jones, an instructor at the federal penitentiary in Lexington, Ky.

Psychic costs: Penal authorities have also become more sensitive about the psychic costs to kids. Some children feel guilty about their parents' predicaments—imagining, for example, if they hadn't opened the door for the cops, Mom would be free. The Huron Valley Women's Facility in Ypsilanti, Mich., provides kids with therapy after visits. "If we are going to lock up these mothers, we have to take some responsibility for those children," says Marilyn Marshall, a vocational counselor at the prison. "They will certainly be our next generation of prisoners unless we pay attention now."

women have taken to crime to support their families as economic conditions have worsened. In Florida last year, more than two thirds of the men were working at the time of their arrest, while 73.8 percent of the women were jobless.

New Breed: Women prisoners have always been easier to manage than the men—they're more prone to verbal than physical abuse. But that may be changing. Some penologists worry that the lack of space will not only exacerbate existing problems—for example, fights stemming from lesbian jealousies—but provoke the women into new forms of aggression. "The recidivism, as well as the level of violence, seems to be directly linked to the amount of overcrowding," says Rebecca Jurado, an attorney with the ACLU of southern California.

Drugs, in particular, have stimulated violent outbreaks. More than half the women in the federal system were convicted on drug charges. And the problem doesn't stop at the prison gate. Mary Vermeer, a deputy warden in Perryville, Ariz., says new inmates are delighted to discover that, despite efforts to stem the flow, the drug pipeline makes it almost as easy to get a fix inside as out. At Frontera, crack houses and shooting galleries operate in portable toilets in the yard. Old-timers complain about the new breed of "druggie." "They don't care about nothing," says Delores Lee, 37, who is doing 25 years in Florida on a murder conviction. "They steal; they break things."

AIDS also contributes to the crisis atmosphere in American prisons. So far, there are no national figures measuring the disease among the convict population. An official Massachusetts study based on 400 inmates who volunteered to be tested found that 35 percent of the women were HIV-positive, compared with 13 percent of the men. In California, any woman who tested positive was put into a segregated AIDS unit—whether or not she was actually ill. As a result of a discrimination lawsuit, many HIV inmates at Frontera have been mainstreamed during the day—but must return to their separate quarters to sleep.

Though few would argue that male convicts are socially well adjusted, penal experts tend to agree that female inmates require—and desire—more psychological counseling. Many women feel enormous guilt about their kids. "When men get arrested, they ask for a lawyer," says Brenda Smith, an attorney at the National Women's Law Center in Washington, D.C. "When women get arrested, they ask about their children." The children effectively serve as hostages on the outside, ensuring that the women make few demands. "The No. 1 issue for women is getting their kids back," says Sarah Buel, a battered-women's advocate in Massachusetts. "The unwritten rule is, don't make a fuss and we'll help you get [them] back."

Prison officials have begun to acknowledge the enormous disparity in the treatment of men and women. In a number of recent lawsuits, women plaintiffs have accused the system of gender bias. A major problem is "overincarceration." Because of a lack of facilities, many low-security inmates have landed in medium-security penitentiaries. Many of the women have been subjected to greater restrictions, such as strip searches, than their crimes warrant—and which their male counterparts are largely spared.

Some social critics believe the states should help inmates break the cycle of abuse and poverty that led many of them into crime in the first place. They also argue that the system should recognize that women generally pose less of a threat to public safety than men and deserve more lenient sentences. "Assuming that we want to help offenders, the best place to do this is not in prison," says Nicole Hahn Rafter, author of "Partial Justice," a history of women's prisons. That attitude is unlikely to win much support, particularly now that public opinion favors strict penalties. But it is clear that the overcrowded conditions and lack of rehabilitation programs doubly punish women—and do little to advance the society's interests.

ELOISE SALHOLZ with LYNDA WRIGHT in Los Angeles, CLARA BINGHAM in Washington, TONY CLIFTON in New York, GINNY CARROLL in Houston, SPENCER REISS in Miami, FARAI CHIDEYA in Boston and bureau reports

You're Under Arrest— AT HOME

With a jail's daily operating costs of $35-$125 per prisoner, home detention represents big savings for hard-pressed correction officials.

Fred Scaglione

Mr. Scaglione is a New York free-lance writer.

NOBODY wants a prison in his or her neighborhood, but don't be surprised if that split level next door is already a jail cell. As the nation's penal system staggers under the weight of an ever-rising inmate population, corrections officials are taking a new, high-tech look at an age-old technique—house arrest. Jurisdictions in 32 states now are sending almost 2,000 offenders to their homes, rather than to traditional lock-ups, and outfitting them with an array of electronic equipment to ensure they stay there. "We believe this is an important enhancement to a criminal justice system that is already overburdened," says James K. Stewart, director of the National Institute of Justice (NIJ).

Offenders accepted into these programs are given a daily schedule, allowing them to leave the house for work, approved counseling sessions, and religious services. Some are fitted with continuously signaling anklets or wristlets which broadcast to a second unit attached to their home telephone lines. If the offender leaves the house and takes the transmitter out of the broadcast range, the telephone-based receiver automatically calls the program's central monitoring station. There, a computer programmed with the offender's daily schedule determines if the absence is authorized or if a violation report is warranted.

Other jurisdictions use a computer-generated random calling system, requiring the offender to verify his presence in a variety of ways each time the phone rings. The central schedule monitoring station works the same in both cases. Neither system eavesdrops on the offender's conversations or activities, nor can they track him if he leaves the house. "The monitor is the baby sitter and I'm your mom," explains In-House Arrest Officer Trish Dosset to new program participants in Palm Beach County, Fla. "For the next 30 days, you don't go anywhere without asking me first."

The programs also require regular face-to-face meetings, verification of employment and hours worked, telephone checks, and occasional site visits at the offender's home and workplace. Clients with drug and alcohol problems may be required to attend counseling sessions and undergo randomly scheduled urine tests.

Inmates may be the nation's fastest growing community group. By June, 1986, there were over 750,000 residents of Federal, state, and local penal institutions, twice the number of 10 years earlier. The American Correctional Association ex-

pects the population to double again by soon after the year 2000, as legislators continue to demand longer sentences generally and mandatory imprisonment for specific offenses.

Law enforcement officials have been unable to accommodate their burgeoning clientele. Prisons in Connecticut, California, and Ohio, for example, were 83%, 76%, and 69%, respectively, above their designed capacities in 1986. Almost one-quarter of all city and county jails now have court orders limiting their populations.

Efforts to expand the prison system have been devastatingly expensive. The average construction cost of a new jail cell is estimated at $75,000. Jurisdictions then go on to pay operating costs ranging from $35 to $125 per night. It's not surprising that correctional expenses are now the fastest growing segment of state government spending.

Electronic monitors, on the other hand, cost anywhere from $2 to $10 per day for each offender, depending on the type of equipment and the size of the program. Staff costs will vary according to the level of personal supervision a program specifies. Clackamas County, Ore., estimates

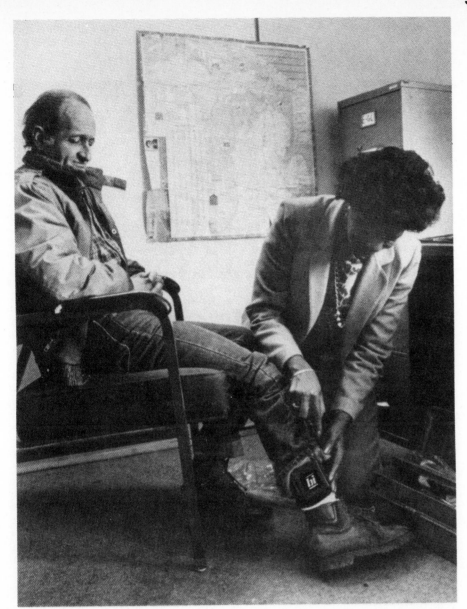

A continuously signaling device is installed on the ankle of a man under house arrest. A telephone-based receiver will call authorities if his body transmitter is taken out of broadcast range.

to visit him. He gets to know his wife and kids, stops drinking or doing drugs, saves his money, and works around the house. Nine months later, they take off the monitor and he still comes home at night. He's got a job, a bank account, and a whole new relationship with his family. The monitor and house arrest have made him healthy, wealthy, and wise.

If it sounds like a law-enforcement fairy tale, it is. However, for certain offenders it's also true. "I now own my own deli," says a 25-year-old man after five years on cocaine, six months in prison, and 10 months on the New Jersey ISP program. "I do not do drugs and I will not go back to doing drugs. This program was a lifesaver for me."

An auto mechanic, also in his mid-20's and convicted on drug charges, stands in the service station where he works, talking about his wife, baby, and the five-year sentence he started serving in state prison. "I'm going to make it," he asserts, explaining how he's regained much of the weight he lost to drugs. "That cost me $2,800," he adds, pointing to a large metal tool cabinet. "I never could save up to buy decent tools before."

"We've had people who, for the first time in their lives, are working. They're going home and they're providing some kind of support for their family," says Ingrid Lewis, administrator of the house arrest program in Clackamas County. "They're at home and they have to take care of responsibilities at home," explains Capt. Ken Lane of the Fairfax County, Va., Sheriff's Office. However, corrections officials, perhaps out of experience, are quick to burst their own bubble. They are cautious about predicting success or prescribing monitoring programs for too many offenders.

Many of the plans which have sprung up in recent years mirror the two original Palm Beach County models established in 1984. Approximately one-third of all participants throughout the county are traffic offenders, predominately drunk-drivers. Some jurisdictions extend participation to work-release inmates and to those convicted of low-level property crimes. A history of violence, drug abuse, or sexual misconduct often will disqualify an applicant. White-collar criminals also make appearances in many of the local programs. In July, 1987, for example, a Los Angeles court sentenced a local slumlord to house arrest in one of his rat-infested buildings.

Growth also has come through monitoring a wide range of offenders with varying,

total costs at $12 per day; Utah officials quote $17.

No matter how you add it up, home detention represents big savings for hard-pressed corrections officials. "We're buying additional jail beds for $10," says Marie Whittington as Orange County, Calif., prepares to expand its house arrest program from 25 to 75 slots.

New Jersey, with 400 felons on pre-release from its overcrowded prison system, estimates that its Intensive Supervision Probation (ISP) program is saving approximately $6,700,000 in direct expenditures annually. In addition, working program participants usually make a wide range of payments that further offset the costs of supervision; most programs collect a fee from participants to cover the cost of monitoring equipment. Palm Beach County's PRIDE, Inc., for example, charges the fairly typical amount of $7 per day. Offenders also pay taxes, fines, and restitution as required. They often are obligated to work on community service projects as well. New Jersey estimates that these payments and activities add up to an additional $1,400,000.

Life-saving programs

Yet, these programs may be saving more than money. They may be saving lives. Success stories are depressingly rare in the world of correction, but many administrators of home detention programs like to tell one—the same one. It's about the offender who comes to their program near the end of his personal rope. He's sick—busted in more ways than one. He gets a monitor and a curfew, and goes to work every morning and comes home every night. He stops seeing his friends on the corner or at the bar and they don't bother and more serious, backgrounds. Clackamas County, for example, assigns offenders convicted of violent felonies like armed robbery and manslaughter. They are also one of the few programs to accept sex offenders. "We look at the individual, not just the crime," says Ingrid Lewis.

As the technology has grown more reliable, a number of states have incorporated monitoring into pre-release programs aimed at freeing up bed space in crowded prisons. Inmates agree to a variety of conditions, including monitoring and curfews, in exchange for the chance to get out of prison early. Michigan, for example, began providing monitors to convicted felons in its Extended Furlough Program in April, 1987. It now monitors nearly 1,000 offenders.

About 90% of all participants successfully complete home-monitoring programs. "I'm continuously amazed with the level of compliance that prisoners give us," states Jim Putnam of the Michigan Department of Correction. However, there still is relatively little hard data to support the gut feelings of administrators that these successful graduates go on to live crime-free lives. A recent survey of 327 offenders who completed the New Jersey ISP program since 1984 did find that only four percent had been rearrested in the state, an excellent result compared with typical studies of recidivism. The National Institute of Justice is funding a series of tests to follow offenders randomly assigned to electronic monitoring as opposed to other programs.

Of the 10% who fail to complete the programs, the majority are sent back to jail for violating in-house rules—missed curfews, refusal to attend counseling sessions, or failed urine tests. A small fraction are sent back because of new arrests. In county-run programs, these tend to be relatively infrequent and for minor offenses.

State-run pre-release programs generally have a greater return rate with more serious rearrests despite screening out 70-80% of all potential candidates. The New Jersey ISP program, for example, has returned approximately seven percent of its participants to prison because of new charges, with approximately two-thirds of those for felonies. Michigan's program recently suffered a murder/suicide by one of its participants, the most serious crime committed by a monitored offender to date. Incidents such as these appear inevit-

able when offenders are sent back into the community. Yet, so far, electronically monitored home detention seems to have drawn high marks in protecting the public safety.

If anything, administrators, particularly on the local level, have been criticized for being too cautious in their selection of offenders. "Judges are gun shy," says Joan Petersilia of the Rand Corporation, a research/consulting firm in Santa Monica, Calif. "They're picking people who they are fairly sure won't embarrass the program." If this means that monitoring is used for offenders who wouldn't normally draw jail time and pose little risk to the public safety, she argues that the program is self-defeating. "It's costly. It's intrusive. I don't think we can afford to do those symbolic punishments anymore."

Monitoring probation

However, there is a group now walking the streets of society for which electronic monitoring is appropriate, Petersilia believes. The nation's overflowing prisons have swelled the probation caseload to over 1,800,000, more than twice the number incarcerated. At the same time, dwindling resources have reduced routine probation supervision to an exercise in paper-shuffling. "Half of all people now on probation are convicted felons," she states, "and a quarter of them are convicted of violent crimes." A recent Rand study found that 65% of California probationers are rearrested within 40 months, 75% for serious crimes. This population, she feels, is much too dangerous to be receiving nominal probation supervision. "The system must develop intermediate forms of punishment more restrictive than routine probation, but not as severe or expensive as prison."

Electronic monitoring may be at least part of the answer. Some officials worry, however, that monitoring will become a popular and counterproductive crutch. "I'm concerned about programs that put too much emphasis on the equipment and not enough emphasis on a balanced program of equipment and personal supervision," says Marie Whittington, director of Orange County's Work Furlough Program. "The monitors are only a back-up," agrees New Jersey ISP officer Mike McCree. "What makes this program work is close personal contact."

In fact, New Jersey puts electronic mon-

itors on only 20 problem cases out of its total of 400 participants. Another 200 receive computer-generated nightly telephone calls, but are not required to wear a bracelet to verify their identities. Unlike many jurisdictions which require only one office visit per week, New Jersey's program averages 27 contacts per month, many of them face to face in the offender's home. Participants attend weekly rap sessions, special ISP-sponsored drug counseling sessions, and 16 hours per month of community service. They also must maintain an up-to-date diary and personal budget.

"We get involved in every aspect of their lives," McCree says, adding with a smile, "I've been to two or three weddings and we've got a wall full of baby pictures."

Although offenders with monitors may certainly feel that Big Brother is watching, the American Civil Liberties Union (ACLU) has yet to take issue with any of the house arrest programs. "The overarching problem in correction is overcrowding," says Ed Koren, an attorney with the ACLU's National Prison Project. "We'd like to see this happen if it can get people out of prison." Therefore, while it remains sensitive to the threat of abuse through overutilization and to possibilities of discrimination in selection and offender contribution requirements, the ACLU basically is watching as the strategy continues to develop.

While programs similar to those already in existence are likely to continue to grow rapidly, new technological developments are offering the possibility of even more comprehensive electronic surveillance. One manufacturer has added a blood alcohol-level monitoring system to its house arrest equipment. At least two others are developing methods to track an offender's position geographically as he travels throughout a metropolitan area and report it back to a computerized central control station for comparison with his approved daily schedule.

Some corrections officials respond favorably to this prospect of expanded surveillance. Others, however, are skeptical. "I think the technology is a long way off," says Joan Petersilia, "but I think the public acceptance of that is an even longer way off." Nevertheless, electronic monitoring and house arrest clearly are here to stay as correctional strategies. "The future of this is very bright," concludes the NIJ's Stewart.

Difficult clients, large caseloads plague probation, parole agencies

Randall Guynes

American probation and parole systems now face an increasingly difficult clientele despite less adequate resources. Despite greater financial resources, personnel increases are not keeping pace with rising caseloads of clients with serious problems. These are some of the major findings of a survey of State and local probation and parole officers conducted as part of the National Assessment Program (NAP) sponsored by the National Institute of Justice.

This *Research in Action* describes survey results from 49 State probation and parole directors and 339 local offices. Of the local offices, 43 percent provide probation services only, and 21 percent are parole field offices. The remaining 36 percent are responsible for both probation and parole and are referred to as "combined" agencies throughout this publication.

The primary aim of the National Assessment Program is to identify key needs and problems of local and State criminal justice practitioners. To accomplish this, the National Institute of Justice (NIJ) contracted with the Institute for Law and Justice, Inc., to conduct a national survey of approximately 2,500 practitioners from a

The Institute for Law and Justice, Inc., Alexandria, Virginia, conducted the 1986 National Assessment Program for the National Institute of Justice. Under a subcontract, the Institute for Economic and Policy Studies, Inc., conducted the surveys of correctional officials, including this report by Randall Guynes on the survey of probation and parole agency directors.

sample of 375 counties across the Nation. Included were all 175 counties with populations greater than 250,000 and a sample of 200 counties having less than that number.[1] Persons receiving surveys in each sampled county included the police chief of the largest city, sheriff, jail administrator, prosecutor, chief judge, trial court administrator (where applicable), and probation and parole agency heads. In addition, surveys were also sent to State probation and parole agencies to obtain their viewpoints.

The survey covered five general areas: agency background, criminal justice problems, caseload, staffing, and operations. The results for each of these areas are discussed in detail in the following sections.

Background

Organizational Units. Using political subdivisions to sample probation and parole agencies obviously results in a diverse set of respondents including directors of county probation departments, heads of branch offices for State agencies, and agencies responsible for several counties. Yet this reflects the diversity of organizational arrangements in probation and parole generally (see Exhibit 1).

In about 25 percent of the States, probation is primarily a local responsibility, with the State accountable only for functions such as providing financial support, setting standards, and arranging training courses. This locally based approach accounts for about two-thirds of all persons under probation supervision in the United States.[2]

The governmental branch responsible also varies. A State or local department may be in the judicial or the executive branch of government, and supervision of probationers may cross branches or levels within branches. Despite these variations, agency functions are similar: supervising and monitoring persons; collecting and analyzing information for decisionmakers; and performing other duties such as collecting fees, fines, restitution, and child support payments.

Staffing and budgets. For the agencies responding, the median numbers of employees are 32 for combined agencies, 47 for probation, and 62 for parole. The respective medians of cases monthly are 934, 1,225, and 885. Probation directors indicate a median of 129 presentence, revocation, diversion, or other investigations monthly, compared to 75 for parole and 94 for combined agencies.

As expected, parole cases are generally classified at higher supervision levels than cases handled by either probation or combined agencies. Parole reports the highest proportion of intensive (11 percent) and maximum (35 percent) cases and the lowest median caseload (65 cases per officer). The other two groups indicated from 22 to less than 4 percent in intensive and maximum supervision categories and had correspondingly higher median caseloads (probation 109, combined 99). However, 27 percent of the parole caseload is classified as "unsupervised."

A larger proportion of parole agencies (29 percent) report budget increases in excess of 30 percent over the last 3

Difficult clients, large caseloads plague probation, parole agenices

Exhibit 1
Probation structures, National Assessment Project

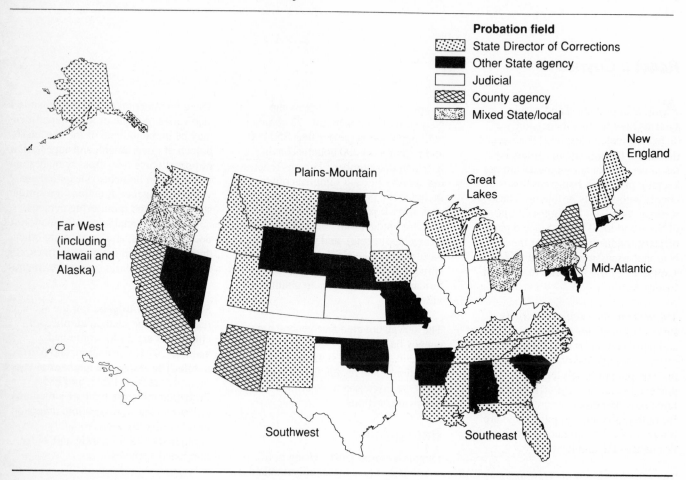

Staff shortage is clearly the dominant problem for all agencies. It has the highest average rank for probation and combined agencies and second highest for parole. Prison crowding also rates high among parole agencies and combined agencies. Similarly, State

years than did probation (22 percent) and combined agencies (16 percent). More than two-thirds of the directors of combined offices rate their financial resources as inadequate, while 55 percent of probation respondents and 48 percent of parole respondents rate their resources as inadequate.

Criminal justice problems

Based on the previous National Assessment Survey in 1983,[3] the current survey asked respondents to rank the severity of seven criminal justice problems within their systems: lack of staff skills, prison crowding, agency management, staff shortages, jail

crowding, coordination among agencies, and the public's lack of understanding of criminal justice agencies. Respondents ranked these items from most serious (1) to least serious (7). Exhibit 2 shows the average ranking for each issue by type of agency. The percentage of "number 1" responses appears in parentheses.

probation and parole directors (not shown in Exhibit 2) rank prison crowding and staff shortages as the most significant issues.

After staff shortage, probation respondents see the criminal justice system as being troubled almost equally by coordination problems, a lack of understanding by the public, and both jail and prison crowding. Coordination is significant to probation officers because the regular performance of their duties requires them to work with judges, law enforcement personnel, jail managers, and sometimes prison officials. As for crowding, probation officers are affected by both jail crowding, as local governments attempt to control jail populations with probation supervision, and prison crowding, as courts and legislatures attempt to control prison populations through increased probation.

In most of the remainder of the survey, respondents were asked to rate problems and needs on a scale of 1 to 4 with a rating of 1 representing "Not at all" and 4 representing "Major" problem or need. In the discussion that follows, the ratings of 3 and 4 combine to indicate a significant problem or need.

Agencies were asked to rate the degree to which eight factors had contributed to increased caseloads over the past 3 years (see Exhibit 3). All respondent groups identified increased supervision needs of offenders as the first or second greatest reason for caseload increases. Other significant contributors to caseloads were jail and prison crowding, slow growth in residential options, and time required for investigations and reporting. Increased supervision terms were rated low by all groups. In general, directors of parole field offices rated all contributing factors higher than did directors of other agencies. Parole and combined agencies reported prison crowding and early parole release as important contributors to caseloads—a result in agreement with their views on significant criminal justice problems.

Reflecting their different perspectives, 63 percent of parole directors, but only 28 percent of probation directors, gave a high rating to the related issue of early parole release. State agency directors considered slow growth in community residential beds as less significant than did directors of local offices. However, State directors gave more emphasis than other respondents to investigation and reporting time as a contributor to caseloads.

There were significant regional variations in how much crowding, early parole release, and increased supervision terms affect caseload. From 80 to 100 percent of probation or parole directors in the Southeast and Plains-Mountain regions considered prison crowding an important factor in increasing caseloads. They were joined

Exhibit 2
Most serious criminal justice problem (average ranking by type of agency)

Average rank	Probation only agencies	Probation and parole agencies	Parole only agencies
1.0			
2.3			
2.4			Prison crowding(41%)
2.5			
2.6			
2.7	Staff shortage(48%)		
2.8		Staff shortage(38%)	
2.9			
3.0			Staff shortage(30%)
3.1		Prison crowding(25%)	
3.2			
3.3			
3.4			
3.5	Coordination(9%)		Jail crowding(6%)
3.6	Jail crowding(16%)	Jail crowding(10%)	
3.7	Lack of public understanding(13%)		
3.8	Prison crowding (11%)	Lack of public understanding(11%)	
3.9			
4.0			
4.1			
4.2		Lack coordination(10%)	
4.3			Lack of public understanding(10%)
4.4			Lack coordination(1%)
4.5			
4.6			
4.7			
4.8		Management(8%)	Management(10%)
4.9			
5.0			
5.1			
5.2	Lack staff skill(4%)		
5.3			
5.4	Management(1%)	Lack staff skills(3%)	
5.5			Lack staff skills(3%)
5.6			
7.0			

Note: The number in parentheses is the percentage of persons assigning rank of 1 to the problem.

For example, among probation and parole agencies, "staff shortages" was given an average seriousness of 2.8 on a scale of 1 down to 7, but 38 percent ranked it as a number 1 problem.

by parole agencies from New England and probation agencies from the Southwest. The greatest concern with early parole release was expressed by Southeast (93 percent) and Southwest (78 percent) parole directors.

As shown in Exhibit 3, increased supervision terms is rated lowest as a contributor by all groups of respondents. However, an interesting regional variation is that respondents from the Southeast and Southwest consider

Difficult clients, large caseloads plague probation, parole agenices

Exhibit 3
Caseload contributors

Reason	State agencies	Probation agencies	Parole agencies	Combined agencies
Increased supervision needs	75%	82%	80%	79%
Staff increases not keeping pace	73	79	74	73
Prison crowding	79	68	86	79
Local jail crowding	63	62	61	63
Time for reports and investigations	60	59	57	64
Early parole release	55	28	63	61
Residential options not keeping pace	53	57	64	52
Increased supervision terms	42	37	51	35

longer supervision terms as a very significant contributor to caseload increases (93 and 100 percent respectively). Generally, respondents from the Southeast and Southwest express greater concern on more items affecting caseloads than those from other regions.

Responses to caseload management problems

Respondents were asked to list projects in their jurisdictions that have improved personnel and operational problems. Projects listed to improve caseload management speak to changing times in probation and parole. Responding agencies exhibited creativity in managing increased and more difficult caseloads with little or no increases in human resources. Almost one-third of the projects mentioned involve differential supervision, including intensive, minimum, and unsupervised. Another third were examining their workloads or developing liaisons with other key criminal justice system actors (usually court officers) as precursors to reducing supervision levels.

About 10 percent of the respondents who listed projects used early terminations and about 25 percent relied on

alternative program assignments (e.g., pretrial diversion and drug treatment programs). Other approaches included streamlining paperwork assignments while acknowledging that presentence investigations consumed considerable time. Interestingly, only one respondent cited reduction in service levels as a solution.

The two major reasons for increased caseloads were disproportionate growth in increased supervision needs of offenders and staffing levels. These reasons imply that personnel and case management issues will continue to be major operational concerns for probation and parole agencies.

Operations and procedures

Agencies were asked questions about their needs to improve operations and procedures in five general categories: classification, community resources, scheduling, management information systems, and private sector contracting. As explained in the sections that follow, the last three are the most salient concerns for the respondents.

Classification. When asked to list projects that have improved classification, almost half the respondents stated that they had developed an evaluative

technique incorporating risk. Less than 40 percent of each respondent group indicated a need to improve initial and subsequent classification of offenders' risks or needs.

Scheduling. Since field services organizations are dependent on others to complete many of their tasks, it was hypothesized that scheduling with other criminal justice agencies might be a problem. Respondents were asked to rate the degree to which scheduling is a problem for each of the following groups or activities:

- Court hearings (sentence and revocation hearings).
- Prison officials (investigations).
- Timing for sentence investigations.
- Clerk of court (fines and fees).

From this list, only scheduling problems with regard to sentencing and revocation hearings were rated high. More than 50 percent of local directors and 47 percent of State directors noted this as a problem. Combined agencies indicated this was a more severe problem (68 percent) than the other agencies.

Management information systems. The analysis of the questions on management information systems suggests that the use of these systems is limited. Only about 15 percent of the agencies have automated systems to support classification. The overwhelming majority of respondents either (1) did not have a system in place, (2) were just in the process of developing such a capability, or (3) limited the use of their system to minor applications such as word processing.

Respondents generally wanted historical data, such as criminal record and substance abuse information on their clients, to be computerized. The computerized system would further enhance the classification procedures and make the client information readily available for other uses. A need was also expressed for information on referrals for service to be used in the ongoing management of cases. Greater concern for referral information was reported by probation offices in the New England, Mid-Atlantic, and Far West areas. Interestingly, most groups did not place a priority on improving information on management supervision assignments and levels.

The needs expressed for management information reflected different collection strategies. Historical data on criminal records and substance abuse generally depended on information from other criminal agencies and the clients, supplemented by information from families and friends. In contrast, referrals for service and associated dates could generally be found within the agency—at least during the supervision period—and were easier to maintain within a system.

Community resources. Probation and parole rely on public and private resources outside their agencies to supply many services to offenders. Directors were asked to rate the degree to which they see the need to improve or create nine types of community services (Exhibit 4). In general, parole agencies rated the items as more significant needs than the other groups.

One-half or more of the directors reported that the number of residential options were not keeping pace with offenders' needs, and at least three out of four believed increased supervision requirements were contributing to caseload management problems. Given the higher levels of supervision now required, one respondent from the Northeast argued that halfway houses and other options were needed to "restore probation and parole as legitimate sanctions." In addition to current needs for residential programs, one director noted that the challenge of the next 3 years will be "development of new programs to divert those currently in jails awaiting transfer to prison custody—to the extent that the community is not jeopardized."

Other differences appeared to reflect the stage of the criminal justice process at which offenders were referred. For example, 80 percent of parole agencies reported a need for housing referral services, compared to about 62 percent of other field offices. In contrast, there were few differences among agencies regarding the need for job readiness training, which was cited by 65 to 73 percent of the field offices. Vocational education services were reported as a need by 74 percent of parole and 61 percent of probation agencies, and 56 percent of combined agencies.

Exhibit 4
Needs for new or improved community resources

Community resources	State agencies	Probation agencies	Parole agencies	Combined agencies
Residential programs	80%	72%	83%	73%
Housing referral services	57	63	80	62
Job readiness training	65	68	73	69
Mental health services	72	60	71	67
Drug programs	81	63	79	62
Employment referral services	50	70	66	61
Alcohol programs	62	50	73	54
Vocational education	62	61	74	56
Adult basic education	31	33	60	33

There were several regional variations in perceived need for improved or expanded community resources. Although adult basic education was the lowest priority for everyone, directors in the Great Lakes, Mid-Atlantic, and Southwest rated the problem considerably higher than their colleagues. Drug programs were of more concern to parole directors in the Mid-Atlantic, Southwest, and Far West than in other parts of the country. Probation offices in New England (83 percent) and the Far West (91 percent) reported a greater need for mental health services than probation offices overall (60 percent).

Contracted services. Residential, drug, job readiness, and mental health programs can be provided internally or through arrangements with public or private service providers. Recent attention given to contracting in corrections and the reduction in government-supported social service programs suggests that the demand for privately sponsored arrangements may increase. Probation and parole officials were asked to indicate whether they currently purchase none, some, most, or all of eight specific services.

The most prevalent service currently provided under contract is staff training. At least four-fifths of the respondents contract for some or all of their staff training. In contrast, emergency food is provided under contract to fewer than one-third of parole agencies and in less than 15 percent of other field offices.

The private sector is used less overall in the Southeast than in other regions. All local directors in the Southeast report fewer purchases of drug testing and medical services. Single-function agencies contract for staff training less frequently than combined agencies. Only 7 percent of local parole offices and a lower percentage of combined agencies use the private sector for residential centers or emergency housing.

Fewer than 35 percent of Great Lakes parole directors contract for any staff training, urinalysis, mental health services, emergency food, or housing. Approximately the same percentage of probation agencies in the Great Lakes, Mid-Atlantic, and Plains-Mountain regions contract for medical services. Only about two-fifths of the Far West offices responsible for both probation and parole purchase any medical or halfway house services.

Staff recruitment and retention

As reflected in Exhibit 2, staff shortages were rated high as a problem by all three groups of agencies. The results from the recruitment and retention sections of the survey provided insights into this problem.

Recruitment. Among the most significant recruitment problems are low salaries, locating qualified professional staff, shortages of qualified minority applicants, hiring freezes, and poor image of corrections work.

In general, State directors saw fewer recruitment problems than did local officers and considered a shortage of minority applicants the most important

Difficult clients, large caseloads plague probation, parole agenices

Exhibit 5
Recruitment problems

Issue	State agencies	Probation agencies	Parole agencies	Combined agencies
Low salaries	33%	50%	53%	68%
Shortage of minority applicants	48	44	41	50
Locating qualified staff	31	46	52	49
Hiring freeze	29	47	38	40
Poor image of corrections	21	27	43	37
Entrance requirements too high	17	22	28	19

recruitment issue (Exhibit 5). In contrast, 50 percent of the local probation directors, 53 percent of the parole directors, and 68 percent of the combined agency directors considered low salaries an important recruitment problem. Approximately 45 percent of local agencies reported problems recruiting minorities.

Restrictions on hiring significantly affect recruitment for more than 47 percent of local probation directors, but only 38 percent of their counterparts in parole. In contrast, the poor image of corrections work was a significant problem for 43 percent of local parole agencies.

Retention. Agency directors were asked to rate the degree to which seven items contribute to staff turnover: salary increases, burnout, inability to use leave time, poor image of corrections work, substance abuse, inadequate career incentives, and excessive overtime. Career incentives were considered the number one staff retention issue by State directors (58 percent), local parole (70 percent), probation (60 percent), and combined agencies (71 percent). Salary increases and burnout were cited as serious by 40 percent or more of all four groups, with the remaining problems receiving substantially lower

ratings. The salary problem was considered a major issue by 68 percent of the combined agencies.

Forty-seven percent of the probation offices and 67 percent of both parole field offices and combined agency directors rated burnout as a serious retention problem. "Burnout" is used to encompass a variety of situations, from personal crises unrelated to occupation, through systemic dysfunctions in organizations, to uncertain environmental conditions. Its causes may be personal, organizational, environmental, or (more frequently) a combination. Within the limits of this survey, it was not possible to determine the specific causes of burnout at the local level. Interestingly, from other survey responses, burnout is apparently not being caused by excessive overtime (rated as a problem by only one respondent in five) or employee substance abuse (rated as a problem by less than 2 percent of all respondents).

Responses. It is clear that compensation, including "career incentives," is perceived as essential for both attracting and holding probation and parole staff. What is unclear is whether salaries are considered inadequate relative to similar occupations and other public service jobs in terms of skill levels

required and risks involved. Addressing these staffing issues tests the ingenuity of agencies facing increased demands with constrained resources. Few agencies, for example, cite new funding as the way they are trying to solve their personnel problems. Instead, evaluation and reorganization of workload are used as the major way of alleviating staffing burdens. Frequently cited recruitment methods (reported by over one-half of all those responding) included special minority recruiters and outreach in the community and at colleges.

Training. Respondents were asked to rate their agencies' interest in several training topics (Exhibit 6). Consistent with the finding that "increased supervision needs" increased caseload problems, at least 76 percent of all groups reported they need to upgrade staff skills to handle special problem offenders. Six other topics interested at least half of all local agencies: offender monitoring techniques, counseling, stress management, legal liability, report writing, and caseload management.

While overall training needs were high (with parole reporting the highest overall), responses varied substantially by agency function. Consistent with high burnout, stress management training was a greater need in parole and combined agencies, with almost 70 percent of agencies significantly interested. Probation agencies rank handling special offenders highest (80 percent), followed by case management (63 percent), offender monitoring (57 percent), and liability (57 percent).

There were also interesting differences between State and local perceptions of training needs. State directors reported a somewhat greater degree of interest in training in counseling techniques (61 percent) than did local offices (about 50 percent). Forty-one percent of State directors favored training in report writing, compared to 53 percent of local directors. Caseload management skills were among the most wanted training for local respondents, but among the least significant for State directors. If training policy and resource allocation were influenced primarily by State officials, these results suggested a need to reconcile local and State perspectives.

Exhibit 6
Training needs

Training area	State agencies	Probation agencies	Parole agencies	Combined agencies
Handling special problem offenders	79%	80%	86%	76%
Caseload management	49	63	71	61
Offender monitoring	57	57	58	58
Liability issues	53	57	67	55
Report writing	41	54	63	53
Stress management	54	52	68	69
Counseling techniques	61	52	56	57

There are also some notable regional variations. Report writing was considered significant by parole in the Mid-Atlantic region and by parole and combined agencies in the Plains-Mountain States. Sixty-seven percent of directors responsible for both probation and parole in the Great Lakes region considered training in investigative techniques a significant need.

Legal liability training was deemed more serious by both probation and parole in the Plains-Mountain, Southwest, and Far West, where from 83 to 100 percent of agency directors considered this an important training topic.

What makes these results more striking is that monitoring, counseling, and report writing are fundamental to probation and parole functions. Along with investigations (a high priority only for parole respondents), there are the set of activities generally labeled "case management." Yet, probation and parole officials generally reported a significant need for training in these basic skills areas.

When acute basic skills deficiencies are considered along with workload, recruitment, and retention problems, they make a gloomy scenario for probation and parole. Staffing levels are not keeping pace with a growing caseload. At the same time, supervision needs are increasing. Recruitment is made difficult by low salaries that will not attract enough qualified applicants, and, once hired, employees are discouraged by poor career incentives, small salary increases, and burnout.

Conclusion

In broad strokes, the NAP survey painted a picture of America's probation and parole systems as facing unprecedented challenges. Despite recent budget increases of more than 20 percent for many agencies and major improvements in risk management, more than 75 percent of all agencies said staff increases are not keeping pace with the number of offenders.

Compounding this increase in staff-to-client ratio is the fact that at least three-fourths of the respondents believe offenders' supervision needs are greater now than in the past. Thus, not only are the numbers larger, the offenders are also a more difficult group to manage.

Fifty to sixty-eight percent of all local probation and parole offices report that salaries are too low to attract qualified applicants. Once hired, personnel did not find financial and other incentives sufficient to stay in positions where burnout is a major problem.

Employees in general have extremely high training needs, even in such basic skills as counseling, report writing, offender monitoring, and caseload management. Fifty-five to seventy-five percent of all local directors rate one or more of these as a significant need. In addition to training in basic skills, training in handling special problem offenders, stress management, and legal liabilities are also needed by the majority of respondents.

Unlike institutions, probation and parole agencies depend on a supply of community resources to carry out their core responsibilities. Today, over half the local offices report a need to expand or improve all types of community resource efforts, including drug programs, residential programs, housing referral services, vocational education, job readiness training, and mental health services.

Over the last 15 years, probation and parole agencies have expanded their domain from primarily presentence investigations and offender supervision to pretrial diversion, halfway houses, alleviating institutional crowding, and a host of other activities. "Dealing with an increased number and variety of alternative programs in an effective manner" was cited by one director as the most serious management problem over the next few years.

Data submitted by these 388 professionals suggested that not only must this type of growth stop or slow dramatically, but also that serious questions must be raised about the system's present capacity to absorb additional offenders. Large and difficult caseloads coupled with a lack of staff and a shortage of community resources reflect a criminal justice subsystem strained to its limits.

Notes

1. The random sample was drawn from counties with populations greater than 50,000 and less than 200,000.

2. *Juvenile and Adult Correctional Departments, Institutions, Agencies, and Paroling Authorities*, College Park, Maryland, American Correctional Association, 1987.

3. The 1983 National Assessment Survey was conducted for the National Institute of Justice by Abt Associates, Inc., Cambridge, Massachusetts.

NCJ 113768

Life Without Parole: The View From Death Row

Julian H. Wright, Jr.

Julian H. Wright, Jr., Joint Program in Law and Divinity, Vanderbilt University, Nashville, Tenn.; former Editor in Chief, Vanderbilt Law Review.

This article considers the suggestion that capital punishment be replaced with the sanction of LWOP and discusses this proposal from all available perspectives, especially those of the people on death row. The author first covers some of the theoretical and practical problems inherent in applying capital punishment and then briefly describes LWOP. Next, the methodology of a Tennessee survey that included specific questions about LWOP is explained and the results of the survey examined. The author concludes with an analysis of what these views reflect about LWOP and the death row inmates themselves.

Like most Americans, Tennesseans seem to support overwhelmingly the concept of capital punishment in the abstract.[1] Having murderers pay for their crimes with their own lives seems only appropriate to most Tennesseans, especially when those murders were heinous or especially brutal or involved some degree of depravity of mind.[2] Like most states, however, Tennessee flinches when it comes right down to killing someone. Tennessee has not executed anyone since William Tines in 1960.[3] And a case currently before the Supreme Court of Tennessee, *State v. Black*,[4] may throw out the sentences of the eighty-five people currently on Tennessee's death row and force the General Assembly to take another long, hard look at capital punishment in Tennessee.

In *Black*, the defense has challenged Tennessee's death penalty statute as violating the state constitution. Specifically, the sentencing law provides that a jury "shall" sentence a defendant to death if aggravating circumstances in the murder outweigh mitigating circumstances.[5] A rather obscure provision of the Tennessee Constitution, however, provides that a jury "shall have a right to determine the law and the facts, under direction of the court, as in other criminal cases."[6] Essentially, the defense argues that Tennessee's death penalty statute, as worded, impermissibly interferes with the discretion guaranteed a Tennessee jury. The Supreme Court of Tennessee is seriously considering the issue.

Should the court overturn the current death penalty statute, the Tennessee General Assembly would likely move to replace it with an acceptably worded statute as quickly as possible. Even a successful appeal in *Black* will not be the end of capital punishment in Tennessee. What form such a new statute might take, however, remains anyone's guess. On the other hand, even if the Supreme Court of Tennessee affirms Black's conviction, it will not mean that Tennessee's system of capital punishment does not face serious problems. The odds remain in Black's favor that he will not be executed, and he will still have the opportunity to appeal his decision for years in the federal courts.[7]

Tennessee's system of capital punishment, like all U.S. systems that impose the death penalty, has substantial problems that deserve to be evaluated in light of serious alternatives for punishing violent murderers. As former Tennessee Chief Justice Ray L. Brock wrote in an early dissent against Tennessee's current death penalty statute: "Society would be adequately protected from . . . condemned murderer[s] by [their] permanent imprisonment; killing [them] is not necessary." Justice Brock added: "Life imprisonment without parole is an alternative that serves the functions of severely punishing the criminal and permanently protecting the society from the possibility of a repeated offense."[8] The time has come both for Tennessee and all of society to reconsider Justice Brock's suggestion for replacing capital punishment with the sanction of life without parole (LWOP) and to consider this proposal from all available perspectives, even those of the people on death row.

Reprinted from *Criminal Law Bulletin*, Vol. 27, No. 4, July/August 1991, pp. 334-357. *Criminal Law Bulletin*, published by Warren Gorhorn Lamont.

Need for a Death Penalty Alternative

Since the 1976 decision in *Gregg v. Georgia*[9] initiated the modern era of capital punishment in the United States, nearly 4,000 persons have been sentenced to die.[10] Thirty-six states, the federal government, and the U.S. military all authorize capital punishment as the ultimate penalty for especially heinous or diabolical murderers.[11] Recent public opinion polls indicate that 80 percent of Americans support the use of capital punishment against convicted murderers, the highest figure in this century.[12] Yet, both despite and because of this tremendous support for the idea of killing people as a punishment for killing people, U.S. criminal justice systems have executed "only" 143 people since 1976.[13] Approximately 2,400 condemned persons currently languish on U.S. death rows.[14]

A variety of theories explain why the U.S. system of capital punishment so seldom effects an execution. The Ad Hoc Committee on Federal Habeas Corpus in Capital Cases, chaired by former Justice Lewis Powell, identified as the single most important reason the dual system of collateral review of all capital cases in both state and federal courts.[15] Particularly in the federal courts, piecemeal and repetitious litigation drags on for years, resulting in unnecessary delay and frustrating both the retributive and deterrent purposes of capital punishment.[16] The lack of qualified attorneys to handle death penalty cases at every stage of litigation also exacerbates the problem and leads to later, time-consuming habeas corpus proceedings brought under an incompetent-representation-by-counsel rationale.[17]

Such habeas corpus proceedings have a startlingly high success rate in federal courts and often result in a death sentence's being vacated.[18] Paradoxically, the solution to eliminating numerous, costly habeas corpus proceedings and the resultant overturning of death sentences lies not in restricting capital defendants' and inmates' rights to counsel at each stage of capital litigation, but rather in ensuring that they have the best possible counsel at each stage in order to reduce procedural errors and later appeals.[19]

To explain why so relatively few executions take place in the United States despite the death penalty's popular appeal, other critics attack the institution of capital punishment itself on a variety of grounds. Some commentators argue that capital punishment has no deterrent effect.[20] Others find fault with its discriminatory application.[21] Certain scholars maintain that capital punishment brutalizes society, resulting in more violent crimes being committed instead of fewer.[22] Other critics demonstrate the exorbitant financial costs of imposing the death penalty on so relatively few murderers.[23] Others point out the even higher costs of an inherently flawed system of capital punishment that at least occasionally executes an innocent person.[24] Ultimately, the constitutional requirements of due process and judicial review under which the U.S. system of capital punishment must operate and the underlying flaws that plague both capital punishment as an institution and the U.S. system in particular combine to produce a system of capital punishment that "[f]ew would argue . . . is satisfactory."[25] Indeed, many would argue that, despite its widespread popular support, the system is a disgrace.

Alternative of Life Without Parole

Given the realities of a capital punishment system that seldom achieves its ultimate end and the myriad flaws within the system, several jurisdictions have begun to consider alternatives to capital punishment. An alternative to capital punishment that currently receives at least some attention in academic literature and policy debates is the sentence of life imprisonment without the possibility of parole, or LWOP.[26] LWOP is a sentence that generally means exactly that: Inmates so sentenced spend their natural lives behind bars without even being considered for parole. It is the penultimate penalty. LWOP inmates are not killed by the state; they are locked up to live the rest of their lives as punishment in a controlled environment where they are unable to harm society at large.

At least thirty states currently have some form of LWOP in their sentencing schemes to punish the types of murderer each state deems most severe.[27] Some states use LWOP as their sternest punishment for murder, instead of capital punishment.[28] Other states may give sentencers a choice of sentencing options for capital murderers that includes LWOP.[29] In several states, sentencing jurors or judges may choose only between the death penalty and LWOP in the sentencing phase of a bifurcated capital trial.[30] At least one state requires its chief executive to impose LWOP on any murderer sentenced to death to whom the executive grants clemency, even though the LWOP sentence is not an option at trial in the state's capital sentencing scheme.[31] Still other states effectively have LWOP even though the sanction is not in their sentencing statutes because these states' parole laws specifically preclude from parole eligibility any inmates serving regular "life" terms for murder.[32]

Punishment for Crimes Other Than Murder

LWOP is also used as a punishment for crimes other than murder. Several states impose LWOP as the penalty for repeatedly convicted "habitual offenders."[33] Other states and the federal government use LWOP against traffickers in large amounts of narcotics and other drug "kingpins."[34] The most prevalent use of LWOP, however, remains as an option to capital punishment for murderers. And the use of LWOP itself is becoming more prevalent. One study indicates that over 10,000 inmates are serving LWOP in U.S. prisons, although the study does not indicate specifically how many of those inmates are serving the sentence for murder.[35] The figures represent a 21 percent increase from 1988 to 1989 alone.[36]

New York Debate

The debates about the death penalty in general and the use of LWOP, instead of capital punishment, in particular currently rage most bitterly in the State of New York. For several years, the New York legislature has passed legislation authorizing the resumption of capital punishment in the state, only to have Governor Mario Cuomo veto the measure each time.[37] Cuomo favors a LWOP sanction for murderers. The governor maintains that a life behind bars is a tougher penalty than death and refers to LWOP as "death by incarceration."[38] Whatever Cuomo's personal or political reasons for opposing capital punishment and supporting LWOP, his stance could presage future activity in other states. Simply because of New York's size and the magnitude of the publicly perceived problem of violent crime in the state, events in New York will be closely watched by other states wrestling with the problem of how best to respond to violent crime.[39]

From a purely political perspective, Governor Cuomo and other supporters of LWOP appear to be on solid ground. A variety of evidence indicates that a majority of persons in several states, even states that have the death penalty, favor LWOP over death as a means for punishing murderers. In Georgia, the state with the fourth highest total of executions in the country since *Furman v. Georgia*,[40] a Georgia State University poll indicates that 53 percent of Georgians surveyed would vote to abolish the death penalty if state law provided for a murder sentence of LWOP for at least twenty-five years (not even a natural life term), combined with some kind of restitution program.[41] Even in Florida, generally considered the state that can execute virtually any inmate that it desires, 54 percent of persons surveyed by Amnesty International, U.S.A., said that they would be less likely to support capital punishment if assured that dangerous murderers would be imprisoned for life with no chance for parole.[42] Some 58 percent of Nebraskans polled favor the abolition of capital punishment if the alternatives of LWOP for at least twenty-five years and a restitution program are offered.[43] A nationwide Gallup poll demonstrates that support for capital punishment across the United States fell from 72 percent to 55 percent when respondents were told of the alternative of LWOP.[44]

In New York itself, even though polls indicate that at least 72 percent of New Yorkers favor capital punishment, that support is exceptionally soft. When New Yorkers are asked whether they prefer the death penalty or LWOP with any of the incarcerated inmate's potential earnings going to the victim's family, 62 percent favored the latter alternative while only 32 percent favored the death penalty.[45] Some surveys show that, even without the restitution element, a majority of New Yorkers would favor LWOP over capital punishment.[46]

Rationales for Support

There are many reasons for the grass roots popularity of LWOP. Many of them stem from LWOP's contrasts with capital punishment. It is a sure penalty.[47] It is a sanction that incapacitates violent murderers without the moral cost of killing them. It preserves the innocent life that may be prosecuted and punished in an imperfect system of justice and allows for mistakes to be corrected later at a cost of years lost instead of lives. The sanction has its problems as well,[48] but generally, it accurately reflects the disdain that society at large has for the violent taking of human life.

Most importantly, LWOP has been embraced by advocates from across the political spectrum and by professionals throughout U.S. criminal justice systems. More traditionally liberal opponents of capital punishment may support LWOP as a means of sentencing fewer persons to death row.[49] More traditionally conservative adherents of law and order may also support LWOP, used in conjunction with or as an alternative to the death penalty, because of LWOP's sternness and its preferability to a regular life sentence that still allows for parole.[50] Within criminal justice systems, prosecutors favor LWOP because the sentence places violent murderers "in an atmosphere where it limits the persons they can hurt."[51] Defense counsel favor LWOP as a means of keeping clients alive, but many acknowledge concern over the potential psychological cruelty of LWOP.[52] Concern also exists that, in a system that previously only had regular life or death alternatives for capital murders, the insertion of a LWOP alternative will result not in fewer inmates being sentenced to death row, but rather in more inmates who previously would have gotten an eventual chance at parole never getting that opportunity and thus serving longer sentences. Some advocates of LWOP, however, consider this eventuality to be a beneficial fine-tuning of capital sentencing that better allows each punishment to be tailored to fit a particular crime.

No one disputes that the routine of confinement over a forty-, fifty-, even sixty-year period could be physically or psychologically traumatic for LWOP inmates. In this era of prison overcrowding and frequent use of parole, a seven-year sentence is considered "long-term" incarceration.[53] These long-term inmates have their own special needs in terms of health care, programming, recreation, and security. One can only imagine how these special needs will be exacerbated by multiplying the length of incarceration seven, eight, or nine times. Studies of significant numbers of inmates incarcerated for such long times simply are not available.

Numbers of inmates already serving LWOP in various jurisdictions indicate how brutal prison life can be and how devastating an effect it can have over a number of years. As convicted murderer and Alabama LWOP inmate Ted McGinnis states: "All I see every day is hate, confusion, people hanging themselves, lying in bed with one another, raping one another. . . . You have to adjust to keep from going crazy. You just have to accept things."[54] But how much can a person adjust, and for how long? Unlike death row inmates, who face their own unique struggles on death row but are isolated from the rest of prison life,[55] LWOP inmates are not isolated from parolable inmates. LWOP inmates must live with these other inmates and put up with the same and additional pressures without even the anticipation of being released.

Apart from the potential threats of psychological cruelty or insanity, LWOP inmates must also come to terms with growing old behind bars. Most prisons simply are not designed and do not have the programming to cope with increasingly large numbers of elderly inmates. Infirmaries and prison hospitals cannot become old-age wings in penal institutions and still perform their assigned tasks of caring for sick and injured inmates. If LWOP becomes an increasingly common sentence, planners for large correctional departments will have "to begin to think in terms of maximum security convalescent homes."[56]

Concern also exists that such an extended stay behind bars might make LWOP inmates more dangerous prisoners. Some corrections officials worry specifically that inmates may become greater security risks the longer they are in prison and thus pose a threat to other inmates and the prison staffs who must oversee them.[57] Surprisingly, evidence indicates that LWOP inmates commit fewer disciplinary infractions than other inmates and that LWOP inmates may actually be the best-behaved inmates in a prison because they are the most institutionalized.[58] Thus, a number of corrections officials support the use of LWOP.[59] This view is echoed by law-enforcement officers who call for life sentences to be imposed without the possibility of parole.[60] Furthermore, despite these potential concerns, the constitutionality of LWOP has been sanctioned by the United States Supreme Court,[61] and commentators have called for increased use of the sanction as an alternative to capital punishment.[62]

Opinion of Death-Row Inmates

In the ongoing discussions about LWOP, however, the views of at least one group of persons have not been solicited. While a host of inmates serving LWOP have been asked what they think of LWOP, the question has never been asked systematically of death row inmates.[63] Despite the fact that their bleak existence on

death rows across the country stands as probably the most eloquent testimony to the failure of the U.S. system of capital punishment, few, if any, makers or influencers of policy ever have bothered to ask death row inmates about what they would consider effective or just alternatives to capital punishment. The simple truth is that many of these inmates are locked away on death rows precisely because much of society would rather forget about them and what they might have to say.

Methodology of the Survey

As part of a larger project entitled "A Survey of Death Row Inmates' Opinions on Justice and Ministry Needs,"[64] Tennessee's death row inmates were given the opportunity to respond to a question comparing the death penalty and LWOP. Questions on the larger survey included comparisons of different definitions of justice, what the inmates need in living from day to day on death row, and whether death row populations should ever be mixed with regular prison populations. The specific LWOP question asked: "Which would you consider to be the harsher punishment, the death penalty or LWOP?" LWOP was defined for the inmates as "a natural life imprisonment term with no chance of ever being let out on parole." The inmates were also asked to explain why one penalty was worse than the other.

Because only 38 percent of all inmates admitted to Tennessee Department of Corrections institutions in 1989 had a high school diploma or the equivalent, the survey provided answers in a multiple-choice format as well as space for the inmates to explain their choices if they desired.[65] On the LWOP question, inmates could indicate whether (1) LWOP is much worse than death; (2) LWOP is a little worse than death; (3) they had no opinion; (4) death is a little worse than LWOP; or (5) death is much worse than LWOP. The inmates were also informed that their identities would not be disclosed unless they specifically allowed it and that they were free to explain their answers in any way they desired, or not at all.

Cover letters explaining the survey's purpose, how to answer the questions, and how to return the results were attached to each copy of the survey. Tennessee Department of Corrections staff at Riverbend Maximum Security Institution and the Tennessee Prison for Women agreed to distribute the surveys to the seventy-six inmates on death row as of January 12, 1990.[66] The surveys were actually distributed during the week of February 5, 1990. By the end of March 1990, thirteen inmates had completed and returned the surveys. A fourteenth inmate claimed that he did not receive the survey from the Department of Corrections until late March and, because of his illiteracy, requested an oral interview.[67] This inmate completed the survey with the author on April 20, 1990. Representatives of the Department of Corrections maintain that the 18 percent completion rate of the survey is generally higher than figures for participation by death row inmates in most other voluntary activities.[68] Those inmates responding to the survey provide an interesting and representative cross-section of opinions.

Results of the Survey

Of the fourteen inmates responding to the survey, exactly half considered LWOP a worse penalty than death. One inmate considered LWOP a little worse than death, and six inmates felt LWOP to be much worse than capital punishment. Another six inmates maintained that the death penalty is still much worse than LWOP and would have preferred being sentenced to life in any form instead of death. One inmate indicated no opinion on whether one sanction is worse than the other. This inmate based this response on the belief that "the court system is so messed up now they railroad people who haven't did anything wrong like myself. . . . [They] [m]ove you from one institution and add more charges to your case. . . ." The inmate added: "The world is coming to [an] end real soon because of all the low-down people in charge of others. . . . God knows the truth."[69]

Assuming that the debates about capital punishment and LWOP continue into the foreseeable future, the comments of Tennessee's other death row inmates provide valuable insights into the advantages and disadvantages of the two sanctions.

LWOP: A Worse Sanction Than Death

Generally, those seven inmates maintaining that LWOP is a harsher punishment than death seem to agree with Governor Cuomo's assessment that LWOP represents "death by incarceration."[70] An inmate incarcerated for eight years on death row specifically stated that "while a man is in prison he is the same as a dead man."[71] An inmate incarcerated there for five years argued that, at least on death row, he was able to maintain a part of his human qualities as he battled against his sentence. With little left to lose, he perceived himself as being in a struggle in which he at least could take sides and form his own opinion. He maintained that LWOP would be an even worse sentence than death precisely because LWOP would be a total denial of freedom, a denial even of his struggle to maintain life.[72]

Some commentators embrace LWOP specifically because they favor a harsh penalty that does not let a murderer off as "easily" as a quick death in the gas chamber or electric chair. One commentator, for example, calls for the fifty state governments to reinvent Dante's *Inferno* in the form of a "giant maximum-security prison in the desert."[73] Murderers would be

sent there to face a hopeless, barren existence, languishing and forgotten by all Americans.[74] The commentator has no problem with inflicting suffering on murderers; the commentator just does not want himself or his society to be guilty of the exact crime for which the murderer is punished. As he puts it: "Ted Bundy is dead. Would that he were sitting in an empty cell contemplating his crimes for the next 40 years."[75]

Doubtless, many more Americans reflect the two sides of this opinion, specifically that dying is too easy for some particularly vile murderers and that murderers should be punished harshly but not with a cost measured by the amount of blood on society's own hands. At least two of Tennessee's death row inmates echo these sentiments. An inmate incarcerated for nine years considers LWOP worse than death because "the person must live with his guilt and be separated from his loved ones. The death penalty only ends the offender's suffering!"[76] A seven-year veteran of death row maintains that "when you *know* that you would never be with your family and friend again that's worse than death. Why death is only a few seconds away. Life without parole is longer and more painful."[77] Some current supporters of capital punishment might embrace LWOP specifically because it is longer and more painful as a purely retributive punishment, but imposing it need not occasion pangs of hypocritical conscience.

Harshness as a Rehabilitative Factor

At least one inmate, drawing on thirteen years of experience on death row, agrees that LWOP is "worse" than death because it is harsher but believes this harshness can also be effective in beginning a process of rehabilitation for convicted murderers. As the inmate writes:

> *Real* change comes from within! When a person is removed from society, then they can be free to see themselves & society clearer. For a person to be locked in a cell for the rest of there [sic] life . . . knowing that there is a world of life going on and they can never be part of it again. . . . THAT'S PUNISHMENT! When enough time has passed, (it will be different for each person) they will see that they have no one to blame for being where they are except themselves. Then change has a chance to *come about*![78]

Although perhaps not as eloquently, the Supreme Court of New Hampshire issued essentially the same opinion in *State v. Farrow*.[79] In a widely cited decision, the court upheld the state constitutionality of New Hampshire's LWOP statute on a variety of well-reasoned grounds.[80] The defendants attempted to argue that LWOP would reduce them to "caged animals," without a reason to reform, to "the lowest level of existence," and doom them to "the dismal spectre of gradual annihilation" and the "ultimate degradation unsurpassed in enormity."[81] The court, however, found that the defendants had the hope of increased privileges within prison, the opportunity for vocational and educational training, and the chance for executive pardon or commutation, should their behavior improve to a remarkable degree.[82] Instead of a doomed existence on death row, the defendants had the still bleak but preferable opportunity to live and to change in prison.

This view of LWOP harshness stresses that its severity, along with the passage of time, results in the possibility of change and rehabilitation in an inmate. Should such rehabilitation not occur, the inmate remains securely locked away. Because of the possibility of real change, however, and an executive pardon or commutation, LWOP need not always mean a natural life behind bars.[83] Ultimately, the sanction remains harsh. Whether this harshness is viewed from the perspective of providing more effective retribution or a meaningful spur to rehabilitation, at least some inmates staring directly at the alternative of death view LWOP as being even worse.

Death Penalty: Worse Than LWOP

The views of the 43 percent of the inmates who feel that death is worse than LWOP mirror the arguments made by many of capital punishment's opponents. For example, critics from George Bernard Shaw to Henry Schwarzchild have argued that it makes little sense to punish people for killing people by killing even more people. Shaw condemned capital punishment as "the worse form of assassination because it is invested with the approval of society. Murder and capital punishment are not opposites which cancel one another—but similar."[84] In testimony before Congress, Schwarzchild stated:

> What does the death penalty, after all, say to the American people and to our children? That killing is all right if the right people do it and think they have a good enough reason for doing it! That is the rationale of every pathological murderer walking the street: he thinks he is the right person to do it. . . . How can a thoughtful and sensible person justify killing people to teach that killing is wrong?[85]

An inmate incarcerated for eight years on death row simply states that "if you kill for killing you are only perpetuating the same wrong."[86]

The Futility-of-Death Factor

Commentators also have noted that death is different from other punishments because of its sheer finality. If a mistake is made and an innocent person executed, no remedy exists to right the wrong. As Anthony G. Amsterdam states: "[C]apital punishment not merely kills people, it also kills some of them in error, and these are errors which we never can correct."[87] As an eight-year death row inmate puts it: "[Death] is final, there is always the hope of legal relief

in life (the pendulum swaying back to a liberal way) or maybe a chance to climb a fence."[88] A five-year inmate writes:

> Death is irrevocable, and there is to[o] much of a chance with our system of sending an innocent man to his death. It has happened. If he is given a life without parole at least he has that time to continue to try to correct the wrong done him, but once you execute him there is no chance of that even if he is . . . later proven to be innocent.[89]

This same inmate also maintains that LWOP would be more of a deterrent than capital punishment. He acknowledges: "I may be wrong, but the men I have talked to would think about that [LWOP] more than the death penalty. No one wants to die but at the same time we seldom think we will anytime soon."[90] A variety of commentators have observed that the death penalty often fails to deter murderers because murderers generally kill during moments of great emotional stress, when they are in fear or under the influence of alcohol or drugs, and when logical thinking has been suspended.[91] In clear cases of cold premeditation, no severity of punishment could be expected to deter an individual who plans out a murder for the express purpose of not being caught, convicted, or punished.[92] The inmate's evidence for his claim is purely anecdotal, but his statement that no one wants to die but that we seldom think we will strikes close to a fundamental truth. How many people, in whatever situation, actually think that their actions will result in their own deaths? And if most of the death row inmates surveyed, who obviously were not deterred from committing murder by the threat of capital punishment, maintain that LWOP is a worse sanction than death, does it not stand to reason that the penalty that is perceived as being the harshest will have been the greatest deterrent effect, whatever that effect might be?

Degradation of the Inmate

Former Justice Arthur Goldberg argues that "[t]he deliberate, institutionalized taking of human life by the state is the greatest conceivable degradation to the dignity of the human personality."[93] An inmate incarcerated for four years on death row describes the degradation in different terms. This inmate considers the death penalty worse than LWOP "because the accused isn't the only one to suffer; his family does too . . . were as [sic] the victim's family only pained for a short time. But the accused has to '*live*' with people *planning* his death, and setting dates to tell him *when* he's dying."[94] One certainly could debate the assumption that victims' families only suffer a "short time," but one cannot deny that death row inmates' families also suffer through the agonizingly slow process of watching the system grind toward a loved one's execution.[95] This inmate also demonstrates the inherent cruelty in the U.S. system of capital punishment of not only killing an inmate, but of making the inmate wait for years on death row contemplating his eventual fate. [96] Many of capital punishment's supposed advantages accrue only when the punishment is carried out swiftly and surely. Given the current U.S. constitutional system, the death penalty is never carried out in such a fashion. [97]

Professor Jack Greenberg sums up a career of opposition to capital punishment by debunking any supposed moral or practical advantages that U.S. systems of justice and government gain by implementing the death penalty. He states that, in terms of using death as a penalty for killing, "the moral force of any retribution argument is radically undercut by the hard facts of the actual American system of capital punishment," principally that it is haphazard, regionally and racially biased, and not used often enough to achieve its own moral aims. [98] Because of the moral costs of the death penalty and the killing that it only perpetuates, the United Nations has also affirmed resolutions about the desirability of abolishing capital punishment, and virtually all of the civilized countries in the world have already abolished the sanction. [99]

How the United States Ranks

Remarkably, in an era of expanding global liberty, the United States places itself in the company of nations such as Chile, China, Iran, and South Africa by continuing to embrace the use of capital punishment. [100] An inmate incarcerated for nine years on death row maintains that death is a much worse punishment than LWOP and castigates governments for their shortsightedness in imposing capital punishment. He states:

> I avoid, however, associating death with punishment. When someone is put to death, all the entity is doing is displaying gigantic ignorance [sic], idiotcy [sic], stupidity. And that same ignorance, idiotcy, stupidity will show up in other areas of the entity. In short, I think it (Death penalty) weakens an entity (government). [101]

As Americans struggle with the problem of violent crime and how best to respond to it, they should remember that all responses exact a cost. For Tennessee death row inmates, this cost is measured in terms of their lives. For all Americans, however, the toll of continuing to implement any system of capital punishment is measured not only in terms of lives, court costs, and dollars, but also in terms of the message that it sends about what our system of justice should accomplish. Americans also lose opportunity costs by relying too easily on capital punishment to solve problems of violent crime, instead of pursuing the real roots and causes of crime and working to alleviate them.

One ten-year veteran of death row maintains that he and his colleagues could be part of a larger solution if sentenced to LWOP, instead of the harsher penalty of death. [102] LWOP sentences would allow for these inmates to progress through certain levels of behavior and self-discipline in prison, and once a certain level was attained, "we [LWOP inmates] could actually talk to kids in schools who were going bad. Talking to them. Telling them about our mistakes. That's the key to success."[103] Instead of reacting in a knee-jerk way to violent crime after it happens, U.S. criminal justice systems should explore more preventive measures, and LWOP inmates who have sufficiently turned their lives around behind bars could be a valuable preventive resource.

A variety of reasons exists for acknowledging that LWOP need not be as harsh a penalty as death. Many of these reasons parallel the arguments about why the U.S. system of capital punishment functions so poorly. To a remarkable degree, the statements of those death row inmates who still consider death a worse punishment than LWOP echo the arguments made by numerous commentators for abolishing capital punishment.

Conclusion

Although faced with the ultimate penalty, exactly half (and the largest number of Tennessee death row inmates surveyed) consider the penultimate penalty of LWOP a worse alternative. One might argue that these inmates have a vested interest in convincing others that a penalty that preserves life is a harsher punishment than death. Such a cynical argument, however, credits these generally uneducated inmates with the construction of a sophisticated theory of reverse psychology. The survey results do not indicate any more or any less than the fact that many, even half, of the inmates sentenced to death believe it would be worse to live out the rest of their natural lives behind bars than to have the state prematurely end their lives for them.

The argument that death row inmates could be expected to espouse LWOP as being harsher than capital punishment because such a position somehow advances their interests also ignores the reality of these inmates' situations. First, they have precious little, if any, interest to be advanced. They are sentenced to die, and no answer that they circle on a graduate student's survey can be expected to alter their fate. Even if Tennessee should pass a LWOP statute at any point in the future, the law need not apply retroactively to these inmates. Granted, if a death row inmate preferred retaining life in any form to dying, then such an inmate would want a chance to be resentenced or commuted to a sentence of LWOP. Anonymously filling out a survey, however, will not advance this interest directly, and Tennessee's death row inmates have little motivation for dishonesty.

Second, by maintaining that LWOP is a *harsher* sentence than death, the seven death row inmates who responded in this way implicitly assert that they would *rather* be put to death than languish behind bars for thirty, forty, or fifty years. The six inmates who responded that death is still a harsher sanction than LWOP are the individuals who would prefer being kept alive. They affirm death as the worst alternative and actively seek to live. If the seven inmates who implicitly stated that they prefer imminent death to LWOP are attempting some sort of reverse psychological ploy, why are not the other six who clearly would prefer life trying the same ploy? Little can be gained by overanalyzing data that, in the first place, is not particularly scientific. Given the fairly even split and range of responses, it seems more reasonable to accept the statements of the inmates at face value. These statements indicate that many death row inmates would embrace their fate in the gas chamber or electric chair rather than be kept alive behind bars for the rest of their natural lives, thus coming to terms with their crimes, and perhaps eventually serving a useful purpose.

If the purpose of capital punishment is to punish murderers as severely as possible, it makes little sense to kill them when they are more apprehensive of "death by incarceration."[104] The U.S. institution of capital punishment suffers from a variety of problems. Limitations, errors, and prejudices plague its application. Supporters of the death penalty, however, have always been able to take a grim satisfaction in each execution that has taken place.[105] Every murderer that dies at least is a murderer punished, and would-be murderers can recognize that such a fate might eventually befall them. The survey results, however, indicate that executed murderers are not punished in the way that murderers and would-be murderers would consider most severe. Granted, when compared to LWOP, the death penalty's alleged swiftness might satisfy a crowd's immediate thirst for violence and vengeance, but it does not punish the murderer as harshly as other murderers claim LWOP would.

Finally, the breakdown of what death row inmates think about LWOP fairly mirrors what society at large thinks of the sanction. Even the inmate's statements, both for and against LWOP, reflect the same general arguments advanced by various commentators in the nonprison population. For persons working with death row inmates, the fact that the views from death row parallel the views of society at large comes as no surprise. For most of the United States, however, the feeling runs deep that somehow death row inmates are fundamentally different than the rest of "us." "They" are dangerous, flawed, and expendable. "They" can be killed precisely because "they" are so different they do not deserve even to live in a cage. Granted, death row inmates are different. Courts have found that they

have killed with premeditation and violence. Those crimes, however, need not make them so different that they do not deserve to live. For better or, more accurately, for worse, those inmates are part of our society with opinions, thoughts, and feelings that mirror everyone else's. How the rest of our society treats them indicates much about the value our society places on human life.

FOOTNOTES

1. See, e.g., "Grand Jury Supports Death Penalty," Nashville Tennessean, Sept. 4, 1989, at 1B, col. 3. Generally, 80 percent of all Americans favor capital punishment for murderers. See text accompanying note 12 *infra*.
2. See Williams, "State Justices to Wrestle With Death Penalty," Nashville Tennessean, Feb. 24, 1991, at 10 (remarks of Johnson City, Tenn., prosecutor David E. Crockett that "the only appropriate punishment is that the person should forfeit his life for that crime").
3. *Id.*; see also State v. Bomer, 205 Tenn. 572, 329 S.W.2d 813 (1959) (quashing Tines's final writ of habeas corpus); Tines v. State, 203 Tenn. 612, 315 S.W.2d 111 (1958) (upholding Tines's conviction for rape and sentence of death). Note that current death penalty statutes, including Tennessee's, apply only to first-degree or capital murders and that, today, William Tines would not get the death penalty for committing rape.
4. State v. Black, Davidson County Crim. Appeal No. 01-S-01-9002-CR-00007.
5. Tenn. Code Ann. § 39-2-203(g) (1982) (stating that "[i]f the jury unanimously determines that at least one statutory aggravating circumstance or several statutory aggravating circumstances have been proved by the state beyond reasonable doubt, and said circumstance or circumstances, are not outweighed by any mitigating circumstances, the sentence shall be death").
6. Tenn. Const. art. I, § 19.
7. Of the 3,778 people sentenced to die across the United States since 1976, only 143 have been executed. NAACP Legal Defense and Education Fund, Inc., *Death Row, U.S.A.* 1 (Jan. 21, 1991) (hereinafter *Death Row, U.S.A.*). In addition, 1,078 people have had their convictions or sentences reversed, 62 have had their sentences commuted, 30 have committed suicide, and 53 have died of other causes while awaiting execution. *Id.* The odds of a fate other than Tennessee's electric chair are in Black's favor. For more on Black's opportunities to appeal through the federal court system, see text accompanying notes 15–19 *infra*.
8. State v. Dicks, 615 S.W.2d 126, 138, 139 (Tenn. 1981) (Brock, C. J., dissenting).
9. 428 U.S. 153 (1976). *Gregg* and its companion cases—Roberts v. Louisiana, 428 U.S. 325 (1976); Woodson v. North Carolina, 428 U.S. 280 (1976); Jurek v. Texas, 428 U.S. 262 (1976); and Proffitt v. Florida, 428 U.S. 242 (1976)—definitively upheld the notion that capital punishment could be administered in ways that were not cruel and unusual in their capriciousness.
10. *Death Row, U.S.A.,* note 7 *supra* (3,778 persons sentenced to die).
11. *Id.*
12. See Malcolm, "Capital Punishment Is Popular, But So Are Its Alternatives," N.Y. Times, Sept. 10, 1989, at E4, col. 1 (citing a 1989 Gallup poll).
13. *Death Row, U.S.A.,* note 7 *supra.*
14. *Id.*
15. See Judicial Conference of the United States, Ad Hoc Committee on Federal Habeas Corpus in Capital Cases, *Committee Report and Proposal* 1–2 (1989) (hereinafter *Powell Committee Report*), *reprinted in* "Report on Habeas Corpus in Capital Cases," 45 Crime. L. Rep. (BNA) 3239 (1989) (hereinafter "Report on Habeas Corpus").
16. *Powell Committee Report*, note 15 *supra*, at 2, *reprinted in* "Report on Habeas Corpus," note 15 *supra*, at 3239.
17. See *Powell Committee Report*, note 15 *supra*, at 3–4, *reprinted in* "Report on Habeas Corpus," note 15 *supra*, at 3240. See also

6. PUNISHMENT AND CORRECTIONS

Berger, "The Supreme Court and Defense Counsel: Old Roads, New Paths—A Dead End?" 86 Colum. L. Rev. 9 (1986); Mounts & Wilson, "Systems for Providing Indigent Defense: An Introduction," 14 N.Y.U. Rev. L. & Soc. Change 193 (1986); and Mikva & Godbold, "You Don't Have to Be a Bleeding Heart," 14 Hum. Rts. 22 (1987). See generally Lardent & Cohen, "The Last Best Hope: Representing Death Row Inmates," 23 Loy. L.A. L. Rev. 213 (1989). Even when adequate numbers of lawyers are provided in capital cases, no guarantee exists that the lawyers will have the skills and experience needed to defend life in the ultimate trial. See Herron, "Defending Life in Tennessee Death Penalty Cases," 51 Tenn. L. Rev. 681 (1984); Goodpaster, "The Trial for Life: Effective Assistance of Counsel in Death Penalty Cases," 58 N.Y.U.L. Rev. 299 (1983). See generally American Bar Association, *American Bar Association Guidelines for the Appointment and Performance of Counsel in Death Penalty Cases* (1989).

18. Mello, "Facing Death Alone: The Post-Conviction Attorney Crisis on Death Row," 37 Am. U.L. Rev. 513, 520–521 (1988) (estimating that the success rate from 1976–1986 in federal capital habeas proceedings was between 60–70 percent).

19. See Coyle, Strasser & Lavelle, "Fatal Defense," Natl L.J., June 11, 1990, at 33–40; Recent Development, "Meaningful Access for Indigents on Death Row: *Giarratano v. Murray* and the Right to Counsel in Post-Conviction Proceedings," 43 Vand. L. Rev. 569, 590–591 (1990).

20. See, e.g., Fox & Radelet, "Persistent Flaws in Econometric Studies of the Deterrent Effect of the Death Penalty," 23 Loy. L.A.L. Rev. 29 (1989); Carrington, "Deterrence, Death, and the Victims of Crime: A Common Sense Approach," 35 Vand. L. Rev. 587, 594–599 (1982).

21. See, e.g., Baldus, Woodworth & Pulaski, "Arbitrariness and Discrimination in the Administration of the Death Penalty," 15 Stetson L. Rev. 133 (1986); Gross & Mauro, "Patterns of Death: An Analysis of Racial Disparities in Capital Sentencing," 37 Stan. L. Rev. 27 (1984). But see McCleskey v. Kemp, 481 U.S. 279 (1987) (even assuming the death penalty was imposed disproportionately on blacks and other minority groups, such imposition was effectively harmless error).

22. See, e.g., W. Bowers, *Legal Homicide: Death as Punishment in America, 1864–1972*, at 271–336 (1984).

23. See Spangenberg & Walsh, "Capital Punishment or Life Imprisonment? Some Cost Considerations," 23 Loy. L.A.L. Rev. 45 (1989); Comment, "The Cost of Taking a Life: Dollars and Sense of the Death Penalty," 18 U.C. Davis L. Rev. 1221 (1985); Von Drehle, "Bottom Line: Life in Prison One Sixth as Expensive," Miami Herald, July 10, 1988, at 12A, col. 1.

24. See Bedau & Radelet, "Miscarriages of Justice in Potentially Capital Cases," 40 Stan. L. Rev. 21 (1987); Bedau & Radelet, "The Myth of Infallibility: A Reply to Markman and Cassell," 41 Stan. L. Rev. 161 (1988); Giarratano, " 'To the Best of Our Knowledge, We Have Never Been Wrong': Fallibility v. Finality in Capital Punishment," 100 Yale L.J. 1005 (1991) (authored by a former Virginia death row inmate who recently had his sentence commuted).

25. *Powell Committee Report*, note 15 *supra*, at 3, *reprinted in* "Report on Habeas Corpus," note 15 *supra*, at 3239. For a comprehensive treatment of the problems of imposing capital punishment in America, see Tabak & Lane, "The Execution of Injustice: A Cost and Lack-of-Benefit Analysis of the Death Penalty," 23 Loy. L.A.L. Rev. 59 (1989).

26. See Cheatwood, "The Life-Without-Parole Sanction: Its Current Status and a Research Agenda," 34 Crime & Delinq. 43 (1988); Stewart & Lieberman, "What Is This New Sentence That Takes Away Parole?" 11 Student Law. 14 (1982); Note, "Life-Without-Parole: An Alternative to Death or Not Much of a Life at All?" 43 Vand. L. Rev. 529 (1990).

27. See Note, note 26 *supra*, at 540–547.

28. See, e.g., R.I. Gen. Laws § 11-23-2 (1978) (establishing that first-degree murder in Rhode Island will be punished by life imprisonment and that the sentencer may decide if such penalty will be with or without parole); Haw. Rev. Stat. § 706-656(2) (1980) (establishing that all of Hawaii's most severe murderers will be punished with a mandatory LWOP sentence).

29. See, e.g., Md. Ann. Code art. 27, § 412(6) (1987) (authorizing the three sentencing options of death, LWOP, or regular life for capital murders in Maryland); Ala. Code § 13A-5-46(e) (1975)

(authorizing the two sentencing options of death or LWOP for capital murders in Alabama).

30. See, e.g., Ark. Stat. Ann. § 5-4-601(b) (1) (1981).

31. See S.C. Const. art. IV, § 14; S.C. Code Ann. § 16-3-20(A) (Law. Co-op. 1983).

32. See, e.g., Wyo. Stat. §§ 6-2-101(b), 7-13-402(a) (1988). Sentencing schemes such as Wyoming's raise serious questions about what a juror may or may not know about a state's parole law in deciding whether to impose death or a sentence of life imprisonment that still provides for parole. See Paduano & Smith, "Deathly Errors: Juror Misperceptions Concerning Parole in the Imposition of the Death Penalty," 18 Colum. Hum. Rts. L. Rev. 211 (1987); Note, "The Meaning of 'Life' for Virginia Jurors and Its Effect on Reliability in Capital Sentencing," 75 Va. L. Rev. 1605 (1989).

33. See, e.g., Ala. Code § 13A-5-9 (1975) (Alabama's Habitual Offender Act). See also Cheatwood, note 26 *supra*, at 48.

34. See, e.g., Ala. Code § 13A-12-231 (Supp. 1989); 21 U.S.C. § 848 (1982) (providing that a conviction for continuing criminal enterprise in narcotics will be punished with a term of imprisonment up to life without probation being granted or parole laws being applied). See also United States v. Gonzalez, 922 F.2d 1044 (2d Cir. 1991); United States v. Levy, 904 F.2d 1026 (6th Cir. 1990) (both cases applying the federal statute).

Michigan currently imposes a LWOP sentence on even a first-time offender for possessing cocaine in an amount over 650 grams. Mich. Comp. Laws Ann. §§ 333.7401(2)(a)(i)-333.7401(2)(a)(ii) (West Supp. 1990). The Court of Appeals of Michigan has affirmed this severe sentence (People v. Harmelin, 176 Mich. App. 524, 440 N.W.2d 75 (1989)), although the United States Supreme Court is currently considering an appeal of the sentence on proportionality grounds. Harmelin v. Michigan, 110 S. Ct. 2559 (1990).

35. See Medland & Fischer, "Life Without Parole Offered as Alternative to Death Penalty," Crim. Just. Newsl., Jan. 16, 1990, at 4–5 (quoting a study by the Criminal Justice Institute of South Salem, New York).

36. *Id.* at 5.

37. See Cuomo, "Vetoing the Death Penalty," in 9 Hospitality at 3, 5 (1990) (text of the speech delivered by Governor Mario Cuomo on March 20, 1989, vetoing death penalty legislation in New York), *reprinted from* 46 Lifelines at 4 (July–Dec. 1989) (the newsletter of the National Coalition to Abolish the Death Penalty); Kolbert, "As Vote on Death Penalty Nears, Cuomo Advocates Life Sentences," N.Y. Times, June 19, 1989, at B10, col. 1. See also Kramer, "The Political Interest: Cuomo, the Last Holdout," Time, April 2, 1990, at 20.

38. See Medland & Fischer, note 35 *supra*, at 5 (quoting Governor Mario Cuomo).

39. As former Justice Arthur J. Goldberg has stated, opponents of capital punishment must now look to Congress, state legislatures, state courts, and governors for relief from and alternatives to capital punishment. See Goldberg, "Introduction to the Death Penalty Approaches the 1990s: Where Are We Now?" 23 Loy. L.A.L. Rev. 1, 3 (1989) (symposium issue). Tennessee is an example of a state that does not have LWOP for capital murderers but may be considering its adoption in the future. See text accompanying notes 1–8 *supra*. For more information on alternative strategies for battling capital punishment, see Acker & Walsh, "Challenging the Death Penalty Under State Constitutions," 42 Vand. L. Rev. 1299, 1300–1302 (1989).

40. 408 U.S. 238 (1972) (capricious imposition of death penalty amounted to cruel and unusual punishment).

41. R. Thomas & J. Hutcheson, Center for Public and Urban Research, College of Public and Urban Affairs, Georgia State University, *Georgia Residents' Attitudes Toward the Death Penalty, the Disposition of Juvenile Offenders, and Related Issues* 24–25 (Dec. 1986) (prepared for the Clearinghouse on Georgia Prisons and Jails). See also *Death Row, U.S.A.*, note 7 *supra*, at 3, 18 (14 executions have occurred since 1973, and 112 persons are on death row in Georgia).

42. Cambridge Survey Research, *An Analysis of Attitudes Toward Capital Punishment in Florida* 18 (June 1985) (a public opinion survey prepared for Amnesty International).

43. Bureau of Sociological Research at the University of Nebraska—Lincoln, *The Nebraska Annual Social Indicators Survey* (Jan. 1981) (prepared by David R. Johnson and Alan Booth).

44. Gallup Reports 244, 245, Jan./Feb. 1986, at 10–16.

45. See Tabak & Lane, note 25 *supra*, at 127–129.

46. *Id.*; see also Milligan & McCoy, "Life-Without-Parole Favored," N.Y. Daily News, May 23, 1989, at 15, col. 1; Gallagher, "Death or Life Without Parole?" Gannett Westchester Newspapers, June 25, 1989, at A1, col. 4.

47. See Note, note 26 *supra*, at 556–557.

48. These problems include what amounts to a lack of knowledge of the long-term effects of the sentence and what extensive use of LWOP might mean for prison overcrowding, prison discipline, and the need for more facilities for elderly inmates. See *id.* at 559–565. See also text accompanying notes 53–57 *infra*.

49. See, e.g., Lieberman & Stewart, "Life Without Parole Successful in 19 Other States," Atlanta Const., Feb. 15, 1982, at 7A, col. 7 (quoting Laughlin McDonald, Director, Southeastern Regional Office, American Civil Liberties Union).

50. See, e.g., Stewart & Lieberman, note 26 *supra*, at 16 (remarks of Assistant Alabama Attorney General Ed Carnes).

51. *Id.* at 17 (quoting Nevada Deputy Attorney General John Meyer).

52. See Note, note 26 *supra*, at 553 n. 157 & 557–558.

53. See, e.g., Wilson & Vito, "Long-Term Inmates: Special Needs and Management Considerations," Fed. Probation, Sept. 1988, at 21.

54. See Note, note 26 *supra*, at 550 n. 140 (quote from a Birmingham Post-Herald newspaper interview).

55. See, e.g., Abu-Jamal, "Teetering on the Brink: Between Death and Life," 100 Yale L.J. 993 (1991) (written by a Pennsylvania death row inmate describing life on death row).

56. Cheatwood, note 26 *supra*, at 55. Some of these potential problems with LWOP can be eliminated by adequate planning and the use of executive clemency and commutation powers. Virtually all jurisdictions that have LWOP provide for executive clemency and commutation, thus giving even an LWOP inmate a potential mechanism for release. *Id.* at 48–50. Pardons and commutations can either be a "safety release" mechanism in dire situations or a potential "carrot" to hold out to LWOP inmates to encourage them to behave. See text accompanying note 83 *infra*.

57. See, e.g., Stewart & Lieberman, note 26 *supra*, at 39 (remarks of Anthony Travisono, Executive Director, American Correctional Association); Note, note 26 *supra*, at 553 n. 159.

58. See Note, note 26 *supra*, at 549–550, 564–565.

59. See, e.g., Stewart & Lieberman, note 26 *supra*, at 16–17 (remarks of Jerry Springborn, Clinical Services Supervisor, Illinois Department of Corrections).

60. See Milligan & Beneson, "Lawmen Call for No Parole," N.Y. Daily News, June 24, 1989, at 5, col. 1.

61. See Schick v. Reed, 419 U.S. 256 (1974); Note, note 26 *supra*, at 534–535.

62. See, e.g., Brill, "Throw Away the Key," Am. Law., July-Aug. 1987, at 3; Snellenburg, "Is There a Reasonable Alternative to the Death Penalty?" 71 Judicature 5 (1987) (calling for LWOP, with the first five years of each sentence spent in solitary confinement, as an alternative to capital punishment).

63. Generally, LWOP inmates vehemently disapprove of their sentences. See, e.g., "Inmate Keeps His Store of Hope Alive," Birmingham Post-Herald, Jan. 21, 1983, at 1B, col. 4 (telling the story of Alabama LWOP inmate Ted McGinnis); Medland & Fischer, note 36 *supra*, at 5 (quoting Louisiana inmate Wilbert Rideau).

64. See J. H. Wright, Jr., A Survey of Death Row Inmates' Opinions on Justice and Ministry Needs (1990) (unpublished manuscript on file with the author) (hereinafter Death Row Survey Results). All of the surveys completed by the inmates are on file with the author and are cited as Death Row Survey Results. All quotes attributed to the inmates come from the surveys and are presented in unedited form.

65. See Death Row Survey Results, note 64 *supra*, App. A, at 4 (a copy of the original survey). See also Letter from Susan C. Mattson to Julian H. Wright, Jr. (Dec. 8, 1989) (discussing survey proposal).

66. See Tennessee Department of Corrections, Totals—Death Row Inmates (Jan. 12, 1990) (unpublished document) (available from the Tennessee Department of Corrections and on file with the author). Both Riverbend and the Prison for Women are located in Nashville, Tenn.

67. Letter from Gerald Laney to Julian H. Wright, Jr. (Mar. 7, 1990) (discussing request for an oral interview at the Riverbend facility). See also State v. Laney, 654 S.W.2d 383 (Tenn. 1983).

68. Telephone interview with Susan C. Mattson, Director, Planning and Research, Tennessee Department of Corrections (Mar. 15, 1990).

69. See Death Row Survey Results, note 64 *supra*.

70. See text accompanying note 38 *supra*.

71. See Death Row Survey Results, note 64 *supra*.

72. *Id.*

73. Cohen, "Politicians, Voters and Voltage," Time, Feb. 13, 1989, at 96.

74. *Id.*

75. *Id.*

76. See Death Row Survey Results, note 64 *supra*.

77. *Id.*

78. *Id.*

79. 118 N.H. 296, 386 A.2d 808 (1978).

80. *Id.* at 301–307, 386 A.2d at 811–815.

81. *Id.* at 303, 386 A.2d at 813.

82. *Id.* at 304, 386 A.2d at 813.

83. The federal government and forty-six states allow the chief executive to commute LWOP sentences to provide potentially for inmates to be released on parole. Martin, "Commutation of Prison Sentences: Practice, Promise, and Limitations," 29 Crime & Delinq. 593, 597 (1983). South Carolina and Alabama provide only limited powers for their executives to commute death sentences, and Vermont and Rhode Island do not provide for any means of commutation. *Id.* Normally, commutation is an option that can always be held out to LWOP inmates, and it provides a release mechanism in crises or special situations. Some states mention commutation specifically in their LWOP statutes. See, e.g., Iowa Code Ann. § 902.1 (West 1979); Wash. Rev. Code Ann. § 10.95.030(1) (Supp. 1989). Thus, even LWOP need not mean a life behind bars if an executive intervenes, although the executive can be forbidden constitutionally from intervening. See generally Note, note 26 *supra*, at 550 n. 141 & 562.

84. E. B. Block, *And God Have Mercy* 165 (1962).

85. Schwarzchild, "In Opposition to Death Penalty Legislation," in H. Bedau, *The Death Penalty in America* 364, 369–370 (3d ed. 1982) (taken from excerpts from the July 19, 1978, Hearing on H.R. 133660, Sentencing in Capital Cases, before the Subcomm. on Criminal Justice of the House Comm. on the Judiciary, 95th Cong., 2d Sess. (1978)).

86. See Death Row Survey Results, note 64 *supra*.

87. Amsterdam, "Capital Punishment," in H. Bedau, note 85 *supra*, at 346, 349.

88. See Death Row Survey Results, note 64 *supra*. A variety of inmates sentenced to LWOP have threatened escape attempts, but generally, such threats are never carried out. See, e.g., Note, note 26 *supra*, at 529 nn. 1–3.

89. See Death Row Survey Results, note 64 *supra*.

90. *Id.*

91. See, e.g., Bedau, "The Case Against the Death Penalty," in P. Jerslid & D. Johnson, *Moral Issues and Christian Response* at 280, 281 (4th ed. 1988).

92. *Id.*

93. *Id.* at 286.

94. See Death Row Survey Results, note 64 *supra*.

95. See generally S. Dicks, *Death Row: Interviews With Inmates, Their Families and Opponents of Capital Punishment* (1990). See also Amnesty International, U.S.A., *The Death Penalty* 171–172 (1987).

96. See, e.g., Amnesty International, U.S.A., note 95 *supra*, at 108–109. Albert Camus once observed that, for capital punishment truly to be a fate for the murderer equal to that of the victim, "the death penalty would have to punish a criminal who had warned his victim of the date at which he would inflict a horrible death on him and who, until the moment murdered, had confined him at his mercy for months. Such a monster is not encountered in private life." See A. Camus, "Reflections on the Guillotine," in *Resistance, Rebellion and Death* (1960).

97. See, e.g., Greenberg, "Against the American System of Capital Punishment," 99 Harv. L. Rev. 1670, 1670–1678 (1986).

98. *Id.* at 1677.

99. See U.N. ECOSOC Supp. (No. 1) at 36, Official Records 58th Sess. (1971), reaffirmed in 1977 by the General Assembly.

100. See Amnesty International, U.S.A., note 95 *supra,* at 228–229.

101. See Death Row Survey Results, note 64 *supra.*

102. *Id.*

103. *Id.* Death row inmate Gerald Laney suggested that "trying to keep other kids from making my mistakes is about all I can hope to do." Interview with Gerald Laney, Tennessee Death Row Inmate (Apr. 20, 1990). See text accompanying note 67 *supra.* Many critics might scoff at the idea of LWOP inmates being effective anticrime spokespersons, but one of LWOP's distinct advantages over capital punishment is that it allows for possibilities of rehabilitation, growth, and change by inmates. Their stories and experiences could be quite compelling.

104. See text accompanying note 38 *supra.*

105. Some supporters of capital punishment display more than grim satisfaction when executions are carried out. For example, when the State of North Carolina electrocuted Velma Barfield in 1984, a mob of death penalty supporters gathered outside the penitentiary to celebrate and chant: "Kill the bitch! Kill the bitch!" on the night of her execution. See Ingle, "Final Hours: The Execution of Velma Barfield," 23 Loy. L.A.L. Rev. 221, 236 (1989). See generally J. Ingle, *Last Rights: Thirteen Fatal Encounters With The State's Justice* (1990).

US: World's Lock-'Em-Up Leader

Crime statistics and strict sentencing policies account

for the nation's high incarceration rate

Cameron Barr

Staff writer of The Christian Science Monitor

BOSTON AND WASHINGTON

MORE people, per capita, are in jail in the United States than in any other country on earth, according to a recent report by the Sentencing Project, a Washington-based research group.

It used to be that South Africa and the Soviet Union kept more of their citizens in jail than did the US – that was the finding of a landmark 1979 study on international rates of incarceration by the National Council on Crime and Deliquency. But now the US heads the list. For every 100,000 people in the US, 426 are sentenced to prison or are being held in pretrial detention. The US also imprisons black men at a rate four times higher than that of South Africa (see chart).

Rates of incarceration aren't available for all countries – China is notably absent from the Sentencing Project's report.

The Sentencing Project report doesn't analyze the reasons why the US leads the world in this dubious arena, other than to observe that US crime rates are higher than in other countries and that US criminal justice policies have favored imprisonment.

American murder rates, for instance, are at least seven times higher than in most of Europe. And the report says that "thousands are in prison due to policy choices – as a result of mandatory minimum sentences, restrictive parole policies, sentencing guidelines, and other policies."

The US rate, says Alabama corrections commissioner Morris Thigpen, reflects a "philosophy that all of us have allowed to become so [entrenched]: that the way we handle criminals is by totally removing them from society, by locking them up."

"I think," he says, "that people are beginning to question whether that really solves anything," although he stresses firm support for imprisoning violent criminals. "Some people realize now that just to routinely turn to incarceration [in cases of property and nonviolent crimes] is an unwise decision."

To slow the rate of incarceration the report advises the repeal of mandatory sentencing laws, that those fighting the "war on drugs" redefine drug abuse as a public health and not a criminal justice problem, and that law-enforcement officials focus more on community needs and crime prevention. It also urges wider use of alternatives to incarceration and, for those in prison, easier access to education and, job training.

But most of all, the Sentencing Project urges widespread discussion of crime and punishment. Reaction to their report shows why national dialogue is needed: While corrections officials like Mr. Thigpen viewed the new statistic with grim foreknowledge, the press coverage, conveyed with a tone of dismay and shock, suggested that the public would greet the news with surprise.

The report is a simple publication, without fancy printing or binding. It consists of a few tables and 15 pages of recommendations and comments. But it drew an impressive blast of press attention. Some 700 newspapers have written about the findings, and more than 50 papers have editorialized on the subject, according to Marc Mauer, assistant director of the Sentencing Project and the author of the report.

The US wins "The Grand Slammer Award," opined the Blade of Toledo, Ohio. It's a "shameful world record," said the Oakland Tribune. The US is "At the Top of Wrong List," pronounced the Washington Post.

There wasn't much surprise on the part of those in the business of incarcerating US lawbreakers and alleged criminals – state-corrections commissioners, wardens, and other law-enforcement executives. In interviews, some of these officials said the Sentencing Project's report, and the reaction it caused, are signs that a longstanding political consensus that crime should be battled with long prison terms may be waning.

When Bob Watson, Delaware's corrections commissioner, began his career in 1953, he saw rehabilitation programs losing ground to a heavy emphasis on law and order and punishment. Now, he says, "I think we're seeing that the pendulum has swung as far in [that] direction as it can go."

Among Alabama politicians, judges, and media, commissioner Thigpen also sees changes in attitudes. Thigpen says that at a recent state legislative conference political leaders "were acknowledging openly that we've got to

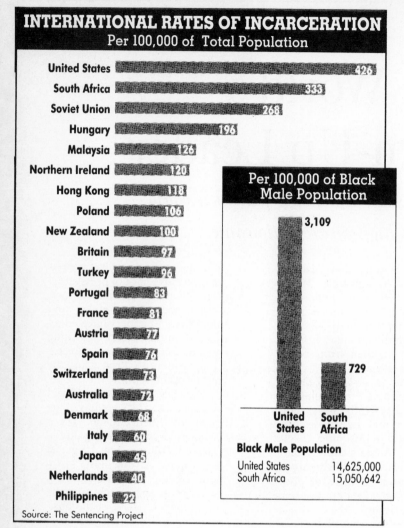

INTERNATIONAL RATES OF INCARCERATION
Per 100,000 of Total Population

United States	426
South Africa	333
Soviet Union	268
Hungary	196
Malaysia	126
Northern Ireland	120
Hong Kong	118
Poland	106
New Zealand	100
Britain	97
Turkey	96
Portugal	83
France	81
Austria	77
Spain	76
Switzerland	73
Australia	72
Denmark	68
Italy	60
Japan	45
Netherlands	40
Philippines	22

Source: The Sentencing Project

Per 100,000 of Black Male Population

United States: 3,109
South Africa: 729

Black Male Population

United States	14,625,000
South Africa	15,050,642

Only when those criteria are in place, Rufo says, should the corrections community go much further toward alternative sentences.

RUFO'S situation isn't much different from that of any other corrections official. He's seen his jail's annual population go from 3,400 in 1977 to more than 15,000 projected for this year. But he doesn't cite society's sharp-edged moral focus or mandatory sentencing laws to explain that increase.

"The reason for that is pure and simple," he says, "the proliferation of drugs in our society. The availability of drugs, cheap drugs, has infected our young people's minds to the point where they do not want to work, they've lost their self-esteem, they have no drive, they have no work ethic, for the most part, they just want to get high and hang out and then get in trouble."

But ask James Rollins, warden of a maximum-security state prison in Baltimore how he reacts to the knowledge that the US is a world leader in his line of work, and he'll say it's because American society has become selfish.

"From the inmates that I talk to it's all *I* ... it's all taking care of *my* needs." Some will tell you, he says, that they "had very little opportunity to have the materialistic things that people have in life, so they choose the quick money." To him it seems impossible that his state will be able to continue building prisons and taxing the public for the necessary funds.

Only when the public refuses to pay will society address the "causes and effects of incarceration," says Warden Rollins.

Getting the public to look at the big picture is Marc Mauer's mission at the Sentencing Project. Says Mauer, "What we've done in some small way, I think, is to help people to take a step back ... [and] look at the cumulative impact of all [the] day-to-day decisions, and the cumulative impact is ... unbelievable – that the wealthiest country in the world is the world leader in incarceration. I mean, how can that be?"

look for some other way of dealing with this problem."

Delaware's Mr. Watson says there's "a valuing of freedom ... reflected in [high US and state] incarceration rates – that when someone breaks our laws we're quick to lock them up."

"We have in this culture," he explains, "a right/wrong, black/-white, good/bad, true/false [mentality]. We don't have much tolerance for in-betweens." He says this sensibility has influenced the application of mandatory prison sentences for certain violent and drug-related crimes.

But Watson says he's been encouraged by the growing awareness that the higher the quality of a state's public education system, the lower its rate of incarceration is likely to be. He says he hopes that politicians and the public may want to spend funds on improving educational opportunities, rather than on constructing new prisons.

In his dual role as politician and jail administrator, Robert Rufo views the national corrections picture a little differently. The elected sheriff of Suffolk County, Mass., Mr. Rufo presides over the Nashua Street Jail, a pretrial detention facility for Boston with an average daily count of 470 prisoners. He is in the trenches of the prison-overcrowding controversy; the US Supreme Court has agreed to decide whether Rufo can modify a 1979 consent decree, approved by a judge, by putting two inmates in some of his cells.

"I understand the concept that we can't ... build our way out the crime problem, and I do not believe that every person, every first-time incarcerant, should be [put] behind bars.... But I think that what we have to do as a society, and we are beginning to do this, is to carve out certain criteria ... for the types of people that really should not be [at large]."

Criminal Treatment

Kenneth F. Schoen

PUNISHING criminals is a provocative subject that arouses deep feelings of anger, compassion, frustration, and fascination. Millions of tourists have trooped through the remaining buildings of the now defunct Alcatraz, chilled at the thought of being caged in a claustrophobic underground dungeon, gripped by tales of escapes, and intrigued at the sight of the cells of Capone and the Birdman.

The public's fear of criminals was exploited by the Bush campaign, which made Willie Horton the symbol of who is to be feared. In another vein, state-budget officers stand frustrated as they watch swelling inmate populations drain the state coffers. Alabama's finance director recently observed that if the increasing cost of the state's corrections system is not stemmed, the state will have no money for schools, welfare, or highways.

Princeton professor John DiIulio has produced another book on America's policies of punishing criminals. While "No Escape—The Future of American Corrections" will attract few readers from the ranks of the Alcatraz visitors, it isn't because the author buries the reader in arcane or slow-moving verbiage. Written in plain and appealing English, DiIulio delves into matters that worry wardens who preside over increasingly crowded prisons. He examines issues that finance directors and lawmakers must weigh, including the need for expansion and the privatization of prisons and alternatives to these institutions. The book is a series of op-ed type essays, peppered with "I's," "me's," and "my's."

DiIulio is crystal clear on his position on several major corrections issues, presenting an unveiled critique of what is and what should be. His conclusions are heavily influenced by the many correctional practitioners he has observed and interviewed, from wardens to guards to probation officers. He holds high value for advising the policies and practices of punishing offenders and thus, himself an academic, avoids being impaled on his own sword when he declares his disdain for academics and other "elite penal reformers."

But the author's promise of a Delphic glimpse into the future of corrections falls short. He briefly predicts that the trends of recent years will persist: The corrections population will continue to grow, more prisons and jails will be built, and institutions will continue to be overcrowded. He may be right in the short run – the United States is now the world's leader in the rate it incarcerates its citizens – but policies eventually have to change. A recent projection by the Brookings Institution found that at the increasing rate the US is locking up offenders, over one-half of all Americans will be in prison by 2052. Long before, the fiscal bite inflicted on the states and counties will force a reduction in imprisonment and expansion of the use of alternative punishments.

The author includes chapters on managing prisons and jails (he feels they can be), alternatives to incarceration (only a few programs work well, with few good available candidates), rehabilitation (some treatments work), and judicial intervention (an episode in correctional history with mixed results). He makes clear which programs and administrators measure up and often lists by name those he likes and dislikes. For example, wardens and corrections directors who avoid becoming chair-bound and who manage by mingling with staff and inmates are more likely to be associated with smooth-running regimes. DiIulio makes a useful observation when he warns that overcrowding or poor facilities are easy scapegoats for disorder when lousy management is often the real culprit. (During a visit to an uncrowded and reasonably maintained but nevertheless, violence-ridden Michigan prison a few years ago, I found the inmates did not know the warden's name or what he looked like; guards rarely saw him.)

DiIulio's unreserved esteem for certain administrators and systems clouds his objectivity and invites dispute. His assertion that the Texas system was "hailed as one of the nation's best" is not a universal opinion—not held by me, for one. The judge who presided over the litigation that found conditions in Texas prisons to be wanting was not the injudicious jurist DiIulio classified him as being. Faced with the same corrupt system, the judges in the New York and Alabama prison cases, to whom he gives good grades, would probably have behaved like the Texas judge. Indeed, a Texas jury found one inmate, who had drowned the warden in a water-filled roadside gutter, not guilty of murder when they learned of the brutality in the prison.

DiIulio's central argument, coined in the book's title, is that in the final analysis there is no escape from the reality that "whatever the 'experts' say, write, or do, and whatever the public demands, the future of American corrections is in the hands of the practitioners." This is an important observation, but is not reason to dismiss the reflections and efforts of the academic and reform-minded communities.

The institutions that manage criminals do not possess self-healing qualities and, if left alone, tend to become cynical about their clientele and their mission. Alabama judges with the nicknames of "Maximum Braxton" and "Black Death," and a couple dozen of their colleagues, sit in classrooms with Yale law students and professors and reconsider their sentencing practices. By the judges' testimony, the experience has significantly boosted their interest in alternative punishments for selected offenders. Bridging the gap between penal practice and theory offers an escape from the dismal conditions that beset the nation's penal system.

■ *Kenneth F. Schoen, director of the justice program at the Edna McConnel Clark Foundation, is a former commissioner of the Minnesota Department of Corrections.*

"Boot Camp" Programs Grow in Number and Scope

Doris Layton MacKenzie

Doris Layton MacKenzie, Ph.D., is an associate professor at the University of Maryland and a visiting senior research associate at the National Institute of Justice.

Boot camp prison programs are being used increasingly as a sentencing option for young drug offenders and others convicted of nonviolent offenses.

The number of such State programs for adults now operating throughout the country has grown to 21, up from 14 a year ago, according to an NIJ survey. Seventeen States now use boot camps—also known as shock incarceration—compared to 11 States in May 1989. Three States have begun programs in 1990: New Hampshire, Maryland, and Arkansas. Another three are planning to begin programs before the year is out: Connecticut, Pennsylvania, and Wyoming. County and juvenile jurisdictions are also considering shock programs. Figure 1 and table 1 give the latest statistics contrasted with those published in *NIJ Reports* a year ago.

Most shock incarceration programs are designed for young, nonviolent

Figure 1.

Shock Incarceration Programs in the United States, July 1990

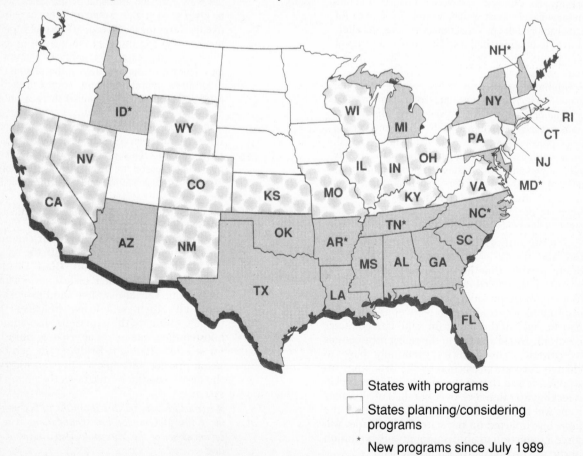

States with programs

States planning/considering programs

* New programs since July 1989

From *NIJ Reports*, November/December 1990, pp. 6-8. *NIJ Reports*, the bimonthly journal of the National Institute of Justice. Reprinted by permission of the author and *NIJ Reports*.

Table 1.

Characteristics of Shock Incarceration Programs, May 1990

State	Year Programs Began	Number of Programs	Number of Participants (Male/Female)	Number of Days Served	Maximum Age Limit	First Felony?	Non-Violent Only?
Alabama	1988	1	127 male [a]	90	none	no	no
Arizona	1988	1	150 male [a]	120	25	yes	no
Florida	1987	1	100 male [a]	90 [b]	25	yes	no
Georgia	1983	2	250 male [a]	90	25	yes	no
Idaho	1989 [c]	1	154 male	120	none	no	no
Louisiana	1987	1	87 male [a] 1 female	120	39	no	yes
Michigan	1988	1	120 male	120 [d]	25	no	no
Mississippi	1985	2 [a]	225 male [a] 15 female	110 [e]	none	yes	yes
New York	1987	5 [a]	1,500 male [a] 102 female	180	30	yes	yes
North Carolina	1989 [c]	1	54 male	93	24	yes	yes
Oklahoma	1984	1	150 male	90 [f]	25	yes	yes
South Carolina	1987	2	98 male [a] 13 female	90	24	yes	yes
Tennessee	1989 [c]	1	42 male	120	30	yes	yes
Texas	1989	1	200 male	90	25	yes	no

References

[a] Indicates increase since May 1989.
[b] May 1989: Average 101.
[c] Program new since May 1989.
[d] May 1989: Average 90.
[e] May 1989: Average 180.
[f] May 1989: Average 120.

States planning or considering programs: California, Connecticut, Indiana, Kansas, Missouri, Nevada, New Jersey, New Mexico, Pennsylvania, Wisconsin, Wyoming. States that began programs in 1990: Arkansas, Maryland, New Hampshire.

These data appear in greater detail in the September 1990 issue of *Federal Probation*.

offenders serving time on their first felony convictions, although the programs are not limited to these individuals. Some criminal justice officials view shock incarceration as a promising approach for controlling offenders who would otherwise be sentenced to probation.

The overall picture that emerges from a review of existing programs is that of a common core based on the military atmosphere, discipline, youth of the offenders, and a common goal of providing punishment without long-term incarceration.

However, programs differ as to who is responsible for placing offenders in the program—the judge or corrections department—whether offenders may enter the program or drop out of it voluntarily, the location of the program, and the supervision of offenders upon release. Programs also differ greatly in the number of hours devoted to physical training, drill, work, education, and counseling. But frequently offenders in these programs spend more time in rehabilitative-type activities such as education or counseling than they would in a regular prison.

Growing knowledge

Some conclusions are emerging from NIJ research:

• Programs vary greatly, and any evaluation must begin with a description of the program and its objectives.

• There is some evidence that the boot camp experience may be more positive than incarceration in traditional prison.

• There is no evidence that those who complete boot camp programs are angrier or negatively affected by the program.

• Those who complete shock programs report having a difficult but constructive experience. Similar offenders who serve their sentences in a traditional prison do not view their experiences as constructive.

• Boot camp recidivism rates are approximately the same as those of comparison groups who serve a longer period of time in a traditional prison or who serve time on probation.

• Programs differ substantially in the amount of time offenders spend in rehabilitative activities.

• Success may be contingent on the emphasis on rehabilitation—giving offenders the training, treatment, and education needed to support new behavior—during incarceration and on aftercare during community supervision.

On the basis of early research results, visits to programs, interviews with staff and inmates, and reviews of related research, several observations can be made.

Some evidence suggests that offenders change in a positive way during their brief incarceration. Parolees who complete the programs are generally much more positive about their experiences than those released from regular prison. However, those who are not ready to change may drop out of the program.

Research also suggests that returning to the home environment may present such overwhelming difficulties for offenders that positive changes during incarceration cannot be sustained. New York, with the largest shock incarceration program of any State, has identified maintaining positive change as a possible problem and has developed an "after shock" program to help offenders while they are under supervision in the community.

Most of these programs are not merely a time of punishment through hard labor and exercise. In almost all shock programs, offenders receive more treatment (through counseling or edu-

cation) than they would in the general prison population. One question raised by research is whether the boot camp atmosphere enhances the effect of treatment or whether an intensive treatment program alone would have the same effect.

However, physical training, drill, hard labor, and the boot camp regime may be important in several ways. Offenders who are near the end of their time in shock incarceration report that these activities result in their "getting free" of drugs and becoming physically fit. They also mention the advantage of learning to get up in the morning and being active all day.

The radical changes these activities produce in everyday living patterns may have other effects. They shake up the offenders, creating stress at a time when offenders may be particularly susceptible to outside influences. This is an excellent time for them to re-evaluate their lives and change their thinking and behavior.

'THIS MAN HAS EXPIRED'
WITNESS TO AN EXECUTION

ROBERT JOHNSON

ROBERT JOHNSON *is professor of justice, law, and society at The American University, Washington, D.C. This article is drawn from a Distinguished Faculty Lecture, given under the auspices of the university's senate last spring.*

The death penalty has made a comeback in recent years. In the late sixties and through most of the seventies, such a thing seemed impossible. There was a moratorium on executions in the U.S., backed by the authority of the Supreme Court. The hiatus lasted roughly a decade. Coming on the heels of a gradual but persistent decline in the use of the death penalty in the Western world, it appeared to some that executions would pass from the American scene [cf. *Commonweal,* January 15, 1988]. Nothing could have been further from the truth.

Beginning with the execution of Gary Gilmore in 1977, over 100 people have been put to death, most of them in the last few years. Some 2,200 prisoners are presently confined on death rows across the nation. The majority of these prisoners have lived under sentence of death for years, in some cases a decade or more, and are running out of legal appeals. It is fair to say that the death penalty is alive and well in America, and that executions will be with us for the foreseeable future.

Gilmore's execution marked the resurrection of the modern death penalty and was big news. It was commemorated in a best-selling tome by Norman Mailer, *The Executioner's Song.* The title was deceptive. Like others who have examined the death penalty, Mailer told us a great deal about the condemned but very little about the executioners. Indeed, if we dwell on Mailer's account, the executioner's story is not only unsung; it is distorted.

Gilmore's execution was quite atypical. His was an instance of state-assisted suicide accompanied by an element of romance and played out against a backdrop of media fanfare. Unrepentant and unafraid, Gilmore refused to appeal his conviction. He dared the state of Utah to take his life, and the media repeated the challenge until it became a taunt that may well have goaded officials to action. A failed suicide pact with his lover staged only days before the execution, using drugs she delivered to him in a visit marked by unusual intimacy, added a hint of melodrama to the proceedings. Gilmore's final words, "Let's do it," seemed to invite the lethal hail of bullets from the firing squad. The nonchalant phrase, at once fatalistic and brazenly rebellious, became Gilmore's epitaph. It clinched his outlaw-hero image, and found its way onto tee shirts that confirmed his celebrity status.

Befitting a celebrity, Gilmore was treated with unusual leniency by prison officials during his confinement on death row. He was, for example, allowed to hold a party the night before his execution, during which he was free to eat, drink, and make merry with his guests until the early morning hours. This is not entirely unprecedented. Notorious English convicts of centuries past would throw farewell balls in prison on the eve of their executions. News accounts of such affairs sometimes included a commentary on the richness of the table and the quality of the dancing. For the record, Gilmore served Tang, Kool-Aid, cookies, and coffee, later supplemented by contraband pizza and an unidentified liquor. Periodically, he gobbled drugs obligingly provided by the prison pharmacy. He played a modest arrangement of rock music albums but refrained from dancing.

Gilmore's execution generally, like his parting fete, was decidedly out of step with the tenor of the modern death penalty. Most condemned prisoners fight to save their lives, not to have them taken. They do not see their fate in romantic terms; there are no farewell parties. Nor are they given medication to ease their anxiety or win their compliance. The subjects of typical executions remain anonymous to the public and even to their keepers. They are very much alone at the end.

In contrast to Mailer's account, the focus of the research I have conducted is on the executioners themselves as they carry out typical executions. In my experience executioners—not unlike Mailer himself—can be quite voluble, and sometimes quite moving, in expressing themselves. I shall draw upon their words to describe the death work they carry out in our name.

DEATH WORK AND DEATH WORKERS

Executioners are not a popular subject of social research, let alone conversation at the dinner table or cocktail party. We simply don't give the subject much thought. When we think of executioners at all, the imagery runs to individual men of disreputable, or at least questionable, character who work stealthily behind the scenes to carry out their grim labors. We picture hooded men hiding in the shadow of the gallows, or anonymous figures lurking out of sight behind electric chairs, gas chambers, firing blinds, or, more recently, hospital gurneys. We wonder who would do such grisly work and how they sleep at night.

This image of the executioner as a sinister and often solitary character is today misleading. To be sure, a few states hire free-lance executioners and traffic in macabre theatrics. Executioners may be picked up under cover of darkness and some may still wear black hoods. But today, executions are generally the work of a highly disciplined and efficient team of correctional officers.

Broadly speaking, the execution process as it is now practiced starts with the prisoner's confinement on death row, an oppressive prison-within-a-prison where the condemned are housed, sometimes for years, awaiting execution. Death work gains momentum when an execution date draws near and the prisoner is moved to the death house, a short walk from the death chamber. Finally, the process culminates in the death watch, a twenty-four-hour period that ends when the prisoner has been executed.

This final period, the death watch, is generally undertaken by correctional officers who work as a team and report directly to the prison warden. The warden or his representative, in turn, must by law preside over the execution. In many states, it is a member of the death watch or execution team, acting under the warden's authority, who in fact plays the formal role of executioner. Though this officer may technically work alone, his teammates view the execution as a shared responsibility. As one officer on the death watch told me in no uncertain terms: "We all take part in it; we all play 100 percent in it, too. That takes the load off this one individual [who pulls the switch]." The formal executioner concurred. "Everyone on the team can do it, and nobody will tell you I did it. I know my team." I found nothing in my research to dispute these claims.

The officers of these death watch teams are our modern executioners. As part of a larger study of the death work process, I studied one such group. This team, comprised of nine seasoned officers of varying ranks, had carried out five electrocutions at the time I began my research. I interviewed each officer on the team after the fifth execution, then served as an official witness at a sixth electrocution. Later, I served as a behind-the-scenes observer during their seventh execution.

The results of this phase of my research form the substance of this essay.

THE DEATH WATCH TEAM

The death watch or execution team members refer to themselves, with evident pride, as simply "the team." This pride is shared by other correctional officials. The warden at the institution I was observing praised members of the team as solid citizens—in his words, country boys. These country boys, he assured me, could be counted on to do the job and do it well. As a fellow administrator put it, "an execution is something [that] needs to be done and good people, dedicated people who believe in the American system, should do it. And there's a certain amount of feeling, probably one to another, that they're part of that—that when they have to hang tough, they can do it, and they can do it right. And that it's just the right thing to do."

The official view is that an execution is a job that has to be done, and done right. The death penalty is, after all, the law of the land. In this context, the phrase "done right" means that an execution should be a proper, professional, dignified undertaking. In the words of a prison administrator, "We had to be sure that we did it properly, professionally, and [that] we gave as much dignity to the person as we possibly could in the process....If you've gotta do it, it might just as well be done the way it's supposed to be done—without any sensation."

In the language of the prison officials, "proper" refers to procedures that go off smoothly; "professional" means without personal feelings that intrude on the procedures in any way. The desire for executions that take place "without any sensation" no doubt refers to the absence of media sensationalism, particularly if there should be an embarrassing and undignified hitch in the procedures, for example, a prisoner who breaks down or becomes violent and must be forcibly placed in the electric chair as witnesses, some from the media, look on in horror. Still, I can't help but note that this may be a revealing slip of the tongue. For executions are indeed meant to go off without any human feeling, without any sensation. A profound absence of feeling would seem to capture the bureaucratic ideal embodied in the modern execution.

The view of executions held by the execution team members parallels that of correctional administrators but is somewhat more restrained. The officers of the team are closer to the killing and dying, and are less apt to wax abstract or eloquent in describing the process. Listen to one man's observations:

It's a job. I don't take it personally. You know, I don't take it like I'm having a grudge against this person and this person has done something to me. I'm just carrying out a job, doing what I was asked to do....This man has been sentenced to death in the courts. This is the law and he broke this law, and he has to suffer the consequences. And one of the consequences is to put him to death.

I found that few members of the execution team support the death penalty outright or without reservation. Having seen executions close up, many of them have lingering doubts about the justice or wisdom of this sanction. As one officer put it:

I'm not sure the death penalty is the right way. I don't know if there is a right answer. So I look at it like this: if it's gotta be done, at least it can be done in a humane way, if there is such a word for it. . . . The only way it should be done, I feel, is the way we do it. It's done professionally; it's not no horseplaying. Everything is done by documentation. On time. By the book.

Arranging executions that occur "without any sensation" and that go "by the book" is no mean task, but it is a task that is undertaken in earnest by the execution team. The tone of the enterprise is set by the team leader, a man who takes a hard-boiled, no-nonsense approach to correctional work in general and death work in particular. "My style," he says, "is this: if it's a job to do, get it done. Do it and that's it." He seeks out kindred spirits, men who see killing condemned prisoners as a job—a dirty job one does reluctantly, perhaps, but above all a job one carries out dispassionately and in the line of duty.

To make sure that line of duty is a straight and accurate one, the death watch team has been carefully drilled by the team leader in the mechanics of execution. The process has been broken down into simple, discrete tasks and practiced repeatedly. The team leader describes the division of labor in the following exchange:

the execution team is a nine-officer team and each one has certain things to do. When I would train you, maybe you'd buckle a belt, that might be all you'd have to do. . . . And you'd be expected to do one thing and that's all you'd be expected to do. And if everybody does what they were taught, or what they were trained to do, at the end the man would be put in the chair and everything would be complete. It's all come together now.

So it's broken down into very small steps. . . .

Very small, yes. Each person has *one* thing to do.

I see. What's the purpose of breaking it down into such small steps?

So people won't get confused. I've learned it's kind of a tense time. When you're executin' a person, killing a person—you call it killin', executin', whatever you want—the man dies anyway. I find the less you got on your mind, why, the better you'll carry it out. So it's just very simple things. And so far, you know, it's all come together, we haven't had any problems.

This division of labor allows each man on the execution team to become a specialist, a technician with a sense of pride in his work. Said one man,

My assignment is the leg piece. Right leg. I roll his pants leg up, place a piece [electrode] on his leg, strap his leg in. . . . I've got all the moves down pat. We train from different posts; I can do any of them. But that's my main post.

The implication is not that the officers are incapable of performing multiple or complex tasks, but simply that it is more efficient to focus each officer's efforts on one easy task.

An essential part of the training is practice. Practice is meant to produce a confident group, capable of fast and accurate performance under pressure. The rewards of practice are reaped in improved performance. Executions take place with increasing efficiency, and eventually occur with precision. "The first one was grisly," a team member confided to me. He explained that there was a certain amount of fumbling, which made the execution seem interminable. There were technical problems as well: The generator was set too high so the body was badly burned. But that is the past, the officer assured me. "The ones now, we know what we're doing. It's just like clockwork."

THE DEATH WATCH

The death-watch team is deployed during the last twenty-four hours before an execution. In the state under study, the death watch starts at 11 o'clock the night before the execution and ends at 11 o'clock the next night when the execution takes place. At least two officers would be with the prisoner at any given time during that period. Their objective is to keep the prisoner alive and "on schedule." That is, to move him through a series of critical and cumulatively demoralizing junctures that begin with his last meal and end with his last walk. When the time comes, they must deliver the prisoner up for execution as quickly and unobtrusively as possible.

Broadly speaking, the job of the death watch officer, as one man put it, "is to sit and keep the inmate calm for the last twenty-four hours—and get the man ready to go." Keeping a condemned prisoner calm means, in part, serving his immediate needs. It seems paradoxical to think of the death watch officers as providing services to the condemned, but the logistics of the job make service a central obligation of the officers. Here's how one officer made this point:

Well, you can't help but be involved with many of the things that he's involved with. Because if he wants to make a call to his family, well, you'll have to dial the number. And you keep records of whatever calls he makes. If he wants a cigarette, well he's not allowed to keep matches so you light it for him. You've got to pour his coffee, too. So you're aware what he's doing. It's not like you can just ignore him. You've gotta just be with him whether he wants it or not, and cater to his needs.

Officers cater to the condemned because contented inmates are easier to keep under control. To a man, the officers say this is so. But one can never trust even a contented, condemned prisoner.

The death-watch officers see condemned prisoners as men with explosive personalities. "You don't know what, what a man's gonna do," noted one officer. "He's liable to snap, he's liable to pass out. We watch him all the time to prevent him from committing suicide. You've got to be ready—he's liable to do anything." The prisoner is never out of at least one officer's sight. Thus surveillance is constant, and control, for all intents and purposes, is total.

Relations between the officers and their charges during the death watch can be quite intense. Watching and being watched are central to this enterprise, and these are always engaging activities, particularly when the stakes are life and death. These relations are, nevertheless, utterly impersonal; there are no grudges but neither is there compassion or fellow-feeling. Officers are civil but cool; they keep an emotional distance from the men they are about to kill. To do otherwise, they maintain, would make it harder to execute condemned prisoners. The attitude of the officers is that the prisoners arrive as strangers and are easier to kill if they stay that way.

During the last five or six hours, two specific team officers are assigned to guard the prisoner. Unlike their more taciturn and aloof colleagues on earlier shifts, these officers make a conscious effort to talk with the prisoner. In one officer's words, "We keep them right there and keep talking to them—about anything except the chair." The point of these conversations is not merely to pass time; it is to keep tabs on the prisoner's state of mind, and to steer him away from subjects that might depress, anger, or otherwise upset him. Sociability, in other words, quite explicitly serves as a source of social control. Relationships, such as they are, serve purely manipulative ends. This is impersonality at its worst, masquerading as concern for the strangers one hopes to execute with as little trouble as possible.

Generally speaking, as the execution moves closer, the mood becomes more somber and subdued. There is a last meal. Prisoners can order pretty much what they want, but most eat little or nothing at all. At this point, the prisoners may steadfastly maintain that their executions will be stayed. Such bravado is belied by their loss of appetite. "You can see them going down," said one officer. "Food is the last thing they got on their minds."

Next the prisoners must box their meager worldly goods. These are inventoried by the staff, recorded on a one-page checklist form, and marked for disposition to family or friends. Prisoners are visibly saddened, even moved to tears, by this procedure, which at once summarizes their lives and highlights the imminence of death. At this point, said one of the officers, "I really get into him; I watch him real close." The execution schedule, the officer pointed out, is "picking up momentum, and we don't want to lose control of the situation."

This momentum is not lost on the condemned prisoner. Critical milestones have been passed. The prisoner moves in a limbo existence devoid of food or possessions; he has seen the last of such things, unless he receives a stay of execution and rejoins the living. His identity is expropriated as well. The critical juncture in this regard is the shaving of the man's head (including facial hair) and right leg. Hair is shaved to facilitate the electrocution; it reduces physical resistance to electricity and minimizes singeing and burning. But the process has obvious psychological significance as well, adding greatly to the momentum of the execution.

The shaving procedure is quite public and intimidating. The condemned man is taken from his cell and seated in the middle of the tier. His hands and feet are cuffed, and he is dressed only in undershorts. The entire death watch team is assembled around him. They stay at a discrete distance, but it is obvious that they are there to maintain control should he resist in any way or make any untoward move. As a rule, the man is overwhelmed. As one officer told me in blunt terms, "Come eight o'clock, we've got a dead man. Eight o'clock is when we shave the man. We take his identity; it goes with the hair." This taking of identity is indeed a collective process—the team makes a forceful "we," the prisoner their helpless object. The staff is confident that the prisoner's capacity to resist is now compromised. What is left of the man erodes gradually and, according the officers, perceptibly over the remaining three hours before the execution.

After the prisoner has been shaved, he is then made to shower and don a fresh set of clothes for the execution. The clothes are unremarkable in appearance, except that velcro replaces buttons and zippers, to reduce the chance of burning the body. The main significance of the clothes is symbolic: they mark the prisoner as a man who is ready for execution. Now physically "prepped," to quote one team member, the prisoner is placed in an empty tomblike cell, the death cell. All that is left is the wait. During this fateful period, the prisoner is more like an object "without any sensation" than like a flesh-and-blood person on the threshold of death.

For condemned prisoners, like Gilmore, who come to accept and even to relish their impending deaths, a genuine calm seems to prevail. It is as if they can transcend the dehumanizing forces at work around them and go to their deaths in peace. For most condemned prisoners, however, numb resignation rather than peaceful acceptance is the norm. By the account of the death-watch officers, these more typical prisoners are beaten men. Listen to the officers' accounts:

A lot of 'em die in their minds before they go to that chair. I've never known of one or heard of one putting up a fight. . . . By the time they walk to the chair, they've completely faced it. Such a reality most people can't understand. Cause they don't fight it. They don't seem to have anything to say. It's just something like "Get it over with." They may be numb, sort of in a trance.

They go through stages. And, at this stage, they're real humble. Humblest bunch of people I ever seen. Most all of 'em is real, real weak. Most of the time you'd only need one or two people to carry out an execution, as weak and as humble as they are.

These men seem barely human and alive to their keepers. They wait meekly to be escorted to their deaths. The people who come for them are the warden and the remainder of the death watch team, flanked by high-ranking correctional officials. The warden reads the court order, known popularly as a death warrant. This is, as one officer said, "the real deal," and nobody misses its significance. The condemned prisoners then go to their deaths compliantly, captives of the inexorable, irresistible momentum of the situation. As one officer put it, "There's no struggle. . . . They just walk right on in there." So too, do the staff "just walk right on in there," following a routine they have come to know well. Both the condemned and the executioners, it would seem, find a relief of sorts in mindless mechanical conformity to the modern execution drill.

WITNESS TO AN EXECUTION

As the team and administrators prepare to commence the good fight, as they might say, another group, the official witnesses, are also preparing themselves for their role in the execution. Numbering between six and twelve for any given execution, the official witnesses are disinterested citizens in good standing drawn from a cross-section of the state's population. If you will, they are every good or decent person, called upon to represent the community and use their good offices to testify to the propriety of the execution. I served as an official witness at the execution of an inmate.

At eight in the evening, about the time the prisoner is shaved in preparation for the execution, the witnesses are assembled. Eleven in all, we included three newspaper and two television reporters, a state trooper, two police officers, a magistrate, a businessman, and myself. We were picked up in the parking lot behind the main office of the corrections department. There was nothing unusual or even memorable about any of this. Gothic touches were notable by their absence. It wasn't a dark and stormy night; no one emerged from the shadows to lead us to the prison gates.

Mundane considerations prevailed. The van sent for us was missing a few rows of seats so there wasn't enough room for all of us. Obliging prison officials volunteered their cars. Our rather ordinary cavalcade reached the prison but only after getting lost. Once within the prison's walls, we were sequestered for some two hours in a bare and almost shabby administrative conference room. A public information officer was assigned to accompany us and answer our questions. We grilled this official about the prisoner and the execution procedure he would undergo shortly, but little information was to be had. The man confessed ignorance on the most basic points. Disgruntled at this and increasingly anxious, we made small talk and drank coffee.

At 10:40 P.M., roughly two-and-a-half hours after we were assembled and only twenty minutes before the execution was scheduled to occur, the witnesses were taken to the basement of the prison's administrative building, frisked, then led down an alleyway that ran along the exterior of the building. We entered a neighboring cell block and were admitted to a vestibule adjoining the death chamber. Each of us signed a log, and was then led off to the witness area. To our left, around a corner some thirty feet away, the prisoner sat in the condemned cell. He couldn't see us, but I'm quite certain he could hear us. It occurred to me that our arrival was a fateful reminder for the prisoner. The next group would be led by the warden, and it would be coming for him.

We entered the witness area, a room within the death chamber, and took our seats. A picture window covering the front wall of the witness room offered a clear view of the electric chair, which was about twelve feet away from us and well illuminated. The chair, a large, high-back solid oak structure with imposing black straps, dominated the death chamber. Behind it, on the back wall, was an open panel full of coils and lights. Peeling paint hung from the ceiling and walls; water stains from persistent leaks were everywhere in evidence.

Two officers, one a hulking figure weighing some 400 pounds, stood alongside the electric chair. Each had his hands crossed at the lap and wore a forbidding, blank expression on his face. The witnesses gazed at them and the chair, most of us scribbling notes furiously. We did this, I suppose, as much to record the experience as to have a distraction from the growing tension. A correctional officer entered the witness room and announced that a trial run of the machinery would be undertaken. Seconds later, lights flashed on the control panel behind the chair indicating that the chair was in working order. A white curtain, opened for the test, separated the chair and the witness area. After the test, the curtain was drawn. More tests were performed behind the curtain. Afterwards, the curtain was reopened, and would be left open until the execution was over. Then it would be closed to allow the officers to remove the body.

A handful of high-level correctional officials were present in the death chamber, standing just outside the witness area. There were two regional administrators, the director of the Department of Corrections, and the prison warden. The prisoner's chaplain and lawyer were also present. Other than the chaplain's black religious garb, subdued grey pinstripes and bland correctional uniforms prevailed. All parties were quite solemn.

At 10:58 the prisoner entered the death chamber. He was, I knew from my research, a man with a checkered, tragic past. He had been grossly abused as a child, and went on to become grossly abusive of others. I was told he could not describe his life, from childhood on, without talking about confrontations in defense of a precarious sense of self—at home, in school, on the streets, in the prison yard. Belittled by life and choking with rage, he was hungry to be noticed. Paradoxically, he had found his moment in the spotlight, but it was a dim and unflattering light cast before a small and unappreciative audience. "He'd pose for cameras in the chair—for the attention," his counselor had told me earlier in the day. But the truth was that the prisoner wasn't smiling, and there were no cameras.

The prisoner walked quickly and silently toward the chair, an escort of officers in tow. His eyes were turned downward, his expression a bit glazed. Like many before him, the prisoner had threatened to stage a last stand. But that was lifetimes ago, on death row. In the death house, he joined the humble bunch and kept to the executioner's schedule. He appeared to have given up on life before he died in the chair.

En route to the chair, the prisoner stumbled slightly, as if the momentum of the event had overtaken him. Were he not held securely by two officers, one at each elbow, he might have fallen. Were the routine to be broken in this or indeed any other way, the officers believe, the prisoner might faint or panic or become violent, and have to be forcibly placed in the chair. Perhaps as a precaution, when the prisoner reached the chair he did not turn on his own but rather was turned, firmly but without malice, by the officers in his escort. These included the two men at his elbows, and four others who followed behind him. Once the prisoner was seated, again with help, the officers strapped him into the chair.

The execution team worked with machine precision. Like a disciplined swarm, they enveloped him. Arms, legs, stomach, chest, and head were secured in a matter of seconds. Electrodes were attached to the cap holding his head and to the strap holding his exposed right leg. A leather mask was placed over his face. The last officer mopped the prisoner's brow, then touched his hand in a gesture of farewell.

During the brief procession to the electric chair, the prisoner was attended by a chaplain. As the execution team worked feverishly to secure the condemned man's body, the chaplain, who appeared to be upset, leaned over him and placed his forehead in contact with the prisoner's, whispering urgently. The priest might have been praying, but I had the impression he was consoling the man, perhaps assuring him that a forgiving God awaited him in the next life. If he heard the chaplain, I doubt the man comprehended his message. He didn't seem comforted. Rather, he looked stricken and appeared to be in shock. Perhaps the priest's urgent ministrations betrayed his doubts that the prisoner could hold himself together. The chaplain then withdrew at the warden's request, allowing the officers to affix the death mask.

The strapped and masked figure sat before us, utterly alone, waiting to be killed. The cap and mask dominated his face. The cap was nothing more than a sponge encased in a leather shell with a metal piece at the top to accept an electrode. It looked decrepit and resembled a cheap, ill-fitting toupee. The mask, made entirely of leather, appeared soiled and worn. It had two parts. The bottom part covered the chin and mouth, the top the eyes and lower forehead. Only the nose was exposed. The effect of a rigidly restrained body, together with the bizarre cap and the protruding nose, was nothing short of grotesque. A faceless man breathed before us in a tragicomic trance, waiting for a blast of electricity that would extinguish his life. Endless seconds passed. His last act was to swallow, nervously, pathetically, with his Adam's apple bobbing. I was struck by that simple movement then, and can't forget it even now. It told me, as nothing else did, that in the prisoner's restrained body, behind that mask, lurked a fellow human being who, at some level, however primitive, knew or sensed himself to be moments from death.

The condemned man sat perfectly still for what seemed an eternity but was in fact no more than thirty seconds. Finally the electricity hit him. His body stiffened spasmodically, though only briefly. A thin swirl of smoke trailed away from his head and then dissipated quickly. The body remained taut, with the right foot raised slightly at the heel, seemingly frozen

there. A brief pause, then another minute of shock. When it was over, the body was flaccid and inert.

Three minutes passed while the officials let the body cool. (Immediately after the execution, I'm told, the body would be too hot to touch and would blister anyone who did.) All eyes were riveted to the chair; I felt trapped in my witness seat, at once transfixed and yet eager for release. I can't recall any clear thoughts from that moment. One of the death watch officers later volunteered that he shared this experience of staring blankly at the execution scene. Had the prisoner's mind been mercifully blank before the end? I hoped so.

An officer walked up to the body, opened the shirt at chest level, then continued on to get the physician from an adjoining room. The physician listened for a heartbeat. Hearing none, he turned to the warden and said, ''This man has expired.'' The warden, speaking to the director, solemnly intoned: ''Mr. Director, the court order has been fulfilled.'' The curtain was then drawn and the witnesses filed out.

THE MORNING AFTER

As the team prepared the body for the morgue, the witnesses were led to the front door of the prison. On the way, we passed a number of cell blocks. We could hear the normal sounds of prison life, including the occasional catcall and lewd comment hurled at uninvited guests like ourselves. But no trouble came in the wake of the execution. Small protests were going on outside the walls, we were told, but we could not hear them. Soon the media would be gone; the protestors would disperse and head for their homes. The prisoners, already home, had been indifferent to the proceedings, as they always are unless the condemned prisoner had been a figure of some consequence in the convict community. Then there might be tension and maybe even a modest disturbance on a prison tier or two. But few convict luminaries are executed, and the dead man had not been one of them. Our escort officer offered a sad tribute to the prisoner: ''The inmates, they didn't care about this guy.''

I couldn't help but think they weren't alone in this. The executioners went home and set about their lives. Having taken life, they would savor a bit of life themselves. They showered, ate, made love, slept, then took a day or two off. For some, the prisoner's image would linger for that night. The men who strapped him in remembered what it was like to touch him; they showered as soon as they got home to wash off the feel and smell of death. One official sat up picturing how the prisoner looked at the end. (I had a few drinks myself that night with that same image for company.) There was some talk about delayed reactions to the stress of carrying out executions. Though such concerns seemed remote that evening, I learned later that problems would surface for some of the officers. But no one on the team, then or later, was haunted by the executed man's memory, nor would anyone grieve for him. ''When I go home after one of these things,'' said one man, ''I sleep like a rock.'' His may or may not be the sleep of the just, but one can only marvel at such a thing, and perhaps envy such a man.

No Reversal of Fortune for Blacks on Death Row

Justice Department reports a disproportionate number of blacks are awaiting execution

Michael J. Sniffen

The Associated Press

WASHINGTON—Amid a congressional debate on how to impose the death penalty, the Justice Department reported yesterday that blacks still make up a much larger share of Death Row inmates than of the nation's population.

The department's Bureau of Justice Statistics said that as of Dec. 31, 1990, blacks made up 40 percent of prisoners awaiting death penalties. The 1990 census found the U.S. population is 12.1 percent black.

In 1987, the Supreme Court ruled that statistical evidence of discrimination is insufficient to render death-penalty statutes unconstitutional.

That ruling came in the case of Warren McCleskey, a black man who was executed last Wednesday in the Georgia electric chair for the killing of a white Atlanta policeman during a 1978 furniture store robbery.

Last week, the House Judiciary Committee approved and sent to the House floor a bill allowing legal challenges to death sentences based on statistical showings of race discrimination. The Senate rejected a similar provision.

Bush Expanding Death Penalty

Under prodding from the Bush administration, both House and Senate crime bills would greatly expand the federal death penalty—to cover some 50 new crimes.

The Justice Department study found 2,356 prisoners awaiting death penalties at year-end, up 5 percent from the previous year. Thirty-two of them were women, and the median age was 34.

At the time of the study, 34 states and the federal government had death penalties on the books, but Colorado's has since been struck down by the state supreme court.

Of those condemned to die, 1,375, or 58.4 percent, were white, 943 or 40 percent were black, 24 or 1 percent were American Indian and 14 or 0.6 percent were Asian. Those of Hispanic ethnic origin totaled 172, or 7.3 percent. In the prison study, as in Census compilations, people of Hispanic origin are counted in other racial categories: black, white or other.

The 1990 Census found that the U.S. population was 80.3 percent white, 12.1 percent black, 0.8 percent American Indian, 2.9 percent Asian and 3.9 percent other races. Within those various racial designations, 9 percent are of Hispanic origin.

The study released yesterday did not attempt to calculate what percentage of the overall U.S. federal and state prison system population is comprised of black people.

Death penalties were overturned in the United States by the Supreme Court's 1972 Furman decision, because of arbitrariness and evidence of race discrimination. Beginning in 1976, the Supreme Court has upheld a series of death penalties, redrawn to address the concerns of the Furman decision.

Worse for Blacks in 1971

Before Furman, blacks were even more disproportionately represented on death row. At the end of 1971, Justice statistics show there were 620 inmates waiting to die. Of these, 325 or 52.4 percent were black; 291 or 46.9 percent were white and 4, or 0.006 percent, were other races.

Diann Rust-Tierney, director of the American Civil Liberties Union's capital-punishment project, said there were two main reasons the Furman decisions and subsequent ones had not done more to eliminate racial disparities.

"Going back to 1972, the focus is on

what happens at the trial," Rust-Tierney said in an interview. "There is no regulation of how prosecutors choose cases for death penalties. If you're only selecting black defendants, then the use of aggravating or mitigating factors at sentencing isn't going to overcome the bias in the selection."

"In McCleskey's appeal, they showed that those who killed white victims were four times more likely to get death sentences than those who killed black victims. The risk of getting a death

---

'The risk of getting a death sentence if your victim is white is greater than the risk of getting heart disease from smoking, but the Supreme Court in 1987 said that wasn't enough to make it unconstitutional. They're asking for the kind of absolute proof that doesn't exist—like prosecutors confessing discrimination.'

—**Diann Rust-Tierney, director, capital punishment project, American Civil Liberties Union**

---

sentence if your victim is white is greater than the risk of getting heart disease from smoking, but the Supreme Court in 1987 said that wasn't enough to make it unconstitutional. They're asking for the kind of absolute proof that doesn't exist—like prosecutors confessing discrimination," she said.

Rust-Tierney said the other reason was "economic—the quality of counsel. Most people who go on trial for their lives have lawyers most of us wouldn't want in a traffic case."

Bureau of Justice Statistics Director Steven D. Dillingham noted that since 1976 there have been 3,834 people sentenced to death, but that only 155 have been executed since the penalty was resumed in 1977.

CRIME CLOCK
1990

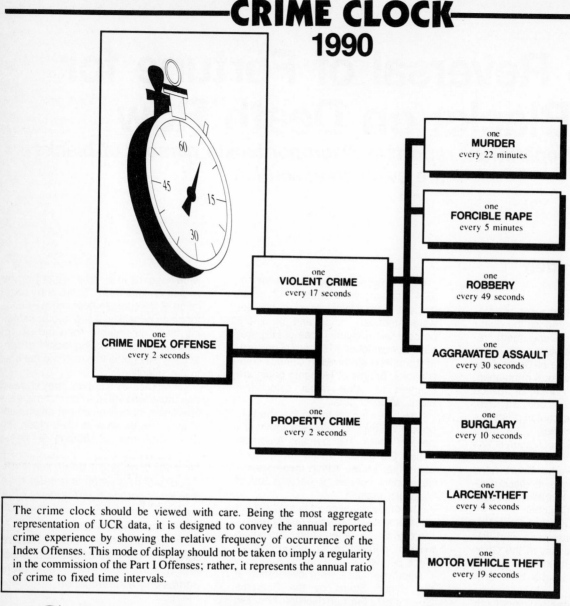

one **MURDER** every 22 minutes	
one **FORCIBLE RAPE** every 5 minutes	
one **VIOLENT CRIME** every 17 seconds	one **ROBBERY** every 49 seconds
	one **AGGRAVATED ASSAULT** every 30 seconds
one **CRIME INDEX OFFENSE** every 2 seconds	
one **PROPERTY CRIME** every 2 seconds	one **BURGLARY** every 10 seconds
	one **LARCENY-THEFT** every 4 seconds
	one **MOTOR VEHICLE THEFT** every 19 seconds

The crime clock should be viewed with care. Being the most aggregate representation of UCR data, it is designed to convey the annual reported crime experience by showing the relative frequency of occurrence of the Index Offenses. This mode of display should not be taken to imply a regularity in the commission of the Part I Offenses; rather, it represents the annual ratio of crime to fixed time intervals.

Crime in the United States 1990

Crime Index Total

The Crime Index total rose 2 percent to 14.5 million offenses in 1990. Five- and 10-year percent changes showed the 1990 total was 10 percent above the 1986 level and 8 percent higher than in 1981.

From 1989 to 1990, overall violent crime showed an 11-percent increase. The number of property crimes increased less than 1 percent for the 2-year period.

The largest volume of Crime Index offenses occurred in the Southern States which accounted for 37 percent of the total. Following were the Western States with 23 percent, the Midwestern States with 21 percent, and the Northeastern States with 18 percent.

Crime rates relate the incidence of crime to population. In 1990, there were an estimated 5,820 Crime Index

offenses for each 100,000 in population nationwide. The violent crime rate was 732, and for property crime, it was 5,088 per 100,000.

Regionally, the Crime Index rates per 100,000 inhabitants ranged from 6,405 in the West to 5,102 in the Midwest. The South registered a rate of 6,334 per 100,000 inhabitants, and the Northeast, 5,193.

National estimates of volume and rate per 100,000 inhabitants for all Crime Index offenses covering the past decade are set forth in Table 1, "Index of Crime, United States, 1981-1990."

Table 2, "Index of Crime, United States, 1990," shows current year estimates for MSAs, rural counties, and cities and towns outside metropolitan areas (other cities). See Appendix III for the definitions of these community types.

Table 1.—Index of Crime, United States, 1981-1990

Population[1]	Crime Index total[2]	Modified Crime Index total[3]	Violent crime[4]	Property crime[4]	Murder and non-negligent man-slaughter	Forcible rape	Robbery	Aggra-vated assault	Burglary	Larceny-theft	Motor vehicle theft	Arson[3]
				Number of Offenses								
Population by year:												
1981-229,146,000	13,423,800		1,361,820	12,061,900	22,520	82,500	592,910	663,900	3,779,700	7,194,400	1,087,800	
1982-231,534,000	12,974,400		1,322,390	11,652,000	21,010	78,770	553,130	669,480	3,447,100	7,142,500	1,062,400	
1983-233,981,000	12,108,600		1,258,090	10,850,500	19,310	78,920	506,570	653,290	3,129,900	6,712,800	1,007,900	
1984-236,158,000	11,881,800		1,273,280	10,608,500	18,690	84,230	485,010	685,350	2,984,400	6,591,900	1,032,200	
1985-238,740,000	12,431,400		1,328,800	11,102,600	18,980	88,670	497,870	723,250	3,073,300	6,926,400	1,102,900	
1986-241,077,000	13,211,900		1,489,170	11,722,700	20,610	91,460	542,780	834,320	3,241,400	7,257,200	1,224,100	
1987-243,400,000	13,508,700		1,484,000	12,024,700	20,100	91,110	517,700	855,090	3,236,200	7,499,900	1,288,700	
1988-245,807,000	13,923,100		1,566,220	12,356,900	20,680	92,490	542,970	910,090	3,218,100	7,705,900	1,432,900	
1989-248,239,000	14,251,400		1,646,040	12,605,400	21,500	94,500	578,330	951,710	3,168,200	7,872,400	1,564,800	
1990-248,709,873	14,475,600		1,820,130	12,655,500	23,440	102,560	639,270	1,054,860	3,073,900	7,945,700	1,635,900	
Percent change: number of offenses:												
1990/1989	+1.6		+10.6	+.4	+9.0	+8.5	+10.5	+10.8	-3.0	+.9	+4.5	
1990/1986	+9.6		+22.2	+8.0	+13.7	+12.1	+17.8	+26.4	-5.2	+9.5	+33.6	
1990/1981	+7.8		+33.7	+4.9	+4.1	+24.3	+7.8	+58.9	-18.7	+10.4	+50.4	
				Rate per 100,000 Inhabitants								
Year:												
1981	5,858.2		594.3	5,263.9	9.8	36.0	258.7	289.7	1,649.5	3,139.7	474.7	
1982	5,603.6		571.1	5,032.5	9.1	34.0	238.9	289.2	1,488.8	3,084.8	458.8	
1983	5,175.0		537.7	4,637.4	8.3	33.7	216.5	279.2	1,337.7	2,868.9	430.8	
1984	5,031.3		539.2	4,492.1	7.9	35.7	205.4	290.2	1,263.7	2,791.3	437.1	
1985	5,207.1		556.6	4,650.5	7.9	37.1	208.5	302.9	1,287.3	2,901.2	462.0	
1986	5,480.4		617.7	4,862.6	8.6	37.9	225.1	346.1	1,344.6	3,010.3	507.8	
1987	5,550.0		609.7	4,940.3	8.3	37.4	212.7	351.3	1,329.6	3,081.3	529.4	
1988	5,664.2		637.2	5,027.1	8.4	37.6	220.9	370.2	1,309.2	3,134.9	582.9	
1989	5,741.0		663.1	5,077.9	8.7	38.1	233.0	383.4	1,276.3	3,171.3	630.4	
1990	5,820.3		731.8	5088.5	9.4	41.2	257.0	424.1	1,235.9	3,194.8	657.8	
Percent change: rate per 100,000 inhabitants:												
1990/1989	+1.4		+10.4	+.2	+8.0	+8.1	+10.3	+10.6	-3.2	+.7	+4.3	
1990/1986	+6.2		+18.5	+4.6	+9.3	+8.7	+14.2	+22.5	-8.1	+6.1	+29.5	
1990/1981	-.6		+23.1	-3.3	-4.1	+14.4	-.7	+46.4	-25.1	+1.8	+38.6	

[1]Populations are Bureau of the Census provisional estimates as of July 1, except 1990 which are the decennial census counts and are subject to change.
[2]Because of rounding, the offenses may not add to totals.
[3]Although arson data are included in the trend and clearance tables, sufficient data are not available to estimate totals for this offense.
[4]Violent crimes are offenses of murder, forcible rape, robbery, and aggravated assault. Property crimes are offenses of burglary, larceny-theft, and motor vehicle theft. Data are not included for the property crime of arson.
All rates were calculated on the offenses before rounding.

CRIME INDEX OFFENSES REPORTED

MURDER AND NONNEGLIGENT MANSLAUGHTER

DEFINITION

Murder and nonnegligent manslaughter, as defined in the Uniform Crime Reporting Program, is the willful (non-negligent) killing of one human being by another.

TREND

Year	Number of offenses	Rate per 100,000 inhabitants
1989	21,500	8.7
1990	23,438	9.4
Percent change	+9.0	+8.0

Volume

Reaching an all-time high during 1990, the total number of murders in the United States for the year was estimated at 23,438 or 1 percent of the violent crimes reported. More persons were murdered in July than any other month, while the fewest were killed during February.

Murder by Month, 1986-1990

[Percent of annual total]

Months	1986	1987	1988	1989	1990
January	7.7	7.7	8.2	8.1	7.9
February	7.0	7.9	7.2	7.1	7.0
March	8.3	8.2	7.7	7.8	8.0
April	8.0	7.6	7.7	7.9	7.4
May	8.2	8.6	7.8	7.8	8.1
June	8.3	7.8	7.7	8.2	8.4
July	9.4	8.6	8.9	9.1	9.6
August	9.4	8.9	9.5	9.0	9.3
September	9.1	8.3	8.9	8.8	9.2
October	8.3	8.8	8.9	8.9	8.8
November	8.0	8.3	8.2	8.5	7.6
December	8.4	9.1	9.2	8.7	8.8

When viewing the four regions of the Nation, the Southern States, the most populous, accounted for 43 percent of the murders. The Western States reported 20 percent; the Northeastern States, 19 percent; and the Midwestern States, 18 percent.

Trend

The murder volume was up 9 percent nationwide in 1990 over 1989. The Nation's cities overall experienced an increase of 11 percent, with upward trends recorded in all population groupings. Of the cities, those with populations under 10,000 registered the greatest increase, 19 percent. Suburban counties recorded a 5-percent rise, and the rural counties registered a 4-percent increase.

All regions experienced more murders during 1990 than in 1989. The number of murders was up 11 percent in the West; 10 percent in both the Northeast and South; and 4 percent in the Midwest.

The accompanying chart reveals a 14-percent rise nationally in the murder counts from 1986 to 1990. The 10-year trend showed the 1990 total 4 percent above the 1981 level.

Rate

A murder rate of 9 per 100,000 inhabitants was registered nationwide in 1990. Two-, 5-, and 10-year trends showed the 1990 rate was 8 percent higher than in 1989 and 9 percent above the 1986 rate but 4 percent below the 1981 rate.

On a regional basis, the South averaged 12 murders per 100,000 people; both the West and the Northeast, 9 per 100,000; and the Midwest, 7 per 100,000. Compared to 1989, murder rates in 1990 increased 10 percent in both the West and Northeast; 9 percent in the South; and 6 percent in the Midwest.

The Nation's metropolitan areas reported a 1990 murder rate of 11 victims per 100,000 inhabitants. In the rural counties, the rate was 6 per 100,000, and in cities outside metropolitan areas, the rate was 5 per 100,000.

Nature

Supplemental data provided by contributing agencies recorded information for 20,045 of the estimated 23,438 murders in 1990. Submitted monthly, the data consist of the age, sex, and race of both victims and offenders; the types of weapons used; the relationships of victims to the offenders; and the circumstances surrounding the murders.

Based on this information, 78 percent of the murder victims in 1990 were males; and 90 percent were persons 18 years of age or older. Forty-nine percent were aged 20 through 34 years. Considering victims for whom race was known, an average of 49 of every 100 were black, 49 were white, and the remainder were persons of other races.

FORCIBLE RAPE

DEFINITION

Forcible rape, as defined in the Program, is the carnal knowledge of a female forcibly and against her will. Assaults or attempts to commit rape by force or threat of force are also included; however, statutory rape (without force) and other sex offenses are excluded.

TREND

Year	Number of offenses	Rate per 100,000 inhabitants
1989	94,504	38.1
1990	102,555	41.2
Percent change	+8.5	+8.1

Volume

During 1990, there were an estimated 102,555 forcible rapes in the Nation. Rape offenses comprised 6 percent of the total violent crimes. Geographically, the Southern States, the region with the largest population, accounted for 38 percent of the forcible rapes reported to law enforcement. Following were the Midwest with 25 percent, the West with 23 percent, and the Northeast with 14 percent.

Monthly totals showed the greatest number of forcible rapes were reported during the summer, with July recording the highest frequency. The lowest total was registered in February.

Forcible Rape by Month, 1986-1990

[Percent of annual total]

Months	1986	1987	1988	1989	1990
January	7.1	7.2	7.4	7.4	7.6
February	6.7	6.8	7.3	6.3	6.7
March	7.9	8.1	8.0	7.7	7.9
April	8.1	8.2	8.0	8.3	8.1
May	8.8	8.9	9.0	8.6	9.1
June	9.2	9.3	8.7	8.9	9.0
July	9.8	9.7	9.9	10.0	9.6
August	10.2	9.8	9.8	9.5	9.4
September	9.1	8.9	9.0	8.8	9.1
October	8.4	8.1	8.4	8.9	8.4
November	7.8	7.7	7.6	8.3	7.7
December	7.0	7.3	6.8	7.3	7.4

Trend

Compared to the previous year, the 1990 forcible rape volume increased 9 percent nationwide. In the cities collectively, the total was also up 9 percent. The rural counties recorded a 7-percent increase and the suburban counties, a 10-percent rise. City trends ranged from a 4-percent increase in cities with populations of 1 million or more to a 14-percent increase in cities with under 10,000 inhabitants.

Geographically, all four regions reported higher forcible rape volumes in 1990 than in 1989. The increases were 11 percent in the Southern States, 8 percent in both the Midwestern and Western States, and 2 percent in the Northeastern States.

National trends for 5 and 10 years show that the forcible rape total rose 12 percent over 1986 and 24 percent above 1981.

Rate

By Uniform Crime Reporting definition, the victims of forcible rape are always female. In 1990, an estimated 80 of every 100,000 females in the country were reported rape victims, an increase of 8 percent from the 1989 rate. Since 1986, the female forcible rape rate has risen 10 percent.

Female forcible rape rates for 1990 showed there were 89 victims per 100,000 females in MSAs, 64 per 100,000 females in cities outside metropolitan areas, and 44 per 100,000 females in rural counties.

Regionally, the highest female rape rate was in the Southern States, which recorded 88 victims per 100,000 females. Following were the Western States with a rate of

87, the Midwestern States with 83, and the Northeastern States with 56.

Nature

Of all reported forcible rapes during 1990, 84 percent were rapes by force. The remainder were attempts or assaults to commit forcible rape. A 10-percent increase was registered in the number of rapes by force, and a 1-percent increase for attempts to commit rape.

Clearances

Nationwide, as well as in the cities and suburban counties, 53 percent of the forcible rapes reported to law enforcement were cleared by arrest or exceptional means in 1990. Rural county law enforcement agencies cleared 54 percent of the offenses brought to their attention.

Clearance rates for the regions ranged from 47 percent in the Midwestern States to 58 percent in the Southern States. In the Northeastern States, the clearance rate for forcible rape was 53 percent, and in the Western States, it was 50 percent.

Of the total clearances for forcible rape in the country as a whole, 12 percent involved only persons under 18 years of age. Rural counties recorded a 13-percent involvement of this age group, while 17 percent was recorded in suburban counties. In the Nation's cities, only persons under age 18 accounted for 11 percent of the forcible rape clearances.

Persons Arrested

The number of arrests for forcible rape rose 8 percent nationwide and in the Nation's cities and suburban counties from 1989 to 1990. Arrests for this offense rose 6 percent in the rural counties. For the 5-year period, 1986 to 1990, total forcible rape arrests increased 9 percent nationwide. Those of adults and of persons under 18 years of age increased 10 percent and 3 percent, respectively.

Of the forcible rape arrestees in 1990, 44 percent were persons under the age of 25, with 29 percent of the total being in the 18- to 24-year age group. Fifty-five percent of those arrested were white, 43 percent were black, and the remainder, other races.

ROBBERY

DEFINITION

Robbery is the taking or attempting to take anything of value from the care, custody, or control of a person or persons by force or threat of force or violence and/or by putting the victim in fear.

──── TREND ────

Year	Number of offenses	Rate per 100,000 inhabitants
1989	578,326	233.0
1990	639,271	257.0
Percent change ..	+10.5	+10.3

Volume

Accounting for 4 percent of all Index crimes and 35 percent of the violent crimes in 1990, robbery was estimated at 639,271 offenses for the year. Robberies occurred most frequently in December and least often in April during 1990.

Robbery by Month, 1986-1990

[Percent of annual total]

Months	1986	1987	1988	1989	1990
January	8.7	8.9	8.6	8.8	8.7
February	7.7	8.1	7.9	7.4	7.3
March	8.2	8.2	8.0	8.0	8.1
April	7.6	7.5	7.3	7.3	7.2
May	7.7	7.5	7.6	7.6	7.7
June	8.0	7.6	7.6	7.6	7.8
July	8.4	8.3	8.4	8.4	8.5
August	9.3	8.7	8.7	8.6	8.8
September	8.6	8.5	8.7	8.6	8.6
October	8.7	8.8	9.1	9.2	8.9
November	8.3	8.5	9.0	9.0	8.7
December	9.0	9.2	9.2	9.3	9.6

Distribution figures for the regions showed that the most populous Southern States registered 32 percent of all reported robberies. Following were the Northeastern States with 28 percent, the Western States with 22 percent, and the Midwestern States with the remainder.

Trend

Nationally, the 1990 robbery volume was 11 percent higher than the 1989 level. In the Nation's cities overall, robbery jumped 12 percent, the greatest increase being in those with populations of 500,000-999,999, 19 percent. The suburban counties experienced a 6-percent increase, while the rural counties recorded the only decline, 1 percent.

Two-year trends show the number of robberies in 1990 was up in all four regions as compared to 1989. The increases were 9 percent in both the Northeast and the South, 11 percent in the Midwest, and 14 percent in the West.

The accompanying chart depicts the trend in the robbery volume, as well as the robbery rate, for the years 1986-1990. In 1990, the number of robbery offenses was 18 percent higher than in 1986 and 8 percent above the 1981 total.

Rate

The national robbery rate in 1990 was 257 per 100,000 people, 10 percent higher than in 1989. In metropolitan areas, the robbery rate was 322; in cities outside metropolitan areas, it was 63; and in the rural areas, it was 16. With 1,139 robberies per 100,000 inhabitants, the highest rate was recorded in cities with a million or more inhabitants.

A comparison of 1989 and 1990 regional rates per 100,000 inhabitants showed the rates of 199 in the Midwest and 263 in the West were each up 12 percent. The rates were 237 in the South and 353 in the Northeast, both up 9 percent from 1989.

Nature

In 1990, a total estimated national loss of $501 million was due to robberies. The value of property stolen during robberies averaged $783 per incident. Average dollar losses ranged from $341 taken during robberies of convenience stores to $3,244 per bank robbery. The impact of this violent crime on its victims cannot be measured in terms of monetary loss alone. While the object of a robbery is to obtain money or property, the crime always involves force or threat of force, and many victims suffer serious personal injury.

As in previous years, robberies on streets or highways accounted for more than half (56 percent) of the offenses in this category. Robberies of commercial and financial establishments accounted for an additional 22 percent, and those occurring at residences, 10 percent. The remainder were miscellaneous types. By type, all categories of robbery showed increases from 1989 to 1990. The increases ranged from 4 percent for convenience store robberies to 18 percent for bank robberies.

Robbery, Percent Distribution, 1990
[By region]

	United States Total	North-eastern States	Mid-western States	Southern States	Western States
Total[1]	100.0	100.0	100.0	100.0	100.0
Street/highway	56.1	64.7	58.9	49.1	52.8
Commercial house	11.5	8.6	9.8	13.0	14.2
Gas or service station	2.7	2.4	3.4	2.8	2.5
Convenience store	6.1	2.0	3.7	11.2	5.9
Residence	9.8	9.4	8.9	11.9	8.0
Bank	1.5	.9	1.0	1.3	2.8
Miscellaneous	12.4	12.0	14.3	10.7	13.7

[1]Because of rounding, percentages may not add to totals.

AGGRAVATED ASSAULT

DEFINITION

Aggravated assault is an unlawful attack by one person upon another for the purpose of inflicting severe or aggravated bodily injury. This type of assault is usually accompanied by the use of a weapon or by means likely to produce death or great bodily harm.

TREND

Year	Number of offenses	Rate per 100,000 inhabitants
1989	951,707	383.4
1990	1,054,863	424.1
Percent change	+10.8	+10.6

Volume

Totaling an estimated 1,054,863 offenses nationally, aggravated assaults in 1990 accounted for 58 percent of the violent crimes. Geographic distribution figures show that 38 percent of the aggravated assault volume was accounted for by the South, 25 percent by the West, 20 percent by the Midwest, and 18 percent by the Northeast.

The 1990 monthly figures show that the greatest number of aggravated assaults was recorded during July, while the lowest volume occurred in February.

Aggravated Assault by Month, 1986-1990
[Percent of annual total]

Months	1986	1987	1988	1989	1990
January	6.8	7.3	7.2	7.5	7.4
February	6.3	7.0	7.0	6.6	6.7
March	8.0	7.8	7.9	7.9	7.8
April	8.1	8.1	8.1	8.1	8.2
May	9.1	8.9	8.9	8.9	9.0
June	9.7	8.9	9.0	8.9	9.4
July	10.0	9.5	9.8	9.6	10.1
August	10.0	9.5	9.8	9.2	9.3
September	8.8	8.7	9.0	8.8	8.9
October	8.3	8.5	8.4	9.1	8.3
November	7.6	7.9	7.5	7.9	7.4
December	7.4	7.8	7.5	7.5	7.5

Trend

In 1990, aggravated assaults were up 11 percent nationwide. Upswings in volume were evident in all regions and population groups as well, 1990 versus 1989. All cities collectively recorded a 10-percent increase, with cities of populations from 50,000 to 99,999 recording the greatest rise, 17 percent. The suburban counties registered an 8-percent increase and the rural counties, a 9-percent rise for the 2-year period.

During the same time period, the South registered a 16-percent upswing in its aggravated assault volume, and the Midwest, a 12-percent rise. Increases of 7 and 5 percent were recorded in the West and Northeast, respectively.

Five- and 10-year trends show aggravated assaults up 26 percent above the 1986 level and 59 percent over the 1981 experience.

Rate

Up 11 percent above the 1989 rate, there were 424 reported victims of aggravated assault for every 100,000 people nationwide in 1990. The rate was 23 percent higher than in 1986 and 46 percent above the 1981 rate.

Higher than the national average, the rate in metropolitan areas was 478 per 100,000 in 1990. Cities outside metropolitan areas experienced a rate of 357, and rural counties, a rate of 163.

Regionally, the aggravated assault rates ranged from 491 per 100,000 people in the West to 346 per 100,000 in the Midwest. The rate in the South for 1990 was 472, and in the Northeast, 366. Aggravated assault rates rose in all geographic regions in 1990 over 1989. The increases were 16 percent in the South, 13 percent in the Midwest, 5 percent in the West, and 4 percent in the Northeast.

Nature

In 1990, 32 percent of the aggravated assaults were committed with blunt objects or other dangerous weapons. Of the remaining weapon categories, personal weapons such as hands, fists, and feet were used in 26 percent of the offenses; firearms in 23 percent; and knives or cutting instruments in the remainder.

Assaults with firearms showed the greatest increase from 1989 to 1990, 14 percent. Those committed with personal weapons and with knives or cutting instruments were each up 7 percent, and those involving blunt objects or other dangerous weapons increased 10 percent.

Aggravated Assault, Type of Weapons Used, 1990

[Percent distribution by region]

Region	Total all weapons[1]	Fire-arms	Knives or cutting instruments	Other weapons (clubs, blunt objects, etc.)	Personal weapons
Total	100.0	23.1	19.5	31.9	25.5
Northeastern States	100.0	17.4	22.6	34.0	26.1
Midwestern States	100.0	25.6	19.7	34.1	20.5
Southern States	100.0	26.4	21.0	31.4	21.3
Western States	100.0	20.6	15.3	29.6	34.5

[1]Because of rounding, percentages may not add to totals.

BURGLARY

DEFINITION

The Uniform Crime Reporting Program defines burglary as the unlawful entry of a structure to commit a felony or theft. The use of force to gain entry is not required to classify an offense as burglary.

TREND

Year	Number of offenses	Rate per 100,000 inhabitants
1989	3,168,170	1,276.3
1990	3,073,909	1,235.9
Percent change ..	−3.0	−3.2

Volume

An estimated 3,073,909 burglaries occurred in the United States during 1990. These offenses accounted for 21 percent of the total Crime Index and 24 percent of the property crimes.

Distribution figures for the regions showed that the highest burglary volume occurred in the most populous Southern States, accounting for 42 percent of the total. The Western States followed with 22 percent, the Midwestern States with 19 percent, and the Northeastern States with 17 percent.

As in previous years, more burglaries occurred in August than any other month. The lowest number was reported in February.

Burglary by Month, 1986-1990

[Percent of annual total]

Months	1986	1987	1988	1989	1990
January	8.4	8.4	8.4	8.8	8.8
February	7.5	7.8	7.8	7.3	7.5
March	8.3	8.3	8.1	8.2	8.1
April	7.9	7.6	7.5	7.7	7.8
May	8.1	8.0	8.1	8.4	8.1
June	8.1	8.0	8.0	8.3	7.9
July	8.9	8.8	8.8	9.2	8.9
August	9.0	9.1	9.3	9.3	9.0
September	8.5	8.4	8.6	8.6	8.3
October	8.4	8.4	8.5	8.5	8.5
November	8.1	8.4	8.4	8.1	8.3
December	8.8	8.8	8.5	7.8	8.7

Trend

Nationwide, the burglary volume decreased 3 percent in 1990 from the 1989 total. By population, decreases were registered in all city groupings with the greatest decline in cities of 250,000-499,999 in population, 7 percent.

Geographically, three of the four regions of the United States reported decreases in burglaries during 1990 as compared to 1989. The declines equaled 4 percent in the Western, Midwestern, and Southern States. The only increase in burglary volume occurred in the Northeastern States with a 1-percent rise.

Longer term trends show burglary down 5 percent from the 1986 volume and 19 percent below the 1981 level.

Rate

A burglary rate of 1,236 per 100,000 inhabitants was registered nationwide in 1990. The rate fell 3 percent from 1989 and was 25 percent below the 1981 rate. In 1990, for every 100,000 in population, the rate was 1,356 in the metropolitan areas, 1,053 in the cities outside metropolitan areas, and 671 in the rural counties.

Regionally, the burglary rate was 1,498 in the Southern States, 1,304 in the Western States, 1,020 in the Northeastern States, and 983 in the Midwestern States. A comparison of 1989 and 1990 rates showed decreases of 6 percent in the West, 4 percent in the South, and 3 percent in the Midwest. A 1-percent increase was reported in the Northeast.

Nature

Two of every 3 burglaries in 1990 were residential in nature. Seventy percent of all burglaries involved forcible entry, 22 percent were unlawful entries (without force), and the remainder were forcible entry attempts. Offenses for which time of occurrence was reported were evenly divided between day and night.

Burglary victims suffered losses estimated at $3.5 billion in 1990, and the average dollar loss per burglary was $1,133. The average loss for residential offenses was $1,143, while for nonresidential property, it was $1,110.

Both residential and nonresidential burglaries showed declines from 1989 to 1990, 4 and 3 percent, respectively.

Clearances

Geographically, 14 percent of the burglaries brought to the attention of law enforcement agencies across the country were cleared in 1990. In the South, the clearance rate was 15 percent; in the West and Northeast, 13 percent; and in the Midwest, 12 percent.

Rural county law enforcement cleared 16 percent of the burglaries in their jurisdictions. Agencies in suburban counties cleared 14 percent, and in cities, 13 percent.

Adults were involved in 81 percent of all burglary offenses cleared, and only young people under 18 years of age were offenders in the remaining 19 percent. Similar to the national experience, persons under age 18 accounted for 19 percent of the burglary clearances in cities. Rural county law enforcement agencies reported 20 percent of their burglary clearances involved only juveniles, while suburban county agencies registered 21 percent. The highest degree of juvenile involvement was recorded in the Nation's smallest cities (under 10,000 in population) where young persons under 18 years of age accounted for 26 percent of the clearances.

LARCENY-THEFT

DEFINITION

Larceny-theft is the unlawful taking, carrying, leading, or riding away of property from the possession or constructive possession of another. It includes crimes such as shoplifting, pocket-picking, purse-snatching, thefts from motor vehicles, thefts of motor vehicle parts and accessories, bicycle thefts, etc., in which no use of force, violence, or fraud occurs.

TREND

Year	Number of offenses	Rate per 100,000 inhabitants
1989	7,872,442	3,171.3
1990	7,945,670	3,194.8
Percent change ..	+ .9	+ .7

Volume

Estimated at nearly 8 million offenses during 1990, larceny-thefts comprised 55 percent of the Crime Index total and 63 percent of the property crimes. Similar to the experience in previous years, larceny-thefts were recorded most often during August and least frequently in February. When viewed geographically, the most populous Southern States recorded 37 percent of the larceny-theft total. The Western and Midwestern States each registered 23 percent; and the Northeastern States, 17 percent.

Larceny-Theft by Month, 1986-1990

[Percent of annual total]

Months	1986	1987	1988	1989	1990
January	7.8	7.6	7.6	8.0	8.2
February	7.2	7.5	7.5	7.2	7.4
March	8.3	8.3	8.2	8.2	8.2
April	8.2	8.0	7.8	8.0	7.9
May	8.4	8.2	8.3	8.6	8.3
June	8.6	8.5	8.5	8.7	8.3
July	9.1	9.1	9.0	9.2	8.9
August	9.3	9.2	9.5	9.5	9.1
September	8.4	8.4	8.5	8.3	8.2
October	8.5	8.6	8.7	8.6	8.7
November	7.9	8.1	8.2	8.0	8.1
December	8.3	8.4	8.3	7.7	8.4

Trend

Compared to 1989, the 1990 volume of larceny-thefts increased 1 percent in the Nation and less than 1 percent in all cities collectively. The suburban and rural counties showed increases of 2 percent and 3 percent, respectively.

Regionally, volume upswings of 2 percent were recorded in both the Midwestern and the Southern States. The Northeastern States showed a 1-percent increase, while the Western States registered a 1-percent decline.

The 5- and 10-year national trends indicated larceny was up 9 percent over the 1986 total and rose 10 percent above the 1981 level.

Rate

The 1990 larceny-theft rate was 3,195 per 100,000 United States inhabitants. The 1990 rate was 1 percent higher than in 1989, 6 percent above the 1986 level, and 2 percent above the 1981 level. The 1990 rate was 3,533 per 100,000 inhabitants of metropolitan areas; 3,559 per 100,000 population in cities outside metropolitan areas; and 1,024 per 100,000 people in the rural counties.

Regionally, the rates of 3,471 in the South and 3,024 in the Midwest were up 2 and 3 percent, respectively, over 1989 levels. The Northeast's 1990 rate of 2,598 per 100,000 inhabitants was up less than 1 percent, while the rate per 100,000 inhabitants in the West, 3,515, was 3 percent lower than the year before.

Nature

During 1990, the average value of property stolen due to larceny-theft was $480, up from $462 in 1989. When the average value was applied to the estimated number of larceny-thefts, the loss to victims nationally was $3.8 billion for the year. This estimated dollar loss is considered conservative since many offenses in the larceny category, particularly if the value of the stolen goods is small, never come to law enforcement attention. Losses in 24 percent of the thefts reported to law enforcement in 1990 ranged from $50 to $200, while in 36 percent, they were over $200.

Losses of goods and property reported stolen as a result of pocket-picking averaged $355; purse-snatching, $278; and shoplifting, $115. Thefts from buildings resulted in an average loss of $791; from motor vehicles, $541; and from coin-operated machines, $147. The average value loss due to thefts of motor vehicle accessories was $319 and for thefts of bicycles, $215.

Thefts of motor vehicle parts, accessories, and contents made up the largest portion of reported larcenies–37 percent. Also contributing to the high volume of thefts were shoplifting, accounting for 16 percent; thefts from buildings, 14 percent; and bicycle thefts, 6 percent. The remainder were distributed among pocket-picking, purse-snatching, thefts from coin-operated machines, and all other types of larceny-thefts. The accompanying table presents the distribution of larceny-theft by type and geographic region.

Larceny Analysis by Region, 1990

[Percent distribution]

	United States Total	North-eastern States	Mid-western States	Southern States	Western States
Total[1]	100.0	100.0	100.0	100.0	100.0
Pocket-picking	1.0	3.6	.7	.4	.5
Purse-snatching	1.0	2.1	1.0	.8	.7
Shoplifting	16.2	13.6	13.6	16.8	19.6
From motor vehicles (except accessories)	22.0	22.8	18.8	19.7	27.6
Motor vehicle accessories	14.9	15.1	15.0	16.4	12.4
Bicycles	5.6	5.7	5.1	4.6	7.4
From buildings	14.1	18.5	19.0	10.5	12.0
From coin-operated machines	.8	1.2	.6	.8	.6
All others	24.4	17.5	26.1	29.9	19.2

[1]Because of rounding, percentages may not add to totals.

MOTOR VEHICLE THEFT

TREND

Year	Number of offenses	Rate per 100,000 inhabitants
1989	1,564,800	630.4
1990	1,635,907	657.8
Percent change ..	+4.5	+4.3

Volume

An estimated total of 1,635,907 thefts of motor vehicles occurred in the United States during 1990. These offenses comprised 13 percent of all property crimes. The regional distribution of motor vehicle thefts showed 31 percent of the volume was in the Southern States, 25 percent each in the Western and Northeastern States, and 18 percent in the Midwestern States.

The 1990 monthly figures show that the greatest numbers of motor vehicle thefts were recorded during the months of July, August, and October, while the lowest count was in February.

Motor Vehicle Theft by Month, 1986-1990

[Percent of annual total]

Months	1986	1987	1988	1989	1990
January	7.9	7.9	8.0	8.3	8.5
February	7.1	7.5	7.6	7.3	7.6
March	8.1	8.4	7.9	8.1	8.4
April	7.8	7.9	7.4	7.5	7.9
May	8.0	8.0	7.8	8.0	8.1
June	8.2	8.1	8.0	8.2	8.1
July	8.9	8.8	8.8	8.8	8.8
August	9.5	9.0	9.4	9.0	8.8
September	8.7	8.4	8.7	8.5	8.4
October	9.0	8.8	9.0	9.0	8.8
November	8.5	8.5	8.7	8.7	8.3
December	8.3	8.7	8.7	8.5	8.4

Trend

The number of motor vehicle thefts increased 5 percent nationally from 1989 to 1990. This upward trend was evident in all city population groupings with those having populations of 500,000 to 999,999 showing the largest increase, 11 percent. The rural counties showed an increase of 3 percent, while the suburban counties recorded a decline of less than 1 percent.

Geographically, all four regions experienced motor vehicle theft increases. The increases were 6 percent in the Northeastern Region, 5 percent in the Midwestern Region, 4 percent in the Southern Region, and 2 percent in the Western Region.

The accompanying chart shows that the volume of motor vehicle thefts in 1990 increased 34 percent over the 1986 volume.

Rate

The 1990 national motor vehicle theft rate—658 per 100,000 people—was 4 percent higher than the rate in 1989. The rate was 30 percent higher than in 1986 and 39 percent above the 1981 rate.

For every 100,000 inhabitants living in MSAs, there were 801 motor vehicle thefts reported in 1990. The rate in cities outside metropolitan areas (other cities) was 232 and in rural counties, 121. As in previous years, the highest rates were in the Nation's most heavily populated municipalities, indicating that this offense is primarily a large-city problem. For every 100,000 inhabitants in cities with populations over 250,000, the 1990 motor vehicle theft rate was 1,693. The Nation's smallest cities, those with fewer than 10,000 inhabitants, recorded a rate of 257 per 100,000.

Among the regions, the motor vehicle theft rates ranged from 818 per 100,000 people in the Northeastern States to 501 in the Midwestern States. The Western States' rate was 778 and the Southern States' rate, 598. All regions registered rate increases from 1989 to 1990. In both the Northeastern and Midwestern States, the increase was 6 percent; in the Southern States, 4 percent; and in the Western States, less than 1 percent.

An estimated average of 1 of every 119 registered motor vehicles was stolen nationwide during 1990. Regionally, this rate was greatest in the Northeast where 1 of every 82 motor vehicles registered was stolen. The other three regions reported lesser rates—1 per 105 in the West, 1 per 135 in the South, and 1 per 163 in the Midwest.

Nature

During 1990, the estimated value of motor vehicles stolen nationwide was over $8 billion. At the time of theft, the average value per vehicle stolen was $5,032.

Eighty percent of all motor vehicles reported stolen during the year were automobiles, 15 percent were trucks or buses, and the remainder were other types.

Motor Vehicle Theft, 1990

[Percent distribution by region]

Region	Total[1]	Autos	Trucks and buses	Other vehicles
Total	100.0	79.7	14.5	5.8
Northeastern States	100.0	92.7	4.4	2.9
Midwestern States	100.0	84.3	9.9	5.8
Southern States	100.0	74.9	18.5	6.6
Western States	100.0	69.9	22.7	7.4

[1]Because of rounding, percentages may not add to totals.

Bibliography

Abraham, H., *The Judicial Process,* Oxford University Press, 1968.

Adler, F., *Sisters in Crime,* McGraw-Hill, 1975.

Allen, H. and C. Simonsen, *Corrections in America,* Glencoe Press, 1978.

Amos, W., *Delinquent Children in Juvenile Correctional Institutions,* C.C. Thomas, 1966.

Atkins, B. and M. Pogrebin, *The Invisible Justice System,* W.H. Anderson, 1978.

Balton, M., *European Policing,* John Jay Press, 1978.

Bartollas, C., S. Miller, and S. Dinitz, *Juvenile Victimization,* Sage Publications, Inc., 1976.

Bartollas, C. and S.J. Miller, *Correctional Administration: Theory and Practice,* McGraw-Hill, 1978.

Bartollas, C. and S.J. Miller, *The Juvenile Offender: Control, Correction and Treatment,* Allyn & Bacon, Inc., 1978.

Bayley, D., *Police and Society,* Sage Publications, Inc., 1978.

Beigel, H., *Beneath the Badge,* Harper and Row Publishers, Inc., 1977.

Bell, J.B., *Time of Terror: How Democratic Societies Respond to Revolutionary Violence,* Basic Books Inc., 1978.

Bequai, A., *Organized Crime,* Lexington Books, 1979.

Bequai, A., *White Collar Crime,* Lexington Books, 1979.

Berkeley, G., *The Democratic Policeman,* Beacon Press, 1969.

Berkley, G., *Introduction to Criminal Justice,* Holbrook, 1980.

Berns, W., *For Capital Punishment: Crime and the Morality of the Death Penalty,* Basic Books, Inc., 1979.

Best, A., *The Politics of Law Enforcement,* Lexington Books, 1974.

Bittner, E., *The Functions of Police in Modern Society,* U.S. Government Printing Office, 1970.

Bittner, E., and S. Krantz, *Standards Relating to Police Handling of Juvenile Problems,* Ballinger Publishing Co., 1978.

Blumberg, A.S., *Criminal Justice: Issues and Ironies,* New Viewpoints, 1979.

Bond, J., *Plea-Bargaining and Guilty Pleas,* Clark Boardman Co., 1975.

Bouza, A., *Police Administration,* Pergamon Press, Inc., 1979.

Bowker, L., *Women, Crime, and the Criminal Justice System,* Lexington Books, 1978.

Bowker, L., *Prison Victimization,* Elsevier, 1980.

Bracey, D.H., *''Baby-Pros''—Preliminary Profiles of Juvenile Prostitutes,* John Jay Press, 1978.

Butler, A., *The Law Enforcement Process,* Alfred Publishing Co., Inc., 1976.

Carlson, D.L., *Criminal Justice Procedure,* W.H. Anderson, 1979.

Carrington, F., *The Victims,* Arlington House, Inc., 1975.

Carte, G., *Police Reform in the United States,* University of California Press, 1975.

Carter, R. and L. Wilkins, *Probation, Parole and Community Corrections,* Wiley, 1976.

Challenge of Crime in a Free Society, The, Presidential Commission on Law Enforcement and Administration of Justice, 1967.

Chambliss, W., *Law, Order, and Power,* Addison-Wesley Publishing Co., 1971.

Chevigny, P., *Cops and Rebels: A Study of Provocation,* Random House, Inc., 1972.

Clinard, M.B., *Cities with Little Crime,* Cambridge University Press, 1978.

Cole, G., *The American System of Criminal Justice,* Duxbury, 1976.

Collins, M.C., *The Child-Abuser,* Publishing Sciences Group, 1978.

Conklin, J.,, *''Illegal But Not Criminal'': Business Crime in America,* Prentice-Hall, Inc., 1977.

Conley, J.A., *Theory and Research in Criminal Justice,* W.H. Anderson, 1979.

Conrad, J., *Crime and Its Correction,* University of California Press, 1965.

Conrad, J., *The Dangerous and the Endangered,* Lexington Books, 1978.

Conrad, J. and S. Dinitz, *In Fear of Each Other: Studies of Dangerousness in America,* Lexington Books, 1977.

Cook, J.G., *Constitutional Rights of the Accused, The,* Lawyers Co-Operative Publishing Co., 1972.

Cotte, T.J., *Children in Jail,* Beacon Press, 1978.

Creamer, J., *The Law of Arrest, Search and Seizure,* W.B. Saunders Co., 1975.

Cressey, D., *Criminal Organization,* Harper & Row Publishers, Inc., 1972.

Davis, K., *Discretionary Justice,* University of Illinois Press, 1971.

Delin, B., *The Sex Offender,* Beacon Press, 1978.

Devine, P.E., *The Ethics of Homicide,* Cornell University Press, 1979.

Dowling, J., *Criminal Procedure,* West, 1976.

Drapkin, I. and E. Viano, *Victimology,* Lexington Books, 1974.

Empey, L.T., *American Delinquency: Its Meaning and Construction,* Dorsey, 1978.

Falkin, G.R., *Reducing Delinquency,* Lexington Books, 1978.

Felkenes, G., *Constitutional Law for Criminal Justice,* Prentice-Hall, Inc., 1977.

Felkenes, G., *The Criminal Justice System,* Prentice-Hall, Inc., 1973.

Felkenes, G., *Criminal Law and Procedure,* Prentice-Hall, Inc., 1976.

Felt, M., *The FBI Pyramid,* G.P. Putnam's Sons, 1979.

Field, H.S. and N.J. Barnett, *Jurors and Rape,* Lexington Books, 1978.

Folley, V.L., *American Law Enforcement,* Allyn & Bacon, Inc., 1980.

Fogel, D., *The Justice Model for Corrections,* W.H. Anderson, 1979.

Foucault, M., *Discipline and Punish,* Pantheon Books, Inc., 1978.

Fox, J.A., *Forecasting Crime Data,* Lexington Books, 1979.

Fox, J.G., *Women in Cages,* Ballinger Publishing Co., 1979.

Frankel, M., *Criminal Sentences,* Hill & Wang, 1972.

Freeman, J.C., *Prisons Past and Future,* Heinemann, 1979.

Gardiner, J. and M. Mulkey, *Crime and Criminal Justice,* Heath, 1975.

Gaylin, W., *Partial Justice,* Knopf, Inc., 1974.

Geis, G., *Not the Law's Business,* NIMH, 1972.

Geis, G. and R. Meier, *White Collar Crime,* Free Press, 1977.

Gerber, R., *Contemporary Punishment,* University of Notre Dame Press, 1972.

Germann, A., et al., *Introduction to Law Enforcement,* C.C. Thomas, 1973.

Gibbs, J., *Crime, Punishment, and Deterrence,* Elsevier North-Holland, Inc., 1975.

Gifis, S.H., *Law Dictionary,* Barron's, 1975.

Glaser, D., *Adult Crime and Social Policy,* Prentice-Hall, Inc., 1972.

Glaser, D., *Crime in Our Changing Society,* Holt, Rinehart & Winston, Inc., 1978.

Goldsmith, J. and S.S. Goldsmith, *Crime and the Elderly,* D.C. Heath, 1976.

Goldstein, A., et al., *Police Crisis Intervention,* Pergamon Press, Inc., 1979.

Goldstein, H., *Policing a Free Society,* Ballinger Publishing Co., 1977.

Gottfredson, M.R. and D.M. Gottfredson, *Decision-Making in Criminal Justice,* Ballinger Publishing Co., 1979.

Greenberg, D., *Corrections and Punishment,* Sage, 1977.

Greenwood, P., *The Criminal Investigation Process,* Rand McNally Co., 1975.

Grosman, B., *New Directions in Sentencing,* Butterworths, 1980.

Gross, Hyman, *A Theory of Criminal Justice,* Oxford University Press, 1978.

Guide to Criminal Justice Information Sources, National Council on Crime and Delinquency, 1977.

Hahn, P.H., *Crimes Against the Elderly,* Davis, 1976.

Hahn, P.H., *The Juvenile Offender and the Law,* W.H. Anderson, 1978.

Haskell, M.R. and L. Yablonsky, *Crime and Delinquency,* Rand-McNally Co., 1978.

Hemphill, C.F., *Criminal Procedure: The Administration of Justice,* Goodyear Publishing Co., Inc., 1978.

Heumann, M., *Plea-Bargaining,* University of Chicago Press, 1978.

Hills, S., *Crime, Power and Morality,* Chandler, 1971.

Jahnige, T., *The Federal Judicial System,* Holt, Rinehart and Winston, Inc., 1968.

James, H., *Crisis in the Courts,* McKay, 1971.

Johnson, N., *The Human Cage: A Brief History of Prison Architecture,* Walker, 1973.

Johnson, R.E., *Juvenile Delinquency and Its Origins,* Cambridge University Press, 1979.

Johnson, T.A., G. Mizner, and L.P. Brown, *The Police and Society,* Prentice-Hall, 1981.

Jones, D.A., *Crime and Criminal Responsibility,* Nelson-Hall Publishers, 1978.

Jones, D.A., *Crime Without Punishment,* Lexington Books, 1979.

Kalven, H. and H. Zeisel, *The American Jury,* Little, Brown and Co., 1966.

Kamisar, Y., et al., *Criminal Law and Procedure,* West, 1974.

Kassebaum, G., *Prison Treatment and Parole Survival,* Wiley, 1972.

Killinger, G. and P. Cromwell, *Penology,* West, 1973.

Killinger, G.G. and P.F. Cromwell, *Corrections in the Community,* West, 1978.

Klein, I., *Law of Evidence for Police,* West, 1973.

Klein, M., *The Juvenile Justice System,* Sage Publications, Inc., 1976.

Klotter, J. and J. Kanovitz, *Constitutional Law for Police,* Anderson, 1977.

Kratcoski, P. and D. Walker, *Criminal Justice in America,* Scott, Foresman and Co., 1978.

Kratcoski, P.C. and L.D. Kratcoski, *Juvenile Delinquency,* Prentice-Hall, Inc., 1979.

LaFave, W.R., *Principles of Criminal Law,* West, 1979.

LaPatra, J.W., *Analyzing the Criminal Justice System,* Lexington Books, 1978.

Levin, M., *Urban Politics and the Criminal Courts,* University of Chicago Press, 1977.

Lewis, P.W. and K.D. Peoples, *The Supreme Court and the Criminal Process,* W.B. Saunders Co., 1978.

Lipton, D., R. Martinson, and J. Wilks, *The Effectiveness of Correctional Treatment,* Praeger Publishers, Inc., 1975.

Loeb, R.H., *Crime and Capital Punishment,* Franklin-Watts, 1978.

MacNamara, D. and F. Montanino, *Incarceration,* Sage Publications, 1978.

MacNamara, D. and E. Sagarin, *Perspectives on Correction,* Thomas Y. Crowell Co., 1971.

MacNamara, D. and E. Sagarin, *Sex, Crime, and the Law,* Macmillan-Free Press, 1977.

MacNamara, D. and M. Riedel, *Police: Problems and Prospects,* Praeger Publishers, Inc., 1974.

MacNamara, D. and E. Sagarin, *Corrections, Punishment and Rehabilitation,* Praeger, 1972.

MacNamara, D.E.J. and L.W. McCorkle, *Crime, Criminals and Corrections,* John Jay Press, 1982.

Marmor, J., *Homosexual Behavior: A Modern Reappraisal,* Basic Books, 1979.

Mathias, W., *Foundations of Criminal Justice,* Prentice-Hall, 1980.

McDonald, W., *Criminal Justice and the Victim,* Sage Publications, 1976.

Menninger, K., *The Crime of Punishment,* Viking Press, 1968.

Miller, F., *The Correctional Process,* The Foundation Press, 1971.

Miller, F., *Prosecution,* Little, Brown and Co., 1970.

Mitford, J., *Kind and Usual Punishment,* Knopf, Inc., 1973.

More, H., *Effective Police Administration,* West, 1979.

Morris, N., *The Honest Politician's Guide to Crime Control,* The University of Chicago Press, 1970.

Morris, N., *The Future of Imprisonment,* The University of Chicago Press, 1974.

Munro, J., *Administrative Behavior and Police Organization,* W.H. Anderson, 1974.

Nagel, S., *Modeling the Criminal Justice System,* Sage Publications, 1977.

Nagel, S., *The Rights of the Accused,* Sage Publications, 1972.

Nagel, S. and H.G. Neef, *Decision Theory and the Legal Process,* Lexington Books, 1979.

Navasky, V. and D. Paster, *Law Enforcement: The Federal Role,* McGraw-Hill Book Co., 1976.

Neary, M., *Corruption and Its Management,* American Academy for Professional Law Enforcement, 1977.

Netter, G., *Explaining Crime,* McGraw-Hill Book Co., 1978.

Neubauer, D., *Criminal Justice in Middle America,* General Learning Press, 1974.

Newman, C., *Probation, Parole and Pardons,* C.C. Thomas, 1970.

Newman, G., *The Punishment Response,* J.P. Lippincott Co., 1978.

Niederhoffer, A., *The Ambivalent Force,* Ginn and Co., 1970.

Niederhoffer, A., *The Police Family,* Lexington Books, 1978.

O'Brien, J.T. and M. Marcus, *Crime and Justice in America,* Pergamon Press Inc., 1979.

Ohlin, L.E., *et al., Reforming Juvenile Corrections,* Ballinger Publishing Co., 1979.

Packer, H., *The Limits of the Criminal Sanction,* Stanford University Press, 1968.

Platt, A., *The Child Savers: The Invention of Delinquency,* The University of Chicago Press, 1977.

Platt, T. and P. Takagi, *Punishment and Penal Discipline,* Crime and Social Justice Press, 1979.

Price, B., *Police Professionalism,* Lexington Books, 1977.

Quinney, R., *Critique of the Legal Order,* Little, Brown and Co., 1974.

Rawls, J., *A Theory of Justice,* Harvard University Press, 1971.

Reid, S.T., *Crime and Criminology,* Holt, Rinehart, & Winston, Inc., 1979.

Reiss, A., *The Police and the Public,* Yale University Press, 1971.

Reppetto, T., *Residential Crime,* Ballinger Publishing Co., 1974.

Reppetto, T., *The Blue Parade,* The Free Press, 1978.

Rich, V., *Law and the Administration of Justice,* Wiley, 1979.

Rieber, R.W. and H.J. Vetter, *The Psychological Foundations of Criminal Justice,* John Jay Press, 1979.

Rifai, M.A., *Justice and Older Americans,* D.C. Heath and Co., 1977.

Ross, R. and P. Gendreau, *Effective Correctional Treatment,* Butterworths, 1980.

Rossett, A. and D. Cressey, *Justice by Consent,* J.P. Lippincott Co., 1976.

Rothman, D., *The Discovery of Asylum,* Little, Brown and Co., 1971.

Rubin, S., *Law of Criminal Correction,* West, 1973.

Rush, G.E., *Dictionary of Criminal Justice,* Holbrook Press Inc., 1977.

Sagarin, E., *Deviants and Deviance,* Praeger Publishers, Inc., 1976.

Sagarin, E., *Criminology: New Concerns,* Sage, 1979.

Saks, M.J., *Jury Verdicts,* D.C. Heath and Co., 1977.

Sanders, W., *Detective Work,* The Free Press, 1977.

Saunders, C., *Upgrading the American Police,* The Brookings Institution, 1970.

Schultz, D.D., *Modern Police Administration,* Gulf Publishing Co., 1979.

Schur, E., *Crimes Without Victims,* Prentice-Hall, Inc., 1965.

Senna, J. and L. Siegel, *Introduction to Criminal Justice,* West, 1978.

Shanahan, D.T. and Whisenand, P.M., *Dimensions of Criminal Justice Planning,* Allyn & Bacon, Inc., 1980.

Sheehan, S., *A Prison and a Prisoner,* Houghton Mifflin Co., 1978.

Sherman, L.W., *The Quality of Police Education,* Jossey-Bass, Inc., 1978.

Sherman, L.W., *Scandal and Reform: Controlling Police Corruption,* University of California Press, 1978.

Silberman, C., *Criminal Violence—Criminal Justice,* Random House, Inc., 1978.

Simon, R., *Women and Crime,* Lexington Books, 1975.

Simon, R., *The Jury System in America,* Lexington Books, 1979.

Simonsen, C.E. and M.S. Gordon, *Juvenile Justice in America,* Glencoe Press, 1979.

Skolnick, J. and T. Gray, *Police in America,* Little, Brown, 1975.

Snortum, J. and I. Hadar, *Criminal Justice,* Palisades Publishers, 1976.

Stanley, D., *Prisoners Among Us: The Problem of Parole,* The Brookings Institution, 1975.

Stead, P.J., *Pioneers in Policing,* Patterson Smith, 1977.

Strasburg, P., *Violent Delinquents,* Monarch Books, 1978.

Strickland, K.G., *Correctional Institutions for Women in the United States,* Lexington Books, 1978.

Stuckey, G.B., *Evidence for the Law Enforcement Officer,* McGraw-Hill Book Co., 1979.

Szasz, T., *Psychiatric Justice,* Macmillan, 1965.

Toch, H., *Living in Prison,* The Free Press, 1977.

Turk, A., *Legal Sanctions and Social Control,* NIMH, 1972.

Ungar, S., *F.B.I.,* Little-Brown and Co., 1976.

Ulviller, H., *Adjudication,* West, 1975.

Van Dyke, J.M., *Jury Selection,* Ballinger Publishing Co., 1977.

Vetter, H. and C. Simonsen, *Criminal Justice in America,* W.B. Saunders Co., 1976.

Viano, E.C., *Victims and Society,* Visage Press, 1976.

Von Grimme, T.L., *Your Career in Law Enforcement,* ARCO, 1979.

Von Hirsch, A., *Doing Justice: The Choice of Punishments,* Hill and Wang, 1976.

Walker, A., *A Critical History of Police Reform,* Lexington Books, 1977.

Warren, E., *The Memoirs of Chief Justice Warren,* Doubleday, 1977.

Weaver, S., *Decisions to Prosecute,* M.I.T. Press, 1977.

Weinreb, L., *Leading Constitutional Cases on Criminal Justice,* Foundation Press, 1978.

Wheeler, R. and H. Whitcomb, *Judicial Administration,* Prentice-Hall, 1977.

Whisenand, P., *Crime Prevention,* Holbrook Press, 1977.

Weiss, J.A., *Law of the Elderly,* Practicing Law Institute, 1977.

Wice, R., *Bail and Its Reform,* National Institute of Law Enforcement and Criminal Law, 1974.

Wilkins, L., *Evaluation of Penal Measures,* Random House, 1969.

Wilson, J., *Varieties of Police Behavior,* Harvard University Press, 1968.

Wilson, J., *Thinking About Crime,* Basic Books, 1975.

Wilson, J., *The Investigators: Managing the FBI and Narcotics Agents,* Basic Books, 1978.

Witt, J.W., *The Police, the Courts and the Minority Community,* Lexington Books, 1978.

Wolf, J.B., *The Police Intelligence System,* John Jay Press, 1978.

Wolfgang, M.E., *Prisons: Success and Failure,* Lexington Books, 1978.

Wolfgang, M.E. and F. Ferracuti, *Diagnosis in Criminal Justice Systems,* Lexington Books, 1978.

Wootton, B., *Crime and Penal Policy,* Allen & Unwin, 1978.

Wright, E., *The Politics of Punishment,* Harper & Row, 1973.

Zimring, F. and G. Hawkins, *Deterrence,* University of Chicago Press, 1973.

Glossary

Abet To encourage another to commit a crime. This encouragement may be by advice, inducement, command, etc. The abettor of a crime is equally guilty with the one who actually commits the crime.

Accessory after the Fact One who harbors, assists, or protects another person, although he knows that person has committed a crime.

Accessory before the Fact One who helps another to commit a crime, even though he is absent when the crime is committed.

Accomplice One who is involved in the commission of a crime with others, whether he actually commits the crime or abets others. The term *principal* means the same thing, except that one may be a principal if he commits a crime without the aid of others.

Acquit To free a person from an accusation of criminal guilt; to find "not guilty."

Affidavit A written declaration or statement sworn to and affirmed by an officer having authority to administer an oath.

Affirmation To swear on one's conscience that what he says is true. An *oath* means that one calls upon God to witness the truth of what he says.

Alias Any name by which one is known other than his true name. *Alias dictus* is the more technically correct term but it is rarely used.

Alibi A claim that one was in a place different from that charged. If the person proves his alibi, he proves that he could not have committed the crime charged.

Allegation The declaration of a party to a lawsuit made in a pleading, that states what he expects to prove.

Amnesty A class or group pardon (e.g., all political prisoners).

Appeal A case carried to a higher court to ask that the decision of the lower court, in which the case originated, be altered or overruled completely.

Appellate Court A court that has jurisdiction to hear cases on appeal; not a trial court.

Arraignment The appearance before the court of a person charged with a crime. He or she is advised of the charges, bail is set, and a plea of "guilty" or "not guilty" is entered.

Arrest To take a person into custody so that he may be held to answer for a crime.

Autopsy A post-mortem examination of a human body to determine the cause of death.

Bail Property (usually money) deposited with a court in exchange for the release of a person in custody to assure later appearance.

Bail Bond An obligation signed by the accused and his sureties, that insures his presence in court.

Bailiff A court attendant whose duties are to keep order in the courtroom and to have custody of the jury.

Bench Warrant An order by the court for the apprehension and arrest of a defendant or other person who has failed to appear when so ordered.

Bill of Rights The first ten amendments to the Constitution of the United States which define such rights as: due process of law, immunity from illegal search and seizure, the ban on cruel and unusual punishment, unreasonably high bail, indictment by a grand jury, and speedy trial.

Bind Over To hold for trial.

"Blue" Laws Laws in some jurisdictions prohibiting sales of merchandise, athletic contests, and the sale of alcoholic beverages on Sundays.

Booking The procedure at a police station of entering the name and identifying particulars relating to an arrested person, the charges filed against him, and the name of the arresting officer.

Burden of Proof The duty of affirmatively proving the guilt of the defendant "beyond a reasonable doubt."

Calendar A list of cases to be heard in a trial court, on a specific day, and containing the title of the case, the lawyers involved, and the index number.

Capital Crime Any crime that may be punishable by death or imprisonment for life.

Caseload The number of cases actively being investigated by a police detective or being supervised by a probation or parole officer.

Change of Venue The removal of a trial from one jurisdiction to another in order to avoid local prejudice.

Charge In criminal law, the accusation made against a person. It also refers to the judge's instruction to the jury on legal points.

Circumstantial Evidence Indirect evidence; evidence from which the principal fact can be proved or disproved by inference. Example: a finger-print found at the crime scene.

Citizen's Arrest A taking into custody of an alleged offender by a person not a law enforcement officer. Such an arrest is lawful if the crime was attempted or committed in his presence.

Code A compilation, compendium, or revision of laws, arranged into chapters, having a table of contents and index, and promulgated by legislative authority. Criminal code; penal code.

Coercion The compelling of a person to do that which he is not obliged to do, or to omit doing what he may legally do, by some illegal threat, force, or intimidation. For example: a forced confession.

Commit To place a person in custody in a prison or other institution by lawful order.

Common Law Law that derives its authority from usage and custom or court decisions.

Commutation To change the punishment meted out to a criminal to one less severe. Executive clemency.

Complainant The victim of a crime who brings the facts to the attention of the authorities.

Complaint A sworn written allegation stating that a specified person committed a crime. Sometimes called an *information*. When issued from a *Grand Jury,* it is called an *indictment*.

Compulsion An irresistible impulse to commit some act, such as stealing, setting a fire, or an illegal sexual act.

Confession An admission by the accused of his guilt; a partial admission (e.g., that he was at the crime scene; that he had a motive) is referred to as "an admission against interest."

Confinement Deprivation of liberty in a jail or prison either as punishment for a crime or as detention while guilt or innocence is being determined.

Consensual Crime A crime without a victim; one in which both parties voluntarily participate (e.g., adultery, sodomy, etc.).

Conspiracy A secret combination of two or more persons who plan for the purpose of committing a crime or any unlawful act or a lawful act by unlawful or criminal means.

Contempt of Court Behavior that impugns the authority of a court or obstructs the execution of court orders.

Continuance A delay in trial granted by the judge on request of either the prosecutor or defense counsel; an adjournment.

Conviction A finding by the jury (or by the trial judge in cases tried without a jury) that the accused is guilty of a crime.

Corporal Corporal punishment is pain inflicted on the body of another. Flogging.

Corpus Delicti The objective proof that a crime has been committed as distinguished from an accidental death, injury or loss.

Corrections Area of criminal justice dealing with convicted offenders in jails, prisons; on probation or parole.

Corroborating Evidence Supplementary evidence that tends to strengthen or confirm other evidence given previously.

Crime An act or omission prohibited and punishable by law. Crimes are divided into *felonies* and *misdemeanors;* and recorded as "crimes against the person" (murder, rape, assault, robbery) and "crimes against property" (burglary, larceny, auto theft). There are also crimes against public morality and against public order.

Criminal Insanity Lack of mental capacity to do or refrain from doing a criminal act; inability to distinguish right from wrong.

Criminalistics Crime laboratory procedures (e.g., ballistics, analysis of stains, etc.).

Criminology The scientific study of crime and criminals.

Cross-Examination The questioning of a witness by the party who did not produce the witness.

Culpability Guilt; *see also mens rea.*

Defendant The person who is being prosecuted.

Delinquency Criminality by a boy or girl who has not as yet reached the age set by the state for trial as an adult (the age varies from jurisdiction to jurisdiction and from crime to crime).

Demurrer In court procedure, a statement that the charge that a crime has been committed has no sufficient basis in law, despite the truth of the facts alleged.

Deposition The testimony of a witness not taken in open court but taken in pursuance of authority to take such testimony elsewhere.

Detention To hold a person in confinement while awaiting trial or sentence, or as a material witness.

Deterrence To prevent criminality by fear of the consequences; one of the rationalizations for punishing offenders.

Direct Evidence Proof of facts by witnesses who actually saw acts or heard words, as distinguished from *Circumstantial Evidence.*

Direct Examination The first questioning of a witness by the party who produced him.

Directed Verdict An instruction by the judge to the jury to return a specific verdict. A judge may not direct a guilty verdict.

Discretion The decision-making powers of officers of the criminal justice system (e.g., to arrest or not, to prosecute or not, to plea-bargain, to grant probation, or to sentence to a penal institution).

District Attorney Prosecutor; sometimes County Attorney, (U.S. Attorney in Federal practice).

Docket The formal record maintained by the court clerk, listing all cases heard. It contains the defendant's name, index number, date of arrest, and the outcome of the case.

Double Jeopardy To be prosecuted twice for the same offense.

Due Process Law in its regular course of administration through the courts of justice. Guaranteed by the 5th and 14th Amendments.

Embracery An attempt to influence a jury, or a member thereof, in their verdict by any improper means.

Entrapment The instigation of a crime by officers or agents of a government who induce a person to commit a crime that he did not originally contemplate in order to institute a criminal prosecution against him.

Evidence All the means used to prove or disprove the fact at issue.

Ex Post Facto After the fact. An ex post facto law is a criminal law that makes an act unlawful although it was committed prior to the passage of that law.

Examination An investigation of a witness by counsel in the form of questions for the purpose of bringing before the court knowledge possessed by the witness.

Exception A formal objection to the action of the court during a trial. The indication is that the excepting party will seek to reverse the court's action at some future proceeding. *Objection.*

Exclusionary Rule Rule of evidence which makes illegally acquired evidence inadmissible; see Mapp vs. Ohio.

Expert Evidence Testimony by one qualified to speak authoritatively on technical matters because of his special training or skill.

Extradition The surrender by one state to another of an individual accused of a crime.

False Arrest Any unlawful physical restraint of another's freedom of movement. Unlawful arrest.

Felonious Evil, malicious, or criminal. A felonious act is not necessarily a felony, but is criminal in some degree.

Felony Generally, an offense punishable by death or imprisonment in a penitentiary.

Forensic Relating to the court. Thus, forensic medicine would refer to medicine in relation to court proceedings and the law in general.

Grand Jury A group of 16 to 23 citizens of a county who examine evidence against the person suspected of a crime, and hand down an indictment if there is sufficient evidence to warrant one.

Habeas Corpus (Writ of) An order that requires a jailor, warden, police chief, or other public official to produce a person being held in custody before a court in order to show that they have a legal right to hold him in custody.

Hearsay Evidence not originating from the witness' personal knowledge.

Homicide The killing of a human being; may be murder, negligent or non-negligent manslaughter, or excusable or justifiable homicide.

Impeach To discredit. To question the truthfulness of a witness. Also: to charge a president or governor with criminal misconduct.

Imprisonment The act of confining a convicted felon in a federal or state prison.

In Camera In the judge's private chambers; in secrecy; the general public and press are excluded.

Indictment The document prepared by a prosecutor and approved by the grand jury which charges a certain person with a specific crime or crimes for which that person is later to be tried in court. Truebill.

Inference A conclusion one draws about something based on proof of certain other facts.

Injunction An order by a court prohibiting a defendant from committing an act.

Intent A design or determination of the mind to do or not do a certain thing. Intent may be determined from the nature of one's acts. Mens Rea.

Interpol International Criminal Police Commission.

Jail A short-term confinement institution for the detention of persons awaiting trial and the serving of sentences by those convicted of misdemeanors and offenses.

Jeopardy The danger of conviction and punishment that a defendant faces in a criminal trial. *Double Jeopardy.*

Judicial Notice The rule that a court will accept certain things as common knowledge without proof.

Jurisdiction The power of a court to hear and determine a criminal case.

Jury A certain number of persons who are sworn to examine the evidence and determine the truth on the basis of that evidence. Grand jury; trial jury.

Juvenile Delinquent A boy or girl who has not reached the age of criminal liability (varies from state to state) and who commits an act which would be a misdemeanor or felony if he were an adult. Delinquents are tried in *Juvenile Court* and confined to separate facilities.

L.E.A.A. Law Enforcement Assistance Administration, U.S. Dept. of Justice.

Leniency An unusually mild sentence imposed on a convicted offender; clemency granted by the President or a state governor; early release by a parole board.

Lie Detector An instrument which measures certain physiological reactions of the human body from which a trained operator may determine whether the subject is telling the truth or lies; polygraph; psychological stress evaluator.

Mala In Se Evil in itself. Acts that are made crimes because they are, by their nature, evil and morally wrong.

Mala Prohibita Evil because they are prohibited. Acts that are not wrong in themselves but which, to protect the general welfare, are made crimes by statute.

Malfeasance The act of a public officer in committing a crime relating to his official duties or powers. Accepting or demanding a bribe.

Malice An evil intent to vex, annoy, or injure another; intentional evil.

Malicious Prosecution An action instituted in bad faith with the intention of injuring the defendant.

Mandamus A writ that issues from a superior court, directed to any person, corporation, or inferior court, requiring it to do some particular thing.

Mens Rea A guilty intent.

Miranda Warning A police officer when taking a suspect into custody must warn him of his right to remain silent and of his right to an attorney.

Misdemeanor Any crime not a *Felony.* Usually, a crime punishable by a fine or imprisonment in the county or other local jail.

Misprision Failing to reveal a crime.

Mistrial A trial discontinued before reaching a verdict because of some procedural defect or impediment.

Modus Operandi Method of operation by criminals.

Motions Procedural moves made by either defense attorney or prosecutor and submitted to the court, helping to define and set the ground rules for the proceedings of a particular case. For example: to suppress illegally seized evidence or to seek a change of venue.

Motive The reason for committing a crime.

N.C.C.D. National Council on Crime and Delinquency.

No Bill A phrase used by a *Grand Jury* when they fail to indict.

Nolle Prosequi A declaration to a court, by the prosecutor that he does not wish to further prosecute the case.

Nolo Contendre A pleading, usually used by a defendant in a criminal case, that literally means "I will not contest."

Objection The act of taking exception to some statement or procedure in a trial. Used to call the court's attention to some improper evidence or procedure.

Opinion Evidence A witness' belief or opinion about a fact in dispute, as distinguished from personal knowledge of the fact. Expert testimony.

Ordinance A statute enacted by the city or municipal government.

Organized Crime The crime syndicate; cosa nostra; Mafia; an organized, continuing criminal conspiracy which engages in crime as a business (e.g., loan sharking, illegal gambling, prostitution, extortion, etc.).

Original Jurisdiction Trial jurisdiction.

Over Act An open or physical act, as opposed to a thought or mere intention.

Pardon Executive clemency setting aside a conviction and penalty.

Parole A conditional release from prison, under supervision.

Penal Code The criminal law of a jurisdiction, (sometimes the criminal procedure law is included but in other states it is codified separately).

Penology The study of punishment and corrections.

Peremptory Challenge The act of objecting to a certain number of jurors without assigning a cause for their dismissal. Used during the *voir dire* examination.

Perjury The legal offense of deliberately testifying falsely under oath about a material fact.

Petit Jury The ordinary jury composed of 12 persons who hear criminal cases. Determines guilt or innocence of the accused.

Plea-Bargaining A negotiation between the defense attorney and the prosecutor in which defendant receives a reduced penalty in return for a plea of "guilty."

Police Power The authority of the legislation to make laws in the interest of the general public, even at the risk of placing some hardship on individuals.

Post Mortem After death. Commonly applied to examination of a dead body. An autopsy is a post mortem examination to determine the cause of death.

Preliminary Hearing A proceeding in front of a lower court to determine if there is sufficient evidence for submitting a felony case to the grand jury.

Presumption of Fact An inference as to the truth or falsity of any proposition or fact, made in the absence of actual certainty of its truth or falsity or until such certainty can be attained.

Presumption of Law A rule of law that courts and judges must draw a particular inference from a particular fact or evidence, unless the inference can be disproved.

Prima Facie So far as can be judged from the first appearance or at first sight.

Prison Federal or state penal institution for the confinement of convicted felons. Penitentiary.

Probation A penalty placing a convicted person under the supervision of a probation officer for a stated time, instead of being confined.

Prosecutor One who initiates a criminal prosecution against an accused. One who acts as a trial attorney for the government as the representative of the people.

Provost Marshal Military police officer in charge of discipline, crime control and traffic law enforcement at a military post.

Public Defender An appointed or elected public official charged with providing legal representation for indigent persons accused of crimes.

Reasonable Doubt That state of mind of jurors when they do not feel a moral certainty about the truth of the charge and when the evidence does not exclude every other reasonable hypothesis except that the defendant is guilty as charged.

Rebuttal The introduction of contradicting testimony; the showing that statements made by a witness are not true; the point in the trial at which such evidence may be introduced.

Recidivist A repeater in crime; a habitual offender.

Recognizance When a person binds himself to do a certain act or else suffer a penalty, as, for example, with a recognizance bond. Release on recognizance is release without posting bail or bond.

Relevant Applying to the issue in question; related to the issue; useful in determining the truth or falsity of an alleged fact.

Remand To send back. To remand a case for new trial or sentencing.

Reprieve A stay of execution or sentence.

Search Warrant A written order, issued by judicial authority in the name of the state, directing a law enforcement officer to search for personal property and, if found, to bring it before the court.

Sentence The punishment (harsh or lenient) imposed by the trial judge on a convicted offender; major options include: fines, probation, indeterminate sentencing (e.g., three to ten years), indefinite sentencing (e.g., not more than three years), and capital punishment (death).

Stare Decisis To abide by decided cases. The doctrine that once a court has laid down a principle of law as applicable to certain facts, it will apply it to all future cases when the facts are substantially the same.

State's Evidence Testimony given by an accomplice or participant in a crime, tending to convict others.

Status Offense An act which is punishable only because the offender has not as yet reached a statutorily prescribed age (e.g., truancy, running away, drinking alcoholic beverages by a minor, etc.).

Statute A law.

Stay A stopping of a judicial proceeding by a court order.

Subpoena A court order requiring a witness to attend and testify in a court proceeding.

Subpoena Duces Tecum A court order requiring a witness to testify and to bring all books, documents, and papers that might affect the outcome of the proceedings.

Summons An order to appear in court on a particular date, which is issued by a police officer after or instead of arrest. It may also be a notification to a witness or a juror to appear in court.

Suspect One whom the police have determined as very likely to be the guilty perpetrator of an offense. Once the police identify a person as a suspect, they must warn him of his rights (Miranda warning) to remain silent and to have legal advice.

Testimony Evidence given by a competent witness, under oath, as distinguished from evidence from writings and other sources.

Tort A legal wrong committed against a person or property for which compensation may be obtained by a civil action.

Uniform Crime Reports (U.C.R.) Annual statistical tabulation of "crimes known to the police" and "crimes cleared by arrest" published by the Federal Bureau of Investigation.

Venue The geographical area in which a court with jurisdiction sits. The power of a court to compel the presence of the parties to a litigation. See also *Change of Venue*.

Verdict The decision of a court.

Victimology Sub-discipline of criminology which emphasizes the study of victims; includes *victim compensation*.

Voir Dire The examination or questioning of prospective jurors.

Waive To give up a personal right. For example: to testify before the grand jury.

Warrant A court order directing a police officer to arrest a named person or search a specific premise.

Witness One who has seen, heard, acquired knowledge about some element in a crime. An *expert witness* is one who, though he has no direct knowledge of the crime for which the defendant is being tried, may testify as to the defendant's sanity, the amount of alcohol in the deceased's blood, whether a signature is genuine, that a fingerprint is or is not that of the accused, etc.

Credits/ Acknowledgments

Cover design by Charles Vitelli

1. Crime and Justice in America

Facing overview—The Dushkin Publishing Group, Inc., photo by Pamela Carley Petersen.

2. Victimology

Facing overview—United Nations photo by John Isaac.

3. Police

Facing overview—Drug Enforcement Agency.

4. The Judicial System

Facing overview—EPA-Documerica.

5. Juvenile Justice

Facing overview—United Nations photo by Paulo Fridman.

6. Punishment and Corrections

Facing overview—National Archives.

ANNUAL EDITIONS ARTICLE REVIEW FORM

■ NAME: _____ DATE: _____

■ TITLE AND NUMBER OF ARTICLE: _____

■ BRIEFLY STATE THE MAIN IDEA OF THIS ARTICLE: _____

_____

_____

_____

_____

■ LIST THREE IMPORTANT FACTS THAT THE AUTHOR USES TO SUPPORT THE MAIN IDEA:

_____

_____

_____

_____

_____

_____

■ WHAT INFORMATION OR IDEAS DISCUSSED IN THIS ARTICLE ARE ALSO DISCUSSED IN YOUR
TEXTBOOK OR OTHER READING YOU HAVE DONE? LIST THE TEXTBOOK CHAPTERS AND PAGE
NUMBERS:

_____

_____

_____

_____

_____

_____

_____

■ LIST ANY EXAMPLES OF BIAS OR FAULTY REASONING THAT YOU FOUND IN THE ARTICLE:

_____

_____

_____

_____

_____

■ LIST ANY NEW TERMS/CONCEPTS THAT WERE DISCUSSED IN THE ARTICLE AND WRITE A
SHORT DEFINITION:

_____

_____

_____

_____

_____

ANNUAL EDITIONS: CRIMINAL JUSTICE 92/93
Article Rating Form

Here is an opportunity for you to have direct input into the next revision of this volume. We would like you to rate each of the 45 articles listed below, using the following scale:

1. Excellent: should definitely be retained
2. Above average: should probably be retained
3. Below average: should probably be deleted
4. Poor: should definitely be deleted

Your ratings will play a vital part in the next revision. So please mail this prepaid form to us just as soon as you complete it.
Thanks for your help!

Annual Editions revisions depend on two major opinion sources: one is our Advisory Board, listed in the front of this volume, which works with us in scanning the thousands of articles published in the public press each year; the other is you—the person actually using the book. Please help us and the users of the next edition by completing the prepaid article rating form on this page and returning it to us. Thank you.

Rating	Article	Rating	Article
	1. An Overview of the Criminal Justice System		24. Public Defenders
	2. What Is Crime?		25. Abuse of Power in the Prosecutor's Office
	3. Are Criminals Made or Born?		26. These Clients Aren't Fools
	4. Crime's Impact on Blacks Makes for a Bleak Picture		27. Convicting the Innocent
	5. The High Cost of Crime		28. Improving Our Criminal Justice System: Can We Borrow From Europe's Civil Law Tradition?
	6. The Men Who Created Crack		29. Alternative Sentencing: A New Direction for Criminal Justice
	7. The Mobster Who Could Bring Down the Mob		30. Criminal Rulings Granted the State Broad New Power
	8. Computer Ethics		31. Handling of Juvenile Cases
	9. The Fear of Crime		32. The Evolution of the Juvenile Justice System
	10. The Implementation of Victims' Rights: A Challenge for Criminal Justice Professionals		33. Girls' Crime and Woman's Place: Toward a Feminist Model of Female Delinquency
	11. Hunted: The Last Year of April LaSalata		34. Teenage Addiction
	12. A Vicious Cycle		35. Correcting Juvenile Corrections
	13. Tougher Laws Mean More Cases Are Called Rape		36. Kids Who Kill
	14. Even the Victim Can Be Slow to Recognize Rape		37. Sentencing and Corrections
	15. The Unbearable Loss		38. Women in Jail: Unequal Justice
	16. Police Response to Crime		39. You're Under Arrest—AT HOME
	17. The Police in the United States		40. Difficult Clients, Large Caseloads Plague Probation, Parole Agencies
	18. Cops Under Fire		41. Life Without Parole: The View From Death Row
	19. Law and Disorder		42. U.S.: World's Lock-'Em-Up Leader
	20. New Faces, and New Roles, for the Police		43. "Boot Camp" Programs Grow in Number and Scope
	21. Not Just Old Wine in New Bottles		44. 'This Man Has Expired'
	22. Law Enforcement Officers Killed, 1980–1989		45. No Reversal of Fortune for Blacks on Death Row
	23. The Judicial Process: Prosecutors and Courts		

(Continued on next page)

ABOUT YOU

Name_____ Date_____

Are you a teacher? ☐ Or student? ☐

Your School Name _____

Department _____

Address _____

City _____ State _____ Zip _____

School Telephone # _____

YOUR COMMENTS ARE IMPORTANT TO US!

Please fill in the following information:

For which course did you use this book? _____

Did you use a text with this Annual Edition? ☐ yes ☐ no

The title of the text? _____

What are your general reactions to the Annual Editions concept?

Have you read any particular articles recently that you think should be included in the next edition?

Are there any articles you feel should be replaced in the next edition? Why?

Are there other areas that you feel would utilize an Annual Edition?

May we contact you for editorial input?

May we quote you from above?

ANNUAL EDITIONS: CRIMINAL JUSTICE 92/93

BUSINESS REPLY MAIL

First Class   Permit No. 84   Guilford, CT

Postage will be paid by addressee

The Dushkin Publishing Group, Inc.
Sluice Dock
DPG **Guilford, Connecticut 06437**